W9-BVG-077

J.J. Strauss
1967

PHILLIPS BROOKS

PHILLIPS BROOKS

1835–1893

MEMORIES OF HIS LIFE
WITH EXTRACTS FROM HIS
LETTERS AND NOTE-BOOKS

BY

ALEXANDER V. G. ALLEN

AUTHOR OF

"LIFE AND LETTERS OF PHILLIPS BROOKS"

NEW YORK
E·P·DUTTON & COMPANY
PUBLISHERS

PREFACE.

The Life and Letters of Phillips Brooks was published in 1900, some seven years after his death. Since then an abridgment has been frequently and urgently called for, on the ground that a large number of people who would like to know Phillips Brooks have not the time to read so full a biography, whose cost also is in many cases prohibitive. In reducing the work some parts have been rewritten in order to condensation, but care has been taken to preserve everything of importance bearing on his development, and to maintain the perspective of his career. The very kind and generous reception accorded to *The Life and Letters of Phillips Brooks* is here most gratefully acknowledged. It indicates how deeply he had stamped his personality upon the American people, and what enduring impression he had left by his unprecedented power in the pulpit. The love and devotion which went out toward him in such unstinted measure while living have not ceased with his death. He is still speaking to the world he loved—the world whose growth he wanted to live in order that he might see. His message has not been, and cannot be, outgrown. He had solved in his capacious mind and heart the issues which still confront us. In extraordinary manner he combined a love for the historical Christ and insight into His life and teaching with a devotion so rare to the essential and eternal Christ, whom the Church has worshipped, that he seems to belong to what are called the "Ages of Faith" rather than to the world of doubt in which he lived. Among his large utterances which tend to reconcile and encourage, this was one of the foremost,—that all humanity constitutes, according to the divine ideal, the body of Christ; and another was that the words of Christ "I am come not to destroy but to fulfil" applied not only to the spiritual aspirations and movements of His own age, but to those of every age and country.

iii

PREFACE

My chief indebtedness in making this abridgment is to my wife, without whose aid it could not have been accomplished. A pupil of Phillips Brooks, she had drunk deeply of his teaching and she has been a most valuable and indefatigable collaborator in this effort to make him more widely known.

CAMBRIDGE, September 30, 1907.

CONTENTS

CHAPTER I.

1835–1855.

CHAPTER II.

1855–1856.

CHAPTER III.

1856–1857.

CHAPTER IV.

1857–1858.

CHAPTER V.

1858–1859.

♥

CONTENTS

CONTENTS

CHAPTER X.

1869–1872.

CHAPTER XI.

1873–1877.

CHAPTER XII.

1877–1878.

CHAPTER XIII.

1877–1880.

CONTENTS

CHAPTER XVIII.

1886.

CHAPTER XIX.

1887.

CHAPTER XX.

1888.

CHAPTER XXI.

1889.

CONTENTS

CHAPTER XXII.

1890.

CHAPTER XXIII.

CHAPTER XXIV.

1891.

CHAPTER XXV.

1891–1892.

CHAPTER XXVI.

1893.

CHAPTER I.

1835–1855.

ANCESTRY. BIRTH AND EARLY LIFE. BOSTON LATIN SCHOOL. HARVARD COLLEGE.

THE two families represented in the name Phillips Brooks trace their origin to the earliest days of New England history. They migrated from England in the seventeenth century—the Rev. George Phillips in 1630 and Thomas Brooks in the same decade—and were associated in the parish at Watertown near Boston, of which Rev. George Phillips was the first pastor. While both families are Puritan in their antecedents, they differed as widely as doctrinal Puritans differed from political Puritans in the conflicts of the age of migration. In the Phillips family, there was from the first a transcendental idealism which was handed down substantially unchanged in the successive generations, an intense religious devotion, an ascetic view of life. But combined with these in organic relationship was an interest in political affairs, and in the secular relations of business and trade.

The Rev. George Phillips was prominent in the Puritan councils of his time; he helped mould the ecclesiastical polity of New England and in some respects may be called its founder. Each of the three generations following was represented by a Puritan minister, the most distinguished being the Rev. Samuel Phillips, pastor of the Old South Church in Andover, Massachusetts (1711–1773),—a masterly man in whom the dignity of the Puritan minister was embodied. His descendants went into trade, but remained profoundly religious. Among them the most prominent, in whom the family attained high distinction, was Judge Samuel Phillips of Andover (1752–1802), who became Lieutenant-Governor of Massachusetts, and was even more distinguished as the founder of Phillips Academy and the Andover

Theological Seminary. To these institutions he gave a large part of his fortune. For nearly thirty years he took an important part in all the measures of the State. He possessed great business capacity, with high statesmanship and patriotism as well as devotion to the cause of learning and religion. He was the great-grandfather of Phillips Brooks. His grandfather was a man like minded, John Phillips, who, living a less public life, made sacrifices in the cause of religious and theological education. To his daughter Mary Ann Phillips, the mother of Phillips Brooks, was transmitted the family endowment unimpaired—the great capacity for religion. In her deep nature, the example and teaching of her ancestors found congenial soil for further growth and expansion. She pondered these things in her heart.

When we turn to the Brooks family we are conscious of a difference in the religious and social atmosphere. There is no special sympathy with doctrinal or experimental Puritanism. In tracing the line of descent, there are seen no religious leaders. Only one of its members entered the ministry; nor did Harvard College claim the same relative contingent as in the Phillips family. They were rich farmers, with the inherited English love for the land. They became more exclusively identified with trade, counting in their numbers opulent merchants; they showed devotion to country, some of them rising to high positions in the army or in offices of the State. They cultivated integrity of character, in each generation possessing some representative who was trusted and honored. As a family they became identified with the town of Medford, as the Phillips family was identified with Andover.

In the schism which befell the Puritan churches, the Brooks family became Unitarian. Their sole clerical representative in the eighteenth century, the Rev. Edward Brooks (1733–1781), having become entangled in the mazes of error—so they were deemed—of the rising Arminianism, was forced by his strict Calvinistic parishioners to resign his place as pastor. He left the Church for the army, where he rose to be acting adjutant-general in the battle of Monmouth. It was through his marriage with a daughter of the house of the Rev. John Cotton that Phillips Brooks became a lineal descendant of that famous divine, whose name was in all the churches; whose coming to New England from old Boston, in Lincolnshire, had been regarded at the time as a signal favor of Divine Providence.

One of the sons of this Edward Brooks was Peter Chardon Brooks (†1849), reputed in his day to be the richest man in Boston. His life has been described by one of his descendants: "he was simply a merchant coining money as he had opportunity, making investments, sending out cargoes, negotiating bonds, pursuing a just course, yet he did his full share of public good, and left a name that his descendants are proud to bear." He is entitled to mention here because, at an important moment in their lives, he stood *in loco parentis* to William Gray Brooks and Mary Ann Phillips, the father and mother of Phillips Brooks. To Mary Ann Phillips he was related through his marriage to her mother's sister; and William Gray Brooks was the son of his older brother. Peter Chardon Brooks had a large family of sons and daughters. The sons went out into the world to make for themselves honorable names; of the daughters, one married Edward Everett, another Charles Francis Adams, and a third the Rev. N. L. Frothingham. To the hospitable mansion of her uncle, Mary Ann Phillips often resorted from the old homestead in North Andover, and thither came William Gray Brooks who was in Boston for the purpose of establishing himself in business.

After their marriage in 1833, they lived for several years at the house No. 56 High Street, then occupied by residences. Here Phillips Brooks was born December 13, 1835. In 1842 the family removed to No. 3 Rowe Street. The change was necessitated by the encroachments of business, and in part by the needs of a larger house for the growing family. Rowe Street has since disappeared from the map of Boston, merged into Chauncy Place, of which it was the continuation, while Chauncy Place has been extended to Summer Street. When Rowe Street was finally demanded for the expansion of trade, the family moved once more and took up its abode in Hancock Street.

In this modest household with its unconscious accumulation of ancestral tendencies and forces, we are struck by one marked characteristic,—its strong family feeling, the glad recognition of that bond which unites the members in living relationship. To this result its isolation contributed, for it did not enter the world of fashionable society, but devoted its somewhat limited resources to its own interior development. The education of the children became the supreme motive. The home life shut them up with the parents as in some sacred enclosure, a nursery for great opportunities in the future. The father and mother appear as ruling with diligence and unquestioned authority, while beneath their authority runs the principle of self-sacrifice, and they seem to live only for the welfare of the children. They were interested, not so much for themselves in the increase of their own joy in life or in their own cultivation, as in making a larger life possible for the children whom God had given them.

It need hardly be said that this was a religious family. The usage of family prayer was observed, in the morning before going forth to the work of the day, and again in the evening at nine o'clock. The evenings were spent by the whole family together around the common table in the "back parlor," the father busy at literary tasks which his interests and ingenuity imposed on his leisure; the mother with her sewing, and with her deeper meditations, and the boys at their books preparing the lesson for the next day. Visitors came in occasionally for a call or to spend the evening, but this was rare; the avocations of the family were pursued without interruptions. There was abundance of hilarity, and boisterous demonstration, but the undercurrent flowed in a channel of serious and direct endeavor. This home for the children was interesting, and not monotonous or dull. The boys did not fret at exclusion from richer interests in the world outside or long to escape the narrow routine. The evenings at home were made attractive in some way, the newest books were read aloud, the fulfilment of duty was in itself a pleasure. But the concentration of parental love upon the children must after all have been the secret of the charm which bound the children to their home. Such a sacrifice had its reward. The home became to the children their choicest treasure, to which they reverted in after years, when its diviner meaning was more apparent. When Phillips Brooks left home for the first time he was followed by letters which always assured him that he was constantly remembered, and never at any moment forgotten. He responded to this affection by carrying about with him the memory of the home circle as a picture stamped upon his soul in colors ineffaceable. At heart he always remained a "child in the household" until father and mother were withdrawn from the world. The vision of that unworldly, self-sacrificing life was before him at home or in his wanderings abroad, nearer to him than any other experience.

More important than the fixing of the domicile was the determination of the religious question and the choice of a place of worship. By the year 1833 the schism had been completed between the "Orthodox" and the "Unitarian" parties in the churches of Massachusetts. The Brooks family at Medford under the pastoral care of Dr. Osgood had become Unitarians, and in this faith the father of Phillips Brooks had been reared. He had the characteristics of his family, with its devotion to affairs, its interest in this present world; he was religious also, and reverent, but not given to introvertiveness or contemplation, nor seeking the assurance of an inward experience. Like his ancestors, he illustrated the gospel of the secular life, faithful in the performance of duty, quick to recognize all obligations. It was his ideal to become a citizen alive to civic and social relationships. He had sympathy for all things human; he watched the movements affecting the interests of Boston with keen interest; he studied men and his judgment of men and movements was characterized by sobriety and sanity. He identified himself with Boston and in those days it seemed as if Boston were identified with Unitarianism.

The mother of Phillips Brooks represented another tendency. She carried in her heart the ancestral history of the Phillips family. She was not an intellectualist, or a controversialist in theology, but she was no stranger to the purpose for which her father and grandfather had labored and sacrificed in founding the institutions on Andover Hill,—the purpose to maintain the old Puritan faith in its integrity. Her religion moved in the grooves of the ancient piety. The cognitive power of feeling was the source of her knowledge, for she was no wide or discursive reader. She had an interior life more real than the phenomena of the passing world. If her range of interests seemed narrow in comparison with the outlook of her husband, yet her aspiration, her ambition, had a world-wide scope, for she would have all men everywhere brought under the control of her dominant purpose. The subject that most absorbed her imagination was foreign missions, for whose success she hungered and prayed. She had, too, a powerful will for the accomplishment of great ends, though the sphere was restricted for its manifestation. The study of her family history afforded her a picture of life, where tragedies in the loss of children had saddened its successive generations. Something of the sadness which had become a family characteristic was written on her features, the face of one subdued by the possibilities of infinite loss in an uncertain world.

When the father and mother with their contrasted tendencies, which were also supplementary to each other, set up their home in Boston, they chose the First Church, then situated in Chauncy Place, as their place of worship. Its situation was convenient; its pastor, Rev. N. L. Frothingham, was their kinsman; its first pastor at the time of its foundation was also an ancestor, the Rev. John Cotton—a consideration of no slight importance. For six years this arrangement continued, with a growing restiveness on the part of Mrs. Brooks. Religious controversy over the points at issue between "Orthodoxy" and "Unitarianism" was then at its height, disturbing the peace of congregations. She was familiar with the staple features of the controversy from her childhood. She grew more and more dissatisfied with the teaching at the First Church. Lines which at first were vaguely drawn were more sharply drawn, and she was forced to come to a decision. Dr. Frothingham was known as a conservative Unitarian, with no sympathy for the newer mood in religion represented by Dr. Channing. The doctrine of the dignity of man, and the sufficiency of human reason he condemned as "the apotheosis of human nature," as leading man to "the last delusion, the worship of himself." He maintained a reverence for Holy Scripture as the authority for religious faith. But on the other hand, he taught with emphasis that the Bible gave no sanction to the system of doctrine known as Calvinism or "Orthodoxy." It was too much for Mrs. Brooks to be told that her religious faith and that of her ancestors had no warrant in Scripture. Her capacity for devotion, her possibilities of enthusiasm, the powerful will, the longing for immediate conscious relationship with God, the desire to give herself in complete self-sacrifice to Christ,—these religious instincts found no satisfaction in the gentler but unheroic gospel, as proclaimed by Dr. Frothingham.

When the moment came for a readjustment of ecclesiastical relations, she did not seek to return to the Orthodox party of the Congregational order. Her husband's feelings were to be considered as well as her own. The compromise was the Episcopal Church, where the familiar gospel was preached without the painful reminders of controversy and schism. To St. Paul's Church, on Tremont Street, she turned as affording the best possibilities of a religious home for herself, and especially for her children. Her husband notes the change in his journal as an important movement, under the date October 18, 1839. For himself, he confesses his indifference, his regret at leaving his accustomed place of worship. He had given up his own inclinations to please his wife, for, as he remarks, "women make religion more a matter of conscience and heart, than men do." But a year later, he records in his journal that he does not regret the change. He finds the morning service rather long and at times tedious, but has no desire to return to the church he had left. At the time when the change was made, Phillips Brooks was four years old, unable to remember any earlier religious associations than those connected with St. Paul's Church, as the church of his infancy. The mother's anxiety for the religious welfare of her husband did not cease, until he had become like herself a communicant, and not merely an attendant on the worship. His confirmation took place, in 1847, when he had reached the age of forty-two. The elder children must have been present as witnesses of the transaction, Phillips Brooks being then a boy of twelve. We may also picture the mother, now becoming anxious that her sons should soon follow their father in this deed of self-consecration. To her it meant inexpressible depths of gratitude, and hope, and yet the endless solicitude.

It might have seemed as though in throwing in her lot with the Episcopal Church, Mrs. Brooks was breaking violently with the Puritan traditions. But to her the differences seemed un-

important. In the preaching of Rev. Dr. J. S. Stone, then
rector of St Paul's, she found the cultus of an inward experience,
the presentation of the personal Christ as the motive power of
true religion. Under his guidance she studied the Prayer Book,
and found solution for the problems which confronted her.

The coming of Dr. Vinton to St. Paul's was a great event in
the Brooks family, destined to influence its fortunes in the case
of all the children, no less than the religious life and belief of
the parents. In the year 1842, when he began his rectorship,
Phillips Brooks was six years old, and from that time until he
graduated from Harvard College and entered upon the preparation for the ministry, he was under the influence of this strong
personality. Dr. Vinton had a majestic appearance in the
pulpit. As an imposing representative of the clerical profession,
he was imaged in bronze upon the Soldiers' Monument on
Boston Common, in the act of blessing the troops on their
departure for the war. In the Episcopal Church he stood as its
foremost preacher, influential also in its administrative councils.
He, too, like Dr. Stone, was of the evangelical school, enforcing
the atonement of Christ as the supreme doctrine of the gospel,
urging also an inward conversion as the condition of its acceptance. He had the evangelical conception of the pastor's
office, a great ideal, which he had left the medical profession in
order to serve.

Among the features of his ministry at St. Paul's, one of the
most important was a Bible class, where he explained Christian
doctrines, or commented on the Epistle and Gospel for the day,
or at times took up the books of Scripture. To the sessions of
this Bible class Mrs. Brooks went regularly, going with a purpose,
in order that she might better teach her children. She gave
to them in her own impressive way what Dr. Vinton had given
to her. In this task of teaching her children religion she was
indefatigable, laboring with a concentrated purpose in season
and out of season, never for a moment forgetful of her mission,
quick to seize the passing moment which seemed fertile for
opportunity, but withal gentle and alluring, and making religion
attractive. The children's earliest remembrance of her was
at their bedside, repeating to them Bible stories as they were
going to sleep. She did not relax her sense of religious respon-

sibility when childhood passed into youth. Even after her sons had entered the ministry, she continued to watch and guard them as if they were in danger of beguilement with false doctrines.

On Sundays the rule was to go to church twice. It was also the custom of the children to learn hymns every Sunday, to be recited at the family gathering in the evening. When Phillips went to college there were some two hundred that he could repeat.

The life of the children was diversified by visits to their uncle's home in Medford, and especially in the summers to the old homestead in North Andover, where the grandmother was still living, venerated and beloved. Left a widow at a comparatively early age, with the responsibilities of a large family and the trials of a small income, she had maintained herself in honor and dignity, making her home an attractive spot, the centre of interest and devotion to the scattered and expanding family, until her death in 1856. Susan Phillips formed an important part of the household from the first, and was greatly endeared to all her nephews.

When he was four years old Phillips was sent to a private school on Bedford Street kept by Miss Capen. At the age of eight he went to the public grammar school, known as the Adams School, situated on Mason Street. A schoolmate writes of him, that, when school was out, he never went with the other boys to the near-by Common for games, but took his way down West Street, across Washington, down Bedford to his home. From the Adams School he passed at the age of eleven to the Boston Latin School in Bedford Street, remaining there for five years until his preparation for college was completed. Mr. E. S. Dixwell was the head-master when he entered, and was succeeded by the late Mr. Gardner in the last year of Phillips's attendance. It may have been the case that he was not over diligent as a pupil at first, or that the parents at home lamented some lack of devotion to his studies. Here is a document preserved, a scrap of paper, recording a great resolution:

"I, Phillips Brooks, do hereby promise, and pledge myself to study, henceforward, to the best of my ability.

"P. BROOKS.

"March 8, 1848."

At this time he was growing rapidly, having reached, when he was fourteen, the height of five feet eleven inches, a circumstance recorded in his father's journal. He is recalled as carrying his height awkwardly, leaning to one side as he walked, or holding to his older brother's arm. The Latin School gave to him the full benefit of its famous training in the classics, as well as the taste for their study. But it is in his literary work that the interest chiefly centres, where may be traced the first signs of his distinctive power. His essays are preserved, each one carefully written in his best style of penmanship. His handwriting closely resembled that of his father, who attached importance to these things; while his mother was more indifferent, writing rapidly and carelessly from a full heart, only anxious to make her meaning clear.

In his early essays may be seen the characteristics of the future man. His favorite illustration of the sunlight of truth is here. There is a desire to get all the aspects of the subject. There is moral purpose, a consciousness as if he were responsible for the well-being of the whole world, and were aiming at nothing else; the determination to secure the completest self-culture. He gives the rein to his enthusiasm, his vocabulary grows richer, his confidence in his powers increases. There is still formality of expression and a certain old-fashioned conventionality, the limited range of a schoolboy's information. But his own thought and observation of life, whether gained by books or by experience, are uttered with a deep emphasis, as though he would have been driven to speak by the impelling power of his own emotion. One can discern that he is writing better than he knows. He is uttering sentiments which will be the staple of his teaching as a mature man. It is unreal, for there is no experience behind it, and yet it is prophetic, giving one a reverence for the early stages of his growth. His rank in his class was third, when he graduated, and he was one of six to take the Franklin medal, which stood for excellence in the final examinations. What the Latin School had been to him, is best told in his "Address at the 250th Anniversary," on the occasion of the dedication of its present building, after the lapse of thirty years since he left it.

In 1851, when he was still some months short of his sixteenth birthday, Phillips Brooks entered Harvard College according to the custom of his ancestors. As he went simply from Boston to Cambridge, it was not like leaving home for college. The time from Saturday to Monday in every week was spent with his family. He attended St. Paul's Church, and was under the same parental and pastoral influences which had followed him through the Latin School. Harvard had not then begun to develop into a university. Its distinction lay in its age and its traditions. It possessed distinction in its corps of teachers; literature was represented by Longfellow, the natural sciences by Agassiz and by Asa Gray; Benjamin Peirce was teacher of mathematics; Sophocles and Felton stood for the classics, and Bowen for metaphysics; Child and Lane and Cooke were young men, beginning their long and honored careers as teachers in English, in Latin, and chemistry. The president of the college from 1852 was Dr. James Walker, who exerted a strong influence on the young men, both in the pulpit and the classroom, whose high character was recognized, admired, and imitated.

The total number of students in the college in 1851 was 304, and in all the departments, 626. The library contained 60,000 volumes. Attendance at prayers was required twice every day and once at church on Sundays. The hour of daily morning prayers was seven o'clock from September to April, and six o'clock from April to the close of the college year. Three recitations were made each day with sufficient intervals between for the preparation of lessons: from eight to nine, from twelve to one, and from five to six.

Phillips Brooks became a Harvard man at once, throwing himself into college life, reflecting that peculiar quality with which Harvard stamps her children. He became a member of the Institute, of Alpha Delta Phi, the Hasty Pudding Club, and of Phi Beta Kappa. He took his part in the Pudding theatricals, but his cast was generally determined by his height, which according to his father's measurement on his entering college was six feet three and one half inches. The studies in which he excelled were the languages. In Greek he took uniformly the highest mark, and was very close to the highest in Latin. Of French he had a good reading knowledge but paid no attention to its refinements. German he took as an elective and became able to read it with comparative ease. He does not appear to have aimed at high standing in his class, but to have been fitting himself for a teacher's profession, where his preference would have been the Greek language and literature. In other studies, his standing was not a high one, but he had a peculiar gift which always enabled him to succeed at an examination. Whatever might have been his grade mark for the daily recitation, his mark at an examination was apt to be a high one, not seldom the maximum.

His grade was not as high as one might have expected in such work as forensics and themes, nor did he give any sign of becoming an orator. It is recalled of him in his college days that he despised elocution as at war with naturalness and simplicity. But he could not have been wholly unattractive or without impressiveness as a speaker even in his college days, though still awkward and embarrassed by shyness. His earliest delivery was identical in manner with his latest, marked by the same extraordinary rapidity of utterance. This rapidity of speech was constitutional; it was not adopted to cover any natural defect, such as stammering; it was the natural expression of the man.

His standing when he graduated was thirteenth in a class numbering sixty-six. His concentration on the classics, taking easily the other work required, enabled him to turn to literature, where his reading was large and wisely chosen. Here he was pursuing an independent development unshackled by prescription or authority. Inspiring as were his teachers, there was no dominating influence, carrying him away captive to some other power than his own. The work he was doing for himself was quite as important as that done for him. He did not at first turn to the great writers who were then moulding the thoughts of their generation, but to the older school represented by Walter Scott and Washington Irving. To the writers of the eighteenth century he seems to have been particularly drawn, to Boswell's *Johnson*, Johnson himself, Goldsmith, Dryden, Swift, Leigh Hunt, Hume, and others. The poets of the eighteenth century and of the early nineteenth had for him a special charm. He read Shakespeare and books illustrating his age. He took up Lamb and Southey, but did not so early discover Milton, Coleridge, or Wordsworth. There was a calming influence in these writers of the eighteenth century, with their simple world, at wide remove from the desire for reforms, the agitation, the aspirations, the new interpretations of the age into which he was born. Here lay something of the preparation for his life work. He gained a picture of life in another age, which afforded a basis for comparison and criticism when he should come to the work of his own time. He learned to know and to honor the purely human amidst the disguises of past generations. These writers of the eighteenth century harmonized with his favorite classics, reflecting their influence and something of their outlook on life.

Later in his college course he turned to writers of his own age. Among the books which left an impression was Carlyle's *Life of Cromwell*. It created a deep interest in the names associated with the Puritan struggle. From that time he began to be at home with its personages, with Milton and Baxter and Jeremy Taylor; measuring its issues and growing stronger by their contemplation. In after life it was his ambition to write a Life of Cromwell, for which he made preparation by collecting materials in his visits to England. Carlyle's *Heroes and Hero-Worship* became a handbook for a time. The *French Revolution* he admired to the last, as a masterpiece of art, but for *Sartor Resartus* he came to have a feeling of contempt as a hollow and superficial cry. He read Emerson, but there are no traces of an influence upon his mind, such as Carlyle produced. The writer who exerted the strongest influence was Tennyson. *In Memoriam* had been published in 1849. From the time he read it, it kept running in his head; he imitated its metres and its subjects in poetic efforts of his own.

A classmate of Phillips Brooks at Harvard recalls his physical inactivity. He took no part in games or athletic sports. He did not care much for walking; it was hard to drag him out for a walk. But on the other hand his "intellectual faculties were in course of rapid yet not too rapid development. He read largely and, though not superficially, yet with an extraordinary speed. He was endowed with a marvellous gift of very rapidly taking in a printed page." His intellectual force is revealed in a series of essays, written to be read before the various societies to which he belonged. In them may be seen unusual gifts of expression, a varied vocabulary, together with insight and maturity of thought. Among other characteristics here disclosed is the power of observation,—the gift of seeing clearly and distinctly, and of seeing things in their relations. What he learned from books and teachers was important but was a small part of his equipment compared with what he gained from the observation of life. To this gift was joined another, the power of imagination, enabling him to enter wide realms of experience, through no experience of his own. He was gaining that knowledge of the world of which Goethe has remarked that it is "inborn with the genuine poet, so that he needs not much experience or varied observation to represent it adequately."

One of these college essays deserves to be mentioned, for it took the first Bowdoin prize in his Junior year,—"The Teaching of Tacitus regarding Fate and Destiny." Here he may be seen delving in the sources, and drawing his own conclusions, reconstructing a distant age by his imagination, analyzing a personality, applying to Tacitus and his age the law of human development. To the *Harvard Monthly* of 1854, he contributed a paper on "The English Table Talkers," which has one sentence worth citing in view of his career: "Men like to be talked to better than to be preached at; they prefer the easy chair to the pulpit." The point with which he is mainly concerned is that the secret of charm in all these talkers lies in their unveiling of themselves, so that we see the simple, natural, unaffected men, "the least artificial of men in their least artificial mood." In this same essay, when speaking of Walpole, he gives his estimate of the value of letter writing: "Men do not drop true genius into the post-office or trust the evidence of a great soul to the letter bag." To this judgment, he seems to have adhered throughout his life, with some few notable exceptions.

When we turn from literary influences to inquire what forces were acting upon his religious life, we are met with reserve and an almost unfathomable silence. He kept no journal to record his impressions or his aspirations. It could not have been long before he felt the expansion of his religious horizon, in whose unaccustomed vastness many familiar landmarks must have shifted their relative positions. In these years great changes were taking place in the religious world. But New England differed widely in its distinctive religious development from the mother country. Harvard was a stranger to any such religious reformer as John Henry Newman. Phillips Brooks does not seem to have heard of Newman while in college. Next to Emerson, who to some extent was one of his religious teachers, the most potent influence disturbing familiar convictions was Theodore Parker. Since 1852 he had been preaching in the Boston Music Hall. In 1852 he published his *Ten Sermons of Religion*, and in 1853 his *Theism, Atheism, and the Popular Theology*. He was at once the delight of some, but the terror of the many. There was sensitiveness on the subject in the Brooks household. The mother was alarmed at the growth of his influence. Whether Phillips Brooks listened at any time to Parker's preaching, or had at this stage of his life read any of Parker's sermons, is not known.

It was the essence of Parker's teaching that the divine revelation must be submitted to the tribunal of human reason. No external authority must be allowed to overawe the soul of man made in the divine image, with the capacities of the divine nature, and endowed by the divine will with insight and authority. This was the clash and struggle of the middle of the century, On the one side, Newman, pleading for the submission of the soul, without examination, to external authority, and on the other hand, Parker, demanding the soul's emancipation from obedience or even deference to any tradition.

Connected with this conflict was that phenomenon so common in this period, what is called "religious doubt." It affected young men in the universities wherever thought had been awakened. Tennyson had illustrated it in his *In Memoriam*. For those to whom it would be moral and intellectual suicide to submit to Newman's guidance, but did not feel competent to sit in judgment upon the issues of the traditional faith, Tennyson became for the time a religious teacher, as well as the truest of poets.

In the soul of Phillips Brooks there was some disturbance. He delayed presenting himself for the rite of confirmation. His ancestors had gone through religious experience while in college, which ended in joining the Church, at an early age. But he continued to postpone the decisive act during his years in college. There was a religious society in the college, the Christian Brethren, in which one of his ancestors had been prominent, but of this he was not a member. His college essays reveal no tendency to dwell upon the subject of religion. This is in contrast to his theses in the Latin School. His earlier boyish efforts expressed religious faith based on the home teaching, in emphatic and even enthusiastic form, but it was premature and unreal. A profound and independent process was required before it became in the realest sense his own. When he returned to the formulas, so easily accepted at first, it would be with a consciousness of appropriation, making them new. We may surmise the working of his spirit at this moment. There were depths in his nature which had not been reached by the ministrations of his pastor. There was a reconciliation to be accomplished between what he had been taught by others and what he was learning by himself.

When he graduated at Harvard in 1855 he was but nineteen, his twentieth birthday being six months distant. He was still a boy in feeling and manner. How he then appeared to a timid Freshman, looking up to the Seniors with too great deference, is told by one who sat at the same table with him, observing the grace of his ways and fascinated by the wonderful charm of his face. He would take the opportunity to push dishes to the end of the table, where the Freshmen sat, who would otherwise have failed to get their rightful share. He took one of the Freshmen aside on one occasion, and solemnly urged him to greater self-assertion. The college, he said to him, really belonged to the Freshman class, who were just entering and had their college life before them, rather than to the Seniors, like himself, who had had their day and were about to leave.

A prominent feature in the character of Phillips Brooks, throughout his life, was his reserve. It manifested itself at Harvard in refusal to talk of himself or of his purpose in life. His manner is remembered as quiet and undemonstrative, not particularly noticeable in any way. Among his friends he displayed that fine capacity for trifling which certainly did not diminish in his later years. One of his classmates, Mr. G. C. Sawyer, contributes this picture from memory:

"Phillips Brooks, though a quiet man in college days, was the brilliant writer, taking prizes for English essays and doing the best writing at all times in the various societies to which he belonged. At the same time it was, I remember, noticeable how, outside of this literary vein so markedly brilliant, he did not, except occasionally, let himself out in conversation. He was playful, even boyish, at times bright and witty in his speech. He distinctly refused, as in later years, to be drawn; and I call to mind one time when an importunate classmate, more obtrusive than considerate, had forced him to a long walk for the too manifest purpose of drawing him into literary or philosophic converse, came back, to the amusement of those of us who knew Brooks's moods better, quite discomfited at having got from him little but the persiflage which on occasions he understood so well how to use.

"Thus early in life he was distinguished by nothing more than by a dislike of show and of putting himself or his opinions forward. At the same time there never was a doubt in the minds of his college friends or his instructors that underneath lay a rich vein, so deep down that it promised when worked to be developed into products of marvellous value. Even then he had, I may say, his worshippers, who foretold great things of him. But then, as afterwards, he was always noticeable for putting aside anything that looked like adulation even from friends. His best efforts seemed to come easily and naturally.

"The lines of Wordsworth come to me in thinking of those youthful days when, with his great powers still in their formative state, he went in and out among us, 'moving about in worlds not realized.'"

Whether he had thought of the Christian ministry as his future vocation is uncertain. He was aware of the prevailing sentiment among young men of his age, that the Church did not offer the prospect of the highest usefulness. But the result of his years at Harvard had been of a nature to prepare him directly for his sacred calling. "He was that rare and blessed creature," as was said of Arthur Hallam, "anima naturaliter Christiana." Much yet remained to be done before his preparation would be complete. When he left college, he was a humanist, dwelling on the sacredness, the beauty, and the joy of the secular life. The tendencies inherited from his father's family were uppermost. But there was another inheritance from his mother and his stricter Puritan ancestry, the God consciousness with which he must reckon in the future. Signs of its presence were not wanting; its latent force may have deterred him from too easily making the formal profession of the Christian life. But he himself is the best commentator on the significance and result of these early years. In a sermon on the "Sacredness of Life" (1882) he has given a glimpse of his autobiography at this turning point in his career. No one realized more intensely than he the significance of the landmarks of life.[1]

[1] Cf. *New Starts in Life, and other Sermons*, by Phillips Brooks, pp. 108*ff.*

CHAPTER II.

1855–1856.

FAILURE AS A TEACHER IN THE BOSTON LATIN SCHOOL.
EXTRACTS FROM NOTE-BOOK. BEGINNINGS OF
RELIGIOUS EXPERIENCE. DEPARTURE FOR THE
THEOLOGICAL SEMINARY OF VIRGINIA.

AFTER leaving college, Phillips Brooks took the position of a
teacher in the Boston Latin School, beginning his work there
in September, 1855, not yet having reached his twentieth birthday. It does not appear as a mere temporary expedient, adopted
until he could look about for some other and better opening in
life. He had formed a plan of remaining for a while in the Latin
School to gain experience and then to go abroad for study in
order to fit himself for a professorship. Beneath the nonchalant
tone of college talk there existed a high ideal. He writes to
one of his classmates, soon after he had entered on his work:
"Seriously, I like the life. Is n't there a sort of satisfaction
and pleasure in knowing that you are doing, or at least have the
chance of doing something. At Cambridge it was all very well,
but we had only ourselves to work on. Here we have some
twenty, thirty, or forty on whom we can bring to bear the authority and influence of a superior position and see what we can make
out of them and watch all their workings. You think this is a
funny way for me to talk, but I really think so." He was well
fitted for his position so far as intellectual equipment went. He
taught Greek and Latin, the studies he had specially cultivated
while in college; but he found it necessary to acquire a more
competent knowledge of French, which he had taken easily.
In this he did not succeed so well as he wished. He speaks
of his teaching French as slip-shod work, which he would like
to escape from to firmer ground. For the first two months or

more, things went pleasantly with him; "everything," he writes, "is working in the quiet regular way in which it has settled for the winter." But hardly had the winter opened when trouble set in, serious trouble, since he could write to his college friend and say of the class he was teaching, "They are the most disagreeable set of creatures without exception I ever met with"; or again, speaking of himself, "I am tired, sick, cross, and almost dead." In a letter dated January 19, 1856, it is evident that the situation is a strained one, and that failure is impending:

"I am very much obliged to you for your last letter and the sympathy which you express with the laboring ruler of my rebellious subjects. I have had very considerable trouble, but matters have lately been getting a little better. Things have settled down into a strong feeling of quiet hate, which is eminently conducive to good order and rapid progress. In all my experience of schoolboys and schoolmasters I cannot recall a single teacher who was honored with such an overwhelming share of deep, steady, honest unpopularity as is at this moment the lot of your harmless and inoffensive friend. I believe they consider me just now as a sort of dragon with his claws cut, a gigantic ogre who would like to eat them, but has n't the stomach to do it. If I should adopt your plan of weekly receptions I should deem it safe first to procure a complete suit of chain armor to be privately worn so that not a heel might be exposed to the assassin's knife of some bloody members of the Third Class of the Public Latin School. It may be needful to explain that I have changed my class. The one I had before were splendid little fellows; these are tough old sinners with the iniquity of some sixteen springs, summers, autumns, and winters on their grim hoary heads. I am teaching them French which they don't, Greek which they won't, and Virgil which they can't understand or appreciate. . . . The idea of asking me whether I have read any books! I work like a dog in school and out, and the Lord knows where it is going to end. You must excuse this very selfish letter. It is a great relief and pleasure to talk with you even on paper and on so poor and trite a subject as a discomfited usher. Let me hear from you when you can, and if you know of a profitable school anywhere in the country just drop a line to your downtrodden friend."

By February, 1856, the trouble had culminated and he was obliged to abandon his place. Under the date February 8th, his father records in his journal:

"An occurrence took place to-day that has given us some anxiety, that of son Phillips's inability to maintain his position as usher in the Latin School. It was entirely for the want of discipline. He was not enough of a disciplinarian to maintain the necessary good order, and he was put at the head of a class of thirty-five boys that were rowdy and unruly and had already had two masters who had left them. Not receiving the necessary assistance and advice from the Principal, I was obliged to advise his resignation. The class of boys were from fifteen to seventeen years of age, and he is but twenty. The task was too much for him, and he is now looking for work."

The failure of Phillips Brooks on the threshold of life was conspicuous and complete, momentous also, and, it may be said in view of his later career, providential. The following reminiscence communicated to the Massachusetts Historical Society, after Brooks's death, by its president, Mr. Charles Francis Adams, shows the impression the event made on others:

"I cannot remember the time when I did not know Phillips Brooks. He was my second cousin, for his father and my mother were cousins-german. So, at almost the first school I ever went to,—a little dame school kept in a small wooden house then standing on Bedford Street, immediately in the rear of Church Green, as the enclosure on Summer Street was called whereon stood the New South meeting-house, in which Dr. Alexander Young then ministered,—in this antiquated little wooden edifice, long since removed, Phillips Brooks and I learned our letters; both of us, I take it, then being about the age of five or six. Some eight or ten years later, I next met him at the Boston Latin School, where he was one year in advance of me. Later on we were in college together; he still a year ahead, graduating in 1855. Of him at Cambridge I retain a distinct and pleasant recollection, for we were in many of the same societies, and he had already evinced that peculiar facility of written expression in which afterwards he won renown, and he was always chosen as a matter of course to deliver society orations and read literary papers. . . . Those were indeed golden, precious days,—those days passed in the June sunshine of the college grounds with young men who seemed in no way unusual in our every-day eyes, but who in fact were filled, as the result soon showed, with infinite possibilities, the Bayards and Sidneys and Bossuets of the fast-coming years,—days I failed, as under like circumstances we all of us always fail, to appreciate at the time, and so grasp them and delight in them as they pass. . . .
"After Brooks graduated, he became one of the ushers at the

Boston Latin School, then presided over by Francis Gardner,—a man whom many here will remember, rough and harsh in exterior, but not without a kindly side for those whom he liked. To those he did not like a harder and less charitable man it would not be easy to find; and those who knew both Francis Gardner and Phillips Brooks would feel instinctively at once that Francis Gardner could never have taken kindly to Phillips Brooks. . . .

"While Phillips Brooks was thus earning his living as usher at the Boston Latin School and waiting for the future to reveal itself to him, I was studying law in the office of Richard H. Dana. I soon learned that Phillips Brooks was in trouble. The master complained that the usher had in him no single element of a successful school-teacher,—that he was unable to maintain order among the boys in his room, and, in short, that the good of the school peremptorily required an immediate change. The change accordingly was decided on, and Brooks's resignation called for. But the young man selected to take his place was not immediately available, and a question arose as to what was to be done during the intervening time,—a period perhaps of two or three weeks. Moved, probably, more by the humor of the thing than by any other motive, and not unwilling to try my hand in a new field, I suggested that I should make the experiment of taking charge of Brooks's room until the new master came. Years before I had been in Mr. Gardner's classes, and he saw fit to receive the suggestion with favor, though at first somewhat amused by it, as he had never looked on me as a possible instructor of youth; but I am led to believe that he expressed his conclusions in terms not necessarily complimentary to either Brooks or myself, intimating in his usual rough way that any change, no matter what, could hardly fail to be for the better. He thought, however, that in common decency the opportunity should be given Brooks to remain until his successor appeared, though he hardly believed he would do so. But in this Master Gardner was mistaken. Phillips Brooks, though both discouraged and cut to the quick by his failure, did wish to remain until his successor appeared; and as my services were thus dispensed with, I never occupied an usher's chair.

"Now comes the point of my reminiscence. Shortly after this, as I was told at the time and have since seen no occasion to disbelieve, Phillips Brooks—humiliated, discouraged, utterly broken down, indeed, by his complete failure at the threshold of life, not seeing well or at all in what direction to turn or to apply his hand—went despondently to some man in his family acquaintance of assured success, and in the depth of his disappointment and mortification asked him for advice,—could he suggest any way in which it would be possible for him, the recent graduate and the future great preacher, to earn a living! . . .

" This experience of Phillips Brooks, the memory of which I do not doubt he carried with him to the end,—and he, too, I fancy, like myself, though for other reasons, felt a sense of satisfaction, approaching relief, when that gloomy, ugly Latin School edifice in Bedford Street was levelled with the ground and a thoroughfare made to occupy the site where it stood, for it recalled no pleasant memories to either of us,—that early, mortifying Latin School experience, I say, Phillips Brooks doubtless carried freshly with him to the grave."

It seems to have been an accident which defeated Brooks's purpose to make teaching his profession in life. If he had not been transferred from the charge of one of the younger classes to a class which had made itself a reputation for mischief and turbulence, and had already succeeded in ousting his two predecessors; or if he could have had the proper backing from the head-master in efforts to control it; if he had possessed age and experience and self-discipline, instead of coming directly to his difficult task from the spontaneity and irresponsibility of college life; or if he had been less quick in his sense of humor, or not so embarrassed by a constitutional shyness—if these and other conditions are granted, it can be conceived that his work might have been successful. But it is the misery of such failures as this that they cannot at the time be explained.

It was then a catastrophe complete, final, and humiliating. To have sought for another similar position under the circumstances was hopeless. The head-master had offered consolation to Brooks after his discomfiture, in the remark that he had never known any one who failed as schoolmaster to succeed in any other calling.[1] It was an event calling for comment among a large circle of acquaintances, who had expected great things. Nothing was wanting to make the sense of mortification supreme. And no one could know at the time, that in the failure lay the germ of his later triumph. It was as if the world spirit had already fastened upon him for its own, and resented the possibility of his loss to its own mysterious purpose. He did not see it at the time, perhaps he never fully acquiesced in the verdict of the power that makes of men what they do not contemplate,

[1] For Phillips Brooks's estimate of Mr. Gardner, *cf.* "Address at the 250th Anniversary of the Boston Latin School," in *Essays and Addresses*, pp. 419–422.

that carried him away and bore him aloft, but first took him into the wilderness, till it had been shown him what he must do.

The letters of Phillips Brooks in the six months after his resignation from the Latin School have an indifferent tone; they are couched in the dialect of a college student, who has not yet recovered from the thraldom of college life; they show how deeply and completely he had entered into its spirit. It had been to him a time of emancipation from the law of the household, when he had enjoyed his independence, when the mere pleasure of living had been a sort of intoxication. He had seen college life in its varied phases, associating with all sorts and conditions of men, watching what is called the Bohemian temperament, while scorning its lower manifestations and its false conception of life. His identification with the standards and fashion of the college world was the more complete because of his quick sensibility to external influences. His reserve would have prevented him from showing the more serious purpose within, even had that purpose begun yet to stir his spiritual nature. He was struggling against the temptations of youth, fighting his battle with the passions of his nature, and the strength of the conflict was greater in proportion to his greater capacities for good and evil. But even this conflict he disguised, wearing his mask so well that to some who knew him his life at moments seemed like a rudderless ship, whose sails hung idly, flapping with the breeze, as though it were uncertain what his decision would be. No strong and avowed religious consecration kept him from falling, but rather the habit of Christian nurture, the unconscious virtue, the respect for moral traditions. His fall came, or what corresponds to it, when he was put to the test of actual life and succumbed in the struggle with a class of turbulent boys. Although he had chosen the calling of a teacher in sincerity and with a high ideal of its possibilities, yet he still lacked the highest fitness and the inward consecration, for he was postponing the deeper spiritual issues of life.

One who read himself as he did, and was so alive to all that was passing within, could not have been unaware of a great issue postponed. But we encounter here a reserve so deep that it is impossible to do more than surmise. This much seems to be clear, that he had not been reached by the religious teaching at

St. Paul's Church, and to a certain extent was in revolt against it. While in college he had listened with a critical mind. He is still remembered as he sat in the family pew, at the end of the pew, where, crouched down with his head between his shoulders, one could not tell whether or not he were paying attention to the preacher. But it is evident that he heard, and from some of the teaching dissented. The Christian life, as presented by the Evangelical school, of which Dr. Vinton was a representative, called for a renunciation of much which he knew or believed to be good. The denunciation of the intellect as a dangerous guide, and of wealth as a thing to be avoided, the condemnation of the natural joy in life and its innocent amusements, the schism between religion and life,—against all this he inwardly protested. If this was what devotion to the law of God demanded, he was not ready to make the sacrifice of his will.

In this interval of waiting, Dr. Vinton, meeting his father, sent word to Phillips to come and see him. His father replied that Phillips would not then see any one, but that after he got over the feeling of mortification in consequence of his failure he would come. His first step toward recovery was to lay his case before the president of Harvard College, to whom he had listened occasionally in the college chapel on Sunday evenings. Dr. Walker was a confessor to souls by an inward divine appointment. He encouraged him to study for the ministry. "He encouraged me," said Brooks, alluding to the incident in later life, "but he was not enthusiastic; he was not an enthusiastic man." President Eliot, at that time a tutor in the college, recalls how he met Brooks at the door coming from the interview and was struck by his appearance.

The six months after leaving the Latin School were a gloomy period, when the depression of his spirit reached its lowest degree. He read and studied, mainly classical writers, and kept up his reading of German, perhaps from habit, or the necessity of doing something, or as though there were still some possible prospect in the future of his becoming a teacher. He wandered through the streets of Boston, meeting now and then a classmate or college friend. He made a list of the names of his class, jotting down against each name what occupation he had found, for what profession he was planning. The mortification of failure rested like an incubus on his proud and sensitive spirit. College experience had not yet relapsed into its true perspective. He was still hanging about the place of the gay assemblage when the guests were gone and the lights were out. We can hardly exaggerate the trial he was passing through. He had made his first essay at real life and had been defeated. He had been shut out from his Eden by a stern decree; a flaming sword confronted him which turned every way to keep him from his chosen vocation. In his desperation he had resolved to give up ambition for himself, to be content with the lowest and humblest place at the feast. He was much impressed with a book which had then just appeared, Souvestre's "Attic Philosopher" (*Un Philosophe sous les Toits, Journal d'un Homme Heureux*), the story of "a man who, in the midst of the fever, the restlessness and ambition which racks society in our time, continues to fill his humble part in the world without a murmur, and who preserves, so to speak, the taste for poverty. With no other fortune than a small clerkship, which enables him to live within the narrow limits separating competence from want, our philosopher looks from the heights of his attic upon society as upon a sea, of which he neither covets the riches nor fears the wrecks. Too insignificant to excite the envy of any one, he sleeps peacefully, wrapped in his obscurity." So impressed was he with the lesson of the book that he wrote a short story, working up the experience of the sisters Frances and Madeleine, in his own way, with a conversation upon it, where different speakers express their judgments upon life.

The need of expression was imperative, and yet there was no one to whom he could unburden himself; he hardly knew what the burden was. In walking the streets of Boston he was alone as if in the desert, for the waste of his experience was a veritable Horeb, and like the prophet, he was receiving a revelation within. He now began to commit his thoughts to writing, and in so doing gained a clearer vision and a new courage. There is reserve here, even to himself; but as we read we become aware that we are listening to the cry from the depths, *suspiria de profundis*, the breathings of an awakening soul, the confessions of an inquiring spirit.

"' How pure in heart, how true in head,
With what divine affections bold,
Must be the man whose soul would hold
An hour's communion with the dead !'

"These, I think, are exactly the feelings with which we should
approach the study of a life which has been lived here on earth.
I think that in our democratic grouping of mankind we recognize
too little the individualities of individual human natures. We
read too little the infinite variety of the human mind. I think
the man never yet lived who could fully, sympathetically, and
understandingly appreciate any other man. Each mind and soul
in the fulness of its powers and its weaknesses, its capacities and
its deficiencies, is more or less a riddle unread and unreadable by
every other mind and soul. . . ."

" Mind, intellect, we can measure only by original thought.
Knowledge may show a man's application, wealth may declare
his industry, power may prove his tact (his smartness, we call it
here); this alone can establish the depth and worth and power of
his mind. If Plato or Aristotle were to come on earth to-day
just as they left it some twenty centuries ago, you or I could take
them to school; we could teach them new facts in science, new
truths in religion, new events in history, new lessons in worldly
wisdom, but would we therefore boast of greater intellect, truly
speaking, greater knowledge, than Plato or Aristotle? Our pupils
would take our teachings even from our lips, but how soon we
should find that they had passed into them with a power that they
never had in us; that what we had learned and taught as new
they were using as gods, and our facts and truths, events and
lessons, growing pliant in those old hands, would melt and mould
in purer and stronger shapes of symmetry and truth."

" It seems sometimes as if the world had to come back every
little while and prove its first principles. Those primary truths
which are constantly in use grow, as if by friction, smooth and
tame and dull. Men build their heavy structures of religion,
policy, and law on what they honestly and earnestly believe a firm
foundation, and then taking their foundation for granted they forget it for a while and go on with their superstructure. But the
world's little or large waves are beating, heard or unheard, down
below, till some son or son's son dreams that the basis which his
father laid is safe and sound after all, and he goes down and tries
it again and once more begins the bulky work. The world comes
forever back to Pilate's question, What is truth? What do I
believe and why do I believe it? It has proved that our fathers
were mistaken about the planets; let us see whether they knew

about the soul. These investigations are occasional, and (it is both a good and a bad sign) they seem to grow more frequent. Is not one going on now? There was one in Luther's time, another in the later mythologists', and still another in the prophets'; all were more partial and more reverent than this last."

" How often we are made to feel that there is very much in us which our nearest friends do not and cannot know. I do not think there is a man living, however base or weak or dull or commonplace, who does not in some waking moment of his dim life feel, perhaps with no more fulness than we may suppose an infant to enter into man's life, that he has more in him than he dares or cares or is able to show out, more of feeling, good or bad, more of power, more of manhood. How little we know of ourselves! How we are forever making discoveries in our own characters, tearing off disguises, tearing down old idols, tearing to pieces old rules and canons which were once like Heaven's truth to our blind hearts. Then we are always or often (not often enough) finding in ourselves new capacity and appreciation for goodness and beauty and truth, new rooms for knowledge and new desires to fill them. We do not know ourselves. And when I profess my ignorance of what I am, shall another pretend to teach me? Knowing far more than any one else knows of me, and knowing that I know it, I think we may learn from it a lesson of self-dependence or rather of independence of others; for here may we not see one of the secrets of man's need and craving and demand for a God, for something to trust to? I and you know neither ourselves nor each other; every day we feel it more and more. But not to be all unknown we may find one who knows us both; and while in self-distrust and mutual ignorance we are separated from each other, let us rest with Him and make through Him a surer union for ourselves. We may love God not only because He made us and guards us and supports us, but also because He knows us, and thus our love to Him will be essentially different in kind from that which any human creature has ever excited, or can ever excite, in any other. The fulness of know- ledge, where no richer or deeper can be hoped, will be to know then, just as we may feel or find comfort in the feeling that we are known now."

" How much power is lost or impaired in this world by being in the wrong hands. I suppose every man has often felt that he has capacities in him which another man would turn (perhaps only from their combination with other qualities) to honor, or profit, or power of some kind, yet feeling all the while that in his own hand these selfsame capabilities are lying and probably wil*l* always lie unused. If this be so may we not suppose that we all possess, though they be not useful in us, all the germs or seeds, if not of all capacities, yet of many more than we are in the habit of using every day, and so hope that in a fuller and completer estate of being, when that which is in part shall be done away, this partialness of our own development and use may become obsolete, and we may awake and know ourselves, our powers, our abilities, our uses, and rise to new lives, new aims, new ends of being?"

"Most men read other men's lives as they would spell out a language of which they are ignorant, but which somewhat resembles their own. With the help of a word here and there, which looks a little like one with which they are familiar, they go bungling, stumbling, doubting through, reading a little, guessing at more, and letting the rest go altogether. Let such pray for a moral gift of tongues, a mental Pentecost which shall teach them the strange language in which their neighbors' lives are written. No one can ever know how far he is a fair specimen of his race, how well he embodies its average endowments and may serve as a sample to judge humanity. We may hope that we are none of us so,—an average man; a sample human must be a miserable creature."

"With how much clearness and precision we can often trace the steps by which a man has mounted to some leading principle, the mental ladder by which he has climbed to some great idea. The materials lie in everybody's hands; the only difficulty is in the ingenuity necessary for building them into shape, and the strength of head which is required to mount without dizziness from stage to stage. Every man must build his own ladder. We cannot use each other's. And it depends upon a man's own clearness and soundness of head whether, having reached the summit, he can cast off the steps by which he mounted, or needs them still to rest his eye on them for confidence and support."

"Some leading, settled, authoritative truth is a treasure to a man. The mind probably does not know what it needs while it is without it, but it soon feels that it is stronger and firmer the moment that it is gained. A thought once fully examined and weighed and approved, whose soundness is acknowledged, whose value is unquestioned, whose place is fully established, becomes from that moment a standpoint for the soul; other thoughts come to its confessional for approval or advice; like a magnet it draws the scattered fragments of other thoughts around it, binding them to itself and to each other, giving them a part of its own life, its own power, its own truth. Under such a thought the soul's government is firm, energetic, full of life, for it has a prerogative and a pre-established authority like a king's; and then if that kingly thought dies, with no other full grown and ready to succeed, an interregnum must ensue, and be, as always, vacillating, weak, and witless."

"A stranger's thought is to no one like his own. He may adopt, it and cherish it and call it his, but his blood is not in its veins nor the stamp of his likeness on its features. Not that we may not have the same thought for the beacon or the basis of our lives, but it must be natural and home-bred for each. You must not borrow it from me, nor I from you. Because it serves your life it is no sign either that it will or will not serve mine. That we must try for ourselves; and if we find it will not serve, then away with it, not as useless, but as useless for us. I may grant the beauty in which your soul as well as your body is dressed, but that soul garment of yours would fit and would become me not a whit more than your body's clothing. Another lesson of independent thought. I must have and must demand not only beauty and sublimity and power, but fitness and adaptability as well."

"A spark of original thought, a gleam of an idea which is his own, which he does not know to have visited another being, strengthens a man's feeling of individuality, but weakens his sense of race. It is an inspiring, ennobling, elevating, but not a social thing. But what a kindly power, what a warm human family feeling, clusters around a thought which we find common to our mind and to some old mind which was thinking away back in the twilight of time. The common idea binds us to that dead man with a friendship of the soul as warm and full and free as any which holds us to our living companions. So when we recognize a common impulse, or rule of life, or instinct of love and hate, we must feel humanity in its spirit bearing witness with our spirits that it is the offspring of a common divinity. When I find the great and poor, and wise and weak, of all ages, just such in some point as I am to-day, I cannot be an atheist. Hence the value of books. What a power is in them! What cosmopolites they are and make of us! Hence the beauty and the use of a perfect biography, the perfection of a perfect book. It consoles our weaknesses, for it casts them on humanity; it destroys our boasts and vanities, for it shares them with mankind. It makes us happier, purer, truer men by making us more human. To make a perfect biography a man's own self-knowledge ought to be united to a stranger's calm, impartial, disinterested judgment, a thing not likely to be seen on earth."

"Is it not almost time for some men to learn that their incessant railing at earthly riches and power and learning is doing far more harm than good, that men are really convinced on reasonable grounds that these things are good, worthy objects of ambition and endeavor, and that if they have higher and worthier advantages to offer, their way to recommend them must not be to decry and depreciate what little good man already possesses? Such men may thank merely the weakness of their cause and of themselves that their efforts are not productive of more serious effects. Once convince men that wealth, power, and learning are mean and despicable and wrong, and you have crowned inefficiency and ignorance, brutality and stupidity, as the monarchs of our race forever."

"The attempts to control and change belief by arbitrary commands, which appear so absurd and impossible as they were attempted at the time when the Reformation was going on, are perhaps not so strange after all, or rather the strangeness and false judgment lay not so much in the thing undertaken as in the manner in which the attempt was made. It has been done for ages, by Popes and Saints, by direct, open, undisguised, undoubting dictation. It is done now, and has been done ever since, by ministers and writers, by the quieter, but scarcely less arbitrary demands of personal influence, social custom, apparent logic, and blind individual reverence. Now the error of those who attempted this same thing and failed in the sixteenth century, as King Henry VIII. in England and others elsewhere, would seem to be that, living in a changing age, their age was a little in advance of them, they were passing from the old to the new way of receiving belief. They still clung to the old way of impressing it, and hence arose the trouble."

"How strangely at times we wake up to a new meaning or a new beauty in an old, dry commonplace that has been growing rusty on the lips of men for years,—one of those didactic heirlooms that father has handed down to son through long generations of stupidity. We have received it as stupidly as any before us, either stupidly thinking that we felt its force, or as stolidly scorning it as trite and lifeless. But sometimes a thought will come like an angel to the pool; our souls are troubled, and the old dead axiom finds its place as a living working thing; light breaks from its eye; its heart begins a human beating, its tongue is loosed, and the dumb speaks oracles. It is only another instance that man may hold power in his hands and not know it, another proof of life and energy that is passing for death all around us, because we are so far from perfect that we cannot make use even of all our imperfections."

" I may learn from the general indifference with which I am apt
to regard the private acts of other men outside of the narrow
circle of a few friends, that my deeds and words are not matters
of such interest to them as I am sometimes apt to dream, that
they comment upon them for a moment and then forget what is
of infinite importance to me forever. And so I may begin to
ponder less upon how my conduct strikes them and more on how
my duty urges me. And heeding them less in the present I may
also heed my own past less. "Let the dead past bury its dead."
Good or bad, it is gone now, and I have only to read its lessons
as far as I may learn to profit and grow by them; as we solemnly
and sadly close the eyes and draw the veil over the face of some
dear dead friend, and go out into the world, to live by his advice
and his memory a better and purer life."

" The choice of a profession is to a great extent the choice of a
life, for nothing can be more different than the habits, associations, relations of life into which the different professions cast us.
By one single decisive act all these are to be settled for all the
future. Up to the time of choice all have been general, common
to us with all young learning men, but now the broad, clear, open
road breaks and separates; its paths diverge in every direction
and bear all manner of appearances at their starting. Which
shall we take? And first one word as to the importance and the
difficulty of the choice. Whatever be our selection we shall probably never know it if we are wrong. Our dissatisfaction in the
pursuit which we have chosen will not prove that another would
have suited better. And as to trying them all and so satisfying
ourselves of the wisdom of our choice, it is impossible simply because we have only one short life and not three or four to live.
And again men who have made the choice years ago are little
more qualified to assist us than we are to help ourselves. Each
has tried only his own pursuit, and is unqualified, except on the
general grounds which we all possess, to speak of the pursuits of
others. If he has wasted his life in trying to test them all, he is
probably all the less qualified to speak of either. Again the conviction of the wisdom of my neighbor's choice will not assist me
in making mine. I may be sure that he is wise and right in
going to the bar, and yet know all the while perfectly well that
the most foolish thing I could do would be to stupidly follow him
there, walking in his steps because they are his steps, not because
they mark the pathway for which I was made. It is no place for
fashion. A wise man may follow his neighbors in the cut of his
coat, or the style of his manners; no one but the rankest fool will
give up his life to be moulded and modelled by their hands. We
must cast off then, once for all, all regard to the preferences or
prejudices of our friends if our selection is to be at all a wise

one. If I am to choose a life for *myself*, which I am to live and for which I am to answer, let the choice be *really mine*, let me say to my advisers: I receive your advice, but no dictation. Without presumption or vanity, humbly, earnestly, and firmly, I claim my own human and divine right to my own life. Likewise we must regard not at all those professional prejudices which, magnifying one pursuit, would make it the test of capability for success in all. I have heard an excellent schoolmaster say (or heard of his saying) that he never knew a man who failed in teaching to succeed in anything else. I humbly believe it was the schoolmaster and not the man who spoke. I have failed myself most signally in teaching school, but I am not yet quite ready to acknowledge myself wholly unequal to all this wide world's work."

"The *professions* as the term is generally used are three: Law, Medicine, and Theology. The protection of a man's rights, of his body, and of his soul, the three great barriers which, while he is hedging and ditching and tilling in his busy, bustling fields, are keeping out the destroying waters that would waste him and all his together. Law, the pledge of man's social being, the common friend that takes man's hand and placing it in his neighbor's bids him trust in social honor, integrity, and justice, embodying at once the sternest workings of human vengeance and the purest and most merciful spirit of human love, drawing its charter from the holiest source, God's eternal law, and making that charter the blessed agent for smoothing the world's rough roads alike for the clumsy feet of human governments and the humblest steps of common men who cannot but jostle each other in the rugged way,—Law, so often made powerless by debased humanity, is almighty in the inherent diversity of its nature. And Medicine, man's humbler but his truer friend, more immediately visible in the good it gives, standing by the sick-bed where the poor man lies tossing with his fever, wiping his clammy brow, moistening his parched lips, soothing and calming the racking of his exhausted frame, man's first visitor and his last, the most direct, the most efficient, the most apparent, of his benefactors all through his life. And Divinity, the most revered of professions or the most despised, which is either everything to man, or worse, far worse than nothing, either the most solemn and the most Godlike of truths or the most fearful and devilish of lies, whose very perversions and disgraces and abuses show its native worth, the nearest, dearest, most familiar of messages from God to man, which men reverence while they sneer at, and honor and worship in its nature when they most shudder and shrink from the dresses, all soiled and stained and of the earth, with which it sometimes claims that it is clothed,—surely, looking at the three thus in their purest and whitest abstraction, this last is not unworthy."

" Shelley at the age of seventeen writing *Queen Mab* seems to me, whatever we may think of the religion, the politics, and the ethics of that poem, to be one of the most remarkable sights on which we can ponder. It is not merely a boy of genius, like Chatterton or Byron or Keats. It is a boy man with all a boy's fire and young strength and young zeal and all a man's earnestness of purpose and belief. I must say the blasphemy, for we must use the word, of that strange poem has done more to make me a Christian than many a wise homily. How he stands with his young face intent to seize all the great converse of God and Nature which is ever speaking between earth and heaven And O, how sad to see him catching only Nature's half of the dialogue and thinking earnestly, indignantly, that he has heard the whole, and then with all the martyr spirit of a Huss, madly crying to religion and government, and commerce and marriage and God, that they are utter lies. I do not envy the man who can read the poem and, through all his horror at the sacrilege, and disgust and disapproval of the false morality, false logic, false history, and false hopes that fill it, not feel a thrill of honor and pity and love for the poor, pure world-wretched man who wrote it. How many men there are who have no truer light than he, but who can be content in darkness, which he could not, who want only his depth of feeling and height of genius to be what he was."

" Of the *Revolt of Islam* it seems to me to be the purest conception and embodiment of his creed as conceived and embodied by the purest soul that ever believed in the power of mere human love and joy and virtue to regenerate the world. And the great answer to his theory seems to be just where he was too pure to find it, in his own purity. Laon and Laone hardly lived in the earth, or even the stuff of which Laon and Laone might be made, outside of the mind of Shelley. The creed then which they could make, and which should then guard, guide, and comfort them, was a creed for them, not for mankind. . . . Shelley's error throughout seems to me too low an estimate of man's actual and too high a faith in man's (unaided) possible.

" The last sentence of the *Prometheus Unbound* should surely forever entitle the aspirations and longings of that poem for a purer world to respect and reverence. . . . If purity of heart and earnestness of purpose and perfect poetry of life and hopes and universal being be things to honor and revere, then we must give to Shelley full honor and esteem. . . . Who would not give months of our common, stale, dead days for one of his fullest, happiest, richest, silver, spirit-crowded days "

" The laws, especially those of early nations, consist much less of commands than of prohibitions. Man is more ready to do the good which is in him than to leave undone the evil. I think it is more to his credit than if the reverse were the case; this shows a want of self-restraint; that would argue positive malignity, and predilection for the wrong."

" The great analogies of nature are fossilized in the language of mankind. The clear stars give a name to the clearness of an eye; the ruddy roses to the blushing of a cheek; and even in more lofty moral things, the purity of the evening sky, the fresh nakedness of morning, the calm beauty of summer, and the stern majesty of winter give us terms and titles for the pureness, the energy, the calm devotion, or majestic duty of men's lives. The fullest, richest, and yet the truest of figurative language is what the tongue, untaught but capable of eloquence, learns among the woods and brooks and birds."

" Humanity has no sterner judge than human nature; mankind no stricter master than man. The great difficulty of the contemporary historian is to judge rightly where the tidemark of time will run, how high the waves will rise, what must be covered and what points will stand out to tell future men where the firm ground of his age once stood. All that is to be remembered must group round these points; all that can make its mark on them will tell. The greatness of the memory of things often differs much from the greatness of their reality in kind. The great glaciers that went crushing and crashing and crumbling over our continent uncounted ages ago are known and remembered to-day by a few faint scratches on a few old rocks. No historian will be perfect till he shall have fully learnt the perspective of history. Then he will be an artist with his art complete."

" We speak with enthusiasm of originality, but too seldom distinguish between its different kinds, between originality as a habit and originality as a life. One sparkles out here and there in a strangeness of thought or oddity of action, is often entertaining, sometimes awakening and so improving, but not generally very estimable. The other is a genuineness and self-reliance of the whole man. There may be no thought or act which has not been thought or done over and over again by men before. The peculiarity consists in its being home-bred and original over again, after all its triteness, with this new man; and in its new strength he is strong."

" Let us cultivate and reverently cherish the honest indignations of our nature, for they are the life and fire that is in us. God has given them, and the man is most happy who has them the warmest, the truest, the least wrenched by prejudice, the least dulled by sense and sin."

"The mind that never consciously repeats itself, that finds fresh thoughts and feelings always prompt when fresh occasions rise, never having to go back and take old dresses and recut, refit, and make them over to suit new needs, is blessed of God. It is hard to have to look to old emergencies to meet the new exigencies of life, demanding of the past not only memories and teaching which it owes us, but also the present powers and present resources which the present ought to furnish."

"With what care we should cherish each waking thought that bears a trace of nobleness or purity or strength, tend, foster, and watch it, 'for by so doing many have entertained angels unawares.' It may be our angel. We may soon see its bright wings unfold and the bright smile of heaven spread over its face, and it may take our hands and lead us over the rough, hard road, giving us hope and strength and purpose, when without it all would have been despondency and weakness."

A study of these reserved, almost impersonal utterances of Phillips Brooks discloses the birth of a new religious experience. In familiar religious parlance, it is the story of a conversion, but unlike any other recorded in the biographies of religious men. He appears in revolt against methods and principles in which he had been trained, but already he has begun the process of their reinterpretation, while some he rejects altogether. He is responding to what was distinctive in his age, but he is in no blind subjection. That he is contemplating the Christian ministry is apparent, also that he is reconciling himself to it. Great obstacles still confront him. There are traditions of talks with his fellow-students, to whom it seemed like throwing one's self away to enter the Church. This fear he undoubtedly shared himself, and it left its influence upon him. It was a fresh surprise to him throughout his life that the ministerial profession instead of limiting the range of human interests was a perpetual enlargement. He never spoke to young men on this subject in later years without telling them how full and free, how inexpressibly rich, was the clerical calling. But all this was yet to come to him in the slow course of years. That the reverse might be true was the danger that haunted him in this first crisis of his religious experience. Another objection, keenly felt by many, was the indifference of the Church to the humanitarian movement calling for the abolition of slavery. The inference was easy that the Church had ceased to keep pace with human progress. The appeal to throw in his lot with the cause of moral reform came with strength to one in whose blood ran the Puritan motive. But on the other hand was a conviction that traditional Christianity had not yet spent its force; that inherent in it was an unsuspected power yet to be revealed.

One other incident in this waiting period from February to October, in 1856, remains to be mentioned. He called upon Dr. Vinton, to ask what steps should be taken by one who proposed to study for the ministry. According to his own report of the conversation at a later time, Dr. Vinton said that it was customary to have received confirmation before becoming a candidate for orders, and also remarked that conversion was generally regarded as a prerequisite for confirmation. To this Phillips Brooks replied that he did not know what conversion meant. But Dr. Vinton rose above conventionalities. He approved of the plan to study for the ministry, and recommended the seminary of the Protestant Episcopal Church at Alexandria in Virginia as the place where the preparation should be made. Phillips Brooks seems to have left home suddenly for Virignia some weeks after the term had opened. Beyond his father and mother, he took no one into his counsels. To a remonstrance for his want of confidence in not telling his friends of the step he contemplated, he wrote in reply: "Please let all that matter drop. I said scarcely anything to any one about it but Father and Mother. Consider me here at the seminary without debating how I got here."

He closed the record of his thoughts on the eve of his departure with these words:

"*As we pass from some experience to some experiment, from a tried to an untried scene of life, it is as when we turn to a new page in a book we have never read before, but whose author we know and love and trust to give us on every page words of counsel and purity and strengthening virtue.*"

CHAPTER III.

1856–1857.

THEOLOGICAL SEMINARY AT VIRGINIA. NATURE AND EXTENT OF READING. EXTRACTS FROM NOTE-BOOKS.

"It is the five years after college which are the most decisive in a man's career. Any event which happens then has its full influence. The years which come before are too fluid. The years which come after are too solid." This remark of Phillips Brooks, when speaking of his friend Richardson, the architect, was based on his own experience, as a study of his years in the Virginia seminary will reveal. A unique interest attaches to his work as a theological student. He was making accumulations, fixing his methods, laying the foundations of his future greatness.

In his decision to enter a theological school, there was included a large tentative element. He had determined to give it a trial, but with grave misgivings about the result. He was chiefly afraid for himself that he should deteriorate and become content with some lower standard. On the other hand he had safeguards, which were qualifications for his work: a sense of humility, and the growing consciousness of a vocation. The following passage from a sermon, preached in 1879, may be taken as the commentary on his state of mind as he left home to begin the study of his profession:

" With regard to that time [the period of professional preparation], I think that all of us who have seen many men will bear witness that it is just there that many men grow narrow, and from being broad in sympathies, large, generous, humane, before, even in all the crudity of their boyhood, the moment of the choice of their profession seems to make them limited and special, shuts them up between narrow walls, makes them uninteresting to all the world outside their little work, and makes all the world ou side their little work uninteresting to them. . . . Where shall the larger spirit come from? The spirit of an act comes from its motive. There must be a larger motive then. And the largest of all motives is the sending of God, the commission of Him who is the Father of us all. . . . The true salvation from the sordidness and narrowness of professional life comes only with a profound faith that God sent us to be the thing that we are, to do the work that we are doing." [1]

It must have been an exciting and busy moment in the Brooks family when Phillips left home for the first time,— the mother's first call to this peculiar experience. When it came a second time, in the case of her son George, she spoke in a letter to Phillips of the pain it gave her, and how it had reminded her of his departure from home. The love which bound the household together was intensified by this event, so common, so familiar, and yet ever new. We speak of these things because no one could attach more importance to them than Phillips Brooks. From his childhood he recognized the mystery which broods over meetings and partings. But he was young, not yet twenty-one; it was like going to a new world; he was to see on the way the places he had long heard of and had been eager to see, the larger cities of his own country. He had in him the making of a traveller, and this was his first experience. His face was set towards the future, and beneath it all was the conviction, weak indeed, and yet growing, that God was sending him.

On his arrival at Alexandria, November 7, 1856, he wrote letters giving his first impressions:

" My lordly apartment is a garret in an old building called the Wilderness. Its furniture at present consists of a bedstead and a washstand. I looked in for a moment, threw down my carpet bag, and ran. I suppose I 've got to sleep there to-night, but I 'm sure I don't know how. There seem to be some fine fellows here. They are very hospitable, and would kill me with kindness if I would stand it. They are about half from the North and half from the South. I 'm in a perfect wilderness of names, for they 've been introducing me all around and I sha'n't know half of them again. I have seen the head, Dr. Sparrow, who is a thin, tall gentleman, with not much to say. So Buchanan is our next President. . . . Of course there is nothing of the

[1] *Cf. New Starts in Life and Other Sermons*, by Phillips Brooks, p. 12.

brutality of slavery here, but the institution is degrading the country just as much. All the servants are slaves. Those in the seminary are let out by their masters for so much a year, paid of course to the master just as you 'd pay for a horse hired. . . . I had a stunning time in New York: saw most of the lions, and almost walked my feet off all over the city. I passed through Baltimore while the fight was raging, and heard the whole town in an uproar. Philadelphia I liked very much, so far as I saw it. Washington is a sort of a skeleton affair, splendidly laid out and about half grown. The public buildings strike me as decidedly shabby. The Potomac is a splendid river; we can see it plainly from the seminary, as also the Capitol and Monument, etc., at Washington. The seminary has about 100 acres of ground, mostly covered with oak and hickory. The cedar and locust trees are very plenty in this neighborhood. I had to get my watch put twenty minutes back in Washington, which convinced me that I was getting some way from home. It is about three miles to Alexandria, and a very pleasant walk. I am a stronger Fremont man than ever, since seeing Buchanan and Fillmore States, and know nothing that I would not do to change the result. The only hope now is that he will make things bad enough to call forth a louder and wider indignation at the next election."

" I am looking for everybody whom I have any claim to write to, for an answer to a letter is a perfect boon in this remote place. You will find on consulting your map the dirty little city of Alexandria, about seven miles down the river Potomac from Washington, and about two miles back from the river behind Alexandria, on a high hill in the woods, stands this institution. It is a lonely, desolate sort of a place, with about forty students. . . . It is beautifully situated, overlooks the river and Washington. . . . I am beginning to buck into Hebrew pretty slowly, and like it extremely. It is the queerest old language I ever saw. I live almost entirely by myself, see little or nothing of the other students. . . . I imagine they don't think much of me. The course here is three years. I suppose I shall stay that time. The country and weather here is glorious. I never saw such moonlight nights in all my life. But the people are wretched, shiftless, uninteresting, lazy, deceitful. I suppose it is one of the best places to see the sad effects of slavery on the white population, degrading and unmanning them. I don't feel much like saying anything of the election [of Buchanan]. The people around here are delighted with the result, and crowing and exulting as if they had saved the land. There are crowds of slaves about here: very many of them, however, are hired from other parts of the State, and from other States, of their

masters They are a jolly-looking set of people. . . . I
have spent considerable time since I have been here over in
Washington sightseeing. There is ever so much to look at, and
next month, when Congress is sitting, it will be very lively.
At present it is dull enough so far as company is concerned. I
have just been invited to join a students' party in a sailboat to-
morrow, down the river to Mt. Vernon, and am going, but expect
it will be mighty slow. It is as unlike college as anything can
be. . . . I saw Sanborn shortly before I left Boston, and
had a long walk with him one Sunday afternoon. He was still
hopeful about election. I wonder how he feels now. He said
that if Buchanan was elected he went in dead for a dissolution of
the Union. Did you see the account of the riot in Baltimore
on election day? I came through there on that day, and the
whole city was in an uproar. I stayed there about an hour, and
was earnestly importuned to vote, in spite of non-residence and
everything else, many times. I sha'n't go near Mr. James
Buchanan's inauguration, although it is so near."

The years in which Brooks was at Alexandria saw events
rapidly moving toward civil war. One of them was the election
of Buchanan, accomplished by the Southern States with the aid
of Pennsylvania, New Jersey, Indiana, and Illinois. He had
been travelling to Virginia on election day. His letters are full
of political allusions, indicating that he shared in the anti-
slavery sentiments. He found it hard to adjust himself to a
country where slavery existed. What was going on in the
country at large was reproduced among the students in the
seminary, who were about equally divided in sentiment regarding the issues of the hour. There were suspicions rife at
Alexandria and in the seminary of a threatened insurrection
among the negroes, which had led to some manifestations of ill
feeling on the part of the Southern students against those who
came from the North. The latter had probably been active in
teaching the negroes to read and write, or had held religious
services for them. A member of the seminary at the time
writes of this affair:

"The 'dear old seminary' was not a very comfortable place
then for anti-slavery men, such as a few of us were, especially
if we exercised and claimed the right of free speech. When one
of our fellow-students was notified that he would be 'tarred and
feathered' if he did not leave, Phillips stood nobly by him, and

declared that the men of the North must all leave together and
publicly declare their reasons for withdrawing, unless they were
assured of protection and the liberty of free speech.   A petition
was sent to the faculty, and what we asked was granted; and
even public discussions were allowed in 'Prayer Hall.'   Slavery
was thoroughly reviewed in its political, moral, and religious
aspects, and leading Southern men frankly acknowledged that
they had known but little of the *animus* of the institution [sla-
very] until they heard these discussions; their views and feelings
were greatly modified."

To this description is added Phillips Brooks's comment in a
letter to his father:

" The affair of which I spoke in that letter, although it seems
pretty certain that it was all a groundless panic, is having a bad
effect.   It has excited much jealousy among the Southern students and the town people against the Northerners.   One Northern student, who has held a meeting once a week for the servants
of the seminary and the neighbors, has received notice that it
must be given up, or he will have to suffer. . . .   Another who
has preached some in the neighborhood, has been informed that
there was tar and feathers ready for him if he went far from the
seminary.   And in general they have been given to understand
that their tongues were tied and they were anything but free.   A
pretty style of life, is n't it? . . ."

The tone of his letters in other respects shows him dissatisfied
with his surroundings, depressed, and anxious to get away.   He
admits that if he were not twenty-one, he should say he was
homesick.   One striking peculiarity was his susceptibility to the
influence of the weather.   He was made miserable, incapable
even of work by a hopelessly rainy day.   Not until several years
later does he seem to have outgrown this peculiarity.   The
Christmas holidays were spent in Virginia, but were enlivened
by a visit from his mother and his brother William.   Connected
with the visit was the circumstance that he made his first communion on Christmas Day, kneeling by his mother's side at St.
John's Church in Washington.   He had not yet been confirmed,
but from this time it may be inferred that he was "ready and
desirous."   He also took steps to become a candidate for orders.
But there is some reluctance to do what will commit him to the
ministry as a profession.   At least he sees no reason for immediate action.

As the months went by, he does not seem to have become reconciled to the situation. He expresses a strong desire to leave and try his fortunes elsewhere. The teaching he complains of as most inadequate, as not what he needs or wants. Judged by the standards at Harvard, with which he compares it, it seemed greatly inferior. So far did he go under the influence of this mood, that one of his friends was induced to write to the president of the Andover Theological Seminary, asking for the terms of admission there. Something might have come out of this appeal for relief, had not the Andover authorities delayed too long with their reply. And when the answer came, it was not altogether encouraging. He was told that if he and his friends came to Andover, they would be expected to attend the college chapel. He characterizes the letter as "short and very stuffy and to my ideas a very ungentlemanly note." In almost every letter he bewails his condition. The instruction he receives is useless, it is doing nothing for him. He has heard of a new seminary to be established in Philadelphia, which he thinks may be better but cannot be worse. He has a scheme of condensing the three years into two and spending a third elsewhere. He also remarks, "if it had not been for something done outside our regular course, I should not have known what study was."

Among his trials was the sense of isolation, the loss of connection with the large world of human interests through lack of reviews and periodical literature, the deprivation of great libraries. To overcome the want he sought to establish a reading-room; but want of funds and of any general interest prevented its success. In later years he saw the meaning in this temporary separation from the world and was wont to enlarge upon its purpose when addressing students for the ministry.

It should be said in relation to the Virginia Seminary, that at the time when Brooks was there, it was most highly regarded and as a little better than any other theological school in the Episcopal Church. It had done great things for the Church. To many it seemed like a Mecca, because of its sacred associations. But Brooks was right in thinking of Andover as having at the time a higher standard. Princeton and Union seminaries also could have given him what Alexandria and other schools in the Episcopal Church did not and could not. But the real guidance for which he sought could have been found nowhere. Had he gone elsewhere he would have been dissatisfied still, and possibly that other work he was doing for himself would not have been done. The misery of his situation was the divinely appointed condition of his growth. For the rest, he suffered in being transplanted from one social climate to another. His devotion to Harvard was an obstacle in the way of acclimation. But by the close of his first year away from home, he had begun to take root in the new soil; the process of wilting had been survived; though he did not realize it, a new life was circulating in his veins.

The students in the seminary contemporary with Brooks have left on record their impression of him: "He was without a rival as a writer of beautiful English and a poetical thinker," says Bishop Randolph; "we felt the charm of originality in his thought and the sympathy in his voice; . . . a beautiful mind was among us . . . of singular purity and strength." The following extract gives interesting detail in regard to life at the seminary as well as the peculiar characteristics of Brooks.

"It was in November of the year 1856 that I first met Phillips Brooks. The term had already begun at the Alexandria seminary. . . . Brooks, coming late, and finding the best places taken, was billeted in an attic room above us, where he could not stand at his full height. It was already as great, perhaps, as afterwards, but his frame was spare and did not fill out to its full proportions for some years.

"There were no very recent Harvard men then in the seminary, and Phillips Brooks came unheralded. . . . He made no immediate impression on us. He was modest, quiet, reserved, with rather more of the Massachusetts frostiness than he exhibited in later years, after contact with various men. . . .

"The seminary life was simple and primitive. Many of us sawed our own wood, made our own fires, and did nearly all of our own chores. The driver of the mail wagon did our few errands and made our few purchases at Alexandria, some four miles distant. Our clothes were not always of the latest cut, nor in the freshest condition. We took our meals, abundant but not luxurious, in a basement, half under ground. . . . Adjoining the dining-room was Prayer Hall, a large uncarpeted room, with a desk and long wooden benches for its only furniture. The ceiling was low, the walls were whitewashed; I think no picture of any sort relieved their blank surfaces. Here some of the recitations were said; here we met for prayers and for a weekly gathering known as faculty meeting, when a professor made a few remarks bearing on the cultivation of spiritual life, and the other professors—there were but three—took up their parable in turn and emphasized the lesson. The talk was devout, earnest, tending to be pietistic, but mainly useful and simple. Another evening in the week a debating society met in the same place, when papers were read, topics discussed, and criticism offered. . . .

" I do not remember that Phillips Brooks took any part in our debates, made any cutting comments, or displayed any of the extemporaneous power which afterwards distinguished him. But from the first his writing stamped him as no common man. It had the ease and charm of a master. . . . There may have lingered something still of the overluxuriance of springtime, but it was a graceful luxuriance, not a wasteful and ridiculous excess. Harvard severity of taste had already nipped some straggling shoots and repressed some exuberances. Brooks loved to tell how Professor Child had damped his pristine ardor. He had begun a college composition by an elaborate flourish of trumpets, and had carefully inserted a purple patch of which he was not a little proud. What was his consternation, when the paper came back, to find at the close of his labored introduction the penciled comment, 'Begin here.' . . .

" It was an uninspiring life for the most part which we led at the seminary, something very unlike the eager throbbing life of our great theological schools to-day. . . . There were no lectures to supplement the text-books. The recitations were hardly calculated to impart knowledge; they seemed designed rather to betray how little we had acquired. There was much fervor and piety among us, less enthusiasm for scholarship. Good men were not sensitive to failures in the classroom. There was little serious thinking, little outside reading, either in theology or literature. The library was small, merely, I think, a dumping-place for the collections of departed Virginia ministers. . . .

" Still, with whatever imperfect apparatus and unstimulating atmosphere, those who had a mind to work worked on in their own lines with neither encouragement nor opposition. . . . Brooks was a faithful student in and out of the required course. He had brought from college a sound knowledge of Greek and Latin, and used it in a very considerable amount of reading in the Church Fathers, of whom by some unexplained accident there chanced to be in the library the Abbé Migne's edition. . . .

" I do not think that Brooks in any way took our hearts by storm or extorted an immediate admiration except for his ability as a writer. He was liked, as others were. There was no special brilliancy in his talk, there was no visible superiority in his character to that of others about him. His piety was real, but not demonstrative. When he offered prayer at any of our meetings you could not but feel that God was very near and living to him. In his most serious moments there was no appalling gravity about him. He was not perpetually prying into his own soul or ours. He was alive and growing and took it for granted his fellows were, without stopping to pull up their roots or his own to see. He was very human then and always. I do not remember that he told good stories in those days. Certainly he enjoyed them. A quiet humor bubbled up through all his talk. Some of our happiest moments were after the midday meal, when he would often stray into another student's room for a cup of digestive coffee. . . .

"It was understood that we were always welcome at the houses of the professors. Once or twice a year, perhaps, we used our privilege. It was our chief dissipation. As the chairs were pushed back from the tea-table, we sat in our places, family prayers followed, and the discreet did not linger too long after the benediction. The roads were dark, the mud deep, the dogs loud-mouthed, the neighbors were scattered and we saw little of them. It was pure cloistral life for the most part. In one of Brooks's letters in the year that he outstayed me at the seminary, he writes of 'another winter's mental and moral bleakness on that poor hill,' and in another occurs a revealing sentence, 'When are you coming to see us? Leave your intellect behind; you won't need it here.'

"The churchmanship of the time and place was not advanced. The ritual was simple to barrenness. The music was a repeated martyrdom of St. Cecilia. It was not uncommon for the professors to appear in the chancel in their overcoats, and lay down gloves and muffler in the font or on the communion table. The architect of a new chapel of a nondescript form of Gothic had ventured to relieve the dead level of the pews by a modest trefoil or poppy-head rising at the end of each, a little above the rest. A lively imagination might see a foliated cross in them. Bishop Meade had such an imagination. Bishop Johns had winked at them, but the elder Bishop would not trifle with his convictions. He arrived to dedicate the building. He inspected it the night before. A carpenter was summoned and every poppy-head was laid low before the opening service. The erring excrescences were treasured *in memoriam* in the rooms of wailing students. Yet the number of extreme ritualists proceeding from the Virginia seminary, strange to say, is small."[1]

Neither the letters of Phillips Brooks during his first year in the seminary nor the reminiscences of his friends give us the

---

[1] Rev. C. A. L. Richards, in *Remembrances of Phillips Brooks by Two of his Friends*. Boston. Printed for the Members of the Clericus Club, 1893

whole man. There is fortunately a third source, where he continues to reveal himself as he had begun to do in those waiting months of depression, before he made up his mind to theology as a possible opening in life. From the moment that he reached Virginia, he began the practice of keeping note-books. They can hardly be called journals, in the ordinary sense; they are not exactly commonplace books. They are "notes of the mind" or "notes of the soul," containing evidence of intellectual and religious growth. But it is religious life of no ordinary kind. It does not assume the familiar aspect of meditation or self-examination. Sentiment and feeling do not predominate, but rather an intellectual and ethical tone. It is a record of thoughts, so he seems to regard them, floating down to him from the open heavens.

When he went to the theological seminary he seems to have made a determination to do hard and thorough work. He had a misgiving that his years in Harvard had not been improved to the utmost. It was a blessing in disguise that he now found himself compelled to take his theological education in a measure into his own hand. He was free to inquire, he had leisure to read and ponder, above all to study himself. If a theological seminary offers that opportunity, it is, for those who can appreciate it, accomplishing one of the highest purposes of education.

The first thing which impresses one in turning over these note-books is the capacity shown for scholarship. In his classical proficiency, he had attained a source of power for the enlargement of his life. The moment had come when Greek and Latin were at his disposal, as means of entering into other worlds of human experience. It was a thrilling moment when this revelation flashed over him, turning what had before been drudgery into pleasure, the consciousness, as it were, of new faculties. Thus in the first few months after he reached the seminary, we find him reading Herodotus and Æschylus, and among Latin writers, Plautus, Lucretius, and Lucan; of ecclesiastical writers, Augustine, Tertullian, and the Venerable Bede. Tertullian attracted him with a singular charm, as though he found in that vehement, passionate soul something akin to his own moods. From all these writers he was making extracts, sometimes in the original, or translating as an exercise for the mastery of the language. He kept up his French and was tempted to try his hand at a translation of Schiller's *Wallenstein*.

Next to the study of the classics and early ecclesiastical writers comes his devotion to English literature. He was reading many books. Coleridge, Wordsworth, and Shelley, Shakespeare, Milton, Robert Browning and Mrs. Browning, Emerson, Cowley, Waller, Henry Taylor, Landor, Keats, Southey, Johnson, Piers Plowman, Chaucer, Barry Cornwall, Whittier, Sir Thomas Overbury, Ossian, Pope, Swift, Charlotte Brontè, Kingsley, Holmes, Dryden, Chatterton, Lowell, Carlyle, Cowper, Shaftesbury, Ruskin, Jones Very,—the Salem mystic; these are the authors into whom he is dipping at will, from whom also he is making extracts in his note-books. His quotations reveal his own tendencies, becoming part of his mental furniture. There is here disclosed a hunger after the best thought of the world.

Another decided taste was for books descriptive of ancient peoples and their customs. In this list are found Layard's *Nineveh and its Remains*, Heeren's *Nations of Antiquity*, Becker's *Gallus* and *Charicles*, Wines's *Lectures on the Ancient Hebrews*, Kane's *Arctic Explorations*, Josephus's *Jewish Wars*, Prideaux's *Connections*, *Asiatic Researches* by Sir William Jones. He mentions also Stirling's *Cloister Life of Charles V.*, Prescott's *Ferdinand and Isabella*, and Coxe's *House of Austria*.

There are traces of English theological reading,—Bishop Butler's *Sermons*, Milman's *History of the Jews*, Heylin's and Fuller's histories of the English Church, Hengstenberg's *Christology*, Olshausen's *Commentary*, which yielded many suggestive hints; and for religious and devotional reading, Kingsley's *Sermons for the Times* and Huntington's *Sermons for the People*. This is indeed meagre compared with his other lines of reading, but must be supplemented by his study of the Church Fathers and by the work of the classroom, his study of the Old Testament in Hebrew and of the New Testament in Greek, and another work now hardly known, Knapp's *Systematic Divinity*.

One of the striking features of the note-books is the large amount of verse. Most of it appears to have been written rapidly without effort at correction; or if he corrects he rarely improves upon his first utterance. He did not study the laws of metre or of rhythm; he wrote for his inward satisfaction, under compulsion to give form or restraint to emotion. In an address on poetry, delivered at the Howard School, near Alexandria (1859), he justifies its production on the ground that "all men may be and ought to be poets all the time." "There are times when it is good for any man to perpetrate a page or two"; but he adds, "There is a good deal of poetry that is perfectly justifiable to write but utterly inexcusable to show when written." Of the mood which justifies the poetic effort he says:

"There are times when the dullest souls among us fledge unguessed-of wings and turn to sudden poets. There are books whose singing is contagious, and sunrises which turn all live men into Memnon statues. We find poems written in the world that we cannot help reading and singing. Out of as prosaic a car window as your road can boast, I saw God write a gorgeous poem this very morning. With a fresh sunbeam for a pencil, on a broad sheet of level snow, the diamond letters were spelled out one by one till the whole was aflame with poetry. I could have defied the deadest soul in that hot car to have looked out of that window and not heard that song of the Almighty sing itself within his brain. . . .

"This creative power of making a world of beauty in the soul out of the beauty of the earth outside of us, is what makes one young man stronger and purer than his fellows. . . . It comes the nearest to being superhuman, to getting outside the chafing humanities, the weaknesses, the limitations, the hard harness of routine."

Another persistent feature in the note-books is the cultivation of form and style. He states his idea, expands and illustrates it, and clothes it in most fitting language. It looks as if he were testing himself in advance, anticipating the preacher's task in the presence of an invisible audience. Incidental to this purpose is the accumulation of ideas, striking phrases, or epigrammatic statements. The rich and graceful style, the literary wealth and suggestiveness, the abounding metaphors, —these features which marked his style came by the hard effort of years of preparation. A native gift in this direction had been cultivated to the utmost of his ability. There are also many hundreds of similes collected here, which afterwards reappeared in his preaching. In this study

of the simile as an art, there is a philosophical method. He
quotes from Olshausen's *Commentary on Romans* a passage that
met his approval:

" Men are wont to say that parables prove nothing.   Nevertheless comparisons often teach by depth of meaning infinitely more
and better than all abstract arguments, seeing they are devised
from nature, the mirror of the glory of the unseen God, living
demonstrations, as it were, of the Most High God Himself."

We are watching here in the springtime of a rare soul, admitted into the secret process of its growth.   But of this process,
the books that he browsed over do not form the largest part.
They were the conditions under which his spirit was taking
wings for its independent flight.   He was becoming conscious
of the possession of creative power.   His spirit grew stronger
within him, and he had moods of inward joy and triumph.   He
was awakening to the beauty of outward nature; his soul thrilled
at some exquisite landscape; there was a perpetual consciousness of the glory of sunrise or sunset; he watched the
brooks, and meditated on the meaning of flowers and fields, of
all that met his vision.   Wordsworth was doing his part in this
dawning revelation of the spiritual significance of the natural
world, and Shelley also; but they brought their message to a soul
preordained for its reception.   From his childhood, and through
all his years, the simple, elementary consciousness of being alive
and on this earth, the open eye for the special revelation given in
the coming of each new day, the delight in observing the power
of the sun to beautify and glorify the creation,—these simplest
of the natural sensations never lost the novelty of their charm,
as if each new day was a fresh miracle, as if each day he saw the
wondrous phenomenon for the first time.   In his sermons will be
found the ever-recurring allusion to the sun as the symbol of
the spiritual life.   Such was the foundation on which he reared
the superstructure of his appeal.

Immediately on reaching Virginia, he began his self-imposed
task, and for three years continued it, unaware of its profound
import, but conscious of some power within, first revealed in
the days of his failure and disappointment.   Of the work he
was doing he spoke to no one.   In his new abode, solitary among

strangers, in an inconvenient room, with a bed too short for him, with no "armchair" or any of the comforts and conveniences of life, with only the light afforded by a tallow candle, he sat down at the earliest moment to catch and portray the images floating in his mind.

"November 14, 1856. For our virtue should not be a deed or a work, but a growth,—a growth like a tree's, always rising higher from its own inner strength and sap; not a work like a building patched upon by foreign hands, with foreign substance, and so when done unreal, foreign itself, and not our own. Or it should be like a statue worked slowly out of the hard old grain of the native stone; not like a painting, a cheat of foreign color with all its artificial beauties of perspective, foreshortening, and shadow."

"December 1, 1856. To many minds a ceremony or a form comes with all the force of a principle or a fact. Not 'what man has done man may do,' but what man has done man must do is their creed, which cramps their limbs and chills their blood and makes them fail of the little good they are seeking. For no man by sheer imitation has yet reached his pattern. Even if in native power he is more than equal to the task, and so in outward deeds even excels his example, the flush and glow of original achievement, which made the model a living, warm, breathing thing, is wanting to the copy which is cold and stiff and dead."

"December 3, 1856. Suppose a single day of perfect sincerity, a day with no falsehood, no sham, but only purest truth, when a lie should be an impossibility and a cheat unheard of from the rising to the setting of the sun. How earth's eyes would open before that day was done! What golden shrines it would pull down and show the hideous gibbering idol that grins within! What Esau-skins it would tear off, what good men it would turn to knaves and knaves to very devils! How long before the noon of that day men would go crying for the rocks and hills to fall on them and hide them from a sincere world and themselves! But oh, it is cheering to think that there are characters which would show brighter for that day, characters that would stand like unruined ruins, hung over with moss and ivy, and heaped in rubbish of old dead forms and dry ceremonies, which would shake off all this defilement, to stand out in their simple, honest, beautiful, native beauty, in the clear light of the world's truest day."

"December 5, 1856. Wholly deprecating any morbid weakness over the past, I still say that we are too much afraid to look the lives we have been living in the face. We are ashamed and shrink from owning and claiming our past selves. They have been weak and wicked, and we, whose their wickedness and weakness really are, have not the manliness to bear the shame. We turn with a shudder from the poor offspring of our lives, and say with Hagar, Let me not see the death of the child. Oh, if we can only hear God's angel calling, 'Fear not, for I have heard the voice of the lad where he is,' 'Arise, lift up the lad, for I will make him a great nation,' and we do arise and take our old poor weak lives in our hands and go forth to train them by God's strength into richness and power."

"December 7, 1856. The danger with a cherished idea is simply the same as with a graven image, that it will cease to become a symbol and become a god, that our mind, long bent down to the thought, however great, will become stiff and strong in its bending and no longer spring up to the Father of thoughts. Thus the purest reason, which is the purest religion, turns to rationalism, which is idolatry. For reverence is the eyelash that lets us endure the sun, which lost, we must make up our minds to darkness for the rest of our lives, and give up forever all thoughts of the vigor and health and pure richness of life which sunlight only gives."

"December 9, 1856. If a sense of duty were made the measuring requisite of mental strength, if just in proportion as a man earnestly recognized the work there was to do on earth his share was measured out to him, and mind and strength was given him to do it, how with a will and a stir earth's labor would go on. *This is what we need,—to bring the will to meet the power.* There is enough of both, but they lie in different hands, and oh, how often the men who hold the power stand like savages on some new-found golden coast, holding out their priceless treasures, and proud and eager to barter them for some childish trinket or poor worthless toy."

"December 20, 1856. If a thought comes and offers its service question it like a man. What can you do? Are you a worker? Can you sow and dig and build? Are you a schemer? Can you scheme, divine, invent? Are you a teacher? Can you show us better ways to live and better ways to die? Are you an artist? Can you clothe our lives with more beauty, making them know more of holiness and purity and love and God? Ask these questions, and let no thought enter your service that cannot answer them freely and well, and the mysticism of thought is gone and the thinker is the most practical of men."

"December 21, 1856. Yes, Originality is a fine thing, but first have you the head to bear it? Can you walk under it without reeling and staggering about the world, catching at every weak support to keep you steady, with a whole pack of little minds hooting and jeering and pelting you with mire all the way? And have you the heart for it? Can you wear it within as well as without, be warmed to the core with the fire of its life? It is so easy to be a John the Baptist as far as the wilderness and goat's hair and leathern girdle and the locusts and wild honey go, but the glowing heart to speak from and the holy words to speak are a different thing. The average chance is that it will be better in the long run for you and me to stay at home and work as our fathers work, counting that very work a fortune in itself. Besides it is dangerous, this trifling with novelties. It requires hazardous experiments before we can be at all sure that they will answer our purpose."

"January 1, 1857. How we grow more and more to see that it is the will and the feelings, far more than any thought, upon which almost all our life and loved opinions rest. How much of our faith is obstinacy, how much of our devotion sentiment, how much of our religion pride; how much working strength there is in a blind determination and how little in a clear-eyed thought. Mohammed knew all this and built Mohammedanism upon sentiment and will, and stamped the marks of shrewd sense upon it when he forbade the Islamite to dispute on his religion."

"January 11, 1857. A noble cause cannot of itself make a man noble. We must despair of growing great, unless we can feel that we are given to the cause to work for it, and not it to work for us. In the old torch races of Pan, the rule was that each runner should hold his torch as long as it kept its light, but when he flagged he must hand it to another who stood ready girded to follow up the race. And so it must be with us. We must recognize the great end of all this panting and running and toiling, not that you or I should reach the goal, and be rich or honored in men's mouths, but that the torch of truth that was put into our hands when we started should reach the people at the end all alight with truth as when we took it. Let it be our hands, if we can, that bring it there, and then the honor shall be ours; but that must not be our end, and when we see it sinking and going out, let no petty conceit or unfledged pride keep us from giving it to a fresher and stronger man, with a hearty Godspeed to run the next stage of the same great journey. Thus we win a broadness and deepness and fulness of character that sinks all little human ventures like the sea."

"February 6, 1857.   What has become of all that blessing of
Christ which He left with His people on earth on that 'first day
of the week, when the doors were shut where the disciples were
assembled for fear of the Jews, and Jesus came and stood in the
midst, and said unto them, 'Peace be unto you'?   Has it with-
ered in the scorching heat of the world's fiery hopes and more
fiery fears, and rage and scorn and ignorance and pride?   Or is it
still bright with the everlasting freshness of its miraculous youth,
making humble hearts more holy, and holy lives more happy
wherever there is a clear eye, or better still a clear heart, to see
its beauty and great power of making blessed?   When He sent it
on earth in a few weak men's hands and it floated down on weak
men's breath, as centuries before the hope of Israel had drifted in
a bulrush cradle down the Nile, till some unthinking and unknow-
ing hand could take it up and nurture it and make it strong and
noble in the high places of the land, He sent it with a power to
insure its life. . . ."

"February, 1857.   In spite of all the mischief that over-credu-
lous delusion has always done, I still say we need more faith upon
earth.   We have not the trust that we ought to have in God and
nature, in human hopes and dreams and bright stray thoughts
that have wandered from their homes in heaven, with light and
glory and unproven truth still glorifying them, and come and ask
us to take them in from the cold world where they feel strange,
and shelter and cherish them while they shall lighten our hearts
and homes.   We turn them away, for we do not believe in them.
We do not trust to poetry or art, to our neighbors or ourselves.
'Lord, increase our faith.' . . . I would trust in human goodness and purity and truth as I do in the yearly return of May, a
day or two later perhaps, one or two more cold storms or dead
dull frozen days in one year than another, but sure to come at
last, unable in any event to fail of coming as long as this world
in this world, and nature what it has always been.

"It is not for us to make our lives artistic, we can only make
them true.   If we give ourselves to a weak attempt to build them
for effect, to place ourselves where some critical observer might
stand and fashion them to suit his point of view, we shall surely
make them wretched failures.   It is not thus that nature works.
There is no studied symmetry, no measured perspective, no conscious foreshortening in her great original.   All this is left to the
observer's eye, and nature declines to be accountable for the powers, or infirmities, or refinement, or clumsiness of his vision. . . .
Just this then is our duty by our lives.   Give them room to grow
to truth, and they will grow to symmetry; give them leave to
ripen, and they will richen too.   Let each day's commonest act

be an act that has an aim and does it, and it shall make us wonder to see us dignified by that aim and cured of all its commonness, taking its place of its own true instinct in the true, fresh, glowing pictures of our life."

" In the great temple where the singers of old are sleeping their quiet sleep, where Homer's gray tranquillity, and Shakespeare's still, calm forehead, and Milton's peaceful, sightless face lie, undisturbed, as if they looked on inner sights and listened to some inner voice, while the noisy, heedless world is wrangling and chattering and fighting without, above each minstrel's tomb hangs the harp to which he sang, still strung and tuned for singing. But well may men tremble, as they walk through the temple and stand and look and think upon the dead, to take down their harps and draw presumptuous hands across the strings. Yet let us look with indulgence and hope when, in the strength of young poetry, some hand is timidly reached to touch those old chords and try if perhaps the old music that lies in them may answer to another than its master's call."

" We must learn the infinite capacity of truth to speak to every human mind, and of every human mind to hear, and more or less completely understand, the truth that speaks. It may come like a poor and shambling thing, and impart in its stammering Galilean tongue the great message that it has to give, but all the multitude will catch the words, and, whatever may be their tribe, Romans, Medes, Parthians, and Jews, shall hear in their own tongue, like that Whitsunday congregation, the wonderful works of God. Let us then reverence our neighbor's way of finding truth. If by his life and faith we can clearly see that he is finding it indeed, let us not turn away because he hears it in another tongue than ours. The speaker is the same. If he can read in a stormy sky, or a sunny landscape, lessons for which we must go to books and sermons, so much the better for him."

" When we gain a victory moral or mental, when we subdue a passion or achieve a thought, let the conquest be decisive. Let the question be settled, the idea mastered, the doubt decided forever. Let there be no fear of future difficulty. If the serpent lie across our path and we must kill it to pass, let the blow be struck straight and strong; let us lift the body and see that it be really dead, lest when we pass this way again to-morrow it may lift its foul head and hiss and frighten us from the pathway out among thorns and briers, wandering from our way, torn and tired with our struggles, ashamed of the wretched shiftlessness which is only a specimen of our moral and mental lives."

" There lies in earth a secret note to which her harmony should be and was at first attuned, but from which her degenerate discord wanders. Her slow ear has forgotten that old first note, and she chants her daily song unconscious of the wandering of her voice, till, once in an age, some great soul comes and reaching forth a master's finger touches life's keynote, and all earth trembles when she hears the harmony, and knows at one sudden shock how far her mortal song has strayed from the old angels' anthem from which she learned it first."

"Until we have learned the universal language of human sympathy, how can we hope to speak so that all may hear us and be drawn to us by what they hear? While we speak thus, each in the selfish tongue of our own interest or passions, our words will come sealed to the ears of our fellows, and all the consciousness that we are heard and understood by others, or the sweeter feeling that the world is better for our words, will all be lost."

" The world claims of us, as Nebuchadnezzar did of the Chaldeans, not only to solve, but first of all to discover her problems. The man who has learnt thoroughly what it is that is wonderful and inexplicable, where the hard questions lie, in the constitution and habit of the world and of his fellow-men, even if his steps have been very few towards the explanation of those wonders, has reached not a little knowledge of men and things."

With these passages may be connected another from his book *The Influence of Jesus*, where, after many years, he commented on the way by which he had been led:

"Who of us has not bowed his will to some supreme law, accepted some obedience as the atmosphere in which his life must live, and found at once that his mind's darkness turned to light and that many a hard question found its answer? Who has not sometimes seemed to see it all as clear as daylight, that not by the sharpening of the intellect to supernatural acuteness, but by the submission of the nature to its true authority, man was at last to conquer truth; that not by agonizing struggles over contradictory evidence, but by the harmony with Him in whom the answers to all our doubts are folded, a harmony with Him brought by obedience to Him, our doubts must be enlightened ? "

The summer of 1857 was passed with his family in the home on Chauncy Street, Boston,—the first home-coming after a long absence. Upon his arrival, he took the long-deferred step, in the language of the Church, of "ratifying his baptismal vows."

He was presented by Rev. Edward L. Drown, and confirmed by the Rt. Rev. Manton Eastburn at St. Mary's Church, Dorchester, Sunday, July 12, 1857. Among his mother's papers found after her death was this memorandum:

"Sunday, July 12, 1857.

"This has been a most happy day in which I have witnessed the confirmation of my dear son Phillips, aged twenty-one, at Dorchester.

"I will thank God forever that He has answered my lifelong prayers in making him a Christian and His servant in the ministry.

"Oh, how happy this makes me! May God continue to bless my dear boy and make him a burning and shining light in His service."

CHAPTER IV.

1857–1858.

SECOND YEAR AT THE ALEXANDRIA SEMINARY. HOME LETTERS. EXTRACTS FROM NOTE-BOOKS.

THE summer of 1857 was spent at home. It was not an idle one, for work of some kind was the law of the family. It was the custom of the father when he came home in the evening to ask the boys what they had been doing through the day. Phillips had known what it was to have days when he had nothing to report; when, as he confesses, he sought to keep out of his father's way. Now that the long study for its own sake and for an ulterior end had been established, there was no possibilty of idleness. He began another note-book with extracts from his summer reading. Much of his time was spent in the Boston Public Library, then situated on Boylston Street. He was led by some instinct to the works of Lord Bacon, cultivating his Latin at the same time by translations from the *Novum Organum*, the *Nova Atlantis*, and the *De Sapientia Veterum*. The latter work encouraged what was characteristic of Brooks's later work in preaching,—a tendency to go beneath the form, in order to discover some deeper meaning some analogies in things unlike. He kept up his German by reading Schiller, his French by Montaigne's essays, whose apology for Raimond de Sabonde left an enduring impression. He was reading Browning and Matthew Arnold for the first time, and was browsing over Ruskin, in one of whose sentences he found food for thought: "Landscape seems hardly to have exercised any strong influence, as such, on any pagan nation or artist."

When he left Virginia for his holiday he had some vague hope of going elsewhere to complete his theological course, but the plan was abandoned and in the fall he returned to Alexandria.

He had in reality struck root there, and had formed friendships too valuable to be sacrificed. The year 1857–58 is remembered as a year of financial depression, causing the most severe trial to business interests the country had ever known. Following the financial distress came a religious awakening which for depth and extent and abiding results can only be compared with the "Great awakening" of the eighteenth century. The political situation was full of excitement, indicating that the trend of sentiment in the country was against Buchanan's administration. The question was before Congress whether Kansas should be admitted into the Union under the Lecompton Constitution, so called from the place where it had been drawn up,—a constitution which recognized slavery, and had never been submitted to the people of the Territory. It was a great event when Mr. Douglas, the rival of Mr. Lincoln, committed himself by a speech against the proposal to adopt this constitution. To this speech Brooks alluded in one of his home letters, dated March 23, 1858:

"I have just returned from Washington, where I spent the greater part of last night, from seven till eleven, standing on a very little bench in a very large crowd, listening to Douglas's anti-Lecompton speech in the Senate. You have seen it. I suppose, in the papers. It was n't a very great speech, but as I had never heard him I was glad to have the opportunity. I never saw such a crowd before. It was almost impossible to get in, and once in, it was utterly out of the question to get out again. Toombs replied in a fiery speech.

"Mr. Everett was lecturing in Alexandria last week, and everybody is admiring him. I did not hear him."

The home letters riveted more closely the family ties. Both father and mother follow the absent son with parental anxiety and sense of responsibility. It was taken for granted that he had not outgrown the need of a father's care or the saving influence of a mother's love. He was still to be watched over, and warned and stimulated to greater exertions. These letters deserve to be mentioned because they constitute formative influences more potent than any other. Thus his father thought it necessary to write:

"Remember what I have often told you about the seminary,

that after all, dull as it is, the most depends on your individual exertions, and these I know never will be allowed to rust with you. I wish other things were equal, and that you found it more pleasant and congenial.

". . . . Do you go to Washington much? a rowdy place I should not advise visiting much! What a disgraceful drunken scrape that was last week among them!"

The new *Atlantic Monthly* had not been accorded a kindly reception at the seminary. Referring to this and to his son's allusions to politics, the father writes:

"Boston, December 21, 1857.

". . . I note your remarks on politics, etc. All very well to keep posted on such matters, but I want you to be aware (for I am afraid you are not) of the importance of acting discreetly on all matters between the North and the South, remembering it is a delicate subject on both sides. I do not think it was wise or discreet in the *Atlantic Monthly* to publish such an article in such a magazine, but they must abide by the result. Standing here on Northern soil, it is all well enough, but I can see how the South would view it and I wish to impress it earnestly upon you not to enter into the discussion there. It can do you no good, and may do you much harm, if not positive evil. You know I have expressed this before, but the tenor of your letter impresses me with the idea that you are too regardless of consequences. . . . It was a very small and despicable act to remove the magazine from the room, and shows the weakness of their cause; but after the fact was well known, there I should leave it in a Christian spirit, and I believe it would do them more harm than good. *I shall depend on your acting discreetly and cautiously in the matter.*"

"October 20, 1857.

"My Dear Philly,—I am thinking of you continually and we cannot be done missing you, and it is so cheering to get news of you. I wish I could look into your room and see if you look comfortable, and how you have arranged your clothes. . . . I hope you will find some pleasant friends among the new students. Also I hope you will improve this pleasant weather to walk a good deal and enjoy this beautiful weather. . . . Write again soon, and tell us all about yourself, and what you are doing this year in your studies. You *don't know how much* we think and talk of you, and desire your well-doing in every respect Keep *very near* to your *Saviour*, dear Philly, and remember the sacred vows that are upon you, and you will surely prosper. Good-

night, my dear Philly, and pleasant dreams. Whether waking
or sleeping, never forget

> " Your ever loving Mother."

A great tide of love was sweeping through the mother's soul as
she wrote the letter following:

Boston, December 19, Saturday evening.

"My very dear Child,—I have stolen away from the parlor,
and the girls and the boys, and the closing Saturday night cares,
into the nursery to write to you; to send you my wishes for a
happy Christmas, and the enclosed ten dollars for a Christmas
present, and I sincerely wish it was in my power to *double it.*
You must take it as a gift of love from your mother, who loves
you ten thousand times more than she can ever tell you, or than
you can ever know. As Christmas Day returns again I shall
think very much of the pleasant one I spent with you last year,
and especially of the happiness and gratitude I felt on first taking
communion with you. Oh, it was a *happy* day, and my heart
was *full* of gratitude that I had lived to see my child confess his
Saviour before men. God grant that *as long as life shall last*, he
may be His faithful disciple and devoted servant. And although
we shall not be with you this year, Philly, I want you to *enjoy*
the day, and think of us, and therefore I want you for my sake
to go into Washington to church, and, oh, when you take communion, remember your mother. And after church I want you
to go to *Willard's* or *somewhere*, and get a *good Christmas dinner*,
with some of *my present*, and then when the children are enjoying
their *roast turkey*, they can think that Philly *has some too.* Now,
Philly, won't you do all this *for me?*—and I shall think of you
on that day as doing it and enjoying a part of my present. We
shall think and talk much of you on that day, and miss you, and
long to have you with us, and I *know* you will think of us.
Depend on it I think a great deal about you. . . . Philly, I
will say how much you have improved in your character and in
your letters the last year. We both notice it, and I believe you
will be a blessing and honor to us in our future years."

To this and other letters Phillips wrote in reply, deeply moved,
and for once yielding his almost invincible reserve. He explains
why it is he has not yet spoken the words his parents must have
long yearned to hear, but he can write when he cannot speak.
His explanation reveals a feature of his character which to the
last baffled his friends:

"Christmas Eve, 1857.

" Dear Father (and Mother, too, for the mail to-night has brought so much to thank you both for that this note must be a joint affair),—First there is the composite letter of Saturday, enclosing your Christmas presents, which the post office seems to have delayed so as to reach me just in time. I shan't begin to thank you both for your kindness, for in my utter inability to say how much I feel it I should never know where to stop. It is only a piece of the long series of goodness that I have been grateful or ungrateful for, for the last twenty-two years. If I ever can do anything to give pleasure or credit to you, a big part of the gratification to myself will be in feeling that you are gratified, and are so adding to your other kindnesses that of taking my own efforts to help and improve myself as payment for your long labor to help and improve me. You may have thought it a little strange now and then that I have n't said this by word of mouth, but the truth is I can write what I feel deeply much easier and better than I can say it; but the feeling, I at least know, is none the less deep for that. Let this explain a great deal of what you may have fancied is coldness in all my life, and more particularly in my new professon. In truth I do thank you sincerely for your holiday remembrances, and they will certainly make Christmas a great deal merrier to me."

This letter has been indorsed in his mother's handwriting, "A dear letter. Mother." She replies to it:

"January 11, 1858.

" My dear Philly,—I thank you for that letter; it is a treasure to me, it is so full of love and kindness. It tells us all we want to know, that you realize your parents' deep interest in you, and that you promise us the richest reward you can give us,— that of bringing us honor in after life. And also you have convinced us that you have a warm and kind heart, and that your heart is in your profession. Not that I have ever doubted it, for I have always felt that you are too sincere and true-hearted to dare undertake so holy a calling except with your whole heart; but I 've sometimes wished you would make it doubly sure to me by assuring me of it yourself, and I 've felt you owed it to yourself to do so. But, my dear Philly, this letter satisfies me entirely on that point, and I cannot tell you the delight it gives us. Father almost shed tears as he read it."

From this picture of family life, we turn to Brooks's intellectual activity during his second year at the Virginia Seminary.

Out of all the years of his life it stands forth supreme; in no other year did he receive so much from books, from real life, or from himself; in no other year did he leave a fuller record of his genius; every germ and principle of the later expansion is here.

Whatever may have been his own convictions of truth, or however widely he may have been diverging from the teaching of his instructors, he did the required work of the classroom in a conscientious spirit. He read selected parts of the Old Testament in Hebrew, though never with any enthusiasm for the language, and the Greek New Testament; he studied Church history and systematic theology. This was the usual course of study. But at the same time he was living in a world of his own, where his mind was ranging far and wide beyond the imagination of his associates. The routine work calls for no comment beyond the remark that it kept him in touch with received opinions, and enabled him to measure his own divergence. But even here he was engaged in the task of going beneath the formulas to the original purpose which inspired them.

The first impression one gets from his note-books is the wide extent of his reading. The list of books he read or studied, or to some extent became acquainted with, is a long one. Out of this large list from which he makes quotations, there are a few that stand forth with prominence. He went by a sure instinct to the creative minds of the ancient Church, and with them he dwelt till he had appropriated their distinctive quality. He read the Greek and Latin fathers, taking delight in his capacity to read them in their own tongues, but also forced to do so—for translations were not availiable.

His note-books reveal the traces of glowing enthusiasm under the contact of new ideas. Whatever impressed his mind seems to have stirred his whole being. His chief outlet for an aroused, excited soul was at this time the sonnet, for which he shows a decided predilection, whenever he would express the grateful emotion due to any author who had moved him to the depths. He wrote a series of sonnets after reading the tragedies of Æschylus and Sophocles.

Among the ancient authors to whom he was deeply indebted were Philo and Origen, Tertullian, Jerome, and Augustine; among moderns, Lord Bacon, Goethe, Coleridge. The list is an unusual one for a young man to have selected with no guidance but his own will. When these names are studied with reference to the power they exercised over their own world, it must be admitted that he could not have gone more widely in the search for what would minister to his own life, and create enthusisam for those universal convictions which have inspired the Church in the past to its greatest victories, or which underlie modern progress.

From Philo, over whose *De Mundi Opificio* he browsed earnestly, was gained the idea that deep meanings were buried in the old Hebrew laws. Through the study of Origen he was confirmed in this conviction, and learned the quest for himself of some inward sense, imbedded in the page of Scripture. As he mused over Jerome he felt the strange power beneath the ancient creeds. With Tertullian, he could in spirit emerge from the old Roman paganism, with which he was not without sympathy, into the Christian atmosphere; and even Tertullian's inward tumult and contradiction, even his passionate stormy nature, appealed to something kindred in his own soul. For Tertullian he always retained a certain personal affection. Studies like these put him in accord with the most characteristic purpose of historic Christianity. He does not seem to have been engaged in defining his own belief, but rather in finding out what others believed who had exercised the greatest power in the Church, or contributed most to the development of its doctrines or its life. Truths which had helped the race he appropriated as his own. In proportion as he did so he was impersonating in himself the historic Christian ideal, which had subdued the world to Christ.

He was not attracted by speculative or metaphysical studies. Only as they took shape in concrete convictions with a practical relation to life could he give to speculative truths a kindly reception. It was true of him, as it was of Goethe, that a study of speculative philosophy would have turned him in a direction alien to his genius and impeded his development. It should be remarked that he gave no attention to Aristotle. Plato he read and pored over. What chiefly attracted him in Plato was the portrait of Socrates, and the Phædo was his favorite dialogue.

There was one writer, however, Lord Bacon, included among

philosophers, who exercised a lasting influence upon Phillips Brooks. His note-books contain more quotations from Bacon than from any other one author. One reason for the attraction is that which explains also his turning to the masters of the ancient Church—the sense of a power exercised in extraordinary degree at some turning point in history. At that greatest hour in England's career, when after the destruction of the Spanish Armada she came to the consciousness of her destiny in freedom and national independence, Bacon had arisen in the fulness of the rare opportunity, to interpret the world he lived in. Brooks seems to have revelled in Bacon's writings. *The Novum Organum* became his text-book. Out of the many quotations, some translated, others cited in the original, a few deserve to be given, for they are so many mottoes, containing in summary the principles of his life work as a teacher and theologian.

"Interpretation is the natural and genuine work of the mind after obstacles are removed."

"For that is true philosophy which renders most faithfully the voices of the world, and is written, as it were, at the world's dictation; and is nothing else but its image and reflection, and adds nothing of its own, but only repeats and resounds." (*De Sapientia Veterum.*)

"For there is in man a certain ambition of the intellect, no less than of the will, especially in high and lofty minds." (*Nov. Org.,* i., 65.)

"When the human mind has once despaired of finding truth, all things become altogether weak." (*Nov. Org.,* i., 67.)

"There are realities for which there is no name; and there are names with no corresponding realities." (*Nov. Org,* i, 6.)

Brooks never paid much attention to the natural sciences. But from Bacon he gained the principle which put him in harmony with the scientific attitude, and he also learned to believe in the sacredness of secular pursuits, trade and commerce, as agencies for bringing in the Kingdom of God. He quotes from the *Nova Atlantis* an impressive passage, where Bacon claims that commerce has been instituted not for gold or silver or gems or any other such things, but primarily for the creature of God, that is for light, in whatever region it may germinate. Hence the environment of man in this natural world grew rich to his imagination, teeming as it was with untold possibilities.

"We may therefore well hope that many excellent and useful matters are yet treasured up in the bosom of nature, bearing no relation or analogy to our actual discoveries, but out of the common track of our imagination and still undiscovered; and which will doubtless be brought to light in the course and lapse of years, as the others have been before them." (*Nov. Org.*, i., 109.)

Among modern writers he turned to Coleridge, the "true sovereign of English thought," as he has been called, whose gift it was to show "how one may enter into the spirit of a living or departed author without assuming to be his judge." In this capacity, Brooks excelled. At a later time he complained of much current American criticism, that it failed of its true purpose, because it too often mounted the throne of judgment, instead of sitting at the feet of an author to learn. Coleridge's influence combined easily with that of Philo, and Origen, in emphasizing the sacramental view of life, the spiritualization of the whole universe,—"that coherent conception of human life and human culture which recognizes the Divine Spirit as present and operative in all the higher strivings of man."

There are verses in his note-book at this time which disclose, however he may have come by it, a decided Neo-Platonic tendency, where he speaks of the thoughts now springing up so abundantly in his mind, as if they were angelic intelligences descending from God, with whom they had pre-existed and held communion, coming down into the soul with God's blessing upon them. These thoughts he personifies, as carrying memories of the blessed life, and of the heavenly hymn; which, while they come to men in blessing, are themselves yearning for the joys they have left behind them, and so tempt men Godward, as they return to the source whence they came.

Taking the sonnets of Brooks as indications of his grateful recognition to those who contributed to his growth, mention should be made of Dr. Bushnell, to whom a sonnet is also addressed. No books in Brooks's library show signs of harder usage than Bushnell's *Sermons for the New Life*, and Maurice's *Theological Essays*. In the decade of the fifties in the last century, no writers were exerting a stronger or more beneficent effect upon theology.

From this sketch, it may be evident with what discernment and assimilative force he went through the large amount of reading to which his note-books bear witness. Greek and Latin classics, Greek and Latin fathers, the best English literature, especially the English poets, the classics in English theology, the most influential of the then modern writers, all were put under contribution for his enrichment. It is hard to say whether he drew most deeply from contemporary thinkers, Carlyle, Tennyson, Browning, or Ruskin, or from the great masters of antiquity. To him they stood apparently on a common level.

But there are things in these note-books—his own thoughts—not to be traced to any special influence. There are hundreds of passages where an idea is carefully elaborated, which bespeak the native working of his own spirit. It is apparent that one object he had in view was cultivation in the art of expression. Like a true poet, no sooner did he conceive the idea than he set himself, by an inward necessity, to giving it perfect embodiment in words. It was all genuine and spontaneous; he valued his thoughts for their own sake, but also for the artistic form with which he invested them. It seems to have been his plan to work out every day some one or more ideas. At times it looks as if he were preaching to himself, and at other times to an invisible audience, to whom he would commend the truth by artistic impassioned appeal.

He shows also a tendency to personify nature, to think of the earth as alive, conscious, and sympathetic with man, and watching the career of the humanity whom it carries. Its task is a heavy one and he sympathizes with its faithfulness, its weariness, its sad monotony. He personifies time—a living entity growing old and weighted with infirmity, the conviction of sin and failure. His study of Greek literature gave him insight into the inner meaning of Greek mythology, till it seemed like a vehicle for his own emotion. He entered into the religion of nature, whose essence is reverence for the mystery of things. Each new day should be a recurring miracle; each sunrise as fresh and novel a scene as when viewed by the first man for the first time. Each morning God is calling upon the slumbering earth to rise and do his will. "Morning still chases morning, and evening flies from evening round the world." "Each new science is only a new chord in the harp of earth's harmony, each new thought only a new strain in earth's everlasting song of praise." "Prayer and prophecy are the uplifted hand of earth yearning for the heaven that is to come."

"Every sunrise and sunset gives us a new insight into the old belief that the East and the West were blessed lands, with golden rivers and bright hills and warm clear skies and everlasting verdure. How our souls go out into those magic lands, and meet there the old Greek souls who wandered there for beauty, led by a depth of feeling for its worth such as no souls but Greek have ever known."

"Some morning comes to us with a sense of the marvellous beauty of our earth, such as morning after morning all the days of our life have failed to give us. . . . Sometimes a thought seems to have hoarded all the wealth and worth of all our thoughts since thinking first began."

"The still blue sky that has looked in sorrow and in care these six thousand years on sinning, anxious earth."

"Who that did not know by long experience the certainty and richness of God's daily power and love could have imagined that the faint gray hue that we saw this morning dimly dividing between the blackness of heaven and the blackness of earth could have widened and deepened and brightened in these few short hours into perfect day, opening all the great depths of heaven's room, painting all the landscape of earth's loveliness, warming and waking and cheering the cold, dead, dreary hearts of men?"

"Nature is man's best teacher of modesty and of humble doubt, as well as trust of his powers. . . . So long as each day's wisdom and study is perplexed and put to shame by each night's sleep and dreams, let us cease to wonder at what we know, let us stand in silent awe at what we feel, at what we are, and what we dimly discern around us."

"The hymn to Demeter has a noble groundwork of a faith. . . . How the old story must have twined around the city's life, while processions, and ceremonies, and creeds thenceforth made the old myth forever new. . . . Truly humanity yearns for the divine; is drawn by its beauty to the beautiful; catches, while it dreams of the grand, holy, righteous powers of nature, something of their grandeur and holiness and truth."

" Truly there was a clearness and a power in those old eyes and ears that have died out of ours. We hear no voices on the summer wind; no merry faces laugh up their beauty tones from the sunny sea; no Dryads flit away before us down their forest paths. To us the black cloud is a black cloud, and not a power; the clear sky is only a clear sky, and not a smile; our sun is not a god, our stars no happy choirs of singing graces, making night day with the sweet chorus of their perfect loveliness. We have learnt a moral beauty of ethics and of faith, found cheer in sorrow and gladness in despair, but we have lost the daily beauty that fills earth now just as it filled it then."

But nature was more beautiful for the human thoughts it suggested than for itself alone.   He will not admit that man is a blot on the landscape, or that the deeds of man disfigure nature.

" Every earthly scene is imperfect, as Eden was, without man's presence.   Hills and trees and clouds, waves on the seashore, willows by the river's side, fields with their broad green beauty stretching out of sight, lack with all their loveliness one element of poetry, gain it only when a human home stands in their midst, and the signs of human work are seen among them.   Man may mar the beauty of their first creation, spoil or soil them with his clumsy efforts to turn them into use, or even in mere human wantonness take pleasure in turning the usefulness that God has given them into uselessness; but, in spite of all this, earth gains more from human life than she suffers from human mischief.   It gives a point and purpose to her life, gives her that without which all life is death."

Many other passages might be quoted to illustrate his discernment of analogy between the life of the spirit in man and the phenomena of the external world.   He was impressed by Tertullian's argument connecting the resurrection of the body with the process of nature: "The whole, therefore, of this revolving order of things bears witness to the resurrection of the dead." (*De Res*. xii).

The true interpretation of nature sanctions the moral ideal; the natural order is an illustration of moral duties.

" We believe in the same power of nature to join a broken life as to unite the pieces of a broken bone.   Error, ignorance, care, pride, or prejudice has struck our life and it has yielded to the shock, but bring the jagged ends together and leave them to the quiet influence of time, and nature's moral laws will do their silent work, and our life rise up to do its part again among the busy lives of men."

"While this morning sunrise is rosy with the memory of last night's sunset, while noon looks longingly down the eastern sky that it has travelled, and onward to the night to which it hastens, while month links in with month, and season works with season, and year joins hand with year in the long labor of the world's hard life, there is a lesson for us all to learn of the unity and harmony of our existence. Let us take the lesson, and, with it in our hearts, go out to be more tolerant, more kindly and more true in all the social strivings of our fellow-men. Let us carry it back with us to history, and forward with us in our dreamings of the years to come."

"If nature is twenty years building our bodies, let us grudge no needful time to build our minds. If she is content to spend the slow months of a long sunny spring and summer in painting the flower's petal and an insect's wing, which the quick decay of autumn is to make as if it had not been, let us shrink from no length of labor, or minuteness of finish, or conscientious thoroughness of every part of every work that is entrusted to our hands."

In these earlier years the intellect holds the ascendency, for a work was to be done by the critical function in order to adjust the individual reason with the reason of humanity. This task, which confronted him in college, still occupies the foremost place in his consciousness. He yearns for "more capacity to learn of all that has truth to teach."

"We may judge of thoughts as of other guests. If they come frankly up and strike boldly at our doors, and bid us admit them and welcome them for the message that they bring, ready to speak freely with us, ready to be questioned, ready to claim and prove kindred to other thoughts which we have taken to our hearts in other days, then we may take them by the hand and lead them in and grow stronger for their presence."

"Our gradual learning of our powers is a blessed thing. Suppose that we woke with one sudden thrill . . . into the full noon of intellectual being, how could the body or the mind endure it?"

"One single thought has power to keep our strength alive."

"Trains of thought that are strong cords to bind the loose bundles of our life together."

" Our best and strongest thoughts, like men's earliest and rudest homes, are found or hollowed in the old primeval rock. In some cleft of truth we find shelter, and all the strength that has been treasured up in meeting the storms of centuries is made available for our protection. Not till our pride rebels against the architecture of these first homes, and we go out and build more stately houses of theory and speculation and discovery and science, do we begin to feel the feebleness that is in us, how doubt makes the joints of our structure weak, and prejudice spoils all its fair proportions, and our ignorance is stronger than our skill at every step."

" After all, it is in a few great tracts of hard granitic truth, the deep accumulations of dead years, that this whole modern world of ours rests, waiting for the manifold change of time. In their clefts and ridges lies the alluvium of modern theory and thought, wherein we plant and tend the bright flowers and sunny fruits of our daily life; but when we would found a system-structure that shall *stand*, how we dig deep till we find the solid rock and build on that; . . . when we would read the moral history of our earth, how we find it written in the piled stones of those dark foundations."

Nowhere in these note-books does Phillips Brooks regard himself as a pioneer in search of new thought. It is evident enough that he is passing through some sort of crisis; but his method of allaying doubt or attaining conviction is distinctively his own. He does not test truth by individual experiences, but by the larger experiences of humanity. All that he asks is to enter more deeply into the meaning of familiar truths that have been waiting to be understood. His ruling idea is that *history* contains the material with which the intellect must deal; the agency or coin we must offer in order to transfer it into our own being is *faith*. Of things in the past, freely offered to the reason and soul of man, there is this condition only for their reception: Believe and thou shalt have them for thine own. The secret of power was to enter, and ever more deeply, into the meaning of old familiar things. In this lay the principle of progress; this was Christian radicalism.

" I believe in these things because I know that they have helped my race. I look to them as I look to the sun with a faith that all the centuries of sunlight forbid me to disown. I hear them from the Bible claiming my allegiance, as from all nature I hear

God's voice demanding that I should give reason room to grow to trust and love."

" Every identification that a man can make of himself with his race is so much power gained. He multiplies his life eight hundred millionfold. The world was made and sun and stars ordained and salvation sent to earth for him. The history of the race becomes his experience, the happiness of the race his glory, the progress of the race his hope."

" The awakening to an old truth may be worth more to us than the discovery of a new. For, in spite of our dulness and deadness to it, it has still been slowly ripening our nature for its reception and the final heart-acknowledgment of its truth. This preliminary process we do not feel, but when the day of our awakening comes, then old dreams half remembered take at once their proper places, and we recognize the growth that has been going on within us and now has brought this precious truth to birth."

" Sometimes with a touch of vulgar circumstance we wake to a thought that we have been thinking, or a faith that we have been feeling, for long years and known it not; how the phenomena of our life are torn aside, and we look down into its substance on whose broad bosom all our hopes and plans and loves have been built all through these years of hating, planning, loving, hoping, when we were proud and conscious of the living, but knew nothing of the life. For thought and faith lie too deep within us for our blind eyes to see or our weak hands to grasp them."

" We do not speak alone; all honor and virtue of antiquity bear witness to our truth, all its struggles for a purer life, all its clingings to a truer faith. And the future sends its voice to plead for us, all the hopes of posterity, all the longings of our race, all the dim glimpses of truth yet to be revealed and blessing yet to be attained . . . The whole world with its histories and hopes reasons with every soul, and adjures it to judge wisely and be firm and true."

" When Solomon's great temple to the Lord was done, he brought in the things which his father had dedicated. We build our temples of duty and devotion to the Lord our God. We suit them to our growing needs, to the changing demands of new times and seasons; but with our new modes and means of worship, we may set up in them too our fathers' holy things, their true old faith and fervent prayers, the fragrant memory of their good lives, the censers with the incense of their praise still about them. So their dead worship shall give life to ours; so with our Christian prayers shall mingle the noble conservatism that treasures up a Christian past."

"Our hope is in this Christian radicalism, which, through the myriad shows and semblances of Christian life, goes down directly to the root of things, and clings to Charity, and says, 'Lo, out of these shall grow a Christian church for all the world, and out of them a Christian experience for me!'"

In his vocabulary the word "truth," like the word "life," is of frequent recurrence. Truth is personified as a Deity dwelling in a shrine where men may worship, but also comes out of her pillared temple, and descends into the common world of human life:

"Truth lives and thrives in her fair house of Learned Theory. But its grand, pillared front is too high, its wide doors too rich and ponderous; her form as she moves within too fair and proud and queenly for common men to dare to come and enter her great gates and ask to learn of God and Nature and their own humanity from her lips. Rather will they stand without forever. looking from far away upon the towers of her wondrous home and see the great Mistress walking with a few bold scholars through the greenness of her trees, deeming it all a thing in which there is no part for them. So then, fair Truth, that she may claim her right to govern from her readiness to help all men, lays by her gorgeous robes, takes the plain white mantle of most simple faith, comes down from her great house, and goes along the crowded street and close lanes of poor men's homes, with a lesson and a smile for each, a soothing touch for the sick child's forehead, a helping word for the poor workingwoman, a passing look that makes the strong man's heart more strong and happy, long after she has passed back to her house."

"Crown the truth supreme in every department and office of your soul. Set it on the throne with all the majesty of kingliness about it. Stand it in your temples and let the incense of your daily prayers rise up in all the beauty of God's holiness about it. Make it your guide and friend in all your hourly business: truth of design and truth of expectation, truth of plan and purpose and labor, truth of taste and judgment, of time and place—let them blend to make your whole life true and worthy of His service who is the Way, and the Truth, and the Life. Whoever will not bow before this monarch you have crowned, let him be rebel to you."

"We do not understand our life. Truth has laid her strong piers in the past eternity and the eternity to come, and now she is bridging the interval with this life of ours. . . . Controversies grow tame and tiresome to the mind that has looked on truth. . . . We walk the bridge of life. Can we not trust its safety on the two great resting-places of God's wisdom?"

He asks why it is the great truths, that possess the power of regenerating the soul to a higher life, should become trite and lose their appeal:

"We may make it a rule that whenever there is triteness there is some lack of truth; some falsehood, open or concealed, in speaker or hearer, wherein the triteness and tediousness consist. If, when a man is preaching what the whole gospel of nature and revelation forbids us to believe untrue, we yet find it dry and tame, it may be well for us to pause and ask for the seat of the untruth we may be sure there is somewhere. It may be in him. The words he says may be tinged with the insincerity of the mouth that says them. . . . Or it may be in us, for our frivolity may be so estranged from earnestness or moral truth that it does no even know its own footstep. . . . Or again it may be in circumstances and relations. For there is a truth of time as well a truth of purpose and fact. But one thing is certain: the triteness must be in some falseness somewhere, for truth is never trite. We pray the prayer and read the Bible of the old fathers with as much fresh comfort and delight as we see the old sun rise every morning."

"The vessels that we call empty are full to overflowing of earth's common air, and the hearts that seem to us most dull and vacant have their true share, we may remember, of true humanity, human motive, human prejudice, and human faith. Thinking thus we may win for them something of that active regard which, recognizing in them powers like our own, wills, hopes, capacities of truths, may go on to feed their hopes with noble aims, point their wills to worthy deeds, and fill their souls as full of truth as they are able to contain it."

One dominant motive running through these closely written note-books is intellectual, indicating birth into a world of fresh thought. There is a tone of mastery and sense of power, the realization that he was stepping into a rich heritage. Closely accompanying this attitude is another mood, never far away, demanding reconciliation of the activity of reason with the con-

duct of life.   To this end everything seems finally to converge.
He does not collate ideas for the purpose of comparison or discussion.   He dwells on the issue of life and how thought and truth
are related to it.   How ideas are to be brought into organic relationship with the will is still his problem, as it had been when
he first became aware of his intellectual power.

" A fresh thought may be spoiled by sheer admiration.   It was
given to us to work in and to live by.   There is more of clearness
in our eyes than of skill and readiness in our hands.   It is because every thought should minister to the work of life that it
deserves and claims our reverence.   It will give its blessing to
us only on our knees.   From this point of view, thought is as
holy a thing as prayer, for both are worship."

" We need new standards of usefulness and use.   There is a duty
incumbent on us to recognize and be grateful for the slightest
wedge that began the opening up of our lives.   Faith and faculties both need strengthening; conscience can help the first, long,
earnest daily care can help the second."

" Life is developing the energies of thought, while thought is
working out the richness that lies hid in life."

" Every past deed becomes a master to us; we put ourselves in
the power of every act.   A deed simply conceived and planned
belongs still to the heritage of thought, but when it passes into
act there comes a personality to it, we gain ownership in it, and
men will give us credit for its good and hold us responsible for
its ill."

" Even in the old superstitions, the amulets and charms, saints'
medals and saints' bones, bits of the cross and thorns from the
crown, there was some power of strength in weakness and safety
in alarm, because there was belief in them, and belief always
ministers to power."

" In the long years when great principles are busily clothing
and arming themselves for their work, our short-sighted weakness thinks them idle."

" Some great true principle must inspire our work.   There must
be no stint of labor where labor will tell for our neighbors' happiness, but no wasteful extravagance of it where it will not profit.
Our study must regulate itself by the principle of profusion that
is not waste.   And so most of all must our *faith*.   We have be-

lief enough to buy all needful truth.   That must be our first care.
Then if there be any left we may spend it afterwards as taste and
conscience lead.   But it is at once foolishness and wickedness so
to lavish it upon the luxuries of metaphysics and of science
that when we come to the providing of great household truths
—religion, morals, and the practical sense whose needful offices
fill up each day—we must stint them of the profusion that is their
due."

"It is a very happy but not at all a merry thing to pass from
another's mastery, and so more or less another's responsibility,
into our own."

"We carry all our interests with us, if we did but know it, into
all our work.   There is not enough of us, mind, heart, or brain,
to make many men of, hardly enough to make one well.   Every
scene and thought and habit weaves itself with every other to
clothe our life."

"Remember we are debtors to the good by birth, but remember
we may become debtors to the bad by life, and both sides of
service and allegiance must be paid alike."

"If we could find some soul so pure that we might say of its life,
Here is a spirit that has made the flesh its helper and its slave,
not its partner and its lord, then we might test our own life by
that soul's working, know that deeds of which he was capable were
pure and holy, unstained by fleshly corruption.   But no human
life can give us such a test.   By approximation only can we
make such use of human lives.   We must use our truth the other
way.   This deed must be deed for carnal and not saintly minds,
because I find what spirituality there is in me, what energy of
spirit there is in all our human race, protesting against it, shrink-
ing from it, growing weak or dead when it has yielded to its
power."

"There are truths which the moral state feels that it must have,
but which it still discredits—truths with ungracious offices, the
common executioners, as it were, who live in darkness till their
help is needed in the last resort.   Such is the old stern truth that
pain and death must follow human sin and suffering, is linked to
crime by crime's own nature and the charter of our life."

He deems it a false theory that we ought not to criticise defects in our neighbor's life unless we have the purity and truth
in ourselves we demand in him:

"It is false because it ignores that self-criticism which every honest man is far readier to bring in judgment to his own heart than to his brother's life. A true man's ideal once worthily set up, it is as much a sin against that standard to overlook another's failure as to flatter and disguise our own. In no malignant, or envious, or unworthy sense, our own imperfection is ever crying in our ears that our neighbors are imperfect too."

The absence of anything like a personal tone is a characteristic of these note-books. In reality they are confessions, the records of inward aspiration and experience. Here is a passage which, despite the impersonal form, reveals the reserve which throughout his life he wore as a garment, and also indicates something of its motive:

"If we talk with any weak companion that we meet of religion, of friendship, and truth, then friendship will cease to be beautful and religion to be holy, and truth will turn to falsehood, the trust and honor of our life be turned to doubt and baseness. In course of time we come to the knowledge of this mental domestic economy."

No summary will do justice to the wide range of thought and observation which these records of Brooks disclose; yet an imperfect summary may give a hint of what it is impossible to present in full quotation. He was meditating upon the fundamental appearances of things, the sun and the sunlight, the hills and the mountains, the rocks, and their crevices, the ocean, the waves, the tide, the green fields and the rivers; the phenomena in the life of man, his toil, his suffering, his evil and sin; but the aspiration also,—the hunger and the thirst for good; the city streets, the traffic, the cares of business, country lanes, the flowers, the sabbath bells, the churches; the Christian festivals and the divisions of time, the lapse of ages, the roll of past centuries, the great works of the past, the hopes of the present, human progress, its faith, its hopes and fears. He is impressed with finding that in past ages there were the same doubts, the same mysteries, that oppress humanity to-day, but meanwhile the world progresses. God meant it so to be, that each succeeding age should draw new strength and use from its doubts and sense of the mystery of things. The idea of perpetual growth is the ruling idea of religion and moral culture.

He meditates upon study and its relation to the coming years. It is simply putting the human powers at interest, in order to draw their accumulations hereafter. The thought of death, its meaning, its relation to life, is before him. There are unuttered thoughts in every man that give unconscious motive to action, like the Jewish name of God which was not pronounced. Historical facts and situations become parables with a wider application. He muses over Tertullian's challenge to the ancient world which has lost its faith in the worship of the gods of Olympus: "Quid ergo colunt, qui talia non colunt?" A new and higher reverence must always await the decline of the old faith. The crusades of the Middle Ages point to the constant necessity of spiritual search for Christ in his native land and country. One reason why men cling to the old machinery after it is useless is their dread of the first cost of introducing the new. It is shiftless housekeeping to fill the attics with rubbish thinking it may some time be useful. He meets in Coleridge the familiar passage which speaks of every man as a born Platonist or an Aristotelian. He does not apply it to himself, or ask which he may be, but he comments on the deduction that all the great questions of the mind are broader than they seem, how great men are bound most closely to their race. The daily questions of interest or truth win wider scope, and are part of the development of eternity.

Throughout the note-books are interspersed condensed statements of great truths, or epigrammatic sentences. "There is no mystery," he writes, "but waits to have an axiom; the wider grows our knowledge, the wider grows our store of axioms." Some of these brief statements are given in illustration:

"Many men have found a blessing and gone in and enjoyed it, other men may search their footprints and find where they went in. . . . We gain something of the prophet's inspiration if we stand in the doorway and cry, Ho! every one that thirsteth, to the thirsty thousands as they pass."

"There are two kinds of benefits that we may leave for men to thank us for: we may set up new wonders in the museum of knowledge, or we may merely make the doorway wider and access easier to the already crowded halls."

"Age is so apt to sneer when youth pronounces a judgment upon it. Is it then so sure that youth may not judge of age as age of youth? The one sees by hope, the other by memory; the one by faith, the other by experience; the one by the direct light of his own fresh nature, the other by the reflected light of his own dead years. I believe that a man of thirty knows more of what he will be at sixty than of what he was at twelve."

"It must be not what the world can do for me, but what I can do for the world. Surely God never meant that conscious weakness should lessen conscious duty. All nature, all life, all gospel truth, is full of the lesson, that the more we measure ourselves against the world the more we shall see that, little as we are, there is still great work for us to do in it."

"Let us think there is some noble economy we do not understand that makes you and me as necessary for our places here on earth as Paul and Moses were for theirs. Unless we learn to feel our lives essential we shall never live them well. If the world does not need my work, there is little enough of motive in myself to work for."

"Surely it shows a weak and false sense of the nature of true power that the great church rulers had to forge for pious use such scores of miracles about their saints. . . . We have outgrown the need of miracles like those. A moral miracle is growing more and more the test of saintship."

"No book has made itself fairly the possession of the race until it has made itself an unconscious necessity of men's life . . . . Almost every man has some book which is . . . not his master or his slave or his friend alone, but part of his own self."

"One great evil of the sin that we are full of is that it takes away our right to be indignant when other people sin, and so in time our standard of thought is lowered to their scale."

"A community is not safe or happy unless among its store-houses and dwellings and schools there is a church somewhere; and in our little world within there is a want that will be felt till we have built a sanctuary there."

"There are moments in the midst of life that have a power almost as marvellous as death. . . . These little deaths that we die daily catch some of the wonder of the death that we say so often we are all to die."

" Now and then we seem to catch some glimpses of that ideal world which Philo thinks God made in his own thought, before he made this world of sea and land we live in."

" If I knew that I had fathomed all the love or all the wisdom of God, how faith and reverence and trust would fall away from a being that such powers as mine could grasp."

" You and I go out to-night and look at the heavens all aflame with stars and call it beauty; but the wise man in his tower studies these same bright heavens and proclaims it law."

" Much of our principle and knowledge lies by us all unemployed, not a treasure because not a use."

" In earth's great armory hang each man's arms and the commission that contains his labors."

" No doubt that haunted you along the way has any right to trouble your convictions when the truth is found."

" We have no more right to confound doubt and disbelief than mystery and falsehood."

" The gracious mercy that binds omnipotence a willing servant to every humble human prayer."

" These constant forces, faith, conscience, religion, are everywhere consciously or unconsciously at work."

" Only by an identification of duty and delight will life grow up into manly grace."

"Every new sympathy according to its fulness makes us richer by more or less of a neighbor's life."

" Faith could once shake mountains; mountains now shake faith."

" We must answer for our actions; God will answer for our powers."

"There is a limit to our achievement; but none to our attempt."

" We are builders, not architects of history and life."

The principle underlying the fragmentariness, the wide reading, the studies and deeper meditations of which these note-books of Phillips Brooks are the evidence, is the value of the human soul. It is this which gives unity to the mass of quotations and reflections. He heard much in the Virginia Seminary of the love of souls as the motive of the Christian ministry. He had heard it from his childhood. It was the motto of the Evangelical school. It was now becoming the motive of his own life. But he followed his own method in making that motive a conscious possession. Before the human soul could be loved, it must be known. He turned to literature and to history as constituting together the biography of man. He wandered up and down its highways, he turned into its bypaths; but wherever he went, from great writers or those less known, heathen and Christian, ancient and modern, he never failed to extract judgments of value, unsuspected revelations of the beauty, the dignity, the greatness, the worth, of the human soul. He saw also the dangers with which the soul of man was surrounded, the sin, the evil, the curse, and the tragedy of life. He gathered a new and larger conception of what the salvation of such a soul must mean.

But to know the human soul he must enter into its experiences, its convictions, study their formulas, and somehow make them his own. He did not undertake to sift experiences or choose those agreeable to his mood. To sit in judgment upon the records was not for him, but rather, assuming that all was genuine, to enter into the meaning. The experience of the race was to be his experience. His object is to penetrate here and there, wherever the way is open, into the secret of the life of man. Whether he understands or not, whether he can appreciate what he has been called to appropriate as his natural heritage, is another question. He is willing to wait. As he pursues his search, he comes to Christ as the greatest figure in the records of human life. There are in his note-books indications that already he was drawn to that study of His life and teaching which was to be in the future his one preoccupation. But it was not until some years after he had left the seminary that he discerned the significance of the personality of Christ, in history, in the life of institutions, and in individual experience. Meantime, he recognized the value of that traditional presentation of His person with which he had been familiar from childhood, and sought to clothe it in impressive forms of appeal. Among the texts chosen for

his first sermons was one which became in later years the leading
motive of his preaching: "Have I been so long time with you,
and yet hast thou not known me, Philip?" (John xiv., 9).

In the souls of great men, the issues of the age in which they
live come to a focus. All that was characteristic of the nineteenth century was rising into the consciousness of Phillips
Brooks at the age of twenty-two. The issues the century had
raised came up before him for solution at the moment when he
was claiming his spiritual heritage. There was doubt and conflict
before he gained the victory. Differing epochs have differing
types of the process known as conversion. What may be called
his conversion differs from that of an Augustine or a Luther, but
the emergency was no less sharply distinguished. A new world
had been revealed to him, of which Augustine and Luther did not
dream. He was reading the new revelation in the world of outward nature, exploited by the labors of science or by the insight of
great poets. The conception of humanity anticipated by Herder
and Rousseau had been unfolded in its deeper significance, in its
details and as a whole, and laid before him, by the researches of
many students, as never hitherto in any age. And again, the
great body of modern literature, that had been produced with
such marvellous fertility, a consequence of the Protestant Reformation, still waited for its adjustment with Christian faith. In
these directions he could not wander without making the effort
to bring them into unity, to reconcile them with faith in God and
obedience to the divine will. In a word, the product of the centuries since the Reformation, in which must be included the
opening up of the history of humanity and the bringing together
of dissevered worlds, was handed to him with the injunction to
make it subservient to some higher unifying truth. He loved it
all; it was no question any longer of abandonment, but of reconciliation and appropriation in some deeper way.

In this process he struggled, haunted by doubts and negations, by disintegrating influences, whether bred by science or
by literature,—the substitution of impersonal law for a righteous
intelligent will, the worship of humanity in the place of Christ,
the fatalism in literature which was paralyzing moral effort and
inducing moral degeneracy. To be true to himself, to renounce
nothing which he knew to be good, and yet bring all things cap-

tive to the obedience of Christ, was the problem before him. He hesitated long before he could believe that such a solution was possible. His heart was with this rich, attractive world of human life, in the multiplicity and wealth of its illustrations, until it was revealed to him that it assumed a richer but a holier aspect when seen in the light of God. But to this end, he must submit his will to the divine will in the spirit of absolute obedience. Here the struggle was deep and prolonged. It was a moral struggle mainly, not primarily intellectual or emotional. He feared that he should lose something in sacrificing his own will to God's will. How the gulf was bridged he could not tell. He wrote down as one of the first of the texts on which he should preach, "Thy people shall be willing in the day of thy power," with the comment that "willingness is the first Christian step." Thus the conversion of Phillips Brooks becomes a representative process of his age. So far as the age has been great, through science or through literature, its greatness passed into his soul. The weakness of his age, its sentimentalism, its fatalism, he overcame in himself when he made the absolute surrender of his will to God. All that he had hitherto loved and cherished as the highest, instead of being lost was given back to him in fuller measure. To the standard he had now raised there rallied great convictions and blessed experiences, the sense of the unity of life, the harmony of the whole creation, the consciousness of joy in being alive, the conviction that heaven is the goal of earth. He was submitting himself in the spirit of a childlike docility to receive every lesson which the divine Instructor of humanity would impart. To use the familiar metaphor, he was like a lyre played upon in quick responsiveness by the spiritual forces in the universe, whether in nature or in the history of man, anxious to miss no chord of the heavenly harmony. Out of this process was born the preacher who in turn was to play upon humanity as a lyre, evoking from it the same response which his own soul had rendered back to the choir of the immortals. Beneath the rich contents of his mind and heart, there was a deeper simplicity. There was but one rule to follow: he must be the man that he ought to be, and was made to be, to do always the thing that he ought to do, and then labor to bring the world which he loved to his own standards.

CHAPTER V.

1858–1859.

LAST YEAR AS STUDENT. THE FIRST SERMON. ORDI-
NATION. CALL TO PHILADELPHIA. EXTRACTS FROM
NOTE-BOOK.

As Phillips Brooks was leaving Virginia in 1858 for the long
summer vacation, he admits that the second year in the seminary
had been a happy one. He liked the Virginia people, but, as he
remarks, he still hated Virginia, which meant that he could not
become reconciled to a land where slavery existed. He was
filled with joy at the thought of going home, sending word to his
mother to be on the doorsteps to meet him. The summer was
passed partly at the old Phillips homestead in North Andover,
and for the rest, with occasional excursions to Nahant and elsewhere, in Boston, in the usual way with the family. Much of his
time was devoted to his younger brothers, who looked up to him
as an example and guide, wondering at the new life on which he
was soon to enter. With his brother Frederick, who was to
enter Harvard in the fall, he took up again his college text-books,
and read over favorite Greek and Latin authors. It was a circumstance in the family history when his father purchased a
share in the Athenæum Library, enabling him to resort to
its rooms, with the latest books on its tables. The chief event
in his intellectual life was making the acquaintance of Goethe.
To one of his friends he writes: "I have just finished a book
that has held me very close ever since I began it, that is Lewes's
Life of Goethe. I had always rather shrunk from it till I took it
up quite by accident and liked it so much I found, or made, time
to put it right through." How deep the impression made by
Goethe is evident from a sonnet indited to him, beginning,
"Once in long ages God sends such a soul"; and further from
the numerous citations in his note-book.

"It is never well to put ungenerous constructions when others, equally plausible and more honorable, are ready; and we shall do well here to follow the advice of a thoughtful and kindly writer, to employ our imagination in the service of charity."

"Our strength is measured by our plastic power. . . . Bricks and mortar are mortar and bricks until the architect can make them something else."

"Make me feel what I have not yet felt, make me think what I have not yet thought, then I will praise you. But shrieks and noise will not supply the place of pathos."

"Art, says Lewes, enshrines the great sadness of the world, but is not itself sad. . . . Goethe could not write *Werther* before he had outlived Wertherism."

"Aujourdhui l'homme désire immensément mais il veut faiblement."

"The shout of freedom rouses them to revolt; no sooner are they free than the cry is 'Whom shall we obey?'"

"The roll of drums has this merit at all events, that it draws men from their library table to the window, and so makes them look out upon the moving, living world of action, wherein the erudite may see a considerable sensation made even by men unable to conjugate a Greek verb in Greek letters."

"Let mental culture go on advancing, let science go on gaining in depth and breadth, and the human intellect expand as it may, it will never go beyond the elevation and moral grandeur of Christianity as it shines forth in the Gospels."

These following sentences, extracted from Goethe's letters, may be assumed to have a personal application:

"I have a purer delight than ever when I have written something which well expresses what I meant."

"The happiest thing is that I can now say I am on the right path, and from this time forward nothing will be lost."

"I find in the Christian religion virtually the foundation of the highest and noblest; and the various manifestations of the same in life appear to me only therefore so repugnant and insipid, because they are failed representations of the highest." (Extract from letter of Schiller to Goethe.)

Brooks entered deeply into Goethe's conception of life, and gained from him an insight into the relations of art to the highest development of man; but he also makes a protest against the one-sidedness of Goethe's estimate of culture. Goethe had said, "We know that we exist when we recognize ourselves in others"; Brooks's comment runs, "Nay, we do not fairly know of our existence till we recognize ourselves in God."

"Gradually, as we study the divine nature, there comes out from it impulse after impulse that enters into our own hearts and finds some impulses akin to itself doing the blind work there. Gradually we catch some glimpse within ourselves of God's image in humanity. . . . We leave the pagan theology that makes God but a great man, and reverently study the divine to learn of it what truth and beauty God has planted in the human."

The abiding influence of Goethe may be traced in the controlling principle of Brooks's preaching that the Christian life involves spiritual culture, an exigent opportunity for the development of the perfect man according to a divine ideal.

On his return to Alexandria in the fall he was invited to take charge of a new department of the seminary, where students were to receive a preliminary training before entering upon the study of theology. The experiment was afterwards abandoned, but at the time it was regarded as an important undertaking, and for the person to whom it was intrusted it was a mark of confidence and esteem as well as recognition of scholarship. It had a further significance for Brooks—it meant success in a line where before he had met with failure. The salary was small, but sufficient to meet his expenses—a consideration with him of no small importance. The time had come when he should be independent. He disliked to call on his father for money. His apology when he did so was met with remonstrances that he should be so sensitive. The home correspondence indicates the possibility of a strain on both sides, the parents slowly relinquishing the authority which the sense of responsibility begets. His mother was the first to yield. But habit had a stronger hold upon the father, who writes to his son that he is willing he should act for himself in the matter of this invitation to take the preparatory school. In other ways the father clung to the authority traditionally maintained in Puritan households. Years afterwards he complained in his journal that he had not been consulted about an important event in his son's career.

But the mother was also passing through a trial of her own in consequence of her son's invincible reserve. Her letters to him met with no response, letters displaying such depth of love that they cannot be read without emotion. No lack of affection for his mother caused this seeming neglect. It was simply impossible for him to answer such letters. Of the effect they produced on him, silence was the only, perhaps the most fitting, expression. Neither then nor throughout his life did he freely give himself to any one in unrestrained intercourse or personal communion. What he gave he did in impersonal ways. About his inner life or religious experience he was dumb. He resembled his mother in boundless capacity for affection, whose outlet was at last to be found in preaching.

The father's letters were those of a man of affairs, conversant with the world, more interesting because rich with the interests of actual life. They could be answered by the son without committing himself to any utterance regarding his inner self. When a young man is entering upon life, the father naturally steps forward as his guide, with practical suggestion, while the mother recedes for a moment into the background. But this moment passes away, and the mother resumes her ascendency. It seems to have been so in the case of Phillips Brooks.

At last he broke his reserve, the accumulated silence of a year, in a letter to his brother William:

"Saturday evening, November 6, 1858.

"This letter is going to be all about myself, and forgive it accordingly. Somehow the work I am at begins to look very different and strange to me. Do you know I feel as I never felt before, to find myself here within eight months of the ministry? Whether it is this getting at sermon-writing that makes me feel more than ever how weak I am to go about the world's greatest work, I certainly do feel it fearfully to-night. But yet I tell you, Bill, I can't recall many pleasanter hours than those that I have spent in writing my two or three first poor sermons. It seems like getting fairly hold of the plough, and doing something at last. I always have been afraid of making religion professional, and turning it into mere stock in trade when I approached the work, but I have never felt more deeply how pure and holy and glorious a thing our Christianity is, what a manly thing it is to be godly, till I sat down to think how I could best convince other men of its purity and holiness. I do enjoy the work, and, with all my unfitness for it, look forward to a happy life in trying to do it. Somehow I have never been quite frank with you; as much with you as anybody, but not thoroughly with any one, I think. But I am beginning to own up more fairly to myself. Every day it seems as if the thing I have got to do stood up plainer before me and forced me into frankness. My ideas of a minister are a different thing from what they were two years ago, poor and unworthy enough yet, but I think growing purer and more worthy. It seems to me every day more and more as if it were treason to his work for him to neglect any part of his whole nature that is given to that work, and so I think the broadest mental outline, and the deepest moral truth and the purest spiritual faith are more and more the demands, one and all of which Christ makes of his workmen, growing to *perfect men* and so to perfect Christians, to the measure of the stature of the fulness of Christ. I have just been writing a sermon on that subject, the 'Manliness of Faith.'

" I have undertaken this year to preach plain sermons to a small congregation of from fifty to seventy-five people at one of the stations near the seminary, and feel that I am better for the work, more and deeper in sympathy with simple, honest men, and have a clearer light into what common men's minds are doing, and how they may be taught to do better and nobler things.

" PHIL."

The letter was most exceptional; there is hardly another to be compared with it for self-revelation in all his correspondence. Could the family at home have had the opportunity of knowing his inner life any anxieties would have been removed as to the sincerity and genuineness of his religious purpose, or any doubts as to his success in the ministry. Meantime this personal letter, read by all the family, was the source of profound pleasure and satisfaction. His mother was silent, interpreting more accurately how such a letter should be met. His father wrote in reply:

" It was so exactly what I have been wanting to hear from you so long, it breathed the spirit which I have so long wished and prayed for in you, and I am confident you will hereafter feel happier in your own mind. Do go on, my very dear son, and cultivate that feeling, prayerfully and strongly. I am pleased, too, that you find your situation at the seminary pleasanter and more to your satisfaction. . . . I would not be so selfish as to lead you to think that I am expressing only my own feelings; by no means; we all rejoiced at it, and your mother was exceedingly gratified. It was a family letter, and only considered as such. Do write so often, my dear son, and express your feelings freely. You cannot imagine how it would gladden your parents' hearts."

The last year at the Virginia Seminary was a full one, though somewhat disturbed by the nearer approach to the reality of the ministerial life. It was well that the best part of his work of preparation had already been done, the foundation securely laid, and the main direction of his life work clearly discerned. During the last years it was the custom to require written sermons of the students, which were read before the class and the faculty for criticism. So Phillips Brooks came to his first sermon, which seems to have marked a definite moment in his experience. The family at home were also greatly moved, as by some decisive event, which would determine whether life was to be a success or a failure, as if it would reveal the result of the years of preparation about which he had been so reticent. The father was bold to ask that the sermon be sent him for perusal, with the understanding that it should be sacredly kept private. The word "private" was written on the manuscript above the text. The son in turn asks for his father's opinion:

"Tell me how it struck you? How it would have struck you had you heard a strange young man, of six feet four, preach it in your own pulpit; what you would have said about it when first got home? Be indulgent with it, it is my first."

The sermon did not elicit any enthusiasm from his father or mother, but, as the expression goes, it seems to have given "good satisfaction." The father thought it "sound," the mother recognized in it "the Gospel" and was especially pleased because Christ was made prominent. On the other hand, in the seminary it made a deep impression—the prophecy of the great preacher. Brooks himself referred to it in his later years:

"I well remember the first sermon that I ever achieved. The text was from II Corinthians xi., 3, 'The simplicity that is in

Christ,' and a cruel classmate's criticism of it was that 'there was very little simplicity in the sermon and no Christ.' I am afraid that he was right, and I am sure that the sermon never was preached again. Its lack of simplicity and lack of Christ no doubt belonged together. It was probably an attempt to define doctrine instead of to show a man, a God, a Saviour." [1]

But the sermon was a noteworthy utterance. It was his manifesto, and revealed his orientation, and the process by which it had been reached. There are signs in it of his rejection of favorite Evangelical shibboleths, while retaining, undiminished, the Evangelical principle of knowing nothing but Christ. Beneath the utterance lie the struggles of the years when he had been ridding himself of the conventional language of a religious party. As the Evangelical school, like every other, passed into its decline, it was disturbed by fears lest its young men should accept principles endangering the creeds, or weakening the hold of familiar doctrines whose external clothing was identified with the essence of the divine revelations. It was tacitly assumed, or so it seemed, that salvation depended on holding "sound views." It had become customary to speak of the pride of the intellect as the greatest foe to faith; to "preach Christ" was to renounce intellectual activity. On the other hand, Phillips Brooks had feared that if he became a Christian minister it meant the sacrifice of the rich and ennobling influences of literature, the withdrawal from the large human directions of the intellect and the imagination. When he left home to begin his study for the ministry, it was with the words of some friend or classmate ringing in his ears, that Christianity meant the lessening of a man, the narrowing of the range of human interests. He may have seen something of this in those whom he knew, and have feared it in himself. He had determined to know for himself whether it was true.

The note which he strikes at the opening of his sermon springs from the deep conviction that the great positive valuable lines of human activity converge in Christ. His doctrine is positive, negations are absorbed in larger affirmations: not the abnegation or suppression of the reason, but its consecration to Christ

[1] *Essays and Addresses*, p. 74. The greater part of the sermon is given in the same volume as an essay, with the title "The Centralizing Power of the Gospel."

is his message. What is true of the intellect applies also to feel-ing and to will. So long as consecration to Christ is the ruling endeavor, there is no danger of license or anarchy within the Church. There will be developed a larger Christian Church for all the world, whose mark will be unification and simplicity. There is something solemnly heroic in this one central purpose standing calmly in the midst of the feverish anarchy of the world.

Such was the substance of the first sermon. As a sermon it was overcrowded with thought, ending with a momentous conclu-sion, where he gives the rationale of faith, worked out for himself in the seclusion of his soul. But it is here only hinted at in a few sentences:

"This new Christian simplicity is not perfect till it recognizes the world's hope in its own. Then there comes the true 'liberal-ity' of our religion. The man begins to identify himself with the race, and wins a share in its collective faith and power. He multiplies his life eight hundred millionfold. The world was made, and the sun and stars ordained, and salvation sent to earth alike for humanity and him. The history of the race becomes his experience, the happiness of the race his glory, the progress of the race his hope. He begins to say, '*We* shall do this and thus, win new secrets from nature and new truth from God,' for this man goes hand in hand with humanity down the highways of its life, till they stand together before the throne of God in heaven. He says of Christ's truths: 'I believe in these things because I know that they have helped my race. I look to them as I look to the sun, with a faith that all these centuries of sunlight forbid me to disown. I hear them from the Bible claiming my alle-giance, as from all nature I hear God's truth demanding that I should give reason room to grow to love and faith.'"

Brooks had felt his isolation at Alexandria, and was forced to strike out for himself; yet he owed a great debt to the school in Virginia for what it did for him. It was something that he could write in his note-book this paragraph, indicating his grow-ing respect for that which at first he resented:

"It is a noble and beautiful thing to feel ourselves growing out of our own contempt; to recognize each day that something which we have been weakly despising as mean and poor is high and pure and rich in worth and beauty."

He also took his first lessons in the doctrine of tolerance.   Individual conviction must go hand in hand with the recognition of the same privilege for others.   Thus in his note-book he writes:

" You have a rock down somewhere in your soul, and that is the rock for you to build on.   Beware how you borrow a fragment of some other man's and plant it on your sandy places and try to build on that.   Dig deep, dig well, dig till you find the proper basis of your strength."

" Poor feeble creatures in a feeble world, we each must catch what is most comfort to his feebleness.   Believe in mine for me; I will believe in yours for you.   Surely we each have quite enough to do to hold our own, without this cruel folly of saying to another, 'Your comfort is a cheat, your hope a heresy, the earnest life that you are living all a lie.'   If you can give him something better, do it in God's name.   If you can only sneer away his peace and pleasure you belie your manhood when you do it."

" Surely we might make more allowance for the roads we walk in if the great ends we aim at are the same.   Our paths through life are like the great tracks men map out on the seas.   They say they go the same way that the ships of old have gone; they mean they seek the same harbor, round the same headlands, shun the same quicksands, read the same silent constant stars.   But the waves they plough have changed a myriad times; the great unrest or circumstance has broken into confusion the unquiet road they travel, but they call it still the same, because by the same great eternal sureties, it points them to the same old heaven.   So by the sure witness of faith we pass over the restless path of human accident to the great truth harbor that we seek."

In the case of such a pupil as Phillips Brooks, no theological training school could have been found adequate, nor could teachers have been found to direct his course.   He had the vision of a perfect teacher, but must have known that he did not exist, nor was it desirable that any student should have so easy a solution of the problems of life.   This passage is from one of his early note-books:

"A man that you could come to with the results of your speculation, come to him confidingly and truthfully, and say: ' Here, see what I have done; take and try what truth, what reality, or what solid stuff there is about it; weed out for me the weak; test how much strong remains, how strong it is, what use it is good for;

try it unsparingly and thoroughly, for you are wiser and more trustworthy than I.' "

Among his teachers was a man who still lives as a tradition by the power of his personality. Brooks had been attracted to Dr. Sparrow from the first, speaking of him in a letter as "a splendid man, . . . clear as daylight, and fair and candid, without a particle of dogmatism or theological dry rot." In after life he paid his tribute to him as "one of the three or four men whom I have known whom I look upon with perpetual gratitude for the help and direction they have given my life, and whose power I feel in forms of action and kinds of thought very different from those in which I had specially to do with them."

It was also of great service to him that he was forced by the routine of the seminary to become familiar with the belief of other ages, and to know the history of Christian doctrine. It was sometimes said of him in his after life that he seemed blind to theological distinctions or that he had an inborn deficiency for theological statements. It would be truer to say that by some native instinct he shunned them. But he was familiar enough with the history of religious formulas to know where the pitfalls lay, and sagacious enough to avoid them. He was never guilty of proclaiming as if it were new truth some old exploded heresy. So well was he indoctrinated by theological training that he did not err through ignorance or make theological blunders. When he was once urged to read more carefully the old theological writers he replied that he knew beforehand all they had to say.

The custom in the seminary of calling for essays from the students led to Brooks's expression of himself on various controverted points. These papers still exist. They may not indicate his final judgment in all cases and yet there is no evidence in his later work of any material change. What he saw he saw clearly. He had difficulties with infant baptism which were not at once overcome. In an essay on the question why Christianity should not have taken a stronger hold on the world, his answer is that it has done all that could have been expected from it, confirming its divine origin and giving promise of a great future. In discussing the creeds he meets the objection that they fetter the intellect and hinder mental ability and progress. He thinks they have been abused by a kind of intellectual idolatry among the cold intellectual races of the North, as sensual image-worship has been among the Southern races. But, on the other hand, the presentation of truth in clear and sharply defined propositions, as in a creed, has a value for the mind in its first activity. It satisfies a certain human natural desire for clearness, and overcomes the natural distrust of vagueness. "Without the creed each man must have the original force in himself to select and build his own position, deriving no help from others' previous endeavors, with no historical ground to build upon and no historical support to look to. It is demanding of ordinary minds an originality which we have no right to presuppose." But even granting that men had this ability, yet the rejection of the creeds "is taking out of truth the social elements that God in setting up his Church infused so strongly in it."

The most liberal Christianity among us,—practically what have we seen its rejection of formal confessions of faith amount to? Its masses—its men that correspond to those who in the style of much-abused servility give in their matter-of-course assent to old systems of doctrine—have simply rejected that assent, to say, as servilely and with quite as little candid judgment, 'I believe in this or that preacher or divine.' Servility has been transferred from systems to individuals, and liberality has but bound the new freeman in a close and more unquestioning adherence to his sect or some traditional leader of that sect."

In another essay he finds that the Thirty-Nine Articles revolve around the doctrine of justification by faith as their central theme, and that errors which the Articles condemn spring from their denial of this central conviction. The Articles are not a string of fragmentary utterances, but are grouped into unity by a great common belief. He studied the deeper issues of the Pauline theology,—the distinction between gospel and law,—asking why it was that Jewish and Christian Churches should be tempted by the shallowness of the Pelagian heresy. He writes on the propitiatory sacrifice of Christ, taking for a text the words of Bishop Butler and confirming their truth: "By the general prevalence of propitiatory sacrifices over the heathen world, the notion of repentance alone being sufficient to expiate guilt appears to be contrary to the general use of mankind."

He comes to the conclusion that the principles of Christian

theology must in their origin have struck their roots in the life and confession of humanity, uncontrolled by an external conventional authority. Not only in regard to the idea of sacrifice, but of the doctrines of the fall and of the incarnation, does it hold true that they were believed by the race of man; and especially was the Incarnation—the union of God with man in some divine-human being—longed for and earnestly desired, even anticipated in crude ways in the heathen world. As such, these doctrines form part of the necessary experience of man; they reveal the characteristic essence of the human soul; they are not badges of bondage, but the conditions of human freedom, by which the race has risen to the realization of its divine heritage.

All these theological essays show a conservative tendency of mind; they reveal study and were carefully written; but although conservative they disclose an independent and original character; the conclusions are his own and not adopted to please his teachers. What most impresses one is the capacity and the character of the scholar. Especially is this scholarly habit manifest in an essay on the New Testament Greek, and in another on the prevalence of the Greek language in the time of Christ. He made an elaborate study of the Fourth Eclogue of Virgil, as a prophecy of the Incarnation.

There is in the note-books a somewhat curious and vague statement as to how Brooks looked upon much of the current religious thought and expression to which he submitted. It was written during his second year at the seminary, earlier than many of the essays alluded to, before his outlook had been enlarged by further study. But it is a characteristic passage, in that it contains a prophecy or anticipation of his future work:

"These things may be true or false that we are saying and believing every day about the daily points that are always coming up for us to think or speak about. We cannot but fear that very many of them are very far indeed from truth; but still it is well for us to believe them, and to say them, too, for it is these words and faith that really make a life for us which otherwise we could not have. It will not do to turn our whole existence into a prudent suspense. We must be ready to say promptly and firmly, ' Yes, that is right and that is wrong, this is wise and that is foolish, and this is strong and that is weak.' Then, when we reach the end of each stage of our journey and look curiously back to see what sort of work we have made of it, we shall see something more than a bare, broad, safe plain. There will be marks of our labor all over it, a well dug here, a fort raised there, a garden or two planted, and a forest or two cleared away,—much work clumsily, no doubt, and rudely done, perhaps some few trees felled that should have been left standing, and some few wells dug where a wiser head might have told us there was no water to be had; but on the whole, the field is better for our toil, it will be easier for future travellers; and we too are better for it, and the rest of our journey will be easier to us for the health and muscle that this early work has given us."

The word "believe" is here used in the sense of assent. If we may interpret a passage like this, somewhat vague and tentative, it might be said that he appears as acquiescing in many theological statements of whose meaning he was not certain; he was comparing the Church to some vast mansion with its surrounding estate, built in generations long gone by, and adapted for use and the needs of a later age. But it was better to dwell in it as it was than to destroy and rebuild from the foundations. "It will not do to turn our whole being," he writes, "into a prudent suspense, for in the meantime we should be homeless and without the things that make for life. But it is possible in this mansion, or the estate where it is planted, to make some changes or improvements, adapting it to the demands of a larger and fuller life."

It was the crowning glory of the Evangelical school that it was the first to recognize the claim of foreign missions. The missionary spirit prevailed among the students of the Virginia Seminary to an extent unequalled elsewhere in the Episcopal Church. Since 1835 its graduates began to work in foreign fields, till fifty-five years later there were enrolled over thirty missionaries. Each year witnessed the enthusiasm of the students as they bade farewell to classmates. On these occasions, Phillips Brooks was taking lessons in the power of foreign missions to test the reality of the life and faith of the Church. If the call had come to him, it would have satisfied the aspirations of his mother, who never wearied of holding up to her children the examples of great missionaries as the noblest the world could offer. But the Spirit called him to another work, where heroism and self-sacrifice could be illustrated as well as in a foreign land.

There were other ways in which the theological seminary in Virginia exercised upon Brooks a strong and beneficent influence. He found himself on his arrival there plunged into a fervent religious atmosphere whose warmth of devotion was in contrast with the colder reserve of New England. He has left a record of his first impression and the inference he drew for his guidance:

"I shall never forget my first experience of a divinity school. I had come from a college where men studied hard, but said nothing about faith. I had never been at a prayer-meeting in my life. The first place I was taken to at the seminary was the prayer-meeting; and never shall I lose the impression of the devoutness with which these men prayed and exhorted one another. Their whole souls seemed exalted and their natures were on fire. I sat bewildered and ashamed and went away depressed. On the next day, I met some of those men at a Greek recitation. It would be little to say of some of the devoutest of them that they had not learned their lessons. Their whole way showed that they never learned their lessons; that they had not got hold of the first principles of hard, faithful, conscientious study. The boiler had no connection with the engine. The devotion did not touch the work which then and there was the work, and the only work, for them to do. By and by, I found something of where the steam did escape to. A sort of amateur preaching was much in vogue among us. We were in haste to be at what we called our work. A feeble twilight of the coming ministry we lived in. The people in the neighborhood dubbed us parsonettes." [1]

To combine thorough intellectual culture with the intensity of religious devotion became from this time his ideal. The prayer-meeting helped to overcome the reserve which, however invincible in his relation with individuals, disappeared when he entered the pulpit. One of his fellow-students bears this testimony to his power of extemporaneous prayer:

" Another, more sacred, thought of him goes back to the class prayer-meeting, held each week in one of our rooms. We had never heard such prayers, so fervent, trustful, simple, so full of what we should not have guessed was in him till he testified beside us on his knees. He had learned a lesson which the books could not teach, worth more to him and to those he knelt with, then and afterwards, than the cultured scholarship he brought

[1] *Lectures on Preaching*, p. 44.

from Harvard, or the systematic theology that Alexandria gave us."

The endowment which we call feeling had come to Phillips Brooks by inheritance in an extraordinary degree; a talent improved, but originally given as by free grace, as to the man that had already ten talents.   Only one who has had the privilege of poring over his mother's letters can realize how rich and wonderful was the gift she had transmitted.   His father wrote to him when he had important news to communicate.   But the mother wrote when her heart was full of a mother's love which knows no bound.   She longed for him, she thought of him every hour and minute of the day, she counted the weeks and the days till she should see him; sometimes she was so impatient that she feared that she could not wait for his coming, but must fly to him.   It was this element in Phillips Brooks that formed one large constituent of his strength.   Those who knew him knew that his capacity for deep feeling was like the ocean in its majesty; that ideas, experiences, the forces of life, which appealed to him, roused him as a whirlwind, and feeling became a torment until it had found expression.

The cognitive power of feeling was one of the truths borne in on him from his arrival at the seminary.   He enters the statement in his earliest note-book—as if he had discovered some new power of determining his growth—that "feeling is a teacher." But the intellectual faculties were on the whole in the ascendant in these earlier years, and he frequently alludes to problems which he has not solved.   What he wants is some principle of unity; he is still haunted with the unpossessed secret process by which intellect and feeling shall be transmuted into fuel for the will.   He has visions of Christ in some moment of transfiguration, and would fain penetrate more closely into the strange, bewildering mystery of His power.

"There is the old city child's difficulty in thinking of his city as a whole.   He knows this street and that street, but never recognizes the organic town standing surrounded by others like it, acting as an individual with concrete purposes and thoughts.   I do not know that other children have this difficulty, but it always troubled me.   And there is something of the same kind, I think, to most of the minds new born into the world of thought when they try to conceive of each man's separate life."

"As behind the sun, and clouds, and silent stars, lies the great eternity of space, so behind this man's or that man's living, or thinking, or enjoying, lies the immensity of life, that we try to measure by these planets that God has stationed in it."

"There is one magic word somewhere, if we can find it, with which we can tame these truths, as the old magicians subdued the spirits to their will. Called by that word they come to our confessional and tell their secrets. The power that was in them passes into us, and we become their masters, as they once were ours. They go to do our bidding in humility, and own our sovereignty now by that magic word."

"I could not but be struck to-day in our Virgil class with the contrast of the heaven of the *Æneid* with the heaven of the Revelation. 'Solemque suum, sua sidera norunt,' says the poet (*Æneid*, vi., 641). 'And the city hath no need of the sun, neither of the moon, to shine in it; for the glory of the Lord did lighten it and the Lamb is the light thereof' (Rev. xxi., 23). So speaks the Evangelist of what he saw on the Lord's Day in Patmos. Once get the Bible idea of Deity and we feel that it needs something more than a new earth to make a heaven."

He was now anticipating with a mingled sense of joy and of fear the work he was soon to begin. Visions of the profession of a teacher seem to have faded away for the moment. Life was rich in its promise, with the feeling of his days before him; but there is no trace of any sense of superiority, no consciousness of gifts that raised him above other men, or expectation of distinction which if not satisfied would beget the soreness of disappointed ambition. His outlook was in humility of spirit. There was a consciousness of inward harmony which began to be reflected in the symmetry of his person. The happiness within was stamped upon the features, in place of a certain anxious look which some of the early photographs display. He was looking forward to his own marriage as he chronicles the marriages of his friends, but as yet in a general way. He felt no call to a celibate life. He wrote love songs and was cherishing an ideal dream of human love, most rare and sacred. To one of his friends who asked him for the conditions he would make, he replied, in a humorous way, that in the first place she must be small; in the second place she must be beautiful; in the third place she must not know too much, and he added in the fourth place, as if an afterthought, she must of course be good. He was rather exigent in his demand for personal beauty of form and figure, as though an injury had been done him where it was wanting. His letters contain many allusions of this kind after the manner of all young men. This is a specimen:

" I received the other day an invitation to dinner from one of the nabobs of Alexandria, which, as I afterwards found, I owed entirely to his having been rather intimate with Uncle Brooks and his family when he was at college in Cambridge thirty years ago. Of course I went, and had a very pleasant time. So you see our rich relations do us some little good sometimes after all. He lives in great style, keeps a grand house, sets a splendid table, and has one of the prettiest girls (age about eighteen years one month, I should say) for a daughter that I ever saw. She is the prettiest girl I have seen in Virginia, and that is n't saying much. But she is really quite stunning—dark hair and eyes, fine complexion, dresses tastily, lively, full of fun, and cordial on first acquaintance, as all Southern ladies are."

For some time there had been rumors of possible calls to parishes. His old friend and pastor Dr. Vinton, who had become rector of the new Church of the Holy Trinity in Philadelphia, had expressed a wish that Brooks should become his assistant. The opening seemed attractive, the church ranked among the strongest and most influential in the city, and the association with Dr. Vinton was alluring. Other positions of a similar kind had been mentioned. He was weighing the question whether it was better to begin as an assistant in a large parish, or to strike forth independently and from the start assume complete responsibility. It was a Sunday afternoon in March, 1859, that two strangers appeared in the little chapel of the Sharon Mission, some three miles from the Seminary, where Brooks was officiating as a lay-reader and preaching extemporaneous sermons. Whether he had won any recognition as a preacher by these early efforts is uncertain; the testimony seems to vary. After the services on this Sunday afternoon were over, the two strangers came forward and gave him the call to become the rector of the Church of the Advent in Philadelphia.

He was now for the second time confronting the entrance upon life, and the old memory of his failure in Boston was before him.

If allusion to this incident were omitted the narrative would be incomplete. At this time the sensitiveness of his constitution was so great that he was almost made ill. He gave up his work on the following Monday; on Tuesday he complained of headache and of the weather, and for the rest of the week he was wretched. In one of his letters he says, "I have n't passed such a week for three years"; and again, "I have just been driven crazy this last week between a need of thinking and these recitations that do n't leave a minute to think in." Such extreme susceptibility, followed by nervous exhaustion, may seem extraordinary, in contrast with his heroic powers of endurance in later years, when no amount of excitement seemed to tell on his vigorous frame. But it was not so in the earlier years. After his first day's experience as an usher in the Latin School, he attempted, as he told a friend, to take a walk, but found himself so exhausted after a few minutes that he was unable to continue it. It may be that in this peculiarity of his physical make-up lay one of the conditions of his power.

The call to Philadelphia created as much excitement in the quiet household in Boston. It was a family affair, in which his parents and brothers shared as by divine right. The solidarity of the family life found expression in the numerous letters that came and went. There were conditions to be considered: Dr. Vinton's wishes in the matter, the will of the bishop of Massachusetts, whose consent must be gained. One thing seems to have been taken for granted, that he would not return to Massachusetts to begin his ministry. There is a tone of excitement and confusion in the letters; the dread of making a mistake is apparent. It seems a momentous task at the age of twenty-three to assume the complete charge of a church. The issue was finally decided by a compromise; he declined to accept the formal call to become the rector, but agreed to officiate for three months; when that time had expired the vestry were to be at liberty to give him a permanent call, or he was at liberty to withdraw. So the issue of his life was decided. He had gone to the theological school as an experiment, uncertain what the result would be. These years of quiet and seclusion had done their work and had resolved the tentative mood into a glowing enthusiasm for the work to which he now believed himself to be called. How he regarded the prospect is told in a letter to his brother, where he seems to defend himself against anything like indifference, or suspicion that he was acting in a perfunctory way:

"THEOLOGICAL SEMINARY, Thursday evening, March 17, 1859.

". . . As to Advent, let me be frank. I feel, I believe, more fully than you can the responsibility and labor of the place. I know, too, more deeply than you can my own deficiencies, and yet I have engaged to go there, at least for a temporary supply. One thing I am sure of,—it was not accepted from any ambitious desire of occupying a conspicuous or responsible place. I am going honestly, as I believe, in a sincere feeling that I *ought* to go, in an earnest conviction that there is work there to be done, and that by a strength above my own I shall be helped to do it. The ministry has been growing a new thing to me this year; and most of all this direct presentation of a field of work has, I believe, sent me outside of myself to look for direction and for strength where it is promised to us all. I believe I am going at last in humility to tell the Bible story to those people. I have told them that that story was all I had to bring, in all its simplicity and truth, and I hope to find strength to tell it plainly and distinctly at least. In all this I have weighed the solid facts. From what experience I have had, I do not feel afraid of two plain sermons in a week. I have gained considerable facility in extempore speaking, and shall do that much. The other work, visiting, etc., I am unused to, but do not look forward to with dread. They are kind and simple people, and ready and anxious to make their minister's life a pleasant one."

It was decided he should begin his rectorship of the Church of the Advent on the second Sunday of July, 1859. But as this would deprive him of a vacation after a hard year of labor, he asked for leave of absence in order to have a month at home to recuperate. And this home-coming meant much to him. He had retrieved the failure of three years before, when the world looked blank to him, without opening or opportunity. He took a humble view of it all, for the lesson in humility had penetrated the recesses of his spirit. On his journey he stopped by the way at Philadelphia, where he met the vestry of the Church of the Advent and surveyed the scene of his future labors. While he was in Boston he seems to have been diligent in attending religious services, dividing his time with the Athenæum and the new books.

The great event after his return was the ordination to the diaconate. There were many visitors to the "Hill" in view of the sacred festivities impending, among them his own father, who with his eye for men and affairs enjoyed all that came under his observation. He writes home that his father made a fine impression. Thursday, June 30, was the Commencement Day, when, in the presence of his future church warden, his father, the large audience, and the ecclesiastical dignitaries, he delivered his thesis on "The Centralizing Power of the Gospel." The next day, Friday, was Ordination Day, ushered in with a prayer-meeting. Then came Bishop Meade of Virginia. At nine o'clock was the interview appointed when the young candidate for orders should hear what the bishop had to say to him. Bishop Meade was held in high reverence in Virginia as the founder of the theological seminary, a preacher as well as administrator, and a leader in the counsels of the Evangelical school in the church. The services in the chapel began at eleven o'clock, and the sermon was preached by the Rev. Mr. Gibson of Petersburg, Va.

The next day he started for Fredericksburg, Va., to pay a visit to his friend the Rev. A. M. Randolph (now the bishop of Southern Virginia), who had offered him his pulpit for the following Sunday. Bishop Randolph has contributed this account of the memorable day:

"In thinking of my impression of the two sermons and of the way they were spoken, and also of the impression made upon the many intelligent people who listened to them, I am reminded of these characteristics of his preaching, which all who ever heard him will recognize,—a singular absence of self-consciousness, a spontaneity of beautiful thinking, clothed in pure English words, a joy in his own thoughts, and a victorious mastery of the truth he was telling, combined with humility and reverence and love for the congregation. I have heard him often since, and the impression was always the same."

The story of the ordination and of the last week at the theological seminary may fitly close with a letter from his father, written at Philadelphia, where he stopped on his journey home and while the scene was still vivid which had so deeply moved him:

"PHILADELPHIA, Sunday evening, July 3, 1859.

". . . I can hardly realize the events of the past week. They have been too great and too delightful to my feelings, Phillips, to be yet fully realized. I do thank God for the many things I have seen and heard, and for you, my dear son, that you have given your friends such good impressions as were expressed to me at the seminary. Depend upon it, my heart has been gladdened and made happy beyond what I dare express or can express. I only wish your anxious and loving mother could have been with me and seen all I did, also. At times I have thought it too much to realize. You perhaps little thought when you were having that last meeting in Strong's room, and the music of your voices sounded in my ears so sweetly, I was in spirit with you. And to-day, while kneeling at the chancel rail where you are to assist in dispersing the elements of the communion, how full my heart was, and how earnestly I prayed that you might have the power of the Holy Spirit showered upon you, to be faithful and devoted in all your great and responsible duties in that sacred place. This last week I shall never forget. That ordination day will remain foremost among all the scenes of my future life."

And so the period of his preparation ends. The long stretch of his life was before him, the seemingly endless years. It is a characteristic of the young that they dwell upon death and its meaning, more than those who approach old age, or are bearing the burden and heat of the day. He was wont at this time to ponder upon the awful secret, as throwing light upon the meaning of life. But he made no effort to bring before his imagination the intervening years. It was of these, however, that his father and mother were thinking, and more particularly his mother, as she forecast the future in the anxiety of her love. Her one prayer for him was that he should lead the rest of his life according to this beginning. It is not possible for the young to look at things from the point of view of those who are older. It may have been so with him. And yet the refrain of the letters his mother wrote must have lingered in his mind,—the earnest invocation to be faithful to the end in order that he might receive at last the crown of rejoicing before God: "Be thou faithful unto death, and I will give thee the crown of life."

CHAPTER VI.

1859–1862.

FIRST TWO YEARS IN THE MINISTRY. CHURCH OF THE
ADVENT. PHILADELPHIA. EARLY RECOGNITION OF
HIS POWER AS A PREACHER. EXTRACTS FROM LET-
TERS AND NOTE-BOOKS. BEGINNING OF THE CIVIL
WAR. CALL TO CHURCH OF THE HOLY TRINITY IN
PHILADELPHIA.

PHILLIPS BROOKS began his ministry July 10, 1859, at the
age of twenty-three, in the Church of the Advent, Philadelphia.
It was not what is called a prominent church in the city; its
seating capacity was five hundred and it numbered one hundred
and fifty communicants. The church was situated on the corner
of York Avenue and Buttonwood Street, and is still standing,
though its interior arrangements have been modified. He took
rooms in the neighborhood at 701 Vine Street. His first sermon
was on the " Law of the House." (Ezek. xliii., 12.) His advent to
the city was chronicled in the newspapers, with an account of his
sermon, and with flattering allusions to his appearance and
ability. He began his work with great zeal, writing two sermons a week, and visiting diligently his congregation. He constantly remarks on the kindness of the people. But he was
lonely and somewhat depressed. When alluding to these first
Sundays at the Advent, many years afterward, he recalled a
circumstance of which there is no hint in his letters at the time.
To a clergyman who humorously complained that he was drawing
away his congregation, as of all the other churches in Boston, he
replied, "We all of us have to go through this." He then went
on to say that he had engaged to supply the Church of the Advent for three months, leaving them at liberty to call him as rector at the expiration of this time. But one Sunday evening, as he
was going home from church with one of the vestrymen, he said

to him that perhaps he had better leave at once and not wait till the three months were out. All that his companion could say in reply was, "As long as you have begun, you had better stay out the time for which you were hired."

But the young minister was really succeeding, as is seen by his letters. His church was full at the evening service; there was an increasing demand for pews; he liked the people and it soon became evident that they wanted him to remain. In October (1859), the three months of probation having expired, he became the permanent rector. The attendance at the services had continued to grow, and he speaks of the church as crowded. In the early weeks of October he preached at the large church of the Holy Trinity, taking Dr. Vinton's place. He mentions in his letters rather dreading the preaching in the big church and "filling the great man's place," but thought he "got through it pretty well." His reputation had not by November, at least, extended throughout the city. In making an exchange he experienced mortification arising from the lack of pulpit fame. It was at the Church of our Saviour, in West Philadelphia, as he related the incident, that he officiated in the morning of Sunday, November 27. He was about to close the service from the chancel when he noticed a member of the congregation approaching through the main aisle with some message for him. And the message was this: Was he to preach again at the evening service? When the messenger was told that the exchange was only for the morning, he replied, "Will you please give notice that the rector himself will preach in the evening?"

Among his experiences was preaching for the first time in the presence of Dr. Vinton, whom he looked up to with reverence, as the greatest preacher in the Church. Dr. Vinton's comment was: "He preaches better sermons than I did at his age, or have ever done since." Dr. Vinton pronounced him an "orator," and thought that a great part of his power lay in his voice.

As he followed political affairs, he was greatly moved by the death of John Brown, enclosing in his diary with a border of black lines these words: "Friday, December 2, 1859, 10.15 A.M., John Brown hung at Charlestown, Va." The execution took place under the administration of Governor Wise of Virginia, whose son was a friend of Brooks, and was at that time the rector of a

Church in West Philadelphia. He comments on this event in his letters:

"December 3, 1859. What a death for such a man. It makes me mad to hear the way some of our Northern conservatives talk about him. I believe Governor Wise himself does him more justice than they do.

"As to his being crazy, of course excessive lack of prudence, judgment, and foresight, which every one admits that he showed, is craziness in its very definition, and so every rash man is crazy; but his heroic devotion to what he thought was right is surely not to be confounded with the craziness that he showed in judging whether it was really right and best. What do people say about it all in Boston?"

"December 9, 1859. Wise took tea with me last night, and for the first time we had a long talk about Harper's Ferry troubles, John Brown, etc. Of course we did n't coincide, but it gave us both a chance to define our positions, and I was pleased to find him not quite so radical as I had thought. He is drawing great crowds here, and preaching splendid sermons."

His father took alarm at the tone of his son's comment; perhaps he had misgivings about the Phillips blood. He had already seen enough of his son to know that he was more pronounced than himself in his opposition to slavery, and in one of his letters had described to him a recent meeting in Fanueuil Hall, where "your friends the anti-slavers mustered in force, and your kinsman Wendell Phillips expressed a wish that the prayer 'God save the Commonwealth of Massachusetts' should be changed to read, 'God damn the Commonwealth of Massachusetts.'" Now he wrote to his son more emphatically:

"I see you allude to the Harper's Ferry affair. All well enough to have your private opinions on all such matters, but I must beg of you don't carry such things as politics into the pulpit. Leave all such at 701. . . . Let others trumpet the exploits and virtues of 'old Brown.'"

These first years of his ministry in Philadelphia were full of interest. He had deep satisfaction and joy in his work; it was more delightful than he had anticipated. He had been received by his congregation with open hearts and hands. His diary presents an attractive picture. His mornings were given to study and sermon-writing, his afternoons to visiting his parishioners. The clergy of the city made him welcome. He enjoyed the society of many friends in Philadelphia and the vicinity. Relations with Dr. Vinton became very close. Through him, he became acquainted, as he says, with the "upper ten of Philadelphia," receiving many invitations he was unable to accept. Among his new friends was Dr. Weir Mitchell, destined to eminence as a man of letters. One of his closest friends was Rev. Charles D. Cooper, rector of St. Philip's Church, a man of wealth who kept open house—a rendezvous for clergy of kindred minds.

In the midst of many engagements runs the constant reference to sermon-writing. It does not appear as an easy task; he labored over his sermons; a rainy day made it impossible for him to write. He complains of being "terribly tired" after a Sunday's work. Some relief was found in the habit of clerical exchanges of which he took full advantage. What is called "church work" was then almost unknown, and there was but little complexity in the organization of a parish; the sewing circle and the Sunday-school divided the labors and interests of pastor and people. There was of course the standing difficulty with the choir, and to this the Church of the Advent was no exception. At times, Mr. Brooks grew weary with the incessant demands of the endless routine. He writes to a friend:

"The everlasting whirligig of visiting and sermon-writing keeps up its revolutions; no weddings, not even a baptism to break the monotony. But it's a pleasant life. . . . You would have been amused to see me presiding at the first meeting of my sewing circle the other day, to choose officers, etc. The way women won't be bound by parliamentary rules is very funny."

The ritual of the church was also simple in those days, nor had the movement known as ritualism yet begun. The minister faced the congregation in the reading of the service, the boy choir was almost unknown, and in the pulpit it was the prevailing custom to wear the black Geneva gown. It created a commotion when, soon after the new rector came, the "black gowns" were stolen from the vestry. It did not then occur to them that the surplice might be used as a substitute, and immediately they were replaced. The Morning and the Evening Prayer constituted the Sunday service, with the administration of the Lord's Supper on the first Sunday of the month. But the great attraction was the sermon.

Both as a boy and as a man, Brooks attached importance to the commemoration of birthdays and Thanksgiving days. It was with a sense of regret that he realized the time-honored New England Thanksgiving Day had become for him a thing of the past. His first commemoration of one in Philadelphia called for a sermon in his church, but he remarks that "people have n't learned here yet the true Puritan style."

His home letters show how strong was the tie binding him to home and the family life. As he grew into manhood, he could not put away these things. So long as the home still existed, his heart leaped up at the thought of it. The tie of blood relationship had in it something for which no friendship was a substitute. These words may be taken as a specimen of many of his letters: "I feel kind of homesick this evening, sick of seeing nothing but these stranger faces; and it would be a treat to look in at the red-clothed back parlor table for an hour or two." Still he was happy in his work. February 9, 1859, he says: "Things are going much as usual down at Advent, quietly and pleasantly. The church is well filled and most of our desirable pews rented. I don't think I could have happened upon a more satisfactory little place if I had had my pick out of all the country. I have been here seven months to-morrow."

But a small cloud was now rising which portended change. The congregation was contented with its rector, and the gentlemen who had visited Sharon Mission, near the seminary, to hear him had been justified in their report that he was the man for the place. Never in the history of the church had the attendance been so large. All would have been well but for the appearance one Sunday of mysterious strangers who came to listen to the preacher, empowered to give him a call to St. John's Church, Cincinnati, after hearing him. Already he had declined one call from St. Stephen's Church, in Harrisburg, feeling sure that he was rightly placed. The call from Cincinnati became known in his parish and in the city and it caused disturbance. It was an urgent call, with a petition containing many signatures, and it meant increase of income to one who was somewhat hampered by the meagreness of his salary. It was declined, but it had begotten as a result uneasiness about the future of the Church of the Advent. They met the emergency as best they could, offering their rector such additional attractions as were in their power. Most of the congregation were persons of limited means, but they did what they could. The women at once employed themselves in carrying out long-needed reforms. At their expense the vestry of the church was repainted, recarpeted, and new furniture was added. The men grappled with the long-standing debt of $8000. If this were paid some $500 would be set free to add to the salary.

The incident did not escape the attention of the newspapers. From this time the eyes of the world began to be upon him. In the comment of the press he was praised for having declined the call, but a lesson was read to wealthy parishes, who sought to seduce the clergy from their allegiance by pecuniary temptations.

The ordination to the priesthood took place on the morning of Whitsunday, 1860, at the Church of the Advent, in the presence of the congregation, and of his father and mother and his brother George. Bishop Bowman preached the sermon, Dr. John A. Vaughan presented him, and Bishop Alonzo Potter administered the sacred rite. In the evening he preached, and his mother listened to him for the first time. His brother George was also an attentive hearer, drawing his own conclusions. He had not yet been confirmed, and the delay was the heaviest burden his mother carried. An extract from his mother's letter after her return finds here a fitting place:

"Thank you, my dear child, for the joy you have given me in devoting your life to the service of Christ. It was the desire of my heart from your birth, and I gave you up to Him, and I thank Him for accepting my offering. My dear Philly, when I hear of your faithful labors in the ministry, I thank God, and feel that I have not wholly lived in vain.

"I suppose you feel gratified that you have had those two calls, Philly; but don't let it make you proud. Keep humble like Jesus, . . . plead mightily for Christ.

"Father is very happy in your success, and I wish you could know how glad it makes your mother's heart."

The sermons, more than the note-books, now become the record of his intellectual and spiritual life. He was reading Robertson's sermons with an eagerness which cannot be understood by those who read them to-day, when their thought has become widely diffused. He continued to read Bushnell, but remarks that he is not entirely in agreement with him. A few extracts from the note-book follow:—

"The great good of reading history or biography is to get a glimpse of men and nations and ages doing their duty."

"What a relief the purely intellectual is sometimes! Stripping off pride and prejudice, and dogmatism which is the growth of them, keeping the soul at rest for a little while; just for a little while letting the mind be master and pursue in purest dominion its own peculiar way. It does rest the tired soul and give it time for refreshment."

"Is not all positiveness of necessity partiality? To say, 'This is true, I know it,' and to leave no room for the limitations and qualifications that we cannot know, for all those outside influences of unseen truth which we must be working on and drawing from this fact that we have found,—is there not some folly here? Is not the true wisdom something like this?—I know so far as it goes this truth is sacredly and wholly true, but that very truth forbids me to believe that it has not developments and ramifications reaching far out into the universe of associated truth with which it is connected. Now I *know*, and I prize my knowledge as the gift of God and hold it sacred; but 'I know in part,' I wait till that which is in part shall be done away."

"It seems sad and strange to see how now and then in history, now and then even at the present day, must come protests of the soul against the Christian Church. It is not strange if we look at it rightly. I do not think that it is even sad. It is the best and purest part of human nature crying out against the false humanities that have fastened themselves upon a system whose divinity they cannot cloak, but whose efficacy they deform. I do not think that it is sad, for in it I see a new wonder of the care of God, that has arrayed against the possible falsifications of His truth the inherent truth and earnestness of moral life; because I see in it new room to think that the Church thus cared for, whose purification has thus been thought worthy of the wisdom of Omnipotence, has surely high and holy work to do on earth, and till that work be done I shall live to do it."

"'As a Christian, humiliation before God was a duty the meaning of which he knew full well; but as a man moving among other men, he possessed in that moral seriousness and stoic scorn of temptation which characterized him a spring of ever present pride, dignifying his whole bearing among his fellows and at times arousing him to a kingly intolerance.' (Said of Milton, Masson, i., 237.) The two perfectly compatible, and their compatibility solving many a problem which I have often felt."

"The world ruled and managed so often by its little and not its greater men. Is it not the same principle that reappears when a weaker and not a stronger motive settles our conduct, when a slighter and not a more weighty argument, or when a whim and not an argument at all, decides our belief?"

"How fortunate that ideas are not confined in their development to the developing capacity of the mind that first conceives them."

"Beginning to allow ourselves insincere pretensions of belief is like beginning to take opium."

He was reading at this time Quinet's *Histoire de mes Idées*, and quotes this passage as expressing his own experience:

"Ce que j'ai aimé je l'ai trouvé chacque jour plus aimable. Chacque jour la justice m'a paru plus sainte, la liberté plus belle, la parole plus sacrée, l'art plus réel, la realité plus artiste, la poésie plus vraie, la vérité plus poétique, la nature plus divine, le divin plus naturel."

The year 1860 was broken by the usual holiday, spent with his family in Boston. He occupied his old room in the house on Chauncy Street, kept as he had left it when he first went from home. It was characteristic of him that he wrote the sermon to be preached on the Sunday after he should return. It gave the impression that he did not need to work as others did, making him free when others were in the toils of labor. The year that now followed was prolific in sermons. In addition he gave a weekly lecture on Wednesday evenings, and on Saturday evenings met a Bible class composed of members of his congregation. To his large Sunday-school he gave a large part of his time and interest. He still complains of being "fearfully tired" after the Sunday work; his letters contain apologies for delay. These things disappeared so entirely in later years, when he was in the full swing of his power, that it seems surprising it should have been otherwise. He reached the age of twenty-five on the 13th of December, 1860, and records his weight as one hundred and ninety-five pounds. But, with his great height, he gave the impression of being slender in his figure.

Hardly had he begun his second year at the Church of the Advent when urgent calls were received to other parishes, which it was necessary, at least, that he should consider. A committee waited on him with a call from Trinity Church, Newport. Another invitation was to a vacant parish in Providence, R. I. Still a third call came from San Francisco. There is something remarkable in the way the knowledge of him had travelled. These invitations were declined. But in April 1861, there came a call louder and more peremptory, to which he long refused to listen. When Dr. Vinton resigned the rectorship of the Church of the Holy Trinity in Philadelphia he recommended Brooks as his successor and the unanimous call immediately followed. His connection with the church had been a close one through his relations to Dr. Vinton. He had not only preached there frequently, but the members of the congregation of Holy Trinity at times formed a considerable part of his audience at the Church of the Advent. It had become the fashion in Philadelphia for people to wend their way to the neat little church on the corner of York Avenue and Buttonwood Street. "It was not an unwonted sight on a Sunday evening to see the streets in the neighborhood of the church filled with carriages." All through the year 1861 the question was pending whether Phillips Brooks would leave the Church of the Advent for the large Church of the Holy Trinity. It was settled apparently by a letter to its vestry on April 9th, when he declined the call on the ground that he could not then leave the Church of the Advent in view of its condition and the circumstances of his connection with it. But the subject had only been postponed, and was soon to come up again for more serious consideration.

It was in the spring of this year, 1861, that the Civil War began. Events had been rapidly moving toward this result from the time of Lincoln's election. Mr. Brooks had recorded in his diary for November 6, 1860, this sentence, with a line drawn about it isolating it from other sentences to make it appear as prominent on the page as it loomed up significant to his mind,—"Abraham Lincoln chosen President of the United States." For the next four years his letters, his sermons, his public addresses, show how the tragedy and its issues entered and quickened his personality. His letters became a chronicle of the war. They contain nothing new; he had no special source of information; there are thousands of such letters, but these have value as coming from him. So far as they are used here, it will be, not to supplement histories of the war, nor to revive its painful memories, but as part of the story of a life sinking its individuality in the national purpose, till the soul of the nation seemed to pass into his own. He emerged from this experience with a deeper devotion to the cause of humanity. He received its teaching as a message to himself, fusing his powers into more intense and consecrated endeavor. In one sense the war gave him his opportunity. He was roused by it to the highest pitch of enthusiasm; he became its representative and mouthpiece to the city of Philadelphia and finally he spoke to the country at large in a memorable way.

September 27, 1860. "I am regularly assessed and my name on the voting list. . . . Everybody is talking politics, and it is the exception when there is n't at least one political procession within hearing. There go the caps and capes and torches, up Franklin Street, through the rain.

"The wigwam up at Sixth and Brown is open every evening, and you can't get into a street car without being reminded that it's within a few weeks of Old Abe's election. No danger of a man's forgetting to vote in such times as these. Almost all Advent go with the rector. I don't know but one or two Democrats among them, and hardly a Bell man."

December 7, 1860. "What a time you had in Boston Monday! I see Sanborn was in the thick of it. I don't believe in John Brown, but I don't believe either in that way of choking down free speech. It looks too much like the way they have of doing things down in South Carolina. What do people up there say about the message? Poor old J. B. [President James Buchanan.] He 's on his last three months, luckily."

December 21, 1860. "So the Union 's gone if South Carolina has the right to go; but I believe we shall see brighter times yet, and don't believe the country five years hence will repent of the Republican victory of 1860."

Fbruary 25, 1861. "What do you think of the President-elect's sudden run from Pennsylvania hospitalities? Next week at any rate is close upon us, and then 'we shall see what we shall see.' I saw 'Abe' on Thursday. He is a good-looking, substantial sort of a man, and I believe he 'll do the work. At any rate it 's a satisfaction to have an honest man there, even if he can't do much."

March 25, 1861. "As to Holy Trinity I have about concluded not to go, and have signified as much to Dr. Vinton. I think there are many reasons why I ought to go, but I don't see how I can properly leave Advent just now. I enclose you a paragraph that was handed to me yesterday, cut from the Sunday *Dispatch*,—a 'flash' paper of this city. It shows how absurdly the thing has been talked about here."

April 2, 1861. "Does n't it seem wonderful [he writes to his younger brother Frederick, on the occasion of his confirmation] always to look back on the way that God has led us and to trace back His guidance ever so far before we began to have any idea that we were under it? How completely it makes one feel that the whole work is in God and not in us, from first to last that He has done it not we. And how much more than satisfied we are that it should be all His doing. What a happy confidence it gives us that, as He began it in spite of our indifference, so He can carry it on in spite of our feebleness. I am thankful that you can write and feel as you do."

April 29, 1861. "What times these are! Is n't it great to see people in our degenerate days willing to go to work for a principle as our people are doing now? How splendidly old Massachusetts is doing. She has evidently got the old blood left in her yet. The feeling here is just as deep as ever. Not quite as much noise, but everybody doing what they can. Our lecture room at Advent has been a tailor's shop for the last week, with the ladies making clothes for the volunteers. This morning a company attended service at Advent and had an appendix to the sermon for their benefit. To-night there is to be a baptism in Advent of two young men who are ordered off to-morrow, and cannot wait till confirmation time. Everything now has something to do with the war.

"Wise left town last Monday; his furniture has been sent off, and he will probably never return. He made himself somewhat obnoxious before leaving, and was turned out half-shaved from a black barber's shop on Monday morning because he used his tongue too freely.   His church is in a quandary.

"We see people here from Baltimore every day.   I met a lady last night just from there, who said that half the city would rejoice to have a U. S. army of 30,000 men come and occupy the city.   Why don't they do it?   The administration will be forced to do it yet by the strong popular pressure.   You have asked once or twice about the Holy Trinity and my reasons for not going there.   I had but one real reason,—I could n't see that I could leave Advent.   If I had been wholly free I should have gone, and think from the peculiar nature of that parish I could have got along. . . .   The war fever has overshadowed all these church excitements.   I had an offer yesterday to go to San Francisco, to Grace Church, salary from $5000 to $6000.   If ever I move, I am not sure but that would be a good direction, but for the present I said I could n't think of it. . . ."

"Franklin Square you would n't know.   It is a drill yard from morning to night, and at this moment there is a whole company on the sidewalk opposite to 701."

April 29, 1861.   " 'The war is inevitable, and let it come.   I repeat it, sir, let it come.   It is in vain, sir, to extenuate the matter.   Gentlemen may cry, Peace! Peace! but there is no peace! the war is actually begun.'   We are in the midst of recruiting and drilling and arriving and departing of troops.   We see the Massachusetts men as they pass through on their way to Baltimore, and in a few hours we hear of their being bruised and beaten and killed in a city that claims all the benefits of being on our side.   There can be but one party in the North now.   There is but one in Philadelphia.   The excitement is intense.   Several young men of my congregation have enlisted and are going on high religious motives.   Who dare say that it is n't his duty to go when the duty is so urgent and the cause so sacred?

"Of course nothing else is talked of here, and it 's hard to fix down to work of any kind.   I was in New York on Monday and things were the same there.

"Everything goes well at Advent.   They have just voted to raise my salary to $2000, beginning next month.   Our confirmation has just been fixed for the 15th of May."

May 4, 1861.   "War still; quieter just now, but yet, as we all think, a fight certainly coming.   How your last letter bubbled and boiled with patriotism!   Is n't it a grand thing to see how the mind of the whole country has risen up to the demand of the times?   Does n't it prove, what in a long time of peacefulness we are apt to forget, that the heroic qualities are true elements in human nature, and will always be developed with the recurrence of any exigency that calls for their exhibition and employment? Does n't it renew and enlarge our faith in our race?

"But I'm not going to write war again. To be sure, there's little else. It's hard to get away from it in sermon-writing or letter-writing."

May 13, 1861. "What of the war? Is n't it grand? Your enthusiasm is no doubt as great as ours, and your confidence as strong that just the thing our land has been needing for ever so long to clear it, first of its corrupt government and ultimately of the hateful curse of slavery, has come about at last. The Seminary is broken up and probably Northern students will never be on its roll again. Sparrow and Packard have gone South, May has returned North. The Northern money that has gone into those buildings is sunk. . . . At Advent all goes much as usual. I have been busy getting ready for confirmation, which comes next Wednesday evening. There are twenty-seven or twenty-eight candidates."

May 18, 1861. "It is only two weeks now before I shall be on my way in your direction [Boston], unless Jeff Davis is in Philadelphia before that time, in which case, as he may like to attend service at Advent and hear what we think of him there, I should have to stay and tell him.

"I had a letter from Father the other day full of red-hot war spirit and making much of Governor Andrew. It seems after all the *Courier* said that his was an election quite fit to be made. How well our Yankee general Butler comes out too. Massachusetts is ahead yet in the war.

"Last Wednesday evening we had our confirmation at Advent. Bishop Potter officiated, and the church was crowded. There were thirty-one candidates. It is encouraging to feel that some work is doing. I have enjoyed this last year exceedingly, and if I can only feel that the people get as much good as I do pleasure out of our connection, I shall be well satisfied."

June 26, 1861. "Things don't seem to get ahead much in the war, do they? This new talk about compromise I am convinced will come to nothing, but it is a bad symptom, and ought to be stopped. I am glad to see that Massachusetts has come down handsomely with ten more regiments."

June 29, 1861. "Another blunder down South yesterday in the death of Captain Ward. One of these days, perhaps, we shall do something to brag of, but we don't seem to have done it yet.

What will Congress do is the question. People are getting dreadfully poor here, and even ministers are beginning to economize. Where will it end?"

September 14, 1861. "When is the great battle coming? Everybody says now before another week is over, but I believe McClellan knows what he is about, and won't fight till he's ready, and then will whip them terribly. Philadelphia brags loudly of her son and has forgotten Patterson in her delight over McC.

"How comfortably the traitors are getting housed in Lafayette. Boston has contributed nothing yet. You must have some old *Courier* men that you would like to spare that you could send to keep our precious townsmen company."

September 27, 1861. "We are just through the President's Fast Day, and I have never seen a weekday kept as it has been. Our stores almost without exception were closed; the churches thronged. We had service at Advent in the morning, and in the evening and afternoon joined with Mr. Cooper's and Dr. Newton's congregations for union services. The churches all three times were overflowing, and unable to hold all that came, and so it was with all the churches, I believe, all over town.

"I had no sermon, only a short address. The only restraint was a feeling that I could not speak out as fully as I wished on the one great sin which is beyond doubt the chief reason of this calamity being on us, and which has got to be removed before the calamity can be lifted off. It is useless to talk round and round it, when we know and are sure that slavery, its existence in the South and its approval in the North, is the great crushing, cursing sin of our national life and the cause of all our evils. I spoke of it freely yesterday, and so far as I know without giving offence.

"How strange this continual mismanagement is! What is hampering our soldiers and statesmen? Another defeat and another brave man useless out in Missouri, and all apparently for want of foresight and prudence. Here's a noble letter about the war and the country. Well, you'll excuse it, for there isn't much worth thinking or talking of besides in times like these."

October 1, 1861. "I got last night the *Transcript* with its cut at Dr. N——. He deserved it, and more too. The man who can insult a Northern congregation nowadays by standing up and laying the whole blame of these troubles on the North deserves all the dislike and distrust he gets."

October 20, 1861. "Another defeat and another butchery. Where are we drifting to, and when is the tide to turn? I have n't a doubt that it will turn, but it is tedious waiting for it, and meanwhile we are losing time and men.

"We have been busy and excited this week in the choice of a bishop. The papers have told you, no doubt, that Dr. Stevens was elected. I voted against him, and was sorry that he was elected simply because I do not think in the present state of things, and with the prospects that are before us, any man of Southern sympathies and connections, even though he may be just now professedly loyal, ought to become the mouthpiece of a Northern diocese. However, he is an able and a good man, and I shall hope the best of his administration. It was a very long and excited canvass.

"There is nothing new in my own church relations. I have had an interview with the Holy Trinity people in reference to their giving a new call, and have discouraged it, at least until they have made trial of one or two persons who have been for some time before them. What will be the upshot of it I can't tell."

November 8, 1861. "I went to hear your senator last night, Charles Sumner, on the war. He was n't very great. He has grown fat and clumsy, and has not the same fire that he used to have Where is the fleet? Are we ever to hear from it, or has it drifted out into infinite space or gone over to secession or gone down Armada fashion in one of these gales? I have faith still, but things look badly, especially in Missouri. What a pity that Fremont's removal came just at this time, though, independently of that, no doubt it was a good move, or rather it was a bad one ever to put him there."

The Church of the Holy Trinity, after waiting for six months, renewed its call to Mr. Brooks and the call was accepted On November 18, 1861, he wrote to his parents:

"Monday, November 18, 1861.

"DEAR FATHER AND MOTHER,—I have resigned the Advent to-day, and shall accept the Holy Trinity to-morrow. You will not think it strange that I have not written you about this before. I wanted to have it fixed and settled before I troubled you with it again.

"The call from the Holy Trinity came two weeks ago, and since then I have been in a wretched state, weighing my desire to stay with the Advent people against my apparent duty to go and work this larger field. I never want to pass another such two weeks.

I went on a week ago to-day and passed two days with Dr. Vinton. After coming back from there the matter has had much serious and prayerful thought, and has resulted finally in a clear conviction that I ought to go. The Advent people are very much hurt and very indignant about it. I am sincerely sorry to leave them, more so than I can tell, but what can I do?

"And now about the details. My resignation is to take effect after the first Sunday in Advent. I have n't the heart to go right to Holy Trinity the next Sunday, and so shall accept then to begin the 1st of January. Most of the intervening time I shall spend with you in Chauncy Street, if you will take me in. I say 'most' because I may be kept here a few days after I leave Advent to make arrangements about moving, etc., and also because I have partly promised to spend the second Sunday in December with Dr. Vinton. At any rate I shall be at home to keep George's birthday and Christmas."

The motives which induced Mr. Brooks to accept the call from the Church of the Holy Trinity were of a practical character. It need not be said that no sordid element was among them. Some things had become more apparent as the months went by and he was obliged to face the actual situation. His church was crowded with worshippers, but they brought no strength to the parish; they came to listen, but not to identify themselves with the congregation. He was ministering to the members of other parishes. If he must preach to crowded churches, as seemed to be his destiny, it was better that he should do so in a larger edifice, capable of accommodating fifteen hundred hearers, than in one with a capacity of only five hundred. He needed a stronger vantage ground, a more prominent position. That part of the city where he ministered was changing, the trend of the population was away from the neighborhood, and the possibilities of growth were limited. The case of the Church of the Holy Trinity was laid before him in a statement by an eminent jurist, one of the members, and the pleas there urged coincided with his own sober judgment. During the two years and a half that he had been at the Advent, there had been developing a struggle between him and the larger church. He had preached there too often not to have created a bond between him and its people. So long as he was a possibility they could unite on no one else. Dr. Vinton's opinion and advice also weighed heavily with him. On the other hand, his own people were not willing to let him go. They refused to accept his resignation. He seemed to belong to them by divine right. They had no great jurist among them, but they stated their case in a way to move the strongest heart. They recited the story of how they had discovered him when he was unknown, how their hearts had gone out to him from the first, how much he had been to them and to their children, how the church had grown and prospered under his care. In all this they saw the moving of a divine spirit.

He was distressed and sore at heart, as his letters show, in reaching his conclusion. It was unfortunate that social distinctions should have complicated the issue, but that was inevitable. The subject was discussed in the newspapers, with the suggestion that the decision turned on personal ambition, or other unworthy motive.

Whichever way he decided, there would be great rejoicing and great sorrowing. It had become evident from repeated calls that he would not be left in peace where he was. The desire grew upon him to be permanently fixed, where he could do his work undisturbed, and to better advantage.

Before his resignation should take effect came Thanksgiving Day. How to interpret the dark hour, when a nation was involved in the horrors of a fratricidal war, so that gratitude to God might still be the undercurrent of its being, was the problem to be faced. He took for his text the verse of a familiar Psalm, "I will sing of mercy and judgment." The sermon was reported in the daily newspapers with the preface, "The neat little Church of the Advent was filled to its utmost capacity yesterday morning." He referred in his sermon to the recent Fast Day services:

"The shadow of that day will give color to this. God's two hands—His hand of blessing and His hand of caution—are laid on us together, and if we sing at all to-day it must be a double strain, like that which David announces in our text, 'I will sing of mercy and of judgment.'"

On December 6th he started for Boston, staying for a few days in New York. It was his intention during his absence to refrain from preaching. How well he kept his purpose is shown by the records of his Sundays during the month of December. On the 8th he preached in the morning at Trinity Church,

New York, and in the afternoon at St. Mark's. On the 15th he was in Medford, preaching at Grace Church, morning and evening. On the 22d—and this was a memorable day for him and his family—he preached at St. Paul's Church, Boston, in the church to which he had gone as a child since he was three years old, with his family in the old pew, No. 60, in the broad central aisle. His text was St. John iv. 28, 29: "Come, see a man who told me all things, that ever I did; is not this the Christ?" In the evening he preached at St. Mary's, Dorchester, where his uncle, Mr. John Phillips, resided. On the 29th he preached for the first time in Trinity Church, Boston, while Bishop Eastburn read the service. In the evening of the same day he preached at St. James's, Roxbury. On the 13th of December he kept his twenty-sixth birthday.

One would like to know what judgment his parents passed upon his preaching as he stood before them, or what Bishop Eastburn, the stalwart Evangelical divine, thought of the unfamiliar utterance as he listened from the chancel. The father was a severe critic of preachers as they passed before him in review at St. Paul's. He admired the slow deliberate oratory, with the rotund sonorous voice. It must have seemed to him as though his son defied every rule of oratory, or was incapable of classification according to accepted principles. Indeed, the new preacher gave his audience no time to think about his voice, whether it were fine or not; there was a rush of sentences, one tumbling after another, and the audience had all it could do to follow, for somehow he made them intensely eager to follow and to catch each spoken word, as though something essential would be lost if their attention should be diverted. There must have been surprise and even amazement at something so unlike what they had ever heard before. Not only was the preacher's delivery unfamiliar, but his thought was new; the old familiar gospel was in his sermons, but it came with a new meaning and force, stripped of the old conventionalities of expression. When he preached at Dorchester, one who heard him thought the congregation was rather amused than impressed with the rapid manner, the stumbling over sentences, the occasional entanglement of words from which he extricated himself with difficulty. There is a tradition also that his uncle, when he first heard him, did not feel sure that he would succeed as a preacher, but thought him a young man possessed of genius.

During the first six months of the new rectorship the time was so occupied with making the acquaintance of his parish and gathering up the lines of work that he found little time for study. The record shows that he wrote but two sermons and was obliged to fall back upon extemporaneous preaching. He was making and receiving calls morning, afternoon, and evening of each day. The hospitality of his congregation was boundless, the social festivities at which his presence was desired were innumerable.

His new position entailed other and wider responsibilities. He was taken at once into the confidence of the venerable men who were charged with duties to the Church at large, the leaders of the Evangelical party, who at that special moment felt that a crisis was impending in the Church, which called for strenuous efforts if the faith was to be maintained. From this time he was a constant speaker at meetings and anniversaries of the American Church Missionary Society, the Evangelical Knowledge Society, and to these was now to be added a third, the Evangelical Education Society. The seminary at Alexandria having been closed in consequence of the war, and its professors and students scattered, the need was felt for a central school of theology with the advantages which proximity to a large city could confer. As the rector of Holy Trinity, Mr. Brooks became one of the overseers of the new divinity school, giving freely of his time to the many preliminary meetings which the new enterprise demanded. By the leaders of the Evangelical school, he was welcomed for his high position, and the social influence he represented, but chiefly for that eloquence which gave a new and potent charm to the cause so dear to them. These older men must even then have recognized some difference in the presentation of the truth as they held it, but they were wise and large-hearted, penetrating beneath the surface and recognizing that at heart, and in all the essential quality of the gospel, he was at one with them. From this conviction they never wavered.

It was characteristic of him in his youth that he met those new and larger obligations with the gravity of age, throwing himself into every speech he made on representative occasions, so that the occasion should not fail through any fault of his. He was now sought after for such special events as ordinations and consecrations of churches, because his presence and the word he spoke were felt to be necessary to the fitness of these solemnities. It was almost too much for any man to be called on to endure with safety. But the admiration, the adulation which now went forth towards him, the enthusiasm his presence created, he seemed to regard as a shadow from which he would fain escape. If he was *in* this world of social and ecclesiastical functions he was not *of* it. Those who knew him well can bear witness to another peculiarity; he was only too glad to leave the scene of his triumph to get once more with a few well-chosen friends, as though the honor and applause which came to him were unimportant compared with the privilege which friendship brought, and he were tacitly entreating his friends to forgive these accidental distinctions of popularity and fame as having no intrinsic significance. After every public function, he hastened away to this social communion. Sometimes it left the impression that he was hardly responsible for or but slightly related to his work in the pulpit, that the value of life was to be found in social fellowship. To make the quick transition from the spiritual exaltation of the pulpit to the ordinary converse of life was easy for him and seemed essential to his peace of mind. While others were still too deeply moved with what he had been uttering to think of anything else, he appeared to have forgotten it or to regard it as an ordinary circumstance. To those who knew him the impression was not misleading. He was bearing testimony to the truth of his own experience, that the joy of living, the pleasure of social converse, the talk which turned upon little things, the wit and the humor natural to man, were not incompatible with religion; that to turn from one to the other, to be ready for either, was only to recognize the unity of man's existence in a world which was temporal while conjoined with the eternal. He may seem to have carried his defiance of conventional religious manners to an extreme, but, if so, he may have felt that the singular power which he exerted in the pulpit was a source of danger, unless it were counterbalanced by participation in the ways of common life.

"January 11, 1862. I like them (my new people) more and

more the more I see of them. They are kind, cordial, and full
of will to work. There is a good deal of disagreeable fashionable life among them, but many of them are earnest and devoted
people. My first Wednesday evening lecture came off last
Wednesday night. The lecture room was thronged, but both
then and last Sunday there were many strangers. I am not
ambitious of a crowd and am satisfied to have the church well
filled."

"February 3, 1862. All is going swimmingly at the new church.
Mr. C—— tells me he rented the last pew on Saturday, and the
church is all taken now for the first time. Yesterday I began my
plan of having evening service once a month, with a service for
the children instead of the regular afternoon service. It went
first-rate; both afternoon and evening were overcrowded. Our
Wednesday evening lectures are always much more than full.
So you see that we are doing well and have every reason to hope
for the future. Dr. Vinton was here last week and seemed to
think things looked prosperous. . . .

"I want you and Mother to make your plans to come on here in
the spring."

"February 8, 1862. Everything with us is going as quietly as
if there were no war. I am getting easy in my new seat, and
have about all the reins picked up and fairly in my hands for the
long drive. Our church is very full and all rented. They are
beginning to whisper of enlargement, but it won't be done so
long as we owe $60,000. . . . To-morrow I am going back to
Advent for the first time. I am going to take charge of their
Sunday-School Anniversary in the afternoon and to preach for
them in the evening. It will feel queer; some of them did n't
want me to come, but I think probably the best way to break
down that feeling is just by going."

To his brother Frederick he writes, urging on him the claims
of the ministry, and congratulating him on his election into the
Hasty Pudding Club at Harvard:

"February 9, 1862. Have you ever thought about your profession? It is almost time to choose. The ministry of Christ
needs men terribly; so much to do, so few trained and cultivated
men to do it. What do you say? Write to me about this too,
and be sure that all you say shall be to me alone.

"When is it [the initiation] to come off? Please write me word
that I may make my plans if possible to be there. I bid you
welcome into our little fraternity, and shall be glad to sit with
you at our musty board and glory once more in my silver spoon."

" March 3, 1862. What with sermons, and lectures, and meetings, and dinings-out, and making five or six hundred new acquaintances, the time has gone very pleasantly, but very hurriedly. I find the new parish all that it was promised. There is a very great deal of wealth and luxury, but also a large amount of intelligence and refinement as well as of earnestness and devotion. The church is all taken up, and we are slowly providing for our debt by the sale of pews. Some $3000 has been sold since I took charge. The contributions in these two months are something over $2000. Then we are doing a large work among the poor, over two hundred of them being in our classes and societies. Our meetings are all overcrowded, especially our Wednesday evening lectures, for which our lecture room is much too small. . . .
" How well the war goes on, but now the elements are against us once again, and I am afraid the great Virginia 'Advance' will suffer from this frightful weather."

His mother's letters were not so frequent as when he was at Alexandria. She was at this time concentrating her interest and anxiety upon George, the third son, who had not yet been confirmed. For years she had been praying and working for this consummation, and George, who had reached the age of twenty-three, gave no sign of an awakening to the things of religion. But she was also moved, as was every member of the family, by the reports which were brought to Boston through friends who had been visiting Philadelphia, and who went with great expectations to hear the young preacher. The homage he seemed to be receiving gave his father and mother a sense of disquietude lest some injury should be done to his character. His mother now wrote: "I am glad you are prospering so well in your church. I hope you will always be faithful and *humble*. Some-times I fear, Philly, that the praises of your friends will make you proud, for you are human; but do not let it." His father was also moved to warn him against the evils of flattery: "You are in a dangerous situation for a young man, and I cannot help warning you of it. Keep your simplicity and your earnestness, above all your devotion to your Master's cause, and don't let these flattering demonstrations you see about you withdraw you from them. Keep on in the even tenor of your ways, so that when there is a lull in the excitement it will find you the same."
But mingled with parental fears was pride in the son's career.

His mother writes to him: "What a delightful work you are engaged in, and you seem so happy in it! No wonder. How different it seems from my life's work, so humble and so laborious. But far be it from me to complain, while God is honoring me in letting my children preach His glorious gospel. I wish He would call every one of them for His servants." But she was not unconscious that she had some share in the result. She encloses a short extract from a newspaper, which may have more than one application: a prospective look for him, as well as retrospective in her own case:

"It is often a matter of surprise that distinguished men have such inferior children and that a great name is seldom perpetuated. The secret of this is often evident: the mothers have been inferior,—mere ciphers in the scale of existence. All the splendid advantages procured by wealth and the father's position cannot supply this one deficiency in the mother, who gives character to the child."

In response to his parents' caution, he writes:

"Wednesday, March 12, 1862. I thank you for your congratulations and also for your cautions. I hope my letters have not looked as if I were getting conceited. You must let me know just as soon as they do. Seriously, though, there is so much to humble one every day in the sense of the imperfections with which the work is done, that it seems to me there is but little chance for a man to get puffed up with the mere outward manifestations of success. I am abundantly and devoutly thankful for all the fruits I see, but they are so out of proportion to the needs and capacities of the field that there is enough to humiliate as well as to elate. . . .

"How the news comes in this morning from the war! [1]—It seems rather hard to understand as yet. Either there is a general cave of the great rebellion, or else they are laying deeper plots than ever before. We shall see in a few days now. What a narrow escape we had in the Merrimac affair. . . ."

From this time there were constantly appearing, in the newspapers, descriptions of the preacher and of his preaching. A

[1] The capture of forts Henry and Donelson by General Grant, which gave the Union armies possession of the Tennessee and Cumberland rivers, the highway to the Southern States of Alabama and Mississippi.

clerical correspondent of the *Christian Times*, who visited Philadelphia from New York, writes:

"It is no common sight, even in this precocious age, to see so young a man ministering with such ability and acceptableness to a congregation that will rank among the most numerous and influential in the land. . . . In appearance he is tall and commanding, but not over-graceful; his style of elocution is rapid even to discomfort, many of his glowing periods being lost through the quickness of their utterance. His composition is marked by striking originality and comprehensiveness. . . . Whether due to Mr. Brooks's personality or the character of the people, we noticed that the church was as well filled in the afternoon as in the morning,—a statement that could hardly be predicated of any of our own churches."

But on the other hand, so long as he remained at the Church of the Holy Trinity he was subjected to a certain petty and malignant criticism; his motives were impugned, reports circulated which were untrue but which travelled far and wide, causing no little embarrassment. One of these reports (intended to be amusing) was the story that he had been presented with one hundred and fifty pairs of slippers. The motive of these attacks seems to have been resentment at his leaving the Church of the Advent.

Amid the pressure of parish duties, so heavy and exacting as to leave little time for study or for sermon writing, even the war itself seemed remote. But in the spring of the year, General McClellan began his movement toward Richmond. Phillips Brooks was one of the many who put faith in McClellan and looked for a speedy termination of the war. After Lent was over he made a visit to Washington, of which he writes:

"I saw all there was to be seen, and although there is no army in that region now, yet the forts and camps and the general look of the country on the other side of the Potomac are very interesting. Our old seminary is a hospital now, and the place is terribly altered. The woods are all cut down, fences gone, and the roads completely obliterated. The whole country for miles around is trodden down with a perfect desolation."

McClellan's movement ended in disastrous defeat but there was encouragement in the capture of New Orleans by Farragut, the battle of Shiloh, and the taking of Corinth (May, 1862), which gave to the North the greater part of the Mississippi River, threatening the South with the loss of Tennessee, Alabama, and Mississippi. General Grant was now first heard of in the West. His name had not yet become familiar to the people, but the battle of Pittsburg Landing revealed his character and method. The record of killed, wounded, and missing was 24,000. While these events were occurring, Mr. Brooks made his first visit to Niagara Falls.

" It was dark when we got there, and so I slept all night with the roar of the cataract, which I had not yet seen, preparing me for the morning sight. When I woke up, full in the view from my room window, there it was! Greater than any dream I ever formed of it. More wonderful and awful than any sight I had supposed our world could furnish. Of the next two days I can't tell you much. They were spent in an incessant wandering, learning the miracle from every point of view,—under the falls and over the falls, up the river and down the river, from the Bridge and the Island and the Tower, and what is after all the view I remember most vividly,—that grand sweep that you see from the front piazza of the Clifton House. We went everywhere, and got ourselves full of the glory and beauty of Niagara. The most wonderful thing to me, I think, was the color, both of the falls and of the river, its changes, and depths, and brilliancy. I never knew what water was before. The last day of our stay was at the Cataract House, though we had been over on that side before."

The impression made on him by Niagara found expression in a sonnet:

> "O Christ, whose truth once spoke from winds and seas,
>   Hast thou not still for wretchedness and sin,
>   Some message speaking out of scenes like these?"

This year his vacation was a more elaborate one; he made his first visit to the White Mountains, stopping at Newport on the way to Boston where he spent a week with one of his parishioners. While there in the first week of July he heard the news of McClellan's defeat before Richmond. He records the purchase, while in Boston of many books. His tramp in the White Mountains was a very enjoyable one, for he had friends with him, and met others. But he was not fitted for severe climbing, his

9

strength gave out, and he finally succumbed to a sprained ankle.

The chief event of the summer was connected with the war, which now came close to his family. The future was looking dark, after McClellan's defeat with heavy slaughter; but Boston was girding itself anew to the fearful task, no longer under any illusions about McClellan, or fond anticipations that the end of the struggle was near. Instead of dreaming of an easy victory over the South, it began to look as though the South might prolong the contest indefinitely, if not finally secure its independence. A great meeting had been held at Faneuil Hall, to aid in the work of enlistment, where Edward Everett was one of the speakers, and Phillips Brooks was present to hear. The excitement was intense, and under these motives, that the need was pressing and that the call had come to him, George Brooks had enlisted as a soldier in the ranks.

CHAPTER VII

1862–1863

THE CIVIL WAR. LINCOLN'S PROCLAMATION. GENERAL
CONVENTION OF THE EPISCOPAL CHURCH. DEATH
OF HIS BROTHER. PARISH WORK. THREATENED
INVASION OF PHILADELPHIA. BISHOP HOPKINS'S
BIBLE ARGUMENT FOR SLAVERY. INTEREST IN THE
FREEDMEN. THANKSGIVING SERMON.

SOON after his return to his parish in September, Mr. Brooks
was asked to consider a call to St. Paul's Church, Brookline,
Mass. There came also an invitation to the rectorship of Christ
Church, Fifth Avenue, New York. He was advised by a good
judge in these matters to accept this latter call, on the ground
that, as he must be destined for the metropolis, he might as well
go at once. He had returned to Philadelphia with the determination to rescue more of his time for study and sermon writing. For this purpose he now kept a room at the church. He
had creative moods in the work of sermon writing. One of
these was from 1862 to 1865, when he lived in a state of intellectual tension as well as of moral fervor as a result of the
influence upon him of the Civil War. During these years it was
wonderful how he poured himself forth and apparently without
effort, never disappointing expectation or falling below himself.
One of his youthful hearers has described the effect upon him:

"Many a Sunday afternoon when the wide doors of that church
were thrown back, and the crowds flocked out into the open air,
it seemed to those listeners coming out into the street again as if
the very heavens were on fire, not because the sun was setting
across the Schuylkill, but because the preacher had projected a
light into the open sky of the heavens,—the light of the mystic,

the light of the prophet, the light which never was on sea or land.''

He had now won the confidence of his hearers to such an extent that whatever he might say, even if it were unimportant, or trite, gained an added effect from the force of his personality. He exerted a mysterious charm the secret spring of which neither he nor his hearers could understand.

The autumn months of 1862 were the darkest in the history of the war. McClellan had been outgeneralled, his army defeated with immense loss of life, while the Southern forces, gaining new hope and energy, had begun to act on the offensive, with the intention of carrying the war into the North. The prospect of bringing the war to an end by the capture of Richmond vanished into the remote future. If it was to be done at all, it must be by the conquest of the whole Southern territory, the Northern army gradually closing in upon the Confederate capital from the west and south as well as from the north. To do this, required not only the indefinite prolongation of the war, but would be attended by an appalling slaughter of human lives. The total loss in the engagements between the two armies which had ended in the defeat of McClellan (June 26–July 2, 1862) was 36,000 men, and this was but a foretaste of greater destruction yet to come. It is not to be wondered at that the country trembled at the prospect, or that many in the North who had hitherto supported the war should draw back, seeking some compromise by which the slaughter, too terrible to be contemplated, might be averted, even at the expense of Southern independence.

At this time President Lincoln was contemplating his proclamation of the emancipation of the slaves. It was to be a war measure and justified on that ground, not on any principle of the inherent wrong and evil of slavery. The object of the war was the preservation of the Union. If it would embarrass the South in the prosecution of its purpose to free the slaves, then the act of emancipation would be justified. On political grounds it might have been questioned whether such an act would be constitutional. As a war measure, put forth in an emergency, it assumed a different aspect.

To have put forth his proclamation immediately after the

disastrous defeat of the Northern army before Richmond would have been impolitic,—a cry of distress or an acknowledgment of inability on the part of the Union forces to cope with the enemy on equal terms. Lincoln therefore held it back until some victory of Union arms should constitute a more fitting opportunity. On September 22, 1862, the public announcement was made that on the first day of January, 1863, the slaves should be declared free in every part of the country at war with the United States.

It was one of the traits of Phillips Brooks that he never failed to share in the popular convictions, sheathing his critical faculty where the people's faith was concerned, clinging even to those faiths when evidence was against them. Thus he found it hard to give up his faith in McClellan, thinking that if he had been let alone he might have done the great things which were expected of him.

On his return to Philadelphia, he writes, to his father, under date of September 12, 1862:

" Found everything here a good deal excited; troops starting off for Harrisburg under the governor's orders, and some people trying to make out that Philadelphia is in danger. Of this latter, however, there is no fear, and business, with the exception of the withdrawal of a great many men for military service, goes on as usual. Every one is counting much on the heavy rain of last night, which has made a tremendous flood, and it is hoped has hemmed in the enemy between impassable rivers. At any rate everybody here is confident and full of faith in the government and in McClellan."

" September 15, 1862. It is hard to think that we have been in such danger as some people imagine, but no doubt all the precautions taken were wise, and the enthusiasm they have stirred up will do much to help on enlistment. Almost all the able-bodied men of my church are off to Harrisburg."

" September 19, 1862. So the rebels, as we hear to-night, have got off again in Virginia. I am sorry for it, for I have been in hopes that they were going to make an end of them in Maryland. Then Harper's Ferry was a bad business, and so is this which we hear to-day from Mumfordville. Still McClellan has won a victory, and we are a little nearer the end than we were. I heard yesterday that I was to be asked to the chaplaincy of a new regiment now raising here. If I am I think I shall go."

"September 26, 1862. What a week this has been in the history of the country,—the greatest in one point, I believe, since the country was born. We have heard the Proclamation of Freedom promised from the President's chair. I am sure for once we may go with the 'Tribune' and say, God bless Abraham Lincoln. What do they say about it in Boston? Our troops are fast coming back to Philadelphia, who have been off to the Border and into Maryland, for the protection of the State. They have done well, and deserve the welcome they are getting on their return. It comes pretty hard to buckle down to work again in times like these."

"I am sincerely glad to see the President's Proclamation. We have been getting ready for it for a year. It remains to be seen whether we are wholly ready for it now. If we are as I hope we are, then it is the greatest and most glorious thing our land has ever seen. We have broken off at last our great iniquity and may go on our way with some hope of a blessing."

In October Mr. Brooks went to New York in order to see for the first time the Protestant Episcopal Church assembled in General Convention. He was at this moment meditating a great purpose under the growing conviction that it was the duty of the Church and of a Christian minister to sustain, by sympathy, by act, and spoken word, the government of the country struggling in mortal throes. On these points the sympathies of the delegates were greatly divided. The Bishop of Michigan, in his opening sermon, had declared that the introduction of politics into a religious synod would be "high treason against God."

Resolutions offered declaring the sympathy of the Church with the government were tabled. The alleged reason for refusing to act was that the Church was a purely religious organization, and in that capacity knew nothing of the State or its concerns. There was also a feeling that if the Convention refrained from any action, the reconciliation would be easier with their Southern brethren when the war should be over. It may be said in explanation of this attitude of the Episcopal Church that its membership was, to a large extent, in the Democratic party, with whom the question of State rights was the chief political issue involved in the war. There were many who conscientiously held that any State had a right to secede from the Union, and that the action of the government in attempting to restrain such a step was unconstitutional. The Episcopal Church during the war, and for some years preceding, had become a house of refuge for those who disliked political preaching. For a time it seemed doubtful which way the General Convention representing the Episcopal Church would move. As the days went on, the party which stood for sympathy with the government grew stronger. The politics which had been so deprecated had exerted their influence upon the delegates. The time was drawing near for the annual elections, and the Hon. Horatio Seymour, candidate for the governorship in New York, was a member of the lower house. It would damage the Democratic party and its candidates in New York and elsewhere if the Episcopal Church should refuse to speak, for such refusal would be interpreted as sympathy with the rebellion. Resolutions at last were passed, very moderate in tone, almost colorless, but they answered the purpose. In the House of Bishops, despite its outward decorum, there was more aggressive activity as well as a clearer conception of the situation than in the lower house.

It had fallen to the lot of Bishop Hopkins of Vermont, as the presiding bishop, to draft the Pastoral Letter, wherein the bishops, according to custom, address the Church at large. After he had read to the bishops the letter he had prepared, in which the issues of the hour were studiously waived, Bishop McIlvaine of Ohio presented another letter, which was offered as a substitute, and accepted by the bishops, committing the Church to sympathy with the government in the prosecution of the war. Bishop McIlvaine deserves to be remembered in this connection. He had been one of the three commissioners sent to England for the purpose of explaining the situation, and conciliating English sentiment in high circles toward the North. Bishop Hopkins did not submit quietly under this condemnation of his attitude. He published a protest against the Pastoral Letter of the House of Bishops, which was sent broadcast through the country. All this was at a moment when the depression throughout the country in consequence of Northern defeats was at its lowest, when to many the prospect seemed almost hopeless.

"October 24, 1862. I own that we are in the darkest moment of the war and that our elections and some others do look wretchedly, but is n't our cause just as good as it ever was, and does n't it seem as if all through the war there had been a design of Providence to put off the settlement so that when it did come it might be thorough? Certainly if we had conquered at the first Bull Run, we should have been only too likely to have put things back on essentially the old basis, on some Crittenden compromise or something of that kind, and in a few years had the whole work to do over. We hope for better things than that. I agree with you perfectly about the Convention. Its shilly-shallying was disgraceful. It was ludicrous, if not so sad, to see those old gentlemen sitting there for fourteen days, trying to make out whether there was a war going on or not, and whether if there was it would be safe for them to say so. However they may represent the learning of the church, they certainly don't represent its spirit. Some few men, however, stood out well, Vinton and Goodwin and Clarkson, Randall and others, and the House of Bishops has put out a capital letter, written by Bishop McIlvaine. I am going to read it to my people to-morrow morning. . . . No, don't give up the old church yet. She 's got a thick crust of old-fogyism, but she 's all right at the core, and I hope will show it yet."

Whether in consequence of the excitement caused by the war, or for other reasons, Mr. Brooks seems to have been somewhat restless and dissatisfied with his position. He would have liked to do something heroic. He talked of going to California, "to evangelize the country there." It appeared to him as offering great attractions.

"November 8, 1862. It seems almost wrong to be going on with parish work here when there is so much of a more stirring kind going on everywhere, but I have not succeeded in getting a place as chaplain, and with this parish on my hands do not think I have any right to give up the ministry and go into the ranks."

On Thanksgiving Day he spoke his mind on the subject of slavery, despite the conservatism of the General Convention,— and committed himself and his congregation so far as it was in his power to the support of the nation. His text was Zechariah xiv. 6, 7: "And it shall come to pass in that day, that the light shall not be with brightness and with gloom: but it shall be one day which is known unto the Lord; not day, and not night: but it shall come to pass, that at evening time there shall be light." He had now lost his faith in McClellan, but out of the depression of the hour, there was springing up a more deeply rooted faith in the Divine will.

"November 21, 1862. I believe in the removal of McClellan, because, much as he has done for us, he seemed to be incapable of doing the last great thing, putting out the rebellion by an earnest, vigorous campaign, and, much as I like him, I think no man ought to be allowed to stand between us and peace by victory, which is our great object now."

A few weeks later he saw General McClellan at a reception to him in Philadelphia, and gives this estimate:

"I saw considerable of the general, and am not a stronger McClellan man for having seen him. He does n't look like a great man. His face does n't show, either, special refinement. He is pleasant and affable, and the soldiers collected to greet him were very enthusiastic. He looks like a good, sensible, bright engineer and not much more."

To his brother George, on his way to his regiment in North Carolina, he had written:

"November 7, 1862. How strange it seems for two of us to be in correspondence at such queer places. It did n't look much like it when we used to be growing up so quietly in Chauncy Street. If your experience is like mine you will find yourself wondering about your own identity sometimes; wondering whether you are yourself or whether you are n't somebody else. The best way when you get into such a condition is to go to work and reassure yourself by writing a long letter to some member of the family (me, for instance), and so get yourself back where you ought to be as one of the Brooks Boys.

It looks now as if there were work cut out for you to do on your arrival in North Carolina. The papers this very morning tell of an expedition from Newbern of 12,000 men, probably to Goldsboro. I hope something will come of it all. McClellan seems to be pushing on slowly but certainly in Virginia, and altogether, in spite of the elections, things look better. . . .

"Of course your eyes are all where ours are,—on Burnside.

What a job he has in hand.   Everybody has great faith in him,
though Philadelphia is sore about the removal of her pet son,
McClellan.   Things certainly look more encouraging and hopeful; and next Thanksgiving Day I trust we may be all safe at
home, rejoicing in victorious peace.

" Things at home seem to be going on pretty much their usual
course.   I had a long letter from Mother the other day.   They all
miss you terribly there.   My own impression, strengthened every
day since I first left the paternal roof, is that we have one of the
happiest homes the world can show.   Don't you begin to think
so? "

" December 5, 1862.   We had an anti-slavery sermon at Holy
Trinity on Thanksgiving which does n't seem to have done any
special harm.   The church was very full, and I had the satisfaction of alluding in praise to the Bishop's letter before that old
rebel, ——, who was present.   What do you think of the
President's message?   It's badly put together, but a very plain,
straightforward, understandable document, it seems to me.   If
all our government was as true as he is, we should see different
success, but with Washington full of corruption and treachery
no wonder if it takes us two or three times as long, and costs us
two or three times as much, as it ought to."

The year 1862 closed with widespread despondency among
the people.   The fall campaign had been unfavorable to the
Union arms.   The loss also of life had been enormous.   At the
battle of the Antietam, September 17, 1862, where victory
was left doubtful, 22,000 men had perished, and of these
12,000 belonged to the Union army.   Burnside had been defeated near Fredericksburg on the Rappahannock, December 13,
1862, with a loss of 12,000, and a Confederate loss of 4000.
Again, in Eastern Tennessee, at the battle of Murfreesboro,
December 31, 1862, where the Union army under the command
of Thomas and Sheridan at least held its own and repelled the
assault of the Confederates, out of 80,000 men engaged, 23,000
was the number of the killed and wounded.   The situation was
appalling, and as yet the beginning of the end was not visible.
The fall elections had been discouraging to the Republican
party.   Some who had hitherto supported the government were
now in favor of intervention from abroad or compromise at
home.

The Emancipation Proclamation issued by President Lincoln

on the first day of the New Year, 1863, was an event of high importance to Phillips Brooks. As he interpreted its meaning, the war had for its purpose a moral issue. God was in the conflict. There was now to be evidence afforded of a progressive movement in human affairs. The doctrine of an increasing purpose in the life of humanity, he had hitherto gathered from the records of history. Now it was to be made visible before his eyes. There followed a deeper faith, a vaster enthusiasm, a stronger sense of the reality of spiritual things, the concentration of the will on the great issue, in the confidence that God's will was thus subserved. He was taking a great step forward in his own experience. The consciousness of power and authority marked his utterances. He had no longer misgivings about the result of the protracted struggle. The tone of despondency disappears, to give way to exultation. The failure of this or that leader, disasters and defeats, were no ground for depression. He had completely vanquished the lower mood in which he had trusted to any one man to become the saviour of the country. To his father he writes on the 15th of January: "I cannot feel as blue about the war as you do. Nor is it time to look out yet for the effects of the Emancipation Proclamation. Military success is the first thing we want. We have had it already in Tennessee, and we shall see it yet at Vicksburg." This was written nearly six months before General Grant won his victory there. When Burnside was removed he wrote, "There is this comfort at least, that the more we try and find to be the wrong ones, the nearer we must be coming to the right one all the time." He had no longer any illusions about McClellan. "What did you think of Lincoln's letter to McClellan that came out in the court martial and was published in the papers of this morning [January 17th]? It looks as though Old Abe was just as good a general as the young Napoleon after all."

There are but few allusions to the fortunes of the war in the letters written at this time by the mother of Phillips Brooks. Her mind was preoccupied by one absorbing issue—the spiritual history of her son George, who had now reached the age of twenty-three, without presenting himself for confirmation. He was the third son, born in 1838, and if any son was a favorite with his parents more than another it was he. He was attractive in his personal appearance, manly and sincere, with a singular mixture of sweetness and strength. In making his start in life, he had met with several disappointments and bore them without complaint and with no diminution of courage. But on the subject of religion, he made no sign, as the years went by, resembling Phillips in the reserve with which he guarded himself. After his enlistment and just before he joined his regiment, he was confirmed at Trinity Church, September 28, 1862. That event counted with his mother for more than the victories or defeats of armies.

After his confirmation, the veil of reserve removed, George spoke freely of his religious experience. The change to him had been momentous and thorough. His religious life was deepened by the events of the war. In his Company, a prayer-meeting was held daily morning and evening conducted by the Captain. "He told me," said the Chaplain of his Company, "that he had never had full assurance of his pardon and accept-ance till he became a soldier; that in the battle of Kingston, under the terrible fire of the enemy, his Saviour came to him as never before, declared His presence, revealed His love, and held his soul in His hands."

Phillips Brooks was now to be called into another experience, which hitherto had been far away from him. His father unex-pectedly appeared in Philadelphia on his way to the South, summoned by tidings of the dangerous illness of George Brooks. But even before the father had started on his journey the end had come. The telegram that his brother had died of typhoid pneumonia on February 10th reached Phillips on the 16th, and he started at once for home. In the darkened house they waited for a week in silence, no word reaching them from the father, who was slowly making the journey home with the body of his son. With these days of waiting was associated the lines of Tennyson, the prayer for the ship bearing the loved remains:

> " Sphere all your lights around, above;
> Sleep, gentle heavens, before the prow;
> Sleep, gentle winds, as he sleeps now,
> My friend, the brother of my love."

While they waited at home Phillips Brooks wrote a sermon on the text (Luke xxiv. 18), "Art thou a stranger in Jerusalem, and hast not known the things which are come to pass there in these days?" On returning to Philadelphia, he wrote at once to his mother:

"Tuesday afternoon, March 3, 1863.

"MY DEAREST MOTHER,—I am back here again and trying to collect myself to go to work again to-morrow morning. Ever since I left you my thoughts have been with you all at home and I feel like a stranger here among the things that were so familiar only two weeks ago. These two weeks seem to me like a strange sort of dream, and it is hard to realize that such a change has come over our family life since the last time I was sitting here at my desk. And yet I find it hard to be sad or mournful about it. I cannot think that George himself, as he looks at us, wishes us to be sad or mournful. I have been looking over and over again, all last night and this morning, the whole life that we have lived with him. I cannot remember one moment whose memory is painful to me. I cannot recall a single quarrel that I ever had with him, and I suppose the other boys would say the same. I cannot bring back one look that was not all kindness, or one act that was not pure and good, or one word that was not bright and truthful. I envy him his life and death. I would gladly lie down and die to-night if I could look back on such a spotless life as his, and find my faith as simple and secure for the future as his was. How beautiful his religion was. He has taught me for one, as I never knew before, what Jesus meant when he told of 'receiving the kingdom of God as a little child.' Such a perfect trust as his I know is in the power of any of us to reach as he reached it, and yet I do not dare to expect it ever perfectly for myself, but am determined to live and pray and struggle for it, and shall rejoice if I can have a seat at last somewhere in sight of the perfect happiness and glory which he is in to-day and will be in forever. My thoughts of home will always be different now. I shall always think of George as there among you. I do not care about Mount Auburn. I don't care ever to go there again, till I am carried as he was yesterday. I want to think of him as being about the old house and always one of your group, making it happier and holier by his memory and influence, just as he always made it beautiful and bright when he was in the body. And I want to feel him there too, helping me and making me fitter for every duty with his own courage and cheerfulness and blessed faith.

"I find work enough waiting for me, and shall go about it happily, but always looking for the time when it will be all done, and we shall be with Christ and him.

"God bless you all,
"PHILL."

During the following week he was thinking much of George, his life and death. The confirmation of Arthur Brooks, the fifth son, on Easter day, at the age of seventeen, was to him the fruit of George's experience, and as though he were speaking to them from heaven. Into the work of his parish he now entered with greater zeal, taking on additional work. Connected with the parish was a night school, held in the chapel on week-day evenings, a mothers' meeting, and an outside Bible class, taught by ladies connected with the parish. To these he gave his personal presence and oversight. He continued to hold the deep interest of his Bible class on Saturday evenings, he lectured Wednesday evenings in the church to large congregations, and he gave a preparatory lecture for the monthly communion. On the first Sunday of each month came children's church in the afternoon. To the Sunday-school he gave special attention. He prepared his candidates for confirmation, not only in a series of lectures, but made it an obligation to call upon each candidate for personal conversation. Each week he tried to rescue as much time as possible for reading and study. Each week as a rule he records the writing of a sermon. Rarely a Sunday passed that he did not preach three times, very often reading the service twice in addition. If he found himself disengaged on Sunday evenings, he went to church somewhere for the purpose of hearing others preach. In the spring of this year, 1863, he was engaged in soliciting subscriptions for the purchase of a neighboring church in order to make it a chapel for Holy Trinity. To those who looked on he appeared to carry his work with ease; there was an air of spontaneity about his preaching, as though it came without effort or anxiety. But he writes: " You have no idea how fatiguing this work of speaking in public is. It does n't look like much to talk for half an hour to a room full of people, but it often leaves me tired out in mind and body and good for nothing."

The service in his crowded church on Fast Day was marked by unusual solemnity and impressiveness. "The congregation listened with the most profound attention, and apparently gave a sincere and hearty response to his remarks." The burden of his prophetic soul was the sin of slavery.

" It was not timely or proper to preach [so ran the report of his remarks], but would it not be a mockery before God to say that we have sinned, we have broken Thy laws, we have polluted Thy Sabbath and received in vain Thy grace, without alluding to the greatest sin of all,—the blackest stain upon our country and the cause of all the ruin and bloodshed and affliction that have been visited on our land,—the black sin of slavery? Have we not that duty to perform, to pray for the removal of that great crime, that dark spot upon our country's history? And was this all? Were there not here among us persons whom we meet daily in social intercourse who give not even a faltering support to the administration of the laws, who are not using the means that God has given them for the suppression of rebellion and treason; men who deprecate the extermination of the evil that has caused all our troubles? Was it not as much our duty to pray for the rebuke of those traitors in the North as for the discomfiture of the openly declared enemy in the South? It was the duty of the congregation to cultivate that firm, unwavering loyalty to the government that would recognize no distinction between the open foe and the secret enemy.''

Among the phases of the larger ministry to which Phillips Brooks was impelled was his protest against the indifference, even the avowed hostility, toward the government in the prosecution of the war. He had written under date of March 23, 1863:

"I have been away two days this week preaching in New Jersey. It was disheartening to see the state of public feeling there, the apathy or opposition to the administration that has made that little State disgraceful. But surely things are looking very much better everywhere. It seems as if the more we suffer the more we must feel ourselves committed to finish completely the great work we have undertaken."

It was said of an Episcopal church in Philadelphia that "in the war-time the clergyman could not read the prayer for the President without causing a rustle of silken skirts, worn by the ladies who insisted at this point upon rising from their knees." [1] A Philadelphia clergyman, writing of Mr. Brooks's relation to the war, says:

"The Union League [Club] was founded to counteract this baneful influence of society. I accompanied Phillips Brooks to the

[1] *Phillips Brooks*, in Beacon Biographies, by M. A. De Wolfe Howe, p. 26.

opening meeting (February, 1863), and he made one of those bold Union speeches for which he became famous, although his parish was a new organization, heavily in debt, and he was in danger of losing some of his most important members by his decided action. When most pulpits were silent and some adverse, his gave forth no uncertain sound. His manly, courageous utterances did much to turn the tide of society in favor of the abolition of slavery and the preservation of the Union."

He does not appear to mind the inevitable opposition he encountered. In a letter dated June 6, 1863, he refers, a rare thing with him, to the criticism he is meeting:

" I have nothing particular to tell you to-day about myself, and so I will let you see what other people say about me by enclosing a slip from our Copperhead journal which some kind friend has just sent me. Is n't it terrible to think of this fearful plot to fill the churches and schools with New England radicals, and gradually seize on all Philadelphia, and make another Boston of it? I suppose a part of our plan must be to get possession of the financial institutions; so just hold yourself in readiness to come on and take a radical cashiership as soon as things are ready for it. This sort of feeling is very strong here, and is making a pretty hard fight, but it can't stand. The world moves. Vicksburg is not ours yet, but everything looks promising, and perhaps we do not know how near we are to the end. At any rate the conviction is stronger every day that, long or short, there 's nothing to be done but fight it out, and ' put down the rebellion.' "

An intimate friend of Brooks, speaking of this phase of his ministry, writes:

" I despair of making the young men of to-day understand what it cost in those days to be lord of one's own soul. Through that weary time, what an overflowing reservoir of moral force, of hope, of courage, of high resolve, Brooks was to all of us Then, as ever, his presence was an inspiration. There were dark days —days when, as we met on a street corner, after some bloody reverse of our armies, he could only wring my hand and say, ' Is n't it horrible?' and pass on gloomily: days when it was easy to take counsel of one's meaner fears and cry for peace at any price, and try to patch up any miserable cabin of refuge from the storm which beat upon our hearts. But his heart never flinched or quailed. His light ever shone out clear."

A victory of General Robert E. Lee, the commander of the

Confederate forces, over the Army of the Potomac in May, 1863, left the North unprotected, and it was decided to carry the war into Pennsylvania. At first it was hard to realize that the State was actually in danger of invasion. Men refused to believe it. War may be wrong and a great evil, the duty of non-resistance may have its place among the Evangelical precepts, but when a city is in danger of invasion something should be done to repel the invaders. So the situation appeared to Phillips Brooks:

"Saturday, June 27, 1863.

"DEAR FATHER,—I suppose you must be wondering a little what is the state of mind in this poor bethreatened city. I wish you could be here and see how dead and apathetic men can be with an enemy almost at their doors. I don't think that Lee is coming to Philadelphia, but there certainly is threatening enough of it to make us get ready if he did come. Nothing is doing here at all. Yesterday the Union League decided that it might oe well to get up a regiment, but as yet, so far as I can learn, not more than 2000 men have gone from Philadelphia, and the men who are protecting the line of the Susquehanna are New Yorkers and New Englanders. I am ashamed of Philadelphia and Pennsylvania, and proud as usual of New England. Or course all our town talk is of the invasion. We do not think that Philadelphia is very likely to be their aim. Evidently they are trying to delude us, and will more likely strike either at Pittsburg or at Baltimore. Some timid people here are a good deal scared. I will let you know if there is any danger. I see George's regiment is after this new raid. How much hard life and terrible work the dear boy has escaped. I think of him always.

"Good-by—one week more (unless I am kept here by danger of a capture) and I am with you. Love to Mother.

"Yours affectionately,
"PHILL."

Cn Monday, June 29, he records in his diary; "Meeting of the clergy of all the churches to offer their services to the Mayor." This remark is illuminated by the following reminiscence:

"From Cooper's study proceeded one movement that the chronicle of those crowded years should not quite lose from view. The enemy was at the gate. Lee's army had invaded Pennsylvania, was before Harrisburg, was threatening Philadelphia. The Quaker City was carrying non-resistance to its last consequence, was folding its hands and shaking in its shoes, and waiting for

Providence or the general government to come to its rescue. It was a panic of stupor akin to a dumb ague. Brooks, Cooper, and the rest of us assembled on a Monday morning in Cooper's study, waxed hot at the local inaction. If laymen would do nothing it was time for the clergy to move. We did move on the moment. We drew up a paper offering our services for the public defence. We would not take up arms, but we could shoulder shovels and dig trenches. Several clerical meetings were in session that noon, and we sent delegates to rouse them. With Brooks and the venerable Albert Barnes at the head of the procession we stormed the mayor's office, a hundred or more strong, and asked to be set at work on the defences of the city. We retired, bought our spades and haversacks, and waited for orders. The example served its purpose."

As the situation still seemed uncertain, Mr. Brooks wrote home that he did not feel at liberty to leave his post for the annual holiday:

"July 4, 1863. The fact is I don't like to leave here while things are just in the present condition; not that I think there is any danger of their coming here, but people are a good deal excited, and till the terrible battle of this week is over, and its results well confirmed, I shall not leave. It will probably be only a short delay, and I will write you next week just as soon as I see my way clear to getting off. Everything to-day looks promising; we are going to beat and bag their army, I believe, and then the war is about over. I am sorry to shorten my vacation, but I must not leave just now."

The events of these weeks culminated in the battle of Gettysburg, where 50,000 men were lost out of 170,000 engaged. The entries in his pocket diary, brief as they are, show the excitement of the moment.

"Saturday, July 4, 1863. Services in Holy Trinity. I read and made a short address. All the forenoon down town. Great news of Lee's repulse by Meade. . . . Evening at Union League. Still good news.

"Sunday, July 5, 1863. Fifth Sunday after Trinity. I read, spoke, and administered the communion. During the communion service news came of Lee's rout, and I announced it to the congregation. God be praised.

"Monday, July 6, 1863. Evening. Started for the battlefield under the auspices of the Sanitary Commission. Arrived at Baltimore about four o'clock the next morning.

"Tuesday, July 7, 1863. Spent all day making arrangements and trying to get off to Gettysburg. Started in freight train at seven o'clock P.M., and spent the night in the cars, arriving at Hanover at seven o'clock the next morning.

"Wednesday, July 8, 1863. Almost all day at Hanover. Left for Gettysburg at five o'clock P.M. Arrived about seven. Slept in loft of a tar-shop.

"Thursday, July 9, 1863, A.M. At Sanitary Commission Tent near the depot. Then all over the battlefield.

"Friday, July 10, 1863. All day at the hospital of the Second Division of the Fifth Corps, distributing clothes and writing letters for the men. Very tired at night.

Saturday, July 11, 1863. To the hospital of the Pennsylvania Reserves. P.M., among the rebel prisoners in the Third Corps. Terrible need and suffering.

"Sunday, July 12, 1863. All day among the rebel prisoners in the Third Corps Hospital.

"Monday, July 13, 1863. All day travelling to Philadelphia. Arrived about 10.30 P.M."

On the 16th of July, 1863, he returned to his home in Boston, where he remained with his family for a few weeks before making another tour of the White Mountains. The first thing was to turn to Mount Auburn on a visit to the new-made grave. Since he was last at home a change had been made by his father's family in their church relations; they had given up their pew at St. Paul's Church and migrated to Trinity Church, then situated on Summer Street. At the invitation of Bishop Eastburn, he preached at Trinity Church the afternoon of Sunday, the 26th of July. It was midsummer, and the congregation was so small as to seem almost invisible. The meagre attendance may have been owing to the circumstance that no announcement had been made that he was to preach. But there was one present who made the occasion the subject of reminiscences in later years. He had called on Bishop Eastburn in his house on Tremont Street opposite the Common, and in the course of the conversation asked the bishop where he should go to church the following Sunday. The bishop answered: "I think you had better go to my church, for I shall have there a young man from Philadelphia named Brooks, who is esteemed to be somebody, and I want you to hear him preach."

"On Sunday morning, therefore, I went to Trinity Church.

which, the reader will remember, was the old Trinity in Summer Street, then a quiet quarter, still retaining many roomy houses occupied by old Boston families. Entering its gray portals I perceived that I might sit where I liked, for there was scarce anybody in the church. . . . When the time for the sermon arrived, a person who had been sitting silent in the chancel, muffled in a black gown, emerged—or rather projected himself—in the direction of the pulpit. A tall, thin figure rushed up the pulpit steps. Before fairly reaching the top of them a voice called out the text, and instantly broke into a speech of most astonishing rapidity, quite beyond anything I had ever experienced or imagined of human utterance. . . . As soon as I recovered from my surprise, and the mind could catch its breath, so to speak, and begin to keep up with the preacher's pace, I perceived that what I was hearing was a wonderful sermon, such as would oftenest be called brilliant, perhaps, but is better described as glowing and lambent. The text was the verse of St. Paul about seeing now "through a glass, darkly, but then face to face," and the discourse contained material for a score of sermons, so rich was it in high thought and apt illustration and illuminative turns of phrase. I fancy that in those days Dr. Brooks used illustrations more profusely than in later years. . . . Possibly I myself might find that sermon too ornate for my maturer taste, but I know the impression it then made upon me was not of over-ornamentation, but of thought intrinsically and aboundingly rich, and I believe that if it shall see the light among any forthcoming collection of Bishop Brooks's literary remains, I shall gain from reading it the same impression that it produced so many years ago."

The writer of this account was impressed with the contrast between the few hearers who listened to Phillips Brooks on that midsummer day in 1863 and the thousands afterwards, in the glorified new Trinity, who dwelt on every note of his voice,—between the young Brooks who was thought to be somebody and the man who became the successor of Bishop Eastburn. But appearances are deceitful. In Mr. Brooks's diary for the following Monday, it reads, "Mr. George Dexter [the senior warden] called to talk about my coming to Trinity Church." For six years the parish had him in view, before the result was accomplished.

A few days were spent in Boston after his return from the mountains, during which he wrote as usual his sermon in order to be ready for his first Sunday in Philadelphia. When he reached Philadelphia on the 5th of September he records his arrival with a sigh, "So vacation 's over!" He found the city "quivering with excitement." The time for the fall elections was near. Governor Curtin, the Republican candidate for governor of the State, was opposed by Judge Woodward as the Democratic candidate. Not only did excitement run high in political circles, but in ecclesiastical, for things were happening which roused the indignation of the Episcopal clergy. The story is now a curious one merely, relating to the action of Dr. Hopkins, the bishop of Vermont, and referred to here because of Phillips Brooks's connection with it.

Bishop Hopkins had resisted the action of the General Convention in 1862, when it gave its approval to the war and its support to the government, as the introduction of politics into a sacrosanct assembly. Among other views, he held that the Bible sanctioned slavery, an opinion to which he had given expression in his *American Citizen*. But, although slavery was a divine institution, yet he thought it should be abolished, and that this was the destiny reserved for it. The Democratic party in Pennsylvania now proposed to make use of him in the heated canvass between Curtin and Woodward. Six gentlemen of Philadelphia had requested his permission to republish his well-known views on slavery, which he had given in a tract issued in 1861, and known as *The Bible View of Slavery*. The original motive in writing this tract had been to cool down if possible the fiery zeal of the abolitionists. Bishop Hopkins gave his consent to the reissue of the tract, and in June, 1863, it had been reprinted by the Society for the Diffusion of Political Knowledge in New York Soon after it was taken up and circulated by the Democratic clubs throughout the country, but chiefly in Pennsylvania, as an electioneering pamphlet.

Such a proceeding could not go unchallenged without committing the Episcopal Church in Pennsylvania to a tacit approval of this extraordinary document. The clergy of Philadelphia were called together by Bishop Potter; a protest was drawn up and intrusted to a committee who should procure signatures to it. Of this committee Mr. Brooks was a member, and by no means an inactive one. Indeed, he was so prominent that he was incorrectly suspected and accused of being the author of the protest. But he did what he could to procure signatures for it, directing circulars with his own hand to be sent broadcast throughout the State. The protest was signed by one hundred and sixty of the clergy, a very large majority of those in the diocese. This prompt and decisive action may have had its influence on the election. Governor Curtin was elected by a majority of 20,000, and Judge Woodward, the defeated candidate, withdrew from the Church of the Holy Trinity. To these and other incidents Mr. Brooks alludes in his home letters:

"October 3, 1863. Last Sunday afternoon I went out and preached to our colored regiment at Cheltenham. It was new sort of work, but I enjoyed it. They are splendid-looking fellows. To-day they have been parading through the city, and seem to have surprised everybody by their good soldierly looks. Have you seen what a stir has been raised up by Bishop Hopkins's slavery letter and by our clerical protest against it? It may look to you like something of a tempest in a teapot, but I can assure you that the letter was doing a great deal of harm, and that our remonstrance has been widely welcomed. One of the Copperhead papers the other day did me the honor to assume that I had a good deal to do with it, and read me a long lecture on the modesty becoming young clergymen."

"October 17, 1863. It is worth another victory of our armies thus to have conquered disloyalty here at the North, and to have got our heel on the neck of the Copperhead. If you had been here I think you would have been as much surprised as I have been at the *radical* character of this campaign which has just closed. And it has not been merely Republican, but anti-slavery; not merely anti-slavery, but abolition all the way through. If this war had n't done anything else so far, at any rate it has made us an anti-slavery people, and begun the end of this infernal institution. I spent Tuesday night at the League House, and have seldom seen such an excitement as there was when the news came in and the result gradually became certain. Judge Woodward has resigned his seat on my vestry, and advertised his pew for sale. I am sorry, for he is a very pleasant man, and has been one of my kindest friends. I presume we shall get along without him, but I wish he could have stayed among us."

A difficult problem in American life had been created when the Emancipation Proclamation of Mr. Lincoln had produced its effect. Hundreds of thousands of negroes were thrown adrift, free, indeed, but unaccustomed to the use of freedom; hitherto cared for, with no sense of responsibility for their maintenance, and now obliged to seek their own support; ignorant, untrained, unfit for the burden placed so suddenly upon them. Mr. Brooks was among the very first to recognize the importance of immediate action. He became a member of the Freedmen's Relief Association. He makes mention of frequent visits to the negro regiment in camp near Philadelphia, watching them on parade, addressing them at their Sunday services. He took special pride in a colored Sunday-school at the corner of 13th and Race Streets. At public gatherings he made important speeches in behalf of the needs and interests of the colored people. He was anxious that the Episcopal Church should be identified with this philanthropic work.

This devotion to their interests by Phillips Brooks was gratefully recognized by the colored people in Philadelphia and elsewhere. It would sometimes show itself in amusing ways, as at evening parties and receptions, when it was understood that no one could expect much attention from the colored waiters if Phillips Brooks were present. Long years afterward his acts of kindness in 1863 were gratefully remembered. When he died, resolutions were passed by the Bethel Literary and Historical Association, of Washington, "recalling his noble and brave words for freedom and enfranchisement in the dark days of the war, the prominent part he took in opening to us the street cars in Philadelphia, and this at the risk both of personal violence and social ostracism."

As Thanksgiving Day approached in 1863, Phillips Brooks was preparing himself to give expression to a people's gratitude, by rising to some mount of vision whence the way could be discerned by which the nation had been led through the years of darkness, of agony, and of sacrifice. Already he foresaw the beginning of the end. The victory of General Meade at Gettysburg, and the capture of Vicksburg by General Grant, in July, followed by the advance of Grant and the significant results at Chattanooga in November, pointed to one conclusion,—the object of the war had been really gained, however long the time which must elapse before its full acknowledgment. The war should have ended here.

Again the great Church of the Holy Trinity was crowded to its utmost capacity, seats were placed in the aisles, and many were standing, as the preacher announced his text: "Therefore, behold, the days come, saith the Lord, that it shall no more be said, The Lord liveth, that brought up the children of Israel out of the land of Egypt; but, The Lord liveth, that brought up the children of Israel from the land of the north, and from all the lands whither he had driven them: and I will bring them again into their land that I gave unto their fathers." (Jeremiah xvi., 14, 15). The next day, November 27, 1863, came the request for the publication of the sermon, signed by some sixty names of the leading citizens of Philadelphia. It was immediately issued with the title "Our Mercies of Reoccupation." There are some features of this sermon which have now only an historical interest, but even in treating these the sentences glow with the splendor of the preacher's deep conviction, his exuberant vitality, his rich imagination. He laments that the Christian Church did not take the lead in the protest against slavery. "Year after year the Church stood back while they who fought the battle went out from her; the whole movement against slavery became not only unchurchly but openly infidel, disowning all interest in every presentation of that Christianity of whose spirit and operation it was nevertheless of itself the legitimate result."

There were those who rejoiced that slavery was disappearing, but "*our* rejoicing," they said, "is for the *white* man; it is not for the negro we care." To this the preacher replied:

"It *is* for the negro we care. It is our fault, and not his, that he is here. It is our fault, inherited from the fathers, that has kept in most utter bondage, and most cruel bondage too, generation after generation of men who have proved themselves the most patient, long-suffering, affectionate, docile race of servants that ever lived, and who now, in the little glimmering of a chance that is given them, are standing between us and the rebels, fighting battles, receiving wounds, dying deaths, that belong more to us than to them, fighting splendidly, working faithfully, learning eagerly, enduring endlessly, laying hold on a higher life with an eagerness that has no parallel in savage history."

He warns his congregation against the fragments of old prejudices still clinging about them:

"Let us get rid of these. If the negro is a man, and we have freed him in virtue of his manhood, what consistency or honor is it which still objects to his riding down the street in the same car with us if he is tired, or sitting in the same pew with us if he wants to worship God?"

But the charm of the sermon, its literary power, its human appeal, lay in the application of its subject, the "Mercies of Reoccupation." The preacher was developing the fundamental principle that the reoccupation, after the loss and deprivation with its accompanying struggle to regain, is greater than was the first occupation. He applied this truth in various ways. He spoke of the reoccupation of the national territory. It was strange that men should talk of the slowness or ineffectiveness of the war in view of what had been gained by the victories of the past year: "It is hard to keep up with telegrams that tell us day by day of the progressive occupation by the power of the government. . . . The great river, which *is* the lordly West, flows open with the light of the Union on it from source to sea . . . . The vast domain west of the Mississippi, with all its untold possibilities, those two States, Kentucky and Tennessee, constituting the keystone of our broad arch, the sweep of Union victory has reclaimed forever to freedom. . . . In our own fair State we have a tale of reoccupation too to tell. The silent graves on that hill front at Gettysburg are voiceful with the promise that, come what will, our Northern soil has felt the last footprint of the oppressor and invader. . . . This reoccupation is to be greater, to make the region which it gives us more distinctly our own, than it was by the first occupation. The nation is just coming to its inheritance. . . . Those who come after us will look back and see that the work of this year was of greater moment in the history of the world than that of any Revolutionary year. They will see that those years inevitably came to be nothing without the completing process of these."

"But infinitely more important than the mere reoccupation of territory is the resumption by this American people in a higher sense, the full occupation of the government of their fathers, the re-entrance into the principles and fundamental truths of the nationality which they inherited, but which up to the beginning of this war they had not begun worthily to occupy and use. . . . More than fourscore years ago this nation declared itself free and independent,—the new ground of a new experiment in national, social, and individual life. . . . How very partially that bright announcement has been fulfilled. We have never half claimed our independence. In our timid regard for foreign opinion, in our blind regard for foreign methods, . . . we have only very slightly made our own the high privilege of independent life. Believe me, it will not be the least of the blessings that God sends us if by any means, by a development of our own powers, by new exigencies leading us into the necessity of untried methods, by the individuality of suffering, . . . by the terrible disappointment which discovers the shallowness of loud-mouthed European phil-anthropy, by the selfishness of the old worlds that will not, or the blindness of old worlds that can not, see how grand and holy a task a younger world is called to do,—if by any means He gives us out of the isolation of our national struggle a larger entrance into the independent life, the separate and characteristic devel-opment of government, art, science, letters, practical religion, and social character, which is the wide domain into which He led our nation, and whose splendid size it has taken us almost a hun-dred years to find.''

There is another reoccupation in the circumstance that party lines in the republic have been broken, and that loyalty to the country has taken the place of all other issues. But the highest of all the reoccupations which by God's grace it has been per-mitted to make this year is the reoccupation of the disused duties and privileges of justice, liberty, and human brotherhood.

''You do not expect me, I do not think you want me, to stand here to-day without thanking God that the institution of African slavery in our beloved land is one big year nearer to its inevitable death than it was last Thanksgiving Day. On that day certain hopeful words were spoken from this pulpit which groped about in the darkness and timidly thought they saw the signs of light. To-day, will any man or woman blame us, as we stand in the anticipation of certainty, and cry above the opened grave of slavery, that only waits till its corpse be brought to it with the decency its reverend age demands, Thank God! thank God! the hateful thing is dead! I am speaking solemnly; I am thinking earnestly; I am speaking as a man whose heart is too glad for utterance, in the washing from his country's robe, even though it be in the red water of her children's blood, of such a stain as she has worn before the nations through these years of her melancholy beauty. What has done it? Not the Proclamation of last New Year's Day, though we ought to thank God, as not the least mercy of these times, that we have had a man to lead us so honest and so true, so teachable at the lips of the Almighty, as to write those immortal words that made a race forever free. Not any public document, not any public act, has done the work; nothing but the hand of God, leading back His chosen people into the land of universal freedom, into which he led the fathers, and out of which the children went so woefully astray. Which God is greater,—He who led the fathers in, or He who leads the children back? At any rate, the Lord grant us to be truer to the new charter of emancipation than (we own it with shamefacedness and contrition) we have been to the declaration of freedom and human equality which the fathers wrote."

One attentive observer who was studying the effect of the sermon noted that the congregation left the church in subdued silence.

The sermon had a large circulation, being placed for sale in the principal bookstores of the large cities. It was recognized as something more than a sermon, or a masterpiece of inspired oratory; it was an event in the history of the times. No such comprehensive utterance was made during the war. The newspapers, in giving abstracts of it and expressing admiration, agreed in commenting upon the fact that such a sermon should have been delivered by an Episcopal clergyman and in one of the wealthiest, most fashionable churches in Philadelphia.

From this public recognition of the sermon one may turn aside for a moment to follow its effect in the home circle. "*I want,*" wrote his father, "*a dozen copies* of that sermon. Don't let your modesty stand in the way; *I want them* and *at least* that number." Happy and proud in the consciousness that he had evidence indisputable of the greatness of his son as a citizen as well as a preacher, the father sent the sermon to his kinsfolk and acquaintances. He had only heard of it when he asked that copies should be sent him, and had not read it. After he had read it, he wrote: "I should have two years ago repudiated much of its doctrine, but now go almost the whole of it." Those to whom he sent it were not all of one mind about its doctrine. He collected their testimony and sent it to his son. Among the congratulations were those of his kinsmen Wendell Phillips and Edward Everett. The Hon. Robert C. Winthrop, in acknowledging the sermon, expressed the hope that it will not be long before Phillips Brooks comes to Boston as rector of one of its churches.

The references to the sermon by Mr. Brooks himself are brief in his home letters. He notes its effect on the congregation:

"All is going on at this church as usual. One pew offered for sale immediately after Thanksgiving Day, and four applicants to buy it at once. We are weeding out fast, and I have now an almost entirely loyal church with not an inch of room to rent. I am glad you liked my sermon. I send you with this the criticism on it of ——, one of our great Copperheads, which appeared in the *Age* a day or two ago. I have just been reading over Dudley Tyng's famous sermon of seven years ago. What a brave thing it was to do! Thank God anybody can do it now."

For some reason, not wholly explained, he was perturbed and at times depressed. To the charge that he was not writing as "jolly" letters as he used to do, he replied: "I am perfectly happy; everything goes with such lovely smoothness that I should be a rascal if I was anything but happy." There are only a few hints as to his reading; he mentions Renan's *Vie de Jesus*, and the writings of Pascal, but without comment. To his older brother he gave a sketch of a week's work, to show how his time was occupied:

"1533 LOCUST STREET, October 31, 1863.
"DEAR WILLIAM,—If there is any cheerfulness in my letter today, it will have to come from inside, and not outside the house. It is raining as hard as Philadelphia only knows how to rain, and all the curtains up hardly give me light enough to write by. Fortunately my sermon is done, or it would be hard to keep it from turning into a very gloomy homily on such a day as this. What shall I write about? Suppose I give you my biography for a week, so that you can know pretty much what all my weeks are. Well, Monday morning I got up pretty tired with Sunday's work, and went down town after breakfast, as I generally do nowadays, to do up my limited business, paying bills, shopping, etc. At one o'clock I went to one of our hospitals to see some Boston men who had found me out and sent to me to help get their discharges; sick and wounded, they needed help and sympathy bad enough. Then all the afternoon I went about making calls in my parish, and spent the evening studying in my room. Tuesday I had a funeral to attend, which took me almost all the morning; then I went, as I always do on Tuesdays, and dined at Mr. Cooper's with Strong and Richards, and spent the evening at Dr. Mitchell's. Wednesday was my morning to receive visitors at my study in the church on all sorts of business, religious and secular, from men begging money to men joining the church. Then I went out and made some more calls, and in the evening made an address to a Christian Work Association in St. Philip's (Mr.

Cooper's) Church. Thursday I went to work on a sermon which I am to preach to-morrow night before the Bishop White Prayer Book Society. It did n't go very well, and I labored over it all the forenoon. I went and dined at Mr. Ashhurst's, and in the evening, after making one call, settled down before my fire and read and studied till twelve o'clock. Friday I went at the sermon again, and, with lots of interruptions which kept taking me away, worked till dinner time. After dinner made a few calls, and went and took tea with a new parishioner. Home by nine o'clock, and at the sermon again for an hour. This morning, being sick and tired of the poor old sermon, I got up and finished it off before breakfast, and since breakfast have got ready my lecture for to-night, and my sermon for the children to-morrow afternoon Pepper that over with lots of people coming to see me on important business, and you have my week's work. It is about a type of all—a quiet, humdrum, and not unpleasant life, with an extra sensation now and then."

Changes were taking place in the family circle. Frederick had left, and the mother had been called again to her task of packing the boxes. Arthur was now in his first year at Harvard. Only John, the youngest son, was left at home. "We are a small figure," so writes his father to Phillips. "It is lonesome indeed after our long table we have enjoyed so many years."

The month of December brought more than its share of anniversaries. After Thanksgiving came his own birthday on December 13, and the birthday of George followed on the 18th. Christmas was the great day of the year. To these he added the night of December 31, keeping it by a vigil in the church. To one who hoarded life as a rich treasure, there was danger of too intense and ever-present consciousness of its flight. He noted too curiously whether the celebration of the feast was adequate, whether he had risen to or fallen short of its demands.

"December 26, 1863.—To-night I have a Christmas tree for the children of a little negro Sunday-school which I started a few squares from my church. We have got about a hundred of the funniest little darkies there that you ever saw. I wish you could be with us. They sing like larks."

The following letter indicates how deep had been the perturbation of spirit:

"December 20, 1863.—I have decided [he writes to Frederick

Brooks], although the decision is not mentioned yet to any one, and you are to accept it in perfect confidence and not mention it to any one, *not even in writing home*, to give up my parish, and take the professorship of ecclesiastical history in the Divinity School. . . . I shall make the change in a month or two. Remember, you are not to mention it to anybody. Let me hear what you think of it."

CHAPTER VIII.

1864–1865.

CALL TO THE PHILADELPHIA DIVINITY SCHOOL. EX-
TRACTS FROM NOTE-BOOK. SPEECHES IN BEHALF
OF NEGRO SUFFRAGE. THE CLOSE OF THE WAR.
THE DEATH OF LINCOLN. THE HARVARD COM-
MEMORATION. DEPARTURE FOR EUROPE.

THE election to the chair of ecclesiastical history in the Philadelphia Divinity School would not have been made without the
knowledge of Mr. Brooks, or if the trustees of the school had not
been encouraged by his tacit approval. And it must be assumed
that he knew his own mind when he decided to accept the call.
At this moment he was at the height of his popularity and success
in Philadelphia; his church was thronged with eager hearers. If
some prominent citizens had left because of his anti-slavery teaching, yet many others were waiting to become purchasers of any
vacant pews. His power as a preacher, or as a platform speaker
on religious or philanthropic occasions, was widely recognized, his
services were in constant demand, and whenever he spoke he
never failed to rouse the enthusiasm of his audience. It had
become almost a commonplace in the newspaper reports to say
that *the* speech of the occasion was by Phillips Brooks. Everywhere he went there was curiosity to see as well as to hear him.
Even in these early years of his career he seems to have taken
the lustre off from other guests or speakers who might be associated with him. There was something strange in it all, and difficult to be accounted for, but it was very real and genuine.

The reasons which he gave for making the change from the
pulpit to the professor's chair are briefly stated in a letter to his
father:

" January 7, 1864.

" DEAR FATHER,—I want to write to you about a very impor-

159

tant matter (to me), probably one of the most important I shall ever have to meet. It has been vaguely in prospect for some time, but not in such a state that I could speak about it until now. You may be sure I have not settled this in a hurry. I want you and Mother to understand just exactly what are my reasons for such a decision.

"In the first place the great need of the Church (you surely know it) is for ministers. And any one who can go to the root of that difficulty, and help to train the right sort of men, is doing a better and more fundamental work than any mere parish minister could do. Then the great need of our seminaries is young men for professors. We have always had old men. We want younger ones, and I have got youth and energy, if nothing else, to give. Again, the parish is much more easily provided for than the chair. Any man they choose to call will take the Church of the Holy Trinity, with its splendid congregation and its $4000 a year. There are not a great many, certainly none with families, who can afford to come to the obscure professorship at $1800 a year.

"Then a more personal reason. I need it for myself. In the whirl of this life which I am living now I get no time for study. Everything is going out, nothing is coming in, and I find myself needing a quieter and more studious life. I shall both do more and get more good in my professor's chair."

Other reasons for the change might be adduced from the knowledge of him gained by his previous history. The intellectual tendency in his nature demanded satisfaction. He saw scholarship as a means to some greater end. He felt the need of a more profound and extensive learning, and felt also that what he gained he must impart. To be a teacher appeared to him as the highest and the most natural calling in life. To do the work of a teacher, quietly and without ostentation, to come in contact with other minds in the intimate relation of teacher and pupil, this, if he had ambition, was his. To the end of his life, his heart rejoiced at the thought of a school or college, above all of a theological school. And further the study of history fascinated him beyond any other, especially ecclesiastical history. For such a position he had unusual qualifications and every reason to expect the highest success. But it seems strange that he did not value the gift of speech with which he was endowed; if he was aware of its possession, he held it in low esteem compared with the reality which he aspired after.

At this point he came in conflict with the world's estimate, which honors most those who have enthralled it with the eloquence of the spoken word. The pressure of opinion was against his preference. His best friends and the best judges of the situation were averse to the change, and felt that his withdrawal from the pulpit would be a public calamity. Preachers, they urged, like poets, were born, not made. "The loss of direct contact with practical life"—so wrote one of his admirers—"might stop some of your sources of intellectual and spiritual supply and freeze over the genial current of your soul." His work in the pulpit was characterized by another admirable judge as of a kind so rare that "it cannot be too highly appreciated and cannot be replaced."

As to the Church of the Holy Trinity, there was painful surprise when it became known that the rector's choice was to abandon the pulpit and become a professor in a theological school. The vestry met at once and sent him "a warm, affectionate, and earnest remonstrance." Then the congregation was summoned as a synod to consider the question and if possible to produce the conviction in his mind that his usefulness required that he should remain in his present position. They came prepared to make great sacrifices. It had become widely known in the parish that there was one thing they could do,—they could refrain from calling upon him during certain hours of the day, thus leaving him leisure for study, and they could excuse him from the necessity of making calls in the parish beyond what necessity demanded. The result of their deliberation was a full and urgent statement of the case as it appeared from their point of view,—a part of which is cited:

"During his occupancy of this position, every day's experience has confirmed our belief in the peculiar fitness of Mr. Brooks for preaching the gospel. His talents seem to us to qualify him in an unusual degree for success, not merely as a preacher, but for the development of those great schemes of church work without which no parish can live or prosper in any sense. His efforts during his incumbency to establish Trinity Chapel and extend the missionary work, and to undertake all those varied labors by which a true Christian life manifests itself in a parish, have met with wonderful success; due in a great measure, it seemed to us, to the sympathetic ardor and enthusiasm of his character, combined in a wonderful and most unusual degree with the wisdom and judgment which has marked all his plans.

" His great popularity and success as a preacher, particularly in the case of those persons of culture and position who have seldom heretofore attended the public services of our church, lead us to the belief and conviction that his influence in extending the power of the Christian church, and in bringing into its fold many who may hereafter become through his agency active and earnest ministers of the church, cannot be overrated. . . .

" Finally we conceive that Mr. Brooks's present position enables him to exercise an immense influence for good as a citizen, which we should be blind and ungrateful not fully to recognize. In view of all these considerations, and of many others equally obvious, which we cannot here enumerate, it is impossible that we should consent to sever the tie which his ability, devotion, and earnest interest have formed between us, and thereby entail a sorrow which we cannot contemplate without the deepest emotion.

" In considering this subject, it seems proper for us respectfully to request that our rector shall set apart certain hours daily, say from ten A.M. until three P.M., or such other hours as he may select, exclusively for his own study, during which he shall be free from any interruption by the congregation, who shall be properly notified of this arrangement."

By January 16th the question was decided, and the congregation was again summoned in formal conclave. The meeting was opened with prayer by Mr. John Bohlen, the founder of the Bohlen Lectures, who offered the following resolution which was unanimously adopted:

"The congregational meeting of the Church of the Holy Trinity, the first ever convened, assembled for consultation in view of the apprehended danger to the congregation which the resignation of the rector would cause, are now called upon, instead of the action proposed before they assembled, to render devout thanks to Almighty God, the giver of every good and perfect gift, that He has been pleased to avert from us this threatened danger, and to renew our assurance of confidence in, and thanks to, our beloved rector, whose ministrations are now to be continued, we trust for many years, to the congregation."

So it was decided that Phillips Brooks should remain in the pulpit and not be lost in a professor's chair. Opinion will differ as to whether he took the right course of action, in this critical moment, when his life was still before him. The wider consensus will acknowledge with gratitude the action of the

Church of the Holy Trinity in Philadelphia, by which the preacher was saved to the Church, to the country, and to the world. But there may be some who will lament that the teacher's chair lost not only an ornament but that the cause of historical theology then suffered a loss which cannot be repaired.

His decision to remain with his church is thus alluded to in a letter to his brother:

"January 22, 1864. I am settled down after my little promise of disturbance, and parish work is going on pretty much as usual, except that by an understanding with my people I expect to get more time for my own study, and to get rid of what I hold to be very unnecessary work, the spending the best part of the day in running about making calls."

While the question of his call to the Divinity School was pending he was induced to consent to the publication of a volume of his sermons. The making of the book had begun, and half of its pages were stereotyped, when he concluded to withdraw it. A few copies were bound up, to give to intimate friends, and at some expense to himself the venture terminated. In a letter to his father he says:

"March 12, 1864. About the book you must say no more. Of course I pay the cost. It won't be much, I don't know just how much yet; Lippincott has not made his calculations yet, but I can stand it. I have n't got boys in school and in college, and though I am not doing a smashing hardware business, I am getting a salary quite sufficient for my wants, and can afford it very well; so no more on that subject.

" The boys' visit still lingers like the odor of an old pipe or an old Andover MS., just which you please. I like the first better than the second. You like the second better than the first. . . . We are in the midst of Lent, and hard at work. My church goes on beautifully, was never so harmonious and so active. I am making it my winter's work to endow a 'Holy Trinity Professorship' in the new Divinity School. It will take $30,000. . . . Money was never so easy to beg as when men are pouring it out in all directions very freely. . . . "

He now laid out for himself a course of reading. The subject which he chose was Mohammedanism. He bought the available books on the subject, and for a year and more pursued his inquiry, returning to his practice of keeping a note-book. We may surmise to some extent the motives of his choice. Carlyle had then interested the world in Mohammed by his essay in *Heroes and Hero Worship*. The nature and secret of Mohammed's power is one of the points turning up in Brooks's comments. It had long been and would long continue to be one of the problems before his mind—the nature of power and its connection with the will. He had always been drawn in his reading to men who had exercised power in the world. It may be also that he felt the need of supplementing studies and influences purely humanitarian, with the idea of God, which was losing its hold on the world of his time. He called his subject Mohammedanism but in reality it was a study of the contrast between Islam and Christianity. In his criticism of writers, he finds that Carlyle overstates and colors his facts, while others labor under rancor and prejudice. These mark the extremes in the method of studying the Arabian prophet. He is not satisfied wholly with Savary's *Abrégé de la Vie*. Gibbon's *Decline and Fall* he read faithfully, alternating in his condemnation and his praise: "How strangely bitter without a bitter word, how malignant with its seeming courtesy to Christianity, is that fiftieth chapter of Gibbon!" He appreciates Renan's subtle and ingenious comments, but thinks him guilty of overstatement. Foster's *Mohammedanism Unveiled* he read with curious interest because of its point of view, drawing much from it despite his repugnance to its methods. He went through Milman's *Latin Christianity* with admiration; it was then a fresh book which all were reading. Many hints he gained from Neander, Gieseler, and Hase, and other German church historians, from Stanley also in his *Eastern Church*, from Maurice's *Religions of the World;* and he did not neglect studies in reviews. He browsed over Weil's *The Bible, the Koran, and the Talmud,* and his *Mohammed der Prophet, sein Leben und seine Lehre.* Of Sprenger's *Life of Mohammed* he remarks that "for careful, thoughtful fact-telling it is worth all the rest together." He would give a good deal if he could get hold of another promised work of Sprenger's, a chronological history of the Koran which will trace the religion philosophically in its growth, for it would give what he can nowhere find. Sale's *Koran with Notes and Preliminary Discourse*, Gagnier's *La Vie de Mahomet*, Washington Irving's

Mahomet and his Successors, Boulanvillier's *Life of Mohammed*, these also were put under contribution to the total picture in his mind. These comments are from his note-book:

"It is curious to ask if the Jews had accepted Mohammed and Jerusalem had continued the Kebla, how far Islamism and Judaism could have coalesced.

"The deficiency in the theistic idea of the Mohammedans, says Neander, was a lack of intimate power of connecting between the human and the divine, robbing Islam on its Hebrew side of any power such as came from a Messiah, and on its Christian side making it impossible to acknowledge a Trinity.

" It made the doctrine of the infinite sublimity of God its basis, as Gieseler says, but in a way so one-sided that an absolute dependence of man on God resulted from it, and ideas of a likeness and an inward union between God and man, and consequently the fundamental principles of all the higher morality, found no place in the system.

" Nothing could convince us like the extreme accuracy of Sprenger's 'Life,' etc., how human Mohammed was, and how divine his descendants thought him.

"Among the picturesque scenes which strike the imagination are the conversation of Mohammed with the Nestorian monk at Bosia; Heraclius, the Roman emperor, receiving Mohammed's letter, and putting it under his pillow; Chosroes, the Persian king, receiving his and tearing it up; Mohammed in the first violent attack of his last illness addressing the tenants of the graves.

"The fine picture of the idols, questioned at the last day whether they or the idolaters were to blame, and the fault cast on the idolaters.

"The Arabs when charged with stealing give for an excuse the hard treatment of Ishmael; they are only getting their rights. Subjective character of sin; its influence by habit.

"Converted slaves become freedmen.

"The dogma of the Immaculate Conception is borrowed from the Koran.

"When Mohammed expelled the images from the holy house, among the banished gods was a Byzantine virgin painted on a column, holding her child in her arms.

"The whole story of the sacrifice of Isaac is told of Ishmael with very great particularity.

"Take these figures, the 'Sun' of Christianity and the 'Moon' of Mohammedanism, and do not their relations in many ways sustain the metaphor?

" The nobleness of Mohammed's last days.

"Why may we not say this about Mohammed? What was true in his faith he believed truly, but it was not his; he found it in the spirit of his people and his time. What was untrue was his, but he never believed it wholly and truly. There was always a mixture of imposture in it. Thus in him, as ever, the eternal difference of truth and a lie is vindicated.

"The state of the Christian Church, with its infinite sects and heresies, when Mohammed appeared would seem to explain much of his perplexity in reducing its doctrine to shape. His epitome of it is in many points certainly remarkable.

"It is a striking fact that the two great powers of the Papacy and Islam should have arisen together, reached their meridian grandeur together, and together have declined, with the rise of Protestantism.

"Look at the Neoplatonism of Ghazzaly, the Plotinus of Islam —how it repeats Alexandria at Mecca, and shows us the eternal sameness of error.

"Ever this new faith touches with the old. It is not a new faith; it is the old. It is another Judaism, more human, less divine. It is the neo-Judaism of decay; and Mohammed is to Moses what Plotinus is to Plato.

"Why should a prophet with miraculous powers have suffered hardship? Jamaly, a mystical poet, gets over this difficulty by representing his life as an allegory. It was a play acted in reality and expressive of the nature of God and the laws of the universe. Not so untrue, O Jamaly, of this man's or any man's life.

"The affinities of Islam with modern Unitarianism, their attempted reunion, and especially that strange story of the visit of Servetus to Africa.

"See Leslie's Works, i. 207, for the celebrated address of the English Unitarians, in the reign of Charles II., to Ameth Ben Ameth, ambassador from the Emperor of Morocco. 'Ce qui distingue le Socinianisme de la religion Mahometane est si imperceptible qu'il n'y a que des intérêts humains qui puissent retenir dans sa secte un Socinien bien instruit.'

"This too is striking. 'The heretical sects of Christianity uniformly incline towards Mohammedanism; the heretical sects of Mohammedanism generally found to incline toward Christianity.'

"I gather from his story this,—that he was at first a religious enthusiast of the practical order, truly, humbly, earnestly attempting the work of reforming the national faith; that his enthusiasm was strong enough to overbear personal difficulties and disgraces and make him unselfish in the consciousness of a mission; that he deduced at that time from the Christianity and Judaism with which he came in contact a scheme of faith wonderfully simple and true when compared with many of the Christian heresies of his time. The change comes with the Hejirah. He loses with the unexpected access of power, first, his intentness, second, his simplicity and singleness of action, third, his unselfishness. Passion of power and self-indulgences keep him unstably into their control, but the better spirit is underneath all the time and will occasionally burst out. The Koran comprises the record of both spirits, and its personal aspects must be judged by his history. All his powers were made weak with unsystematicalness and instability.

"What shall we make of the opposite accounts (cf., for instance, Renan and Carlyle) of the amount of belief of Moslems in Islam. What but this,—that although the amount of special faith in Mohammed and his teaching was but slight and confined to a few, the truth of Islam, its central and more general truth, was needed and seized in a more personal faith by the people who were by God's training ready for it. Mohammed has done vast harm. I should dishonor God if I did not believe that Islam had done good.

" Where did this sublimity come from into the Koran?—

"'The East became too strait for them, notwithstanding its spaciousness,
And their souls became straitened within them;
And they considered that there was no refuge from God,
Otherwise than by having recourse to Him.'

" This is Christianity, come it whence it will."

The study of Mohammedanism left its influence on Phillips Brooks. To get the difference between it and Christianity was to penetrate more deeply the Christian sphere. In these inquiries he also kept in view one distinct purpose of his own, which was to become the unifying principle of his method,—the nature and source of power, how it was to be fed, how ideas and truths and beliefs were to be transmuted into power.

That he was already on the right road for the solution of his problem was shown by an address which he delivered in the spring of this year before the Evangelical Education Society, then recently organized. At a moment when the feeling was rife that the Christian ministry could no longer compete with other agencies for the amelioration of society, he maintained that the pulpit possessed a vast advantage in that it could bring to bear the power of personality, the mightiest force conceivable, in co-operation with the moral appeal. His utterance left an impression on those who listened of a special message for the hour. In many ways this year 1864 was prolific in the spiritual history of Phillips

Brooks. The inner life of his manhood hid with Christ in God he shielded from observation, but it was revealed in the pulpit. He took the world of humanity into his confidence, however reserved in his private conversation. There had been traces of depression in his home correspondence in the previous year, but they seem to have disappeared. There is, to be sure, the same sensitiveness to the weather, the invariable comment on the day or the season as bright or dark; he even dreads a long railway journey. But for the rest, there is freedom and light-heartedness. Life continued to grow richer and fuller, bringing new friendships and expanding in every direction. His brother Frederick had become a member of the Divinity School in Philadelphia, and through him he entered into a close relationship with the theological students, eager to know how their minds were moving in that day of changes in religious thought. It was one of his peculiarities that he would take trouble to hear public lectures. He learned much from living men. He speaks of hearing Goldwin Smith, Edward Everett, Wendell Phillips, Richard H. Dana, and Henry Ward Beecher.

The chief event in the history of the war was the appointment of General Grant, in the spring of 1864, to the command of all the forces of the United States, with the title of lieutenant-general. With the approval of General Grant, the movement of an army of 60,000 men was accomplished under General W. T. Sherman, through the Confederate States from the mountains to the sea, from Atlanta, which was captured, to Savannah; then northward to Charleston in South Carolina, and thence farther northward to Goldsboro, in North Carolina, thus isolating Richmond from the South. General Grant himself now initiated the last stage of the war, but a year was to elapse before the final surrender of the Southern capital. In the months of May and June came the battles of the Wilderness, of Spottsylvania, and of Cold Harbor, in which perished 70,000 men. Activities on a vast scale were projected in the Northern cities, under the auspices of the Sanitary Commission, for the purpose of assisting the government in the care of sick and wounded soldiers. The great fairs in Philadelphia and New York, Boston and elsewhere, were gigantic undertakings, rousing popular enthusiasm, and tending to unify and solidify the Northern sentiment.

Great expectations had been raised when General Grant took command of the army in front of Richmond. The month of May, however, proved to be one of the most fearful months of the long struggle. Even Grant did not meet with success. It began to look as if Richmond were never to be taken. In his diary, or letters, Mr. Brooks records the fleeting impressions of those days of suspense and horror :

" May 7, 1864. We are almost listening to-day for the cannon on the Rapidan. The greatest fight of the war is going on, and God only knows its issue. Before you get this we shall be either close on peace, or way back with half the work to do over again. But we 'll do it, either now or ten years hence, whenever God wills."

" May 8. Good news from Grant."

" May 11. Great excitement all day in receiving news from the army in Virginia."

" May 12. Good news from Virginia. Grant is driving Lee."

" May 16. All day doubtful whether to go to the Army. Had to give it up at last."

" May 21, 1864. I am writing my sermon for the Sunday-school Union. It will be preached to-morrow night. I do not know how it will go. I have told them plainly that it is their bounden duty to teach the children of the country the duty of loyalty and the sin of slavery, that if they shirk that duty they will be in part responsible for some future generations having to go through this fearful education some day again. It will be printed unless they think it is too radical. I will send you a copy.

" Our hopes are all in front of Richmond, and there has been nothing yet to dampen them. God grant there may not be. I am sicker and sicker at heart every day for this fearful loss of precious life. It must bring something. We have not got Richmond yet, nor shall we have immediately. We must be patient. It will come in time, we must believe. Meanwhile we can do nothing but wait and pray."

While he was in Pittsburg, attending the Episcopal Diocesan Convention, he delivered a sermon on the Prayer Book. His text was from Exodus xxv. 22: "And I will commune with thee from above the mercy seat." He maintained that what the skepticism of the day needed was not new proof of abstract truths, but new demonstrations of their personal power; not more study, but more prayer. The Prayer Book furnishes an antidote to secularism in the thought of the Fatherhood of God, making an atmosphere so pure that in it secularism cannot thrive. The Prayer Book makes truth evident, not so much by the clearness with which it defines it, as by the light with which it fills it. It turns the stories of the Bible into the parables of common life. The only way to make men orthodox as to special beliefs is to make the great Christian truths self-demonstrated by the vigor with which they shape themselves into Christian duty and Christian life. The Prayer Book is full of doctrines, and yet fills them through and through with the interest of human life. It never tells men what to believe without telling them what blessing will come from such a belief. He urged a more intellectual study of the Prayer Book, and a higher intellectual estimate of its value. It had in it the eternal power of the Bible to meet all ages, and to suit the newest circumstances of the newest age the best.

"June 4, 1864. I have been to Pittsburg and am home again. . . . Our Convention was a shameful failure. We asked that body of Christian ministers and laymen to say that treason was wicked and slavery a sin. They declined, and substituted some feeble platitudes done up in wretched rhetoric which meant nothing and said it. I was ashamed of my church. Never mind; the salvation of the country does not depend on the Episcopal Church, and glad as I should have been to see her as a body on the right side now, she will have to come there by and by when it will be no honor to herself. Oh, how I hate this miserable conservatism. I almost cried for the church at Pittsburg."

Neither at this time, nor at any time in his life, did Mr. Brooks take an interest in ecclesiastical conventions. He attended them, but it was a burden to his soul. In later years he strove to overcome this repugnance, submitting patiently, keeping his place without intermissions, and occasionally taking part in the discussions. But even so, it was a thing apart from the spirit within him.

The summer had now come, the parish year was over, and he looked forward to vacation and home.

"June 18, 1864. I hope it is n't wrong to travel on the glorious anniversary, but I feel so anxious to get home that I feel it would n't be very wrong to travel on Sunday to get there. We have had Old Abe with us this week at the Fair. He was looking well and seemed to enjoy himself. I heard him speak and shook hands with him. Is n't it good to think that we are going to have him for our next President?

" Our Fair is a great success. It is incessantly crowded, and is making an immense amount of money. The whole city is alive with it, and I think it is going to do good in more ways than one. It keeps people's loyalty alive and their sympathies active. We are having a glorious summer so far, scarcely any warm weather yet, good weather for fighting and for sermon-writing."

The summer was mostly a repetition of other summers, including Harvard Commencement, the Andover homestead, Dr. Vinton at Pomfret, the Athenæum and its alcoves, the great organ, just placed in the Music Hall, the lakes of Maine in August, and as always the sermon written for the Sunday after his return.

"Philadelphia, September 3, 1864. Splendid news from Sherman to-day! Is n't it glorious? A few more steps like this, and we shall have peace earlier than the Copperheads could bring it, and a better one than they want to see. I 've had a splendid vacation. The best part of it what I spent at home."

To his father, who had been guilty of some lapse from his own strict rules, he sends a reprimand:

"PHILADELPHIA, September 12, 1864.

"DEAR FATHER,—Once there was a gentleman in Boston, and he had a son who was a minister in Philadelphia, and he used to upbraid his son and tell him he was an unpractical, unbusinesslike fellow whenever he got a letter from him which did n't have the date in full, and all about the place it was written in, and all that. But one day the minister in Philadelphia got a letter from the hardware merchant in Boston, enclosed in the envelope with the queer direction which you will find with this. And after that the minister did just as he pleased about the dates, and all that, of his letters, for he thought he had got the practical, systematic, businesslike merchant pretty fairly. Don't you think he had?"

A special Thanksgiving Day was appointed by President Lincoln on September 11th, to commemorate the victories of Sherman and Thomas, the capture of the important city of Atlanta, which closed the campaign in the West, and the beginning of Sherman's march to the sea. The entire Union army of some million of men was now at liberty to concentrate its strength on the reduction of Richmond. The chief political event in the fall of 1864 was the re-election to the presidency of Abraham Lincoln. McClellan was the rival candidate, and in Philadelphia had a large following. Pennsylvania went Republican by about 15,000 majority, but a majority of 50,000 had been hoped for and predicted. Excitement ran high in Philadelphia, and Mr. Brooks notes in his diary the great "Copperhead processions," which looked most formidable, and thought the fight would be a hard one. There was enough uncertainty in the situation to make the election of Lincoln seem a triumphant victory. On the evening of election day, November 8th, Mr. Brooks went as usual to the Union League Club to hear the news, and winds up the occasion with the words: "The Union candidates are triumphantly elected. *Thank God!*"

> "Saturday Evening, November 12, 1864.

"What a great week this has been; we shall not forget it soon. I feel too much impressed with its grandeur to go off into raptures about it. Enough that it has saved our country, and you and I will have to thank God for it all our lives. Old Massachusetts did splendidly. I am prouder of her than ever. Oh, if all the country were as true. And yet no part deserves reproach All have done well. Surely Pennsylvania has shown that she is all right. Now we can look ahead and hope. We have thought and talked of little else than the election all this week. Sermons for to-morrow have been crowded into corners."

The sermon on the annual Thanksgiving Day in November was from the text (Ps. cxviii. 27): "God is the Lord who hath showed us light; bind the sacrifice with cords, even unto the horns of the altar." Speaking of his sermon he said, "It is what some people call politics; what I call National Morals." The preacher took what was then regarded as extreme ground in advocating that emancipated slaves should be put in possession of the ballot. He was speaking to the country as he stood that day in the pulpit of the Church of the Holy Trinity. The air was full of excitement. Observers watching the scene were struck with the contrast between the richly appointed church, with its soft cushions, the dim religious light from the stained glass windows, the unobtrusive tones of the organ soothing the worshippers to reverie, the cultivated, fashionable congregation, and the church filled with the vast crowd long before the service began, waiting in eager expectancy; and on the other hand the thrilling uncompromising words of the preacher. The strong sentences seemed out of place, and the stronger sentiments. "The devil of slavery had kissed the strong shoulders of the Republic, and the serpents sprung from the defiling lips were preying upon her life. It was agony to tear them off but it was death to let them remain. Despite our anguish, we had taken courage to rid us of the abomination." The speaker attacked the prejudice against color, rebuking the Street Car Directory, pleading with pathos mixed with satire, and most solemnly, for negro suffrage. "We ought to make, not to be made by, the spirit of the times." In his letters he refers to other efforts in behalf of the same cause:

"November 23, 1864. We had a great Freedmen's meeting at Concert Hall on Monday evening. It rained torrents, but the hall was full. I sent a 'Press' with the report, but beg you most earnestly not to believe that I said all the foolish and contradictory things which the reporter there puts in my mouth. Next Monday I am going to Pittsburg to speak before a meeting of the same character. The western part of our State has done nothing, and we want to wake it up if we can. I had a most interesting visit in Washington, though it was very short; but I saw at once the magnitude and the feasibility of the great work we have undertaken."

The father of Phillips Brooks was anxious lest his son should carry his "radicalism" too far; and in a letter gives the attitude of conservative men in regard to negro suffrage:

"Boston, December 13, 1864.

"We have seen the notices of your Thanksgiving sermon in the 'Independent' and the 'Anti-Slavery Standard.' You seem to be in favor with the radicals of that stamp. Don't go too far. It will require all your best judgment and caution to know just how far to go. Remember you occupy a prominent position and your course will be watched. Don't make it too much 'one idea,' or you will split on the rock so many ministers have before you, of making your situation as a minister of the gospel a secondary matter. How thoroughly has Ward Beecher done this! Do you suppose his congregation go to hear him as a Christian minister? No, it is all for his allusions and quaint expressions upon his one idea, and they are followed up by *applause*. It is sad to see the house of God and the pulpit so debased. Are you not going too fast to advocate the entire freedom and equality of the negro, even to the right of suffrage, as I understand from those notices that you do? I cannot believe that it is best or advisable to introduce another foreign element into our elections; it certainly cannot raise the standards of our right of suffrage or the character of our candidates. Let us keep the ballot box as pure as we can. However you may argue the point of the races being intellectually equal, yet politically to my mind there is no question. I hope I shall never live to see it, and for the sake of my children I hope it will never be done. *Don't go too far.* How many good causes have been injured, nay ruined, by that. Go on in aid of the Freedmen as much as you please, but such a measure as that is not to their aid in the present stage of affairs. . . ."

To this remonstrance Phillips Brooks replied:

" PHILADELPHIA, December 19, 1864.

"You seem quite troubled about my radicalism. Don't let it disturb you. There is no danger. I certainly think the negro ought to be free, and I am sure he is going to be. And I think he ought to vote, and I am sure he will in time; but neither of these things is the subject of my preaching, except on rare occasions. I trust I know my work too well for that. I preach what I was ordained to preach,—the gospel, nothing else; but as a part of the gospel I accept the rebuking of sins, and public sins as well as private. . . . I know not how to work on any other system. My Thanksgiving sermon is not going to be published. It is radical, but quiet, calm, and I think Christian. . . . Republican government [again he writes] does not know such a thing as an unvoting subject. It has no place for Obeyers and Supporters who are not Governors and Directors too. We have got either to eradicate the Negroes or to integrate them. The first we can't do, the second we must."

In his speech at Pittsburg on the 29th of December he gave himself loose rein with glowing earnestness. What he said briefly in his Thanksgiving sermon, he now enlarged upon, and urged with all his power,—the necessity of giving the negro the ballot in order to the completion of his freedom; the responsibility resting upon the North to provide the possibilities of the amplest education; the crisis at hand when, untrained and unaccustomed to care for himself, in his ignorance and laziness, he might become a menace to the country unless the people should give him the conditions of essential manhood; the faith in the negro, as ready to respond with gratitude and devotion, and as having already shown the capacity and the promise for a great future.

He did not forget to comment on the recurring birthday, in a letter to his older brother William:

"December 12, 1864. I am twenty-nine years old to-morrow, just think of it! How we are getting along. Well, there are very few fellows who get to be as old as we are and have such a good time generally all the way along. We had a nice time before we went to school, a nice time at school, and a nice time since we left. Let us hope the rest of our time, till we are fifty-eight and sixty, will go as smoothly as the past, and then we can say Good-by to the world as to a very kind old friend."

On the last day of the year he kept the watch meeting at St. Philip's Church, where he made an address. And so was ushered in the great year in the divine grace, 1865.

The year 1865 was memorable in the history of the republic, memorable also in the experience of Phillips Brooks. In connection with the closing scenes of the war, his personal power reached the climax of its influence and expression. He had become so identified with the national life that other interests, his family, his parish, might seem to be in the background of his consciousness. But the home correspondence went on undiminished in frequency and interest; while incidents also were occurring of no slight importance in his successful career as a parish minister. First among these was the completion of his scheme for endowing a professorship in the Divinity School. Early in the year there came two calls from parishes in San Francisco. These, at once declined, left their effect in the vague longing to be connected with a new country in its new life, free from the trammels of an older civilization.

As he passed into the season of Lent, he remarks that he never had more enjoyed its peculiar work and privileges. He seems, however, to have been annoyed with a circular he had received, giving a list of daily services in a church in Boston.

It was a sign of coming changes in the Episcopal Church, which he did not wholly welcome. "We don't undertake anything like that," he says in reply; "only a Wednesday evening and a Friday afternoon service."

His attachment at this time to Philadelphia was at its strongest and he writes, defending it in a comparative estimate of cities:

"February 20, 1865. Everything here quiet and calm. Philadelphia does n't easily get stirred up. We sit still and look at constitutional amendments, great cities taken, and all that, and are just as glad as anybody if we don't have jubilation meetings or fire a great many cannons. Northern people are apt to sneer at us, but there is no city which has done more for the war, been readier with its regiments, done more for the Freedmen, or kept up the Sanitary and Christian Commissions more splendidly. Don't sneer at Philadelphia. She's a splendid city." [1]

The interest of Mr. Brooks in the freedmen and his activity in their cause continued unabated. He was proud of his aunt Susan for the work she was doing for them in Washington. "What a great character," he writes to his father, "Miss Susan is becoming. I hope her fame won't turn her head." He was very determined about the matter of the street cars, from which in Philadelphia the negroes were still excluded. "A week from to-night (January 13) we are going to have a great meeting here to try to get rid of our special Philadelphia iniquity of excluding the negroes from the cars. I think it will do the work. The meeting will be held either in Concert Hall or the Academy of Music. There are to be a number of speeches, and I have promised to make one."

"March 18, 1865. Last Monday evening I spent at Harrisburg. We held a meeting in the Court House and had a pretty good audience. The cause seems to be growing there. My next work in this line is to be at a big meeting at the Cooper Institute in New York about the first of May. It is to be the beginning of more united action among various societies. Beecher is to speak for the New York Society, Governor Andrew for the Boston and I am to bear the responsibility of ours. A great time is expected.

[1] This tribute to Philadelphia may be taken as neutralizing any reflections on the fame of the city, which might be suggested by his sermons, when he was denouncing indifference or disloyalty to the government in the prosecution of the war.

For Particulars see small bills. Good news this week again. Sherman and Sheridan are doing nobly. It is only a question of time now. Gold is down, but I have n't got any, have you?"

"April 1, 1865. This is All Fools' Day. I have run no risks yet, for I have been sitting still by my table all the morning writing. Perhaps I have made a fool of myself there however. Out of the window I have seen many small boys fastening pieces of paper on to people's backs, and watching mysterious-looking paper bundles that are lying on the sidewalk. I think I remember that we used to be up to some tricks of the same sort ourselves."

In the spring of 1865 all other things were subordinate to the one great event, the close of the war. In the career of Phillips Brooks it was a momentous epoch. To his imagination the war had appeared as a Titanic conflict, as though heaven had entered into a contest with earth, when Freedom and Slavery became the contestants for the possession of American nationality. What he had watched in its incipient stages, as a student in the Virginia Seminary, he was now to behold in its final act.

When the end came at last, it seemed to come suddenly. Events had been moving fast in this direction. On February 20th had come the news of the taking of Columbia, S. C. This had been followed, on February 21st, by the news of the evacuation of Charleston. On the 22d of February Fort Sumter had been retaken. Then there was a pause, while General Grant, with an army larger than ever before had been collected, confronted the stronghold of the Southern Confederacy. On Monday, April 3d, the Union troops entered the city of Richmond. On that night, his young friend Franks, who was staying with Mr. Brooks, remembers how he said before retiring, "Let us kneel down and pray." It was the impromptu thanksgiving of one who was surprised in his joy. On the next day, Tuesday, April 4th, there was a meeting of the citizens of Philadelphia in front of Independence Hall, where Phillips Brooks made the prayer. Among his papers is found a rough draft, which may correspond in some measure with the actual utterance. A few extracts are given:

"O Almighty God, the Sovereign Commander of all the world, in whose hands is power and might which none is able to withstand: we bless and praise, we laud and magnify, Thy glorious name.

"We praise Thee, O God, we acknowledge Thee to be the Lord. All the earth doth worship Thee, the Father everlasting. . .

"Thou hast led us, O our God, by wondrous ways. Thou hast opened the deep sea before us to pass through. Thou hast made the walls of our enemies to fall before us. Not unto us, O Lord, not unto us, but unto Thy name be the praise for Thy loving mercy and Thy truth's sake. . . .

"Not in mere exultation, not in bitter and revengeful malice, not in mere pride and selfishness, but in a solemn reverence, in a profound humility, in an absorbing and controlling sense of Thee, may we bow down our glad heads and thank Thee for the triumph which Thou hast given to Thine own dear cause of Law and Truth, of Human Progress and Human Liberty. Glory! Glory to Thy name. May we stand still and hold our breath and know that Thou hast done it. . . .

"We stand in the presence of this Victory, O Lord, and anew, deliberately and solemnly and to the end, we pledge ourselves to Thee. Take us, our strength, our means, our all, us and our Land, for Thine. We dedicate the country Thou hast saved to a purer life, a more religious, unselfish patriotism, a deeper loyalty to the great kingship of Thy Son. Work out in her, by her, what purposes Thou wilt. She is not ours, but Thine, henceforth. We are Thy servants. Give us willing and patient hearts and hands till Thou shalt create in our country Thy chosen pattern of Christian Government and Christian Liberty, before the nations of the earth. We stand before Thee, and know not how to speak. Read Thou our hearts and see our thankfulness. Thou art our God, and we will praise Thee. Glory to God in the highest, and on earth peace, good will towards men."

The following Sunday had been appointed as a day of thanksgiving by Governor Curtin.

"Friday, April 7, 1865. Began sermon on Luke xix. 40 ["And he answered and said unto them, I tell you, that if these should hold their peace, the stones would immediately cry out"]. . . . Sheridan still pursuing Lee and has routed him terribly."

"Sunday, April 9, 1865. Next before Easter. Thanksgiving for victories. A.M., at Holy Trinity I read, and preached, Luke xix. 40. . . . Ten o'clock P. M., news arrived of surrender of Lee with his whole army to General Grant."

Thus he passed into Passion Week with its daily services. On Monday he records that he was "down town. Great excitement about the news." On Maundy Thursday, in the evening, there

was the administration of the holy communion at the Church of
the Holy Trinity. On Good Friday he preached and began the
writing of his Easter sermon. Early in the morning of Saturday
came the news which turned the joy into mourning.

"Saturday, April 15, 1865. This morning we woke up to hear
that Abraham Lincoln, the President of the United States, was
murdered last night in Washington. The whole land is deep in
sorrow, and there is nothing to do but to pray for help."

"Sunday, April 16, 1865. Easter Day. A sad Easter Day.
A.M., I spoke to the Sunday-school of Mr. Lincoln. Then at
church I read and spoke again of the President."

On this Easter Day the churches were draped in mourning.
The Church of the Holy Trinity was crowded to its utmost
capacity. Mr. Brooks had not intended to make any address,
but when he saw the expectancy of the waiting congregation
he was moved. From a report of his remarks in the newspapers
these extracts are taken:

"I confess that there is one thing which surprised me yesterday
when I read in some of our papers that natural allusion which
occurred to all men,—the correspondence between the day of the
death of our martyred President and the day on which our Lord
was crucified in our behalf; and I saw that the papers, almost
with a tone of apology, spoke as if it were a lack of reverence to
associate the two, as if there were some degradation to the dignity of Christ's nature when we took the day of His death and
called it a fit day for one to lay down his life for a noble cause.
I feel that if there were any day in all the year fit for martyrdom;
if there were any day which one who was to be a martyr for the
cause he loved, might choose above all others, it would be that
Friday which, with all the solemnity and sadness which hung
about it to those who love their Lord and Master, the whole Christian world has risen up in its gratitude and called Good Friday. . . .
For remember what Christ is. Christ was not merely a God
who stood above us; the very meaning of Christ's coming into
this world is that He was a divinely human being in whom every
high quality of man was shown forth in its perfection, so that
all goodness thenceforth was to be but the copy of the life of
Jesus Christ, the perfect man. If there has been any high heroism in the world, any triumph over evil and iniquity, it has been
only a faint repetition of that great work which the perfect man
did when He triumphed once for all over sin, in behalf of His

redeemed world. If there has been any man setting himself earnestly against iniquity as he found it at his especial time and place, it has been only a rebound from that courage with which Christ set Himself against the wickedness that was in the world at His time. And if so be that another Pontius Pilate, as weak as he, is made the agent of an iniquity as deep as that which brought the suffering Saviour to His death, and comes up and strikes at another man pure and good and true to some high object, shall we not say that the day is fit? Do we not know that God has done all things, even the least things that concern Him, well? And then when we pass from Good Friday into Easter Day, shall we say that there is no association when we see that same Christ, martyred for the sins of man, laying down His life meekly and humbly for a great and noble cause, after patiently suffering for it during His three years, rising gloriously from the grave and shedding thenceforth an influence which His mere personal presence would not have attained? And may we not derive example and inspiration from this new martyrdom and look forward to the resurrection that is promised out of it? Thus take, my dear friends, everything out of the parable of those old times, and without a fear of irreverence (feeling that it is the most reverent thing that we can do) apply it to this trial in the midst of which we live, and make it a lesson which shall be the solemnizing strength of all our lives, that henceforth we may be worthy of having lived in the time, and seen the life and death of Abraham Lincoln.

"Of that man it is not time now to speak. We are met to-day not to eulogize the dead, but simply to pour out our tears before the Living God in company with the living. We are met not as those who meet in an assemblage to praise some great man of the world. We are met like children who gather round the hearthstone the night their father dies, to tell one another how they loved him and how they mourn his loss. We are met with a distinctive personal feeling that every one of us has suffered in the loss, not merely of a President who ruled in the interests of our State, but of a man who was to us a friend. If anything struck us as we walked the streets yesterday, it was not the mere solemnity which realized an awful national loss; we also felt how near home that loss had come.

"When the character of Abraham Lincoln comes to be gathered up, it seems to me that this is what shall be said of him, that of all the men who have ever lived in these United States, and come forth into prominence before the world, he was the man most distinctly and in the best and truest sense an American; and he is to stand so before the nations in coming time. . . . In him was represented the majesty of those simplest virtues which all mankind honor and admire, and which so few men are inclined to cultivate and praise by the personal practice of their own lives. . . . If there were anything in this man which shone forth conspicuously to his honor, it was the instinctive love of truth which was in him. Here was a man who had stood before the world, a most searching world, at a singularly eventful period, and up to the day when he laid down his life for the truth . . . he spoke the words which his nature urged him to speak. Bravely and boldly he told it, no matter how men might differ with him or seek to dissuade him. . . . The sublime independence of this man . . . led him to go forward as fast as his conscience drove him and not faster because others would drag him forward. . . . We knew that we had a true man to rely upon. Where shall we find another that shall take his place, having the earnestness with which he rebuked at once the old conservatism and the vast radicalism of our time? . . .

"Shall I say more? Yes, there is more to say, for when we speak of the truth and independence of such a man, they are only vestibules to that higher quality, his reverent fear of God. I believe from my heart that if there be a man who has left on record that he was a Christian man, a servant and follower of Jesus Christ, it is he who lies dead in the coffin to-day. What are the evidences of the service of Christ? If they be a constant submission to His will, an habitual reverence to His authority, an eye that always looks up in danger for deliverance, and looks up in success for thankfulness, an eye that always seeks out a guidance which is not of man but of God, which is always ready to be led and is always afraid of going beyond the commands of a Higher Voice—if this constitutes a Christian character, all this there was in him. We rejoice in the hope not merely of a noble influence for our country, but of a glorious resurrection and an eternal life for him whom we have revered as a father and loved more than we could love any human friend."

On Easter Monday there was a meeting of the Union League, which Mr. Brooks opened with prayer, with thanksgiving to God for the life and character of Lincoln:

"We thank Thee that thou didst put into the hearts of this people to choose such a man, so full of goodness and truth and faithfulness, of patience, serenity, and composure, of such wisdom to perceive the truth and such steadfastness to do it; for the earnestness with which he laid hold upon the great purpose before him, and the calm and wise perseverance with which he followed it. . . . We pledge ourselves anew to Thy service. Hold us up until the great end of Thy Providence be fulfilled, until all the wrong that has cursed our land be righted and the iniquity of our fathers be done away."

This service at the Union League was at twelve o'clock. At one o'clock there was a meeting of the women of Philadelphia in Concert Hall. "It was perhaps," says the report of its proceedings, "the most extraordinary meeting ever held in this city." To this meeting came also Phillips Brooks, and this was the substance of his remarks: "God allowed Abraham Lincoln to stay until he stood at the grave of slavery. God allowed him to stand and look on the land and not see a black face which was not radiant with freedom. Slavery had been blotted out before God called him to his rest. It is for this that we have cause to thank God for Abraham Lincoln. Now the women of America have a duty to perform. They can by their influence shut out from social intercourse those who palliate the great crime of the century. Another thing can be done by women. Never before had we witnessed such frivolities and extravagances as during the last winter. If from this day forth they do not resolve to stop this, it had been better we had not met, and the great loss we have suffered will be in vain."

"Wednesday, April 19, 1865. The whole city in mourning for President Lincoln's funeral. Service in church at the hour of the Funeral, twelve M.
"Friday, April 21, 1865. Began sermon on Ps. lxxviii. 71–73: 'He chose David also his servant, and took him away from the sheepfolds: . . . that he might feed Jacob his people, and Israel his inheritance. So he fed them with a faithful and true heart, and ruled them prudently with all his power.'
"Saturday, April 22, 1865. A.M. Finished sermon on the Character, Life, and Death of Mr. Lincoln. P.M. President Lincoln's remains arrived from Washington, and will lie in Independence Hall all day to-morrow. I went down with the Union League when the body was received, and saw it."

The sermon which was preached on the first Sunday after Easter, April 23d, on the character of Mr. Lincoln, was at once published by request, and must rank among Phillips Brooks's great sermons. It has additional importance as forming a chapter in the biography of Brooks himself. No man can study the life of another, as he was studying the life of Lincoln, or admire as he admired, in gratitude and reverence, without being influenced by the model he had chosen. Among the forces which combined to mould the life of Brooks, a place must be assigned to the character and the career of the great martyr of the civil war. Lincoln became to him the ideal of a man and of an American. When Lincoln died the question was asked by many, who were forecasting the estimate to be made of him by posterity, whether or not he were an intellectual man, or whether his greatness were not exclusively in the moral sphere. There was a tone of resentment in Brooks's soul that such an issue should be raised. Already he had begun to see the solution of what was his own life problem. The following passage has an autobiographic quality:

"As to the moral and mental powers which distinguish him, all embraceable under this general description of clearness or truth, the most remarkable thing is the way in which they blend with one another, so that it is next to impossible to examine them in separation. A great many people have discussed very crudely whether Abraham Lincoln was an intellectual man or not; as if intellect were a thing always of the same sort, which you could precipitate from the other constituents of a man's nature and weigh by itself, and compare by pounds and ounces in this man with another. The fact is that in all the simplest characters the line between the mental and moral natures is always vague and indistinct. They run together, and in their best combination you are unable to discriminate, in the wisdom which is their result, how much is moral and how much is intellectual. You are unable to tell whether, in the wise acts and words which issue from such a life, there is more of the righteousness that comes of a clear conscience or of the sagacity that comes of a clear brain. In more complex characters and under more complex conditions the moral and the mental lives come to be less healthily combined. They co-operate and help each other less. They come more to stand over against each other as antagonists; till we have that vague but most melancholy notion which pervades the life of all elaborate civilization, that goodness and greatness, as we call them, are not to be looked for together; till we expect to see, and do see, a feeble and narrow conscientiousness on the one hand and a bad, unprincipled intelligence on the other, dividing the suffrages of men.

"It is the great boon of such characters as Mr. Lincoln's that they reunite what God has joined together and what man has put asunder. In him was vindicated the greatness of real goodness and the goodness of real greatness. The twain were one flesh. Not one of all the multitudes who stood and looked up to him for direction, with such loving and implicit trust, can tell you to-day whether the wise judgments that he gave came most from a wise head or a sound heart. If you ask them they are puzzled. There are men as good as he, but they do bad things; there are men as intelligent as he, but they do foolish things.   In him goodness and intelligence combined and made their best result of wisdom. For perfect truth consists not merely in the right constituents of character, but in their right and intimate conjunction.   The union of the mental and moral into a life of admirable simplicity is what we most admire in children, but in them it is unsettled and unpractical.   But when it is preserved into a manhood, deepened into reliability and maturity, it is that glorified childlikeness, that high and revered simplicity, which shames and baffles the most accomplished astuteness, and is chosen by God to fill His purposes when He needs a ruler for His people of faithful and true heart such as he had who was our President."

The sermon on Lincoln has been so widely disseminated, that it calls here for no further summary or analysis.   He touched the subject of the origin of the civil war, asking whethei the Northern abolitionists were right or wrong, whether they did harm or good.   He replies that the issue was an inevitable one, the conflict between two different types of civilization, two divergent natures, long advancing to an encounter, meeting at last, and a whole country yet trembling with the shock to bear witness how terrible the meeting was.

The funeral procession of Mr. Lincoln reached New York on the 24th of April, and Phillips Brooks was there the whole of the next day to witness the repetition on a still larger scale of what he had seen in Philadelphia.   His father had been so deeply moved that he wrote, "Oh, my dear son, where are we now!   I am too heartsick to write."   Of the event in Boston, he says:

"A solemn day.   I have never seen one here more so.   I went into the Exchange in the morning; the room was full, but all was hushed and still, where generally we find noise and bustle.   So it was everywhere; the streets were full all day, but all quiet and subdued.   Minute guns were fired, bells were tolled, and with a meeting for prayer and addresses on the Common the day closed. A more general closing of stores I have never seen, even more so than on Sunday."

Phillips Brooks was wondering during these eventful days at the silence of his mother.   In response to his inquiry why she did not write, he received this letter:

"My dearest Philly,—I was delighted to get your letter, and will gladly comply with your request to answer it. I am fully aware of my long silence, but, my dear boy, it is *not neglect;* that is the last sin I shall ever commit towards *you* or any of my children.

"And I know, too, how I used to write to you at the Seminary, but, Philly, things are all changed now. I cannot write letters now that are worth answering, and therefore I hate to tax any one to answer them. My thoughts are *all dead.* Sometimes I really feel that nothing but the Mother's love remains in me. That will never cease, for the dead or the living. And, Philly, often now, truly I don't feel *equal* to writing to you. You have got *before* me now, and this is the course in all nature. The old stalk is good for nothing after it has yielded its fruit. Just so it is with you and me. My work is done, and I am perfectly willing to have it so when the fruit so far excels the parent stock. Now, Philly, I feel all this, and this is one reason, I suppose, I do not write often.

" At the same time I allow no position nor powers nor learning can alter the relation of parent and child. That shall remain dear, precious, holy, invaluable, forever to both of us. And I thank you and love you, dear Philly, for placing such a value on the old stock when it has become such a useless thing. . . ."

There was reaction after the tension and exaltation connected with the death of Lincoln. Circumstances of a trying character were also annoying him to the last degree. But he kept to his work as usual, the sermon-writing, the visiting, and the studies. On the fourth Sunday after Easter, came the Confirmation, when eighty-one candidates were presented. On May 23d he was in Washington, where he spent the whole day in seeing the great review of the Army of the Potomac, before it finally disbanded and the soldiers returned to their homes. He preached the Baccalaureate Sermon before the University of Pennsylvania on Sunday, the 28th of May. On May 29th, he writes: "I had a letter the other day from Professor Child at Cambridge, asking me to make a prayer at the Commemoration of the Harvard soldiers, at Harvard on the 21st of July. I wrote accepting. It will be a great time I expect."

Instead of keeping festival when the war was over, the nation was called by proclamation from Mr. Lincoln's successor to a day of fasting, humiliation, and prayer. Mr. Brooks came once more to the study of Lincoln's life and character. He preached no sermon, but read to his congregation selections from Lincoln's speeches, interspersed with remarks of his own,—the whole constituting an epitome of the war, with Lincoln's words as the commentary on its meaning. Throughout the service Lincoln was speaking,—in his farewell address to the people of Springfield when he invoked the people's prayers, in the Emancipation Proclamation, the address at Gettysburg, and finally the pathetic second inaugural.

The day which had been fixed for the Harvard Commemoration was Friday, the 21st of July, and it was intended that it should be a great day in Harvard annals. The glory and strength of New England were to be there, the sons of Harvard from far and near, and her most distinguished representatives. A great company of returned Union soldiers were to be there to receive a greeting, and in the remembrance of those who had gone forth to return no more, the deep emotions would be stirred which the living feel when contemplating the valor and the sacrifice of the patriotic dead. The day proved to be fine, though exceedingly warm. The buildings were decorated with flags, and a large number of people were assembled in and about the college grounds. At eleven o'clock, the procession moved from the front of Gore Hall passing through the opened ranks of the civil alumni amid great cheering.

After making a tour of the college grounds, the procession marched to the First Parish Church, the galleries and side pews of which were densely crowded with ladies and gentlemen. As the long array of heroes passed up the central aisle, the audience showered upon them repeated applause. General Meade was among the distinguished guests, and General Barlow was singled out for renewed cheering. Others from among the alumni were Major-Generals Force, Devens, Paine, Hayes, and Loring; Brigadier-Generals Bartlett, Eustis, Sargent, Ames, Walcott, Stevens; Colonels Higginson, Savage, Palfrey, Crowninshield, Russell, Huidekoper, and many others. The prayer was offered by Phillips Brooks, and was followed by a hymn written for the occasion by Robert Lowell, and then came the address by Rev. George Putnam of Roxbury. Afterward were addresses by General Barlow, General Devens, Governor Andrew, and President Hill. "Fair Harvard" was played. Poems were read by Mrs. Julia Ward Howe, R. W. Emerson, Dr. O. W. Holmes; and James Russell Lowell read his famous Commemoration Ode.

It is a rare event when a man appears who can utter the word which a great moment demands. Such an event it had been when Lincoln made his address at Gettysburg. Such a word it now was given to Phillips Brooks to speak. When the prayer was over, the people turned and looked at one another. Some of the contemporary comments indicate the impression it left:

"As he stood in all the majestic beauty with which he is endowed by favoring nature, he stood, to mortal eye, confessed of hosts the leader and of princes the king. . . . One would rather have been able to pray that prayer than to lead an army or conduct a state. . . . It is not too much to say that that prayer was the crowning grace of the Commemoration."

"When the 'Amen' came [runs another testimony], it seemed that the occasion was over, that the harmonies of the music had been anticipated, that the poem had been read and the oration already uttered, that after such a prayer every other exercise might well be dispensed with."

"All that I discern [said Dr. W. R. Huntington] as I look into that wholly blurred mirror is the image of Brooks, standing in his black gown in the pulpit of the old Harvard Square Church, his great head thrown back, his face looking as if it might be Stephen's, while there went forth from his lips a fiery stream of thanksgiving and supplication the like of which I never knew. I remember where I was sitting in the crowded north gallery, and I remember Brooks, and I remember my pride in him—these three, the place, the man, and the pride, are all that I remember."

" In the annals of our College, there is a red-letter day, Commemoration Day; when, after years haggard with anxiety, the mother welcomed back the remnant of her children who had escaped 'the pestilence that walketh in darkness, the destruction that wasteth at noonday.'

"On that day words seemed powerless; they did not vent the overflowing of sympathy and gratitude all felt.

"But in the exercises came a prayer, a brief prayer of a few minutes, of one inspired to pour forth the thanksgiving of the assembled brethren.

"From that moment the name of that inspired young man, till then unknown, became a household word." [1]

[1] Colonel Henry Lee in *Proceedings of Mass. Hist. Soc.*, 2d Series, vol. viii., 1892–1894, p. 82.

"It was the most impressive utterance [said President Eliot] of a proud and happy day. Even Lowell's Commemoration Ode did not at the moment so touch the hearts of his hearers; that one spontaneous and intimate expression of Brooks's noble spirit convinced all Harvard men that a young prophet had risen up in Israel."

Of this prayer no record remains. Its glowing sentences have been forgotten. In Mr. Brooks's papers no trace of it is found,— and it is vain to try to reconstruct it. It may seem inappropriate to comment on the eloquence of a prayer to God. But there are different kinds of prayer. There is a conception of prayer, where it does not seem inapt to offer to God the gift of human oratory— what the Germans call the *Andacht*, where, when the most impressive form of human utterance is desired, and the oration and the poem fail in the surging of the tide of human emotions, the orator turns to the living God, who alone sees and knows things as they are, to whom it is becoming to say things which otherwise the presence of no audience would justify. The highest reach of human eloquence is only attainable in prayer.

The experiences of the war left Phillips Brooks a larger man and a different man from what he was before. Henceforth he was no longer his own, but had been bought with a price. He had made the sacrifice of himself,—a confessor though not a martyr. Into that sacrifice he had poured all that made life dear, and a thing to be desired. He did not himself know the depth or the extent of his self-abnegation. The changes and the chances of life went over him at a critical hour, when he was absorbed in a supreme issue, losing himself in God, for country, for freedom and humanity. He had the compensations which belong to the confessor,—the world's honor and love. To that world which he loved and took to his heart he was henceforth to give himself unstintingly till life was done.

The approach of the summer had brought with it a plan of spending a year in foreign travel. The request for absence from his parish was at once granted by the vestry with the continuance of his salary. The break in his life thus afforded, with its opportunity for reflection, and of subsidence into a calmer mood after the excitement and agitation, was an important incident in his life. How much it meant to him in other ways it may be left to

him to express. After Commemoration Day at Harvard, only a
brief time elapsed before he sailed. The days were spent in preparation, and for the rest in the usual manner when at home.
Evidence of excitement over what is before him is shown in the
neglect of his diary, which is now irregularly kept. On the 23d of
July he was at Newport for a short visit, staying with parishioners, and preaching in All Saints' Chapel. There are allusions to
bathing and riding, and to playing croquet while he was there.
It was hard for his mother as she gave her blessing on his purpose.
A parting tribute was paid to him by his parish in Philadelphia.
His great congregation and numerous friends, and the church at
large, were reluctant to miss for so long a period his singularly
powerful and attractive ministrations. He went accompanied
with the prayers of thousands for his happy journeying and his
safe return. On Wednesday morning, August 9th, he sailed from
New York in the steamer *Scotia* of the Cunard Line for England.

CHAPTER IX.

1865–1869.

THE YEAR IN EUROPE. REMINISCENCES. CALL TO
THE EPISCOPAL THEOLOGICAL SCHOOL. NOTES
FROM HIS JOURNAL. LETTER TO DEAN STANLEY.
CALL TO TRINITY CHURCH, BOSTON.

WHILE Mr. Brooks was in Europe he wrote letters every week
to his family and kept an elaborate journal. No American
ever left home for the first time, to travel in the Old World
with a keener appreciation of the value of the opportunity
afforded him. It was a year for realizing the visions accumulated in his preparation for living.

" If everybody who goes to Europe could look back on such a
voyage as we had, Europe would needs be very great to be worthy
of such an admission to it. The entrance way so glorious demands a very glorious structure. I shall never forget those still,
long summer days, steeped full of the sunshine, when with
nothing to do, all care and responsibility of necessity suspended,
we just lived and looked and learned to love the sea for its greatness and gentleness, for a certain large, calm beauty which
took nothing from its grandeur. We had no storms, and only
two foggy nights, when we ran shrieking into the bosom of an
endless cloud, with that wild cry which blends fear for self and
warning for others, and gives both awe and comfort to those
who look out into the white darkness and hear it,—only two
such nights gave us any of the sense of danger from which we
would not have had our voyage wholly free.
  " How strange it seemed at first! That earliest day was simply full of wonder and amusement. One was merely getting *en
rapport* with the oldness of the thing—getting his new atmosphere about him—learning to shape his eyes to the new focus at
which he must bring to his brain things five hundred years old
instead of things fifty. It was not done wholly in one day, but
it was remarkable to see how much the mental process, like the
corresponding physical one, was instinctive."

Dublin was the first city he visited. From Ireland he went to Scotland. Edinburgh appeared to him the queen of cities. Of Mary Stuart and the associations with her of which Edinburgh is full he remarks that "they are of great aid in keeping alive pure romance as distinct from heroism." He made the familiar pilgrimage to Melrose and Abbotsford: "Abbotsford I would have gone to Europe to see alone. The sight of it seemed to make its great master a new and ineffaceable possession." From Scotland he went to the English lakes with thoughts of Wordsworth and Coleridge in his mind, of Dr. Arnold and De Quincey. His enthusiasm was fired anew by these literary associations in combination with the charms of the natural scenery. He describes a Sunday at Ambleside:

"The first Evangelical English Church I have seen. The sermon very poor. The service read. The High Churchmen here intone the service, and the Low Churchmen intone the sermon. How the Englishmen are *at home* in their island. They are so long here, and have it so well 'in hand.' It makes us feel how new we are in America, and how little we have got hold of it yet. Wait awhile."

His first cathedral was Durham. He was delighted with Mrs. Gaskell, the author of the life of Charlotte Brontë, gaining from her information about literary people in England. A letter of introduction given him by Mrs. Gaskell only admitted him to Ruskin's house, for Ruskin himself was away from home. He looked eagerly about the rooms which bore the traces of his presence. On his way to London he took in the eastern line of cathedrals, Ripon and York, Lincoln and Ely, Fountain Abbey also, and Cambridge.

Amidst beautiful English scenery, and the charm of its monuments, he writes, "I had no idea, till I came here, what a tremendous American I was." At Boston he looked with a personal interest at the Cotton Chapel, named after his ancestor. After reaching London, his quarters were at the head of the Strand, near Trafalgar Square and Westminster Abbey. He repeats to himself that he is in London. He was kindly received by his kinsman, Hon. Charles Francis Adams, the United States minister at the Court of St. James. He called on Dean Milman, who received him most kindly, but the deanery was in disorder, cutting short his visit. The dean, however, offered him religious hospitality at the cathedral, and urged him to hear Melville.

" In the afternoon [Sunday, September 17] I went to St. Paul's and heard Melville, the Preacher of the Golden Lectures. Dean Milman told me the night before he was to preach and told me also that he had just lost a daughter and he (Milman) had offered to take his place, but he preferred to do his own regular work. It was a perfect sermon, from 'Now the God of peace grant you peace always by all means.' The division and whole treatment was the simplest and most obvious. The style as clear and exquisite as possible—no action, but the most finished intonation and articulation. He is an old, white-headed man with a noble figure and earnest, kindly face. 'You cannot come out of season to the Tree of Life,' he said, referring to Rev. xx. 2: 'You may bring your season with you, and the tree takes it. You come in autumn, and it is an autumn tree, and bears autumn fruit.' It was the most perfect sermon, all in all, that I ever heard."

Other preachers that he heard were Maurice and Martineau. Of Spurgeon he writes: "A fearful crowd and too long a sermon. But it was good of its kind; and since such a kind always has been and always will be, why, the better it is of its kind, the better."

To one of his friends who had asked for his impressions of Browning, whom he met in London, he writes:

" I can't say anything now except that he is one of the nicest people to pass an evening with in London. He is just what you see him in that picture [a photograph enclosed], a clear-headed and particularly clear-eyed man of the world, devoted to society, one of the greatest diners-out in London, cordial and hearty as a dear old uncle, shakes your hand as if he were really glad to see you. He seemed to me very like some of the best of Thackeray's London men. A full-souled American. . . . As to his talk it was n't Sordello and it was n't as fine as Paracelsus, but nobody ever talked more nobly, truly, and cheerily than he. I went home and slept after hearing him as one does after a fresh starlight walk with a good cool breeze on his face."

While in London he spent much of his time at the National Gallery and the Kensington Museum, where he made the acquaintance of modern English art. Finding the time of the year (September) unfavorable for seeing people he cut short his stay, and left for the Continent, with the intention of returning before his tour was over. Among his final impressions he records his disappointment in cathedrals: "Cathedral life has come to appear to me, with all its elegant retirement, one of the most disagreeable of things, and Cathedral towns the deadest things in England."

From Ostend, where he felt more keenly the consciousness of being actually in Europe, he resumed his journey, stopping at Bruges and Ghent and Brussels, and going out to the battlefield of Waterloo. He made the acquaintance of Rubens at Antwerp, and of Rembrandt at The Hague. And so he came to Germany. He respected, he says, the Dutch, but he liked the Germans. He felt that he was passing an invisible line when he first came in contact, at Cologne, with Roman churches and relics. This brought him to Bonn, where he writes (October 2d) in view of Mayence, Heidelberg, and Frankfort:

"Am I not a lucky chap to see all this? I am splendidly well and keep on the go all the time, and am getting the hang of German enough to be quite at home with the people. I eschew all delicacies and rough it generally. Last night I found a feather bed for covering in my room. I kicked it off and slept like a top without it. The worst thing to me about this travelling is that you can't drink water. Think of my misery. But it is too vile to touch. . . . I would give a dollar for a pitcher of ice water to-night. I think I did right in coming alone, that is as no very intimate friend offered. I find companions everywhere, and see much more of the people than if I were with a party of my own."

Going up the Rhine was a great event, and at Coblentz he stopped, in order to climb to the Castle of Ehrenbreitstein. Luther and Goethe came up before him, first at Worms and Frankfort, and then more vividly as he visited Eisenach and the Wartburg and Wittenberg, and the home of Goethe at Weimar. Of a Sunday spent at Frankfort, he says:

"In the morning I went to the Cathedral and heard some fine German music and a sermon in German from some priest or other which interested me much. It was the most *earnest* preaching, at least, which it has been my lot to hear in the Old World. . . . Then I went and saw the house where Goethe was born. I have liked Frankfort very much indeed. In the afternoon I went again to the Cathedral, and heard the same man preach; and then came the service of [the Benediction] of the Mass, with the most superb congregational singing I ever heard—it rings in my ears now. Those full German voices, every one singing the sonorous German words, produced a wonderful effect. I almost trembled when I saw and felt the power of pure emotion in religious things, and thought I could understand how so many have yielded to the impulse to bow as that splendid procession of the host went by with its thrilling incense and thrilling music, and then by and by bowed to the system of the church that it belongs to."

At Leipsic he was excited by the great bookstores. He went down into Auerbach's cellar, where the Faust scene was laid. He called upon the German professors at Halle, and found them hospitable and interesting,—Erdmann, professor of Hebrew; Hupfeld, with whom he took a long walk; and Tholuck, the friend of all Americans, with whom he spent an evening, talking of theological matters in Germany, England, and America. What interested him most in Germany were the haunts of Luther and Goethe. He lingered over "those old portraits by Cranach, who seems to have been such a character, who at any rate knew how to give Luther to canvas and to the world." He stood before the monument

"in the dead old marketplace at Wittenberg with the noble inscription—Gamaliel's skepticism Christianized into Faith:—

> ' Ist 's Gottes werk, so wird 's bestehen;
> Ist 's Menschens werk, wird 's untergehen.'

And then his tomb under the pavement of the old Schloss Kirche —on whose bronze doors the theses that once were nailed to them in paper have broken forth in bronze—an emblem, as it seemed, of the work they did among men."

He came to Dresden, and with high expectations:

"That room was more like a church than anything I know in Europe where the Madonna stands—to all pictures henceforth what the Bible is to all books. . . . I will not say anything about it, because there is no use trying to tell what a man feels who has been wanting to enjoy something for fifteen years, and when it comes finds it is something unspeakably beyond what he had dreamed."

Then came Munich, with its famous galleries; and by the end of October he was in Vienna, where he hunted up the grave of Paracelsus, and visited the house where Mozart was born. At Vienna he dined with Mr. Motley, the author of the *Dutch Republic*. As he contemplates the prospect before him, he writes to his mother:

" The East, and Italy, and France, and much of England and Switzerland—all this is yet in store. It is two months to-day since I sailed. How they have gone! And to me they have been the fullest months of my life. Not a day without something that I have longed all my life to see. So it will go on till I see the sight that I shall be most glad of all to see, you and Father waiting on the wharf to see me land, as you came down before to see me sail."

All along the way he wrote of the changing aspects of the scenery. At times he fell into verse to commemorate the deeper impressions. He surrendered himself to his moods. He chose to believe that St. John was buried at Ephesus, according to the tradition, and welcomed the first sight of the ruins. He thought of St. Paul "who tried to go in to the people," in the vast amphitheatre. At Messina was the reminder of Tarsus, behind the hills, where St. Paul was born. Damascus was reached on the 3d of December, where Scripture incident is interwoven with natural scenery and human monuments. The deeper significance of what he sees springs from its connection with the supernatural revelation. He was living as if in expectancy of some unearthly light which should dawn on this visible creation. He was anxious to keep a record of every impression.

He notes the street in Damascus, called Straight, where Judas lived, the house of Judas, the wall where Paul was let down in a basket, the house of Naaman the Syrian, and the site of the House of Rimmon. On the walled-up doorway of a Christian church, transformed into a mosque, he read the inscription, "Thy Kingdom, O Christ, is an everlasting Kingdom, and Thy Dominion endureth from generation to generation." He lunched on a spur of Mt. Hermon, drinking the water of the river Jordan. "This is the first spot," he writes, "that we have touched where Christ Himself has been." He rode "through the coasts of Tyre and Sidon," recalling the scene of Christ's meeting with

the Syrophœnician woman. "What city is like to Tyrus, to
the destroyed in the midst of the sea!" He remembered Origen
and his lonely grave, and Frederick Barbarossa, and the place
of Sarepta, where Elijah met the widow. "Think of being in
the dominions of that old Og, king of Bashan, whom we have
always read of in the Psalter." "These last two weeks have
been like a curious sort of dream; all the old Bible story has
seemed so strangely about us." In the plain of Acre, "the
very sight lets you understand" how Asher "dipped his foot in
oil, and his head was fat, and he yielded royal dainties"; the
creeks and the bays recall how Asher lingered, and Deborah
reproached him with "abiding in his breaches." He comes to
Mt. Carmel and to the swift-flowing river, "that ancient river,
the river Kishon." The mountain itself is what it was in
Elijah's time, wooded to the top, looking out on beauty and
richness everywhere:

"What a place for a prophet and what a scene for the great
trial of his faith. Below, the Kishon runs through the plain, as
if still telling of how he took of the prophets of Baal and slew
them there. We sleep under the shadow of Carmel. I am very
tired, and all is still, except the jackal screaming in the distance.
Good-night; I wish I were going to bed in that back room at
home."

As he came to Nazareth, and from that time onward, the
thought of Jesus took possession of his mind and soul:

"It was a strange feeling to ride down through it, and look in
the people's faces and think how Christ must have been about
these streets just like these children.

"We climbed the 'hill on which the city was built,' and saw
what is perhaps the finest view in Palestine. I thought all the
time I was looking at it how often Jesus must have climbed up
here and enjoyed it.

"The sight that His eyes saw farthest off was that line of the
Mediterranean on which His power was to spread to the ends of
the world.

"We lunched at Cana of Galilee. . . . You can picture
Jesus and His mother going out from Nazareth to a near town to
attend the marriage to which they had been invited. . . .
We rode on through a rolling country through which Jesus must
often have walked on his way back and forth between Nazareth

and the lake. The whole country, every hill and valley, seemed marked with His footprints. . . . The Hill of the Beatitudes; another hill where they say Christ fed the multitude.

"Another ridge climbed, and there was the 'Sea of Galilee, which is the Sea of Tiberias.' There it lay in the afternoon twilight, blue among the purple hills. There were the walks He walked, the shores where He taught, the mountains where He prayed. . . . Looking into a house door at Nazareth I saw 'two women grinding together at the mill.'

"This is the 'land of Gennesaret.' This is Capernaum, the home of Christ after Nazareth rejected Him. 'And thou Capernaum!'

"This is Bethsaida, the city of John and James, Peter and Andrew.

"I have had a very pleasant, quiet Sunday here at Nazareth [December 17, 1865]. This morning I went to the Greek church and heard their usual boisterous and disagreeable service. . . . All day the people have gathered round to look at us. It is touching to hear the poor people tell of how they suffered from the locusts in the spring. They came in clouds, covering the ground half a foot deep, as large as sparrows; all the shops and houses were closed for days. Every green thing was eaten up. It sounded like a chapter out of Joel. It is sad, too, to hear them talk of their government. All spirit is gone out of them, and they only wait the inevitable dropping to pieces of the rotten thing, which they all expect."

As he approached Jerusalem, Old Testament history was before his mind, interwoven with the life of Jesus. No incident in the narration seemed to escape him. His head was running with Bible phrases. He read the Old Testament on horseback as he went through familiar places. And so he came to Jerusalem. This passage from his journal sums up his impression:

"'Why seek ye the living among the dead? He is not here; He is risen.' As concerns Jesus, I know nothing which could more adjust our views of Him than a visit to the Holy Land. In fastening the New Testament story in its place by geographical positions it rescues it from vagueness and obscurity and makes the Humanity a clear, palpable fact. At the same time, by the failure of present enthusiasms about the country, by the way in which the power of the religion has outgrown and left behind the places where it had its birth, by the failure of the material to satisfy and account for and accompany the spiritual, it sets us free for a larger and juster grasping of the true Divinity. It is like the relation between an immortal word and the mortal lips that uttered it. . . . Probably it will be even more so at Jerusalem. It seems too as if the same analogy would adjust and state what I hold to be the highest, truest, and most spiritual view of Inspiration, but have never been able to put exactly into shape.

"Of all the associations with Christ, I found most pleasure in Nazareth, Jacob's Well, and the Mount of Olives. The first as the scene of His developing consciousness; the second as that of His highest announcement of truth; the third as that of His completest emotion and mental suffering. I am struck by seeing that it is neither of them as the scene of a miracle.

"Christ is not merely the greatest, but the only presence that fills the landscape in Palestine; not even John the Baptist at the Jordan; some of the Old Testament persons to some extent, but Christ only in the New. John, Paul, and Peter might have lived and written elsewhere as well as here. . . .

"The spirit of all the religions of the East seems to be but one, and that very bad. Its simplicity is not sincerity, but indifference and stupidity. 'God is great' is their only creed because they dare not take the trouble to trace out that greatness of God into its due connections with their own lives and duties. Then again, the secularism of their religion seems to be shown in the way in which they divide themselves and quarrel by religious, which in this case amounts to the same thing as political, names. It bears a sad analogy to the earlier and worse periods of the Christian church, its fifth and sixth, and fifteenth and sixteenth centuries, when men used for political landmarks and rallying cries the sacred words which, whether we make them holier or not, we have at least the sense and shame to keep in their true place in the region of thought and opinion."

After two weeks in Jerusalem, he turned westward. He was anxious to get to Italy. For Egypt he did not greatly care but remained there long enough to visit the Pyramids and meditate beneath the shadow of the Sphinx:

"The Sphinx wonder impressed me more than anything else I have seen. . . . Her calm still face, not stern and not gentle, only self-centred, as if she were too vast either to hate or love the men who worshipped her. The harmony of repose between the features and the form—the great divine pitiless *Rest* of the whole, as if neither human sin could rouse her to anger, nor human goodness tempt a smile—how wonderful she is. The way in which the Egyptian features have been made capable of grand idealization in the face of the Sphinx is very fine . . . the grandeur that always seems to belong to colossal representations of the human face. . . . I think there might be a comparison drawn between the Sphinx and the Dresden Madonna, as the highest art expressions of the two great religions, the East and the West,—Fatalism and Providence, for that they seem to mean. Both have recognized the feminine nature of the religious instinct, for each is a woman. Both have tried to express a union of humanity with something its superior, but one has joined it only to the superior *strength* of the animal, the other has infused it with the superior spirituality of a divine nature. One unites wisdom and power, and claims man's homage for that, the other unites wisdom and love, and says, 'Worship this.' The Sphinx has life in her human face written into a riddle, a puzzle, a mocking bewilderment. The Virgin's face is full of a mystery we cannot fathom, but it unfolds to us a thousand of the mysteries of life. It does not mock, but bless us. The Egyptian woman is alone amid her sands—to be worshipped, not loved. The Christian woman has her child clasped in her arms, enters into the companies and sympathies of men, and claims no worship except love. And so on through many points."

On February 4, 1866, he reached Rome—"Rome at last, the place of all others in Europe that I have most wished to reach. It is exactly as I have always pictured it, only a great deal more interesting." In one of his letters he says, speaking of Rome:

"It was an unceasing and infinite delight. Rome is so much greater and fuller than I had ever dreamed of. I have seen a great deal, but when I think what there is right about me, it seems as if I had seen nothing. I have wandered all through St. Peter's; spent a long day in the wilderness of the Vatican; another in the great museums of the Capitol; and followed the banks of the Tiber; skirted the ruins of the old temples, palaces, and theatres of this wonderful race; roamed through some of the picture galleries of the great palaces; found my way into a few of the numberless gorgeous churches; and to-day have been from one to another of the studios of our own living artists. To a Protestant the Coliseum, like St. Peter's, is too vast and great for Roman sectarianism to keep. They both are among the great religious temples of the race, where all humanity may worship and confess in the presence of all that recalls the exhibitions of mankind's highest and lowest natures.

"One morning I climbed to the roof and galleries and dome of

St. Peter's.　More than ever I seemed to pass beyond the narrowness of the sectarianism of the place, and feel as if it were indeed what one loves to dream it might be, truly Catholic, the great religious home of humanity, where every good impulse, every true charity, every deep faith, every worship, and every benevolence should find a representation,—the great harmony of all the discords of well-meaning and conflicting religious educations and progresses.　In spite of its positive character, its very immensity makes it answer vaguely some such purpose even now to those who go there."

He was too short a time in Rome to do more than the most condensed sightseeing, but it is significant that most of his comment in his journal is on its art, of which "it is hopeless," he says, " to write one's impressions "; but at least he stood before the great masterpieces in wonder and admiration.　Twice he preached before the American Embassy, and on the 22d of February he made an address, which by its language, thought, and rushing eloquence "completely enchained every hearer."

Six months still remained to him after leaving Rome before his year of absence should expire.　Greece was next to be visited.　He had been so eager to get into Italy that he had passed by Athens as if it occupied a secondary place in his affections.　Yet of his first day in Athens he writes, "It was one of the most memorable of all my journey," and again he writes, "Greece has been perhaps on the whole the best and most picturesque success of all my journey."　His visit there revived his youthful classic fervor with the result that he wrote a long letter to his brother Arthur, then a senior at Harvard, giving him an itinerary of his tour:

"Thursday morning, March the 1st, we landed at the Piræus, and took a rickety hack up the dusty road between the almost-gone Long Walls to Athens.　As soon as we were out of the town (Piræus), the Acropolis and Lycabettus and Pentelicus were all in sight.　That day and the three next we spent in the City, with one day's ride out over the Sacred Road to Eleusis, and another's walk to Colonus and the Groves of the Academy and along the Cephissus.　I remember perhaps most of all one afternoon in the newly excavated Dionisiac Theatre just under the south wall of the Acropolis.　Beyond the orchestra the narrow stage, supported by the line of exquisite sculptures, mostly broken and headless, but very beautiful, stands just as when 'Euripides' and 'Æschylus' were performed on it for the first time. The Clergy had front seats at the Theatre in those days. I sat down in the chair Ἱερεὺς Διὸς ᾿Ολυμπίου, and imagined myself the old Reverend who used to occupy it. My brother of Dionysus sat on one side, and his Reverence of Hermes on the other. In front was Hymettus with its deep purple mass, where one almost heard the humming of the bees in the still sunny air. I sat there till they got through one or two plays of the Trilogy, and then got up and went through the Propylæa, past the Erechtheum, with its beautiful Portico of the Caryatides, and saw the sun set from the West Porch of the Parthenon. Another day to the Theseum, the most perfect of ancient temples, which stands at a much lower level than the Acropolis, and is seen very finely as you lie on your back lazily on the Areopagus just over the cavern where the Eumenides had their temple, and just over against the rocky platform at the head of the steps leading up from the old Agora where Paul made his great speech about the temples, with the Parthenon before him for a text. You cross the Agora from the Areopagus, and by a splendid old Pelasgic wall climb up to the Pnyx, and cross it to the Bema, which stands almost as perfect as when Demosthenes was there, and must have been a splendid place to speak from to a great crowd. Last Sunday I preached twice for Dr. Hill in the Church of St. Paul. The doctor is a noble man, and has done more for Greece than all its poor politicians of the last twenty years put together.

"Sunday evening we drove down to the Piræus, and very early the next morning went on board a Greek steamer and sailed for Nauplia. We passed out by the tomb of Themistocles, sailed by Salamis, and kept along close to Ægina, the most beautiful of islands. The classic fleas fed on us through the dewy night. In the morning we started up the Argolid, some more strange countries for to see. We came in half an hour to Tiryns, and did full justice to its vast Cyclopean walls and strange arched galleries, which are so old that it don't make any difference how old you call them. A thousand years or two can't make much difference away back there. Then on, across the grassy plain of horse-feeding Argos, where horses were certainly feeding in plenty as we passed to Argos itself, with its old citadel Larissa, crowned now by a Roman or Venetian citadel. The only remains are an old theatre cut out mostly in the solid rock of the hillside,—a grand old ruin. We kept on across the plain two hours further to Mycenæ, perched between its twin hills. A grand, great citadel with its Gate of Lions and subterranean Treasuries of Agamemnon. It was hard to realize that we were really right in the midst of the scene where that pleasant little family circle of the Atreuses used to carry on such remarkable proceedings. From Mycenæ we rode up a long dark rock glen, delightfully Greek and wild,—

a splendid place for brigands (I forgot to say we took a guard of five Greek horsemen at Argos to defend us from the bloodthirsty),—and came out about dusk into a green plain, some three miles long, with three Doric columns, looking infinitely old, standing towards one end, among the ruins of a temple. This is the place of the old Nemæan games. The lions' cave is still shown in a mountain top overlooking the plain. A little after dark we came to Cleonæ, a wayside station, where we spent the night. The landlord was a jolly Argive, named Agamemnon. Clytemnestra was running about with hair down her back and shoes down at the heel. Fortunately we had our own cook and provisions, and so fared pretty well. Greek cookery is villainous. Early the next morning we were off, and two hours' ride over gray hills brought us to the sight of the blue Gulf of Corinth, the bluest waters I ever saw. The only ruins of Corinth are seven old Doric columns of the Temple of Athena, very striking and terribly old. but I climbed up the Acro Corinthus, the splendid citadel, and saw one of the views that you don't get often in a lifetime. Below, the old town and its columns; then the isthmus, with its two blue gulfs; to the right Megara, Salamis, and Attica beyond, with Hymettus hazy against the sky. To the left the plain of Sicyon and the town itself, with Mt. Cyllene stretching away behind. In front a long line of hills, many of them snowy, to which belong the names Cithæron, Helicon, Parnassus. Just up that hollow to the northwest is Delphi. Behind us are the gray hills of Argolis over which we have come. Is n't that something of a view? I drank at Pyrene, where Pegasus struck water, and then we set out across the isthmus, passing in sight of Cenchrea where Paul landed, and close by the ruins of a vast temple of Poseidon, where the Isthmian sanctuary was. And this is my story about Greece.

"Are you very tired of all this? Well, some day you will come here yourself, and then you will understand how anybody here gets carried away with this delicious country, and gets garrulous and persuades himself that other people will be as glad to listen as he will be to talk about it. It stands out as very different from all the rest of my trip, and one of its most complete successes. Anybody who comes to Europe and not to Greece is a very much Donkey—tell him so when you see him."

From Greece he returned to Rome, to spend an additional month. It was hard to tear himself away. In pure enjoyment the time spent in Rome surpassed all else in his tour. He cultivated the artists in their studios, and was the recipient of social attention from the American colony. The itinerary of his route after he should leave Rome promised him much that appeared as most rich to his imagination. He was not tired, nor had he exhausted his capacity for new impressions.

"I shall leave [he writes] and go by way of Foligno and Perugia to Florence; then to Bologna, Parma, Modena, Ferrara, Padua, and Venice; then to Verona, Milan, the Italian lakes, Turin. Genoa, Nice, Marseilles, Lyons, and Paris. Does n't that sound good? I am depending much on Florence and Venice, and indeed all the route is very rich."

At Paris, he met his friend George Strong, a classmate in the Virginia Seminary, and together they went to England. There they were joined by Rev. Henry C. Potter, who had just become the assistant minister of Trinity Church, Boston. From England he went to Switzerland, to spend the summer, of which the story may be read in his *Letters of Travel*. He sailed for home on the 15th of September.

While Mr. Brooks was abroad classical associations seemed almost as important as those of religion. But from this time they pass more into the background and the Evangelical narrative comes into the foreground as the unifying force of his life. Such indeed it had hitherto been, but henceforth with a new emphasis. It was not till later that the Christmas carol, "O little town of Bethlehem," was first printed, but it had been singing in the soul of Phillips Brooks since he was in Palestine. It is beautiful in itself, but it has also a theological significance, —the adjustment between the natural order and the divine revelation.

> "O little town of Bethlehem!
>   How still we see thee lie;
> Above thy deep and dreamless sleep
>   The silent stars go by;
> Yet in thy dark streets shineth
>   The everlasting light;
> The hopes and fears of all the years
>   Are met in thee to-night.
>
> How silently, how silently,
>   The wondrous gift is given!
> So God imparts to human hearts
>   The blessings of His heaven.

No ear may hear His coming,
  But in this world of sin,
Where meek souls will receive Him still,
  The dear Christ enters in."

The Old World had taken such deep hold of Mr. Brooks that it was like the process of taking root again to begin his work in Philadelphia. "The church looks very much as usual," he writes, "and the usual vista of sermons, studies, committee meetings, and Freedmen's Societies is opening before me. It is rather pleasant to feel myself at work again." But he adds, "I am drearily homesick for the Old World sometimes. I know it wouldn't be good for me to go again, and so I try to be as brave as I can and pat myself on the back and call myself contented."

In the political world the method of reconstruction in the South was the issue. Mr. Brooks had faith in Charles Sumner as a leader, sharing the common feeling that the accession of President Johnson was a misfortune. He feared that Congress might lose its temper: "It is bad to see spitefulness when there ought to be wisdom." A meeting was held in November, in behalf of the freedmen, where Chief Justice Chase presided. Again Mr. Brooks exerted his power in an eloquent appeal, advocating the education of the negro to qualify him for a voter. "To many," he said, "it might seem like radicalism, but Christianity is the radicalism of the world. The best way then is to teach pure unadulterated radicalism, for this is the only conservatism." On Thanksgiving Day, the 29th of November, he preached from the text Isaiah xxvi. 15: "Thou hast increased the nation, O Lord"; and his subject was the result of the war in producing a new sense of the significance of nationality:

"Americans have now a self-consciousness of nationality. Irresponsibility and irresolution have been left to the history of our earlier days, and the nation has attained its manhood. Foreign countries had not a true sense of our greatness, and yet they had gained some glimpse of it in their appreciation of our great representative, the lamented Lincoln. In our progress in free ideas, in wealth and size and extent, we have gone forward with gigantic strides. We have now the grandest and noblest nation on earth."

There were demands and appeals to be met besides those of the freedmen. The South, desolated by war, was threatened by famine. The Mayor of Philadelphia called together its prominent citizens, to consider the situation, and Phillips Brooks was the spokesman. He said that at such a time no questions should be asked. What we have to do is to look upon the end of the war as accomplished, and to treat the people of the South as though never estranged from us. We must alleviate the sufferings there, and open the way to happiness, and remove as far as possible the ravages which have taken place. New York has done much, but Philadelphia must outstrip her in gathering contributions and all manner of supplies. This will be the surest means of reconstruction,—the right sympathy of hearts.

"A month after the proclamation of peace [writes Bishop Randolph] I received a letter from him, inquiring of myself, my family, and many of our mutual friends, and telling me to sit down forthwith and write to him, and give him the privilege of helping poor churches that had been crippled by the war and ministers who were suffering the privations of poverty. After spending seventeen years in the city of Baltimore I returned to Virginia thirteen years ago as the Assistant Bishop of the Diocese, and my duties brought me into contact with the people and churches of Virginia, and it touched me to find that many of them had received contributions of money and letters of sympathy and encouragement from him."

In December, 1866, steps were taken toward the completion of the Church of the Holy Trinity by the erection of a church tower. Mr. Brooks had been deputed by the vestry to consult with architects, and determine a plan. But a difference of opinion developed between him and the vestry, whether there should be a massive tower only, or a tower surmounted by a spire. His own preference was for the tower without the spire. That he was clear in his own mind as to what he wanted is evident from a reference to the subject, in a letter: "I have just broken my head against my vestry in an attempt to put a tower harmonious and solid on my church. I have failed. It is to be a spire, taller than anything in town, not bad and not good." In the end, however, he was allowed to have his way, and the lofty tower of Holy Trinity, in Philadelphia, remains a monument to his preference in church architecture.

In the spring of 1867, he received an invitation to become the head of the new Episcopal Theological School in Cambridge, and to be responsible for its organization and the selection of its teachers. The founder of the school, Benjamin Tyler Reed, knew him well; and had frequently entertained him at Lynn, his summer home, where for several successive summers Mr. Brooks had accepted an invitation to preach. Had not the call come so soon after the trial he had gone through in connection with the Divinity School in Philadelphia he might have given the subject greater consideration than he appears to have done. But at this moment, also, the tie which bound him to Philadelphia was stronger than ever. From allusions in his letters, it would seem that he was contemplating marriage at an early moment. To his father he writes:

"April 17, 1867. I have known pretty well how things went on with you at home. The principal events of the winter have been the visits from home, especially those of William, who is going to be married very soon. So runs the story here. I may have the privilege of welcoming you all to the Holy Trinity. Of course you will all come on, from Aunt Susan down to Johnnie, and we 'll charter a car from my house up Walnut Street to the church.

"I rejoice with you all in Johnnie's confirmation last week. Now all the boys are in the Church, and I hope none of them will do her any dishonor.

"I am glad you approve of my decision about Cambridge. I am sure it is all right, although there are some things about the invitation there which tempted me very much. I hope the new school will be well manned and start vigorously. I do not feel that I could leave here for anything now."

To his friend Dr. Richards he writes:

"June 28, 1867. I have just got back from Boston. Arthur, one of those boys who must be all a hazy lump to you, is just graduating, and I am proud of him because he is third scholar in a class of some hundred, and so I went on to his Class Day. It was perfect, Cambridge, with its elms and grass all washed and fresh, and splendid music and luxuriant hospitality, and no end of bright, pretty faces. Do you know I think I am getting more and more susceptible as I grow older. Did you? I should n't wonder if it came to matrimony pretty soon."

The summer of 1867 was spent at Mount Desert, but no

record of it has been kept.   In one of his letters he refers to it as very crowded, and very pleasant, and a hard place to write letters.   As he was beginning in the fall a new year of work in Philadelphia, his two youngest brothers were leaving home.   Arthur went to Andover Theological Seminary to begin his preparation for the ministry, and John entered Harvard College.   Frederick Brooks had been ordained and had accepted a call to St. Paul's Church, Cleveland, Ohio.   His mother writes him: "Nearly all my children have left me, and as I sit alone, I feel lonely. . . . There is but one fault in your letter.   You do not tell whether you are going to preach the Foreign Missions sermon.   Do, and plead strongly the Lord's cause for the heathen."

He still continued, but now only at rare intervals, to record his thoughts in the note-book.   A few extracts are given which belong to this time:

"The shading of character into character we learn by and by, and it is a very confusing lesson.   I can remember well enough how as a child I used to feel as if misers and Sabbath-breakers and infidels were kinds of professions or castes, which you would recognize any moment when you saw them, by their very look. The first time I had an infidel pointed out to me was a wonder. I looked in vain for his badges.   Only by and by you find the misers and the infidels everywhere, nay, even in yourself."

"Any one who travels much and sees the past and the present of the world on a large scale comes, I think, necessarily to attribute a wider and more solid power to *sentiments* and *feelings*, to affections, superstitions, and antipathies in human history,— things that seem shadowy and unreal,—than he was used to do?   What have they done?   Nay, rather, what have they not done?"

"The Mohammedans have the golden gate into the Mosque of Omar heavily walled up.   There is a tradition that if ever they are driven out of possession it will be by the Jews or Christians entering by that gate.   Like this is the way in which many Christians, feeling that attacks upon religion are likeliest to come upon the side of reason, instead of simply arming themselves on that side and keeping watch that the gateway be used only for its proper passers, wall it up altogether and refuse to reason at all about their faith."

"In the order of nature belief always precedes knowledge. It is the condition of instruction."

"The strength of our persuasions is no evidence at all of their rectitude. Crooked things may be stiff and inflexible as well as straight; and men may be as positive and peremptory in error as in truth. (Locke's *Essay on the Human Understanding*, ii., p. 279.)"

"Some men's faith only makes itself visible; other men's lightens everything within its reach. Yet this is not always a difference in the qualities of the two faiths, but may be owing to the conditions of the atmosphere."

"Cicero writes to his brother Quintus of the prosecution of the Consuls (B.C. 52): 'Aut hominum aut legum interitus ostenditur.' Cf. this as a statement of one aspect of the Atonement. *Judex damnatur cum nocens absolvitur.*"

"The great fact of the world, the phenomenon that is to be measured; the responsibility that is to be enjoined, is Tendency."

"The Jesuit ordering pictures from France to use in the Huron Mission wants many souls in perdition (*âmes damnées*) in various styles; of souls in bliss (*âmes bienheureuses*) he thinks that one will be enough. (Parkman's *Jesuits in North America*, p. 133.)"

"A curious argument of the Indians, who believed in the truth as powerful, but drew the inference, not that they had better submit to it, but that it would be better for them not to hear it. (*Parkman, Ib.*, p. 135.)"

"'You do good to your friends,' said Le Jeune to an Algonquin chief, 'and you burn your enemies. God does the same.'"

"It is a strange thing to say, but when the number of any public body exceeds that of forty or fifty, the whole assembly has an element of joyous childhood in it, and each member revives at times the glad mischievous nature of his schoolboy days."

"There are some diseases for which Lacordaire says (he is speaking of morbid solitude) there are but two remedies, Death and God.

"That nameless gift which misfortune adds to the greatest virtues. (*Bossuet.*)"

"The way in which the old army overcoats are still seen about, worn in ignominious work, long after the war is over."

"He cannot force his way in, and so indulges himself with merely banging at the door."

"'*If one's shoes were always being mended, when could they be worn?*' (Masson's *Milton*, ii., p. 276.)"

"' Diogenes the Cynic was a wise man for despising them, but a fool for showing it.' (*Lord Chesterfield's Letters*, p. 74.)"

"' It has been well observed that men's real qualities are very apt to rise or fall to the level of their reputation.' (*Lord Nugent's Memorials of Hampden*, p. 179.)"

He was interested in the Sibylline Oracles, heathen and Christian, and his note-book gives indications of a plan for more thorough study. Niebuhr's *History of Rome* was his guide, but he was led to dip into *Dionysius of Halicarnassus*, *Pausanius*, *Varro*, *Livy*, *Josephus*, *Augustine* [*De Civitate Dei*], *Lactantius*, and *Celsus*. That he should have attempted it shows something of the working of his mind, and where his interest lay.

An incident occurred in connection with the Pan-Anglican Synod, whose first meeting was in 1867, which stirred Phillips Brooks with indignation. As he watched the proceedings in London he wrote: "The great English bishop-show seems to be doing nothing laboriously. Pan-Anglicans are poor things nowadays. My modest impression is that the strength of the Church is in the lower orders of the clergy, backed, of course, by a large-minded laity." One most prominent result of the conference was the condemnation of Bishop Colenso, for his teaching in regard to the Old Testament, an act which seemed to Dean Stanley and others to be fraught with danger to the cause of free inquiry in theology, as well as a violation of the best traditions of the Church of England. For these reasons he refused the request of the archbishop of Canterbury and the bishop of London to use the Abbey in the closing service of the Synod; but, not to be discourteous, he offered it for some service of a general character, which should have no relation to the Pan-Anglican meeting. When this offer was in turn refused, the

14

Dean wrote to Dr. Hopkins, the presiding bishop of the American Episcopal Church, explaining the circumstances, and expressing his desire to show welcome to Americans. Bishop Hopkins in his reply took the opportunity to administer a reprimand to the dean of Westminster for having disobeyed the divine law of the Church in refusing the request of the bishops for the use of the Abbey. To those who knew the usages of the Church of England, and the history of the Catholic Church in the Middle Ages, Bishop Hopkins was making a display of his ignorance; for it was the prerogative of the dean of Westminster that he owed no canonical obedience to any bishop. The letter of Bishop Hopkins was published in the American church papers. When Phillips Brook read it he wrote this letter to the dean of Westminster:

"PHILADELPHIA, November 29, 1867.

"I have just happened to see in the *Church Journal* of New York a letter from you to Bishop Hopkins, our presiding Bishop, with his reply, and I am so mortified and indignant at the impudence and ill-feeling of the Bishop's letter that, whatever may be the liberty I take in doing so, I cannot help sitting down at once and disowning—as I am sure I may do for our whole Church— the spirit and substance of his melancholy letter. It is a little matter to you, but much to us. I, for one, am not willing that my Church should be so misrepresented. I am not willing that you should for a moment think that it is the Church which does what the Bishop of Vermont has done—answer the kind courtesy of your note to him by personal insult and impertinent criticisms of customs with which he had nothing in the world to do. I beg you to believe, sir, that the only feeling in our Church at large on reading the Bishop's letter will be one of sorrow and shame. We would not willingly see any gentleman insulted in our name, and we owe too much to you for all that you have sent us in your books, which we know here as well as any Englishman can, to feel lightly the disgrace of such words as the Bishop of Vermont has written."

In politics things had not been going as he desired to see them. In the enthusiasm of the moment following the emancipation, he had anticipated the end to be reached, not taking into view the intervening years, and the mistakes whose effect would be to retard the progress of the freedmen. From this time he did not regard with such hopefulness as he had done the course of political campaigns and elections. He was giving himself more exclusively to his distinctive work.

"Philadelphia, October 12, 1867.

"DEAR FATHER,—I do not know whether you will take in a letter from a Pennsylvania man after the way in which we have disgraced ourselves this week, But I assure you that I voted the Republican ticket right straight through, and it is not my fault that we have been found patting Andrew Johnson on the back. I did what I could to save the country, but the State is thoroughly demoralized. They try to explain it all by local causes, but it is hopeless to account for it all so. There has certainly been a sad deterioration of public sentiment. And the worst of it is that it seems to be by no means confined to Philadelphia. It seems to have run all over the country. Ohio is bad. Iowa, even, is not up to the mark. You cannot run principles without men, and there are no prominent men for our principles just now."

Phillips Brooks now began to be claimed by other religious communions as a common treasure, in the light of whose message distinctions of creed and polity should become subordinate. We hear of him as preaching, when he is in New York, at the Fifth Avenue Reformed Dutch Church, or in Philadelphia at the First Baptist Church and the Sixth Presbyterian Church, or when he goes to Boston at the Old South Church.

Among those who were first to recognize his unwonted pulpit power were the Unitarians. Since the **days** of Channing, no such voice had appealed to them. They were quick to discern spiritual or intellectual excellence, and ready for the voice of the Spirit bringing a message for humanity. To the utterance of Phillips Brooks, large, rich, and free, they responded with loving confidence. At a meeting of the Unitarian Association in Boston, in May, 1868, one of the speakers was reported as follows:

"I am told that Philadelphia is all alive with the splendid preaching of one of the occupants of the Episcopal pulpit there, who is imparting to that city the fresh life and the new day of the living gospel. When one of his congregation was boasting of his power to a member of our Brother Furness's church, he said in reply, 'Well, do you know the reason? Your preacher was born in a Unitarian home, educated in a Unitarian Sunday-school, grew up under liberal influences, and is giving you the fruit.' (Applause.)   And I say that the faith that can send forth rich, ripe fruit to bless the churches like Phillips Brooks . . . is a living faith, and is doing grand service in the world . . . . My friends, I believe in the providential education of emigration."

It was hardly accurate to speak of Mr. Brooks as having been born in a Unitarian home, for his mother, to whom fell almost exclusively the religious training of the children, was not and never had been a Unitarian, and indeed from her girlhood was pronounced and aggressive in her adherence to what is known as Orthodox Congregationalism.   Nor was Phillips Brooks educated in a Unitarian Sunday-school, but when he went to church and Sunday-school for the first time it was at St. Paul's Episcopal Church on Tremont Street, of which Dr. Vinton was the rector.   Nor can he be said to have grown up under liberal influences, for he continued to sit under Dr. Vinton's ministry until he left Boston for the theological seminary of the Episcopal Church in Virginia.   There is no evidence that up to this time he had read the writings of Channing or of Martineau.   There are, at least, no references to them in his note-books.   There is, however, in the theological antecedents of Phillips Brooks a resemblance to Maurice, whose father was a Unitarian and his mother a Calvinist.   It had been the life work of Maurice to reconcile an inherited theological antagonism.   To some extent Brooks experienced the process through which Maurice passed.   He inherited the twofold tendency, the humanitarian from his father, and the theistic from his mother,—the maternal inheritance being the stronger.   His work resembles that of Maurice in the effort to hold in equilibrium these tendencies which, existing apart, constitute the two wings of New England Puritanism.   Maurice was the writer with whom Phillips Brooks was in deepest sympathy.   He began to study his writings when at the theological seminary; in his last years he recommended him to young men as the greatest theologian of the age.

In April, 1868, the Rev. Henry C. Potter, now the bishop of New York, had resigned his position as assistant minister of Trinity Church, Boston, on the Greene Foundation, and in July Bishop Eastburn had resigned the rectorship.   Then the vestry of the church had immediately been summoned, and a unanimous call had been extended to Mr. Brooks to become the rector.   Mr.

Brooks received the formal document while at Newport on a visit, and thus speaks of it to his father:

"NEWPORT, August 18, 1868.   I want you and Mother and the boys to write to Philadelphia, and tell me what you think of it in full.   Something inclines me to come, but the preponderance is decidedly the other way.   I shall be here till some time next week, probably Tuesday or Wednesday.   Am having a charming time.   Love to all.

"Affectionately,   PHILL."

A problem of a different kind was confronting Phillips Brooks at the time when he received the call, on whose solution hung his destiny,—whether he should or should not leave the city of Philadelphia.   No allusion is made to it, however, in the correspondence relating to his invitation to become the rector of Trinity Church, Boston.   His father, his mother, his brothers, all wrote urging him to accept the call.   Other letters from members of the parish, from the bishop, and from clergymen prominent in the diocese, gave the reasons why he should regard it as a duty to accept the call.   There was great work to be done for the Episcopal Church; he could speak to the whole city, and his voice would resound throughout the Commonwealth of Massachusetts, throughout New England.   He would overcome the negative disintegrating influences which were weakening the churches; he could restore the waning prestige of religion and could save the people from resorting to false guides or from seeking a refuge in sensuous appeals of ritualism.   Trinity Church would be as a throne from which he could sway the multitudes, or, to change the metaphor, a strategic centre, from whence operations could be successively conducted that would alter a situation of weakness into one of strength.   There were other arguments: he could influence young men on a large scale, for Boston with its suburbs was the educational centre of the country.   He owed something to Boston as the place of his birth and education, the home of his ancestry.   It was of course assumed in the arguments that Boston was the most important city in the land, the intellectual centre from whence went forth streams of influence throughout all the country.

To these letters Mr. Brooks gave one brief and almost uniform reply,—that he was not the man to do the work which was described. Any other answer could hardly have been expected from him. To have assumed that he was able to accomplish such a task as these letters prophesied, or that he came to Boston with the intention or expectation of accomplishing it, was to put him in a false position and endanger his usefulness. He asked the opinion of Dr. Vinton, whose judgment shows that he was under no illusion about Boston:

"POMFRET, August 28, 1868.

"MY DEAR BROOKS,—I do not feel competent to advise you in so important a matter with anything like assurance, and can only say in a general way that my impressions are against your removal, on the whole.

"I do not doubt of your success in Boston, but I am more in doubt of your being so useful as in Philadelphia. You are more needed where you are than in a place where the people are more like you.

"You can never have a more devoted parish than Holy Trinity, and when you move from it I think it should be to New York."

When his decision to decline the call was announced, there went up a wail,—from the members of his family, from the church, and from the many who had an interest in his coming to Boston. Mr. George M. Dexter, the senior warden of Trinity, wrote: "Yours, putting an end to all our hopes, came duly to hand. I cannot tell you how much we should have all enjoyed your being able to come to the opposite conclusion. What we shall do I have not the least idea." Dr. Stone, the dean of the new Episcopal Theological School in Cambridge, wrote: "Your letter of the 7th inst. announcing the fact that you had declined the call to Trinity Church, Boston, made my heart sick; I had so longed and hoped for a different decision." Dr. Francis Wharton, a professor in the School and rector of St. Paul's, Brookline, first made the suggestion that the answer be not considered final:

"I must confess that your declination was a great shock to me, and the longer the time that elapses since I heard of it the more anxious the question becomes. . . . My own feeling has been that after the lapse of a year your decision could be reconsidered. Far, far wiser would it be for the parish to wait. . . . Here is really the mainspring of our New England Church, and here will its tone be largely given. You are the one to do this, and to do it with a breadth and power which no one else can approach; and I consider the alternative before us with the greatest anxiety. You are a Bostonian and feel what our want is."

Of these expressions of disappointment, none could have moved him more than the letter from his mother:

" Boston, September 9, 1868.

"My dearest Philly,—.   .   .   It is a dreadful blow to all of us.   I never can tell you how badly we all felt when your long-looked-for letter arrived at breakfast time.   We were all stunned and saddened by it; for your long delay in answering greatly encouraged us to hope, and the disappointment is intense.

" .   .   .   I had thought I should have my boy back again, and the thought of your coming made Father and me very happy, and gave a new impetus to our lives; but I fear we shall never have you now.   We have indulged the proud hope of seeing you change wasted and suffering Trinity into a fruitful field.   Indeed, you could have controlled all Boston.

"It is not too much to say I have been sick at heart ever since I heard it, and I cannot write about it, for I cannot find words to tell you how sorry I feel.   .   .   ."

When he replied to this letter, expressing himself as hurt at the absence of any recognition of his sense of duty in the matter, his mother quickly wrote again, but in a different mood.   She had recovered from her despondency, and was sharing in the growing hope that his decision was not final.

Here the subject of Boston and Trinity Church may be dropped for a moment, while we return to Philadelphia to follow him in the last year of his residence there.   His visit to Boston in October was for the purpose of acting as chaplain on the occasion of breaking ground for Memorial Hall at Harvard.   While in Boston he preached in Trinity Church, which gave him an opportunity for looking at the situation with reference to himself as he had not hitherto done.   During his last year as rector of the Church of the Holy Trinity he was experiencing vicissitudes in human affairs.   The city and the church were not quite the same to him as they had been.   His popularity was not diminished; indeed his power in the pulpit was greater than ever, and his personal prestige something unknown in clerical life.   The devotion of his congregation still attended him.   But nothing could quite compensate for losses which closely affected him.   He was dependent on his friendships.   Gaps had been made in the circle of those with whom he spent his hours of leisure.   The little coterie which had met weekly at dinner under the hospitable roof of Mr. Cooper was sadly reduced. The call to arise and depart could no longer surprise him, strongly as he was still bound to the friends who remained.

At this time he turned much to the younger men who were coming out of the Divinity School. The difference that separated them in age was not great; he had reached in 1869 his thirty-fourth year. His brother Arthur, his junior by fourteen years, was with him, a student at the Divinity School, and between them there grew up an intimate friendship, not always the rule with brothers. Through Arthur, earlier through Frederick, he became acquainted with the theological students, visiting them in their rooms. Whenever a student read a paper in any way notable, he was sure to learn its contents. One of the younger clergy gives this glimpse of him in 1868:

"He was then at the highest point of popularity and fame; he was like a great god, so full of activity and force, and the wonder with me was why such a man cared for me. Yet I had his fullest confidence, and he used to pour out all his contents into my astonished ears. I have known him to come as late as one or two o'clock in the morning, throw snowballs or bits of stick at my windows and give a peculiar whistle, which I, like a game dog, instantly obeyed. He used to make me read my essays and sermons to him."

Some of the younger clergy had formed themselves into a club, called the "Clericus," meeting every month, when an essay was read and discussed. The social element was prominent, for the members were chosen by ballot and one object was to get "clubable" men. They were of similar views, yet not unwilling to add to their membership those who differed from them in opinion, for it gave more zest to their discussions. Although they were young, living at a time which to their elders seemed to abound with omens of evil, when materialism was undermining faith and a Romanizing reaction appeared the only alternative, yet they were fearless, proposing to face science and a critical literature, to overcome the objections and difficulties each in his own way. The club had no constitution, and no specific object, except to meet monthly, when what was uppermost in religious thought found earnest expression. If their purpose could be described, it was an ambition to emulate the spirit of St. Paul: "And now abideth faith, hope, charity, these three, but the greatest of these is charity." They were full of faith and of hope for the Church and for the world. A sense of exhilaration and expectation was in them, as though a great age were to be ushered in, when God in Christ would fulfil his promise: "Behold, I make all things new."

The familiar carol "O little town of Bethlehem," written by Mr. Brooks for his Sunday-school, to which allusion has already been made, was sung for the first time at Christmas, 1868, to the music furnished by Mr. Redner, the organist at Holy Trinity. The hymn with its music at once sprang into popularity, and is now included in all Sunday-school collections.[1]

Those who now met Phillips Brooks for the first time were often perplexed by his manner. The conventional clerical address was wanting; he seemed full of mirth and giving full scope to his talent for nonsense in little things. This manner was on him up to the moment of his going into the pulpit, and he was ready, when the sermon was over, again to resume the bantering, jocular tone. In this there may have been a protest against the conventional melancholy of the clergy. From the Puritan view of human life he was set free. What was good he could retain, and enforce with power unequalled, but the morbid melancholy, the gentle tone of complaint, he felt under no obligation to preserve. In his note-book there is this passage:

"Man is a sort of sunshine in the world, which, falling upon everything besides, calls it out to the flower of its truest beauty and the fruitage of its fullest use. By his touch, nature grows into delight and supply, and all events open into education. And this being true of man at large, it must be true also of each man in his contact with things. He must be a ray of the great

[1] In the Christmas programme for that year was this verse, not afterwards published in any of the hymn-books:

> "Where children pure and happy
> Pray to the Blessed Child,
> Where misery cries out to Thee,
> Son of the Mother mild;
> Where Charity stands watching,
> And Faith holds wide the door,
> The dark night wakes, the glory breaks,
> And Christmas comes once more."

sunshine under whose touch some special flower may open and some special fruit fill itself with healthy and nutritious juice, some little corner of the field grow rich."

This manner of Phillips Brooks, both in conversation and in his familiar correspondence, might mislead any one who did not know him. It did not deceive those who knew him best. One of his friends, a lady with great experience of life, thought that, beneath the merriment and the wild humor, she could always detect "Andover." This peculiarity of manner served as a barrier between his inner life and the curiosity of those who desired to have him talk of himself. He was on his guard lest he should be betrayed into personal conversation or talk intimately of his own experience. There lay his power, that he reserved himself for the pulpit, and refused to weaken himself by admitting any other mode of self-utterance. He never alluded either in letters or conversation to his popularity or to his growing power and influence, although he was daily receiving tributes of admiration and even adulation tending to beget conceit and egotism and arrogance. His high distinction, his personal power, his popularity, his exceptional career tended to constitute a barrier between him and others. In his manner lay his safeguard. It became a sentinel, over his life, over emotions quickly roused into inward tumult. He gained relief by what sometimes seemed an irreverent mirth.

With the opening of the new year 1869 the subject of the call to Trinity Church was reopened by a letter from Hon. R. C. Winthrop asking if there were any immediate or even remote possibility of his coming to Boston. If so they would continue to wait. But if any imperative and inexorable consideration put Trinity out of the question it would not comport with the dignity of either party that such a position should be openly offered and declined a second time so soon. To this question Mr. Brooks replied:

"January 4, 1869. . . . I ought to say at once that I see no possibility of changing the decision to which I came in the fall. My work here is as exacting as ever, and I cannot see any more chance of leaving it. You say very justly that it is not right for Trinity to renew its invitation only to be declined again, and ever since it has been intimated to me in several ways that there was any thought of such action, especially since I received your note, I have tried to see whether it was possible to hope to give any other answer. I cannot see that it is.

"You will judge, no doubt, that for many reasons I should like to come exceedingly. I certainly should. I appreciate fully the value and importance of the parish, and have looked anxiously to see the right man appear for it.

"I do not know after this whether you will still think the proposed interview desirable. But I should like to talk with you about it, because talk is so much more satisfactory than writing."

Mr. Brooks was in Boston on February 14, preaching at Trinity Church morning and afternoon, and in the evening at the Old South Church on Washington Street to a "crowded house," under the "auspices of the Young Men's Christian Association." His text was taken from 1 Corinthians xv., 45. A call would have been extended to him from Emmanuel Church, Boston, made vacant by the election of its rector to the bishopric of Central New York, had he been willing to consider it, but he declined. On the whole he seemed to be settling permanently in Philadelphia, having made at this time an arrangement for joint housekeeping with his friend Rev. C. D. Cooper, who was building a commodious residence with this object in view. But the arrangement did not imply that Mr. Brooks felt himself condemned to a celibate life. In a letter to Rev. George A. Strong, he speaks on the subject of matrimony:

" February 3, 1869. Good luck to you with all my heart, my dear fellow. It is what I have wanted for you for years, and now that it has come, I feel as rejoiced as I could be for anybody except myself. This is a wretched sort of life that we are living now, and when a man breaks out of it as you are going to do, his friends who stay behind must clap him on the back as he departs and congratulate him with all the intensity with which they feel their own forlornness."

The convention of the diocese of Pennsylvania met in May, 1869, and Phillips Brooks preached the sermon. It was published by order of the convention, under the title of "The Living Church." It was a comprehensive sermon defining his attitude at a moment when excitement and alarm existed throughout the Episcopal Church. One demurs a little at the text, taken from Exodus xxviii. 34, 35: "A golden bell and a pomegranate, a golden bell and a pomegranate, upon the hem of the robe round about. And it shall be upon Aaron to minister: and his sound shall be heard when he goeth in unto the holy place before the Lord, and when he cometh out, that he die not." At this stage in his career, he was wont to search for passages in the Bible whose meaning was not at once apparent,—a practice he afterwards ridiculed as clerical affectation. He seeks to connect the text with his theme, but when he is launched into the sermon it disappears. The pomegranate stands for the accumulation of life and its ripening fruit in the soul, the bell for its living utterance and proclamation.

The distinctive character of the sermon lies in putting the living soul before the living Church. The Church is the aggregate of Christian life. Government and symbols are not the Church. There is nothing belonging to the Church in its totality which does not first belong to individual souls. The danger of the ecclesiastical spirit, the danger for all churchmen and for all times to fear, is that there lies a certain vitality in the Church apart from the life of the souls within her. There is danger that the Church may harm the life given to her to cultivate, by stopping the channels through which Christ communicates with souls.

"If a church in any way hinders the free play of human thoughtfulness upon religious things by clothing with mysterious reverence—and so shutting out from the region of thought and study—acts and truths which can be thoroughly used only as they are growingly understood, by limiting within hard and minute and invariable doctrinal statements the variety of the realtions of the human experience to God; if in any such way a church hinders at all the free inflow of every new light which God is waiting to give to the souls of men as fast as they are ready to receive it, just so far she binds and wrongs her children's intelligence and weakens her own vitality. This is the suicide of Dogmatism.

"Or if a church lets any technical command of hers stand across the path, that a command of God cannot get free access to the will of any of the least of all God's people—a system of ecclesiastical morality, different from the eternal morality which lies above the Church, between the soul and God, a morality which hides some eternal duties and winks at some eternal sins,—just so far the Church wrongs her children's consciences and weakens her own vitality. This is the suicide of Corruption.

"Or yet again, if the symbols of the Church, which ought to

convey God's love to man, become so hard that the love does not find its way through them and they stand as splendid screens between the Soul and the Love, or have such a positive character of their own, so far forget their simple duty of pure transparency and mere transmission, that they send the Love down to the soul colored with themselves, formalized and artificial; if the Church dares either to limit into certain channels or to bind to certain forms of expression that love of God which is as spiritual and as free as God, then yet again she is false to her duty, she binds and wrongs her children's loving hearts, and once again weakens her own vitality. This is the suicide of Formalism.

". . . We must come forth into the clear spiritual life of Christ, which desires nothing but to know Him, and obey Him, and feel Him more and more. . . . . The enforcement of a scheme of moral law or good behaviour, making the Church a police system to keep the world in order; the mere introduction of a system of church government and worship, or the compact symmetry of the Church's year, the beautiful order of the Church's education; every sacred rite and every sensuous impression;— all this is machinery through which the life may manifest itself, but apart from the life or power of Christ entering into the Church as truth, guidance, and love, it becomes mere machinery, with the vital fires gone out in the furnaces below. . . . The rites and ceremonies must be clearly significant of truth, and not like the malignant ritualism of our day, significant of error; nor like the tawdry ritualism of our day, significant of nothing, a ghost of dead incantations.

"The world does not hear with any attention the ringing of our golden bells. Men do not listen as we go. Men neither fear the Church nor desire the Church as we sometimes dream they might; as we sometimes think in our reading that once they did. The world in large part goes its own way, and leaves us on one side. We are foreign and unreal to it.

"What is it that is needed? I say by all means that the first need is larger liberty. I think that all of us churchmen are burdened with the consciousness that there is more in the Church than gets out to contact with the world. The Church is better than her utterances. There is a larger thought than our sermons utter. Many a man talks better than he preaches. There are conventionalities and timidities of teaching that restrain the Truth. Does the world guess how the Church loves her Master? Does it imagine, from outside, the reality and intensity of that affectionate dependence which you and I know so well to be real and intense seeing it here within, but which attests itself so feebly, so formally, so artificially in a few stereotyped and narrow ways? There is a deep, spontaneous devotion that lacks the chance of a corresponding spontaneity of utterance and action. Am I not right? I plead for no special methods of liberation. I only point out what we all must know. . . .

"Christ is the Life; first in our souls, to which He enters by His Spirit in knowledge and authority and love, so that 'not we live, but Christ liveth in us'; and then in our Church, where He alone is still the Teacher and the Master and the Saviour, filling it with Himself and clothing it with His righteousness."

Toward the end of May his father wrote him a very personal letter: "I want to ask you whether you have given up all idea of coming to Trinity—a bold question, but not a day, sometimes it appears to me hardly an hour, passes that I am not asked the same question. They are getting anxious and desperate. . . . Let me know whether you would accept if another call was made." To this request he continued to give the same unsatisfactory answer:

"June 1, 1869. I am afraid that I have nothing satisfactory to say. I do not feel ready to intimate in any way that it is more likely than it was last year that I could come to Trinity. Some of the reasons which prevented me last year, it is true, have been removed, but I have not got over the feeling that I am not suited in many respects to Boston and Trinity, and there is still very much to make it difficult for me to leave my present parish. . . . Why don't they look some other way and take their eyes off me? It worries me."

His father's rejoinder was in a desponding tone, dwelling on the wretchedness of the situation; the vestry of Trinity had met and concluded to postpone the subject till the fall:

"I was sorry you got caught by that . . . invitation [to speak at the anniversary in Boston of the Free Religious Association]; it was one of their tricks and only done to catch your name to bolster up their radicalism. Better let them alone and have nothing to do with them; it will surely injure you. Don't get the name of being a Latitudinarian, I beg of you."

He sat down to his task of writing an oration to be delivered before the Phi Beta Kappa Society of Brown University at its coming Commencement. His subject was the "Relation of the Scholar to the World." The peculiar interest of the treatment lay in his development of the power of personality,—a thought now much in his mind. The address was delivered in the First Baptist Meeting House in Providence. Long before the appointed hour, the capacious building was filled with an audience waiting impatiently the advent of the procession which came down the hill from the university grounds. So steep is the hill that "the band of music which accompanied the procession was obliged to play a very solemn march in order to keep the dignified gentlemen from descending too rapidly. This was changed to a livelier strain as the procession gained the level street below and approached the church." Professor George P. Fisher of Yale College introduced the orator of the day, who produced at Providence the same impression as elsewhere, and was followed by the same comment:

"Thought succeeded thought with such rapidity that we were in a condition of intense mental tension through the whole oration, which, continuing an hour, seemed to have no boundary of time to mark its limit."

In the latter part of June he visited his brother Frederick in Cleveland, Ohio, going from there to Gambier, and thence to Cincinnati to be present at the marriage of a friend. On his return he wrote to his older brother:

"July 4, 1869. This is the great Independence Day, which in old time we used to celebrate by a morning's promenade, with ten cents apiece in our pockets to purchase dainties at the stalls around the Common, and by going to the Fireworks in the evening. To-day we will keep it a little differently. I am going to preach a patriotic sermon to an audience of soldiers this morning, and to ride out into the country this afternoon, and spend the night. It won't be so exciting as the old way, but it will be more satisfactory and comfortable for hot weather.

"Besides, I have had my excitement. I have been to see Old Febick [the family name for Frederick]. I found him standing recumbent with his ears up and every sign of vigorous vitality. The new church was on his mind, as it was on that of the whole city and State apparently. It seems to promise a speedy success. I preached for him all day Sunday, and found it screamingly hot.

"Have you read *Old Town Folks*, and is n't it clever and interesting? A New England story to one who lives in this dead Quaker atmosphere has a sort of spring and snap to it that is very refreshing. . . ."

It had been the intention of the vestry of Trinity Church to postpone the renewal of the call till the autumn. But a change had taken place in the situation. The personal issue which had made Phillips Brooks hesitant and vacillating had been determined. He was free to stay or to leave. A sudden visit was made by the senior warden of Trinity to Philadelphia for the purpose of a personal interview. When he returned to Boston, the vestry was hurriedly convened, and on July 6th a second call was extended. What could be done to retain him in Philadelphia was done, but most of the parishioners were away, and there seems to have been a feeling that effort was useless. A church on the defence against such aggressive attacks is at a disadvantage. But the vestry of Holy Trinity met and again made a vigorous protest against the severance of their relations as pastor and people, urging upon him the greatness of his field of influence in Philadelphia and his wonderful success. A prominent clergyman wrote to him:

"I know that you will not stay in Philadelphia, *but don't go to Boston!* Save yourself for New York. That will give you a little longer to your people here, and New York is the place for you. But Boston! What can you do there? They are too much set in their own wisdom. They are too unemotional. You will be cast away there. What you want is a congregation somewhere near the heart of the world, where its pulses are felt and all things stir,—a crowd of new people of to-day is the kind of matter upon which you ought to work."

As the days went on he became aware that he had created the expectation in the minds of people at Trinity that he would come. But a veil of reserve hangs about the whole affair. His letter of resignation implies a struggle. It was sent to his senior warden, at whose house he had been in the habit of dining on Sundays for seven years:

"2026 SPRUCE STREET, July 29, 1869.

"DEAR MR. COFFIN,—At last, with great sorrow, I send you my resignation. Will you please lay it before the Vestry and secure their acceptance of it?

"You do not agree with me, but I beg you to believe me honest and sincere in my desire to do what is right. I have given it thought, carefulness, and prayer, and have tried to decide it in God's fear. I can say no more, and only entreat you to try to think the best of my decision.

"I want to thank you especially, my dear Mr. Coffin, for all your goodness. I owe you more than I can tell. I shall never forget it, but wherever I go my love for you shall always be as warm and fresh as it is to-day.

"As to the time of my resignation taking effect, I want to do exactly what you think best as far as possible. I can come back for the third Sunday in September and can stay a month or six weeks after that, if it is thought best. Please tell me freely what you think about it.

"May God bless you always, you and all of yours.
"Your affectionate friend, P. B."

When it was known that the decision was final there was no delay in action on the part of the Holy Trinity Church. On July 31 the vestry met and accepted the resignation, passing the usual resolutions of regret which attested his eminent abilities, his success, and the cordial relations of minister and people. Letters of regret and deep sorrow, letters of welcome and congratulation, fill up the scene. Mr. John Bohlen writes him, when he learned the decision: "I can only hope, and yet I ought not for their sakes, and do not, that others of the hundreds of families in our church have not suffered with so deep a sense of personal loss as our household has to-day."

He wrote to Dr. Vinton his decision, asking him to "bless him away from Holy Trinity, as he had blessed him to it"; to which Dr. Vinton replied:

"I say with my heart, 'May you be happy.' I suppose I shall see less of you and less of Philadelphia now, and this is my only regret in the matter. . . . When I say my only regret, I mean so far as I am concerned. I regret it mightily for the Philadelphians."

Mr. Brooks spent his vacation in Boston, making a short visit on the way to West Point, where he preached in the chapel of the Military Academy. He went back to Boston, but no longer to the familiar house No. 3 Rowe Street (Chauncy Street), once a street of residences, but now given up to wholesale warehouses. He was a man who loved to preserve old associations unchanged. "And so we've got a new house, and 3 Rowe Street and 41 Chauncy Street will be things of the past. Alas, how the days go by. It never will be natural to eat dinner in Hancock Street.

15

Is the new house fine? I hope not. And will you let common folks come to stay in it?" His mother disliked and dreaded the change. But the father was more cheerful over the prospect: "It is an old house, and there is a good deal to do to it. It is one you will feel just as much at home in as at High Street or Chauncy Street. Nothing 'stuck up' about it; like all our other houses, 'neat but not gaudy'; not like the houses on the Back Bay, where the people go out in the morning to find the doorsteps have sunk out of sight; but it is on the solid hardpan of Beacon Hill, original soil, street named from the old John Hancock."

The short summer over, Mr. Brooks returned to Philadelphia for a few Sundays before his resignation should take effect. On Sunday, October 24, he preached his last sermons as rector of the Church of the Holy Trinity; in the morning from the text Ephesians iv. 30: "And grieve not the Holy Spirit of God whereby ye are sealed unto the day of redemption." In the afternoon he took leave of his congregation with an extemporaneous sermon, when the occasion was one of deep and sorrowful emotion. Thus came to an end his ministry of ten years in Philadelphia.

Among the ties which bound Phillips Brooks to Philadelphia, none was closer than his friendship with Dr. Weir Mitchell, which dates from the time when Mr. Brooks became rector of the Church of the Advent. No one is more competent than Dr. Mitchell to speak of Mr. Brooks during his ministry in Philadelphia.

"In the year 1861, not long after Phillips Brooks came to the Church of the Advent, I first heard him preach. I was struck with the ardor and intensity of the man, and with the imaginative qualities which, in later years, were more or less subjected to the rule of a growing intellect. . . .

"When he became my rector at Holy Trinity he lived quite near to me. Always once, and usually twice, a week he dined with us, and five evenings out of seven was in the habit of dropping in about ten o'clock for a talk and a smoke before the fire in my library. At this time my household was in charge of my sister Elizabeth, a maiden lady, even then in breaking health, some years older than I, and, as Phillips Brooks was much my junior, very far older than he. Between these two people a close friendship arose. . . . She was by nature fond of books, and, with increasing ill health and rare freedom from pain, her appetite for reading grew with what it fed on. In many directions she became singularly learned, but especially so in all biblical literature, and in the history of the Church. Her reading, however, was wide and various. . . . Witty, quick of tongue, picturesque and often quaint in statement, her talk was full of pleasant surprises. She was for years before her death a nearly constant sufferer, but no weakness conquered her. . . . Into this life of humor, learning, and liberal-minded religion, where pain was rarely absent, Phillips Brooks found his way, and as the years went by became her friend. He said to me once that no one had so influenced his opinions as this remarkable woman.

"We made many journeys together, and one summer a long canoe voyage from Moosehead to the sea by the Allegash and St. John rivers. At this time he was a very strong man, and his physical force was a source of admiration to our stalwart guides. It is to be regretted that as years went on he left his great frame without its essential tonic exercise. Upon this question I exerted my influence in vain, and even within the last few years I over and over predicted to him the physical calamities which he was surely inviting. He assured me that he had no time to walk, and that he felt no need for exertion. He was always somewhat annoyed by allusions to his health.

" During these summer journeys Phillips delighted to swim and to use the paddle, and found deep joy in the free woodland life. He neither shot nor fished. I think he had a great dislike to killing even a troublesome insect.

"At one time I asked him to try to speak less rapidly when preaching. He tried it, but found, as I suspected he would, that the speed of his extemporaneous speech had some relation to the rate of his thinking, and that to interfere with the normal rate of delivery of what the mind made ready was fatal. His rate of extemporaneous speech seemed to set the rate for his read sermons, and all effort to alter it became fruitless. As an extemporaneous speaker he was simply matchless. I heard him twice during the war, at public meetings where he was unexpectedly called upon. The effect was such as I have never seen before in any assembly of men.

"When Brooks came to Philadelphia he had been long away from the conventional, either in the Divinity School or in his little up-town church. At first he remonstrated with our efforts to make him see the need for much that he found irksome and destructive of time. He soon yielded, and became in the end careful as to the ordinary social rules and duties.

"He was subject to rare moods of utter silence. I have seen him sit through a dinner party and hardly utter a word; usually he was an easy and animated guest.

"He did not much affect the clerical style or ways, and on our long canoe journey the guides were three weeks before they found out that he was a clergyman.

"He was intellectually sympathetic and liked to talk to men of their own work. As to moral sympathy he seemed to me remarkable. A young mother who had lost her only child once said to me, 'He is the one person who has seemed to me to enter into my grief as if he really shared it,' and yet at this time he had experienced no trouble in life.

"I have known a number of the men we call great,—poets, statesmen, soldiers,—but Phillips was the only one I ever knew who seemed to me entirely great. I have seen him in many of the varied relations of life, and always he left with me a sense of the competent largeness of his nature. Perhaps the most vivid picture I retain of him is as he appeared to me at his Wednesday lectures years ago. Then he used to stand away from a desk, so that his massive figure and the strength of his head had their effect, and from his great height the magic of his wonderful eyes was felt, like the light from some strong watch-tower by the sea. There and thus you got all the impressible emphasis his noble sturdiness gave to the torrent of speech, which at first had, for a little, some air of hesitancy, and then rolled on, easy, fluent, and strong."

It was a good thing for Phillips Brooks—a providential ordering of his life—that he began his ministry in Philadelphia. He had the consciousness of power, but he was shy and sensitive, and of a delicate inward susceptibility which might easily have been hurt. Had he gone to a colder, more critical atmosphere, such as New England is popularly reputed to be, it is possible to imagine that he might have been chilled by rebuffs or not at first understood or appreciated. He might have been driven back upon himself, and in the moment of his first self-expression have failed to take the world into the confidence of his soul. He might have been intimidated by the prestige which from his childhood he had learned to revere in the men and the positions of the place where he had grown up, and have had greater difficulty in adjusting himself as a man to the environment of his early years. But Philadelphia meant freedom from these possibilities. In its warm-heartedness, its rich and genial hospitality, its quick recognition, free from any tendency to overcriticism; in its capacity for real living, without the tendency to introversiveness of the New England character,—in these conditions there was an appropriate climate, where the genius of Phillips Brooks might thrive abundantly.   There was no hostile criticism to repress the utterances of his inner life, but indeed so much encouragement that from the first he poured himself forth freely, and without restraint, and each effort of his genius was an encouragement to further effort, till he quickly came to mastery of himself and of the situation. We may say of his whole ministry in Philadelphia what he said of Dr. Vinton's short pastorate at Holy Trinity, "It was one of the brightest and sunniest pictures which the annals of clerical life have anywhere to show."   In his memorial sermon on Dr. Vinton he thus speaks of Philadelphia:

"Philadelphia is a city where the Episcopal Church is thoroughly at home.   Side by side with the gentler Puritanism of that sunnier clime, the Quakerism which quarrelled and protested, but always quarrelled and protested peacefully, the Church of England had lived and flourished in the colonial days, and handed down a well-established life to the new Church which sprang out of her veins at the Revolution.   It was the temperate zone of religious life with all its quiet richness.   Free from antagonism, among a genial and social people, with just enough of internal debate and difference to insure her life, enlisting the enthusiastic activity of her laity to a degree which we in Boston know nothing of, with a more demonstrative if not a deeper piety, with a confidence in herself which goes forth in a sense of responsibility for the community and a ready missionary zeal, the Church in Philadelphia was to the Church in Boston much like what a broad Pennsylvania valley is to a rough New England hillside."

Among many attempts to describe the impression made by Phillips Brooks's preaching when in Philadelphia, the following account is the best, coming from a most intelligent observer:

"The costly, spacious Church of the Holy Trinity, in Rittenhouse Square, was always filled, crowded in all weathers, whenever it was known that he was going to preach.   And yet to the breathless multitudes who came and went under the spell of his unique eloquence as certainly as the tides, he stood an insoluble puzzle and wonder.   No one could question the genuineness of his eloquence or resist its witchery, and yet no one could touch the secret of his power.   Perhaps there never was developed in any pulpit a parallel experience.   Here were thousands crowding the pews and standing room of the Holy Trinity Church, Sunday after Sunday, and year after year, with growing enthusiasm towards a preacher who himself never seemed overpoweringly moved. . . . He stood impassive, almost statuesque in imperturbable tranquillity, rattling off in a monotone, so swiftly as to tease and half baffle the most watchful ear, swallow flights of thought, feeling, poetry, philosophy, piety, biblical learning, sociological wisdom, trenchant criticism,—in no syllogistic order or sequence, but plainly the legitimate fruition of his theme, held together by a blood tie of spiritual significance; striding, lifting along through the spaces and reaches of the inner world, until the great throngs, in painful, half-breathed, eager silence, seemed beside themselves with a preternatural ecstasy.

"It was something like the glamour of a flying panorama, hour after hour in railway travel; or a deep reverie over the Divina Commedia, or in the grand Duomo itself; and yet unlike anything else having the touch of human artificer. It was not the half mesmeric spell of the mystic and priest, nor the fascination of an artist with an irresistible technique and magnetic individuality. There were no lightning strokes, no stimulating climacterics, no passage of stirring discords in harmonic resolution of transcendental loveliness or grandeur; and yet there was never for a minute any let-up or rallying-place found for the strained and eager sensibility until the last page was turned and the benediction said. Thousands will recognize the truth of this reminiscence stretching through many years, and identify this early mystification and bewilderment which half hid the young preacher from the people."

CHAPTER X.

1869–1872.

TRINITY CHURCH. THE RECEPTION IN BOSTON. CON-
TEMPORANEOUS COMMENTS. RECORD OF WORK.
EXTRACTS FROM CORRESPONDENCE AND FROM
NOTE-BOOKS. SOCIAL LIFE. THE SUMMER IN
EUROPE. FORMATION OF THE CLERICUS CLUB.
DESTRUCTION OF TRINITY CHURCH IN THE BOS-
TON FIRE.

PHILLIPS BROOKS began his ministry in Trinity Church,
Boston, on Sunday, October 31, preaching in the morning
from the text, St. John ix., 4, 5: "I must work the works of
Him that sent me, while it is day: the night cometh, when no
man can work"; and in the afternoon from St. John iv., 34:
"My meat is to do the will of Him that sent me, and to finish
His work." From this moment began the long period of twenty-
two years until he resigned his rectorship.

The church edifice then stood on Summer Street, near Washington Street, one of the relics of an earlier Boston when Summer
Street and the adjacent territory was the scene of residences
with their ample gardens. The church had been built in 1829,
and was regarded as a noble building in its day, equalled by few
in dignity and calm impressiveness. It was the centre and
home of Episcopal traditions and prestige, its organization dating
from the year 1729. During the trying days of the Revolution
it had remained open to its worshippers when most of the Episcopal churches were closed. When the alternatives had been
presented of closing its doors or of omitting the petition, in the
Litany, for King George and all the royal family, it had chosen
the latter with the hope that it would be "more for the interest
and cause of Episcopacy, and the least evil of the two, to omit a

part of the Litany than to shut up the church." It shows the tenacity of the corporate life of the church, that many of its worshippers were descendants of the families who first constituted it.

The new rector brought with him the traditions of the Evangelical school which he had put into successful practice in Philadelphia,—the Wednesday evening lecture, the Saturday evening Bible class, and the communicants' meeting in preparation for the Lord's Supper. Wednesday evening became a sacred occasion. One of the first fruits of his ministry in Boston was to find the chapel of Trinity Church too small for the purpose, and calling for an immediate enlargement. But this did not meet the need, and the service was transferred to the church, where every seat was occupied.

Among the arrangements projected at once for increasing the activity of the parish was a mission on West Cedar Street, where a Sunday school was gathered. There was at this time an Episcopal Church, St. Mark's, on West Newton Street, which, having fallen into weakness on account of the changing population, was no longer able to maintain a rector. This church edifice was purchased at his suggestion and became a dependency of Trinity Church, and the income of the Greene Foundation was devoted to the support of its minister.

Another scheme, broached to the parish during the first year of his incumbency, was the removal of the church to another part of the city, where it could do a greater work and better meet the needs of its parishioners. On this scheme he concentrated his energies. He was studying the city of Boston and the possible directions of its growth, in order to secure the most available site. Permission to sell having been granted by the Legislature, and accepted by the proprietors of Trinity Church, after much deliberation the new site was determined on, and by the close of 1871 the lot was purchased on which the present Trinity Church now stands. The late Mr. H. H. Richardson was chosen as the architect. The building committee were at once impressed with the importance of purchasing the triangle of land which now forms the whole Huntington Avenue front of the estate. The church thus completed its title to the whole domain of over an acre, enclosed by four public streets, and making the church visible in all directions.

When Phillips Brooks came to Boston it became his purpose, as the rector of Trinity Church, to carry out the ideal of a parish minister in all its scope and in all the detail of its relationships. In Philadelphia he had appeared as a reformer, with a work to do outside the pulpit, which rivalled in importance and popular interest his work as a preacher. After he came to Boston he ceased to be identified with any special reform. He was still interested in efforts aiming at human improvement. His interest was recognized and presupposed. He never failed when he was called upon to advocate any good cause. He sympathized with those who devoted their lives to such ends. On occasions in his own pulpit, and especially on Thanksgiving Day, he uttered himself freely on the questions of the hour. But he did not identify himself exclusively with any of them, nor work for them in direct manner. Of all the cities in the land, Boston more than any other was associated with ideas, issues, and moral reforms. It puzzled Boston people, therefore, when Phillips Brooks came among them and began at once to exert his magic influence. They found it impossible to label or classify him. He was neither a moral, a social, nor a religious reformer. It is interesting now to look back at the efforts made to define his position by critical analysis, or by comparison with other men. Boston at last accepted him for himself. But in the earlier years it was not so.

At first there was an inclination on the part of the Unitarians to claim him as their own, as one who, though he might not be conscious of it, must be at heart a Unitarian. They were unfamiliar with the breadth of the national Church of England, as illustrated by Maurice and Stanley and Arnold, Kingsley, Robertson, Thirlwall, and Tait and Temple, who represented liberal theology in the English Church, with whom Phillips Brooks was affiliated in spirit, and at whose feet he had sat as a pupil. Archbishop Tillotson and the liberal theologians of the English Church in the seventeenth and eighteenth centuries had long since been forgotten. It was difficult to believe that such a spirit was indigenous in the Anglican Church, having its roots in the Reformation and in the Book of Common Prayer. However it was, the Unitarians flocked to the new preacher. Against this disposition on the part of Unitarians to "attend the earnest and attractive ministry of Phillips Brooks," the *Liberal Christian*, a Unitarian organ in Boston, gave a most emphatic protest. The editor of the *Christian Register* (Unitarian) went to hear him, and detected in his sermon "the devious ways of theological subtleties," but also came to the conclusion that he was "as rational and independent as an honest man can possibly be while remaining within the Episcopal Church." On this verdict, the *Congregationalist*, an orthodox paper, congratulated Mr. Brooks that he might now "take heart and dismiss his fears." On the other hand, one of the stricter sort of the orthodox who went to hear him complained, that "he did what too many orthodox ministers do in this region,—threw out a sop to the Unitarians"; and also showed his inability for theological subtleties by denying the doctrine of total depravity.

The following testimonies illustrate other differences of opinion:

"Writing from an 'orthodox' standpoint, your correspondent may be pardoned for expressing the joy he felt that Puritan truth is the doctrine of the preacher now most admired and sought after in degenerate Boston. It was most refreshing and hope-inspiring to hear him."

"It is this compound of Broad Church liberality and absolute fixedness and certainty as to points of belief and faith that accounts for Mr. Brooks's wide influence in the community."

". . . It is a significant fact that Harvard, which has been so eminent for the cautious accuracy, careful elegance, and dainty reserve of its orators, should have sent such an unusual representative into the pulpit, and that her representative preacher now is this stalwart Broad Churchman, who preaches the humanity of Channing with the creed of Jeremy Taylor, and strikes at the shirks and shams of our day with the dashing pluck and the full blood of Martin Luther."

"Here and there you will find one who thinks that the Unitarians get a little more comfort out of his preaching than he ought to give them. But there is reason for the remark that such suspicions are mostly confined to those who seldom hear his sermons, if in some instances they are not unaccompanied with what is very near akin to a professional jealousy. I have never heard but one opinion from those qualified by knowledge and impartiality to judge, and that is that the current of his preaching is strongly and warmly Evangelical."

"He has a certain great-heartedness, and a passionate, irrepressible desire to bring others to the Saviour whom he finds so precious that people of all shades of belief, and no belief, are carried along, for the time at least, by the same enthusiasm that seems to possess him. Out of twenty or more of his sermons which we have heard, there has not been one which would have been unsuitable for a revival meeting. Whatever the subject, the central thought is always the cross of Christ—the goodness of the gospel to a sinful soul."

These things recall the Boston of colonial days, where, when a stranger entered its precincts, before he could be accepted, he was questioned and made to give an account of himself. The inquiring looks now directed upon the new preacher, the criticism to which he was subjected, were the Boston greeting. Philadelphia had a different way. It had not the suspicion of the stranger as such. It knew a good thing when it saw it, and did not spoil its enjoyment by over-anxious questioning. It was not perhaps so easy a thing for Boston to bow before Phillips Brooks as it had been for Philadelphia.

The popular verdict on the preaching of Phillips Brooks was more important than the judgment of the critics. He stepped at once into the same relative position he had held in Philadelphia. Trinity Church on Summer Street was crowded with eager hearers. It was almost unseemly the way in which the people claimed him, regardless of the privileges of those whose special minister he was. Precedents and vested rights, distinctions of pewholders, the authority of the sexton, seemed like an impertinence when Phillips Brooks was to preach. It was a trying situation for the parishioners, accustomed to associate worship with calmness and dignity, and with ample accommodation in the high-backed pews. It was no slight annoyance when they sought access to their pews to find them occupied by strangers, whose apologies magnified the grievance. Mr. Dillon, the sexton, strove to rise to an emergency wholly unlike anything he had hitherto known in his long administration. He tried to sort the people who presented themselves for admission, sending some to the galleries, and allowing others, whom he judged more fit, to occupy the waste spaces in the pews on the floor, but his expedients were futile.[1] The people became indignant and vented their anger on "the grim and truculent sexton, who acted as if he owned the church." Complaints found their way to the newspapers, with accounts of the "most disgraceful scenes ever enacted within the walls of a Protestant church." Many who came were unfamiliar with the ways of the Episcopal Church; they regarded the Morning and Evening Prayer as "introductory exercises" before the sermon could be reached. They rejoiced at least that "Mr. Brooks ran it off so rapidly." Mr. Brooks did what he could to facilitate matters. The pews in the galleries were declared free, and after pewholders had taken their seats the church was thrown open to all. But this was no temporary evil to be cured by any expedient. It lasted as long as Phillips Brooks remained the rector of Trinity Church. Bishop Eastburn continued for a while to attend the services at Trinity. But he was not accustomed to see people flocking in crowds to the proclamation of the gospel. He was not altogether sure that the new preacher was "sound in his views," and he betook himself to the roomier spaces of St. Paul's.

The many descriptions of Phillips Brooks and of his preaching, when he made his first appearance in Boston, it is impossible to reproduce, but at least reference should be made to them. The time never came when people tired of portraying him or of writing their impressions. Those who wrote were not more eager to rehearse than were the thousands who had not heard or seen for themselves eager to read what was written. It is part of the story of his life to give him in his relations with the great body of people who were sure that something unknown before in the history of the pulpit was now enacting, and that it behooved them to catch and preserve each slightest accent, as a sacred responsibility. They described his appearance as though in this case the

---

[1] In Mr. Dillon's view of the situation, the end to be aimed at was to reduce the numbers who sought admittance to the church. "He once came to me in the vestry room," said Mr. Brooks, "to tell me of a method he had devised for this purpose, 'When a young man and a young woman come together, I separate them'; and he expected me to approve the fiendish plan."

symmetry of form and beauty of countenance were in some mysterious way the counterpart of the spirit within. Each slightest peculiarity in his manner or bearing—in his dress, or his attitude in the pulpit, the quality of his voice, the glance of his eye—was noted and commented on. All alike were agreed as to the avoidance in his preaching of anything like sensationalism. There was no effort to arrest or to hold attention, no tricks or artifices to produce effect, no attempt whatever to be impressive; indeed according to ordinary rules of rhetoric or oratory he ought to have made no impression, for he defied them and set them at nought. Of his reading of the service it was noted that it was with "a rapid, breathless, almost stuttering delivery, and yet with a certain impulsive and pleading earnestness."

Where was the secret of his power, the hiding of his strength? Those who describe or comment answer the question in various ways. Some thought that he had no remarkable qualities of voice or elocution or gesture, others felt in his voice a wonderful force of appeal. All admired and praised his literary merit, the grace of his style, the beauty of his sentences. But the power of the man did not lie in things like these. "His power consists in his simplicity," said one, "in his earnestness and strength, exhibited in the expression of a theology free from the narrowness and technicalities of those dogmatic schemes which make religion ridiculous and weigh it down." Another said: "Of course he has a fine intellect, but it is the warm, earnest heart guiding the intellect that gives him such influence over his hearers." Still another: "He knows what is in us all. He speaks out of the common experience and comes right to the heart of men." And again thought another:

"His secret does not lie in his thought or his style; not in his utterance, which is rapid almost to incoherency, and marred by an awkward habit of misreading his writing; but in his evident honesty of conviction, sincerity of purpose, and earnestness of desire,—he does not think of himself or of the impression he is making; also, in that he approaches men on the side of their hopefulness. He is a man of exceptionally intellectual abilities, but the moral qualities are so obvious and forceful as to make the other seem secondary."

The secret of his strength may baffle, but of the effect he wrought there could be no doubt:

"His power is what no one less gifted than he can describe to another who has not felt it. It seems to come from a deep, personal experience which gives his message authority. When he preaches you are carried away to the need of men and your own shortcomings, and have no present consciousness of the personality of the speaker. A transparent medium is the purest. You do not think of Phillips Brooks till Phillips Brooks gets through with his subject."

"As he [the preacher] is lifted by his theme into a rarefied atmosphere, and with a marvellous faith catches a glimpse of still higher summits to be reached, like a mountain climber, scaling from crag to crag, you are rapidly borne along with him, till the worries of earth look very trifling from the crest where he pauses."

"When he reaches his sermon and plunges into his subject, as if it were a message from heaven, delivered for the first time to mortals, so fresh and earnest it is that the real height of the man's power is reached."

" The power of the man lies in the fulness of his nature, his thought, his affections, his purpose, and his speech. There is a great deal of him, and he lets himself out without reserve, without affectation, without conceit, without meanness. His sermon flows from its large fountain head in full, continuous course, now in easy talk, and now in swelling volume, and now in dashing force, until it pours into the open sea under the eternal heaven, and carries you on its grand tide to its glorious vision."

The following account by a person belonging to another religious communion who attended the ministry of Phillips Brooks for several months, betrays a most intelligent observer, and is among the most successful attempts to analyze the impression he made:

"Of three points which make this ministry especially attractive we notice, first, an extraordinary mental clearness and precision, which make every word aid in guiding the hearer straight to the point intended; which admits no redundance in its beautiful and finished expression, and, in its most glowing imagery and felicitous illustration, never gives the idea of external ornamentation, but rather deepens the impression of the truth to be conveyed as by the exposition of a purely natural analogy or pre-existing correspondence between things divine and human. And secondly, we are impressed by its rare *persuasiveness*,—a power of taking for granted assent, which almost compels it, an emphasis laid on points of agreement, rather than on those of difference,—so that we find ourselves addressed from the broad ground of a common humanity rather than from the narrow platform of doctrinal distinctions, and are led to recognize the central truths which underlie and comprehend all our diversities of opinion. But once more, and including all the rest, we find in this preaching a depth of thought and purpose, a scorching analysis of character and motive, that cuts clean through the crust of conventionalism (whether of worldliness or religion), and takes us to those depths (shall we say?) or lifts us to those heights where we are set face to face with eternal realities, in whose sight the poor routine of our daily life is transfigured with new hope, made quick with grateful impulse and weighty with sacred meaning."

These testimonies belong to the first years of Phillips Brooks's ministry in the old Trinity Church on Summer Street, while he was making the conquest of Boston. They may suffice to show how the city was moved at his coming. Those were wisest who accepted the situation as inevitable, recognizing that some phenomenal power was in evidence; something that was real and abiding, and as deep and mysterious as the mystery of life in this world. Still, it was a disturbing experience in all the churches. The large congregations were made up of all classes of people.

"The packed congregations of old Trinity [says one] represent the best intellect, the most cultivated minds, as well as the richest families in Boston."

"It is pleasant [says another] to see Phillips Brooks's audience and to analyze it. I had expected that it was exclusively of the more educated classes, but it is not; from the place where I sat last Sunday evening I could pick out easily enough the sewing girls, the Boston clerks, the men of leisure and of study, the poor old women with their worn and pinched and faded, but thoughtful, earnest faces; and it was a dear sight, all those classes and conditions of men riveted to the countenance of Phillips Brooks and hanging on his lips."

There had been some current rumors that Mr. Brooks was dissatisfied in his new sphere, as there were also expectations in Philadelphia that he might return. But in 1872 it had become clear that he was finally identified with the city of his birth.

" It is easy to see that Phillips Brooks has found his true sphere in Boston, and those fond souls that dream of his return to Philadelphia, disappointed with his success here, may safely put away that delusive hope. He has not been long in Boston, but Boston knows how to improve her own advantages, and Phillips Brooks is already a household deity in her complacent pantheon. Harvard has taken him under her wing, and he is already one of her magnates. Boston, secular Boston, quotes him familiarly and scarcely remembers that he ever lived out of sight of Bunker Hill. Philadelphia appreciated and valued him. Boston appropriates and canonizes him, and there is only one thing that Boston will never do with him, and that is to spoil him as an honest, earnest, fearless minister and man."

It had also become clear that he was not to be "Church- or city-limited," that he could not be shut in by any lines. He was claimed as belonging to the Church at large. In the city and in the suburbs he preached in churches of every name. Three times on every Sunday he preached as a rule, and as there were not Sundays enough to go around he preached on week-day evenings, and whenever he preached it was the event of the moment. On the third Sunday evening in January, 1870, he preached for the first time in St. John's Chapel, belonging to the Episcopal Theological School, a memorable occasion, for it was the beginning of a practice to be continued full seven years before it came to an end. On the third Sunday evening in every month, during all this time, he was to be found in the pulpit of the chapel, till his regular appearance became a feature of Cambridge life. From the first Sunday that he preached till the last, the chapel was densely packed, the congregation accommodating themselves in the spaces allotted to the clergy, around and beneath the pulpit, and during the sermon the doorways were thronged with hearers. Long before the service began people were to be seen wending their way toward Brattle Street, willing to wait an hour in the church to secure their seats. The congregation was composed of those who profess and call themselves Christians and of those who do not. Professors and students of Harvard College availed themselves of the opportunity in large numbers. The spectacle was an inspiring one at Trinity Church in Boston, but not more inspiring or significant than that which the seat of Harvard University afforded.

This was the first approach of Phillips Brooks to the students of Harvard College. He did not preach in Appleton Chapel until 1873. In the meantime, from 1870, he took a Bible class in the college, composed mostly of members of the St. Paul's Society.

Quite as striking was his recognition in secular Boston. He rose quickly to the place of a foremost citizen whose presence at every civic function seemed indispensable to its completeness. On such occasions he took his part with dignity and gravity, yet never without the sense of amusing incongruity in the formal association with distinguished citizens to whom as a boy in Boston he had been accustomed to look up with reverence. In February, 1871, he was present at a meeting in Music Hall, whose aim was to awaken public interest in the erection of a museum of fine arts. A distinguished array of leading citizens occupied seats upon the platform; among the speakers were Ralph Waldo Emerson and Edward Everett Hale.

"Mr. Brooks in his remarks maintained that this was a thing of the people and for the people. There was a certain hardness and want of development in American character on its æsthetic side; an art museum would awaken those large ideas of life and nature which nothing but the art feeling can awake,—a boundless good, the new feeling of unworldliness. The passion of our people to go abroad, when we have so much natural beauty at home, was not strange; man needs man's as well as nature's work, and hence Americans flock to the galleries of the Old World. He spoke of what he gained as a Boston boy in the Latin School out of the old room which contained the wonderful casts of Laocoön and Apollo. He thought that an art museum would help every minister in Boston in the effort to lift the people crushed by the dead weight of worldliness to higher things. He spoke [says the reporter] with more than his usual earnestness and eloquence, and was frequently applauded."

He was present as chaplain at the third reunion of the Army of the Potomac, in 1871. In introducing Mr. Brooks, General Meade spoke of the eminent services he had rendered during the war, not only by his eloquence in the pulpit, but by his ministrations in the hospitals to the sick and dying. He attended a large meeting at Music Hall in commemoration of Italian unity, and spoke. He was the chaplain of the Bunker Hill Monument

16

Association at its meeting on June 17, 1871, and in the fall of this year he made the prayer at the laying of the corner-stone of Memorial Hall of Harvard University. When the Grand Duke Alexis visited Boston in 1872, the festivities were concluded with a banquet at the Revere House, at which Hon. Robert C. Winthrop presided, who introduced Mr. Brooks as already a power in the community. Mr. Brooks, in his remarks, dwelt on this feature in Russian history, that all Russian life and government were everywhere pervaded with religion,—a religion different from ours, which had yet a great work to do in the world. He described the growth of the Græco-Russian Church, claiming that the great work it had done for civilization should be recognized.

In 1872 he preached the sermon before the Ancient and Honorable Artillery Company at its two hundred and thirty-fourth anniversary. The sermon, afterwards published, was a notable one, from the text in Revelation xii. 7: "And there was war in heaven." Among the striking passages was this:

"Force has a divine mission. It was not to be invoked save for divine tasks, never for the mere brutalities of selfishness, or ambition, or jealousy, or worldly rage, or for the mere punctilios of national dignity. So far as war had justification in a principle it was this,—that what men think and what men feel should incorporate itself in action. The late civil war was not the manifestation of the military passion, but the passion of civil life, the passion of home, the passion of education, the passion of religion. It was not war but peace that fought, strange as the paradox may seem. This was the claim by which our republic may, with no unreasonable pride, boast to stand among nations as Washington among men, first in war, first in peace; first in war *because* first in peace."

At the Peace Jubilee, Boston commemorated in 1872 the reign of universal peace by erecting a large temporary edifice known as the Coliseum. The music was furnished by a choir consisting of several thousands of voices, with a correspondingly large orchestra. At the formal opening Phillips Brooks was invited to make the prayer.

There were opportunities, however, to take part in civic solemnities which he declined. Such was the invitation by the city of Boston to deliver the oration on the Fourth of July ín 1871. He drew a distinction between the sermon and the oration or lecture. He had come to some resolution to abide by the limitations of the pulpit, if limitations they were. It would have been easy at this moment for him to have been drawn into lines of literary activity. He was received in literary circles in Boston as one of their own number. But when he was urged by the editor to write articles for *The Atlantic Monthly*, the invitation was declined.

Amidst many appeals to his sympathy the cause of children and of young people was most near his heart. The two organizations of the Young Men's Christian Union and the Young Men's Christian Association possessed him as if he were their own. These are included in the educational institutions with which from the first, and in later years, he allowed himself to be identified as he did with no other cause. From the time he came to Boston he proved the teachers' ally and friend, and there was a spontaneity in the action of educational institutions which sought his aid. In 1870 he was elected an overseer of Harvard College. In 1871 he was appointed on the State Board of Education, in which capacity he visited annually the normal schools of Massachusetts. He went to various academies, colleges, and schools to make addresses. As an overseer at Harvard, he was one of the Board of Visitors at the Harvard Divinity School. He soon came into close relations with the Episcopal Theological School in Cambridge. He retained his position as a trustee of the Philadelphia Divinity School, and in 1870 he went to Philadelphia to preach before its alumni. To these many addresses he brought careful and elaborate preparation. He was maturing his distinctive principle, afterwards to appear in books in more impressive and final form; asking himself the fundamental question of his own youthful preparation, How is the power to be brought to bear upon the will? The question of education was only in another form the problem of the pulpit. Thus in one of his note-books he gives hints of the thoughts passing through his mind:

"The whole educational idea needs revision and is getting it. All these years there have been a few influences called education, but others have been doing a large part of the work. The man at thirty—what has made him what he is? Now these are things claiming recognition. The question is how far they can be brought into the methods of a school, and how far a general basis can be found common to all trades. There is hope of this to some extent."

It took a long time, however, before he ceased to hunger for Philadelphia. Indeed he never quite outgrew his longing. Philadelphia remained the city of joy and beauty; it stood for the romance of his life, the home of immortal youth. To his brother Arthur, who asked him as the year 1869 was closing whether he was satisfied that he had done right in coming to Boston, he answered that he would prefer to wait and tell him at the end of another year. Three times within his first three months in Boston he visited Philadelphia. To his friend Miss Mitchell he writes:

"I am afraid I shall be dreadfully jealous of any one who steps into my place at Holy Trinity in spite of my great desire to see it filled, which is very unreasonable and womanly in me of course, but natural. I am seeing my people and like them very much indeed. There are many more young people among them than I had supposed. I do not feel as much as I expected the embarrassment of old associations. . . . My visit was very bright and pleasant. I cannot tell you how pleasant it is to sink out of the strain and tension of this new life into the long-tried friendship of my few kind friends. Two weeks from to-night I shall be at your board again. Till then I am impatient. Christmas has been as pleasant as strangers could make it.

"Trinity is doing beautifully, the church is full, the lecture on Wednesday evenings is crowded, we are just starting a mission, our collections have doubled what they were, the people have a mind to work. There is no opposition worth speaking of to the idea of a new church, and we shall get it very soon. If anybody says that I am disappointed in Boston, tell them from me it is not so. I knew just what to expect, and I have found just what I expected. Last Sunday evening I preached for the first time at Cambridge at the new chapel. It was crowded mostly with students, and all went off very well. I am to go there once a month." (January 20, 1870.)

"The thing that dissatisfies me most this winter is the way I have had to live and work. I have read nothing for three months, and, though I have had a very pleasant time indeed, yet three months is a big slice to take clean out of one's life and give away. But things will be better in this respect by and by, and meanwhile I am getting a whole shelf full of books, that I mean to read in that golden day which is always just ahead when I have leisure enough." (January 24, 1870.)

"I have undertaken what I expect to be very much interested in, a Bible class for Lent in college at Cambridge, where there are a good many young men who desire it, and who came and asked me for it. . . . I can't tell you how much I am depending on my next visit to Philadelphia. . . ."

"Have you read Emerson's new volume [*Letters and Social Aims*]? How delightful it is! I speak not from the point of a Bostonian, but with the mouth of absolute humanity. Is n't it delightful to have a creature so far outside of all our ordinary toss and tumble, describing life as if it were a smooth, intelligible, well-oiled machine, running along without noise on the planet Jupiter, and seen by him with a special telescope and then described to us, instead of being this jarring, jolting, rattling old coach, which almost drives us crazy with its din, and won't be greased into silence? It 's a capital calm book to read at night before you go to bed, but I don't think it would go in the morning right after breakfast, with the day's work before you." (March 9, 1870.)

"Have you read Kent Stone's story [*The Invitation Heeded*] of his conversion? As an appeal it seems to me powerful, as an argument weak. It may touch some people strongly. Poor fellow! there is something dreadfully sad in a man telling himself and the world over and over again that he is happy, as he does for so many hundred pages." (June 8, 1870.)

On June 28 he sailed for Europe, to spend the summer in a pedestrian trip through Switzerland and the Tyrol. He first realized the existence of war by its interference with the Miracle Play at Ober-Ammergau. As to the war, which he regarded as wicked and unnecessary, his sympathies were with Germany, while France seemed to him insolent and arrogant beyond herself. One of the chief drawbacks he experienced in travelling was the shortness of the beds. He writes to Frederick, "You and I are too long; you will have an awful time with the beds when you come into these parts." He speaks of having escaped from bed at an untimely hour, "because I could not stretch out straight or make the narrow bedclothes come over me." He was in Paris on the 28th of August, having met with no obstacles in getting there, though under constant apprehension. The city was still gay, even when the Prussians were believed to be only two or three days distant and the memorable siege was impending. Again he was in Paris on the 5th of September, "too busy and exciting a day to write; there was a bloodless revolution, and we went to bed last night under a republic. I saw the whole thing, and was much interested in seeing how they make a government here."

After his return from Europe he writes:

"I got in New York Stanley's new volume of *Essays*, some of which I have seen before, but all of which are interesting. There is an essay on the 'Religion of the Nineteenth Century' which is the best statement I have seen of the characteristics and prospects of what we call the 'Broad Church' movement. Do read it. His views about Church and State I can't agree with, but it is the only strong ground on which an Englishman can put the question, and for all Englishmen must have weight. What capital English he always writes!" (October 17, 1870.)

"I am reading Huxley's new *Lay Sermons*. How clever it is, how much the man knows, and how brilliantly he writes. But it is like most "Small Books on Great Subjects," most books for the people that popularize science. It is patronizing and mince-meaty, and he is particularly belligerent about the theologians in a way that does not do credit to his discrimination or temper. . . . It does not seem as if it could be only a year ago that I preached my last sermon in Holy Trinity, and we all travelled together to New York the next morning. It seems a half-dozen years at least. My first year here in Boston has been on the whole successful. I have done as much with Trinity as I had any right to expect to do, and we are on a footing to do more now. But it has not been the pleasant life that the old one was, and, while there has been much to enjoy, there has been more anxiety and worry than ever was of old. But I dare say I shall like it better. Meanwhile don't think I am blue." (November 10, 1870.)

"I don't feel theological this morning. It is too near Christmas, which always upsets theology entirely. I have never been able to write a Christmas sermon yet that was in the least a theological satisfaction to me or anybody else. I am so glad that Christmas is coming, and yet I hardly know why. This is the only day whose associations have much power over me. I don't care a great deal about anniversaries, but Christmas, with its whole spirit, into which we all seem to slip so easily year after year, is exceedingly beautiful to me, and, as I go about the streets, the details in these few days beforehand, which are vulgar enough in themselves—men mounting up spruce boughs in churches and men carrying home turkeys by the legs—all give me ever so much pleasure. And I like it more and more as I get older." (December 23, 1870.)

"The lecture Wednesday evening did n't go very well. The night was stormy, and, though I don't care much for a full audience for the name of the thing, I need it for inspiration, and when I see a small audience I lose the impersonalness of the thing. I think of individuals and that always puts me out. But it never is yet the same thing talking in Trinity that it used to be in the old time speaking from the dear old platform." (January 11, 1871.)

"I have been quite stirred upon the subject of prophecy in writing a sermon for last Sunday on Cephas. I am quite convinced that there were two Isaiahs. . . . Queer people come to consult me here. To-day there was a man who had been to England and got into some set of fanatics there and come home calling himself a Christadelphian. To-morrow, like as not, it will be a sceptic of the wildest incredulity." (January 18, 1871.)

"One evening this week I had my Cambridge boys, the fifteen senior members of the St. Paul's Society, in at my room to spend the evening with me, a noble set of fellows, manly and true, and helped instead of hurt by their religion. I take great pleasure in them." (February 3, 1871.)

"I was reading last night one of Robertson's lectures on Poetry, with its extravagant glorification of war, which is so amazing in a right-minded man like him. It seems to have been the last remnant of brutality in a nature which had been almost everywhere cultured and refined far above it. But who can look at the last ten years on both continents and not call war horrible? Let us trust this one is over. Good must come of it, horrible as the process is. Whoever was to blame for it, we surely can't help being thankful that Prussia and not France is to be master in Europe." (February 13, 1871.)

"This is one of the evenings when I wish myself in Philadelphia; not that anything particular is the matter with Boston, but I have an evening to myself and I am tired of reading, and there is nobody in particular that I can go and see without its being a visit, which I don't feel up to. Nobody's house where I can go and smoke and be pleasantly talked to, and answer or not, as I please. I know one such house in another town where

I don't live any longer,　But I am not there, and I must make the best of it."　(March 7, 1871.)

"As to English Church matters, I am thoroughly content with the Voysey decision, and I think the Convocation debate about Vance Smith disgraceful."　(March 15, 1871.)

"This evening I have been reading Tyndall's new book of Alpine stories, which is very charming, bringing back the fascination of that wonderful country and exciting one as all such accounts of venturesome climbing unaccountably do.　The style is charming, and the man, with his splendid health and enjoyment of nature and his current of sentiment, is delightful."　(July 25, 1871.)

"Are all Hutton's essays like the one which I have just been reading?　It is on *The Incarnation and the Laws of Evidence*, and shows a breadth and purity and devoutness of mind which gives one great delight.　I would rather have a Unitarian read it than any book I know; and if one thinks that Broad Churchmanship is necessarily hard or indifferent, of the Whately or the —— style, nothing could better convince him otherwise than the warmth and earnestness of this little book, which has so evidently come out of a man's soul."　(August 10, 1871.)

The summer of 1871 was spent in Boston, in accordance with a rule, though it was not invariable, of taking the alternate summers in Europe.　Throughout the summer he preached regularly at Trinity Church in the morning, and at St. Mark's, West Newton Street, in the evening.　Both churches were free to strangers.　As the season opened in the fall, he wrote:

"The old round of parish duties, which I have gone to afresh every autumn for twelve years, has opened again, and I have been rather surprised at myself to find that I take it up with just as much interest as ever.　I suppose that other men feel it of their occupations, but I can hardly imagine that any other profession can be as interesting as mine.　I am more and more glad that I am a parson."

"How delightfully lazy it was in Philadelphia, and Boston seems so driven and hurried.　People here seem possessed to do something without much care for what they do.　The mere passion of restlessness is in the Yankee blood and partly in the East winds. . . I have had an awfully uneventful life.　Things happen to other people, but not to me.　I am ashamed to look back over any day, though I was never busier in my life. It seems made up of such wretched little details, and yet I would n't be anything else but a parson for the world. I wonder often that the work keeps up such a perpetual freshness when the days are so monotonous."

"I know nothing of the grace of sickness. It seems to me terrible, the whole idea of suffering, but even more of weakness and weariness."

"It is my birthday and I am thirty-six years old. It seems a little strange but not unpleasant, and although I have had a pretty time indeed so far, and would be glad to go back and do it all over again yet I am not miserable that I cannot, and I am still rather absurdly hopeful about the future. To have passed out of young manhood altogether and find myself a middle aged man is a little sobering, but I only hope that all the young fellows who come after me will have as good a time as I have had. . . . We have been seeing the Russian Grand Duke, who appears to be a fine, manly, sensible fellow." (December 13, 1871.)

"Last Sunday I spent at New Haven, and enjoyed it exceedingly. Stayed with Dr. Harwood, who is a fine, studious Broad Churchman; preached for him in the morning, and in the evening preached in his church for the Berkeley Association of Yale College. The church was crowded, and Congregational professors sat in the chancel. I had never seen Yale College before, and was interested in its size and life. It is not equal to Cambridge, but it is a great college still. . . . Have you read Lightfoot's *Commentary on Philippians?* Do get it and read the "Essay on the Christian Ministry." It does seem to me to finish the Apostolic Succession Theory completely."

"The California plan is not settled yet, but I think I shall go. . . . Though it would be folly to talk about being run down, I am conscious of having been on the strain rather too long. I have preached twice every Sunday, and generally three times, since I got home from Europe, a year ago last September. I am preaching badly, and the trip will do me more good now than at any other time."

"I don't think that parsons really are so bad. I suspect that they are human, and I see but little evidence practically of apostolic succession, but I think there are not many who would refuse to see a small-pox patient, or who would give up parish visiting because the small-pox was in town."

"I get so tired of talking with tongue and pen that I don't feel equal to hearing myself in one unnecessary word. To-day, for instance, I have preached a Price Lecture, and attended two funerals, and carried on a mission meeting among our poor folk, and had a regular Wednesday evening meeting (lecture). I am sure that I shall hear my own dreary voice reading the service in my dreams. I have been looking through Hawthorne's *Italian Diary*,—an interesting book that it would have been wicked to publish if it had not been the work of a man who took delight in dissecting himself in public." (March 8, 1872.)

"I have been reading a new book, which is a rare thing with me nowadays. This one delights me exceedingly. It is Dr. Sears's book on St. John (*The Fourth Gospel, the Heart of Christ*). Do get it and enjoy it. It is so rich and true and wise. All that he has written before is excellent, but this is best of all. I have a copy of his *Regeneration*, which you gave me once. . . . Have you read the *Life of Hookham Frere?* It is very interesting. Some of his translations are wonderfully well done."

"I have perfected my plans for Europe now. The 27th of June is the day, and Denmark, Sweden, and Norway are the places, with possibly a little of Scotland thrown in. Judge Gray goes with me. We shall represent to Norwegians that we are insignificant specimens of the Amercan size, and I shall tell them that they ought to see two giants we have at home, called —— and ——, if they want to see the true grandeur of the American pulpit."

"I suppose it is necessary that one should feel that his time is not limited before he can enjoy it thoroughly. At least it is so with me. I hate to be hurried. That will be one great advantage of heaven. . . . We shall have plenty of time for all that our hands find to do. I sometimes have suspicions that if I could live for five hundred years I might come to something and do something here. All is going on beautifully about the new church. Some of the people of their own notion got up a subscription to buy an extra piece of land, and in a few days raised $75,000, and are going on now to make it a hundred thousand, so that the church will be really something very fine. We shall have in all something pretty near half a million to put into it.

The summer of 1872 was spent by Mr. Brooks in northern Europe. Mr. Robert Treat Paine accompanied him and was with him for a month; after that he was alone, dependent on acquaintances made in travelling. The summer included several weeks in Norway. From Norway he passed to Sweden. He was delighted with Stockholm: he went to Upsala for its university and cathedral, and to meditate upon Scandinavian mythology. From Sweden he went to Finland and thence to St. Petersburg, Warsaw, and Moscow, recalling historical associations, commenting on ways and customs, drawing his own inferences, but especially interested in the churches, which he made it a rule to attend on every possible occasion. He returned from Russia to Berlin, stopped at Copenhagen and Hamburg, then went to Paris, where he met his brother, and together they sailed for home. A friend of Mr Brooks contributes this reminiscence of the summer:

"When Brooks was approaching Christiania he heard that Prince Oscar was to come on board the steamer on which he was travelling. As the ship anchored, the royal barge drew near amidst a thunder of salutes from the forts. When the Prince reached the deck he stood for a moment between the sailors drawn up on either side of the gangway, and noticing Brooks, who stood behind the sailors, said in excellent English, waving his hand toward the city, 'Is it not a loyal people?' The prince then retired to the end of the ship roped off for his exclusive use. At midnight, Brooks was smoking a last cigar before turning in, sitting on a part of the deck far removed from the royal enclosure, when a tall man wrapped in a cloak drew near. It proved to be the Prince, who said in English, 'Will you oblige me with a light?' When he had lit his cigar he sat down and entered into a long conversation, asking many intelligent questions about America, especially about the judiciary, the method of administering justice in the courts, etc. He spoke like a man conscious that he had come to a position of responsibility, and anxious to learn all that might be of use to him. The next day the Prince disembarked. Before leaving the ship, as he stood at the gangway, he reached over the line of sailors behind which Brooks was standing, and, shaking hands with him, said, '*Au revoir*. The earth is round and we'll meet again.'"

A few extracts from his note-book give us an idea of the deeper moods of the traveller, in this summer of 1872:

"As we travel, it seems sometimes as if ninety-nine hundredths of the people in this world had so hard a time, could find so little in their lot to enjoy. The reassurance must come from considering that joy in mere life, often dumb, brutish, and unconscious, but very real, which every creature has, the luxury of mere existence to which we cling, for which we slave, and which we really do enjoy.

"As we travel, this impresses us much, I think,—the uniformity of nature under all the endlessly various changes of men and their ways and customs, always the same sky and ground and grass. It is a striking picture of the universality of the primary and simple emotions and affections, beneath the changing aspects of men's more complicated life,—this sight everywhere of the simplest signs of the simplest emotions. The child's smile, curiosity, love, rage, give us the same idea.

"After all, it is the deepest and not the superficial interest of life in which men sympathize most and come together; in religion above all other things, and as regards religion in those things which are deepest, not in forms and ordinances, but in the sense of sin, the sense of God, the hope of perfectness. I was struck with it as I travelled in Norway, where those whom I had not understood, who had lived a different life all the week, seemed as I saw them in church on Sunday to be so perfectly intelligible. The value of Sunday as thus the *common* day, the day of worship."

Out of these reflections was born a sermon on the text, "Until I went into the sanctuary of God":

"The sanctuary of God, the place of solved problems. I think one cannot go into any temple which men have built to worship God in, in however false a way, cannot enter a mosque or the most superstitious of cathedrals in a right spirit, without seeming to feel the influence of some such spiritual illumination on the problems that he has left outside in the hot street. I dare not despise the poor Russian crossing himself, etc."

"I went yesterday into a bookstore to find something to read on my journey hither, and the only legible thing that I could hit on—strange company for an orthodox travelling parson—was a cheap copy of Renan's 'Les Apôtres.' I read it through yesterday, and it was dreadful; the studious putting of the supernatural and the spiritual out of our knowledge, and almost out of our existence, the making of life its own complete solution. I pitied him for his flippant satisfaction, every page I read. What can such an one do with death?"

These journeys of Phillips Brooks constitute the breaks in a somewhat monotonous round of triumph and honors, of numberless engagements, of constantly recurring social functions. They were his only recreation, his only mode of escape from the burdens of the life that now began to press ever more heavily upon him. He had ceased riding horseback; his walking was mainly confined to his round of parish visiting. Occasionally he walked when he went to Cambridge to preach. Now and then he mentions bathing, fishing, and sailing, as when he visits some parishioner. He appeared so well, however, that one would hardly suppose that he was the worse for neglect of exercise. Yet there were hints suggestive of danger. In 1871 he was for several days confined to the house with a bad throat. He wrote describing his illness to Dr. Mitchell of Philadelphia, admitting that he had been alarmed. Here was his vulnerable point. He was putting a burden upon his voice to which it was not equal. Those who were experts in the use of the voice were convinced that he did not understand the right use of the vocal organs. When he was fairly launched in his sermon, in the storm and stress of his great effort, one seemed to hear the voice creaking and groaning, as if overstrained, and the result was sometimes harsh and unmusical. There were fears that his voice might fail him,—fears in which he shared, and which sometimes depressed him as he thought of the future. But the immediate danger passed away, and the voice recovered from its ill usage, though somewhat impaired.

This was the time when he should have married and formed a home of his own. His friends introduced reminders of the subject in their letters, but his reply was only that the coming woman had not yet appeared. When he first came to Boston he took rooms at 34 Mount Vernon Street, but complained of the want of sunlight, and soon transferred himself to the Hotel Kempton on Berkeley Street. He was now creating a new life in the hosts of friends who gathered about him. He made it a rule to dine with his father and mother every Sunday, after morning service. At his older brother's house, he found another home. He was greatly interested in the birth of his first niece as the starting of a new generation in the Brooks family. His youngest brother, John, he attended on his way through Harvard, as he had done with Frederick and Arthur. John graduated in 1872, and then the family succession at Harvard ceased. "Since I entered college," he writes, "in 1851, twenty years ago, we have had one there all the time."

It was a family event of peculiar interest when at the ordination of Arthur Brooks to the diaconate, his two elder brothers in the ministry were present, Frederick Brooks presenting the candidate, and Phillips Brooks preaching the sermon. The event took place in Trinity Church, June 25, 1870, Bishop Eastburn officiating. A brilliant career opened at once to the younger brother. His first parish was at Williamsport, Pennsylvania, where in a short time he witnessed as a result of his labors the erection of a new church. In 1872 he accepted a call to the parish of St. James in Chicago. The following letter was written to him by Phillips Brooks on the occasion of his brother's engagement:

"BOSTON, March 23, 1872. I write at once to say how sincerely and with all my heart I congratulate you upon your great happiness. Of course you are very happy, and you have the best right to be, for a life is a poor, imperfect sort of thing unless a man is married, and engagement is about the same thing. I hope it won't be a long engagement. Do be married and be wholly happy very soon. Life is n't long enough to waste any of it. . . ."

None were quicker than his old college friends and classmates to discern and rejoice in the signs of his greatness, many of them living in or near Boston, some of them his parishioners at Trinity. He felt at first some embarrassment at the revelation of his new and greater self to these associates of earlier years. Hardly had he become fixed in Boston when it seemed as if he were transferring to it his clerical friends of Philadelphia and rebuilding his old environment. Soon after Mr. Brooks came to Trinity, Dr. Vinton came to Boston as rector of Emmanuel Church. In 1870 his clerical friends were associated in a club called the "Clericus," which met on the first Monday evening in every month, organized after the plan of the Clericus in Philadelphia, already mentioned, if it could be called an organization which had no constitution or by-laws. It possessed a clerk who notified the members of the monthly meetings. In the course of years it developed a president in the person of Phillips Brooks, but no one ever knew exactly when or by what process he assumed the office. His right to it, however, was unquestioned. The meetings were held informally for a few years in the houses of the members, until finally Mr. Brooks insisted that they should meet regularly at his rooms. The social element on the whole was the most prominent feature of these evenings, despite the inevitable essay. There were some who thought that the meetings would be more profitable if the members were all required to speak in turn, but to this arrangement the president positively refused to listen. The talk should be spontaneous or not at all. If a member had anything to say let him wait his chance and then hold the floor if he could get it against some one else more anxious to be heard. It was practically Phillips Brooks's Club, and so it came to be generally known. It formed a prominent feature in his life, as it surely did in the lives of all its other members. Those who had the privilege of meeting him there saw him and heard him in familiar and yet impressive ways which will never be forgotten. He was seldom absent from its meetings; he kept track of absent members, and urged their attendance or reproved them for neglect.[1]

The demands upon him were so great even in these early years in Boston that one wondered how he found time for reading or sermon-writing. According to his diary there is rarely a day when he does not mention some dinner engagement. Breakfast was about the only meal that he took at his lodgings. He never gave the impression, however, of one who suffered from the burden of his duties, and never complained, except in familiar letters, that his life was not wholly to his mind. He attended concerts occasionally, especially the Oratorios given in Music Hall. He kept late hours, not generally retiring before twelve o'clock, but was always an early riser, breakfasting at half-past seven. He had one standing engagement where there was no objection to the lateness of the hour,—his Sunday evenings at Dr. Vinton's after his third service was over. If he found "the doctor favorable for conversation" the occasion was a prolonged one. Amid this multiplicity of engagements, he did secure

[1] The founders and original members of the Club were Phillips Brooks, Rufus W. Clark, C. A. L. Richards, Arthur Lawrence, William W. Newton, W. R. Huntington, A. V. G. Allen, James P. Franks, Charles H. Learoyd, George L. Locke, Henry L. Jones, Charles C. Tiffany, Percy Browne, Edmund Rowland, Leonard K. Storrs, Henry F. Allen, Rt. Rev. Thomas M. Clark, Treadwell Walden, James H. Lee, C. G. Currie, E. D. Tompkins, H. C. Cunningham.

time for reading. From 1871 he was a member of the Examining Committee of the Public Library in Boston, which served to keep new literature before him. His own library, already large, was rapidly growing. He continued to make it a rule to read books as they appeared, which every one else was reading, and so kept himself in contact with the literary trend of the moment. In poetry at this time there was Browning's *Ring and the Book* A. H. Clough's poems, Morris's *Earthly Paradise*, Robert Buchanan's poems, George Eliot's *Spanish Gypsy*, etc.; these he read.

"I indulged myself in a little piece of mediævalism in Rossetti's Poems, and as I read over the 'Blessed Damosel' last night I thanked you for it. Have you ever read the Poems? They are Pre-Raphaelitism in verse, very curious and very lovely in their way, but you need to go at them in the right mood, perfectly dreamy, entirely untroubled with practical affairs. . . . Q—— would n't like them because they don't preach the Gospel a bit, and C—— would n't like them because there is not a word of parish work in them; but they are very pretty, nevertheless, when you are a trifle tired with parish work." (December 27, 1870.)

There was different and more substantial reading in Hunt's *Religious Thought in England*, which he greatly admired, or Tulloch's *Rational Theology in the Church of England*. In other books which he was reading we get the reflection of the hour: Lecky's *History of Rationalism*, Darwin's *Descent of Man*, the writings of Herbert Spencer, Huxley, and Tyndall, whose *Prayer Gauge* suggested a sermon on prayer in which he maintained its objective as well as subjective effects; Matthew Arnold's *Culture and Anarchy*, Froude's *History of England*, Stanley's *Westminster Abbey*, and Parkman's *Jesuits in North America;* in biography, the lives of Lacordaire and of Lord Herbert of Cherbury, and the *Letters* of John Adams; in lighter books or novels, *Realmah.* Auerbach's *On the Heights, Wilhelm Meister*, and Lord Chesterfield's *Letters*. One period of history he continued to study with peculiar zest,—the English civil war and the age of the Commonwealth. He read anew *Cromwell's Letters* by Carlyle, taking notes as he read. He read Burnet, Clarendon, Hallam, and Nugent's *Memorials of Hampden.* Masson's *Life of Milton* sent him to Milton himself, and especially to the *Areopagitica.* Another author whom he valued and kept by him was Isaac Taylor. Wordsworth must be mentioned and Shakespeare particularly as writers to whom he was constantly recurring.

In his more distinctively religious reading, he was carrying out some larger purpose. He was studying the Fourth Gospel as the basis of Wednesday evening lectures; he had also begun a systematic study of the life of Christ. After the first six months of his rectorship at Trinity, during which he was making the acquaintance of the parish and wrote but a few sermons, he began with renewed zeal the task of sermon-writing, under a somewhat different impulse from that which had inspired the Philadelphia preaching. The religious situation was changing; the spirit of free inquiry had gone deeper; the difficulties begotten by the scientific spirit were to many overwhelming. These influences he had not felt so strongly in Philadelphia. There his task had been to arouse a living, fresher interest in what men already believed. Now he was called upon to meet the moods of those drifting away from the Christian faith. The question was before him how to be true to one's reason, to be free to accept new truth from whatever quarter, and yet to maintain the historic faith.

Two of his sermons in these early years in Boston were notable, as having an autobiographical value; both of them received his further approval by their choice for publication The sermon entitled "The Young and the Old Christian" from Deut. xxxiii. 16,[1] "The good will of him that dwelt in the bush," written in 1871, has the marks of the earlier Philadelphia manner when he rejoiced in discovering some unfamiliar passage of Scripture, whose meaning was not at once obvious. The thought of the sermon bears on the relation between the beginning and the end of the Christian life; on the process of growth in which the personal Christ becomes clearer to us in the years of mature manhood; so that whatever the years may bring in the accretions of knowledge or wisdom, we shall never be called on to renounce as unreal the vision of youth by the bush side when we first heard the voice of God in our ears. He protests against the nar-

---

[1] The sermon is published in the second volume of his sermons, *The Candle of the Lord, and other Sermons*, p. 39.

rowness and illiberality which many identified with the Christian faith: "Narrowness of view and sympathy is not unnatural in a new believer. It is very unnatural in the maturer Christian life."

"It is too apt to be the case that only by experience does the Christian reach this breadth of sympathy, which comes not from indifference, but from the profoundest personal earnestness. It is something wholly different from the loose toleration which men praise, which is negative, which cares nothing about what is absolutely true or false. . . . At present it seems to be assumed that narrowness is essential to positive belief, and that toleration can be reached only by general indifference. Not long ago I read this sentence in what many hold to be our ablest and most thoughtful journal: 'It is a law which in the present condition of human nature holds good, that strength of conviction is always in the inverse ratio of the tolerant spirit.'"

But if men can only be filled with the spirit of God, we "may still see some maturer type of Christianity, in which new ages of positive faith may still be filled with the broadest sympathy, and men tolerate their brethren without enfeebling themselves." To this end "there must be a larger and larger absorption of truth or doctrine into life."

"We hear all around us nowadays great impatience with the prominence of dogma—that is, of truth abstractly and definitely stated—in Christianity. And most of those who are thus impatient really mean well. They feel that Christianity, being a thing of personal salvation, ought to show itself in characters and lives. There they are right. But to decry dogma in the interest of character is like despising food as if it interfered with health. . . . Before the young Christian lie the doctrines of his faith, —God's being, God's care, Christ's incarnation, Christ's atonement, immortality. What has the old Christian with his long experience done with them? He holds them no longer crudely, as things to be believed merely. He has transmuted them into forms of life. . . . The young dogmatist boasts of his dogmas. The old saint lives his life."

Mr. Brooks was encountering divergent attitudes in regard to Christian faith: some were tenacious and defiant in maintaining the traditional doctrines; others were calling for elimination, or modification, or restatement; others rejected creeds altogether, or if there must be a creed, let it be made anew each day or year to meet the requirements of the passing hour. Under these circumstances he wrote his sermon on the words of St. Paul, "I have kept the faith." [1] During his summer in northern Europe in 1872, when his mind was at leisure to dwell upon his work, the words kept recurring to his mind, "I have kept the faith." He notes in his journal as a popular fallacy "that a man must change his views to show his freedom." He had before him "the danger of making one's opinions matters of faith." The question of training children brings the issue to a test. Shall they be brought up in the traditional faith? What is the result of the experiment which leaves them without religious tenets, until they arrive at maturer years? "What is the meaning of the Collect for Trinity Sunday, which asks of God that *He* would keep us in this faith? Is it merely a prayer that pride and obstinacy may be strengthened, or that He would show us a method of keeping ideas fixed? Exactly what did St. Paul mean by 'the faith'?" It is evident that he meant, whatever else may have been implied, "certain fixed belief," which he had received and not originated. The conclusion is "the possibility of counting some things settled and going on to develop them into life"; and the method is through obedience. No faith is kept except as it is obeyed. There is "a strange mixture of the moral element" in all the passages of the New Testament where "the faith" is mentioned. No faith can be truly kept except by discovering in it relations to life. So it must be with the doctrines of God, of the Incarnation, of the Trinity, of the Atonement, of Immortality.

The sermon was delivered at a moment when people were wondering at his preaching, unable to define his position to their satisfaction. This sermon gives the open secret. There is no bondage in holding to the historic faith as expressed in Christian doctrines, but rather through them lies the way to perfect freedom. The tendency of Christian doctrines is to expansion under the vital process which reveals in them a relation to life.

The impersonal character of entries in his note-book prevents one from discerning the motive out of which they spring. His fellow-traveller in Norway was abruptly summoned home by the death of a child. This is his comment when left alone to his

[1] *Sermons*, vol. i., p. 57.

reflections: "It seems as if a child's death and the keen, bitter pain it brings us let us see much of the feebleness of the intellectual powers to command our love,—of the possibility of that in which the intellectual was not at all developed holding us intensely."

Other extracts from his note-book follow:

"We have no descriptions of Jesus in the Gospels, only stories of what He did. The perfection of Biography. Contrast with novels."

"The difference between suffering and pain. Pain is accidental, suffering is essential. It is right and necessary that we should undergo and accept as our lot whatever comes in our way of work whether it is agreeable or disagreeable (and therefore note that the old Latin and Greek corresponding words were used of 'suffering' or 'experiencing' either pleasant or unpleasant things); but that pain in the sense of discomfort should accompany the acceptance is a mere accident, no more to be called absolutely 'right' or 'necessary' by the ascetic than, on the other hand, pleasure is by the voluptuary."

"'I will walk at liberty because I keep Thy commandments.' The liberty of law, Eden; the passage out of it, a passage into slavery. True liberty is harmony. The slavery of self-consciousness that comes with sin. That is the tree of knowledge. David, so free in his goodness, so cowardly in his sin. Sympathy with a law well kept, that is the best freedom."

"We may not always be consciously thinking of God, only we must think of all things through and in Him, as we do not always look at the Sun and yet see all things we know only by the Sun's shining."

"The danger, the terrible danger of false tests! . . . John Wesley says, 'Infidels know, whether Christians know it or not, that the giving up of witchcraft is in effect giving up the Bible.'"

"O Lord and Sovereign of my life, take from me the spirit of idleness, despair, love of power, and unprofitable speaking." (Prayer of St. Ephraim of Syria, in the Russian Liturgy.)

To Miss Mitchell he writes November 7, 1872:

"I don't like to hear you talk as you have in your last two letters about not living long. Not that I think death is dreadful in the least for the one who goes; he has the best of it; but it is dreadful to be left behind, and find how merely impossible to make new friends that are at all like the old. I am sure, too, that our friends must be more and not less to us in the other world than they are here, and that this world only begins friendships. Otherwise nothing could be more wretched. Only I shudder when I think how one's friends who have believed in him here will find him out there, and see what a humbug he was. I don't believe it will alienate them, though, and no doubt even there the humiliation will be good for him. Promise me that however you find me out to have been a delusion and a sham you won't give me up, for I forewarn you that you don't know me now, and if you ever do the discovery will be a shock to you. Which does n't mean that I ever murdered a parishioner or robbed a house, but only that I know myself better than you know me."

A site had been secured for a new church edifice, the architect had been engaged, and plans were under consideration, when the old edifice on Summer Street fell a prey to the flames in the great Boston fire on the night of November 4, 1872. Mr. Brooks's account of it is given in this letter to Miss Mitchell:

"BOSTON, November 12, 1872.

"We have had terrible days. Last Saturday night and Sunday were fearful. For a time it seemed as if the thing would never stop so long as there was anything left to burn. Everybody has suffered, almost everybody severely. Very many have lost all. Scores of my parishioners have been burned out. But the courage and cheerfulness of everybody is noble and delightful. It began about eight o'clock Saturday evening, and hour after hour it went on, growing worse and worse. Street after street went like paper. There were sights so splendid and awful as I never dreamed of, and now the desolation is bewildering. There was hard work enough to do all night, and though much was lost, something was saved. Old Trinity seemed safe all night, but towards morning the fire swept into her rear, and there was no chance. She went at four in the morning. I saw her well afire inside and out, carried off some books and robes, and left her. She burnt majestically, and her great tower stands now solid as ever, a most picturesque and stately ruin. She died in dignity. I did not know how much I liked the great gloomy old thing till I saw her windows bursting and the flame running along the old high pews. I feel that it was better for the church to go so than to be torn down stone by stone. Of course our immediate inconvenience is great, and we shall live in much discomfort for the next two years. We have engaged the Lowell Institute, a Lecture Hall that seats a thousand people, and shall begin service there next Sunday. . . .

"I can talk of nothing but the fire, and not of that coherently. Some day I will tell you all I can about it, but the horribleness of that night nobody can tell. . . ."

CHAPTER XI.

1873–1877.

ECCLESIASTICAL CONTROVERSIES. RELATION TO THE
EVANGELICAL SCHOOL. EXTRACTS FROM CORRES-
PONDENCE. THE SUMMER IN EUROPE. DEATH OF
FREDERICK BROOKS. SERVICES IN HUNTINGTON
HALL. EXTRACTS FROM NOTE-BOOKS. METHOD
OF PREPARING SERMONS. ESSAY ON COURAGE.
TESTIMONY OF PRINCIPAL TULLOCH. THE NEW
TRINITY CHURCH.

No active part was taken by Mr. Brooks in the controversies
within the Episcopal Church which culminated in the year 1873.
He was an interested spectator, watching the proceedings of
conventions and the trend which things were taking. Although
he was regarded as an Evangelical Churchman, yet so early as
1870 he found himself out of sympathy with the management
of the Evangelical Educational Society, whose object was to
assist young men in their preparation for the ministry. What
had moved his indignation was its policy of sending, to the young
men who wished to become its beneficiaries, a circular letter containing a series of questions or tests which they were required to
answer, in order to show that they were in sympathy with Evangelical tenets. When Mr. Brooks became aware that this policy
was approved by the Board of Managers and would not be abandoned, he wrote to the secretary of the society resigning his position upon the Board, pointing out the inconsistency of holding
the Scriptures as the supreme authority, which was above all tradition, and calling upon its beneficiaries to subscribe to texts,
which were only tradition in another form. He did not feel that
he himself could subscribe to the texts the society imposed. Not

long after this, he came to the conclusion that educational aid societies were undesirable and withdrew from the society altogether. He refused any longer to ask contributions to the society's treasury from his parish or to allow its secretary to make the annual appeal. But he confessed that the question was a puzzling one on which he could see no light. He still continued to aid theological students with gifts or loans of money, but not always with satisfactory results, and in some cases experienced grievous disappointment.

In separating himself from the managers of the Evangelical cause there was no break in his cordial relations with individuals who represented the Evangelical attitude as he understood it. He gave his name as usual to the petition to the General Convention, asking for relief in the use of the word "regenerate," in the Baptismal office, though without the slightest hope that the request would be granted. He proposed that the familiar petition be sent in as before, with the suggestion that it be printed in "Antique Type." He himself had no objection to the word "regenerate" as applied to Baptism.

When Bishop Eastburn died, in 1872, who for more than twenty-five years had been the rector of Trinity Church, Mr. Brooks paid a tribute to his memory from the pulpit, when he took occasion to speak of the Evangelical movement which the Bishop had represented. His words have the apparent tone of one speaking from the outside, but he was still within the circle from which he did not seek escape:

"The Evangelical movement had its zealous men here and there throughout the land. The peculiarities of that movement were an earnest insistence upon doctrine, and upon personal, spiritual experience, of neither of which had the previous generation made very much. Man's fallen state, his utter hopelessness, the vicarious atonement, the supernatural conversion, the work of the Holy Spirit,—these were the truths which the men of those days, who were what were called 'Evangelical' men, urged with the force of vehement belief upon their hearers. They were great truths. There were crude, hard, and untrue statements of them very often, but they went deep; they laid hold upon the souls and consciences of men. They created most profound experiences. They made many great ministers and noble Christians. It was indeed the work of God. To those of you who were his parishioners and friends, who heard him preach year after year, and knew what lay nearest to his heart, I need not say how entirely Bishop Eastburn was a man of this movement. His whole life was full of it. He had preached its Gospel in New York with wonderful success and power. He bore his testimony to it to the last in Boston. A faith that was very beautiful in its childlike reliance upon God; a sturdy courage which would have welcomed the martyrdom of more violent days; a complete, unquestioning, unchanging loyalty to the ideas which he had once accepted; a deep personal piety, which, knowing the happiness of divine communion, desired that blessedness for other souls; a wide sympathy for all of every name who were working for the ends which he loved and desired; these with his kindly heart and constancy in friendship made the power of the long ministry of Bishop Eastburn. The teaching of this parish through twenty-six years was most direct and simple. There was a dread, even, of other forms in which the same awakening of spiritual life was manifest. The High Churchman and the Broad Churchman found no tolerance. But the preacher was one whom all men honored, whose strong moral force impressed the young and old, whose sturdy independence was like a strong east wind, and who went to his reward crowned with the love of many and the respect of all. It seems but yesterday that his familiar figure passed away. His voice is still fresh in our ears. The old Church comes back, and he stands there in its pulpit, as he must always stand, among the most marked and vigorous figures in our parish history. It would not be right to renew our Church life without cordial remembrance of his strength and faithfulness."

It was the custom of the Evangelical clergy in administering the Lord's Supper to invite the members of other religious denominations to remain to the communion. With this custom Mr. Brooks was in sympathy. When his brother Arthur came into collision with the bishop of Illinois, the Rt. Rev. Henry J. Whitehouse, who assumed the right to forbid such notice to be given and to enforce the principle of "close communion" in the Episcopal Church, Mr. Brooks wrote to his brother upon the principle involved in giving the notice:

"May 23, 1873. If there are a considerable number in the parish who object I should discontinue it, but certainly take great pains to say in a sermon at the same time what my real ground was, to explain the perfectly clear position of our Church on the subject, and not to seem to fall low before the footstool of the Bishop at his first assumption of authority.

"The position of our Church is perfectly clear. The Archbishop of Canterbury himself in the Vance Smith dispute distinctly said that the rubric which touches the question applied only to our own people. The more I think of it the more I hope you will continue it unless it is very clearly desirable to drop it. I would not give it up out of mere courtesy to any man. At the same time it is not so absolutely a thing of principle that it might not be omitted if its use would seriously wound many people and injure the parish. You surely have done right so far. . . . What an unpleasant Christian Whitehouse must be. . . . But with all my heart I sympathize with your dread of a controversy and of the cheap notoriety and the disgusting partisanship that comes with it.

"There is only one suggestion I want to make. I do not think the notice is to be in any way considered or to be either attacked or defended as an addition or interpolation in the Service. It is an address by the Minister to the Congregation. It is of the nature of Sermon and not of Liturgy, and considerations of Liturgical integrity have nothing to do with it. If a minister is to be found fault with for doing it, it must be as he would be blamed for any other statement that was considered faulty in his sermon, —on the ground of false doctrine not of rubrical impropriety."

In the early seventies, things were rapidly tending toward a separatist movement in the Episcopal Church. The schism was consummated in 1873 when the Reformed Episcopal Church was organized under the leadership of Bishop Cummins of Kentucky. Despite the restrictive legislation, whose effect was to separate the Episcopal Church from communion with other Protestant churches, Mr. Brooks held it his duty in whatever way was open to manifest his sympathy for the principle of open communion and other modes of Christian fellowship. No canon that had been enacted forbade his preaching in the churches of other denominations. He had the advantage of his brethren in this respect that such opportunities were constantly afforded him. He became conspicuous in representing the affinity of the Protestant Episcopal Church with other Protestant bodies. To these and related points he alludes in his correspondence with Miss Mitchell:

"I have been off for a day down to Ipswich where Dr. Cotton Smith had a clerical powwow for the Dean of Canterbury who has come over to attend the Evangelical Alliance. He is a solid, stolid-looking Englishman, an ecclesiastic from the rosette on his hat to the buckle on his shoes, but a man of learning, reading hard Sanscrit as you and I read easy English, and healthy and wholesome through and through. Several other interesting people are here, especially a few famous Germans, Dorner, the 'Person of Christ' man, and many others. But I do not think the whole occasion promises much, and I shan't go on, though I give it my hearty blessing at this distance." (October 3, 1873.)

"The sermon is just done which is a rare event for Friday. It it about the Evangelical Alliance, which seems to me as it has gone on to have assumed a much larger look than it had at first, and to be really a great and noble thing. It is really so great that it can carry off a great many small faults, speeches here and there in bad taste, and an occasional piece of bad temper. I cannot see how such a meeting can fail to make Christianity stronger and broader." (October 9, 1873.)

"What do you think of the Bishop of Madagascar turning up in New York and writing a letter to Bishop Potter, complaining that the Dean of Canterbury had insulted the Archbishop of Canterbury? There is a roundabout confession and ingenious intricacy about it all which is nuts to the ecclesiastical mind. One may count upon no end of dreary controversy about whether Christ is willing that Dean Payne Smith should eat the Lord's Supper in an Episcopal Church, but not in Dr. Adams's Presbyterian Meeting House. As if all the great questions of faith and morals were settled, and that one minute squabble was the last thing left. Surely not till then will it begin to be of consequence." (October 15, 1873.)

"I don't know anything that makes one feel more genuinely old than to see that great recognizable changes and advances of the current of thought have been made in our time, so that while we see the new we can remember the old as something different. It used to seem as if such changes took a half century at least. Only fourteen years ago when I entered the ministry there were the two old-fashioned parties, the Lows and Highs, over against each other in a quiet, intelligent, comfortable way. Now you can hardly find a representative of either among the younger men except ——, and the Broad Churchmen and Ritualists divide the field. Let us be thankful that we belong to the party of the future." (December 11, 1873.)

"I hear that —— is dead: another of that fading school of Evangelicals who are fast passing away. One of the best of them (the Evangelicals) died the other day, my old professor and friend at Alexandria, Dr. Sparrow, one of the ablest and best men I ever knew, learned and broad, and as simple as a child. I had a letter from the dear old man, dated only two days before he died, in which I was delighted to hear him say, 'I am disposed to regard the prospects of our Church brighter now than they have ever been in my day.' All the old men are croaking and helpless, and it was good to hear one of them sanguine." (January 22, 1874.)

In May, 1874, the first steps were taken toward the establishment of the American Church Congress. The aim of its founders was to bring men together who differed in their convictions, to discuss questions which were subjects of controversy in free untrammelled speech, in the hope that it would lead to a mutual confidence and understanding. Churchmen of all schools of opinion were present, and amid much earnestness and enthusiasm the new institution was organized. Mr. Brooks was placed upon its Central Committee whose task was to select topics for discussion and appoint the speakers.

"Next week we go to New Haven, all of us Broad Churchmen, to see what can be done to keep or make the Church liberal and free. There is a curious sort of sensitiveness and expectancy everywhere in the Church, a sort of fear and feeling that things cannot remain forever just as they are now, and a general looking to the General Convention of next Fall as the critical time. The last impression may be wrong because General Conventions are not apt to be critical, but the other feeling has its foundation, and one wonders what is coming out of it all. Certainly some sort of broad church. A meeting such as this I speak of could not have been possible ten years ago. Then the men could not have been found to go; now men are asking to be invited." (May 12, 1874.)

The Convention of the diocese of Massachusetts which met in May to elect a successor to Bishop Eastburn reflected the stormy times which were passing over the Episcopal Church. The High Church candidate was the Rev. James De Koven of Wisconsin. Mr. Brooks wanted Dr. Vinton to be the Low Church candidate, and when he declined voted for his friend Rev. Henry C. Potter of Grace Church, New York. When it became evident that Dr. Potter could not be elected, a compromise was effected by which the choice of the Convention fell on the Rev. Benjamin H. Paddock of Brooklyn, N. Y. The Convention was a memorable one for the intensity of feeling which prevailed. Among the speeches there was one not easily forgotten by those present, in which the Rev. William R. Huntington of Worcester presented the name of Phillips Brooks, as a man surpassing all others who had been named for the vacant Episcopate. But the time for Phillips Brooks had not yet come. To the bishop-elect, he wrote pledging his support:

"HOTEL KEMPTON, BERKELEY STREET, BOSTON, May 21, 1873.

"REV. AND DEAR SIR,—I have doubted whether I have any right to add another to the multitude of letters which I know you must have received with reference to your election to our episcopate. But I feel so deeply anxious that you should consent to be our Bishop that I venture to add my assurance of cordial welcome and hearty coöperation to all the others which must have come to you. I think I know Massachusetts pretty well, and I am deeply convinced that our Church has a great and good work to do here. She will not do it easily, nor by simply standing still in idle assertion of herself, but if she will work for the people, the people will understand her readily enough. I am sure that all the circumstances connected with your election promise a cordial and unpartisan support of all your plans and labors by both the Clergy and the Laity of our diocese, and knowing this I have ventured to express to you my own sincere and anxious hope that you may be able to come to us.

"I beg you not to trouble yourself to answer this note, but believe me, with much regard,

"Most sincerely yours,
"PHILLIPS BROOKS,
"Rector of Trinity Church, Boston."

These extracts are from his correspondence with Miss Mitchell:

"The worst thing that I see about getting old, or older, is that you get further away from the young people who are the best people in the world. I never see a lot of boys without wanting to be among them, and wishing they would let me into their company and being sure that they won't. I hate to think that boys of sixteen think of me as I used to think of men of thirty-seven when I was their age. Most of the wisdom of old age is humbug. I was struck dreadfully by what you said about the prevalent discontent with life that one hears so much of. It's awful, and is the most unchristian thing one has to deal with. I fancied it was more the fashion here, but I suppose I have forgotten how much of the same thing I used to hear in Philadelphia, or perhaps it did not impress me so much then. I pray God that I may die before I get so tired of living."

"I have just been going again through Hessey's Bampton Lectures. A good conscience is the best guide about keeping Sunday or enforcing it in others. There is very little indeed in the way of positive law to be made out about it. It seems to me there is a strange lack of faith in the way that the strict Inspirationists and the stricter Sabbatarians are always in a panic lest the Book or the Day, which they above all others claim for God, should come to grief."

" 'Keil on the Kings' is a very good commentary as commentaries go, a little overburdened with linguistics, but on the whole telling you (I mean *me*) rather less of what I know already and more of what I don't than most commentaries. But they are all a poor set. Lange has a good deal that is interesting and valuable, but, bless me, who could n't have a few pennies if he swept all the gutters in town and saved all the rubbish."

"I am just come back from Andover where I went to lecture to the Congregational Divinity Students about Preaching. . . . They ask hard questions which you rather despair of answering, not because of the difficulty of the question, but because it shows such a queer state of mind in the questioner. I stayed with Professor Park, who is charming, bright, witty, and genial. . . . Have you read a book about Dissent by an English Bampton lecturer?"

"How interesting and beautiful Tom Hughes's little book is! [*Memoirs of a Brother*.] I wonder whether the brother was as good as he is described. What he (the brother) actually does in the way of letters, etc., did n't strike me much. He is the first man on record, I think, who ever dedicated his life to the health of his Mother-in-law."

"I am busy writing what is a sort of Biographical Oration for what is after a fashion my native town, Andover. It is to be delivered at the opening of their Memorial Hall next week. I don't like the work. Sermons I like to write, the more the better, as many as the deluded folk will sit and hear, but anything else except this weekly letter comes hard. I have a pretty obstinacy when I am asked to do anything right away, but when the task is three months off, I am apt to be feeble and assent, and by and by the day comes on like Fate."

"I have been much interested in reading up about the old Puritan town. What a curious set they were. So estimable and so deadly dull, sober and serious to a degree that is frightful to think of, but strong and tough as granite. The modern religion looks so gentle beside them. I came across this sentence yesterday in that most unpleasant book, Galton's 'Hereditary Genius,' which has just a vexatious amount of truth in it, 'A gently complaining and tired spirit is that in which Evangelical Divines are apt to pass their days.'. . . X—— made a prayer at the new Hall to-day in which he thanked the Lord for the workmen who had been engaged upon the building, that 'He had given his angels charge over them that none of them should strike his foot against a stone.' What do you think of that for a reverent and beautiful use of Scripture?"

"I wonder what *sort* of knowledge we shall have of our friends when we get to the other side, and what we shall do to keep up our intimacy with one another. There will be one good thing about it. I suppose we shall see right through one another to begin with, and start off on quite a new basis of mutual under-standing. It will be awful at first, but afterwards it must be quiet pleasant to feel that your friends know the worst of you and not be continually in danger and in fear that they will find you out. But then with all Eternity ahead there must be a constantly oppressive fear that your friends will get tired of you."

"Nobody can help feeling Agassiz's death. Apart from the scientific greatness, he was such a delightful man, so fresh and joyous and simple. It does surely seem as if he had gone at the right time, falling without decay and setting without twilight. 'T is strange to see how many people knew him here, and how many others feel as if they had known him and mourn his death as a personal loss. It was a good, cheerful, wholesome life.

"Three weeks from to-night I hope to start for Philadelphia. Fix which night you will for me to dine with you, and I will come up to the trial without a flinch. . . . Sunday I shall give to my old Advent folk whom I am proud to find caring for me after so many years. . . . I am glad that the Bible does n't say anything about the idle words which people *write*."

"I have come home from a Wednesday evening lecture, which I always enjoy; the only indication that I have that the people enjoy it is that they come in large numbers. Though they may talk about it among themselves, I myself never get any idea whether I hit them or not. Still I jog on and am very cheerful. I don't care for applause, but I do like to have some idea whether people are interested or not."

"Charles Kingsley is here, and lectured to us on Monday evening. It was good to see the author of 'Hypatia' in the flesh, but the Lecture was n't much, and he is the Englishest of Englishmen.　Then his laudation of this country was overmuch, and we were unnecessarily reminded of how he hated us and hoped good things for the rebellion during our war."

"How sad this sudden news of Sumner's death, and how it makes us realize the lack of great men among us.　And certainly Sumner was in many respects a great man.　The time of his departure like Agassiz's seems to be just what one would wish for him.　Neither of them was a man whom one would like to see crawling about in decrepitude."

"Poor Sumner's funeral was a wonderful outburst of public feeling about a man who had won it by sheer force of character and principle.　He was never popular . . . but true as steel and capable of ideas.　The country is not as bad as you think it.　Certainly no other land offers us anything to envy.　Have you read the book of a Mr. Pater on the Renaissance?　It is wonderfully fresh and full of its subject.　Then I got a book of Masson's the other day on Drummond of Hawthornden, of which I have read a few pages that promise something charming."

"I am in the thick of Lent, with the usual enjoyment of its spirit, and the usual misgiving about the way in which we try to make it useful to our people.　It is trying to see how, just as soon as we attempt to give religion its fit expression, we are instantly in danger of formalism and the mere piety of outside habits.　Yet still there is a great deal in changing habits which mean sad things, for habits which mean good things, for a little while, and some of the meaning does get into people's hearts. . . .
"How hard it is to write an Easter sermon.　The associations of the day are so dependent that it is really difficult to bring it close to people's lives.　But it is remarkable how men like your friend ——, who give up so much about Jesus, still cling to the truth of the Resurrection."

"We have had Principal Tulloch here.　He was at our Church last Sunday, and I spent the evening with him at Mr. Winthrop's. I want you to see him when he comes to Philadelphia.　He is a splendid Scotchman."　(April 30, 1874.) [1]

One incident mentioned in the above extracts calls for some slight expansion,—the address delivered at the dedication of the Memorial Hall in Andover.　Apart from his association with the civil war, or his fame as a pulpit orator, Phillips Brooks

[1] Here closes the correspondence with Miss Mitchell.　She died soon after the letter was written from which this extract is taken.

had been chosen as spokesman for the occasion as the descendant of those connected with the town from its earliest history. He was thus referred to by Professor Park in the prayer which followed the address: "It is of Thy goodness, O Lord, that we have been permitted on this day of our solemnity to hear the voice of one whose godly ancestors our fathers delighted to honor." His address was pervaded with a joyous tone, with the conviction that he had a right to speak, and that in speaking he represented what was uppermost in the minds of his hearers:

"If I wanted to give a foreigner some clear idea of what that excellent institution, a New England town, really is, in its history and its character, in its enterprise and its sobriety, in its godliness and its manliness, I should be sure that I could do it if I could make him perfectly familiar with the past and present of Andover. Nor can one know the old town well and not feel, however, that its scenery has the same typical sort of value which belongs to all its life. All that is most characteristic in our New England landscape finds its representation here. Its rugged granite breaks with hard lines through the stubborn soil, its sweep of hill and valley fills the eye with various beauty. Its lakes catch the sunlight on their generous bosoms. Its rivers are New England rivers ready for work and yet not destitute of beauty. If everywhere our New England scenery suggests to the imagination that is sensitive to such impressions some true resemblance to the nature of the people who grow up among its pictures, nowhere are such suggestions clearer than in this town which is so thoroughly part and parcel of New England."

Phillips Brooks was averse to writing essays, theological or other. The greater interest attaches, therefore, to those he was sometimes compelled to write. In October, 1873, he read before the "Clericus Club" an essay on "Heresy." He distinguished between the New Testament use of the word, and the ecclesiastical, holding the latter conception to be impossible without an infallible church. The moral conception of heresy, which implies personal guilt, no longer applies to the honest seeker for truth who may depart from a certain average of Christian belief.

"In ordinary talk men will speak of heresy as if it were synonymous with error. It may be that the word is so bound up with old notions of authority that it must be considered obsolete, and can be of little further use. And yet there is a sin which this word describes, which it describes to Paul and Augustine and Jeremy Taylor,—a sin as rampant in our day as in theirs. It is the self-will of the intellect. It is the belief of creeds, whether they be true or false, because we choose them, and not because God declares them. It is the saying, 'I want this to be true,' of any doctrine so vehemently that we forget to ask, 'Is it true?' When we do this, we depart from the Christian church, which is the kingdom of God, and the discipleship of Christ. With the danger of that sin before our eyes, remembering how often we have committed it, feeling its temptation ever present with us, we may still pray with all our hearts, 'From heresy, good Lord, deliver us.' "

Among the incidents whose bond of connection is Phillips Brooks, there is one which caused at the moment a flutter in Episcopal circles in Boston,—the occupation of King's Chapel on Ash Wednesday, 1874, by an Episcopal congregation. The famous building was crowded with an eager, curious audience, studying the ancient structure, its chancel and communion table, its reading desk and pulpit, preserved unchanged, unimpaired by modern improvements, since the day when Episcopal rectors presided there, in this first home of Episcopacy in Boston. It had been offered to Phillips Brooks, as the rector of Trinity Church, for the delivery of the Price Lectures, the condition of whose endowment required that the lectures be given either in Christ Church, King's Chapel, or Trinity Church. The kind offer came from the late Rev. Henry W. Foote, then the minister of King's Chapel, a man of beautiful and saintly character, beloved by all who knew him, whose death in the prime of his manhood brought the deepest sense of loss and sorrow. Bishop Paddock had already been invited to deliver the Price Lecture before Mr. Foote had offered the use of his church, and so it came about that a bishop of the Episcopal Church officiated for the first time in King's Chapel.

The summer of 1874 was spent in Europe. He was accompanied by Rev. Arthur Brooks, and for a great part of the summer they were together. Several weeks were given to England. The traditional American prejudice against the English, which he had hitherto shared, to some extent, was disappearing. It was mostly the clergy with whom he mixed, but he remarks that clergymen and laymen have more common interests than in America. They were talking much at this time about the Public Worship Bill at dinner tables and in the newspapers, which surprises him, as things of this kind at home are ordinarily confined to General Conventions. His acquaintance with Dean Stanley was now ripening into friendship. He was invited by the Dean to preach in the Abbey, for the fame of the preacher had reached England, and many were desirous to hear him. The nave of the Abbey was filled. The subject of the sermon was "The Positiveness of the Divine Life," the text taken from Galatians v. 16: "This I say then, Walk in the Spirit and ye shall not fulfil the lust of the flesh." The following comment furnishes a picture of the occasion:

"About six o'clock P.M. we all started for church service at old Westminster Abbey where Phillips Brooks of Boston was advertised to preach at seven o'clock. We went quite early anticipating a crowd, and secured a tolerably good position. The nave of the church where the services are held on Sunday evenings was very soon crowded. There was a choral service by men and boys. Dean Stanley read the Lessons and Mr. Brooks preached. . . . It is a very hard place to preach in . . . but he was distinctly heard, and the sermon was worthy of his reputation. It was a plain, practical enforcement of the great truths of his text, enunciated in simple yet elegant language, and altogether such a style of preaching as those old walls are not accustomed to. There may be better preachers here than the Rector of Trinity Church, Boston, but if so we have yet to hear them. We reached home soon after nine, grateful that we had had the privilege of hearing Mr. Brooks in Westminster Abbey, and still more grateful that God had given to Boston such a man and such a preacher."

From London he passed to the Continent, wandering through Normandy and Brittany, thence to Venice, and back through the Tyrol over the Ampezzo Pass that he had long wanted to see. The sense of vacation, he writes, was complete and made Boston seem far away. The main interest was in looking at churches in Normandy and Brittany; he was gathering suggestions which would afterwards be of service.

"We went up to Rouen and spent a lovely day among its old Gothic architecture. There is nothing more beautiful in Europe. Then we struck off into the country and for a week we have been wandering among old Norman towns . . . each with its churches six or eight hundred years old, some with magnificent cathedrals. . . . For a week we have wandered on through Brittany, looked at old castles and cathedrals. . . . I have been amazed at the richness of the old architecture of the country. In little out-of-the-way villages, reached only by rickety country wagons, we have found glorious and immense churches of rarest beauty,—churches that took centuries to build, and stand to-day perfect in their splendor, with wonderful glass in their windows, and columns and capitals that take your breath away for beauty."

As he wandered he was thinking of the new Trinity Church in Boston that was growing in his absence. To Mr. Robert Treat Paine he wrote:

"Tours, France, August 4, 1874.

" . . . And how's the new Church? I dreamed of it when I wrote to you from London, and now I dream of it again, slowly rising, course on course. I should n't wonder if the robing room were done up to the eaves, but I would give much to step out of the hotel and look in the gorgeous moonlight at that blessed lot on the Back Bay. Sometimes I am very impatient at being away while it is all going on, but I comfort myself with promises of coming home to harder work with the first Sunday in October. . . ."

No traveller returns to his own country, when the long ocean passage intervenes, without some measure of suspense or misgiving, lest bad news await him on his arrival. For Mr. Brooks there was in reserve a great sorrow, in the sudden death of his brother Frederick. The story is told in his father's words, entered in a family record, where he chronicled briefly the events in the lives of his sons:

"In September, 1874, he came to the city to see a young friend who was sick, and who was to take charge of a school at Cleveland. Finding him unable, he went to Lowell for a teacher September 15. On returning from there in the Boston & Lowell train he left the train at East Cambridge, intending to walk home on the railroad bridge. The night being dark he fell through the draw and was drowned. This was about 8.30 p.m. He was thirty-two years of age. The body was not found until the 20th in the Charles River. Funeral services were held September 24, at Emmanuel Church, and he was laid in Mount Auburn."

The friendship between these two brothers was close and beautiful. The older brother had followed with sympathetic interest every step of the younger brother's progress, from his days in the Latin School, and then through Harvard College. Two years they had lived together while Frederick Brooks was at the Divinity School in Philadelphia. For the aid, the sympathy, the brotherly love he received, the younger brother showed his appreciation, as when he wrote to Phillips: "I wish you would let me say what a jump I give to get one of your letters. They are one of the things that help along my year mightily." From the time of his ordination, Frederick Brooks was recognized as a preacher of singular attractiveness. Calls to various parishes had been the evidence that he was believed to have some important work to do. For a time he had been at Des Moines, Iowa, to get a touch of Western life; then he became rector of a prominent church, St. Paul's, in Cleveland, Ohio. To the interests of this church he gave, says his brother, "devoted care, proving himself a rare pastor and preacher, helping and teaching many souls, and building his parish work with singular solidity and power." He became editor of the *Standard of the Cross*, and gave the paper "a marked and noble character." His inherited interest in education led him to establish a school in Cleveland, which should give the best classical preparation.

The loss of his brother and the mode of his death was a nervous shock from which Phillips Brooks did not quickly recover. To a friend sending him a letter of condolence he wrote:

"These three weeks since I came home have been, just between ourselves, pretty wretched. I have tried and tried to get out of my mind the dreadful circumstances of it all. When I can shut them out for a moment and think only of his life here and the life he has begun beyond I am more than happy. I am thankful and full of rejoicing. But almost all the time the terrible scene is before me, and I think I have come nearer to being gloomy and out of heart with life than I ever did before. But I have n't been and I shan't be."

On Sunday the 25th of October Mr. Brooks stood in his brother's pulpit in Cleveland, Ohio, preaching in the morning

from the text, "Are the consolations of God small with thee?"
(Job xv. 11),[1] and in the afternoon another well-known sermon,
with the title, "The good will of him that dwelt in the bush"
(Deut. xxxiii. 16.)[2] Again in the evening he preached, and his
text was, "It became Him, for whom are all things, and by whom
are all things, . . . to make the captain of their salvation perfect through sufferings" (Heb. ii. 10). This was the record of a
day to be remembered by the preacher and his hearers. Another
duty devolved upon him, to visit the deserted room where the
traces of activity suddenly interrupted were all about him. Into
his musings, as he sat there alone with memory, we do not enter.
He looked over the sermons of his brother, and from them
selected a volume for publication. In the preface, he alluded
briefly to the beauty and power of his life. At a later time, when
writing his Lectures on Preaching, he made this terse reference
without further explanation, "To-day I have been thinking of
one whom I knew,—nay, one whom I know,—who finished his
work and went to God."

During more than four years the congregation of Trinity
Church worshipped in Huntington Hall on Boylston Street, de-
prived of the accessories which tend to make religion impressive.
But there were compensations in the heartier and freer worship.
There came a change so marked in the direction and the manifestation of Brooks's power that these years were not remembered as a period of deprivation of ecclesiastical privileges, but
cherished for the richer spiritual influence which they brought.
The secular hall took on a sacred character. The preacher rose
high above disadvantage or limitation. The afternoon service
soon began to be as well attended as the morning, nor were the
accommodations sufficient to meet the demands of the throng-
ing congregation. It was a reminder of the early days of the
Christian Church, when it lacked temples and altars and the sym-
bolic pageantry of the later centuries, when the spoken word
was in itself adequate to reach the intellect and melt the heart.
But it should be mentioned as an instance of his dependence upon
associations, that he sent to Philadelphia for the lecturn or preaching desk at which he had stood when delivering his Wednesday
evening lectures.

[1] *Sermons*, vol. i., p. 98.   [2] *Ibid.*, vol. ii., p. 39.

There was always a curious interest to know the methods by which Mr. Brooks did his work. Every sermon showed the sense of form, together with literary charm, and abundance of thought and illustration; and was marked by spontaneity and ease, as though it had called for no effort in its preparation. Now that we know the process, the secret appears a simple one. Preaching was the exclusive object that occupied his mind,—the message to be delivered and the form it should take. From morning till night, in hours of leisure or apparent relaxation, on his journeys, in vacations, in social gatherings, he was thinking of subjects for sermons, turning over new aspects of old truths, with the purpose of giving better form than had yet been given to old familiar doctrine. In a word, preaching was what he lived for, and for that cause he might almost be said to have come into the world. Beneath the trifling manner, the deep undertone of his spirit was sounding without cessation.

He made careful and even elaborate preparation for every occasional address. In every case the analysis of his remarks may be found in note-books or on detached sheets of paper. It seems to have been a first principle with him not to allow himself to feel that it would be given to him, when called upon, what he should speak. If there seemed to be exceptions to this rule, they were only apparent; it is safe to assume that elaborate preparation had been made some time in advance of the occasion.

After coming to Boston he wrote but one sermon a week and to this sermon devoted the best part of every morning. Before Monday came he had the text in his mind on which he was to write. If he had failed to secure his text or subject before the week began, he knew there was danger of failing to produce a sermon. It was his custom on Monday morning to have his friends about him, for that was his day of rest. But as they sat in his study and the conversation ran on, his mind did not lose sight of the idea which inspired him. On the mornings of Monday and Tuesday he was bringing together in his note-book or on scraps of paper the thoughts or illustrations related to his leading thought, collecting, as he called it, the material for the sermon. Wednesday morning he devoted entire to writing out the plan which he would follow. He took a half sheet of sermon paper, folding it once, thus making four small pages, some seven inches by less than five in their dimensions, which he was to fill. These he invariably filled out to the last remaining space on the last page, as though only in this way he could be sure that he had sufficient material for his sermon. So condensed is the handwriting that each one of these plans will average about one thousand words,—in itself a short sermon. Each plan contained when it was finished a dozen or more detached paragraphs. His next task—and this is the most curious feature of all—was to go over the paragraphs, each of which contained a distinct idea, and was to become, when expanded, a paragraph in the finished sermon, placing over against each the number of pages it would occupy when it had been amplified. Then he added the numbers together. Thirty pages was the limit of the written sermon. If these numbers of assigned pages did not equal thirty he reviewed his plan to see where he might best expand, or where to reduce if he had too many. It was extraordinary that one who gave the impression of such utter spontaneity, whose sermons seemed to come by a flash of inspiration, costing no effort, should have thus limited himself in fixed and apparently mechanical ways.

The hardest part of his work was accomplished when he had completed his plan. Thursday and Friday mornings were devoted to writing the sermon; and as each sermon contained some five thousand words a considerable amount of labor was still required. He wrote with rapidity, rarely making a correction, and in a large, legible, and graceful handwriting. Evidently it was a pleasure to him to write a sermon under these conditions. He came to each paragraph as to a work of art.

The first shape which the sermon took was the brief hint in the note-book. Every sermon may thus be traced in its genesis, even the casual speech on slight occasions. One might have thought that after so many years of preparation it would have been possible for him to make a few minutes' talk after dinner, or to boys in school or college, without first writing down the idea on which he was to touch, and then expanding it into a complete plan. But nothing that he did was without premeditation. He did not trust to the moment to bring him inspiration.

What has been said of his method of preparing a written sermon applies to his extemporaneous sermons. The plan was elaborated and written out and afterwards filed for future reference. There are many hundreds of these plans, but this difference is to be noted, that in making them he used a full sheet of sermon paper, with the handwriting large and bold, clearly with the purpose in view of taking them into the pulpit. He could not thus have utilized the plans of the written sermon, for the handwriting was so small as to have required a magnifying-glass to read it. In this way he cultivated himself in the art of extempore preaching. The practice which he had in amplifying his ideas in the written sermon helped him when preaching without notes, giving him freedom in the pulpit. Often when he was most powerful he had departed from the manuscript before him, or ceased to follow the plan laid out. He was never more effective than when he delivered some written sermon extemporaneously. In such cases he did not use the manuscript for preparation, but went to the plan on which it had been written, coming again under the influence of the original idea which had first inspired him, and then giving to it such fresh treatment as made it seem as if he were delivering a new sermon.

It was characteristic of Phillips Brooks as a preacher that he did not follow the rule enjoined in rhetorical treatises calling for a culmination at the end of the discourse, for which the most effective points or arguments should be reserved. On the contrary he often, perhaps generally, came to his climax as he began. He followed the artist's method, throwing his leading idea upon the canvas in bold outline, holding the gaze of his audience as with an artist's power he filled up the outline and made a living, speaking portrait. What he was doing in every sermon was to reproduce the personal process through which he himself had passed from the moment when he grasped a truth till he had traced out in his own experience its relation to life and to all other truth. This process kept him natural, sincere, and unaffected, preserving his personality in all that he said, and free from the dangers of conventionalism or artificiality. None ever charged him with employing the artifices of rhetoric to accomplish his end, or harbored the suspicion that he moved them by sensational methods. Whatever the rules of rhetoric may require, in real life the strongest argument comes first, and is confirmed by the lesser reasons. This was Phillips Brooks's method. There was a letting down of the audience as he closed from the exaltation with which he began to the sober application of his truth in the realities of life.

A few illustrations are here given from his note-books to show the ideas germinating in his mind, afterwards to be developed into sermons; they also illustrate his preaching and thought at the moment when they were written. One year is as good as another for this purpose, and we fix upon 1874, when he was preaching in Huntington Hall:

"The way the Bible strikes at the average respectability, as in the Elder Brother and Pharisees, yet never would overturn. No socialism; always full of virtue and order, always bringing up the better from below, always making growth the changing force, always developing. That the whole secret of reform. Other systems purely destructive; have tried to appropriate Christianity, but have failed."

"When an end had been made of the people's old religion, of their faith, and of the God-made man of the Gospel, do you know what was substituted? The faith in the God-made man of social-ism. For what is socialism at bottom? It is man believing himself God, in the sense that he believes himself capable of destroying evil and suffering. (Life of Montalembert, vol. ii. p. 112.)"

"*For thus saith the Lord unto the house of Israel, Seek ye me, and ye shall live.* Amos. v. 4. One must be in harmony with the principles of life in order to live; for example, the forces of nature, the laws of the land, the men about us, of all good things. This must be what is meant by seeking God; not His favor, but His nature. This is what is meant by Christ reconciling us to God. The full life of Jesus. . . . There is a rich vitality in the man who has sought God."

"*Elias was a man subject to like passions as we are.* James v. 17. General tendency to think the great men so much greater than we are. What is and what is not common to men (Declara-tion of Independence). Settle it that privilege must belong with character, and then there can be no arbitrary inequality. '*And I will not be judged by any that never felt the like,*' said Richard Baxter on his wife's death."

"*And when he was come into Jerusalem, all the city was moved, saying, Who is this?* Matt. xxi. 10.

"The moved city is the emphasis of ideas by humanity, adding nothing to their inherent reasonableness, but very much to their convincing force.

"*Who is this?* a wonder worker, a truth teacher, a soul changer?

"There must be a Theology, a Christology. Refuge in mere moralism will not do. It is too shallow. If there be a Christ we *must* know Him, think *something* of Him."

"*Giving none offence in any thing, that the ministry be not blamed.* 2 Cor. vi. 3. What the classes are,—Dogmatic bigots; the utterly indifferent; earnest believers. . . .

"What ought to be our feeling towards each?

"The need of having settled principles on which to regulate our life with one another. What are the principles which Christianity brings to bear: 1. God's love for all and guidance of all. 2. The common teachableness. 3. The resurrection and eternal life. 4. The personal conscience. 5. The worth of the soul above the body. All these made manifest by the Incarnation.

"Some time a strong sermon on the Incarnation.

"You cannot carry Christianity everywhere, but you can carry Christ.

"The character of the arguments to which men's minds are open one of the best indications of their calibre."

"*Trouble not the Master.* The tendency of Churchmen to shut up Christ to certain activities, and to lose His spontaneousness and freeness. The causes of such a tendency. Analyze into a care for Him and a lurking, half-unconscious fear of exhaustion; for example, Salvability of the heathen; Forgiveness of very great sins; Salvation of errorists; Few that be saved."

"Sermon on *Forgiveness,* as the purpose of the Gospel. . . . The prerequisites of forgiveness are repentance and faith, . . . not remorse and belief. A reconciled God, the grandeur of that idea. . . . Has it not been done by Christ in the world and in the heart? If men come into the councils of God and dwell there as they could not of old, has not He done it? And by the death of Christ, is not that true also? Sin has been made hideous, obedience lovely, love evident. Then how evident that not by any mere outward works the forgiveness is obtained."

"*But will God indeed dwell on the earth?* Atheism, Pantheism, Deism, Incarnation. Then the spiritual conception of an indwelling God, a God who is *in,* not *is,* the human soul."

"*Say the Lord hath need of him.* God's need of men; the solution of Calvinism. The opposite statements of Spiritual things which may both be true."

"*Humility.* To be gained both by sense of our own weakness and by the bigness of others. . . . Humility and self-respect entirely consistent."

"*That they should seek after God, if haply they might feel after and find Him, though He is not far from every one of us.* God nearer than we think. We are blind to what is nearest to us always. Christ the exhibition of a nearness of God which is already a fact. The difference if we understood it all. God the atmosphere of life."

Two addresses of Phillips Brooks in 1874 and 1875 deserve mention, as illustrating his methods of work, and for autobiographic significance. The first was given in 1874, before the Massachusetts Teachers' Association, on "Milton as an Educator," where he sums up the studies of years on the life and times of Milton, together with his own experience and observation. The address is a remarkable one, suggesting wonder that he should find time for such thorough research into the bearing of his theme. The wonder vanishes, when we find by his note-book that he had given up the previous summer to the needful study, going for himself to the treatises of Locke, Bacon, and Spencer, and then to Quintilian, Montaigne, Comenius, Pestalozzi, and Basedow.

Another address was delivered at the anniversary of the Massachusetts State Normal School, in July, 1875, when his subject was "Courage." [1] The preparation for it was made a long time in advance, and among the writings of Phillips Brooks it occupies a most important place. We are haunted as we read with the conviction that we have before us a chapter from his experience, had he chosen to give it a personal form. He tells us of his method of reading:

"The habit of review reading is hostile to literary courage. To read merely what some one has said about a book is probably as unstimulating, as unfertilizing a process as the human mind can submit to. . . . Read books themselves. To read a book is to make a friend; if it is worth your reading you meet a man; you

[1] Cf. *Essays and Addresses* for both these papers, " Milton as an Educator," p. 300, and " Courage," p. 319.

go away full of his spirit; if there is anything in you, he will quicken it. . . . To make young people know the souls of books and find their own souls in knowing them, that is the only way to cultivate their literary courage."

But the subject itself is most suggestive. If we might fix upon one word to describe the character of Phillips Brooks, it would be courage. It was written in his appearance and manner, showing itself in his sermons and his conversation, the one quality which could not be suppressed or disguised. It had been manifested in Philadelphia when he espoused causes which were unpopular. To preach was an act requiring courage, because he must needs, in order to be successful, unfold his inner self, and speak of the intimate phases of the soul's life in God, when no pressure could have extracted these things from him in ordinary circumstances. When, therefore, he gives the definition of courage, he is imparting the secret of his own experience: *"Courage is the power of being mastered by and possessed with an idea. How rare it is! I do not say how few men are so mastered and possessed; I say how few men have the power so to be."*

The Sundays at Huntington Hall succeeded each other with their unvarying testimony to the preacher's power. No courses of lectures on literature, art, or science with which the hall was associated ever witnessed a greater audience. It would not have been so surprising if on anniversary occasions the crowd had gone forth to meet him; but this was the case Sunday after Sunday, like the sun each day as it rises in its strength, till people became accustomed to it as to the gifts of God, and hardly wondered at the munificence of the feast. A very competent observer has described the preacher at this time, in terms felicitous and true:

"We sometimes read of Schleiermacher and Whitefield and Robertson and McCheyne and Chalmers and Mason, and think it must have been good to live in the times when men preached with their fire and their mighty hold on the heart; but lo! we have the same phenomena in Boston to-day, a man in some respects even more than the equal of some I have named. . . .Philosophic candor, and a large grasp, this separates him world wide from the common pulpit; and those who find themselves always on the guard about the statements of others give Phillips Brooks a ready ear. But with all this, there is in his preaching what one must call the everlasting Gospel; that faithfulness to the conscience, that tender pleading, that dignity of condescension, and yet that brotherliness and sympathy, that fidelity to dogmas, yet that absence of dogmatic expression, that lack of the sensational, ludicrous, and egotistic, and that spiritual quickening, which men sum up in one brief phrase when they say, 'That is what I call preaching.' For myself, I should deem no vacation complete without hearing Phillips Brooks. After hearing Candlish, Dykes, Hamilton, Jones, Binney, Spurgeon, Pressensé, Monod, Krummacher, and Tholuck, not to mention other distinguished divines of Europe, there is no one who so exactly suits me as Phillips Brooks. There is a warmth and life and inspiration and truth from his lips that I have not found elsewhere. And from what I hear mine is not an isolated case."

The late Principal Tulloch of the University of Aberdeen was visiting Boston in the spring of 1874. This was his tribute to Phillips Brooks, in a letter to his wife:

"April 26, 1874. I have just heard the most remarkable sermon I ever heard in my life (I use the word in no American sense) from Mr. Phillips Brooks, an Episcopal clergyman here: equal to the best of Frederick Robertson's sermons, with a vigor and force of thought which he has not always. I never heard preaching like it, and you know how slow I am to praise preachers. So much thought and so much life combined; such a reach of mind, and such a depth and insight of soul. I was electrified. I could have got up and shouted." [1]

There was no living critic who surpassed Principal Tulloch; few who could be said to equal him, in those qualities which go to making up the capacity for final arbitration. The man who could move him to such an outburst had gained some vantage-ground which it is essential to discover. When we turn to the sermon, it is to find that it was no exceptional utterance compared with many others that might be mentioned. And yet it contained in a marked degree that quality which now made all the sermons great. The text was: *Jesus said unto him, Dost thou believe on the Son of God. He answered and said, Who is he, Lord, that I might believe on him? And Jesus said unto him, Thou hast both seen him, and it is he that talketh with thee.*[2] Christ was drawn as the most real, most present power in the world.

[1] Mrs. Oliphant's *Life* of Principal Tulloch, pp. 292, 303.
[2] Cf. *Sermons*, vol. v., p. 194: " The Opening of the Eyes."

Men see Him, talk with Him, but they do not know what lofty converse they are holding. The subtlety of the spiritual imagination enabled the preacher to enter into the mind of Christ and to reproduce the scene, as though Christ were standing in bodily presence before the congregation. What had taken place those centuries ago was repeating itself in the consciousness of many on that Sunday afternoon.

The story of the building of Trinity Church reads like a romance from its first inception, through the difficulties surmounted, till it culminated in the service of consecration. In the accomplishment of the work, the building committee, the architect, the rector, labored together in a spirit of harmony, and under the conviction that "our duty to the parish, to posterity, and to God has been clear, to make the new church fully worthy of the piety, the culture, and the wealth of our people." From beginning to end a deep enthusiasm pervaded the whole undertaking. With Phillips Brooks originated the motives which dominate the edifice. His ideas are written in the structure; he supported and stimulated the genius of the architect, turning it to his own purpose; he possessed the confidence of the building committee and of the members of the parish, manifested by unstinted generosity in giving, in response to increasing appeals. In his judgment the time was ripe to make an attempt in ecclesiastical architecture which, while it retained whatever was effective in traditional methods, should yet be subservient to the expression of the higher aspects of religion. The first condition was to break away from the so-called Gothic style, whose introduction into England and America had been followed by the attempted return to mediæval religion. That type of religion, with its priesthood and confessional, and its emphasis on the sacrament of the altar, had clothed itself in a style of architecture in which the hearing of the word of God was not taken into consideration as affecting the structural necessities of the building art. "Faith cometh by hearing, and hearing by the word of God" was the motive of Phillips Brooks. This was the principle kept in the foreground, as controlling the details of the construction. Even the piers of the central tower, where they are visible in the church, were made smaller than the fitting proportions seemed to demand, failing to represent the massive foundations on which they rest, and even concealing in some measure their structural purpose, in order that the symbolism of the church as a place for the proclamation of the gospel might be more effectually secured.

But in order that the dignity of the sacraments might be secured, and their true significance made prominent, there was added to the chancel end of the church a large semicircular apse, to be devoted to the purpose of the administration of the Lord's Supper. Its motive was to represent the idea of Christian communion and fellowship as one great end which the Lord's Supper was designed to promote. In the centre of the apse stood the Lord's table,—a table according to the original institution of the feast, not a sideboard but a table, whose importance to the Christian imagination was not obscured or dwarfed by other ornamentation. Those who have witnessed the communion of the Lord's Supper in Trinity Church have been impressed by the significance of the divine symbolism. The baptismal font is placed next the chancel, connecting the two sacraments, setting forth the truth that inward purification is the condition for participating in the heavenly banquet.

But it was also the purpose of Phillips Brooks to combine with these features of a Protestant church whatever was of human and enduring significance in the earlier methods of Christian architecture. He would take from the old order the ideas of solidity and of imposing grandeur, of beauty adornment in form and color, which should surpass, if possible, all other beauty, in its costly decoration symbolizing that wealth was worthily employed when it ministered to spiritual ends. Let the complex involutions of the result stand for the rich variety of religious interests. Retain from the old, also, the sense of awe and mystery, that combination of effects in which Milton, though a Puritan, rejoiced, whose result was to dissolve the spirit in religious feeling and bring heaven before the eye.

The completed edifice did not quite represent the original intention of the architect. The walls were to have been several feet higher, and the original design of the tower showed a square lantern with turrets at each corner, much like the present tower, but surmounted by an octagonal portion rising some fifty feet higher. But to carry out this plan of the tower called for walls of such thickness that, in the minds of experts who were consulted, the foundations would not be strong enough to support the weight. To this criticism the architect demurred, but the change was made. The lowering of the walls was partly in obedience to acoustic demands, which were an important consideration, as was also the construction of the ceiling.[1]

It had formed a part of the architect's design that the interior of the church should be decorated in accordance with a large plan embracing the whole and every separate part in its unity of treatment; that this should be done by some creative mind, capable of a task which in this country hitherto had no precedent; that the church within should be rich with the luxuriance of color, as well as with paintings representing angelic intelligences and the great personages of religious history. Into this scheme Phillips Brooks entered with enthusiasm. There was one peculiarity about him, so marked as to be almost extraordinary,— his love of color for its own sake. His susceptibility to color was almost feminine, so quick was he to feel and appreciate. He had become also an adept in the matter of stained glass, studying at factories in Europe the method of its production. It was no indifferent subject, then, to Phillips Brooks, when the architect proposed that the church should be made glorious by the richest effects of color which the best artists could devise.

The interior decoration was entrusted to La Farge, the most eminent of American artists, who gathered about him competent assistants laboring with him, says Richardson, "in a spirit of true artistic enthusiasm for a work so novel and affording such an opportunity for the highest exercise of a painter's talents." Mr. La Farge had a magnificent scheme, but it required time for its fulfilment, a condition which could not be granted. He confined his attention, therefore, to the roof and the walls of

[1] Mr. Brooks had feared that his voice might not be found sufficient for the large edifice, but the first trial proved that the fear was groundless. At this time he had taken no lessons in the use of the voice; his one reference to elocution is of a humorous character: "Of oratory and all the marvellous mysterious ways of those who teach it, I dare say nothing. I believe in the true elocution teacher as I believe in the existence of Halley's comet, which comes in sight of this earth once in about seventy-six years."

19

the central tower in the confidence that if this were completed the rest would follow.

The new Trinity Church at the time of its erection awakened an unusual interest; its progress was followed by the newspapers; architects discussed it at their meetings. This is a report of the impression it produced which will stand for many similar notices:

"A splendid surprise is in store for the worshippers at Trinity Church on the opening to the public for consecration. The interior is impressive in its vast spaces alone, the grandeur of its wide and lofty arches spanning nave and transepts, and the height of the ceiling in the great square tower open to the sight far beyond the vaulted roof. The grand exterior dimensions of the church somewhat prepare one for the spaciousness within. But only seeing can realize the superb beauty of the decoration. . . . Its richness is beyond compare, because there is literally nothing like it this side of the ocean. Trinity is the first church in this country to be decorated by artists, as distinguished from artisans. The result must be to make an era in American art and Church building."

The church was consecrated by Bishop Paddock on February 9, 1877, five years after the destruction of the old edifice. Among the invited guests were the Governor of the State, the Mayor of Boston, clergymen of other denominations, the wardens and vestrymen of other parishes, the architect, the artists, and builders. One hundred and seven clergymen walked in procession from the chapel to the western entrance, where they were received by the wardens and vestry of the church, and together went up the nave, reciting alternately the twenty-fourth Psalm, whose sentences seemed to take on a deeper meaning: "The earth is the Lord's and all that therein is; the compass of the world and they that dwell therein. Lift up your heads, O ye gates; and be ye lift up, ye everlasting doors; and the King of glory shall come in." It was characteristic of Phillips Brooks that he should call about him on such a day the friends of his life who were in the ministry, or who had been associated with him in the theological seminary. Among them was Dr. Vinton who delivered the sermon from the text Revelation xxi. 22: "I saw no temple therein; for the Lord God Almighty and the Lamb are the temple thereof."

On the day after the consecration Mr. Brooks wrote to Mr. R. T. Paine:

"I wish I could tell you, my dear Bob, something of what yesterday was to me, and of how my deep gratitude and love to you mingled with the feeling of every hour. May God bless you is all that I can say. The Church would not be standing there, the beautiful and stately thing that it is, except for your tireless devotion. How often I have wondered at your undiscouraged faith; and all my life as I look back on these years of anxiety and work, I shall see a picture of constancy which I know will make me stronger for whatever I have to do. Your kind words crown the whole and leave nothing to be desired in this complete achievement.

"I am almost appalled when I think what the great work in this new Church may be. I know that I shall have your help and prayers in the part of it which will fall to me to do. Many, many happy years are before us, if God will, and when we leave the great dear thing to those who come after us we shall be near one another, I am sure, in the better life."

At their annual Easter meeting (April 4) the Proprietors of Trinity Church acknowledged to the rector their sense of indebtedness for his contribution to the great achievement:

"We cannot let this great epoch in the life of our ancient Parish pass, without placing on permanent record our sense of the deep obligations of us and our whole people to our beloved Rector, Mr. Brooks. . . . To him in large measure is due the beauty and the glory of the new Church; he has been himself the inspiration of the Architect, Builders, and Committee. . . . The love of our whole people, men, women, and children, is all that we can give him in return."

An incident occurred in connection with the services of consecration to which it is necessary to allude. To the sacrament of the Lord's Supper there came clergymen of other denominations, and among them Unitarian ministers, personally invited to remain for the communion. From two directions followed protests,—a condemnation of the act by a Unitarian who wrote:

"The dignitaries (?) who invited the liberal clergy to partake of the sacrament did what was for them a generous thing. . . . Their eye had caught the vision of a broad church, whose enclosing walls embraced believers of every name. But what shall

we think of the liberals who accepted the invitation?   Were
they looking forward?   Were *their* faces bathed in light?   Were
they straining the line of their traditions?"

   From the other side there came a protest by a presbyter of the
Episcopal Church to the bishop of the diocese against "a grievous
sacrilege" in the admission to the Holy Communion of "those
who avowedly deny the faith once delivered to the saints, even
concerning the fundamental doctrines of our Lord's Godhead."
Such an act was to be regarded as a violation of Scripture, of
"Catholic" custom, and of Christian instinct, as well as contrary
to the letter and spirit of the formularies of the Protestant Episcopal Church.   In the controversy that followed Mr. Brooks
kept silence.   He had made up his mind as to the meaning of the
formularies of the Episcopal Church, he had long since come to
the conclusion that they were not intended to exclude from the
communion those who did not accept her articles of faith or follow her mode of worship.   He distinguished between the ceremonial forms which accompanied the act of Holy Communion
and the simple rite itself, the eating of the bread and the participation in the cup of blessing.   The one essential requisition for
the communion were the words of invitation in the office itself:
"Ye who do truly and earnestly repent you of your sins, and are
in love and charity with your neighbors, and intend to lead a new
life, following the commandments of God, and walking from
henceforth in His holy ways, draw near with faith, and take this
Holy Sacrament to your comfort."

   This comprehensiveness of spirit was obnoxious to some of Mr.
Brooks's brethren in the Episcopal Church; his action was not
forgotten; he was destined to hear from it again after many years.
He had gained, however, the confidence and affection of ministers
and people of every name.   The long and deep-rooted prejudice
against the Episcopal Church in the city of the Puritans was not
to be at once overcome.   But it was a great part of the work of
Phillips Brooks in Boston to lessen the dislike and disarm suspicions.   Among the descendants of the Puritans no one had a more
representative estimate of the situation than the late Rev. Dr.
George E. Ellis, a Unitarian minister retired from active service,
devoting his leisure to historical study and the writing of books,
at a later time the honored president of the Massachusetts His-

torical Society.   He was one of those who went to the communion in Trinity Church.   A letter written by him to Mr. Brooks follows:

" 110 MARLBOROUGH STREET, February 10, 1877.

"MY DEAR MR. BROOKS,—After thoughtfully digesting the noble and appropriate services and the delightful experiences of yesterday in connection with the consecration of Trinity Church, I feel prompted to express to you in this form my sincerest congratulations on the fair completion of an undertaking which must have engaged so deeply your own anxieties and interests.   It has been something more and better than mere curiosity that has led me almost daily to watch the progress of a critical and generous enterprise, from the driving of the first pile to the solemn dedication of the completed sanctuary.   In my view, the distinctive character of your congregation, your own ministry, and the prominent and honored position which you represent before this community conserve the very best elements of religious culture, and of a spirit of Christian comprehensiveness and liberality, associated in my thought with the selectest fellowship of the class of disciples with whom I have been most intimately connected; while at the same time the original deposit of the faith and the fitness of its dispensation have found in you a wiser guardianship than it proved to have with the so-called Liberal denomination as a whole.   So I would venture with much respect to assure you that I am heartily interested in the effective work which, with such modest personal unobtrusiveness and with such power, you are doing among us.

"And I must recognize with a hearty appreciation and gratitude the delightful Christian courtesy shown towards all the miscellaneous company of ministers, including myself, in the arrangement made yesterday for our participation in and enjoyment of the seemly and impressive services, especially the Holy Communion.

"With sincerest respect and regard, I am

"Very truly yours,

"GEORGE E. ELLIS."

The new Trinity Church was not what is technically known as a "free church"; the pews were rented by the Proprietors, and on each pew a tax was laid for the support of public worship.   But the large galleries in the transepts of the church were free in every sense; no tax was laid on them, and no contribution solicited from those who occupied them.   This object had been kept in view by Mr. Brooks when the plans of the church were drawn, and urged by him upon the architect, that such ample accommodation should be provided. The galleries accommodate some four hundred people,—a larger congregation than is found in most churches. It was also understood between the rector and the congregation that at an early moment in the service pews not occupied should be regarded as vacant, to be placed at the disposal of the stranger.

So Phillips Brooks took the place where for many years he was to sway the people with an hitherto unknown power. The enthronement of an ecclesiastical dignitary could possess no deeper significance. He seemed now to stand at the height of his renown. He had other conquests to achieve, but he had accomplished the most difficult, in some respects the most important, of them all,—he had made the conquest of Boston. From this moment his friends watched him with a feeling of pride mingled with awe, while he continued to stride forward and upward, as if there had been placed no limit to his power.

CHAPTER XII.

1877–1878.

RELIGIOUS DOUBT. YALE LECTURES ON PREACHING. THE TEACHING OF RELIGION. THE PULPIT AND POPULAR SKEPTICISM. THE INFLUENCE OF JESUS.

The early years of Phillips Brooks in Boston corresponding with the decade of the seventies were important for the development of his theological attitude. He entered more fully into the possession of himself in his relation to his world. He became the author of important books which revealed him to a larger audience, and in these he found an opportunity of asserting the distinctive truth for which he stood more powerfully than in his briefer utterances in the pulpit. He had a message of his own, which for many years he had been maturing, revolving it in his mind from the time when in the Virginia seminary he had first asked himself what was the source of power, or how the power should be brought to bear upon the will. He was now constantly facing the issue whether Christianity were still to abide as a force in modern life, or had run its course and become an outworn thing of the past. The decade of the seventies was marked by an eclipse of the faith; when men were troubled and walked in darkness. In the long range of Christian experience, there had never been a darker moment. The poetry of Matthew Arnold remains a monument to the distress of the hour. In his "Dover Beach," or in "Obermann once more," one may see how despairing was the mood which the wide-spread skepticism entailed. To such an age, in danger of abandoning faith in God and Christ and the Church, Phillips Brooks now addressed himself, and with hitherto unequalled manifestation of his power.

In the early part of the year 1877, when the building commit-

tee of Trinity Church were making strenuous efforts to hasten
its completion, he went to New Haven to deliver his "Lectures on
Preaching" before the students of the Yale Divinity School. It
was a time of unusual excitement when he was writing the lectures, an excitement and enthusiasm which culminated in their
delivery. So deeply was he moved that for some reason he
could not bear to make the journeys to New Haven alone, and
took with him one of his relatives. The event stirred him the
more deeply because he was unveiling his own personal experience, as he had felt compelled to review it when he sought to
explain the secret which made the pulpit effective. The great
charm of the Yale Lectures, from a literary point of view, is that
they constitute the confessions of a great preacher. The book is
personal throughout. Whether he speaks of himself in the first
person, or veils the revelation, he is giving himself in the most
intimate manner. In the passage following he may be regarded
as speaking out of his own experience:

"There is something beautiful to me in the way in which the
utterance of the best part of a man's own life, its essence, its
result, which the pulpit makes possible and even tempts, is welcomed by many men, who seem to find all other utterance of
themselves impossible. I have known shy, reserved men who,
standing in their pulpits, have drawn back before a thousand eyes
veils that were sacredly closed when only one friend's eyes could
see. You might talk with them a hundred times, and you would
not learn so much of what they were as if you once heard them
preach. It was partly the impersonality of the great congregation. Humanity, without the offence of individuality, stood
there before them. It was no violation of their loyalty to themselves to tell their secret to mankind. It was a man who silenced
them. But also, besides this, it was, I think, that the sight of
many waiting faces set free in them a new, clear knowledge of
what their truth or secret was, unsnarled it from the petty circumstances into which it had been entangled, called it first into
clear consciousness, and then tempted it into utterance with an
authority which they did not recognize in an individual curiosity
demanding the details of their life. Our race, represented in a
great assembly, has more authority and more beguilement for
many of us than a single man, however near he may be. And he
who is silent before the interviewer pours out the very depth of
his soul to the great multitude. He will not print his diary for
the world to read, but he will tell his fellow-men what Christ may

be to them, so that they shall see, as God sees, what Christ has been to him." (Pp. 121, 122.)

The "Lectures on Preaching" possess a further charm because they connect the pulpit with life. The book took its place as a contribution to literature, as well as a treatise on homiletics. It shows the scholar and the man widely read in the world's best books. The work done in the Virginia seminary, as seen in the note-books, is constantly reappearing. The movement is rapid; there is no lingering by the way; every page is full of condensed purpose. There is nothing artificial, no posing for effect; but plainness and great directness of speech, naturalness and simplicity. The book captivates the reader because of the transparency of the soul of its writer, between whom and the reader there intervenes no barrier. And further it is redolent with hope, it encourages and it cheers, and has the effect of reconciling us with life. It abounds in sentences which linger in the mind:

"There must be a man behind every sermon."

"The intercourse with God in history."

"The real power of your oratory must be your own intelligent delight in what you are doing."

"You grow so familiar with the theory of repentance that it is hard for you to know that you have not yourself repented."

"If you could make all men think alike, it would be very much as if no man thought at all, as when the whole earth moves together all things seem still."

"To be dead in earnest is to be eloquent."

"The personal interest of the preacher is the buoyant air that fills the mass and lifts it."

"The sermon is truth and man together. It is the truth brought through the man."

"The temptation from being messengers to be witnesses of the faith."

"Say nothing which you do not believe to be true, because you think it may be helpful. Keep back nothing which you know to be true because you think it may be harmful."

"This value of the human soul is something more than a mere sense of the soul's danger. It is a deliberate estimate set upon man's spiritual nature in view of its possibilities."

"Never allow yourself to feel equal to your work."

"Success is always sure to bring humility. 'Recognition,' said Hawthorne, 'makes a man very modest.'"

In addition to literary charm and autobiographical interest, the "Lectures on Preaching" have further significance in the assertion in a more developed form of the leading idea of Phillips Brooks that truth and moral efficiency are contagious and pass from man to man through the medium of personality. The subject had been long before his mind, and he had given utterance to it on various occasions, so that it had been accumulating in momentum when he went to Yale in 1877. He now placed it in the foreground and gave it a new emphasis. It was the dominant note in his first lecture and sounded throughout the course.

"Preaching is the bringing of truth through personality. . . Jesus chose this method of extending the knowledge of Himself through the world. However the gospel may be capable of statement in dogmatic form, its truest statement is not in dogma but in a personal life. Christianity is Christ. A truth which is of such peculiar character that a person can stand forth and say of it, 'I am the truth,' must always be best conveyed through personality. 'As my Father hath sent me into the world, even so have I sent you into the world.' It was the continuation out to the minutest ramifications of the new system of influence, of that personal method which the Incarnation itself had solved. Nothing can ever take the place of preaching because of the personal element that is in it." (P. 7.)

The principle that truth is made powerful and contagious through personality harmonizes the conflict between the corporate and the individual conception of the Christian life and puts us in right relations with historic Christianity.

"The message can never be told as if we were the first to tell it. It is the same message which the Church has told in all the ages. He who tells it to-day is backed by all the multitude who have told it in the past. He is companied by those who are telling it now. The message is his witness, but a part of the assurance with which he has received it comes from the fact of its being the identical message which has come down from the beginning. . . . All outward utterances of the perpetual identity of the Church are valuable only as they assert this real identity. This is the real meaning of the perpetuation of old ceremonies, the use of ancient liturgies, the clinging to what seem to be apostolic types of government." (P. 18.)

"The religion of Christ had been first implanted as a leaven in humanity by the personality of its founder and from that time had never been without its witnesses —the children of God in every generation."

"The preacher must possess the character which comes from association with Christ."

"Personal piety is the deep possession in one's own soul of the faith and hope and resolution which are to be offered to one's fellow-men for their new life. . . . Nothing but fire kindles fire. . . . To live in Christ and to be His and not our own, makes preaching a perpetual privilege and joy."

The eloquence of the " Lectures on Preaching" culminates in the closing chapter where he describes the value of the human soul. To this exposition he attached high importance. When some correspondent spoke to him of its significance he answered that he wrote the book for the sake of enforcing this truth,—that in the love and reverence for human souls lay the deepest secret of power in the ministry. This was his own characteristic in an extraordinary degree. His love for humanity, his reverence for man as such, grew with his years. He loved places and things, he loved nature, but above all he loved humanity. It made his heart leap up when he beheld the waiting congregation. No one can forget the look that he gave when he had ascended the pulpit, as if to draw in the inspiration for the effect that was to follow before he bent himself with the fervor and tumult of his powerful soul to the communication of his message.

The "Lectures on Preaching" were an event in the history of the pulpit. Phillips Brooks had now added theological students and seminaries to his other conquests. Professors of homiletics were among the first to respond. Letters poured in upon him from every quarter expressing appreciation and deep gratitude. One of these may be taken as a specimen, and it only says what all were saying:

"I believe neither the English language nor any other has anything worthy to stand beside them, treating such a theme,— judging the wide reading, the wit, the wisdom, the mental grasp of the problem, the keenness of the analysis, the profoundness of the insight, or the perfect comprehension of the problems of our day. . . . That book I would lay beside the Bible of every young minister to-day. I would have every preacher read it every year as long as he lives."

The Yale Lectures were followed by a demand for a volume of his sermons, as was to have been expected; and from so many directions as to constitute an imperative call. In response to the demand he selected twenty out of some six hundred which he had written. The principle guiding the selection it would be difficult to determine. What strikes the reader in the titles of the sermons is the large proportion assigned to topics of comfort and consolation: "The Purpose and Use of Comfort," "The Withheld Completions of Life," "The Soul's Refuge in God," "The Consolations of God." One other sermon similar in tone is from the text, "Brethren, the time is short." There seems something incongruous between the prevailing tone of the sermons and the man who, in his letters, or as he appeared in familiar conversation, abounded in humor, in mirth and vitality, as if he had known neither trouble nor sorrow. A person who had gone through great trials and had gained comfort from the reading of the sermons wrote to him.

" 'How did my brother find this out?' 'With a great sum obtained I this freedom.' Are you freeborn, or have you passed all through that way that even He trod, made perfect through suffering? . . . Not since Robertson's beautiful sermons has anything found me, and found me in such deep places (as Coleridge said of the Bible), as your sermons."

In answering this question he never alluded to experiences of his own. He would sometimes say that one could enter by imagination into the experience of others. We also know that he was constantly confronted with the problem of sorrow and suffering. His own personality attracted as by a magnet those who were in trouble. He suffered with them through the tenderness of his own soul and his vast outflow of sympathy.

The other sermons in this first volume had made great impression when they were preached, but they stood the test of the printed book and produced a like impression when they were read. There is one on the Trinity, which shows fine capacity of insight into theological distinctions. The sermon on "Humility" seemed to reveal a new cultus for the highest Christian virtue. "It came upon me like a flood of light," wrote a venerable divine, whose crowning attribute was humility. "The Positiveness of

the Divine Life" enforces the truth which **Chalmers and Bush-**
nell had proclaimed—"the expulsive power of a new affection."
The sermon for All Saints' Day is the only one belonging to his
Philadelphia ministry and is perhaps the most beautiful of all.
He compared the modern with the mediæval conceptions of saint-
hood: "That is the true apostolical saintly succession, the tactual
succession of heart touching heart with fire."

The first volume of sermons met with an extraordinary reception (1878) and reached a sale of more than twenty-five thousand.
The criticism was favorable, more often eulogistic in the highest degree.   This is representative of the best judgment:

"Unlike Robertson, Phillips Brooks constantly reminds us of
him.   He has the same analytical power; the same broad human
sympathy; the same keen knowledge of human nature, toned and
tempered and made more true by his sympathies; the same mysterious and indefinable element of divine life, so that his message
comes with a *quasi* authority, wholly unecclesiastical, purely personal; and the same undertone of sadness, the same touch of
pathos, speaking low as a man who is saddened by his own seeming success."

What the public press said of his sermons was one thing, what
the people were saying to him was another.   In these personal
letters we are listening to the secrets, as it were, of a confessional,
where people are pouring into his ear their sorrows, and are telling
of the relief he has given.   From every part of the country the
letters came, from those who had never heard or seen him, as
well as from those who found a special pleasure in associating his
voice and presence with the reading of the printed page.

"I am sure you will rejoice to hear how my life has been made
richer and fuller through your aid, and my poor blurred sight of
men as trees walking exchanged for clear outlines and effulgent
day."
"You are speaking to *men* as no one else can."
"No book save the Bible gives me so much strength and holy
ambition."
"I covet your method of presenting the truth of the Gospel
more than that of any man living."
" The volume has become my *vade mecum*.   Your sermons are
the highest interpretations of Christian philosophy ever uttered
from an American pulpit."

"You seem to me a person who understands human nature through a close study of yourself, having thoroughly tested all natural and acquired tendencies and resistances, and with sympathetic tenderness can tell others how to live and be victorious."

"They have helped me in a great and almost nameless trial through which I am now passing. Do you know there are trials, compared with which even that of a lifetime of bodily pain and prostration seems almost trivial? I cannot understand how you, who have perfect health and happiness, can know so much about the condition of those who have neither."

"To young ministers of all our tribes they are invaluable. I suppose that scarcely a man among our students will fail to read them, and all who can will own them. To me they are a refreshment for the cheer they give in the assurance that the pulpit is not waning."

The Philadelphia preaching differed in its tone from his Boston preaching. It was quite as mature, and even more rich, more suggestive and interesting, and marked by his peculiar fascination and charm to a greater degree than in his later years. But it was different in tone and purpose and method. Out of the three hundred and seventy-two sermons written in Philadelphia, he chose only five for publication, a small number out of the one hundred sermons to which he gave his approval by printing them. Taking these five as specimens it may be said of them that they are more poetic and imaginative, with a higher literary finish. There is the sermon, already mentioned, for All Saints' Day, 1868, from the text: "After this I beheld and lo, a multitude which no man can number"[1]; and another, 1869, from the text: "And a vision appeared unto Paul in the night: There stood a man from Macedonia, and prayed him, saying, Come over into Macedonia and help us"[2]; the third has for its text: "So speak ye, and so do, as they that shall be judged by the law of liberty"[3]—a sermon preached first in 1864, repeated in many places, and always with an impression which those who heard can never forget; the fourth, written in 1868, based on the passage in Revelation which speaks of "The sea of glass mingled with fire"[4]; and the fifth entitled "The Beautiful Gate of the Temple,"—a sermon first written in 1861, while in his second year in the ministry, but afterwards rewritten in 1873.[5]

[1] Vol. i., p. 117.   [2] Vol. ii., p. 91.   [3] Vol. ii., p. 183.
[4] Vol. iv., p. 110.   [5] Vol. iv., p. 127.

Two causes were operative in Boston to modify his preaching—causes at least which may be traced, whatever other influences may have combined with them. There no longer existed in Boston to the same extent as in Philadelphia the traditional reverence for the clergy in their official character as representing an authoritative organization. The second cause was that strange phenomenon which marked the seventies in the last century,—the decline or loss of religious faith, a falling away from religious beliefs, which may be compared with the ebb of the tide. In Philadelphia it had been Mr. Brooks's method in his sermons to illustrate and enforce old doctrines by fresh interpretation, revealing fuller meaning in old formulas, and some deeper psychological law in the spirit behind the letter. The change in the situation now called for a different method. He gave himself up in one supreme effort, to understand, to meet, and to overcome the evil of the hour. Into this task went the force which had made him great in other ways in Philadelphia.

Among the sermons included in the first volume of his sermons is a notable one, preached on Thanksgiving Day, 1874, from the text, "When the Son of Man cometh shall he find faith on the earth?" In the preamble to this sermon, he remarks: "I am led to think and to speak of the disturbed condition of faith in our time. No subject is more pressing. Even the most careless man's thoughts rest very much upon it. It is discussed and talked of everywhere." And again: "The most noticeable and touching thing about such times as ours is the way in which so many of the best men are silent and will not speak."

The preacher was hopeful, although he offered no panacea for the evil nor had he faith in the panaceas offered by others. "Dogmatism and ritualism are all wrong when they think themselves supremely believing. Both are really symptomatic forms of unbelief." Nor can any relief be obtained by renouncing individual freedom for traditional authority. The peculiar feature of the age is that "it takes its character from its relation to what has gone before and what is to come after rather than from what it contains in itself. This gives it an aspect of restlessness and unquiet. It is full of the sense of having broken with the past and of having not yet apprehended the future that is to come." Great results have been achieved, but the price paid for them has been heavy. "It is a magnificent story how natural science has brought out the starry host of second causes from their obscurity and shown how He who works everything works by everything in the world. This profuse discovery of means, however, has clouded thought regarding the Creator."

Throughout this sermon for the times runs the spirit of hope. He is an optimist because he believes in God. "I do not certainly say that such a time is best, though really in my heart I do not think the world has ever seen a better. There must be better ones to come. The story of the world is not yet told. 'We are ancients of the earth and in the morning of the times.'" He offers no solution of the conflict between religion and science. But it means something that, in the disorder of thought and feeling, so many men are fleeing to the study of orderly nature. He urges his hearers to make much of the experiences of life which are perpetual,—joy, sorrow, friendship, work, charity, relations with one's brethren, for these are eternal. It is not religion itself that is unsettled, but it is only the thoughts about religion that are not clear. Love is at the root of everything. Human souls respond to the appealing nature and life of Jesus Christ. Here is the great certainty. Be sure of God and nothing can overthrow or drown you.

With the religious conflict of the time Phillips Brooks identified himself, watching the phases it assumed, brooding over the subject in hours of leisure, in his walks among men, as he listened to the casual conversation, to the tacit assumptions, which implied more than was said. At the meetings of the Clericus Club the questions of the hour formed the staple element of discussion. He contributed his share to the talk, but among his other endowments he had the capacity of being the best of listeners. Every meeting of the club formed a picture to be studied. He neglected no source of information, and pre-eminently he studied himself in deep sincerity. He was preparing for some larger expression of himself, waiting till the time should come when he could put into form what was uppermost in his heart.

In 1878 Mr. Brooks went a second time to New Haven, giving two lectures before the students of the Yale Divinity School on the "Teaching of Religion." In the summer of the same year he made an address before the alumni of the theological seminary of Virginia, when he took for his subject, "The Relation of the Pulpit to Popular Skepticism."[1] The two themes are closely allied; in both he was dealing with the question,—how to meet the spirit of modern unbelief. There are important statements in his treatment of these themes which are worth recalling. He regarded it as an encouraging fact in an age of religious doubt that Christianity could be taught. As the teacher developed the capacities latent in the pupil, so there was in every man the capacity for religion, which must be evoked by the teacher's methods. Three methods of teaching he criticised; the dogmatic or intellectual, the emotional, and the mechanical: the first, holding that religion is taught when doctrines or truths have been imparted; the second, dwelling on the importance of moving the feelings; and the last, insisting on the confessional and spiritual directorship. The true method of teaching religion is where the personality of the teacher invades the personality of the scholar. The largest idea, which covers every demand of the ministry, consists "in bringing the personal Christ to the personal human nature." He turns this point over and reiterates it in many varying forms of expression: "The object of all the teaching is to bring Christ to men." When this principle is recognized as fundamental, other methods fall into their true relationship; doctrine, emotion, and conduct cease to be counted as valuable in themselves, and are valued as avenues through which Christ, the personal Christ, may come to the soul.

He protests against any tendency to "soften" the truth or pare it down to meet men's wishes: "It is the religion of most demands that has most ruled the world. The easy faiths have been the weak faiths. Always it has been easier to excite fanaticism than to build up a quiet reasonable belief":

"The hope of a large general belief in Christian truth, more general than any that any past age has witnessed, does, no doubt, involve a more reasonable and spiritual presentation of it than the past has seen, but it will never be attained by making truth meagre. . . . The only real assurance against unreal, fantastic,

[1] The first of the two lectures on the "Teaching of Religion" has been published in *Essays and Addresses*, the second is still in manuscript. The essay on the "Pulpit and Popular Skepticism" is also included in *Essays and Addresses*.

sensational, indulgent teaching about Christ is the teacher's own complete conviction, from his own experience, of the perfection and sufficiency of Christ, just as Christ is."

As to religious controversy, though he does not condemn it in the past, yet there are conditions of the public mind when a man must set his face against it. It is bad to cry, "Peace, peace!" when there is no peace. It is just as bad, in some ways it is worse, to cry, "War, war!" when there is no war.

"It seems to me as if, were I a layman in the days when some doctrine had got loose as it were into the wind and was being blown across the Common and up and down the streets, I should go to church on Sunday, not wanting my minister to give me an oracular answer to all the questions which had been started about it, which I should not believe if he did give it, but hcping that out of his sermon I might refresh my knowledge of Christ, get Him, His nature, His work, and His desire for me once more clear before me, and go out more ready to see this disputed truth of the moment in His light and as an utterance of Him. . . . *Preaching Christ!* That old phrase, which has been so often the very watchword of cant, how it still declares the true nature of Christian teaching! Not Christianity, but Christ! Not a doctrine, but a Person! Christianity only for Christ! The doctrine only for the Person!"

There occurs a passage here which is so exact a description of his own preaching, and of his own mysterious power, that it deserves quotation:

"A man comes and stands before a multitude of his fellow-men and tells them a story. It is of something which happened long ago, yet which concerns them. It is of something which happened in one special time and set of circumstances, yet it is universal. As he speaks, his fellow-men who listen begin to change before him. They flush and glow; . . . they tremble in their seats; they almost leap to their feet; tears start into their eyes. It is a most attractive spectacle. It fires the speaker, and he goes on to make yet more intense and glowing the emotion that reacts on him. One who stands by and gazes, though he may not hear a word, is caught with the thrilling, beating atmosphere, and finds himself trembling with mysterious desires. The voice stops, but the spell is not broken. The people rise and go away exalted. They tread the pavement as if it sprang beneath their feet and breathe the air as if it were alive with beautiful and serious thoughts."

While he is not willing to give the foremost place to feeling in religion, he recognizes its true place and importance. In this connection he speaks of music and its function in worship,— his own reflection as he stood in church or pulpit, while the service of song was performed:

"Church music is the general utterance of the melodiousness, the joy, the poetry of religion. And second, it is the special means by which a special truth is fastened on the soul, and a special duty made winning and authoritative. . . . When a great congregation is to praise the Lord and to learn truth and duty by the melody of song, I for one should be sorry to have it lose either of the two exaltations, either that which comes of the great, simple, sublime utterance of its own emotion, or that which comes from listening while voices which the Lord has filled with the gold and silver of His choicest and most mysterious harmony reveal to us the full beauty of truth and the full sweetness and sacredness of duty."

Here is another passage where he speaks of the music of preaching, and throws light upon his own work in the pulpit:

"What I have said of music applies, I think, to all the graces and appealing tones of the preacher's art. There is a music of preaching. What the melody of a hymn is to its words, that the eloquence of the preacher is to his truth. . . . We are afraid of eloquence nowadays. Eloquence of style or gesture has acquired a suspicion of unreality. It has gone out of favor in our colleges. It only lingers in our pulpits here and there. The fact that there is where it lingers makes us sometimes hope that there is where it shall be born into new power."

In the lectures on the "Teaching of Religion" Phillips Brooks followed the conventional method of finding a place in religion for intellect, feeling, and will. But already he is inclined to doubt the value of this method, although he does not yet discard it. The supreme place, however, is assigned to the will as the goal to which come intellect and feeling. He gives his own definition of religion, and among the many definitions it deserves a place for its distinctive quality: "Religion is the life of man in gratitude and obedience and gradually developing likeness to God";

and "the Christian religion is the life of man in gratitude and obedience and growing likeness to God in Christ. Religion is not service simply, nor is it grateful love alone, but gratitude assured by obedience, obedience uttering gratitude." No ancient Roman, pagan or Christian, ever asserted more strongly the claim of obedience to be the highest virtue. A most impressive catena of passages might be selected from his sermons in which he glorifies obedience. It is not the badge of servitude, but of freedom and equality. It is the mightiest of words, because it stands for the final expression of the man in whom the knowledge of Christ has entered, taking possession of the whole range of being. The obedience of Christ was the crown of His glory, the badge of His divinity. And in order to obedience the freedom of the will, in every sense of the word "freedom," is the inalienable prerogative of man.

The essay on "The Pulpit and Popular Skepticism" was published in the *Princeton Review* (1879), and in pamphlet form, and had a wide circulation. In speaking of the deeper sources of unbelief he says:

"It is not the difficulty of this or that doctrine that makes men skeptics to-day. It is rather the play of all life upon the fundamental grounds and general structure of faith. . . . Let this not seem too large or lofty an explanation of the commonplace phenomena of doubt, which are thick around us in our congregations in the world. The reason why my hearer, who sits moodily or scornfully or sadly before me in his pew, and does not cordially believe a word of what I preach to him, the reason why he disbelieves is not that he has found the evidence for inspiration or for Christ's divinity or for the Atonement unsatisfactory. It is that the aspect of the world, which is fate, has been too strong for the fundamental religion of the world, which is Providence. And the temptation of the world, which is self-indulgence, has seemed to make impossible the precept of religion, which is self-surrender; and the tendency of experience, which is hopelessness, has made the tendency of the gospel, which is hope, to seem unreal and unbelievable."

Because this is the character of the skepticism of the time it cannot be overcome by any special skill in proving this truth or disproving that error. The mind of the people and of the clergy is confused and doubtful about the once received doctrines of "verbal inspiration" and of endless punishment. Let the clergy be candid in dealing with these points. "A large acquaintance with clerical life has led me to think that almost any company of clergymen gathering together and talking freely to one another will express opinions which would greatly surprise and at the same time relieve the congregations who ordinarily listen to these ministers." The old talk about holding the outworks as long as possible before retreating to the citadel is based upon a metaphor than which none could be more mischievous. It is a dangerous experiment for parents to try with their children, teaching them what they themselves have long since ceased to believe.

He repeats what he had already said in his lectures on the "Teaching of Religion," that it is a foolish and base idea to suppose that in days like these men want to have Christian truth made slight and easy for them. In this connection he utters what seems like a prophecy that has been fulfilled:

"It would be no strange issue of such times as we are living in, if out of them should come a great demand for difficult doctrine, a time of superstition, a fever to succeed the chill; for the spirit that cries, '*Credo quia impossibile*,' the heroic spirit of faith, is too deep in our human nature for any one century to have eradicated it."

After discussing the question of doctrines, and urging that they must be shown to have some necessary connection with righteousness of character if they are to be re-established in the minds of men, he adds:

"There are doctrinal statements, which puzzle and bewilder, which are in reality excrescences on the faith and must be cast away by the natural and healthy action of the system. There are doctrinal statements, which once were true and did vast good and yet were only temporary aspects of the truth. There are men living by them still, as men are still seeing the light of the stars extinguished in the heavens long ago. The time will come when these temporary statements will disappear, and when their light goes out it will be of all importance that men recognize the sun by whose light these accidental and temporary points of its exhibition have been shining.

"This sun of all truth is the person of Christ. The characteristic of our modern Christianity, which correlates it with all apostolic times, is the substitution of loyalty to a person in place of belief in doctrines as the essence and test of Christian life. This is the simplicity and unity by which the Gospel can become effective. These are the ideas of Christianity which are in conflict to-day,—one magnifying doctrine whose great sin is heresy; the other magnifying obedience. To follow the latter is in these days, I think, the best method of dealing in the pulpit with popular skepticism. The superiority of this method, whose essence is the personal relationship with Christ, lies in this—that it offers 'the highest picture of the combination of stability with progress; while, on the other hand, the intellectual conception is always sacrificing stability to progress or progress to stability.'"

The age of doubt intensified the feeling that if the various bodies into which the Christian world is divided could so subordinate their differences as to consolidate into one imposing organization, the Church could again speak with authority to a distracted age. On this point Phillips Brooks remarks:

"I do not see the slightest promise in any dimmest distance of what is called the organic unity of Christendom on the basis of episcopacy or any other basis. I do not see the slightest chance of the entire harmonizing of Christian doctrine throughout the Christian world,—that dream which men have dreamed ever since Christ ascended into Heaven, that sight which no man's eye has seen in any age. But I do see signs that, keeping their different thoughts concerning Him and His teachings, men, loyal to Christ, owning His love, trusting His love, may be united in the only union which is really valuable wherever His blessed name is known. In that union, and in that alone, can I find myself truly one alike with Peter and with Paul, alike with Origen and Athanasius and Augustine, alike with Luther and with Zwingle and with Calvin and with St. Francis and with Bishop Andrews and with Dr. Channing, alike with the prelate who ordains me and with the Methodist or Baptist brother who is trying to bring men to the same Christ in the same street where I am working. And no union which will not include all these ought wholly to satisfy us, because no other will wholly satisfy the last great prayer of Jesus."

And with this statement he concludes his discussion of the prevailing skepticism:

"My one great comprehensive answer then to the question, What is the best method of dealing in the pulpit with popular skepticism? is really this: Make known and real to men by every means you can command the personal Christ, not doctrine about Him, but Him; strike at the tyranny of the physical life by the power of His spiritual presence. Let faith mean, make faith mean, trusting Him and trying to obey Him. Call any man a Christian who is following Him. Denounce no error as fatal which does not separate a soul from Him. Offer Him to the world as He offered and is forever offering Himself."

These words with which Phillips Brooks concluded his essay on "The Pulpit and Popular Skepticism" are the keynote of the Bohlen Lectures on "The Influence of Jesus" (1879). Its large circulation bears witness to the need it met at the time, but it has also enduring qualities which secure its permanent place in religious literature. There have been many studies in the life of Christ since its appearance, but none that surpasses it in insight, in the reverend appreciation of that divine-human consciousness which no one can ever hope entirely to fathom. Because it was a work designed to meet the special wants of the hour, one inevitably recalls, in reading it, the tendencies of the time when it was written. It was addressed to an age which felt the influence of modern science in creating a new way of looking upon the world. This would have been enough in itself to shake religious beliefs. But combined with this influence was the effect of Biblical criticism in breaking down Protestant scholasticism. The infallibility of the Bible, which had been the basis of Protestant scholastic systems, could not longer be maintained, and with its loss were endangered doctrines such as inspiration of Scripture, the atonement of Christ, the endless punishment of the wicked. For various reasons these doctrines had become obnoxious, and unless guaranteed by infallible authority of some sort their continued hold upon the Christian mind seemed precarious. Under these circumstances, the pressing question was,—where lay the authority, if there was no longer an infallible book? Some fell back upon the authority of tradition expressed by General Councils and long-established usage. The Roman Church was alive to the situation, and the year 1870 was considered opportune for declaring the infallibility of the Pope, in the expectation that a distracted world would be moved by the announcement. Others asserted the inward authority of the soul as divinely endowed to speak with finality upon religious truth—the attitude of what was then known as Transcendentalism. The questionings went further, and it was asked, What is Christianity? What has it done for the world? or is modern civilization so indebted to the Church that it would suffer loss from the decadence of Christian influence? This was the situation when Phillips Brooks came to the task of writing the Bohlen Lectures, or as it had confronted him in his earlier efforts to meet the scepticism of his age. Each successive effort sent him to deeper inquiry, enforcing on him the necessity of seeking some positive substitute for that which had been lost. But he did not come to the inquiry in any scholastic mood, or with the purpose of taking part in theological controversy in order to contribute to the solution of a theological problem. The question of authority resolved itself into the practical issue of the moral and spiritual life.

At first, as he planned his work, he had proposed to answer the question, "How far is the present condition of the social and personal life of Christendom due to Christian faith?" The question answered itself in his mind,—it must be due to the personal influence of Jesus in history. *The Influence of Jesus* was then taken as the title of his book. From the time when he began his preparation for the ministry he had been in search of a stronger religion and a stronger Christ than the age presented. He needed it first for himself and then for others. His tumultuous nature cried out for strength, for some one to obey, whose will would subdue him and bring him into the captivity wherein lies perfect freedom. The outcry of his soul was for a powerful Christ, "a Christ so completely powerful that once perfectly present with a human soul He must master it and it must yield to Him. If the reason why men doubt Him is that they do not, cannot, will not, see Him, then I think it must be certain that what they need is a completer, more living presentation of His personality, so that He shall stand before them and claim what always was His claim, 'Believe in Me'—not 'Believe this or that about Me,' but 'Believe in Me.'" Like all great men and strong natures, Phillips Brooks could live only in contact with strength and greatness. He complains that "Christianity is to multitudes of people a purely abstract system. It has lost its personal aspect. But Christianity is what? The service of

Christ. Its very essence is its personality. It is all built about a person. Take Him out and it all falls to pieces. Just because He *has* been taken out of the religion which many of us call our Christianity, just for that reason is our Christianity a poor thing of the remote brain, bringing no peace to our hearts, and no strength to our hands, no comfort to our sorrows, and no benediction to our joy."

It had constituted an epoch in the life of Phillips Brooks when the book *Ecce Homo* by Professor Seeley appeared in 1865. No book in his library was more worn by frequent usage. It coincided with the whole tendency of his own development. He drew from it profound inferences which the author had not contemplated, but he was one with it in its fundamental contention that Christ was the strongest man in human history. The Christ of *Ecce Homo*, as the author presented the picture, so explained and justified the Christ of history that difficulties about the narratives and sources no longer embarrassed. A strong man, with a clear view of His purpose from the moment He began to teach; no mere teacher uttering placidly his sentiments, but from the first assuming the position of an authoritative lawgiver, enforcing His word by the most powerful of sanctions, calling into existence a society, legislating for that society to the end of time,—this was in outline the Christ in the pages of *Ecce Homo*. "The achievement of Christ in founding by His single will and power a structure so durable and so universal is like no other achievement which history records. The masterpieces of the men of action are coarse and common in comparison with it, and the masterpieces of speculation flimsy and unsubstantial. When we speak of it the commonplaces of admiration fail us altogether."[1]

When Phillips Brooks came to Boston he encountered the impression left by the New England school of Transcendentalists, that no special unique authority belonged to the person of Christ, however great the respect for the ideas he enunciated. It became a commonplace among them to class him with Plato and Socrates and Mohammed, or as one who had contributed to the world's stock of ideas. Mr. Emerson had said, "The soul knows no persons." Theodore Parker had been the chief re-

[1] Cf. Am. ed., p. 354.

ligious exponent of transcendentalism in Boston (1860). For the
religious ideal of Jesus he had the profoundest reverence, but he
could not believe that the truth which Jesus taught depended
on His personality for its propagating power in the world:

"It seems difficult to conceive any reason why moral and
religious truths should rest for their support on the personal
authority of their revealer, any more than the truths of science
on that of him who makes them known first or most clearly.
It is hard to see why the great truths of Christianity rest on the
personal authority of Jesus more than the axioms of geometry
rest on the personal authority of Euclid or Archimedes. The
authority of Jesus, as of all teachers, one would naturally think,
must rest on the truth of his words, and not their truth on his
authority."[1]

Some of Parker's friends and sympathizers were disturbed by
this statement. But he was on fire with his conviction that
every soul should be the judge and arbiter of truth in virtue of
the gift of immediate vision. Painful though the statement
might be, he repeated it in his later *Discourse of Religion*, and
in stronger form: "If Christianity be true at all it would be just
as true if Herod or Catiline had taught it."

Upon this point Phillips Brooks had attained to permanent
conviction at an early period in his ministry. In a sermon written in 1861 he had said:

"I maintain that all such impersonal truth, when it is acquired,
however much it may do for the sharpening and stocking the
brains and improving the outward conditions of mankind, is as
bad as useless as far as any immediate effect upon the character
and temperament is concerned. All truth must be brought, in
order to be effective, through a personal medium. Which of us
can dare to say that he would hold the most effective truths that
he believes in just as much and just in the same way as he does
now, if they had come to him anonymously? . . . We have
some personality behind them all; a mother's voice yet trembles
in them, a father's authority makes them solemn, a teacher's
enthusiasm will not let us count them trivial, and so they first
have gained and so they still hold their great power over us."

The Influence of Jesus is not a controversial treatise. But

---

[1] *Discourses of Matters pertaining to Religion*, p. 244, Boston, ed. 1842.

the following passage from its opening pages shows that the author felt called upon to resist the view that the personal character of the teacher may be disconnected from the message:

"I have been led to think of Christianity and to speak of it, at least in these lectures, not as a system of doctrine, but as a personal force behind which and in which there lies one great and inspiring idea, which it is the work of the personal force to impress upon the life of man, with which the personal force is always struggling to fill mankind. The personal force is the nature of Jesus, full of humanity, full of divinity, and powerful with a love for man which combines in itself every element that enters into love of the completest kind. . . . Every man's power is his idea multiplied by and projected through his personality. The special actions which he does are only the points at which his power shows itself. . . . The power of Jesus is the idea of Jesus multiplied and projected through the person of Jesus. . . . The message entrusted to the Son of God when He came to be the Saviour of mankind was not only something which He knew and taught; it was something which He was. . . . The idea and the person are so mingled that we cannot separate them. He is the truth, and whoever receives Him becomes the son of God" (pp. 12, 13).

And again, in another passage, he makes this more definite allusion: "Not from simple brain to simple brain, as the reasoning of Euclid comes to its students, but from total character to total character, comes the New Testament from God to man"(p. 234).

The lectures were written with great rapidity, for the time at his disposal was short. They were begun at the Christmas season, when the claims of parish and social life were most pressing. He wrote out of his own soul, full of emotion and intellectual fervor. Many of his sermons were here condensed, a sermon in a paragraph; such, for example, as he preached when Principal Tulloch was listening, with its flash of insight and reality. The constant study of the Bible and of the life of Christ, wherein he had gained more than he could give in yearly Bible class or Lenten meditations, or Wednesday evening lectures, was yielding its unsuspected contributions. The book was done in haste, but it was the product of the slow process of years. Some features of the book, in its methods and conclusions, will throw light on the position that Phillips Brooks occupied in his age. In the first place, he attempted the portrayal of a Christ whose mastery was capable of dominating every soul, and of subduing all humanity to Himself. To this end he identified the personality of Jesus with the essence of His religion. By personality he understood the inmost nature and character, that within a man which rules the life. He had brought out this truth in his *Lectures on Preaching*, and elsewhere in his writings. But now he drags it once more into the foreground of a great picture, presenting it with tireless energy and with the eloquence of deep conviction. Everything depends on the prominence which is given to a principle. This is originality, to make a truth supreme through the setting which is given it. Thus it becomes a new truth. It was not enough to present Christ as a moral Guide, uttering ethical precepts worthy of obedience; nor as the Master, imparting knowledge and conveying information about the spiritual world. He was indeed the *Way*, and He was the *Truth*, but He was these because He was first the *Life*.

This principle of the identification of the personality of the teacher with his message might be in danger of becoming a formula, abstract and unprofitable, unless the secret of the personality of Jesus could be unveiled, and become the living possession of humanity. This was the task undertaken in *The Influence of Jesus*, to present the idea which inspired Him, the clue to His divine consciousness, and the motive of His acts. This inspiring idea is "the Fatherhood of God and the childhood of every man in Him."

"Upon the race and upon the individual, Jesus is always bringing into more and more perfect revelation the certain truth that man, and every man, is the child of God. This is the sum of the work of the Incarnation. A hundred other statements regarding it, regarding Him who was incarnate, are true; but all statements concerning Him hold their truth within this truth, —that Jesus came to restore the fact of God's fatherhood to man's knowledge and to its central place of power over man's life" (p. 12).

It had been the usage in the Evangelical school, in which Mr. Brooks was reared, to speak only of the baptized or the regenerate as the children of God. From this view he departs in order to build upon the antecedent truth that every man is the child of God by nature. It is because he is the child by nature that he is capable of becoming the child by grace. In making this truth a first principle in his teaching he was reaffirming what was taught in the standards of the Anglican Church, however it had been obscured,—what Maurice and Robertson and others had brought to light. He differed from them, if he differed at all, in making it the basis of his powerful appeal in the pulpit, as also in making it the central point from which by necessary inference proceeded all other religious teaching. He brought together nature and grace, creation and redemption, in organic relationship. All men alike everywhere inherited in virtue of their birthright the privilege to pray, "Our Father which art in heaven."

"Surely, we cannot be wrong if we say positively that to Christ himself the truth that man was God's child by nature was the great fact of man's existence; and the desire that man might be God's child in reality was the motive of His own life and work" (p. 20).

"To reassert the childhood and fatherhood as an unlost truth, and to re-establish its power as the central fact of life; to tell men that they were, and to make them actually to be, the sons of God —that was the purpose of the coming of Jesus and the shaping power of his life. . . .

"It is more important than we often think, that we should grasp the general idea, the general purpose, of the life of Jesus. The Gospels become to us a new book when we no longer read them merely as the anecdotes of the life of one who, with a great, kind heart, went through the world promiscuously doing good as opportunities occurred to Him. The drifting and haphazard currents gather themselves together, and we are borne on with the full and enthusiastic impulse of a great river which knows itself and knows the sea it seeks. And when the ruling idea is this which fills the life of Jesus, it is doubly true that only by clearly seizing it can we get at the heart and meaning of His life" (pp. 16, 17).

Ethics have often been conceived as separable from religion. Phillips Brooks identifies them:

"The difference between Christian morality and any other which the world has seen does not consist in the difference of its precepts,—for these can be matched in other codes. The motive of all the injunctions in the Sermon on the Mount is the Father, first as the standard of the moral life enforced, and then as the power by which that standard is pursued and attained. There is nothing abstract and cold. Everything shines and burns with personal affection. Be ye perfect even as your Father which is in heaven. Love your enemies, that ye may be the children of your Father. Let your light shine before men that they may glorify your Father. Blessed are the peacemakers, for they shall be called the children of God. The idea of God which fills the great discourse is the idea of the Father." If the question is raised whether this standard be intelligible and practicable, the answer is derived from the first great principle of the Fatherhood of God and the sonship of every man: "It is in the fact that He is your Father, and that you are His child, that the possibility of likeness lies and that the kind of possible likeness is decreed."

The chapter entitled "Influence of Jesus on the Social Life of Man" is written under the conviction that the key to Christ's treatment of men is the constant desire to foster the consciousness of divine sonship by intercourse with those who are fellow-sons of the same Father. The incidents in the life of Christ are brought together with singular felicity in illustration of this truth, that the social nature of man is the provision at once for his most complete self-consciousness and for his fullest activity and efficiency. So important is the social life in the constitution of humanity that it must needs have its analogue in Deity.

"It was by losing His life in the multitude and mass of lives, in the body of humanity to which He belonged, that Jesus at once found His own life and found the lives of the lost, whom He had come to seek. At the very outset He bore witness that not in absolute singleness, not in elemental unity and perfect solitude of being, is the highest existence to be found. He recognized at once in man that multiplicity and power of relationship within the unit of humanity which makes the richness of our human life. If it be so, as we believe it is, that in the constitution of humanity we have the fairest written analogue and picture of the Divine existence, then shall we not say that the human Christ gave us, in the value which He set on human relationships, in His social thought of man, an insight into the essentialness and value of that social thought of God which we call the doctrine of the Trinity? May it not be that only by multiplicity and interior self-relationship can Divinity have the completest self-consciousness and energy? Surely, the reverent and thoughtful eye must see some such meaning when Jesus himself makes the eternal companionship of the life of Deity the pattern and picture of the best society of the souls of the earth, and breathes out to His Father these deep and wondrous words, 'As thou, Father, art in Me and I in Thee, that they all may be one in us.'"

In the latter part of the nineteenth century there was one subject uppermost in the consciousness of thoughtful minds,—how to maintain the goodness of God and a divine Providence against pessimistic tendencies which came at first from speculative thinkers, yet somehow found a response in the common consciousness. The influence of this mood may be traced in the pulpit, in more emphatic and continuous assertions of the goodness, the love, the beneficent providence of God. If this tone of preaching seemed to some an effort to soften the religion, its real motive lay in a more positive purpose,—the justification of the ways of God with men. Men were becoming more keenly alive to the evil in nature and in the moral order. The quickened sensitiveness of an age in which humanitarian sentiment had been so dominant as in the nineteenth century, proved a congenial soil for pessimistic theories of the universe.

To the new necessity Phillips Brooks responded. Before he knew of Schopenhauer and Hartmann he had become sensitive to the issue. He felt the pleasure of living more than most men, but also encountered human suffering on a large scale in the ministrations of the pastoral charge, as well as in his own experience. To this subject he now comes in his third lecture, entitled "The Influence of Jesus on the Emotional Life of Man." He had before him the life of Christ as the ideal expression of humanity; he must enter into the experience of Jesus by the open door of the common experience of humanity.

It tells us nothing, he remarks, about a life to say that it is made up of joy and pain. We discover very early that happiness may mean much or little; that before we can determine the quality of a life we must penetrate the consciousness that lies beneath the sorrow or the joy. The joy and the pain are simply the expressions of emotion:

"The man who lacks emotion lacks expression. That which is in him remains within him, and he cannot utter it or make it influential. And on the other hand the man who lacks emotion lacks receptiveness. That which other men are, if it does not make him glad or sorry, if it gives him neither joy nor pain, does not become his. The emotion of lives is the magnetism that they emit, something closely associated with their substance and yet distinct from it, in which they communicate with one another. There is a condition conceivable in which the emotions should be so delicately and perfectly true to the quality of him from which they issue, that they should furnish a perfect medium of expression. . . . Can any true connection be reliably traced between the way that a man lives and the joy or sorrow his life emits?

"Jesus always thinks of Himself as undergoing the will of God, because God is His father. The pain and pleasure which come to Him in undergoing that will come not simply with their own inherent qualities of comfort or discomfort, but with the values they get from that obedience of which they are the signs and consequences. This is the key to all His attitude towards them. Jesus, with all His sensitiveness to pain and joy, never allows pain or joy to be either the purpose of life or the test of life.

"The sensitiveness of Jesus to pain and joy never leads Him for a moment to try to be sad or happy with direct endeavor; nor is there any sign that He ever judges the real character of Himself or any other man by the sadness or the happiness that for the moment covers His life. He simply lives, and joy and sorrow issue from His living, and cast their brightness and their gloominess back upon His life; but there is no sorrow and no joy that He ever sought for itself, and He always kept self-knowledge underneath the joy or sorrow, undisturbed by the moment's happiness or unhappiness. They were like ripples on the surface of the stream, made by its flow, and, we are ready to imagine, enjoyed by the stream that made them, not sought by the stream for themselves, nor ever obscuring the stream's consciousness of its deeper currents. The supreme sorrow of the cross was never sought because it was sorrowful, and even while He hung in agony it never obscured the certainty of His own holiness in the great Sufferer's soul. These are the perpetual characteristics of the emotional life of Jesus, which our theology has often conjured out of sight, but which are of unspeakable value, as I think; for a clear understanding of them puts the Man who suffered and enjoyed more than any other man that ever lived in a noble and true relation to His suffering and joy, and makes His pain and pleasure a gospel to men in their sadness and their gladness everywhere" (pp. 156, 157).

In the last chapter is treated the influence of Jesus on the intellectual life of man. In tone it is still impersonal, but the writer is disclosing his own method of self-culture and his distinctive attitude towards the theologies of his time. All through the chapter we move in the atmosphere of greatness. But it is the atmosphere of poetry and beauty as well. The ease, the grace, the repose, the transparency of the style, the consciousness of mastery, the sense of finality, the irresistible appeal,—these are the accompaniments of a strain of rich melody.

In the first place he refuses to give the intellect in man the supremacy when taken by itself. He has said this before, but repeats it with deeper conviction. In speaking of the person of Christ, he asks the questions: How does Christ compare in intellectual power with other men? How did he estimate the intellect? Was His intellect sufficient to account for the unique position He holds in the world's history as the mightiest force that has controlled the development of humanity?

He finds the answer by turning to the Fourth Gospel, which gives us most that we know about the mind of Jesus. It is to the other Gospels what Plato is to Xenophon. He does not allude to questions of criticism,—when it was written, or whether it was written by John. He regards the picture as its own vindication. It is the intellectual Gospel, because there is one constantly recurring word,—"truth," which is distinctly a word of the intellect. But in the Fourth Gospel, in every instance, it is employed in a sense different from that of the schools. In its scholastic use it is detached from life and made synonymous with knowledge. But knowledge is no word of Jesus. With information for the head alone, detached from its relations to the whole nature, Jesus has no concern. Truth was something which set the whole man free. It was a moral thing, for he who does not receive it is not merely a doubter, but a liar. Truth was something which a man could be, not merely something which a man could study and measure by walking around it on the outside. The objective and the subjective lose themselves in each other. Truth can be known only from the inside; it is something moral, something living, something spiritual. It is not mere objective unity; it must have in it the elements of character. "To this end was I born," says Jesus, "and for this cause came I into the world, that I should bear witness to the truth. Every one that is of the truth heareth my voice."

21

From this use of the word "truth" is deduced the intellectual portrait of Christ, if we may call it such.   The great fact
concerning the intellectual life in Jesus is this, that "in Him the
intellect never works alone.   You can never separate its workings
from the complete operations of the whole nature.   He never
simply knows, but always loves and resolves at the same time."
To this unity of one's being there is an approximation possible
in every man, as in those moments of exaltation when a man
realizes himself in supreme degree, and the "intellectual action,
without being quenched, nay, burning at its very brightest, blends
with the quickened activity of all the being, and is not even
thought of by itself."   This is the meaning of Lessing's remark, "He who does not lose his reason in certain things has
none to lose."   Or again in the lines of Wordsworth:

> " In such access of mind, in such high hour
>   Of Visitation from the Living God,
>   Thought was not; in enjoyment it expired."

In the further exposition of this principle, he turns to the comparison of Jesus and Socrates, placing the last five chapters of the
Gospel of St. John by the side of the story of the death of Socrates which Plato has told in the *Phædo*.   "Nowhere," he says,
"could the essential difference as well as the likeness of the two
great teachers become more apparent."   To this comparison
he invites "the critics who loosely class Jesus and Socrates together," showing them where their classification fails, where the
line runs beyond which Socrates cannot go, "beyond which the
nature of Jesus sweeps out of our sight."

When he was a boy of fifteen, just leaving the Latin School, it
had been Socrates, the "innocent martyr for truth," who had
fired Phillips Brooks with zeal in the immortal quest.   Now for
twenty years he had been studying the life of Jesus, and, though
he had lost none of his reverence and admiration for Socrates,
there had grown up in his soul a higher and a different reverence,
mingled with love and grateful obedience.

"I know not what to say to any man who does not feel the difference.   I can almost dream what Socrates would say to any
man who said that there was no difference between Jesus and
him.   But how shall we state the difference?   One is divine and

human; the other is human only.   One is Redeemer; the other is philosopher.   One is inspired, the other questions.   One reveals and the other argues.   These statements are doubtless all true. And in them all there is wrapped up this, which is the truth of all the influence of Jesus over men's minds, that where Socrates brings an argument to meet an objection, Jesus always brings a nature to meet a nature,—a whole being which the truth has filled with strength, to meet another whole being which error has filled with feebleness" (p. 243).

In a few words, towards the close of his book, he ventures to sum up the intellectual characteristics of Christ, as He may have impressed them on His disciples:

"A poetic conception of the world we live in, a willing accept- ance of mystery, an expectation of progress by development, an absence of fastidiousness that comes from the possibilities of all humanity, and a perpetual enlargement of thought from the arbi- trary into the essential,—these, I think, are the intellectual char- acteristics which Christ's disciples gathered from their Master; and I think that we can see that these characteristics make, as we set them together, a certain definite and recognizable type of mental life, one that we should know from every other if we met to-day a man in whom it was embodied."

This book, therefore, *The Influence of Jesus*, may be called the Apologia of Phillips Brooks.   It is the defence of himself and of his method, the exposition of his ideal of life, his final answer to the question how to meet the doubt, the weakness, the skepticism of the time.   Although he seemed, and indeed he was, in sym- pathy with his age, yet he saw its defect and had the quality of resisting his environment.   A one-sided intellectualism was the evil which had infected human inquiry.   The things of religion had been hurt by a scholastic tendency.   He pointed out the remedy,—the influence of Jesus tended to the restoration of a lost symmetry.   This was the result of his experience in the first ten years of his Boston ministry, which gives to his preaching in Boston a different tone from the Philadelphia life.   Then he had delighted in exploiting the rich allegorical import of human life and human history, with Christ as its centre and interpreter. The Boston ministry led him to proclaim the stronger Christ, who was powerful enough to subdue the world to Himself.   There are hints in this book that another advance was awaiting him. At times he seems to be tempted to give the primacy to the will. When he speaks of the obedience of Christ, it is clear that he is tending to divinize obedience as the potent faculty in Christ, through which His inspiration came, through which came also the wisdom of God. It is in the sphere of the will that the intimacy is closer than in the intellect. Through the perfect obedience of Christ comes the consciousness of oneness with the Father. Everywhere the inference is that perfect obedience of Christ means not subordination or inferiority, but coequality with the Father. With these eloquent words he closes the book:

"I dare not, I do not, hope that I have succeeded; but I hope that I have not wholly failed. For to me what I have tried to say is more and more the glory and the richness and the sweetness of all life. The idea of Jesus is the illumination and the inspiration of existence. Without it moral life becomes a barren expediency, and social life a hollow shell, and emotional life a meaningless excitement, and intellectual life an idle play or stupid drudgery. Without it the world is a puzzle, and death a horror, and eternity a blank. More and more it shines the only hope of what without it is all darkness. More and more the wild, sad, frightened cries of men who believe nothing, and the calm, earnest, patient prayers of men who believe so much that they long for perfect faith, seem to blend into the great appeal which Philip of Bethsaida made to Jesus at the Last Supper, where so much of our time in these four hours has been spent, 'Lord, show us the Father, and it sufficeth us.' And more and more the only answer to that appeal seems to come from the same blessed lips that answered Philip, the lips of the Mediator Jesus, who replies, 'Have I been so long with you and yet hast thou not known me? He that hath seen me hath seen the Father.'"

CHAPTER XIII.

1877–1880.

EXTRACTS FROM CORRESPONDENCE. INVITATION TO
PREACH FOR MR. MOODY. SUMMER IN EUROPE.
SERMON AT WESTMINSTER ABBEY. DEGREE OF
DOCTOR OF DIVINITY CONFERRED BY HARVARD
UNIVERSITY. COMMENTS ON THE GENERAL CON-
VENTION. VISIT OF DEAN STANLEY TO AMERICA.
ILLNESS AND DEATH OF HIS FATHER. VISIT TO
PHILADELPHIA. CONVENTION SERMON. CORRES-
PONDENCE. THE DEATH OF HIS MOTHER. SER-
MON BEFORE THE QUEEN. WESTMINSTER ABBEY.

THE chief event in the year 1877 was the consecration of the
new Trinity Church. Then had followed the delivery of the
"Lectures on Preaching" before the Divinity School of Yale
University. During the season of Lent, a "revival" was in
process in Boston under the direction of Mr. Moody the evangelist, to which Mr. Brooks alludes in letters to his brother. He
was in sympathy with the movement:

"I have been amused at the way in which the New York clergy
have given us their blessing since we started. Dr. Tyng preached
for us on the afternoon of the first day, and told us that nobody
could be a Christian who did n't believe that the world was made
in six literal days. The Moses up in the new Tower laughed
aloud at the statement. Yesterday afternoon Dr. Morgan of St.
Thomas's in your town turned up and preached an orotund discourse which had quite a good manly flavor to it. In consequence of his appearance, I find myself the surprised possessor of
a discourse which I have never preached, an event which has not
occurred before, except on a Saturday, for years. . . .
"We are in the rush of Lent. One talks until he is tired of the

sound of his own voice, and then he talks some more. There is a good healthy religious influence, I think, and underneath our little work the deep thunder of the Moody movement is rolling all the time. . . . As a sort of variety in Lent I have begun to read Miss Martineau's ' Autobiography.' It is as unlike a Lent lecture as possible. The calm complacency of her unbelief is something wonderful."

While the revival meetings were in progress Mr. Moody was for some reason unable to preach, and Mr. Brooks was invited to take his place. It was a most unusual circumstance, that an Episcopal clergyman, the rector too of Trinity Church, should receive such an invitation. Many doubted whether Mr. Brooks could hold a congregation drawn together by Mr. Moody's peculiar gift of earnest and direct appeal. But he was invited in the confidence that the thousands who were flocking nightly to the tent, or " Tabernacle " as it was called, where the services were held would not be disappointed when they knew of the change. The confidence was not misplaced. It was an event in the history of the revival that Phillips Brooks had taken part in it. On that evening the "Tabernacle" is reported as filled to its utmost capacity. Mr. Sankey sang "The Ninety and Nine." Other hymns were "Just as I am without one plea," and "'Tis the promise of God full salvation to give." The text from which the sermon was preached was the words of St. Paul describing his conversion:" Whereupon, O King Agrippa, I was not disobedient unto the heavenly vision." The preacher was at his best as he unfolded the text, expounding the principle of conversion as he himself had experienced it,—that the vision must come first, to be followed by obedience, when the sense of sin would inevitably ensue, but with the assurance of forgiveness. He condemned the opposite method which sought first to produce the sense of sin, and after the conviction of forgiveness had been attained, held out the prospect of the heavenly vision. He assumed throughout that religion was natural to man, because all men were by creation and by redemption the children of God. They had wandered, they had forgotten or neglected or were ignorant of their birthright; but when the vision came, it appealed to something in every man's constitution, rousing within him the dormant faculties of a divine relationship.

It had now been three years since Mr. Brooks had known a vacation which had brought him rest from preaching. During the summer of 1875 he had preached at Emmanuel Church, Boston, and in the summer of 1876 at Emmanuel in the morning and at St. Mark's in the evening. His congregations were composed of dwellers in the city who could not leave, and of strangers sojourning or passing through, who availed themselves of the opportunity. This free gift of himself met its full appreciation, and was part of the larger ministry to which he was dedicated. But now he had resolved upon a summer in Europe, for, though he does not mention it, the strain had been long and severe. When his intention was known, the following unanimous resolution was taken at a meeting of the Proprietors of Trinity Church, on Easter Monday:

"That the Proprietors of Trinity Church, deeply sensible of the great labors of their Rector during the past year, and of the invaluable services which he has rendered to the Church, desire to express their cordial concurrence in his purpose to seek rest and relaxation in foreign travel during the approaching summer, and that the sum of Two Thousand dollars be appropriated towards defraying the expenses of his tour, with the best wishes of us all that he may enjoy the vacation which he has so richly earned, and return to us with fresh vigor for his work."

Mr. Brooks was entrusted with an important commission in London,—to arrange for the stained glass windows in the new church, in which he took immense interest. He made a visit to Groton, of which he writes to Mr. Winthrop:

"How much I thank you for sending me there. It was a delightful day, and the drive from Sudbury to Groton was very charming. The Rector was most courteous and hospitable, and I saw all that must always make the place very interesting to Massachusetts men."

General Grant was then in England, of whom he writes as the great sensation, eclipsing all other Americans, "as if they [the English] wondered what *we* had come for." He dined at the American Minister's, and met the "great warrior." He saw much of Dean Stanley and was saddened by his appearance, and by the change in the Deanery. On Sunday, July 8th, he preached at Westminster Abbey. Canon Farrar, whose acquaintance he made, wrote to him: "It was a very great pleasure to me to resign the Abbey pulpit to you, and very nobly you used the opportunity." Dean Stanley, who was present, listened with delight to a doctrine after his own heart. The text was from Isaiah lx. 19: "The sun shall be no more thy light by day; neither for brightness shall the moon give light unto thee: but the Lord shall be unto thee an everlasting light, and thy God thy glory." The subject was "The Symbol and the Reality." At a moment when mediæval ritual was urged upon the modern church as though a mistake had been made in abandoning it, when it was argued that an elaborate and gorgeous symbolism was a necessity of the religious life, the conviction was growing stronger in the mind of the preacher that this was not the method which brought the highest result, that no symbol was doing its true work unless it was educating those who used it to do without it if need be. This principle was applied not only to religious symbolism, but to all the symbols of life. Everywhere the letter stands for the spirit, and to give up the letter, that the spirit may live more fully, becomes from time to time the absolute necessity.

While he was in Holland he received the news that Harvard University had in his absence conferred upon him the honorary degree of Doctor of Divinity. On the diploma sent to him it read that the degree was given "in recognition of his eloquence as a preacher, his dignity and purity of life as a minister of religion, and his liberality and large-mindedness as a man." To the Rev. James P. Franks, who first conveyed him the news, he wrote:

"AMSTERDAM, July 15, 1877. I was surprised at it, and of course gratified. I had supposed the College had given up all idea of making any more D.D's, and especially that they would not give the degree to one of their own overseers. But as they have thought good to do it, I am pleased and proud, for a Cambridge man thinks that there are no honors like those which come from Cambridge. Only I won't be called Dr. Brooks, and you may stop that for me when and where you can. . . .

"You are in Salem and preparing to preach the gospel to S——to-day. I honor you, and I am glad I am not in your place. Last Sunday I preached for Mr. Stanley at his church in London, and William and I were much in the little man's company while we were in his town. He is very pleasant and entertaining, but much changed since his wife's death. He has grown old, and seems to be fighting hard to keep up an interest in things. The usual collection of Broad Churchmen was about him, and convocation was sitting in Westminister School almost under his roof. I heard a long debate one day on 'The Priest in Absolution.' On the whole, London was delightful and I was glad to get out of it for the Continent, as I always am. I investigated all the Glass-makers, and found some very interesting men among them."

Mr. Brooks returned to Boston in September to live there henceforth under changed conditions. His father and mother had gone to North Andover to reside in the old Phillips homestead. Forty-four years had elapsed since in the same house to which they now returned they had been married and thence had come to Boston, establishing themselves in the first home on High Street. They had seen six boys go out from them into the world, four of them still living, and now that the youngest had gone from home, they looked to North Andover as a retreat in the decline of life. Mr. Brooks would gladly have had them come to live with him, and would have made any arrangements for that end; he had counted upon it as his pleasure and privilege; but the parents declined to accept such an invitation from him or any of the other sons. It was understood in the family that it was not possible. For many years Mr. Brooks had kept his bachelor quarters in boarding-houses and hotels. He now set up housekeeping for the first time at No. 175 Marlborough Street, taking into employment the servants who had lived with his mother. They served him faithfully and devotedly to the end of his life.

On the voyage home, Mr. Brooks was taken with what the doctor called a slow fever, of which he writes, "It has kept me a good deal shut up ever since. It is the slowest fever that ever was got up. The seat of it is principally in the back of the knees which give way when you have walked about a square. Altogether it is an attack of general good-for-nothingness which I am tired of, and which I am glad to be able to hope is almost over now." His illness prevented him from attending the sessions of the General Convention then sitting in Boston, or from forming any favorable opinion of its proceedings: "There is nothing for them to do, and they are trying hard to make something by bringing up all kinds of ridiculous propositions. I was glad once more to sign the petition about the Baptismal service. It reminded me of good old times, and I hope we shall have it triannually as long as this church stands. It never will be granted of course." In November he went to the Church Congress in New York and after coming back to Boston he wrote to his brother:

"November 7, 1877. I was all the better for it, and am now quite well. Is n't it good to have these show occasions done with and settle down into the steady pull of Parish Life. Last Sunday seemed a blessed relief. There was nobody to be civil to in the Vestry Room, and you could read the service yourself and preach the Gospel which had been bottled up all the time. Now there is a clear field for the winter and I don't mean to have anybody preach for me, except when you come, before next year. . . . I have father staying with me for a day or two. He came down to vote and to attend the Historical Society to-morrow. He seems capitally well and goes out prowling around the town in his old fashion, as if Marlborough Street were quite as good a place as Hancock Street to start from. . . .

"Have you read the new 'Life of Sumner?' I have finished one volume of it and found it interesting. The wonderful reception that he had in England and the sight of the boyhood of these men who are either gone, or are old men now, are very attractive. Then I have been reading Bowen's new book [*History of Philosophy*]. I had forgotten what a queer, familiar, almost jocose style he has, but his expositions of the systems of philosophy are certainly very clear, though one doubts sometimes whether he has got to the bottom of them."

He wrote to Mr. Cooper, who had invited him for the tenth anniversary of the Church of the Holy Apostles, Philadelphia: "Of course I 'll come. Do you think I would let the friends of the Holy Apostles gather and I not be there?" He struck the usual keynote for his birthday, December 13, 1878: "It seems as if everything out of the old times were altered so and things whirl on so fast now, sickness and health, trouble and pleasure chasing each other quickly. The quiet, smooth, unbroken life is all gone. This is not perhaps less happy, but 'the time is short' seems to ring out of everything. And then again the *whole* of things seems of so much more consequence and the details of things of so much less than they used to. I wonder if everybody gets to feel so. I was forty-two last Thursday."

The work in his parish in the year 1878 went on as usual. The Lenten services grew deeper in their interest and power. He asked the Proprietors of Trinity Church for permission to hold free evening services during Lent, and the request was granted unanimously without limit of time. On these occasions the great church was filled. His references to the season of Lent in his letters must be interpreted as meaning that he put his whole soul into the frequent services, but did not care that any one should know with what deep feeling and laborious study he prepared himself for the penitential season. His epistolary references are in contrast with the note-books, where the earnestness of his mood is stamped upon every page. He took up large subjects, in courses of addresses which called for thorough and comprehensive study. In his Sunday preaching the sermons followed each other on the same high level. He did not write many letters, and these inclined to brevity. Of a visit from Dr. Mitchell in February he says: "Weir Mitchell has been here curing all the dilapidated Bostonians. His coming makes a great sensation, for he is a very famous man. I felt as though I were a nerve doctor myself with all the patients that swarmed about the house." He was taking an interest in little things, such as the furnishing of his house, at a time when antique colonial furniture was the fashion. Of a clock which he secured in Philadelphia he writes:

"The clock and the corner cupboard came safely and are both up and running most satisfactorily. I know what time it is and what day of the month and of the week and of the moon. If it only gave the Golden Letter and the Dominical Number and the First and Second Lessons I should feel entirely set up."

In June he was present at the centennial of Phillips Academy, Andover, of which his great-grandfather was the founder, and to Arthur Brooks he writes, June 10, 1878:

"Yes, we did have a good time. I do not know when I have seen a big display go off so well throughout, and we were a sort of quiet centre to the whole thing, we Phillipses, around which it all revolved. We had the glory and they had the work; and that is always fun. . . . It is not often now that all four of us boys get together in one room as we did here in my study the other night. So let us be proud and happy for the way the whole thing was done, and hope for another occasion soon. . . ."

He went soon after this event to Virginia, where he read an essay on "The Pulpit and Popular Skepticism." Of this last visit he writes, July 9, 1878:

"We visited the old Seminary where I read an Essay to the Alumni, and got quite sentimental about old times. The old place seemed to be full of life and turned out a good many parsons of the peculiar Virginia kind, which is n't a bad sort, though one would n't want a whole church made up of them. Then we went down to the Virginia Springs in the Blue Ridge, where we passed three very queer and pleasant days, taking much sulphur both inside and out. Meantime the heat had grown to be something awful in those Northern parts, but down where we were everything was as cool and delightful as possible."

He took a house at Hingham for the summer, going to Boston every Sunday to preach. Of the life at Hingham he writes to Mr. Cooper:

"August 3, 1878. I never had such a profoundly quiet summer as I am having now. I am here in a queer little cottage on an obscure back bay of Boston Harbor, where there is nothing to do, or at least where I do nothing, no sailing, no fishing, no riding, no walking. Nothing in the world but plenty of books and time and tobacco. Nobody to talk to or to talk to me. And I like it first-rate, almost as well as Heiligenblut and Bad Gastein. But it is very different.

"The only thing I really do which I can put my finger on is to prepare my volume of sermons which is coming out in September. Every day some proof comes down which I have to correct and send back. I doubt if they are worth publishing, and I have had a hundred minds about going on or stopping them, but I am in for it now, and will send you a copy when they come out. . . ."

In his seclusion at Hingham, he wrote often to his brother Arthur, in Europe, following his movements with the sympathy of an old traveller:

"August 16, 1878. I am sure you will have a delightful summer, and we shall follow you through it all with our good wishes. It is about the pleasantest thing that people can do in this fallen world.

"I don't think the Pan-Anglican troubled you much, and from all accounts it won't trouble anybody a great deal. I don't hear of anything said or done there which was of the slightest consequence. And it gets to be very funny when in General Conventions and Pan Synods and all sorts of Assemblies of Ecclesiastical people the one thing they can crow over when the meet-

ing breaks up is the 'perfect harmony' of it all,—as if it is a wonder
to sing a Te Deum over, if Churchmen come together without
pulling each other's wigs off and tearing each other's eyes out. . . .
Ben Butler is going to try to be Governor of Massachusetts
this fall, and that will keep things lively here. There has been a
blackguard named Kearney about here preaching low Irish Com-
munism, whom Butler has taken up, and made an ugly mess.
But what do you care for American politics when you are looking
at the Madonna di San Sisto."

The dread of an impending sorrow was hanging over Mr.
Brooks through the summer in consequence of the illness of his
father. He invited both his parents to Hingham, but, as the
change was not beneficial, they soon returned to Andover.
Nothing could exceed the thoughtfulness and tender devotion
which he showed in the now changed relationship,—when instead
of the father watching over the son with anxious affection, it was
his privilege to care for both father and mother. He en-
quired for the best medical skill, in the hope that it might be of
avail. He wrote often to his mother to encourage her; he sent
everything that his ingenious thoughtfulness could devise which
would cheer or help the invalid in his weakness.

The summer passed, and September brought an event of
the highest interest to Mr. Brooks as well as to people throughout the country,—the visit of Dean Stanley to America. No
Englishman ever came whose presence called forth more enthusiasm, nor did any one realize until he came how deep and widespread was the feeling which prompted the people out of pure
gratitude to express their sense of indebtedness in every form
which could do him honor. It was one of the important days
in the history of Trinity Church when, on Sunday, the 22d of
September, he stood in its pulpit, and, with his keen perception
of the romance of history and the picturesque quality inhering
in representative occasions, treated the moment as a meeting
of the East with the West. The sermon which he preached
was afterward printed, and the manuscript given to Mr. Brooks,
who preserved it among the things that he valued.

The year as it came to an end found him in the midst of many
occupations, of which the most laborious was the preparation
of the Bohlen Lectures, to be given in Philadelphia. But he
made time for loving attentions to his father, the thought of

whom was uppermost in his mind. And he found writing the Lectures difficult; "They are a fearful invasion of the legitimate and regular work of the ministry, and the longer I am a Parson the less I think I like special work, the more I like to keep down to the steady humdrum of the Parish Mill."

The experience he had long been dreading, whose import to himself he had been sounding in advance, came on January 7, 1879. These extracts from letters that follow call for no comment as he speaks of his father, and tells the story in its simple and natural pathos.

"BOSTON, January 11, 1879.

"DEAR OLD COOPER,—You are a good kind fellow to write to me about Father and to speak of him so kindly. He was one of the simplest, truest, healthiest, and happiest natures that God ever made. All his life long was a perpetual delight in common things and a quiet, faithful doing of the duties that some men make a fuss about, as if they were the most natural things in the world and everybody did them. His religion was as simple as all the rest of his life, always flowing on serenely, as if to be a religious man and to love God and trust Him were not an exceptional and hard thing, but as true a part of human life as breathing. And at the last he grew simpler and sweeter as his strength faded away, and died at last with calm dignity such as only a child or a strong man can have. But we shall miss him dreadfully. Life will never be again what it has been all these years with him behind us. And poor mother wanders about looking for some one to be anxious about and to take care of, and finding it a dreadful pain that her last anxiety is over, and that she has only to rest in peace till her happiness comes.

"Yes, I shall come in February and lecture. The lectures are poor enough for they were written in the midst of all this derangement and distress, but I shall fulfil my engagement."

To another friend he writes:

"175 MARLBOROUGH STREET, BOSTON, January 18, 1879.

"I have been feeling all these last ten days as I know thousands of men have felt before me when their fathers have died, but feeling it just as freshly as if I were the first man that ever went through it, and with the strong belief that no father ever was to his boys just what ours has been to us. He was so bright and happy and simple and strong through all the long years while our lives revolved around his, and in these last years while he has been failing and we have had the privilege that we could do something for him, he has been so sweet and gentle and childlike and so full of happiness in his constantly narrowing life. And at last he lay down and died with the same quiet dignity with which he had lived. There is nothing that is not good to remember. It was as healthy and true a life as ever was seen, and now I miss him as I never dreamed that I could miss anybody, and it will be so to the end, I know. You knew him a little. He always felt that my friends were his friends, and so he always talked of you as if he knew you well. I know that he would have been glad to think that even so far away, and with so slight a recollection of him, you would care something for his death. . . .

"I am glad that you welcomed Casaubon. He was selected with a little more discrimination than usual, for I had just been reading his life myself, and had been charmed not so much with him as with the Book. . . . I have been lame all winter with a queer weakness of the knee, which the Doctor don't seem to understand. It probably is rebelling at the amount it has to carry. But it is about well now."

At the first meeting of the Massachusetts Historical Society held after the death of their colleague, words of appreciation were spoken by the President, Hon. R. C. Winthrop, and others testifying to the value of his work as a member of the society. The qualities attributed to the father reappeared in the son, with this difference only, that the father had filled no exalted position. But there was a higher tribute to be paid. Such had been the earthly relationship that to the son it bore witness to the nature of the Fatherhood of God. In the year before his father died, speaking to the students of the Yale Divinity School on the best method of teaching religion, Phillips Brooks had said: "For myself, every year that I have preached, that sight, the child and the father in their deepest relationship to one another, has grown an ever clearer and richer revelation of the mystery of man and God." While his bereavement was still fresh, he wrote these words in his Bohlen Lectures on "The Influence of Jesus":

"Beyond all analysis lies the relation which every true son holds to a true father. It is a final fact. You cannot dissolve it in any abstract theory. It issues from the mysterious sympathy of the two lives, one of which gave birth to the other. It has ripened and mellowed through all the rich intercourse of dependent childhood and imitative youth and sympathetic manhood. It is an eternal fact. Death cannot destroy it. The grown-up man feels his father's life beating from beyond the grave, and is sure that in his own eternity the child relation to that life will be in some mysterious and perfect way resumed and glorified, that he will be something to that dear life and it to him forever. All this remains. . . . The joy and pain, all the richness and pathos of his home life, while they keep their freshness and peculiar sanctity, have in them and below them all the multitudinous happiness and sorrow of the larger life in the great household of the world. The child feels something of this truth by instinct. The thoughtful man delights to realize it more and more as he grows older." (Pp. 184, 185.)

The lectures on the "Influence of Jesus" were delivered in Philadelphia in February, 1879. He wrote in relation to them to Rev. W. N. McVickar, his successor at the Church of the Holy Trinity:

"February 8, 1879.

"I was just putting the last words to the last page as your letter came in. There could not have been a better moment. Yesterday it would have seemed like a mockery to talk about the delivery of what looked as if it never would be written. And now I hate to think that I must ever read them again, and especially that I must read them to anybody whom I care about. . . . But I have one or two suggestions to make which are serious.

"1. The lectures are an hour long, each of them. Can it not be arranged that there shall be little or no service?

"2. They are not in the least the things for a popular audience. Not that they are learned, but they are quiet and dry. I want to have them not in the great Church, but in your Lecture Room which will make it much easier for me to read them. I think you will agree with me in this. At any rate I wish it so, and I am sure you will oblige me.

"If you will do both of these things for me I will preach all day for you at Holy Trinity. If not, I will see you at Jericho before I open my mouth in the afternoon.

"And then I want you to let me make a very quiet visit and not go out to dinner anywhere but at Cooper's. I don't feel up to parties, and I want to see you. Won't you say so to any kind people who want to arrange dinners and breakfasts before I come, or who desire to invite me when I am there.

"All this sounds foolish, but the fact is I have had a dreadful winter. These poor lectures have been worried through in all the distress and bewilderment of Father's death. I haven't known what I was writing half the time. Now I want to have a quiet, restful time, and I shall come trusting your good love and tact to get it for me. . . ."

It is needless to say that the great church was thrown open for the purpose, and not the lecture room, as he had demanded. How the lectures were received, and how he appeared as he gave them, is told in a newspaper paragraph of the day.

"Rev. Phillips Brooks of Boston lectured last night in the Church of the Holy Trinity, to an audience that filled every pew in that vast church and left scarcely any sitting room in the galleries. It has been ten years since he left his pastorate of that church to take charge of a parish in Boston. . . . A tall, broad-shouldered man, with a perfectly smooth, open face, strong lines about the mouth, expressive eyes and dark hair, was the *personnel* of the man who came out of the vestry room with Mr. McVickar last evening at eight o'clock, and after the singing of a hymn and the delivery of a brief prayer ascended the high pulpit steps. There was no pause for preparation after he got into the pulpit. He placed the manuscript before him and began the lecture. The delivery of the man was remarkable. He announced the title and introduction in words that came so rapidly that it required the most concentrated attention to keep up with him. He spoke for about an hour. During all that time his tremendous energy of delivery kept up at the same rapid pace, reminding one of a torrent rushing over rocks. The words seemed not to flow out to the audience, but to shoot out. The ground he got over in an hour was equal to that of three ordinary lectures. And when he closed, the attention of the audience was as rapt as ever. Occasionally there would be a stumbling over a word. Then his head would jerk to this side and that impatiently, as though the word must come, despite all impediments. He kept his eyes on the paper almost continuously. Probably four times, certainly not more than half a dozen, he gave a glance out towards the audience. He seemed to lose himself entirely in his subject. His eyes were bent on the manuscript, his whole expression, his features, the twitching of his facial muscles, showed the tremendous concentration of energy put into the effort. There was an absence of all self-consciousness; his hearers lost sight of the man and only saw the ideas, rapid, whirling, and tremendous in their force of utterance, keeping up the idea of the torrent all the time."

Any attempts to save him from the invasion of his friends in Philadelphia were futile. When he returned to Boston he wrote to McVickar: "I counted upon this visit, after this sad and dreary winter, more than ever I did on any other, and it has been to me far more than I had counted on." But he came back tired and somewhat dispirited. "I am back here, and it 's snowing, and I'm lonely; there's work to be done and it 's doleful generally."

In March he accepted the honor of an election to the Massachusetts Historical Society. There began at this time an interesting correspondence with M. Nyegaard, a clergyman of the

Reformed Church in France, at St. Quentin (Aisne), who had been greatly impressed by the "Lectures on Preaching," and asked for permission to translate them into French. The translation was published in 1883. Somewhat later the "Lectures on Preaching" were translated into Dutch. There came an invitation from the editor of *The Atlantic Monthly*, who explained his purpose by saying that he had just been reading the sermon, already referred to, on "The Present and Future Faith." A series of articles of the general tendency of that sermon would find their best audience if clothed in literary form. To this and other invitations of a similar kind he gave a firm refusal. He speaks of Lent as going on most pleasantly: "I have no impatience for it to be over." He was then preaching as usual in many places, three times on Sunday, and often during the week. Easter week he spent in New York. He was at New Haven in April to lecture again before the students of the Divinity School. He seemed to be doing the work of an evangelist, preaching in various towns in churches of his own denomination, but almost as often in churches of other names. There were certain Congregational churches where it seemed to be a settled arrangement that he should appear once at least every year.

At the annual convention of the Episcopal Church in Massachusetts, which met at St. Paul's Church, Boston, May 14, Phillips Brooks was the preacher. The words of his text were the commission of Christ to His disciples, "As my Father hath sent me, even so send I you." He dwelt on the purpose for which Christ had been sent by the Father and in turn had commissioned His disciples. The sermon was one for the times, cutting athwart current ecclesiastical tendencies. From the characteristic words of Christ, four passages were selected as heads for the divisions of the sermon:

I am not come to call the righteous, but sinners to repentance; I am not come to destroy, but to fulfil; He that hath seen me hath seen the Father; He that is not against us is with us.

"We are too apt to speak in church to artificial sins which the great universal human conscience does not recognize, to rebuke the improprieties that are not wrong, and to denounce the honest errors which good men may hold and yet be good, as if they were the first enemies with which we and our Gospel had to fight. . . .

All earnest life which has not reached clear religious faith, all doubt, however radical, which at its heart is truthful and not scornful, all eager study of the marvellous world of nature as if the final facts of our existence must be somehow hidden in her bosom, all glorifying of humanity, as if it were an object for our worship, all struggle to develop society as if by its own self-purification earth could be turned into heaven,—all this is to the Church to-day what Judaism was to Christ, what He came not to destroy but to fulfil. . . . The Christian Church has made and makes to-day too much of settled views of truth which may be dead, too little of the search for truth which *must* be living. One trembles when he sees the Church in any way separating itself from the pure instincts and from the earnest thought of men, and counting itself the enemy to destroy them instead of the missionary to enlighten them.

"*He that hath seen me hath seen the Father.*   There are meanings in these words that can never be true of any other beside Him, not even of the Church which is to perpetuate His mission in the world.   But if they declare what was the great truth of the Incarnation,—that a perfectly pure obedient humanity might utter divinity, might be the transparent medium through which even God might show Himself,—then is there not an everlasting sense in which the words of Jesus may become the words of the Church and the declaration of its highest privilege? . . . When one feels this, he earnestly deprecates, he deeply dreads the 'clericalism' to which the Church is always tending.   It is not by the truth the clergy teach, it is by the lives the Christian people live, that the Church must be the witness of the Father."

He was preaching often at this time in Appleton Chapel, Cambridge, before the students of the University.   One of the sermons which he delivered in May, 1879, exhibited his power in extraordinary manner,—a sermon to the young from the text, "Thou . . . makest me to possess the iniquities of my youth." Some special circumstance had roused him to write it.   His subject was the unity of life, the continuousness of all its experiences. There was no lurid picture of endless torment to alarm his hearers, but even Jonathan Edwards, in his most terrific discourses, could never have produced a more intense or fearful impression.   The sermon was consistent throughout,—the dark side of life under the consciousness of sin.   This is a passage which may serve to illustrate its purpose, but no extract can represent its power:

"It is when some great trouble comes to you, the death of your friend, the failure of your business, the prospect of your own death, then it is you are dismayed to find that under the changed habits of your life you are the same man still, and that the sins of your college days are in you even now. This is what makes men dread any great event in life so strangely. It brings back the past which they want to forget, or rather it compels them to see that the past is still there in the present. It is when you fire a cannon over the pond that the dead body which is sunk there rises."

It was not invective which marked the sermon, but throughout rigorous dissection of the conscience, and a penetration of experiences unspoken. It ended with this sentence: "I know that there are words of comfort which I have not turned aside to speak to-day." He was asked to include the sermon in his printed volumes, but he declined. It might do, he replied, to preach such a sermon occasionally, when judgment without mercy was the theme, but he would not give it a place in the open record.

To a clergyman who had asked him to make an address, he wrote:

"I will be with you on the evening of the 17th. Please state the subject on which you wish me to speak, as you think best, only don't say anything in it about 'workingmen.' I like workingmen very much and care for their good, but I have nothing distinct or separate to say to them about religion, nor do I see how it will do any good to treat them as a separate class in this matter, in which their needs and duties are just like other men's."

In declining an invitation to the annual New England dinner in Brooklyn, N. Y., commemorating the landing of the Pilgrims at Plymouth on December 22, 1620, he wrote:

"It will be quite impossible for me to come. The fact is that Christmas and these Puritans interfere with one another now just as much as they ever did. I believe that they landed just before Christmas on purpose, so that the celebration of their landing might forever interfere with the preparation of Christmas trees and Christmas sermons. So I can't come. I'd rather like to, all but the having to speak. That spoils a dinner."

To a friend he wrote in the Advent season, commending books which he had read, and giving his view of the Second Advent:

"If you ever come across either of the two books which I have just been reading, I am sure that you will like it. One is the *Life of Thomas Erskine of Linlathen*, and the other is the *Life of Bishop Ewing* of Argyle and the Isles. The first is rather a rare book and and a little hard to get; the other you may find. Both of them were noble Christian men of the best type, fair and true, 'without partiality and without hypocrisy,' Broad Church-men of the noblest sort. Every now and then we get a glimpse in the lives of such men of what Christianity yet has to do for the individual and for the race before its work shall be complete. I think I grow to have more and more tolerance for every kind of Christian except one, and he is the Christian who thinks that his Christian faith is *done*, that there is nothing greater for it to do than it has done already. He does not believe in the Second Advent, which is a true doctrine of the Gospel,—not a fantastic idea of a new incarnation and of a visible Christ in Palestine, but a power of Christ over the destinies and institutions and hearts of men more real and spiritual than any that any age has seen yet."

In sending his thanks for a Christmas present of Clifford's writings he says:

"December 23, 1879. I have wanted to see Clifford, heathen though he be, for he is about the best specimen apparently of these men who are telling us that we have no souls, and that there is no God. They must pass away some time if anything that we believe is true. But they will surely leave some mark upon the Faith which they so patiently and ingeniously try to murder, and which will outlive them all. There is something almost pictur-esquely like our muddled time in Clifford being made a Christmas present of. I accept the omen."

There are some letters written in a hurried, anxious tone from Phillips Brooks to his brothers Arthur and John, in the early weeks of 1880, speaking of the illness of their mother. On the 1st of February she died, at the age of seventy-two. To the let-ters of condolence which he received from his friends he replied, but not with the same freedom from reserve as when he spoke of the loss of his father. His grief went deeper. A gentleness and softness of manner came over him, the tenderness which can find its best expression not in words, but in the features. He went heavily, as one that mourneth for his mother.

To Dr. Weir Mitchell he wrote:

"My mother has been the centre of all the happiness of my life. Thank God she is not less my pride and treasure now."

To Mr. Cooper:

"I did not know I could ever be so much like a child again, but to-night the world seems very desolate and lonely. All my life I have feared and dreaded what has come this week. And now that she is with God, I seem to know for the first time how pure and true and self-sacrificing all her earthly life has been. Surely with all these that have gone before it will not be hard to go to Him when our time comes."

To another friend:

"The happiest part of my happy life has been my mother, and with God's help she will be more to me than ever. The sense of God and his love has grown ever clearer in the midst of all this sadness and bereavement."

To his brother Arthur:

"And so the new chapter of life has begun, and the Brooks Boys have got to stand together as long as they are left. Well, we have done it pretty well so far, and I guess we shall do it to the end. May we all get through with the faithfulness and simplicity with which Father and Mother have finished their course."

We must dwell for a moment on the mother of Phillips Brooks. Her strength lay in the depth and power of her emotional nature. She lavished on her family an untold wealth of affection, revealing it in little ways that are pathetic. She concentrated her energies on one single purpose,—the care of her family, first its religious and then its secular welfare. She never accepted an invitation from home for any social function until the youngest child was grown up and no longer needed her care. To this end everything was sacrificed,—the welfare of her children. Phillips Brooks recalled the familiar domestic scene, when he wrote from Germany during his visit to Europe:

"MY DEAREST MOTHER,—You cannot think how strange it seems to be writing in this little German inn, and knowing that you will read it in the old back parlor at home, where you have read my letters from Cambridge, Alexandria, and Philadelphia. Johnnie will bring it up from the post office some night, and Trip will break out into one of his horrible concerts two or three times while you are reading it. Then as soon as it is over, father will get out his big candle and you will put up the stockings, and all go up the old stairway to the old chambers, and to bed. Well, good-night and pleasant dreams to you all, and don't forget that I am off here wandering up and down these old countries and thinking ever so much about you."

She was religious, but the instincts of motherhood predominated, nor did they relax with the years. Even after the boys had grown into men she still felt called upon to exercise her sway. Once when Phillips and Frederick were on a home visit, the one rector of the Church of the Holy Trinity in Philadelphia, and the other rector of St. Paul's Church in Cleveland, she is recalled as putting her head into the doorway of the room from which the noise proceeded, saying, "Boys, remember it is Sunday."

She understood the nature of boys. To a young mother who came to her for advice, she admitted she could say something about the management of sons. This was the substance of her counsel:

"There is an age when it is not well to follow or question your boy too closely. Up to that time you may carefully instruct and direct him; you are his best friend; he is never happy unless the story of the day has been told; you must hear about his friends, his school; all that interests him must be your interest. Suddenly these confidences cease; the affectionate son becomes reserved and silent, he seeks the intimate friendship of other lads, he goes out, he is averse to telling where he is going or how long he will be gone. He comes in and goes silently to his room. All this is a startling change to the mother, but it is also her opportunity to practise wisdom by loving, and praying for, and absolutely trusting her son. The faithful instruction and careful training during his early years the son can never forget; that is impossible. Therefore trust not only your heavenly Father, but your son. The period of which I speak appears to me to be one in which the boy dies and the man is born; his individuality rises up before him, and he is dazed and almost overwhelmed by his first consciousness of himself. I have always believed that it was then that the Creator was speaking with my sons, and that it was good for their souls to be left alone with Him, while I, their mother, stood trembling, praying, and waiting, knowing that when the man was developed from the boy I should have my sons again, and there would be a deeper sympathy than ever between us."

Phillips Brooks resembled in appearance his mother more than his father. The contour of the head, the large dark eyes, the form of the nose, something also in the poise and the carriage of the head, are those of his mother. But the large stature seems to be a remoter inheritance. The indebtedness of Phillips Brooks to his mother in the line of a rich heritage is perhaps the greater, yet what he owed to his father is of such importance that without it he would not have been the man he was. Some of his higher intellectual tastes or habits, his love of historical studies, his taste for architecture, his accuracy, his interest in minute details, his literary sense, and his sober judgments of men and things,— these are traits which his father possessed. They had also a common trait in the love of relics. The father had the constant play of humor without which the highest results in character and achievement are impossible, and these the son possessed in larger measure. Phillips Brooks's almost invariable mood outside of the pulpit was one in which his humor played with all the changes and chances of life. The strict integrity, the uprightness of the perfect man, who could be trusted in all circumstances to do what was right and fitting, was an invaluable paternal legacy. Of the father, the truest words that his sons could speak were these, "The righteous shall be had in everlasting remembrance."

In Phillips Brooks the power of observation, which constitutes the basis of the imaginative faculty, was fused with the vast power of feeling which came from his mother. She had the spirit of the reformer, who is born to set the world right and cannot contemplate with serenity the world as it is. She hungered and thirsted for the righteousness whose coming is so slow. So strong was her will, so intense her nature, that she grew impatient with the obstacles in the way. Phillips Brooks knew the facts of life with his father's eyes, and the hopes and possibilities of life through the eyes of his mother. Had he received by transmission only the outlook of his father without the inspired heroism of his mother, he would not have risen to greatness. But, on the other hand, had he inherited from his mother alone, he might have been known as an ardent reformer, not wholly unlike his distinguished kinsman Wendell Phillips,—a type familiar in New England; but the wonderful fascination of his power for men of every class and degree, the universal appeal to a common humanity, would have been wanting. In his Philadelphia ministry he almost identified the pulpit with the cause of social reforms. When he came to Boston he must have reached the determination to confine himself to preaching. There was danger of life passing away while one was getting ready to live. Some said: "Remove first the obstacles which stand in the way of human progress, and then men will be able to live." He said: "The world, humanity, has already been redeemed by Christ. The opportunities of the divine sonship are open to every man. Live! Live greatly now!"

The mother of Phillips Brooks was a woman of strong theological views with the not unnatural tendency to identify them with spiritual convictions. At one time she was alarmed lest her sons should be influenced by Bushnell's teaching, and she had grave apprehensions about the soundness of *Ecce Homo*. A sermon of Phillips Brooks entitled "The Mother's Wonder" reveals something of his own experience in his treatment of the inevitable divergence of the sons in the household from the parents' dogmatic attitude. But any concern the mother may have felt because of the son's divergence from opinions to which she adhered, ceased to trouble her after he came to Boston. She kept the counsels of her heart about intellectual difficulties and new developments in theology. It was enough that he was preaching Christ with a power and insight she had never known before.

As she went about her household duties, she was brooding over a world to be won for Christ. The possibility filled her with strange unuttered enthusiasm. She thought much about foreign missions. Her heart would have suffered, but she would have bravely bidden farewell to all her sons had they been going forth into heathen lands to carry the Gospel of Christ. "How Mother used to talk to us about Henry Martyn," wrote Phillips Brooks to one of his brothers, when two years later he was in India. The concentration of his powerful will in combination with the brooding love and tenderness for humanity, the yearning for the well-being of humanity, and of individual men, the clear single purpose, from which he steadfastly refused to be turned aside, even by the fascination of intellectual culture or literary creation, the growing devotion to Christ which mastered his whole being,—this we came to know as Phillips Brooks, and this in another form was the spirit of his mother. The words of

Scripture which he directed to be engraven upon the stone that marks her burying-place were these: "O woman, great is thy faith: be it unto thee even as thou wilt." Shortly after her death he preached upon this text in the pulpit of Trinity Church. The sermon contains no personal reference, but it is the son's memorial of his mother.

The reputation of Phillips Brooks as a preacher had now extended into England and Scotland. When his first volume of sermons appeared, it reached a wide circulation in England. A pathetic interest attaches to this first volume because Dean Stanley read it by the bedside of his wife in her last days. A dignitary of the Church of England wrote to a friend who sent it to him:

"January 21, 1879. I must say that Phillips Brooks is of all living divines the one with whom I feel I have most in common,— whose view of Christianity and the Christian life appears to me to be the wisest and the healthiest. I wish I had the chance of 'sitting under' such a teacher. If we could import him into a stall at Westminster what a gain it would be!"

The knowledge of the sermons came to the Queen, who having read them made them a gift to the Dean of Windsor. Her Majesty having expressed a desire to hear him preach when he next visited England, the invitation was conveyed to him by the Dean of Windsor, and on Sunday, the 11th of July, he preached in the Chapel Royal at Windsor Castle. The text of the sermon was Rev. iii. 12: "Him that overcometh will I make a pillar in the temple of my God, and he shall go no more out: and I will write upon him the name of my God, and the name of the city of my God . . . and . . . my new name."[1] As it was the first instance in which an American clergyman had preached before the Queen, Dean Wellesley was naturally interested in the result. Writing to Dean Stanley the next day he says: "Phillips Brooks was a complete success." After the service the Queen sent for him and he had a short interview with her.

On Sunday, the Fourth of July, Mr. Brooks preached at Westminster Abbey, delivering his famous sermon, "The Candle of the Lord." Many felt that the Dean had given a very difficult

---

[1] The sermon is published in *Sermons*, vol. ii., p. 60.

task to an American in asking him to preach on that day in such
a place. The Dean himself felt some anxiety about the result.
Lady Frances Baillie, a sister-in-law of Dean Stanley, has contributed an interesting incident in connection with the occasion.
After the service she slipped out into the deanery by the private
door, and reached the drawing-room before any of the guests
who were to come in from the Abbey. She found the Dean with
tears running down his face, a most extraordinary thing for him;
and as soon as she appeared he burst out with expressions of the
intensest admiration, saying that he had never been so moved
by any sermon that he could remember, and dwelling on the
wonderful taste and feeling displayed in the passage at the end.
This is the passage referred to, appended to the sermon in order
to commemorate the day:

"MY FRIENDS,—May I ask you to linger while I say a few
words more which shall not be unsuited to what I have been saying, and which shall, for just a moment, recall to you the sacredness which this day—the Fourth of July, the anniversary of
American Independence—has in the hearts of us Americans. If
I dare—generously permitted as I am to stand this evening in
the venerable Abbey, so full of our history as well as yours—to
claim that our festival shall have some sacredness for you as well
as for us, my claim rests on the simple truth that to all true men
the birthday of a nation must always be a sacred thing. For in
our modern thought the nation is the making-place of men. Not
by the traditions of its history, nor by the splendor of its corporate achievements, nor by the abstract excellence of its constitution, but by its fitness to make men, to beget and educate human
character, to contribute to the complete humanity, the perfect
man that is to be,—by this alone each nation must be judged
to-day. The nations are the golden candlesticks which hold aloft
the glory of the Lord. No candlestick can be so rich or venerable that men shall honor it if it holds no candle. 'Show us
your man,' land cries to land.

" In such days any nation, out of the midst of which God has
led another nation as He led ours out of the midst of yours, must
surely watch with anxiety and prayer the peculiar development
of our common humanity of which that new nation is made the
home, the special burning of the human candle in that new candlestick; and if she sees a hope and promise that God means to
build in that land some strong and free and characteristic manhood, which shall help the world to its completeness, the mother-
land will surely lose the thought and memory of whatever

anguish accompanied the birth, for gratitude over the gain which humanity has made, 'for joy that a man is born into the world.'

"It is not for me to glorify to-night the country which I love with all my heart and soul. I may not ask your praise for anything admirable which the United States has been or done. But on my country's birthday I may do something far more solemn and more worthy of the hour. I may ask for your prayers in her behalf. That on the manifold and wondrous chance which God is giving her,—on her freedom (for she is free, since the old stain of slavery was washed out in blood); on her unconstrained religious life; on her passion for education and her eager search for truth; on her zealous care for the poor man's rights and opportunities; on her quiet homes where the future generations of men are growing; on her manufactories and her commerce; on her wide gates open to the east and to the west; on her strange meeting of the races out of which a new race is slowly being born; on her vast enterprise and her illimitable hopefulness,— on all these materials and machineries of manhood, on all that the life of my country must mean for humanity, I may ask you to pray that the blessing of God, the Father of man, and Christ, the Son of man, may rest forever.

"Because you are Englishmen and I am an American; also because here, under this high and hospitable roof of God, we are all more than Englishmen and more than Americans; because we are all men, children of God waiting for the full coming of our Father's kingdom, I ask you for that prayer."

In a letter to his brother Arthur, Mr. Brooks gives a short summary of this visit to England and Scotland:

"SCOTLAND, July 25, 1880.

"The Highland journey has been very beautiful and everything has gone well, the weather being exceptionally well behaved. We had almost a week in and about Edinburgh with a little visit to St. Andrew's, where we saw Shairp and Tulloch and the little Divinity School over which the author of the 'Rational Theology' presides. One gets quite interested in theological quarrels here, and listens to the battle which is raging over Robinson Smith and his articles in the 'Encyclopædia Britannica' with a curious sort of sense that he is hearing the roar of an out-of-the-way skirmish of the same battlefield that he is so familiar with at home. The Kirk and the Free Church and the U. P's keep up a perennial turmoil, and divide the people of every little county town among them. . . .

"In London everything was very pleasant. Stanley was very devoted, and put us in the way of seeing lots of pleasant sights and people. I preached for him in the Abbey on the Fourth of July, and was quite shamed with the way in which Farrar in the afternoon outsaid everything that I possibly could have said about America. Then I went down to Windsor and preached. . . . Last Sunday we spent in Edinburgh and heard their great man there, Dr. MacGregor."

Mr. Brooks returned to Boston to take possession of the new rectory of Trinity Church, No. 233 Clarendon Street, the architect, Richardson, having advised with him in regard to the plan. He had at first protested against the purpose of building him a fine house, but he acquiesced in the arrangement, and soon appreciated its advantages. The house on Clarendon Street became dear to him as to his friends. It was part of his recreation to beautify it with pictures and relics and souvenirs of travel, till it took on a personal character and seemed the expression of himself.

Among the letters of this year there is one to his college classmate, the Rev. James Reed, pastor of the New Church (Swedenborgian) in Boston, thanking him for a copy of his book:

"April 29, 1880.

"I am not a New Churchman in the special meaning which the words have for you, but I hope still that I have some small part and lot, as I certainly have the deepest interest and delight, in the great New Church which one feels moving everywhere under the crust of sects and dogmas in these days: the New Church which comes down from heaven and not up out of the earth, and whose power of life and unity is love and loyalty to the personal Christ.

"I thank you with all my heart for your Book, for it has shown me how much there is that is dear to both of us alike, and has helped me I know in faith and life.

"May God bless you always.

"Your old friend,

"PHILLIPS BROOKS."

In the fall of the year he participated in the two hundred and fiftieth anniversary of the First Church in Boston, where his ancestor, John Cotton, had been a minister, and again at Watertown in the commemoration of the founding of the town and church in 1630, in which his ancestor, Rev. George Phillips, had been an important factor. "I am afraid," he writes, "that my ancestors would not approve of the people who are celebrating them."

CHAPTER XIV.

1881–1882.

THE CALL TO HARVARD UNIVERSITY, AS PREACHER AND PROFESSOR OF CHRISTIAN ETHICS. EXTRACTS FROM CORRESPONDENCE. MEMORIAL SERMON ON DR. VIN-TON. DEATH OF DEAN STANLEY. SPEECHES AT CHURCH CONGRESS. SECOND VOLUME OF SERMONS. THE STANLEY MEMORIAL. REQUEST FOR LEAVE OF ABSENCE FOR A YEAR.

ONE of the features of the ministry of Phillips Brooks was its adaptation to all classes of men. In some way he had bridged the gulf which divides the people. He touched the common humanity. For the most part it had been his mission to preach to people of intellectual culture. He made thoughtful men and women realize the power of religion in an age when the current of tendencies ran strongly against religious faith. It is true—so he seemed to be constantly saying,—this religion of Christ; it has a deeper, larger, grander meaning, and a diviner beauty than you knew. It only needs to be seen as it really is and you would receive it with enthusiasm.

It was through his power to meet the needs of those who were seeking to connect intellect with life that he became the favorite preacher to young men in that stage of their progress where the intellect is supreme. Educational institutions recognized his power and asked for his aid. While in Philadelphia he had been called to the presidency of Kenyon College, in Ohio. He had been invited to take the chair of Church History in the Philadelphia Divinity School, and, as we have seen, his impulse had been to accept it. In 1880 he was requested to consider the question of the provostship of the University of Pennsylvania. To

Dr. Weir Mitchell he then wrote that, if he were free, nothing would attract him more, but, he added: "I am a preacher to the end."

But there came a call which shook his resolve to abide exclusively by the pulpit. In the spring of 1881 he was invited to accept the position of preacher to Harvard University and professor of Christian Ethics. It was an opportunity that strangely realized the dreams of his youth, when his highest hopes would have been fulfilled if he had been offered a position in Harvard College. To Harvard his whole heart had been given. On coming to Boston he had been at once elected to the Board of Overseers, and when his first term of service had expired was re-elected for a second term. In this capacity for twelve years he had now served the college.

"In his position as an Overseer [says President Eliot] he supported all changes which enlarged the freedom of the students, simplified regulations, and tended to develop in the young men the capacity for self-control. In his judgment of character and of conduct, he was generous without being weak. He was tolerant of all religious, philosophical, and political views and opinions,—so much so that I never heard him raise a question on any such matter when the appointment of a teacher was under discussion; but he had a strong dislike for the pessimistic or cynical temper, and in a few instances he expressed distrust of College teachers on the ground that they exhibited this quality, in his judgment so injurious to young men."

The call of Phillips Brooks to Harvard produced a widespread and intense excitement. There was much speculation as to its import and possible consequences,—deep searchings of heart when one considered the issues involved. In the minds of some the consideration was foremost that the university was breaking with Puritan traditions in handing over the responsibility for the religious training of its students to an Episcopal clergyman, a representative of the Church of England in America. For two generations the college had been identified with Unitarianism. To call a minister of another denomination must mean at least that the university was swinging away from its position as a sectarian institution. But, on the other hand, the suspicion arose that Mr. Brooks had changed his creed, and under some tacit understanding with the Corporation had been called to the position. In the excitement which prevailed, rumors were magnified into facts. Mr. Brooks himself was so stirred by these reports that he went to President Eliot, and asked if it were understood by those in authority that he was a Trinitarian in his belief. The answer was definite that he had been called with full knowledge of his theological position.

The Corporation of Harvard could not have realized how great would be the interest their action would awaken, how it would stir the city of Boston, the Commonwealth of Massachusetts, and become a question of importance to the country at large. But in the midst of the excitement and the confusion, one thing stood out with clearness,—the university in calling Phillips Brooks had performed an ideal act which was above criticism; they had asked for the one man whom they most wanted, who if he came would fill the vacant place, and bring increasing honor to the institution. They had supreme confidence in the man himself, that under all circumstances he could be trusted to do that which was right in the eyes of all men.

It would seem as though this were a question which a man was entitled to decide for himself, and that Phillips Brooks must insist upon this simple prerogative of his manhood. But here we touch an extraordinary phase in this important experience of his life. He was not to be allowed to decide it for himself. The issues at stake were so momentous, he represented so much more than himself, that he was compelled, as it were, involuntarily to submit the question to be determined by the people while he waited for the verdict. Such is the impression made when the full picture of the moment is gathered in. There came a month of waiting and suspense, filled up with personal interviews, when letters flowed in upon him daily from all parts of the country, from all classes of people, from the governor of the Commonwealth and the president of the university down to the humble serving woman who had found him her consolation in the struggle of life. As one studies this mass of letters, where the question of his going to Harvard is discussed frankly and in all its bearing by scholars and statesmen and thinkers, by lawyers and men of business, by the clergy of all denominations, by women in all ranks of life as well as by men, by those who were his closest friends and by those who had never seen or heard him, there is conveyed to the mind the knowledge of how people are feeling at a definite moment in life, such as one does not get from books or history. Those who wrote and spoke to him broke the customary reticence, and told him what they thought and felt. It was like listening to a long eulogy while he was yet alive. It had its effect. It humiliated him. He was never again quite the same that he had been. There was a change in his face and bearing, as of one who had seen a vision.

It may be interesting to review, now that a generation has gone by, the history of that critical moment in the life of Phillips Brooks. He was the object of a controversy, a battle, between contending parties, not unequally matched. It was the case of the university representing academic interests against the secular world, just as in the Middle Ages it had been the monastery at war with the secular church. Here the university seemed at first to have the advantage in that Brooks felt a strong inclination to accept the call. He had not discarded his early ambition to do some scholarly work. Amid the pressure of duties in a large parish he felt at a disadvantage when questions arose which could be solved only by intellectual research. He liked young men and the associations of student life. He had a special mission to young men at the age when the intellectual is too apt to be divorced from the moral and the spiritual. He was at this time forty-five years of age, not too late to betake himself again to the distinctive work of a student. But it was manifest enough that he had no time to lose. If anything were to be done in this direction it must be now, or he must abandon the dream forever.

And further, he was beginning to be wearied with the burden he had so long been carrying. For twenty years he had stood in the pulpit preaching his matchless sermons. To exert the influence he did was to take the life out of him. With the constant drain on his vital powers it was a marvel that he had endured so long without breaking down. People had come to think of his work as calling for no effort or preparation, welcoming and rejoicing in his appearance as in the sun shining in its strength. In the rich endowment of his nature, he seemed to work with such absolute spontaneity that no one thought of a possible exhaustion, or if they did, postponed it to years in the remote future. Yet there were signs already that he had overtaxed his strength. He

23

knew that he needed some great change, and the opportunity was here presented to him.

These personal considerations were reinforced by earnest appeals from the university, its officers and its students, and by others throughout the land, wherever the interests of Harvard were cherished. A few of these appeals are given here. They came from men of distinction, in varied walks of life:

"I have had an intimate knowledge of the facts for some thirty years, and I speak of what I do know when I say that your power here at this time would exert a greater influence over the educated minds of the country than in any other position however prominent. The one place in the country to fight and overpower the agnosticism which is weakening the religious faith and sapping the manhood of the community is just here. You have a wonderful power, and I do hope you can view this field of labor as I do."

"The College is offering you the very finest chance for working 'Christo et Ecclesiæ' that has ever before been offered to any man in this country."

"The greatest religious opportunity in this country will be lost if you say No."

"And who knoweth [were the words of Scripture quoted to him] whether thou art come to the Kingdom for such a time as this?"

"You can touch the young men at Harvard. I will not say 'you know how to do it,' for I doubt if you do know how you do it. But God helping you, you do it."

"No congregation in this Union can give you such a mighty field of work for God, just where it is most needed, as there. To be the privileged teacher of thousands of men, themselves wellnigh all to be in their future life in some high sense teachers, and of such an institution, will enable you to do a work for the cause of Christ such as is seldom offered to a man. And in this age, when there are such intense mental awakenings and so much silly orthodoxy quailing under them, to have a man who knows how to be true to the essentials and yet not bound in the grave clothes of dead formulas, seems to me one of those providences of God you ought not to regard in any other light or on personal grounds."

"It means more than dozens of Rectorates or even Episcopates. *Accept by all means.* There ought not to be one moment's hesitation, unless merely to enhance the *effect* of your acceptance. Your acceptance will do more to leaven the intellect of the land than can well be conceived of."

Among the incidents of the campaign, as it may be called, was a mass meeting of Harvard students, where speeches were made and a petition signed, expressing not only the hope that he would come, but the conviction that he could not refuse. "It was probably the largest spontaneous meeting of students ever held here," wrote the secretary of the college; "the Chapel was packed, and more were turned away than could find seats or standing room. The speeches, all made by students, were so earnest, so full of confidence in your coming that I wished you could have heard them and seen for yourself what Harvard thinks of your coming."

From the situation in Cambridge we turn to Boston and to Trinity Church. The letters urging him to remain at his post were no less positive in the expression of convictions than those advising his acceptance of the call, but in number they exceeded them in the proportion of ten to one. We learn from them what he had been to Boston in the twelve years of his ministry at Trinity Church. He had become so identified with the city that he had given it a new lustre and reputation. Visitors from all parts of the country and from abroad thought of it as the home of Phillips Brooks. To hear him was an inducement which led strangers to remain over Sunday, or brought them as pilgrims to some sacred shrine. Trinity Church during these years had been like an open cathedral, the common property of the people; or, to change the figure, it had become a confessional, whose spiritual directorship was bringing strength and consolation, faith and hope, to the thousands whom no man can number. The clergy of Boston knew better than most the value of Phillips Brooks's work. They asked him to remain. They said to him, that every church was the stronger for his presence in the city, that they themselves were stronger to do their work, that every agency for good was more effective under the stimulus of his inspiration.

It had been one of the arguments for inducing him to go to Harvard that he would influence the future teachers of others as they passed through the college on their way into the world. He was now reminded that he was doing this work at Trinity. Teachers in the public and private schools of Boston and the vicinity were drawn there in large numbers. He was reminded that he need not go to Harvard to meet young men, for there was a university in his own parish, drawn in part from the college and from the higher institutions of learning and professional schools in and around Boston. Theological students came from their seminaries to listen to the sermons on Sunday afternoons. It would not, therefore, do to assume that it would be no loss to Boston if he went to Harvard. The Governor of the Commonwealth of Massachusetts, Hon. John D. Long, took part in the discussion. He spoke for the city and the State, and the value of his testimony is enhanced in that he was not a member of the same religious communion:

"April 13th, 1881.

"MY DEAR MR. BROOKS,—May I add my sincere word in behalf of your remaining in Boston? It seems to me in the interest of the Commonwealth, with its population accumulating and its young men gathering in its capital, that your close relation to them should not be lost. The Harvard boys do not need you so much. They have everything already. If they develop some wild oats, yet the general surroundings of their college life lead them to higher opportunities and standards sooner or later. But your reach in Cambridge will be nothing compared with what it is in Boston, extending to homes, families, the shop, the counting house, and every fibre of the city. I cannot help feeling that to change would limit and not enlarge your work. I know your own judgment is best, but I think you will pardon my suggestion which is certainly sincere.

"Very truly yours,
"JOHN D. LONG."

The call had been given in the latter part of March, and by the middle of April the excitement had grown to an unprecedented extent. The newspapers in Boston teemed with communications, representing varied points of view. Throughout the country the conflict was watched and commented on as having some undefined import for the higher interests of life. Phillips Brooks was earnestly besought to wait until the question should have been discussed in all its bearings. In the multitude of counsellors there was safety. Both parties felt more secure, if time were taken for the fullest consideration.

As the discussion went on the arguments against accepting the call increased in number and weight. This gift of inspired speech, so divine and so rare, had he any right to endanger its possession for the world by any experiment? The conditions of his place at Trinity Church had favored its expanding power. What would be the result if he were to withdraw into the seclusion of the university town? His power as a preacher might in some way be dependent on conditions which would be lost if he were to abandon the pulpit of Trinity Church: the variety of human experiences absent from student life, of which a great city is full. Did he not carry to students a more valuable message when he went to them with the prophetic burden of a world's needs? And again Trinity Church was so near the University that its students could attend there easily if they wished. It would be only a fraction of the students whom he could reach at Cambridge, for a large proportion spent Sundays at their homes in the vicinity. It was further urged that he would limit his own freedom, trained as he had been in the usages of the Episcopal Church, if he were to accept an undenominational position. The Episcopal Church at large would also suffer in losing a leader who was leavening it with a more comprehensive theology; it would be a calamity, from this point of view, if he abandoned the parish ministry; it might mean that he would sacrifice his identification with the Episcopal Church altogether.

The forces that mustered against the call were too strong to be resisted. If the students of Harvard had a mass meeting to urge his coming, so also a mass meeting was held in Boston in Huntington Hall, at which hundreds of young men raised their voices in protest against his leaving. The entire membership of the Young Men's Christian Association signed their names to a request that he should remain in Boston. There came the same request in a petition from a large business establishment, signed by more than fifty names. Other petitions there were, with the names of prominent business firms appended. It was no slight consideration that the members of his own family were opposed to his going. The wise counsel of the Rev. Arthur Brooks, in whose judgment he placed great confidence, condemned on the whole what seemed a doubtful experiment.   The bishop of the diocese wrote asking him to remain.   And finally Trinity Church spoke in its organic capacity through the wardens and vestry, making it evident that the parish took for granted his duty to remain. In an elaborate and able paper their case was laid before him, closing with the request:

"We ask you to determine nothing until you have heard the representations that will be made by many persons of whose deep and personal concern in your decision you are possibly not now aware; and when you have heard all that can be said by those for whom we speak, we trust and believe that it will be given you to see that it is your present duty not to abandon the field in which God has made it manifest that your power and influence can do a great work for the souls of all conditions of men."

From this time he could have had no doubt as to his place in the hearts of his congregation.   Into the sacred confidences of personal letters, where he was told what he had been to the hundreds of families in his congregation, we must not enter. They have one common feature,—a determination that he should know at last, not merely in a general way but by the unveiling of individual experiences, what his work at Trinity had been to them.

Other suggestions were made, relating to the mysterious working of religion as a motive power in life, to which he could not be insensible—potencies for good which he would lose if he went to Harvard.   But enough has been said to make evident the process by which the verdict was reached, although words will not express the feeling during the long distressing day when the question was pending,—the "terrible earnestness," the "intense anxiety," the "severity of the shock," the "fearful strain," the "sorrow and the gloom," at Trinity Church.

The letters of Phillips Brooks relating to this incident in his life are few and tell little or nothing of what he thought or felt. He was bewildered and hardly knew what to think.   His mind was rent with contradictory impulses.   There was something in him of the feminine mood which led him to go or stay where he was most wanted.   He would like to have gone to Cambridge but he also desired to remain at Trinity.   To go, or to remain meant some inward suffering. He sent for Dr. Vinton to spend Passion Week with him in order that he might get his counsel, heretofore invoked on the changes in his life. Dr. Vinton came up from his retirement at Pomfret,—it was to be for the last time. Then the question was turned over, and the decision reached, that he should stay at Trinity.

To a friend he wrote: "I hope it 's all right, but I 'm awfully blue about it." His call on President Eliot was a severe ordeal; his face was pallid during the short interview, as of a man who saw egress denied him at a critical moment and his life shut up, for his future years, to a work from whose limitations and fearful strain on his vital powers he had dreamed for a moment of escaping. He acquiesced in what seemed to be the popular verdict, but he knew that an opportunity had been lost, which would not return. He did not understand or like his exceptional position, the pedestal on which he was placed. In going to Harvard he might have passed from the glare of publicity into the quiet life he coveted. A tremendous sacrifice was made, when the final decision was reached.

There came another series of letters after the decision had been announced, for the most part of a congratulatory character. Among them is one from the president of Haverford College, in Pennsylvania, who wrote:

"I had pleased myself with a day-dream of you at Cambridge as a better Newman, leading the intellectual hope of the country, not like the Oxford preacher, into the lions' den, but to the promised land. It may be, however, that you will be almost as influential in the University from Boston as from any 'Appleton Chapel,' however enlarged; at the same time your influence over the whole country will be wider from your present post. But wherever you speak, I beg you to feel that you are privileged to command the attention of men at a very critical period in the history of Christianity. Religion and morality itself are menaced by wild and one-sided speculations; but you will continue to teach that there is an eternal, unchangeable moral law, a God in whom we can trust, a Saviour to whom we can cling."

There is a sense in which Harvard University gained in the struggle. The old arrangement was abandoned by which one man ministered to the miscellaneous body of students. A body of chaplains was constituted, of which Mr. Brooks was one, who, coming in from outside, with a wider range in the observation and experience of life, could bring their spiritual force to bear upon the college life. This plan which Harvard was the first to adopt was gradually introduced into other colleges. During the next ten years of his life, Phillips Brooks seemed to have at his command the open door to students' life, throughout the leading colleges in the country. It was Harvard University that was sending him forth with this mission. She had placed her seal upon him as the great university preacher.

On April 26, 1881, Dr. Vinton died at the age of seventy-four. The eulogy which Phillips Brooks pronounced upon him in a memorial sermon preached at Emmanuel Church, Boston, and again in the Church of the Holy Trinity, Philadelphia, was published by request in pamphlet form, but deserves a permanent place among his writings as the description of an ideal which had been before him from his boyhood. He spoke of Dr. Vinton as

" in his true place in that degree of the ministry where preaching is the constant duty. Once or twice they talked of making him a bishop. But it was well, in his heart I think he knew that it was well, that they who formed such plans for him did not succeed.... The great work of the church lies with the presbyters. The deacon saves the presbyter from some details of work that he may be the freer for his tasks. The bishop watches the ramparts of the church and secures for the presbyter the conditions of peaceful and effective labor. But the great work of the church is in the presbyters. And this was our great presbyter. That is his name and honor."

The pastoral office as embodied in Dr. Vinton is thus described:

"I stop a moment and think of that great pastorship, of all it meant to countless souls; and to have lived in it and carried it on as he did seems to me to be an indescribable, an inestimable privilege. A great pastorship is the noblest picture of human influence and of the relationship of man to man which the world has to show. It is the canonization of friendship. It is friendship lifted above the regions of mere instinct and sentiment and fondness, above all thought of policy or convenience, and exalted into the mutual helpfulness of the children of God. The pastor is father and brother both to those whose deepest lives he helps in deepest ways. His belonging to his people is like the broad spreading of the sky over the lives of men and women and little children, of good and bad, of weak and strong, on all of whom alike it sheds its rain and dew."

Dr. Vinton had borne himself well in the trying experience which comes to older men who have been leaders, when the new generation comes in with a departure from time-honored ways,— a model to young men who in their turn must encounter the same difficulty.

"Those years from 1858 to 1861 were interesting years to any minister of our church, because of the new drifts and tendencies of Christian thought which were beginning to become pronounced. Ritualism and rationalism were claiming their places in the church. Especially in the latter of these two directions the movement became vigorous and prominent about that time. The famous 'Essays and Reviews' were published in 1860, and the whole liberal or broad church tendency attracted the interest of thinking men. It would not be right to try to sketch the life of Dr. Vinton, and not to tell how he regarded that movement in which he was, through all the last years of his life, so deeply interested. He mistrusted it and feared it. He disagreed with many of its processes and most of its conclusions. At the same time he never withheld his friendship and his love from those who were most earnestly in sympathy with it, nor ever gave them anything but help and godspeed in their work. He never recoiled from it with horror. . . . For my part, I thank Dr. Vinton for many and many a word even of protest against what I thought was true, which, while it made me more anxious and careful to be sure that what I thought was truth was really true, made me also more earnest in holding it as I became convinced that I was not mistaken. And I am sure that his great soul would not grudge me that gratitude."

There creeps into the correspondence of Phillips Brooks at this time the evidence of physical weariness. He found the sermon on Dr. Vinton one of the hardest things that he had ever undertaken; and he mentions that while he was writing it the weather was atrocious. He declines an invitation to take a journey, which would call for physical endurance, on the ground that he is no longer good for such things. On hearing that one of his clerical friends proposed to take a rest of more than a year he says: "It is getting to be kind of tame and vulgar to plod right on. But it is pleasant nevertheless."

Among the important books which appeared in 1881 was Dr.

Mulford's *Republic of God*, which broke the long silence of the younger men on the religious issues of the day. To a lady who wrote after Dr. Mulford's lamented death, asking his opinion of the book, he replied:

"Dr. Mulford was a most interesting man, and his book is one of the most inspiring and exasperating things that anybody ever wrote. It is as bright and deep and vague as the sky. It will never be much read, but a few men will get out of it what they will interpret to the world. He was not a man for the ecclesiasticism of the Church to make much out of, but he was felt, and his loss nobody can make good."

Mr. Brooks took no vacation from preaching during the summer of 1881. Every Sunday found him in his place in the pulpit of Trinity Church. During the week he visited parishioners in their summer homes. It was a summer to be remembered because of the assassination of President Garfield, when for weeks the country was in suspense waiting for the fatal issue.

"How it brings back that awful Friday sixteen years ago, only this is more wretched because it is not connected with any great issue and has no more dignity than must always belong to death —if it is to be death. The assassin seems to have been the most miserable moonstruck vagabond—and his object nothing more than disappointed spite. I met —— on the street just after we had heard of it this morning, and he told me of an article he had been writing upon the folly of allowing the President of the United States to go about without a bodyguard! Every goose will sting his own sermon into the dreadful tragedy. I saw ——, and he had several delightful and subtle theories about it. But the one thing to do now is to hope that Garfield will get well and that we shall be spared the infliction of Arthur as President. We shall pray for the President to-night at the 'usual meeting previous to the Communion.' "

The summer brought another sorrow, in the death of Dean Stanley, which took place July 18. On hearing the sad intelligence, he wrote to the Dean's sister-in-law, Lady Frances Baillie:

"CLARENDON STREET, July 23, 1881.

"MY DEAR LADY FRANCES,—I hope that I shall not seem to you strangely intrusive if I try to tell you something of my deep sympathy with you and of the deep thankfulness with which I think of our dear friend's beautiful life. It seems to me as perfect a picture of human living as the world has ever seen,—and what it suggests and promises for his great future, for the other life (as we blindly call it) which he has begun, is past all expression. My first thought is all of him, of the rich and sacred delight which has come to that insatiable appetite for truth and that deep love for God.

"But when I let myself think of all his kindness to me, of how he has welcomed me with that beautiful welcome of his which was like no other man's, of how England has been bright and tempting to me, most of all because he was there, the world seems sadly altered now that I shall never see him again.

"I remember so perfectly the first time I saw him. Lady Augusta was with him in the library of the dear old deanery, and before we had loosened hands, it was as if she and he had given me the right to count them friends forever. That was in 1874, and from that day on, with all his cares and interests, he was so full of thoughtful kindness, that he did not even let me think how little right I had to any words or thought of his. But I did give him, and I will give him always, that love and gratitude which is all that such as I am can give to such as he is.

"Surely we cannot lose him. We have not lost him. We are with him in the love of God in which he rests at peace.

"I wish that I could tell you what he was when he was here in America; what friends he made, what a memory of him remains, and what a multitude of hearts are mourning for him, as if he was their friend.

"But more than this is the blessed work that he has done for Christ and for the Church. That cannot die, It will be part of the great future for which he kept such an unfaltering hope, and which we may believe he now discerns with perfect clearness. And it is sweet for us all because he believed in it so.

"Will you forgive me if I ought not to have written, for his sake. I send my kindest remembrance to your daughter, and I am, with truest sympathy,

" Sincerely yours,
" PHILLIPS BROOKS."

In response to a call from the editor of *The Atlantic Monthly*, Mr. Brooks broke the rule to which he had so far adhered and wrote an article on Dean Stanley. He dwelt on Stanley's work in clothing the Bible with a fascinating interest. Although Brooks never felt the charm with which its union with the state invests the English Church, he thought Stanley's *Essays on Church and State* a book every religious student should read. He greatly admired his last volume on *Christian Institutions*, for its wonderful clearness and power, and as showing how in an age of perplexity and disbelief Stanley stood high among the faithful souls who refuse to despair of the Church of Christ. As we read it

"it is as if we heard the quiet word spoken which breaks the spell of ecclesiasticism, and the imprisoned truth or principle wakes and stands upon its feet and looks us in the eye. The flush of life comes back into the hard face of dead ceremonies, and their soul reveals itself. Bubbles of venerable superstition seem to burst before our eyes; and we feel sure anew, with fresh delight and hope, that not fantastical complexity, but the simplicity of naturalness, is the real temple in which we are to look for truth."

He recalled Stanley's personal charm, the charm also of his preaching:

"Apart from the beautiful simplicity of his style and the richness of illustrative allusion, the charm of his sermons was very apt to lie in a certain way which he had of treating the events of the day as parts of the history of the world, and making his hearers feel that they and what they were doing belonged as truly to the history of their race, and shared as truly in the care and government of God, as David and his wars, or Socrates and his teachings. As his lectures made all times live with the familiarity of our own day, so his sermons made our own day, with its petty interests, grow sacred and inspired by its identification with the great principles of all the ages."

The effect of the call to Harvard was to bring Mr. Brooks into closer relationship with the University. He took his turn in preaching at Appleton Chapel and in conducting morning prayers. He felt keenly the responsibility for the spiritual welfare of the students, and in his devotion to the students he did not begrudge the claims upon his time. "I am chaplain this week at Cambridge," he writes, "and go there every morning for prayers. It is very pleasant, but it takes lots of time. I have to leave here at eight o'clock and do not get back till ten."

At the seventh Church Congress, which was held at Providence, in October, Mr. Brooks was one of the appointed speakers on the subject of "Liturgical Growth." The subject was full of interest at the time, for the question of "the enrichment of the Prayer Book" was before the General Convention of the Episcopal Church. He pleaded for extemporaneous prayer on the ground that in a comprehensive church, such as the Episcopal Church claimed to be, this element of power and flexibility should be included. It was not enough that a clergyman was already at liberty to make the extemporaneous prayer at the close of his sermon, a liberty of which he freely availed himself. So long as the rubrics did not authorize it, he felt bound to refrain from indulging his preference, for he was scrupulous in adherence to the prescribed form and order.

The paper on "Liturgical Growth" shows that he keenly felt the restriction which made it impossible to pray with an open heart at critical moments, when the freedom of the soul should be granted. When the city of Chicago was in flames the General Convention, then in session, showed its sympathy and asked the Divine aid by reciting the Litany, while the name of the city and the awful occasion were passed over in silence. Even the Roman Church possessed flexibility in striking contrast with this hard conservatism and immobility. He denounced this conservative attitude as showing lack of faith in the principle of liturgical worship.

Upon one topic he volunteered to speak at this same Church Congress,—a thing unusual, for when people were met to talk it was his custom to be silent. The Revised Version of the New Testament was one of the subjects for discussion. He listened to the objections to it by the various speakers,—its sacrifice of rhythm in style and of familiar expressions which had become dear. He listened till he could bear it no longer, and rose in his majestic presence to make his way to the platform.

"The thing that is really upon trial [he said] is not the Revised Version but the Church. If a man is going to translate a book for me, the one thing I demand is scrupulousness,—the most absolute fidelity to details, the absolute binding of themselves to the simple question how they could most completely represent the Greek in English, letting the question of literary merit take care of itself. That is the one great evidence of faithfulness to their charge which we had a right to ask of those men who undertook this responsible work, which work so far Christendom has stamped with its approval as to its accuracy. If a man came to me to-morrow, and wanted to know what Christianity was, to understand the words of Christ, I should be absolutely bound to give him the New Version and not the old one.

" The great body of new Christians are reading the new book. God grant that our Church may not condemn us to read the old and faulty book in our churches, to the exclusion of the new and corrected one, and so lag behind, as we have done again and again, and only with a tardy run by and by come up abreast of the great dominant sentiment and the prevailing convictions of our fellow-Christians."

In consequence of his bold treatment of both these topics he incurred the strictures of the ecclesiastical press, which, without mentioning him by name, referred to "a brilliant and popular preacher" who had recently been making some rash remarks.

In the fall of 1881 Dr. Brooks published his second volume of sermons, under the title *The Candle of the Lord, and other Sermons*. It met with the same reception accorded to the first volume, reaching a sale of over twenty-one thousand. The titles of the sermon are felicitously chosen, and linger in the memory. Most of them had been written in the seventies in the ordinary course of his preaching at Trinity Church. Out of the twenty-one sermons which the volume contains, the texts of nine are from the Old Testament. If this circumstance has any significance, it lies in showing his gift of the poetic imagination applied to the interpretation of life. He repelled the insinuation, that the Christian pulpit lingers too long among Jewish antiquities. He found in the Old Testament perpetual inspiration, the disclosure of the process by which God reveals His life to the world. The texts of sermons in his second volume taken from the Old Testament recall some of the most abiding impressions of his preaching. The bush which burned and was not consumed stands for the continuity of one's years; the joy of self-sacrifice is typified in ancient ritual, when the "song of the Lord began with trumpets" at the moment of the burnt offering; to lift up one's eyes to the hills is to see all lower sources of comfort and consolation as having their origin in the highest, which is God; the curse which was upon Meroz is the curse upon human inactivity in any age whenever the crises of life are upon men. The accumulation of faith makes it possible to believe that God is as powerful in the present as in the past,—"He could overcome the worldliness of the eighteenth century, He can overcome the materialism and fatalism of the nineteenth century; as in ancient times He not only smote the rock that the waters gushed out, but He also provided bread for His people."

It is hard to speak of some of these sermons without speaking of all. But a few must be specially mentioned, In the sermon on "The Manliness of Christ," which strangely touched the conscience of every one who heard it, he probes the consciousness for the reason why men have failed to see the strength of Christ, and makes apparent the defect, and the cause of the defect, felt in the traditional portraits of Christ.

The sermon on "The Law of Liberty" delivered many times, has in it a reminder of Chalmers and Bushnell, but does not suffer by comparison. In the closing passage, he asks what the result would be of taking off the restraints of education and of social order, leaving each man free to seek his own place.

The sermon on "The Mystery of Light" gives a contrast between the two kinds of mystery, that of light and that of darkness. It is no more possible to measure the depths of one than of the other. Current popular objections to the doctrine of the Trinity are mistaken in considering it as a mystery of darkness, when in reality it is the dazzling, bewildering mystery of light.

This second volume of sermons, like the first, shows traces of the time,—that moment in the history of religious experience when there was a storm on the ocean of life and much wreckage of faith; when Phillips Brooks had stood forth as a commander to the people. On a Thanksgiving Day, when his church overflowed with hearers who anticipated the importance of the message to be delivered, he took for his text the words of the prophet Ezekiel, "Son of man, stand upon thy feet, and I will speak to thee." His subject was the need of self-respect as a condition for hearing the voice of God in revelation.

"If this be a truth, is it not a great truth and one that needs continually to be preached? The other truth is often urged upon us that if we do not listen humbly we shall listen in vain. But this truth is not so often preached, nor, I think, so generally felt, —unless you honor your life, you cannot get God's best and fullest wisdom; unless you stand upon your feet, you will not hear God speak to you. . . . I am sure you know whereof I speak. In large circles of life—and they are just those circles in which a great many of us live, there is an habitual disparagement of human life, its joys and its prospects. Man is on his face. It seems to me that he must hear God's voice calling him to another attitude, or he is hopeless. 'Son of man, stand upon thy feet, and I will speak to thee.'"

The year 1881 as it came to a close brought his forty-fifth birthday. As he entered the forties he had begun to sigh for the youth that was passing, and to realize that something had been lost. When he was reminded of the increasing wealth that came with maturity, the larger vision, the mature ripeness of the powers, he declared there was in them no compensation for that which was gone. In his sermon on "The Manliness of Christ" he is brooding upon this issue:

"It would seem, then, as if this truth were very general, that in every development there is a sense of loss as well as a sense of gain. The flower opening into its full luxuriance has no longer the folded beauty of the bud. The summer with its splendor has lost its fascinating mystery of the springtime. The family of grown-up men remembers almost with regret the crude dreams which filled the old house with romance when the men were boys. The reasonable faith to which the thinker has attained cannot forget the glow of vague emotion with which faith began. . . . Who is not aware of that strange sense of loss which haunts the ripening man? With all that he has come to, there is something that he has left behind. In some moods the loss seems to outweigh the gain. He knows it is not really so, but yet the misgiving that freshness has been sacrificed to maturity, intenseness to completeness, enthusiasm to wisdom, makes the pathos of the life of every sensitive and growing man."

This is one of the passages scattered through his sermons where the preacher is telling of his own experience. When these moods were on him he took them to the pulpit, as to some mount of vision, to test them there. What would not prove a source of strength and elevation could not be true. In his sermon on "The Symmetry of Life," preached on Advent Sunday, he gives the corrective of depressing moods. His text was from the Book of Revelation, in whose imagery he delighted, "The length and the breadth and the height of it are equal."

To his youngest brother he wrote on Christmas Eve:

"How many Christmas Eves we have spent together! Do you remember how we used to go up to St. Mark's and then come back and wander through the toy-shops and look up children's presents, and then how you would go home and find father nailing up Christmas wreaths? Well, that 's all over, and here I am alone with the Christmas festival safely over and the Christmas sermon done, and cheering myself up by looking at the mighty pretty little vase you have sent me, and by thinking how very kind you were to send it."

Watch Night was kept as usual at Trinity Church, and on returning to his house he found a New Year's gift awaiting him from the members of the Clericus Club,—a bronze statue of John the Baptist in the attitude of preaching,—a token of recognition on the part of the club of his hospitality in throwing open his house for its monthly meetings.

In this month of January Mr. Brooks undertook soliciting subscriptions for a memorial of Dean Stanley to be placed in the Chapter House of Westminster Abbey. At a meeting held on December 13, 1881, to commemorate Stanley's birthday, it had been suggested that the opportunity be given to friends of Stanley in America to contribute to the completion of the Chapter House, by supplying one of the windows, for which Stanley had already furnished the designs. The amount required, £1000, came in so quickly in response to Mr. Brooks's appeal that by the month of March some three hundred persons from all parts of the country had sent in subscriptions whose total amount exceeded what was called for by several hundred dollars. In a letter to a friend in England, he spoke of the list of subscribers:

"You will know many of the names: Mr. Winthrop and Mr. Adams among our oldest public men; Longfellow, Holmes, and Whittier among the poets; Parkman and Bancroft among the historians; Emerson, the philosopher, who was most glad to make his contribution; the bishops of Massachusetts, New York, Michigan, Rhode Island, Connecticut, and Nebraska; clergymen of all sorts, Episcopalians, Unitarians, Baptists, Congregationalists; men of business, college students, and professors, and then a great many who have simply read the Dean's books and have personal gratitude for him."

Ash Wednesday fell on the 22d of February. The prevailing usage now called for a multiplication of services till they were held every day of the week, and in Passion week each day was

24

observed by two and even three services. Mr. Brooks accommodated himself to the change, but with some misgivings. He humorously remarks in a letter that he is wearing out the bricks between his residence and the "meeting-house."

"We have got the thing a great deal too full and complicated. No one service amounts to much in the way of exciting thought or feeling, and the whole long stretch of services grows tame if not tiresome. Besides this there has got to be a sort of rivalry between parishes, as if the one which had the most services were the most godly flock and shepherd. Men get each other's 'Lent Cards' and compare them, to see who is doing the most 'work.' There 'll be a great collapse some day."

After Easter Mr. Brooks admitted that he needed a complete change, and a long one; and the subject was mentioned to the wardens and vestrymen of Trinity Church. He had not yet made up his mind definitely how long he should wish to be absent from home, but intimated that he might possibly conclude to ask for an entire year. The answer of the Proprietors of Trinity Church conceding his request was prompt and generous:

"The Proprietors of Trinity Church, deeply grateful for the invaluable services which have been rendered us by Mr. Brooks, during the more than twelve years of his rectorship, and fearing that he may be in need of a longer and more continuous rest from his devoted labors than he has ever yet been willing to allow himself, desire to express their sincere wish that, in going abroad this summer, he may not feel bound to limit his vacation too narrowly, but may be at perfect liberty to linger in other climates for the autumn, winter, and following summer, if he shall deem such a stay more likely to bring him back to us with invigorated health and strength for the work which we count upon so earnestly in future years."

Just before sailing for Europe he wrote this letter to Mr. Cooper:

"June 20, 1882.
"DEAR COOPER,—While I am waiting for the carriage which is to take me to Europe my last letter shall be to you. I got your good kind letter yesterday, and it was like the Benediction I had been waiting for, the last blessing, which I had half hoped to get on board the *Servia* at New York, but your dear old handwriting is the next thing to it.
"What lots of good times we have had together! Race Street

and the mountains and the lakes and the Tyrol and Switzerland and Paris and Boston and Spruce Street for twenty-two years. And now it seems as if you ought to be going with me. The journey does n't look lovely or attractive this morning, but of course it will all brighten up by and by and there will be lots to enjoy, but the best of it all will be getting home again. So keep well and young and strong so that we may have still a lot of talks together.

"Thank you, dear Cooper, for your long friendship and unfailing kindness. May God be good to you as you have been to me.

"Well, well, a year from next September.

"Good-bye, good-bye.

"P. B."

CHAPTER XV.

1882–1883.

PLANS FOR THE YEAR ABROAD. GERMANY. CORRE-
SPONDENCE. EXTRACTS FROM NOTE-BOOKS. INDIA.
EXTRACTS FROM LETTERS AND JOURNAL. RETURN
FROM INDIA. VISIT TO SPAIN. RECEPTION IN
ENGLAND. VISIT TO TENNYSON. LETTERS. EX-
TRACTS FROM JOURNAL.

WHEN it was known that Phillips Brooks was to be absent for
a year and his voice silenced during all that time the people
wondered. It seemed as if no answer to the question, why he
should go away, was quite satisfactory. It was unreasonable,
inexplicable, that he should stop preaching when the world was
waiting to listen. Vague rumors were in the air—fears that
something was wrong. One answer that he gave to the question
why he went was that he had been giving out for a long time
and would like to stop for a moment to take in. But no one
felt it could be true that he was in such need. If his health had
suffered under the long, heavy, and incessant strain, it was not
apparent. There was no diminution in his seemingly boundless
vitality. His very presence had power to carry happiness to
hearts that were heavy. "It was a dull, rainy day, when things
looked dark and lowering, but Phillips Brooks came down Newspaper Row and all was bright,"—was one of the items in a Boston
paper.

The plan for the year abroad included a sojourn in Germany,
India, and England, giving some three months to each country;
and also a short tour in Spain, to glance at its monuments and
churches. It was a plan for study, but from life as well as from
books,—to know for himself, by personal inquiry and observa-

tion, how the world was thinking and living. He found it hard at first to realize that he had a long year before him.

"And so the year of wandering has begun. It is not easy yet to realize that it is more than a mere summer's journey, but every now and then it comes over me that the gap is to be so great that the future, if there is any, will certainly be something different in some way from the past. I don't regret that, for, pleasant as all these past years have been, they don't look very satisfactory as one reviews them; and, although I am inclined to put a higher value on their results than anybody else would be likely to do, they have not certainly accomplished much. I should like to think that the years that remain, when I get home, would be more useful. There is surely coming, and it has partly come, a better Christian Day than any that we or our fathers for many generations have seen. One would like to feel before he dies that he has made some little bit of contribution to it."

He was accompanied by friends on the voyage, and, during the earlier part of his journey, among them Mr. Richardson the architect, with whom he had proposed to visit southern France and Spain. "Architecture under these circumstances must be the main interest," he writes, but "art, life, and scenery shall not be forgotten." The journey included Provence, with its wealth of old Roman remains, Genoa, Leghorn, Pisa, Florence, Bologna, Ravenna, and then Venice. "I think that I enjoyed the re-seeing of old places almost, if not quite, as much as the discovery of new ones. The deepening and filling out of old impressions is very delightful." At Venice the party began to break up. From Paris he wrote of his journey:

"The summer is over, and you have no idea how good it has been. We went down almost to the gates of Rome, and saw the beauty of northern Italy, at its most beautiful. My eyes swim with light and color now. We went also into southern France and saw a great deal of soberer beauty,—quiet old towns, and queer, quaint churches, and kind, dirty people. Richardson was with us till we reached Milan, and then went off into Spain, where he is now. You should have seen the man in Venice! The wonder is that any gondola could hold such enthusiasm and energy, or that he ever, having once got there, came away. . . . You will find him glowing with splendid projects for Trinity. A front porch, a chapter house, and the great piers to be covered from top to bottom with mosaics. You will listen with interest, and dream as I do of how more and more beautiful the dear old church may be made from generation to generation."

While Mr. Brooks was in Germany and India he wrote a large number of letters, many of them long, in which he gives expression to his thought and feeling in an unwonted degree. In his separation from home and friends he felt the necessity of letter-writing for his own satisfaction. Not since he was at the seminary in Alexandria do we get such a complete picture of the man. Some of these letters, but mostly those of a lighter character, have been included in his *Letters of Travel*. Even these, however, are characteristic in their quality. Dr. Oliver Wendell Holmes said that only after reading them did he feel that he knew the man. While he was away he carried the interests of his life close to his heart,—Trinity Church, the Clericus Club, the households of his friends, and the varying phases of ecclesiastical life. His friends charged themselves with the duty of writing to him often, so that he could easily follow the course of events. So voluminous is the correspondence and other material during this year abroad that it would require a considerable volume to contain it. Only a small fraction can be given here.

On August 28, 1882, he writes:

"After three pleasant days together in Paris, they have gone this morning, and I am all alone. It has been a delightful summer, and now I feel as if my work began. A week from to-day I hope to reach Berlin, where I shall stay for some time. I am very anxious to study, and the prospect of unlimited time for reading opens most attractively. I do not feel as if it were a waste of time, or mere self-indulgence, for all my thought about the work which I have done for the last twenty years, while it is very pleasant to remember, makes it seem very superficial and incomplete. I do not know that I can make what remains any better, but I am very glad indeed of the opportunity to try."

To a member of the Clericus Club, Rev. Percy Browne, he commends its interests while he is away:

"You won't let the Club flag this winter, will you? It seems to me that we all owe so much to it; and while we have grown used to it and don't think so much about it as we used to, it has never been better than in these last years. . . . You don't know how pleasant the old life looks from this distance, when one understands that he is to get nothing of it for a year. What good times we have had! and how few the dull and disagreeable spots have been!"

Early in September Mr. Brooks had reached Berlin, taking up his residence there for some two months, but in the meantime visiting other university towns, Giessen, Leipsic, and Heidelberg. These are hints of how he passed his days:

"I am going out to dine at Wansee (which seems to be a sort of Berlin Brookline) with Baron von der Heydt, who is going to have some of the Court preachers to meet me. A good many other people have called on me, and talked about German things and people; so that I see all I want to see of folks, and the days are only too short. Unfortunately, the university is closed, and the professors are all off on vacations, so that I miss many men whom I should like to see.

"I get up in the morning and breakfast at eight o'clock; then I go to my room, which is very bright and pleasant, where I have a lot of books and a good table, at which I am writing now. Here I stay until eleven or twelve, reading and studying, mostly German; then I go out, see a sight or two, and make calls until it is two o'clock. Then I go to Dr. Seidel, my teacher, and take a lesson, reading German with him for two hours. Then it is dinner time, for everybody in Berlin dines very early. They have North Andover fashions here. Four o'clock is the *table d'hôte* time at our hotel, and that is rather late. After dinner I get about two hours more of reading in my room, and when it is dark I go out and call on somebody, or find some interesting public place until bedtime. Is not that a quiet, regular life?

"This week I have been like a college student, going to hear what the great men have to say about theology and other things. I have German enough now to follow a lecture quite satisfactorily, and you do not know how I enjoy it. Of course I have not taken up any systematic course of attendance. My time is too short for that. I only roam round and pick up what I can and fill it out with reading from the books of the same men, a good many of which I have. There are four thousand other students here in Berlin, so that one can go and come in the great university quite as he pleases, and be entirely unnoticed. . . . The thoroughness of these real scholars makes me feel awfully superficial and ashamed."

To the Rev. Arthur Brooks he writes more fully of what he is doing. He had been greatly impressed by reading Lotze:

"On the whole I have been as successful in carrying out my rather vague plans as I could anyway have hoped. I have found people everywhere most accessible, and although very few of the theologians speak English they mostly understand it, and the study I have had here makes their German quite intelligible. Both in such lectures as I have heard here in the last week and in the conversations which I have had with men in various places I have found no real difficulty. In Halle and Heidelberg and Leipsic I have found interesting people and got pretty good ideas of what theologians were at. A thoroughness of exegesis which is beautiful, and an inquiry into the Old Testament history which makes it very living, and a rearrangement of dogmatic statements in philosophical systems—these are their great works. The books which I have read with considerable struggle are the new *Life of Jesus* by Weiss, of Berlin; the *Life of Luther* by Köstlin, whom I saw at Halle, which is the last great work on the Reformation; the *Chrisitan Belief and Morals* of Pfleiderer, of Berlin; and, above all, the lectures of Hermann Lotze on the *Philosophy of Religion* and on the *Foundations of Practical Philosophy.* Then I have dipped into Schleiermacher, of whom I knew nothing before. But Lotze is the most interesting of men. I wish you would get somebody to translate his *Grundzüge der Religionsphilosophie,*—somebody who knows German well, It is a little book, the mere notes of one of his students from his lectures, which has been published this year in Leipsic. If I knew enough German to be quite sure that I was n't making him say just what he did n't mean to I would translate some of it myself, for it is full of as rich sound meat as any book I ever read, and with my poor German knowledge I know I have got at the gist of it. The way that people speak of him here is very impressive. I have heard one or two lectures from his successor Zeller, who is also an interesting man. It is the jolliest thing, this university. There it stands wide open and anybody can go into any lecture that he chooses. I have heard Dillman and Weiss and Pfleiderer, who are the best of the theological people here except Dorner, who is the Nestor of their faculty, but is now very ill and off at Baden-Baden. The city preachers, of whom I have seen several, seem to be very earnest but not very inspiring men. On the whole I feel as if there were not in Germany just the type of man whom we have in England and America,—the really spiritual rationalist or broad Churchman, the Maurice or the Washburn. Their positive men are dogmatists and their rationalists are negative. Such men there must be somewhere,—successors of Schleiermacher on his best side,—but nobody seems to be able to point them out, and except in vague and casual approaches I have failed to find them. Outside of theology I have made some very pleasant acquaintances. I have seen a good deal of

Baron von Bunsen and his family. He is the son of the Bunsen of many books, the Chevalier, and is a very charming man, and his house is always full of pleasant people."

While Phillips Brooks was in Germany he appears to be engaged in a review of his life and experience. He attempts to draw out in order and connection those personal convictions about religious truth which had slowly and separately taken shape in his mind. His mind assumes a devotional tone in dealing with theological problems,—about God and revelation, Christ, the miracle, the Bible, the moral life, personality, the Church, death, eternity. In a beautiful and somewhat elaborate paper he develops each of these ideas, but in a poetic rather than scholastic vein.[1]

The undercurrent of his life was religious. Natural scenery, art, architecture, historical monuments and inscriptions, everything relating to famous men, the customs and manners of people, the course of ordinary life—in these he was deeply interested. But beneath them all he was seeking for the spiritual meaning of human existence. He took the opportunity which his leisure gave him to study the life of Luther, visiting every spot connected with his career. He made himself the possessor of the original editions of the great Reformer's writings, surprised to find that they could be bought so cheaply. Next to Luther in his admiration stood Goethe. He studied the Second Part of *Faust*, and witnessed an attempt to reproduce it in the theatre, which he pronounces a failure. He devoted much of his time to Lessing, making a study of that most suggestive work, *Die Erziehung des Menschengeschlechts*, and writing out in his note-book an abstract of each one of its paragraphs. Much of his time was given to writing in his note-book the thoughts or the impressions he was receiving. Not for many years had he done such systematic work in recording what had passed through his mind. Everywhere interspersed are texts and suggestions for sermons:

"The lateral and terminal moraine,—that refuse of misconception, superstition, etc., which an old institution or faith throws off on its sides as it moves while it is still living, and that which it leaves as refuse at the end after it has exhausted itself and perished."

[1] For this paper see *Life of Phillips Brooks*, first ed. vol. ii., pp. 472–482.

"The sad story of the earnest minister who went to give himself to study so that he might be more useful. And as he learned more and more his faith more and more decayed, until at last he was a learned skeptic, and knew himself that he had destroyed the vessel in filling it with its true wine."

"Apropos of Savonarola,—it is not always the strongest spirits of a time who are most free from its superstitions. The illustrations in one's own time."

"'Show Thy servants Thy work and their children Thy glory,' Psalm xc. 16 (Prayer Book version). One generation doing a piece of the work of God, and the next generation seeing how splendid it is."

"'Lord, not my feet only, but also my hands and my head.' The answer of Christ. The cry of dissatisfied men who only need more impulse and 'go' for a complete change of thoughts and principles; when what they want is only to put to use more conscientiously and vigorously what they have."

"The figure of the 'stream' of time (or life) is true not only in other respects but also in this, that it expresses the constant change along with constant *identity* which life possesses."

"'A little while and ye shall not see me, and again a little while and ye shall see me.' Text for sermon on the passage through darkened periods of life and faith."

"Lessing's *Der Junge Gelehrte* must be more than an amazing farce. In it we certainly can see two things, one temporary and local, the other universal and eternal. The universal teaching is that mere pedantry is not true learning, and that life, no less than books, has lessons for the learning man. The local application must be to a state of Germany in his time, when the studying people, filled with the new enthusiasm of study, were often using it foolishly, as if it were a valuable and noble thing for its own sake,—the crude condition of the ordinary German student in those days, of which we see many signs."

"In all this travelling one is overcome and oppressed with the multiplicity of life. The single point where we stand is so small, yet it is the best and dearest of all. I would not for the world be anything but this, if I must cease being this in order to be that other thing. But I would fain *also* be these other things —these college students, these soldiers in their barracks, these children playing round the old fountain, these actors on their

stages, these merchants in their shops, these peasant women at
their toil, these fine ladies with their beauty; I want somehow,
somewhere, to *be* them all; and the simplicity, the singleness of
my own life, with its appointed place and limits, comes over me
oppressively. Where is the outlook and the outlet? Must it
not be in the possibility, which is not denied to any of us, of getting some *conception* of life which is large enough to include and
comprehend all these and every other form in which men live, or
have lived, or will live forever? And is not such a conception to
be found in Christ's large truth of God the Father? O, to
preach or hear some day a worthy sermon on 'In Him we live
and move and have our being.'!"

"The present condition of our churches is something like an
orchestra tuning up. Each instrument trying itself altogether by
itself. Some time they must all strike in together and the great
Symphony begin. The high unselfishness of the instruments in
an orchestral piece."

"Text: 'Sacrifice and meat offering Thou wouldst not, but
my ears hast Thou opened.' Ps. xl., 8. Sermon on God's love
for intelligent worship and for a desire after the truth upon His
people's part.

"Text: 'This is the victory that overcometh the world, even
our faith.' The absolute creed that only by belief in something
higher should man master the lower. Oh, the necessity of *loving*
purity and great thoughts about great things, not merely being
driven to them. Thus the child's salvation from brutal vice and
infidel cynicism. Point also to the men who are overcome by the
world for want of faith.

"In connection with the above think of the great danger of
abolishing that for which we give no substitute. Sometimes it
must be done, and the development or discovery of the substitute
must be left to wisdom and power greater than ours, but there is
always terrible danger.

"We in America have no complete substitute for the military
training which we rejoice to be free from. The mercantile
rivalry is not a substitute. It lacks the possible self-devotion and
nobleness."

"Text: 'The Son of Man cometh like a thief in the night;
watch therefore.' The whole subject of suddenness; nothing is
sudden, and yet everything is sudden. The value of the knowledge of this in bringing about the true *poise* of temperament.

Expectation without terror, a sense of naturalness and wonder together."

"Luther's protest in behalf of freedom was indeed the opening of a new world, but its real value was measured by the worth of the positive authority to which he appealed. Darwin's protest against the crudeness of popular creationism must be his real claim to remembrance in spite of his saying 'Science has nothing to do with Christ.' It may perhaps turn out after all that science has wiser teachers than the great scientist knew, that Christ's truth of the Father Life of God has the most intimate connection with Darwin's doctrine of development, which is simply the continual indwelling and action of creative power."

"Some people seem to have almost exactly the influence of *Music*. It is an inarticulate influence. It does not communicate ideas, but it creates moods. It is incapable of analysis. Men ask you to give an account of these people's power over you, and you cannot. You tell your story and the listener asks, 'Is that all?' and wonders at your delusion. All that you can do is to say, 'Come and see" as after vainly trying to describe the power of a piece of music you take your friend to hear it. All influence of man over man, however rich it may be in the imparting of ideas and the awakening of the moral sense, seems to be incomplete unless there is in it something of this musical power of creating moods."

"Stein had great contempt for what he called *metapoliticians*, who are, as Seeley in his *Life of Stein* defines it, 'those who stand in the same relation to politicians as metaphysicians to the students of nature.' The same feeling which crudely and coarsely breaks out in our time against the 'scholar in politics,' those 'damned literary fellows.' There are reason and unreason in it both. "

"Text: 'Sir, thou hast nothing to draw with, and the well is deep.' Spoken in perfect honesty. A naïve expression of the worldly man's sense of the difficulty of life and of the inadequate equipment of merely spiritual natures to cope with it. "

"The beasts in a zoölogical garden always trying to get out; their pathetic, brutal inability to be convinced that it is hopeless. You came back after years, and there is that same bear walking up and down just as you left him, trying the same bars, and never giving up the hope that somewhere he may find a gap. It is the dim memory of savage free life—nay, see how even the beasts born in captivity, who have never known by experience the freedom of the desert, they too are at the same endless undiscouraged effort to escape.

"Apply to man's everlasting working away at the problems of existence."

"The Ten Commandments based on the idea of liberty,— 'Thus spake Jehovah who brought you out of the house of bondage,' and issuing in the injunctions of duty and righteousness, 'Thou shalt and thou shalt not'; so Liberty and Duty lie together here."

"We are not called upon to set in opposition the two great conceptions of the results of conduct, one of which thinks of them as inevitable consequences naturally produced, and the other as the rewards and punishments meted out by the superior insight and justice of a ruling Lord. Each conception has its value, which we cannot afford to lose in seeking for the total truth. The first gives reasonableness and reliability to the whole idea. The second preserves the vividness of personality. The time was when the second conception monopolized men's thought. In the present strong reaction from the second to the first conception it would be a great loss if we let the second be denied or fade into forgetfulness."

"I read in a religious paper, 'Nothing short of this can difference the Gospel from any other ethical system in kind.' Do we, then, want to *difference* the Gospel from the ethical systems of the human soul? Is the impulse which makes us want to do so the highest impulse of the soul? Is there not yet a higher and a truer impulse whereby we may rejoice to see the Gospel sweep into itself all of man's moral effort, and prove itself the highest utterance of Him who in the million cravings of man for righteousness has always been, *is* always, making Himself known?"

"There is a stronger and stronger reluctance to have religion treated purely as a regulative force for conduct. That it will surely be, but that it will be most surely if it be primarily considered as the power of a higher consciousness, the power by which the soul knows itself divine, and enters into conscious communion with God. So, if I could do what I would like, I would reveal the power of religion to a soul, and thus it should arrive at lofty contempt for sin, which should be its perpetual safety and strength. And is not this the real thought which was in all the ancient talk about works and faith?"

"The banyan tree, dropping its supplementary branches, which take root; then the main trunk decaying, and the tree supported by these secondary supports. So of institutions and doctrines, and their history and first evidences."

In addition to his letters and the note-book from which these extracts are taken, Mr. Brooks kept a somewhat voluminous journal where he records his impressions of travel. By its aid we may follow him in his wanderings from place to place. Many of the entries are criticisms on paintings and works of art. In modern German artistic manufactures he found heaviness and lack of inspiration:

"'Go to, now, and let us make our furniture beautiful,' they have said, and the result is what we might have expected. The old German work is delightful because it is unconscious and quaint, very little of intrinsic or eternal beauty in it. Take the unconsciousness away and let the race *try* to be beautiful, and they fail just where the Greeks, whom they seem to worship with a sort of despairing adoration, so wonderfully succeeded.

He comments on the picture of George Gisze, the merchant, by the younger Holbein, in the Museum:

"It is a picture perfect in its kind, of the best sort of northern life and mercantile character. No southerner, no dealer with the abstract as the business of his life, ever looked like that. He knew affairs. The lovely green wall, before which he sits, is covered with the apparatus of concrete concerns. He writes and receives letters, which are what fasten men to common, present things. And yet he thinks. Those eyes look beyond his ledgers. And he has suffered. Not idly is his motto written on the wall, 'Nulla sine merito voluptas.'"

"BERLIN, Saturday, September 23, 1882.
"I leave Berlin to-day after a little over two weeks' visit. The people impress me not wholly pleasantly. The enormous power of the army overshadows everything. Great commercial activity is everywhere. Social life is generous and free, and in its best specimens unsurpassed doubtless in all the world, but in its ordinary aspects it is crude and rude. A coarse personality is everywhere, and through the whole community there runs a certain restlessness and fear, a disappointment that the nation has not won, out of the wonderful success of 1870, the advantages which were so confidently looked for; a sense of constant pressure from without, the two great neighbors, France and Russia, never being forgotten for a moment, and a sense of watchful surveillance

within, which makes liberty a partial and *always precarious* possession."

Wherever he went in Germany he thought of Luther and took delight in following his traces.

"WITTENBERG, Sunday, September 24, 1882.

"A delightful Luther Sunday. In the morning at eight to his old parish church, where a dull sermon wearied a quite numerous congregation. The singing was good, and all the time there was the association of his having preached there, and of this having been the place where first, in 1522, the communion in both kinds was given to the laity. How formal an event it sounds, and how essential it really is. The standing of the people while the text is read is very good. The Augustinian Convent, with the great Reformer's rooms, is a perfect monument. And that strange wife of his, who is said to have been so pretty, and looks so ugly in all the pictures, gives a homely reality to it all. His little fourteen-year-old girl's picture, hanging in the chamber where he died, is very pretty. . . ."

"HALLE, Monday, September 25, 1882.

"The University is here, and Francke's Institute. The latter is enormous, and seems as if it must be very difficult to guard from false developments, and perhaps also from corruption. But its look of simplicity is very charming. One is ready very seriously and literally to ask who has left a more enviable name in the world than Francke. I saw the very curious and interesting cast from Luther's face after death, which is made into a sitting statue, and, with his own Bible before him, sits at a window and looks into the market."

"WEIMAR, Wednesday, September 27, 1882.

"The poetic character of this town, with its long worship of Goethe and Schiller, has something artificial, an eighteenth century look about it, but very pretty, and the town suits it perfectly. It is like a very well kept room of an unforgotten but dead friend. One can see Goethe going in and out of Herder's door, and the park all about the town is a beautiful setting for it. And Luther preached here in the Stadt Kirche, they say, on his way to Worms. . . ."

"WEIMAR AND GOTHA, September 28, 1882.

"Of all the pretty Thuringian towns there seem to be none so pretty as these two. Weimar is a monumental town. It is a sort of German Concord, with most characteristic differences. . . .

The Odyssey frescoes of Preller are models of their kind of decorative art. The pale and quiet colors keep the dreamlike vagueness and distance of the whole story. No one can help being interested, but no one can become anxious or excited over the doings or the fate of these far-away people. It is as if the transparent veil of twenty-five centuries were between them and us. Then, in the Bibliotek, you come to the startling reality of Luther's coarse and ragged cloak which he wore when he was an Augustinian monk at Erfurt."

"FRANKFORT, Sunday, October 1, 1882.

"There must have been something in the early Reformation times which tended to bring out the best German character. Luther is constantly interesting. It must have been partly the fresh sense of discovery and the feeling of an opening future, which is always suited to the German mind, and inspires it to its best. It may also have been the presence of conflict, which the German also loves. But, whatever it was, it has strangely disappeared. Modern German Protestantism is the driest thing. It seems to have had no power to develop any poetry or richness. At present it seems to be ground between the upper millstone of a military state and the lower millstone of the learned universities. It was almost a relief to be again in the Catholic worship in the Cathedral here this morning."

"HEIDELBERG, Tuesday, October 10, 1882.

". . . In the early evening on the great terrace, where after all is the finest point of view. I watched the lights gradually kindling in the darkening town, and thought of the Reformation breaking out at point after point in Europe. . . ."

"LEIPSIC, Thursday, October 19, 1882.

"The religious question in Germany has suffered from that fate, which always is disastrous to it, of being made a political question. But leaving aside those whose whole interest in the question is to be explained on political grounds, there remain certain clearly recognizable classes: First, the Virchows and Haeckels, the simply naturalistic people, whose hatred to church and religion is something quite unknown among us. Second, the opposite extreme, the dogmatic churchmen, whose whole theological position is retroactive and obstructive. Third, the liberal church party, who esteem the church purely for its social and police value, and take little or no interest in its missionary aspects. Such are some of the rationalistic preachers. Fourth, there is not clearly shaped nor very prominent a school of thoughtful, earnest, and enlightened men, to whom the real future of Christianity in Germany belongs, the men of reasonable faith like Lotze."

"BERLIN, Friday, October 27, 1882.

"A visit to Dr. Hermann Grimm, the author of the *Life of Michael Angelo*, *Life of Goethe*, etc., translator of some small parts of Emerson, lecturer on art in the university. The picture which, from his point of view, he gives of religion in Germany, and the way in which it has affected his whole feeling about religion, is most interesting. He speaks of all that goes on in the churches as something that does not appeal to him in any way, and so he never goes to church. He claims that there are no men who are what Schleiermacher seems to have been, distinct both from the dogmatists on one side, and from the equally acid rationalists upon the other. And certainly I myself have failed to find any such either in personal intercourse or in reading contemporary books. Professor Grimm then curiously talked of a certain power which distinctly belonged, he said, to the Roman Catholic ceremonial, and made many educated men feel it as they felt nothing in Protestantism. It was historical and it was self-possessed. The priest at the altar, with a certain disregard of the people, busied himself directly with God. He did not attempt to teach what is unteachable, but he stood between the soul and God, and in some vague way made the divine present. Strange enough, surely, to find a man like Professor Grimm feeling all this, and at the same time feeling the power of the preaching of Channing and of Parker, of both of whom he spoke. He speaks hopelessly of religion in Germany, but surely there can be no room for despair until the first trial of a voluntary religion shall be made, and some attempt at a higher priesthood than either the Romanist's or Channing's shall be seen."

"BERLIN, Tuesday, October 31, 1882.

"It is very interesting indeed, in the Dorotheen Burial Ground, to see the two quiet simple monuments of Fichte and Hegel facing each other across the narrow path, which was all wet this afternoon with rain, and covered with dead autumn leaves trodden into the ground."

"DRESDEN, Saturday, November 4, 1882.

"One comes back to the sight of anything which he has seen in his mind's eye, so long as he has seen the Dresden Madonna, with a sort of fear whether, in all these years, the memory has not been deceived by the imagination; whether, dreaming of the world's most perfect picture, his dream has not passed into a region where no actual power of human art can follow it, and so the point from which it started will fail to satisfy one who comes back to it. This is the sort of question which is in one's mind as he passes through the curtained doorway which leads into the shrine of the great picture. And he finds it greater than his dream! A deeper wonder than his memory has been able to carry is in the Mother's eyes. The Child looks into a distance farther than his thoughts have run. The faint, rich heaven of angel faces behind the scene is sweet and holy beyond any conception which his senses have been fine enough to keep. Before the picture begins to open to him again its special treasures of detail, it blesses him with this renewed knowledge of the wonderful power of the highest art."

"One of the things that most impresses me about the picture is the wonderful life that is in it. There is such a stillness in it that it hushes the room in which it hangs, but yet it is all alive. The Virgin is moving on the clouds. Her garments float both with the blowing of the wind and also with her motion. Strangely different it is in this respect from the many pictures in which the Divine Group simply stands and meditates, or gazes from the canvas. The nobleness of the arrangement, too, is most impressive. Every rule of highest art is there, but swallowed up by the sublime intention of the work. The pyramid of figures has built itself. What, one wonders, were Raphael's feelings as he sent his work off to Piacenza? Did he know what a marvel he had done? For among the wonderful things about this picture is the immeasurable degree in which it surpasses everything else of Raphael's."

"VIENNA, Monday, November 13, 1882.

"The first sight of Austria to one who comes from Germany is full of suggested contrasts. The people in Vienna are brighter and handsomer than in Berlin. The whole movement of life is gayer. But at once is felt, what I believe all later observation will confirm, that the people to whom we have come are not the really interesting and respectable people we have left. Germany teems with ideas, conceives of itself as having a mission in the world, and expects a future. Neither of these things is true of Austria."

"VIENNA, Wednesday, November 15, 1882.

"In the Belvedere there is a picture of St. Catherine of Sienna, which, if the story of that very unpleasing person, that canonization of hysterical young womanhood, is ever to be put in paint at all, paints it aright. It is hard and white, but there is a real ecstasy about it, the ecstasy of intense, distracting pain. It is no comfortable damsel, pluming herself on the romance of a celestial lover, and enjoying the *éclat* which her adventure brought her among her earthly friends who were less fortunate. It is the eager, straining, yearning after a mysterious love which is, indeed, more than life to her, for which she would rejoice to die, nay, for which she is dying as we look at her. She does not make the subject pleasing or profitable, but at least it gives the only ideality of which it is capable."

"VIENNA, Thursday, November 16, 1882.

"A figure carved on a gem such as are the most beautiful in the great collection here seems to have reached a sort of apotheosis. It floats in light. When it receives the sunlight through it, it seems to bathe itself in the luminous color, and yet to keep its own brilliant identity and shape, to be a brighter and distincter form of light within the light that bathes it. Somewhat as we conceive of how in the great world of spirit one spirit, while it is part of all around it, has its own special personal glory intensified and made more personal. There is also something in the sense of fineness and eternity combined with the brightness and glory of a gem that makes it beautiful and impressive to the imagination. Size is nothing except to connoisseurs. There is a very small green stone down in the corner of the case hung in front of the window which is glorious."

"VIENNA, Friday, November 17, 1882.

"In the great Treasury there is what seems as if it must be the most glorious opal in the world. It is as large as a small pear, and as it hangs there with the light upon it, it quivers through and through with fire. The flame which you see seems not to come from any surface lustre, but out of its very heart. The mystery of it, and the life of it, every one must feel. Indeed, standing before the whole wonderful collection one feels very strongly the preciousness of precious stones. It is no fanciful or conventional value, but something which springs as truly from a real relation to human nature, though on another side, as the value of a beautiful face or of a noble thought. It does not depend on rarity. If sapphires like that which tops the imperial crown were as plentiful as are gray pebbles, the healthy eye would see their beauty all the more, not less."

"VIENNA, Wednesday, November 22, 1882.

"They may say all that they can about the value of the military discipline in Germany and Austria as a school for raw youths, and we ourselves may sometimes fear lest, in the absence of anything corresponding to it among ourselves, a certain tameness may settle down upon our young men's life, and heroism and obedience to authority may fail; but, after all, when we come to speak seriously about it, words cannot express the privilege we enjoy. Of course its danger and responsibilities come with it. Its dangers are those to which I just alluded. Its responsibilities are summed up in the duty which must rest upon us of finding new and higher cultures for the virtue which the army does no doubt rudely train, and of developing a purer and loftier social life out of a soil which is not cursed and exhausted by the rank weed of military life."

"VENICE, Monday, November 27, 1882.

"Venice has two aspects, one sensuous and self-indulgent, the other lofty, spiritual, and even severe. Both aspects appear in its history, and both are also in its art. Titian often represents the former. The loftier, nobler Tintoretto gives us the second. There is something in his greatest pictures, as, for instance, in the *Crucifixion*, at St. Rocco, which no other artist approaches. The lordly composition gives us an impression of intellectual grasp and vigor. The foreground group of prostrate women is full of a tenderness. The rich pearly light, which floods the centre, glows with a solemn picturesqueness, and the great Christ, who hangs like a benediction over the whole, is vocal with a piety which no other picture in the world displays. And the *Presentation of the Virgin*, in Santa Maria del Orto, is the consummate presentation of that beautiful subject, its beauty not lost in its majesty."

On December 1, he sailed from Venice for India, by the way of the Suez Canal, then a new experience to travellers. The voyage was to be a long one and he had fortified himself with reading in the line of books on India. He amused himself with letter-writing, indulging often in his most nonsensical vein. As he was leaving Venice, he wrote to his aunt in North Andover:

"It is eighteen years since I was here, on my first European journey. Then I was on my way to Palestine. One difference between that year abroad and this I feel all the time. Then the old home in Chauncy Street was still there, and father and mother were both waiting to hear what one was doing, and one of my pleasures was to write to them and to think how I would tell them all about it when I got back. I miss all that part of the interest of travel very much now. Sometimes it is hard to realize that they are not still there, and that I am not to write to them. At this distance all that has come since I was here before seems like a dream."

As the steamship neared Alexandria he wrote commenting on his fellow-passengers:

"So far the voyage thither has gone very well, but has not been particularly interesting. The first days out of Venice were very rough, and many of the passengers were sick and most of them uncomfortable and cross. We took most of our passengers at Brindisi, and since then the weather has been better and the sea more calm, so that the souls of the Englishmen begin to revive and they are growing a little bit more sociable. They are mostly the sort of Englishman who is full of information and intelligence, totally destitute of imagination or of humor, and absolutely determined to bring all the world to his own standard. He makes you mad and amuses you and wins your respect all at once, all the time. . . ."

He speaks of the relief it has been to stop preaching. To a friend whose church had just been consecrated, he writes:

"I am glad the consecration ceremony is safely over, though I can't help feeling as if we consecrated it long ago. But now the Bishop has been there, and he feels better about it if you don't. A large part of our relation to our bishops seems to consist in efforts on our part and theirs to make them feel good. How well I can see the whole scene: Bishop Paddock's arrival with his bag; his breaking up the service into little bits among the clergy like the five loaves and the two fishes, to be set before the people, and his voice beginning the sentences as he went up the aisle, and the sermon and the collation and the Episcopal departure. But, dear me, how far away all that is, and how absurd for me to get mad about it at this distance! It is a lovely forenoon. The stewards are setting the table for lunch, and through the open skylight I can hear the brogue of the Englishmen on the deck. The Lascar sailors, who are all Mohammedans and never heard of Bishop Paddock, are going back and forth in their red turbans, and the wind that comes in through the portholes is like June. Truly the Diocese of Massachusetts need not trouble one here."

On December 13, half way down the Red Sea, he kept his forty-seventh birthday. "I don't believe that many fellows have had a happier forty-seven years than I have had. It seems quite absurd sometimes, when I think how everything has gone about as I should have wished. How good everybody has been to me and how the world has kept its troubles out of the sea. . . . We have been on board now two weeks, and have ten days more of it before we reach Bombay. Everybody has settled down to the life. This morning, as I passed the captain's cabin, he was quietly painting a picture, and the boys and girls are getting up concerts and farces as if they meant to live upon the *Poonah* all the rest of their lives."

On the 23d of December he reached Bombay, and was in India at last. His first act was to telegraph home his safe arrival, and then the vision of the gorgeous pageantry began. Of his first impressions on the day of his arrival he writes:

"We drove about the town and began our sight of Indian wonders: Hindoo temples, with their squatting ugly idols; Mohammedan mosques; bazaars thronged with every Eastern race; splendid English buildings where the country is ruled; a noble university; Parsee merchants in their shops; great tanks with the devotees bathing in them; officers' bungalows, with the handsome English fellows lounging about; wedding processions, with the bride of six years old riding on the richly decorated horse behind the bridegroom of ten, surrounded by their friends, and with a tumult of horrible music; markets overrunning with strange and delicious fruits; wretched-looking saints chattering gibberish and begging alms,—there is no end to the interest and curiosity of it all! And this is dead winter in the tropics. I have out all my thinnest clothes, and go about with an umbrella to keep off the sun. This morning we started at half past six for a walk through the sacred part of the native town, and now at ten it is too hot to walk any more till sundown. But there are carriages enough, and by and by we go to church. I was invited to preach at the cathedral, but declined."

He remained in Bombay for a week, where every facility for seeing what was most important to be seen was afforded him under the best guidance. He lunched, by the invitation of the Governor, Sir James Fergusson, at the Government House. He made excursions to old Buddhist temples in the vicinity, and to the Ellora Caves. But the heat was so excessive that he suffered, and was glad to escape to a cooler climate. From Bombay he went to Ahmedabad. Here he struck Mohammedan influences, and visited the great mosques. From thence he came to Jeypore. The Rajah sent him in a carriage to the entrance to Amber, from whence he made the ascent on elephants to the deserted town, with its splendid palaces and temples. At Jeypore he preached in the English church. On January 8th he reached Delhi. To Mr. R. T. Paine he writes:

"LAHORE, January 15, 1883.

"I wish that I could give you some idea of the enjoyment I have had in the last three weeks. Ever since I landed in Bombay it has been one ever-changing and always delightful picture, but a picture which not only delighted the eye with color, but kept the mind busy with all sorts of interesting thoughts. I cannot begin to tell you about it. That will come in the long evenings when we sit together over your fire or mine, and I tire your patience out and you make believe that you are not bored. But do you know I have seen the Brahmin and Buddhist Rock Temples at Elephanta and Karli and Ellora, in many respects the most remarkable monuments which religion ever wrought? And I have seen the exquisite art of Ahmedabad and Jeypore, and I have been at the great seat of the old Mogul power at Delhi, and I have studied the most perfect mosque that ever was made, with a tower like a dream, at Kittub, and now I am in the land of the Sikhs, and to-morrow I shall see the Golden Temple at Umritsar, and before next Sunday I shall have looked at the Taj at Agra, the gem of all the gems of India. And all the while the most interesting problems of the past, the present, and the future have been crowding on the mind. The efforts of these conscientious, blundering Englishmen to do their duty by the Hindu, whom they don't like, and who don't like them, are constantly pathetic. I have just been spending some days with a household of five young English clergymen at Delhi, who are doing the best kind of missionary and education work. They are splendid fellows, whom you would immensely like. The hospitality of everybody here in India, and the way they put themselves out to make you comfortable and to let you see everything, is a continual wonder and embarrassment."

At Delhi he was invited by the Lieutenant-Governor, Sir Charles Atchison, to a "swell dinner in a gorgeous tent, with about thirty persons, and no end of picturesque servants to wait on us." While he lingered in Delhi he preached in the English church. One who heard him for the first time recalls how he listened with wonder and a sense of awe. As the congregation was leaving the church he heard the comments on every side: "It was a wonderful sermon!" "Who is he?" "He must be some man of high distinction in the world."

From Delhi he went to Agra, visiting the Taj Mahal, the most

beautiful building in India; then to Cawnpore, where he was interested in the mission work, and saw the divinity school; from
there to Lucknow, where he again met with English missionaries;
then to Allahábád, at the meeting of the Jamná and the Ganges.
He was now in the region where Buddhism originated, and made
a pilgrimage to Asoka's Pillar. And so he came to Benares, the
most sacred city in India, with its five thousand temples, one of
the most ancient cities of the globe. Here he paused for a moment and among his letters was one to Herr von Bunsen:

"BENARES, January 28, 1883.

"MY DEAR HERR VON BUNSEN,—Do you really care to know
that this week I have seen the Taj Mahal? It is one of the few
buildings which, like a few people whom one sees in life, make
an epoch. In the midst especially of this Indian architecture
which, rich and interesting as it is, is almost always fantastic
and profane, what a wonder it is to find, as the culmination of it
all, as the perfect flower which has grown out of all this gross and
heavy soil, a building whose one absorbing impression is its
purity. One almost feels that here that essence of pure religion
which is lurking somewhere under all the degradation and superstition of this land has broken forth in an exquisiteness which
surpasses anything that even Christian architecture has attained.
Some day you must come and see it, and get a new memory and
dream for all your life.

"India has interested me intensely. Its past and present and
future are all full of suggestion. I long to see Christianity come
here, not merely for what it will do for India, but for what India
will do for it. Here it must find again the lost Oriental side of
its brain and heart, and be no longer the Occidental European
religion which it has so strangely become. It must be again the
religion of Man, and so the religion of all men. At present the
missionary efforts are burdened with Englishism and American-
ism, and the country does not feel them much; but they are getting broader, and the larger religious life, which I am sure has
begun to come at home, must be felt here."

At Calcutta he remained for nearly two weeks. Here as at
every other point his highest interest culminated in the missionary work. He studied the situation with an open mind, ready
to see things as they were, unbiassed by the exaggerations of
missionary enthusiasm. Immediately on his arrival at Calcutta
he made the long-anticipated call on the Hindu reformer Chunder

Sen. In a letter to Rev. Arthur Brooks he gives the impressions he received:

"February 22, 1883.

"DEAR ARTHUR,—Calcutta itself has not many sights, and so it is the people whom one wants to see. This morning I spent two hours with Keshub Baboo Chunder Sen. And I 'll tell you about him. I told old Mr. Dall, the venerable Unitarian missionary here, that I wanted to see the head of the New Dispensation, and the minister of the Brahma Somaj (which is another name for the same thing) sent back word that he would be at home at nine o'clock to-day. On the Circular Road, one of the chief streets of the city, there is a big house all surrounded on three stories with verandas, standing inside a garden, around which is a high pink-washed wall. On the gate-post is inscribed the name of Lily Cottage, which, I believe, was the title which a previous occupant gave to the place. Driving in under a great *porte cochère*, we were shown up to a very large, high parlor in the second story, where we waited for the prophet. It was furnished comfortably but not tastefully in European style, with rather cheap pictures on the walls. I noticed especially an engraving of the Queen, which had been presented to Keshub by her Majesty; also a very poor little painting of the man himself, sitting on the Himalayas with a woman by his side, he holding a long guitar-like instrument in his hand, and clad in the skin of a tiger. At one end of the room hung a familiar chromo-lithograph of Christ, after Carlo Dolci, holding the sacramental cup, and with the right hand raised in blessing,—a large, cheap Christian picture. While we were looking about, Chunder Sen came in, a rather tall and sturdy man of forty-five, with a bright, kindly, open face, a round head, and black moustache and somewhat short-cut black hair. He wore the Eastern white mantle thrown over his shoulders, and apparently covering a more or less European dress. He gave me a most kindly greeting, and at once began to talk. I asked him questions, and he answered freely and at length. It made me feel very like an interviewer, but it was the best way to get at what I wanted. He said that the central position of Brahma Somaj was pure theism. It stood fairly between Indian pantheism on one side and Indian idolatry on the other, insisting fully on the unity and personality of God, and freely calling Him 'Father,' believing in this God's perpetual and universal presence. It found His prophets everywhere, and aimed to hold all the good and true of all systems and all teachers 'in Christ.' He mentioned, especially, Socrates, Mohammed and Buddha. When you tried to find just what he meant by holding the truth of them 'in Christ,' he eluded you. He constantly asserted that he held Christ to be in unique sense the 'Son of God,' but said he could not any further explain his meaning of that phrase. He rejected all idea of Incarnation. Nor would he own that Christ, in His historic teaching, was in any way the test by which other teachers should be judged. He talked much of 'communion with Christ,' but defined it as such profound contemplation of his character as produced entire sympathy with Him, not allowing anything like personal inter-course with a Christ now living and communicating with us. Still he clung strongly to that phrase 'in Christ.' He described very interestingly the 'pilgrimages' of the Brahma Somaj to Socrates or Buddha or Mohammed or *Carlyle*, which consist of gathering in front of the church and singing hymns and reading some of the great teacher's sayings, and then going inside and sitting still and entering into communion with his character. Besides these, and as something more sacred, they have occa-sionally the Lord's Supper, which is celebrated with Indian sweet-meats and water, and centres in mystic contemplation of the character of Jesus. They have also a baptism, which is quite optional, and strangely keeps association with the Hindu ablu-tions on the one hand and with Christian baptism on the other. He was very interesting in his account of how freely he uses the terms of the old Hindu mythology, talking of Siva and Vishnu and Parvati as different sides of Deity, and hoping so to win the people to spiritual views of what they have long held materially, and to construct in their minds a unity out of the fragments of Divine Ideal, of which their books are full. Thus he hopes some day to appeal to the common superstitious Hindu mind, though thus far the movement has been mostly confined to the higher classes, who have been reached by English education. He said some fine things about the Orientalism of Christ and Christianity, and about the impossibility of India ever becoming Christian after the European sort. At the same time he said unreservedly that the future religion of India would be a Christ religion. The asceticism to which he clings is of a very healthy human sort, rejecting entirely the old ideas of the Fakirs. He pointed to the picture on the wall and said that there he had himself painted as a Vedic Rishi, but had especially taken care to have his wife painted by his side to show that the true asceticism kept still the family life. As to the peculiar worship of their society, he told of the new 'Dance' which has been lately introduced, and which has been much abused. It is, according to him, neither more or less than the Methodist camp-meeting principle of the physical expression of spiritual emotion putting itself into Ori-ental shape. For himself, he eats no meat and drinks no wine, but these restrictions are not enforced nor universal, though they are very commonly observed as a protest against the self-indul-gence into which modern India is largely running as it departs from its old faiths.

"All this and much more was told with a quiet glow and earnestness which was very impressive. The basis and inspiration of it all was intuition. There was no reference to any authority. Indeed he almost boasts that he never reads. Even his Christ seemed to be One of whom he knew not so much by the New Testament as by personal contemplation. He shrinks from dogma and definition, and eludes you at every turn. He is the mystic altogether. As we got up and went out we passed a room where his household and some other disciples were at morning worship. Eight or ten men sat cross-legged on the floor with closed eyes, while one fine-looking fellow in the midst murmured a half-audible prayer. In one corner of the room was a rustic booth devoted to supreme contemplation, in which sat one worshipper, who seemed more absorbed even than the others. At the feet of the men lay drums and other musical instruments, to which they would by and by sing a hymn. We had heard them singing as we sat talking with Keshub Baboo. Behind a thin curtain you could see just the women's fans. Chunder Sen stood and looked in with us at the door and told us all about it, and then bade us a cordial farewell and promised some of his books and a photograph of himself, which he has since sent.

"This is enough, perhaps, of Chunder Sen, but I thought you might care to hear of what has interested me immensely. It is Indian mysticism fastening on Christ and trying to become the practical saviour of the country by Him. They hold in full the idea of special national religions all embraced and included within the great religion of the divine life made known in Jesus. Surely nothing could be more interesting than this. It is not Christianity, but it is the effort of India to realize Christ in her own way,—so far as I know, the only such attempt now being made in any heathen land. . . .

"I am almost ashamed of having written so much, but it does seem to me to be the very kind of thing for which we are all looking. Brahma Somaj is not the end. It is only the first sign of the real working of the native soul and mind on Christ and His truth, which must sometime find far fuller light than it has found yet. The whole movement and its leader believe intensely in the Holy Spirit. And I believe that such embodiments of Christianity as India will sometime furnish, and such as this New Dispensation faintly and blunderingly suggests, will not merely be different from European Christianity, but will add something to it, and make the world of Christianity a completer thing, with its Eastern and Western halves both there, than it has ever been before. These are my views. Sometime soon I will write to you about something else. Now good-night. On Sunday I shall go to the cathedral in the morning and to Brahma Somaj in the afternoon."

While he was at Calcutta he took a long journey for the purpose of seeing the Himalayas, and was rewarded by a most splendid view of the whole range after it had been invisible on account of rain for eight days. In the midst was the "lordly Kinchinjinga, 28,000 feet high, the second highest mountain in the world. Certainly they made the impression of height such as no mountains ever gave me before." On his return to Calcutta, he went to an evening party given by the rajah, in honor of the late British victory in Egypt.

"Of course I went to this, and it was the biggest thing seen in India for years. It is said to have cost the old rajah a lac of rupees, or $100,000. At any rate, it was very splendid and very queer,—acres of palace and palace grounds blazing with lights; a thousand guests, the natives in the most beautiful costumes of silk and gold; a Nautch dance going on all the time in one hall; a full circus,—horses, acrobats, clowns, and all, only after native fashion,—in a great covered courtyard; supper perpetual, and the great drawing-room blazing with family jewels. I stayed till one o'clock, and then came home as if from the Arabian Nights and went to bed."

Leaving Calcutta, he came to Madras. While there he made a trip to the Seven Pagodas, which only needed the company of his friends to have been complete to his imagination. He compensated himself for their absence by humorous letters to his friends, complaining that they were writing sermons when they might just as well have been with him as not. This letter to the Rev. C. D. Cooper gives a specimen of his humor:

"CHEDAMBARAM, February 22, 1883.

"DEAR COOPER,—In case you don't know where Chedambaram is, I will tell you that it is just ten miles from Vaithisvarankoil, and it is hotter than Philadelphia in fly-time. I have been celebrating the birthday of Mr. Washington by firing off bottles of soda water all the morning ever since we came in from our early visit to the wonderful pagoda which is the marvel of this beautiful but benighted heathen town. The only way to see things here in southern India is to start at daybreak, when the country is cool and lovelier than anything you can imagine. The palm-trees are waving in the early breeze. The elephants go crushing along with painted trunks and gilded tusks. The pretty Hindu girls are drawing water at the wells under the banana groves. The naked children are frolicking in the dust of the bazaars. The old men and women are drinking their early cocoanut, and you jolt along on the straw, in your creaking bullock cart, as jolly as a rajah. So we went this morning to do homage to the false gods. Vishnu had gone off on a pilgrimage, and his shrine was empty, but Siva was at home, and the howling devotees were in the middle of the morning service. They must have been at about the second lesson when we arrived, but, owing to the peculiar character of their language, it was not easy to make out just what stage of the morning exercises they had reached. But it didn't much matter, for immediately on our arrival the worship stopped where it was and the officiating clergyman came forward and ridiculously presented us with a lime each, and then tried to put a garland of flowers about our Christian necks. This last attention I refused, with indignation at his making a heathen so summarily out of a respectable presbyter of the P. E. Church from Bishop Paddock's diocese. He gracefully intimated that he didn't mind my being mad but would pocket the insult (or do whatever a fellow does who has no pocket, or indeed anything else except a dirty rag about his loins), provided I gave him the rupee which he expected all the same. While I was doing this there was a noise like seven pandemoniums outside, and soon in through the gate came a wild crowd of savages yelling like fiends and carrying on their shoulders a great platform on which was a big brass idol all daubed with grease and hung with flowers. This was Vishnu, just returned from his sea bath, and in front of him came the craziest band of music, made up of lunatics banging on tom-toms and screeching away on brazen trumpets three feet long. We saw the ugly divinity safe in his shrine, and left the pagans yelling in their joy at getting their ugly image safely home.

"By this time the sun was blazing, as I said, and we came home to the bungalow, which does duty for a tavern, and set a small Hindu to pulling away at a punkah rope at the cost of three cents a day. Then we cut up our sacred limes and poured soda water on the juice of them and made a drink which I advise you to try if ever you have to spend a hot day in Chedambaram. Then we breakfasted on rice and curry and fried bananas, and then I thought I would write to you and send you my blessing out of the depths of this Hindu darkness."

To the Rev. G. A. Strong:

"TANJORE, February 23, 1883.

"It is the loveliest Indian night, and I am sitting on the veranda of a travellers' bungalow, and it is cool, which is more than could have been said of any house to-day since breakfast time. A travellers' bungalow is a sort of government institution which exists in every considerable town in India which has no hotel, and in some that have. It takes you in,—gives you a bedstead. You must bring your own bedding, your own servant, your own victuals, and here you live as independent as a prince, or pack up and are off when you have seen the sights or done your business. The sight of Tanjore is a glorious pagoda,—a vast pyramidal Hindu temple, two hundred feet high, rich with all sorts of grotesque sculpture from top to bottom, and glowing with all sorts of colors,—red and brown and yellow and green and black,—all mellowed and harmonized with ages. Inside there is a hideous shrine with a hideous idol, but the outside is a marvel, and it stands in a great area dotted with palms and guavas, and with a lot of little temples sprouting as if from the roots of the big thing. This is our latest wonder; but every day for the last two months has had its spectacle, and such a sky has been over all all the time as even New Bedford never sees. . . . It has been a great success. Everybody has been very hospitable, and the only wonder has been to find each morning that it was not all a dream and has not vanished in the night. But it is almost over now. Next week we shall be in Ceylon, and on the 7th of March we sail from Colombo to Suez and shall be in commonplace Europe again before we know it. . . And just now it is Lent, I think; I am not sure. A day which I believe was Ash Wednesday I spent up at Darjheeling gazing at the Himalayas. I have no daily service and no confirmation class. All of these things seem like dim memories, but I am glad that some of you are more faithful than I am, and are doing the Gospel work while I am loafing here among these naked heathen. It is wonderful how little clothes an utter absence of the Christian faith can get along with! I have almost wished I was a heathen for this one privilege of heathenism at any rate."

From Madras he went to Ceylon, where he spent a week, visiting the Buddhist shrines, talking with Buddhist priests, interested in the Buddhist schools and in the contrast between Buddhism and Hindu religion. In his spare moments he was reading books on India,—the writings of Hunter and Wilkins. On the religion of India he supplemented what he saw by the works of students such as Max Müller, Barth, and Rhys Davids. Trevelyan's *Cawnpore*, the writings of Meadows Taylor, Macaulay's essays on "Clive" and "Warren Hastings," gave him information to be co-ordinated with his own experience. He mentions *Mr. Isaacs*, a novel by Marion Crawford, which has caught the real life of the people as he himself had seen it, "the atmospheric contrast between the Englishman's sharp, clear concreteness and the Indian's subtlety and mystery very well brought out." He found a new interest in reading again Arnold's *Light of Asia*. On Bishop Heber's *Journey* he dwelt, admiring its spirit, and gaining greater reverence for the man. Into his note-book went some of his reflections regarding Indian religion:

"Hinduism the great stock faith. Its wonderful pliability; philosophical and idolatrous both; subtle and gross at once; neither aspect morally elevating."

"From time to time moral reforms, which afterwards degenerate into either, first, theological differences, like Buddhism, and Jainism, its successor; or, second, political and military movements, like Sikhism."

"These reform movements always taking place, but always being reabsorbed by the superior strength of the great Hindu system."

"The new theism is a stronger movement, because it has affiliations with the two great forces which are moving in the outer world."

"The strongest point of present Hinduism is probably transmigration. Its effect on habits, no meat-eating. Caste is its great social light and safeguard, keeping its central core solid and compact. The true Brahman cannot travel, must prepare his own food, etc."

"Then comes Mohammedanism, sharp, precise, simple, and intolerant,—without philosophy, cutting right through the whole life of the nation, like a wedge. Existing principally in the north."

"Sikhism was originally a sort of attempt to reconcile Hinduism and Mohammedism, but this character has long since gone out of it."

"The Brahmanical doctrine of *Identity*, the assurance that sin and misery alike consisted and resulted in the separation of the personal soul from the *Atman*, the universal self, the absolute existence, and that the struggle of man must be towards, as the reward of man will be in, his reëntrance into the Eternal Identity by the death of his own individual will or desire. The idea also that all the finite world is a delusive dream, a *Maya*, with which the Eternal Being amuses itself, as it were, and which must disappear as the mist disappears above the river which runs on still. All this which we reject entirely as a philosophy, or answer to the problems of existence, has yet in it a wonderful power of appeal to some moods of almost all our natures, which is quite sufficient to make us understand how it could have been, and is still, held by multitudes of souls."

"The three kinds of deities represented in Brahma, Vishnu, and

Siva—the mysterious, the familiar, and the awful—found in all religious systems as the conception of God formed by different nations."

"With all these tremendous exaggerations of space, time, and size, in these Hindu stories, you can get nothing more than the universal and perpetual human passions. Heroes and gods thirty feet high, living ten thousand years, can, after all, only love and hate and wish and dread."

"Siva is pure spirit, although, to render himself perceptible and conceivable, he deigns to assume a body composed 'not of matter, but of force.' The modern sound of this last notion."

"The old Brahman said, 'God is everything, and the earth and all things sensible are illusion (*Maya*).' The modern scientist says, 'The sensible things alone are real, and God is all a dream.' Somewhere these two, getting entirely around the circle, must meet."

"The Hindu triad,—Brahma, only a handful of worshippers; Vishnu supplies a worship for the middle classes; Siva, a philosophy for the learned, and a superstition, cruel and pale, for the lowest classes. Is there not something like this in the Christian's relation to different conceptions of God and Christ?"

"Strange lack of creative power in modern Hinduism; their architecture is all old."

"The endless hope of Brahmanism, which is transmigration, becomes by and by the dread and despair of Buddhism, which only comes to escape from it in Nirvana. The relapse again into the hoplessness in later Hinduism."

"The great pagoda at Chedambaram is the most terrible specimen of pure idolatry. All refinements and subtleties and spiritualizations fade away in the presence of such brutality and darkness. All comparisons with the darker sides of Christian history become mere fallacies."

"The awful state of morals at Delhi; unnatural crimes of the most awful sort. Traceable, perhaps, to the practices of early marriages and early exhaustion, and of the isolation of women and consequent constitution of society solely by men. The country regions better than the city. The absolute failure of Hindu religion to restrain passion. Certainly Occidental morals must come in; and if in the West those morals rest on Christian faith, it must be that the Christian faith shall be brought here as their basis."

As Mr. Brooks passed from India to Ceylon, he received more favorable impressions of Buddhism than of Indian religion. He did justice to its truth, while discerning its weakness. For Buddha himself he had a feeling of reverence.

"As one sees the Buddhists in Ceylon, there is certainly a look of intelligence such as one does not easily find in the ordinary Hindu."

" The three Buddhist notions of (1) *Skandha*, or the composition of each man out of elemental conditions, which disunite at his death, and even if they unite again to make another being, who is his true successor, they do not make him. (2) *Karma*, or the perpetuation of the results of a life in the succeeding being, something quite distinct from transmigration. (3) *Nirvana*, the final falling back of this special phenomenon of life into the mass of universal existence; an anticipation of this in present life, indifference and rest. In all of these a constant extinction of personality both human and divine."

"It is clear enough that the Buddhist did and does draw a distinction, perhaps too subtle for our minds to follow, but still real to him, between Nirvana and personal annihilation."

"Buddha's Bo tree, occupying almost the same place in Buddhism that the cross does in Christianity. It marks the difference. The first religion saves by contemplation, the other by active sacrifice. No such power given to Christ's *temptation*."

"The pathetic connection of Buddha's doctrine of the misery of life, and the hope of ceasing to be, with the miserable circumstances of the special life which he saw about him; with the German pessimist it is all different; a fancy theory."

"The great remonstrance against caste is the noblest part of Buddha's teaching."

"The lapse into the worship of Buddha (a false personal religion) shows where the weakness of his system lay. Original Buddhism a *religion of character*."

"The analogy of the Vedic religions, of Brahmanism, of Hinduism, and of Buddhism, on the one hand, with the primitive Christianity and the early dogmatism and mediævalism and the Reformation on another, and with the patriarchal system and Mosaism and Pharisaism and Christianity on yet another, is illustrative of the whole constantly repeated movement of human nature. The step from Vedism to Brahmanism being associated with the rising authority of the priesthood, and with the loss of the free knowledge of the language of the Vedic hymns, corresponds exactly to the change which took place as the simple substance of the apostolic Christianity passed over into the highly organized ecclesiastical and dogmatic systems of the Latin Church."

"There is much both in Brahmanism and Buddhism that throws light upon the varying understandings of the 'new' or 'second' birth, which have played so large a part in the contentions and speculations of Christendom. Each of these systems, according to its intrinsic nature, has its own understanding of the idea and phrase which both contain. Brahmanism applies it to the boy's formal entrance on a certain period of life, his established manhood. Buddhism, on the other hand, makes it mean the perception of profounder truth which comes with the awakening of the spiritual nature by contemplation. Both of these unite in Christianity with the idea of moral determination (transformation where the nature has been going wrong) to make that complete notion of fulfilled life which is what the phrase is always struggling for, what it means in the supreme use of it by Jesus."

He comments upon the society into which he was thrown,— the Anglo-Indian, the English officials, the civil service, the missionaries whose acquaintance he cultivated:

"England . . . governs the country without sympathy but with careful justice, establishing the most perfect civil service in the world. That service is something at which we never cease to wonder. Highly paid, well selected, free from political subservience, so that a very large part of them to-day are enemies of the present government, they are the most conscientious, faithful, incorruptible body of servants, I believe, that are administering the government of any country anywhere in the world."

"English colonel's statement (at Jeypore), that the more an Englishman sees of other people the more he dislikes them. If this were true, what a great incapacity it would show for the work on inferior races, which in these days seems to be more and more intrusted to the Englishman. There is no love lost between the two races in India."

"The Anglo-Indian has a sort of mental and moral thin-bloodedness which somehow or other the English seem able to bear less than most races. The first-rate Englishman is the best thing in the world."

"The very great assumption of the old Anglo-Indian that he knew more about the worth of missions than the missionary; the liking which he often has for R. C. missions, and even for native idolatries."

"The society of India is either gross heathenism, with its almost total absence of higher things, or English civil life, full of the littleness of officialism, disliking the country, anxious to be away, and with more or less of spite or mutual jealousy. Among these, apart from its direct religious power, how valuably comes in the sweet, unselfish life of such works as the Cambridge Mission.

His final impressions give the missionaries in India and

the English civil service an equal place with the great Hindu temple Taj and the great mountain Kinchinjinga. He had felt some doubts and misgivings about the actual results, as about the methods of missions, when he went to India. These had disappeared, and in their place rose enthusiasm and gratitude and hopefulness.

"These missionaries are really splendid fellows, many, *most* of them. One hears from them far more intelligent talk about religion and the relation of Christianity to other faiths than he would hear from the same number of parsons at home (outside the Club). They and the civil servants of the English government are doing much for India. Oh for a civil service such as this at home! I think, next to the Taj and Kinchinjinga, that is the most impressive sight that I have seen in this strange land.

"The missionaries are as noble a set of men and women as the world has to show. Tell your friends who 'do not believe in Foreign Missions' (and I am sure there are a good many such) that they do not know what they are talking about, and that three weeks' sight of mission work in India would convert them wholly."

He stood in Henry Martyn's pulpit, and the words inscribed upon it, "He was a burning and a shining light," gained a new meaning. Some of his reflections on missions are here given:

"The Bishop of Calcutta (February 3) talking about the foolishness and uselessness of trying to take the Hindu's view,— 'Give them the Englishman's and let them find out their own.' Poor talk."

"Curious article in *Home and Foreign Church Work*, asserting the need of asceticism in India. I do not believe it."

"Missions in India; their naturalness when one is on the ground. The question how missions look to one in a heathen land: intensely practical and absolutely necessary. It brings itself to a personal question, Can this man be lightened with the Light? The great 250,000,000 are a paralysis. This man is an inspiration, and his conversion or the struggle for it keeps hope alive."

"The really unanimous testimony to the Indian's untruthfulness. The awful business of haggling in the bazaars."

"The first sense of tameness in the converts,—loss of their first rude and fierce picturesqueness."

"How much there possibly may be in the Anglo-Indian's statement that the Christian convert is less trustworthy than the Hindu. Possibly something. His associations are broken, and he lacks whatever good influence there possibly may be in loyalty to caste. He has a strong restraint in fellow-men's judgment. His neighbors despise him. Think of old Corinth, and what its magistrate must have said of Paul's converts, 'Have any of the Pharisees believed in Him?'"

"I do not know of any country where religious statistics would mean so little, or, at least, would have to be taken with so much careful reserve as in India. . . ."

"I believe beyond all doubt that the missionaries are doing a great work, and that the time is not far off when it will show; but it must be by some more intimate reading of the thought and genius of the people than has yet been made; not merely plucking brands from the burning, but by putting out the fire."

"The Indians have the primary affections very strong,—parental and filial affections, love of kindred, kindness for creatures, craving for immortality, sense of wonder. These are what Christianity starts with, and what it is to build into completeness."

"After all, the Hindu mind, haunted by the conception of escape and holiness, has something pathetic and sublime about it. No comfortable settling down to life. Somehow the touch needed, which shall move all this power into the region of moral life;—there is where it seems powerless now. The old paradox of much religion and no morality, which we settle far too easily and off-handedly when we decide that the religion is hypocrisy."

"The only advantage in the multitudinousness of denominations in India is the chance that it may leave the question open for the promotion of the national Christianity. Perhaps there was no other possible way for this to come about but by the variety of approach, making the establishment of any one type impossible,—the way this possibly might impress a Hindu."

"Certainly the change to the newer forms of appeals for missions involves the confidence in a higher condition, in the working of better and nobler motives in those to whom we appeal. It may be a question whether men are ready for it, but here, as always, I believe very much in the possibility of making them to *be* by assuming that they *are*. Certainly we see the reverse of this constantly. Men are made unfit for high appeals by the assumption that they can only respond to the lower."

"One high appeal for missions ought to be the need of Christianity for a broader and completer life,—what these other people will do for our Christianity if they become Christians. I think we often understand missions best if we think of the converting power, and that which it tries to convert, as individuals rather than vague masses. Surely one man may say to another, 'I want you to believe my truth, partly in order that by the way in which it influences you and by the form in which your mind apprehends it I may be able to see new sides of it and understand its richness more."

"The reconstruction and simplification of Christian theology is imperatively demanded by missions. Indeed the missionaries are quietly doing it, almost unconsciously doing it, themselves. Christianity as a book religion, resting on the infallible accuracy of a written word, or as a propitiatory religion, providing a mere escape for hopeless culprits, or as a doctrinal religion, depending on the originality of some statements of truth, all of these aspects of it fade; and Christianity as a personal faith revealing *in* Christ, not simply *by* Him, the present living fatherhood of God, becomes the powerful and precious substance of our faith."

The return from India began on the 7th of March. During the three weeks on shipboard, until he reached Gibraltar, he was reading books on Spain, which he found in the ship's library; but his journal shows a mind preoccupied, musing over what he had seen in India. As a corrective for the wild extravagances of Indian religion, he read Robertson Smith on the *Place of the Old Testament in Jewish History*, and his *Hebrew Prophets*. In his note-book he entered these reflections:

"The voyage from India to Spain carries one from the extreme east to the extreme west of the triumphs of Islam. The Moguls of Delhi and the Caliphs of Cordova! what a range of energy, what a history of struggle and suffering, of pride and ruin, is included!"

"As one withdraws from India it is very much indeed as it used to be when one walked farther and farther away from the old Sivite temples, in the southern districts, Madura or Tanjore. Gradually the grotesque details were lost. The dancing and distorted gods became obscure. The crude, hard colors mingled into harmony, the harsh sounds melted into a confused and pleasing murmur, and a quiet mystery, not unmixed with religious seriousness, enfolded and dignified the whole.

"So it is with that mass of legend, allegory, and corrupt tradition, which, taken all together, makes the religion and philosophy of India. It has large masses of color and not ignoble outlines, as one looks back on it fading and mingling into memory."

"Steamship Verona, between Colombo and Aden,
"March 13, 1883.

"Dear Arthur,—I am on the way back from India and you have no idea what soft and brilliant days these are upon the southern seas. And it is a good time to think the whole thing

over, and to get ready for the next scene in the play. The last
thing before we sailed was Ceylon, with its Buddhism. Ceylon
was beautiful beyond all description. Such tropical luxuriance
as one had dreamed of all his life was in its splendor, and made
pictures which one never can forget. And Ceylon Buddhism had
a look of intelligence and decency after the horrible squalor and
coarseness of Hinduism, which was very pleasing. A very different thing it is from the fetish worship of Thibetan Buddhism, of
which we got a sight among the Himalayas. But as for making
of it a great spiritual religion, with any chance in it for the
salvation of the world, it is too hopelessly absurd. Primitive
Buddhism was a philosophy with controlling ethical purpose.
Modern Buddhism has changed it into elaborate ceremonialism,
and invented for it a mythology. But there is no theism in either,
and in spite of the charm of 'Natural Religion,'[1] there is no
powerful faith without theistic basis. What a delightful book
that is! I cannot help thinking that there is a good deal of word-
juggling in it, and that what it needs is a clearer definition.
But to bring out as it does the noble and consecrated side of
'modern thought,' and to show how it gravitates at its best
towards spirituality, is a great boon. One grows very impatient
at the way the selfish trader with a wooden faith is counted a
more spiritual being than the self-forgetful student of truth or
worshipper of humanity. It is good to have such a strong
statement of the other side."

As the *Verona* was crawling through the Suez Canal, subject
to vexatious detentions, Mr. Brooks spent much of his time in
answering letters received from home before leaving India. He
had been kept informed of the incidents at Trinity Church; the
names of the preachers sent to him in advance had enabled him
to reproduce every Sunday "the scene in the blessed old church;"
he read with special interest the list of those confirmed in his
absence. He had followed the meetings of the Clericus Club.
Of the new members elected in his absence he writes:

"You seem to be enlarging the Club with youngsters, so that
one will hardly know it after a year's absence. Every now and
then I feel a touch of intimation that I am growing old, in a bit
of wonder whether these young fellows are good for much; but
generally I am ready to acknowledge their value, and I am glad
that the Church and the Club should get them in. Only in the
Club we never have got much out of the youngest men. They
have generally seemed to be there more for their own sake

---

[1] *Natural Religion*, by the author of *Ecce Homo*, 1882.

than for the Club's. But perhaps your new acquisitions will do better."

Among the items of religious interest was the publication of a volume of sermons by Rev. R. Heber Newton of New York, entitled *Right and Wrong Uses of the Bible*. After reading the sermons he speaks of them as "calm, serious, and conscientious," as saying, "what, in the great mass of it, I have no doubt is true and once accepted by the Christian world must make the basis of a better Christianity. No criticism of small points of style, or discussion of the accuracy of a few details of criticism, can obscure the broad view of inspiration and the relation of the Book both to God and man, which the sermons declare."

"The whole theological world seems to be wakening to the need of a new discussion and settlement about its sacred Book. And no mischief can begin to equal the mischief which must come from the obstinate dishonesty of men who refuse to recognize any of the new light which has been thrown upon the Bible, and go on repeating assertions about it which, if there is such a thing as proof, have been thoroughly and repeatedly disproved. These are the men whom the church in future must look back upon with reproach, and almost with contempt. So the thing looks to me from the Suez Canal."

When he reached Madrid, on his journey through Spain, he learned of the death of two of his aunts, his mother's sisters, who resided in the old house at North Andover. To his brother William he writes:

"MADRID, April 15, 1883.

"It seems as if this great change swept away from the world the last remnants of the background of our earliest life. Even after father and mother went, as long as Aunt Susan lived, there was somebody who had to do with us when we were babies. Now that generation has all passed away. How many old scenes it brings up. This is Sunday morning, right after breakfast, and it seems as if I could see a Sunday morning of the old times in Rowe Street, with a general bustle of mother and Aunt Susan getting off to Sunday school, and father settling down to read to the bigger boys in the front parlor.

"As it may be that before I come home the old house will be left empty, and something have to be done about the property, I want to say that I should like to buy it, and I authorize you to buy it for me, if the chance offers. . . . I should like to hold it as a place where, for the whole or part of the summer, we could gather and have a delightful, easy time, among the most sacred associations which remain for us on earth. A few very simple improvements would make it a most charming place, so do not by any chance let it slip, and hold, by purchase or otherwise, to as much of the furniture as you can. One of these days, when I am a little older and feebler, I should like to retire to it and succeed [Rev.] Augustine Amory at the little church. Is not our window done there yet?"

In Spain the pictures of Velasquez, which he saw in their fulness for the first time, were the principal objects of interest. At Burgos he found in one of the towers of the cathedral what he thought must have furnished the suggestion to Richardson for the tower of Trinity Church, Boston. He speaks of Burgos as a wilderness of architectural delight.

"MADRID, April 28, 1883.

"If you were only here we would begin at once with the Velasquez pictures, which I shall see to-day for the last time and which are famous. They stand away up alongside of Tintoretto's in Venice for every great quality except that high religious exaltation which is in the *Crucifixion* at St. Rocco and one or two other things which we saw last summer in those golden days. As to the rest of Spain it is delightful, but one would rather go to all the other great countries of Europe first. The Moorish work, the Alhambra, and all that, is wonderful; but as for Gothic and the great cathedrals, you who have seen Chartres and Strassburg and Cologne need not worry yourself at all about Seville and Granada and Saragossa and Toledo. . . . We were right last summer and the dear streets of Pisa and Ravenna and Bologna were better than anything we should have seen in sultry Spain. . . ."

On June 8th Mr. Brooks arrived in England. He had received many invitations asking him to preach in London, and especially in the cathedral churches. The Bishop of London sent him a courteous permission to preach in his diocese, expressing, at the same time, the desire that he would accept as many invitations as possible. He was also personally invited by the Bishop of London to preach in St. Paul's Cathedral on Hospital Sunday. His appointments were widely advertised in the London papers. The following extract from a letter by a person unknown to him has a familiar sound:

"A friend and I went twelve miles yesterday to the Savoy Chapel, where you were advertised to preach, but were bitterly disappointed at being unable to get even standing room, although we were at the church door half an hour before the service began. I hope you will pardon my boldness if I ask whether you would be so kind as to let me know by post-card if you are going to preach anywhere during this week; for, if so, we should so much like to make another attempt to hear you."

Dr. Farrar, Archdeacon of Westminster, and others also, made the suggestion that he should be more deliberate in speaking. To the English people his rapidity was more trying than to his compatriots. Yet Dean Stanley saw in it one source of his power, comparing him to "an express train going to its appointed terminus with majestic speed, and sweeping every obstacle, one after another, out of his course." In England, as in America, he was the despair of reporters, owing not only to the rapidity of his utterance, but to the bewildering rush of the thought as well.

Apart from the public honors shown him, Mr. Brooks was the recipient of generous hospitality, combined with a thoughtful kindness and constant acts of courtesy, wholly unanticipated, which made every day of his two months in England a refreshment and delight. He had an invitation to visit one of the most beautiful English rectories, in Surrey, where he might see English clerical life from its highest ideal side, illustrating the best aspect of the union of Church and State. From Lord Aberdeen there came an invitation, giving him a special opportunity to meet Mr. Gladstone, who had been reading his sermons with great interest. He went down to the Tower with a party of government people,—Gladstone and Forster and Bright. He met Browning for the second time; and Mr. Matthew Arnold, whose poetry he had first read many years before.

Mr. Hallam Tennyson (now Lord Tennyson), gave him an invitation to visit his father at Farringford, in the Isle of Wight. He was able to devote only one day to the visit, but in that time he had the poet much to himself. Of his visit he writes: "When the daylight was over, having come to know me pretty well, he wanted to know if I smoked, and we went up to the study,—a big, bright, crowded room, where he writes his Idyls, and there we stayed till dinner time." Then once more,—

"After dinner Tennyson and I went up to the study, and I had him to myself for two or three hours.   We smoked, and he talked of metaphysics and poetry and religion, his own life, and Hallam, and all the poems.   It was very delightful and reverent and tender and hopeful.   Then we went down to the drawing-room, where the rest were, and he read his poetry to us till the clock said twelve,—'Locksley Hall,' 'Sir Galahad,' pieces of 'Maud,' and some of his dialect poems."

The next morning, after breakfast, as Tennyson and Mr. Brooks were taking a walk together, he charged him with secrecy as to their conversation the previous evening.   Tennyson had asked Mr. Brooks to pay him another visit at his home, Aldworth, Haslemere, Surrey.   When he returned there from a voyage to Copenhagen, it was to learn that Mr. Brooks had gone back to America.   He then wrote, saying that he was grieved to know that he had recrossed the Atlantic, and that he should not see him again, closing his letter with a sentence which shows that he liked Phillips Brooks: "The few hours that I spent at Freshwater in your company will always be present with me."   After this, whenever Brooks was in England, he made a visit to Tennyson.

"Brooks was impressed with the way in which Browning threw himself, with gayety and cheerfulness, into the light conversation of the moment, interested in amusing anecdotes current in London society, sharing heartily the pleasure of the hour, but never alluding to any intellectual problems.   On the other hand, he found Tennyson always opening up a large philosophic view of life and its problems, sometimes in tones of sadness, occasionally in a cheerful optimistic spirit, but always philosophizing."

"In speaking of one of his visits to Tennyson, he told how the poet, when reading aloud his own poems, would sometimes praise or criticise them as though they were the work of another.   On one occasion he asked, 'What shall I read?' 'Read "Locksley Hall,"' Brooks replied,—'the poem that stirred us all when we were young.'   When Tennyson reached the lines—

'Love took up the glass of Time, and turned it in his glowing hands;
  Every moment, lightly shaken, ran itself in golden sands,'

he called attention to it as being the most perfect poetic image in his poems.   But when Brooks claimed that the imagery was equally good in the lines:

'Love took up the harp of Life, and smote on all the chords with might;
  Smote the chord of Self, that, trembling, pass'd in music out of sight,'

Tennyson insisted that it was inferior to the other,—lacking, as he said, 'its Greek simplicity and pictured clearness.' 'The figure of the harp of life,' he said, 'is too subjective and complicated in its implications;—no, the other is the best.'

"It was characteristic of Brooks that he should have felt more sympathy with the spiritually suggestive figure of the harp of life than with the 'Greek simplicity of the glass of time.'"

" Brooks mentioned his surprise at Tennyson's confusion and perplexity in speaking of the mystery of the Trinity as compared with the clearness of his ' religious theism,' and his faith in immortality.   He quoted Tennyson as saying that ' matter is more mysterious than mind.   His mind one knows well enough, but cannot get hold of the thought of body.'"

A few extracts from letters follow in which Brooks gives his impression regarding the theological situation:

"Stopford Brooke is declaring in a hearty way that Broad Church is dead and that free thought in the establishment is an impossibility, is talking of giving up preaching and taking to writing a history of English literature, which he would do finely. Meanwhile all the choir boys in England have chanted the Athanasian creed for the last two Sundays, and hundreds of clerical consciences have been torn to pieces.

"I have been spending an hour in Convocation, where that very troublesome creature, the Deceased Wife's Sister, was vexing the souls of deans and archdeacons.   The debates in the House of Lords about her have been very curious.   For the present she is rejected, and we must not marry her.   But, in the end, she will get her rights. "

"In London the other day, at Llewelyn Davies's, I was surprised to hear how dolefully he and other men talked about the prospects of liberal theology in the Church of England.   Davies and Abbott (E. A.) and the bishop of Manchester, who were there, declared the whole Maurician and Broad Church movement a failure; Farrar said the same thing in his cheery, doleful way, Plumptre also, and ——, of whom, perhaps, it might have been expected, and who is the same absurd, inconsequential creature that he was.   The older men of it seemed to be clinging to a remote history back in the days of Frederick Maurice, and the younger men to belong to that school of secularized clergy, which I know you dread as much as I do, and to be clutching at anything,—art, music, ecclesiasticism, sociology, anything to get a power over people which they earnestly wanted, but seemed to see no power in religion to attain.   I went to a meeting of the F. D. M. Club, of which I was made an honorary member.   It was presided over by Mr. Ludlow, and we had Hughes and Davies and Maurice's son for fellow-members, but the whole effect was not inspiring. The debate was about how Maurice would have regarded the modern socialism of Henry George and others, and how they, as Mauricians, ought to stand towards it. Maurice seemed to be a name to conjure with more than an influence upon their thought. Of course, there were many good things said, especially by Davies, whom I though; one of the best and most interesting men that I saw in England."

The London season was over by the middle of July. The year of wandering was drawing to its close, but a month remained before he sailed for America. He had been joined in London by his friend Mr. R. T. Paine, and together they departed for the continent. They stopped at Chartres and Bordeaux, and at Pau, near the Pyrenees. He writes, "The curtain has fallen and risen again; the whole scene has changed." After a "splendid Pyrenean week," including a trip to Lourdes, which reminded him of the Ganges at Benares, he came to Geneva, where he seems to have been chiefly interested in getting impressions of Voltaire. One night was spent at the Grand Chartreuse:

"There are about forty fathers there, Carthusians, in their picturesque white cloaks and cowls. Solitude and silence is their rule. They spend the bulk of their time in their cells, where they are supposed to be meditating. I suspect that the old gentlemen go to sleep. There was a strange ghostly service, which began at a quarter before eleven o'clock at night and lasted until two in the morning. The chapel was dim and misty; the white figures came gliding in and sat in a long row, and held dark lanterns up before their psalters and chanted away at their psalms like a long row of singing mummies. It made you want to run out in the yard and have a game of ball to break the spell. Instead of that, after watching it for half an hour, we crept back along a vast corridor to the cells which had been allotted us, each with its *priedieu* and its crucifix, and went to bed in the hardest, shortest, and lumpiest of beds. In the morning a good deal of the romance and awfulness was gone, but it was very fine and interesting, and the drive down into the valley on the other side at Chambéry was as pretty as a whole gallery of pictures."

From Geneva he went to Mürren, thence to Interlaken and Lucerne, and through the St. Gothard tunnel to Italy. From Italy he came back through the Tyrol, calling up his old associations with the Dolomites. He stopped at Trent and meditated on the famous council. At Brixlegg, a little village near Innsbrück, he was present at the performance of the Passion Play, which he had once failed to see in its more elaborate form at Ober-Ammergau. Then he felt that he was setting his face homeward, as he travelled rapidly from Munich to Paris, and from Paris to London, whence he sailed for America, on September 12.

CHAPTER XVI.

1883.

THE RETURN TO BOSTON. EXTRACTS FROM SER-
MONS. ADDRESS ON LUTHER. CORRESPONDENCE.
EXTRACTS FROM JOURNAL.

MR. BROOKS arrived in Boston on Saturday, the 22d of September; on the following Sunday he stood in his place in Trinity
Church.

"A large number of men and women met him at the Cunard
Wharf in East Boston as the *Cephaionia* arrived. Some of them
had chartered a tug and boarded the steamer off Boston Light.
She reached the pier about half past four in the afternoon; Mr.
Brooks held an impromptu reception on board, and landed about
five. He preached yesterday forenoon to a congregation which
filled Trinity Church to overflowing. He stands vigorous, hale,
and portly as ever, but his head has become plentifully sprinkled
with gray, so that the change strikes one the instant of beholding
him. The text of his sermon was I Cor., i., 6: 'Even as the testimony of Christ was confirmed in you.'"

The text had been in his mind while in India. On the voyage
homeward, as he passed through the Indian Ocean or the Mediterranean Sea, he was writing notes of what he would say. The
sermon was spoken out of the fulness of his heart, as he stood
in the pulpit of Trinity Church, after more than a year of silence.

"I must not seem to be pouring out on you on this first morning
the flood of preaching that has been accumulating through
a whole year of silence. But I have wanted to ask you to think
with me of how the key of the world's life, and of every Christian's experience, lies deep in that Incarnation which it is the
privilege of the Christian pulpit to proclaim and preach. If
what I have been saying to you is true, then that great manifes-

tation of God must be *preaching itself* forever. All history, all life, must be struggling to confirm the Testimony of Christ. . . . I will take up again, enthusiastically, the preaching of that Christ who is always *preaching Himself* in wonderful, and powerful, and tender ways, even to hearts that seem to hear Him least.

"To those who do hear Him and receive Him there comes a peace and strength, a patience to bear, an energy to work, which is to the soul itself a perpetual surprise and joy, a hope unquenchable, a love for and a belief in fellow-man that nothing can disturb, and, around all, as the great element of all, a certainty of God's encircling love to us which conquers sin and welcomes sorrow, and laughs at Death and already lives in Immortality. What shall we say of it that is not in the words of Christ's beloved disciple, who knows it all so well, 'To as many as receive Him, to them gives He power to become the sons of God.'

"Let us say, then, to one another, '*Sursum corda!* Lift up your hearts!' Let us answer back to one another, 'We *do* lift them up unto the Lord'; and so let us go forward together into whatever new life He has set before us."

There was a change, it has been said, in the appearance of Phillips Brooks, when he was seen again in the pulpit, after his long absence. It required an effort to be reconciled to the altered aspect. He was thinner in form, also, having lost weight while in India. He had said as he was contemplating the possibilities which his year abroad presented, "Every now and then it comes over me that the gap is to be so great that the future, if there is any, will certainly be something different in some way from the past." His manner showed the difference, and was not quite the same.

The great change was in his preaching. He was entering upon the third and last phase in his development. In the first, which included his ministry in Philadelphia, he had written his most beautiful sermons, full of the poetry of life, unfolding the divine allegory of human history,—a great artist, himself unmoved as he unrolled the panorama of man. In the second period, he had been at war with the forces which were undermining faith; yet always appearing like a tower of strength. That period was over now. He had felt while abroad a subtle change in the spiritual atmosphere, modifying the situation. There was improvement visible from the highest outlook. The mechanical theory of the world was yielding to the evidences of faith. He met with his old force belated travellers who had not noted the new signs in the spiritual horizon. But to speak to the new age was now his distinctive mission. His preaching changed to correspond to the change within. He addressed himself in his totality as a man to the common humanity, doing greatly whatever he did, and assuming the greatness of those to whom he spoke. He fell back upon the simplest issues of life; the simplest truths were the main themes of his teaching. He illustrated the truth of Goethe's remark, "Whatever a man doth greatly, he does with his whole nature." In his *Lectures on Preaching*, he had said that "the thought of rescue has monopolized our religion and often crowded out the thought of culture." The idea of rescue now became more prominent, but it was the rescue of men from the danger of losing the great opportunity of life. This may have been the ground of his remark that he had but one sermon. He said to one of his friends that he had given up writing essays and was going to preach sermons. It seemed to others that he had been preaching sermons; but he saw deeper depths in sermons, which he proposed to fathom. He had not grown indifferent to the intellectual problems. He followed them with interest and took his part in their discussion. He retained his allegiance to the old formulas of belief. But the full truth was something larger than the intellect could adequately formulate. Meantime the highest duty of man was to live, in the full sense of the word, as apostles and evangelists, as Christ himself, had used it. To help men to live in this sense became his ruling passion in every sermon. There were occasional sermons when his creative genius flashed living pictures upon the canvas, as of old, before his hearers. But these were not so common as before. His method of preaching became more frequently extemporaneous, when he was free to pour himself forth without regard to form of utterance. He allowed more range to the impassioned feeling, and he showed signs of being visibly moved by his own emotion, instead of standing, as in his early years, cool and unmoved, while his hearers were thrilled with excitement. Yet in this latter phase of his life he was listened to more intently than ever; there was an added element of awe, as the man in himself stood revealed in every sermon. He came closer to his world and dearer to the hearts of all the people. There was no longer any question about his greatness. He had made the final conquest. It had dawned upon him that what the people wanted was himself, not his eloquence, or his gifts. There were still before him greater depths of self-abnegation, to be met by an ever larger demand on the part of the people. This was the way in which saints had been recognized in the olden time. The canonization of Phillips Brooks by the people's voice had now begun.

In a sermon preached on September 30th, the second Sunday after his return, we have Phillips Brooks communing with himself as he takes up the burden of life anew. This chapter from his own experience, for such in reality it is, he has entitled " Visions and Tasks; " his text, "While Peter thought on the vision, the Spirit said, Behold, three men seek thee." There was the possibility that the vision might fade as the emotions grew less vivid. The remedy was in action. The picture is that of Peter after the vision has ended, plodding over the dusty hills to meet the men who were seeking him. The practical life is needed in order to complete the meditative life. When a man has had his vision of some great truth which satisfies his soul, the coming of his fellow-men, and their knocking at the doors of his heart, seems at first like an intrusion. "Why can they not leave him alone with his great idea?" So ideas would hover like a great vague cloud over a world all hard and gross and meaningless, if it were not for the man who brings the fire down and makes the whole of nature significant and vocal. He himself had seen a vision which had faded and he was speaking from his own experience:

"It is in the power of man to stand between the abstract truth upon one side and the concrete facts of life upon the other. To this end he must cultivate the two capacities within him,—the gift of knowing and the gift of loving. In some way he must still cultivate the capacity of knowing, whether by patient study or quick-leaping intuition, including imagination and all the poetic power, faith, trust in authority, the faculty of getting wisdom by experience, everything by which the human nature comes into direct relationship to truth. On the other hand, he must cultivate love, the power of sympathetic intercourse with things and people, the power to be touched by the personal nature of those with whom we have to do,—love, therefore, including hate, for hate is only the reverse utterance of love. These two together, the powers of knowing and of loving, must make up the man, and must work together also in all men in order to a genuine manhood. It is not a question of greatness, but of genuineness and completeness. . . . This was the characteristic of Christ, that He was full of grace and truth; no rapt self-centred student of the abstract truth, nor the sentimental pitier of other men's woes. He comes down from the mountain where He had been glorified with the light of God to meet the men who were seeking Him.

"It is the result of some great experience, also, in the life of a man that it makes him a purer medium through which the highest truth shines on other men. Henceforth he is altered; he becomes tenderer, warmer, richer; he seems to be full of truths and revelations which he easily pours out. Now you not merely see him, you see through him to things behind. It is not that he has learned some new facts, but the very substance of the man is altered, so that he stands no longer as a screen, but as an atmosphere through which eternal truths come to you all radiant."

As Phillips Brooks enters upon this new stage of his history he casts a backward glance at the possibilities he has left behind him. He is determined to cultivate the faculty of knowing by every means in his power, but some of the methods of knowing may be closed to him as he follows after the men who are seeking him. In a sermon, also written soon after his return from abroad, he took for his text the words "I know how to be abased." There is something very personal in this extract:

"I must pass on and speak about the way in which a man may know how to be poor in learning. There are many of us who need that knowledge,—many of us who before we have got well into life see what a great world learning is, and also see for a certainty how hopeless it is that we shall ever do more than set our feet upon its very outermost borders. Some life of practical duty claims us; and the great stream of learning, into which we long to plunge and swim, sweeps by our chained feet, and we can only look down into its tempting waters and sigh over our fate. How many practical men, men who seem to be totally absorbed and perfectly satisfied in their busy life, really live in this discontent at being shut out from the richness of learning. Is there a right way and a wrong way, a wise way and a foolish way, of living in that discontent? Indeed there is. The foolish ways are evident enough. The unlearned man who by and by is heard sneering at learning, and glorifying machineries, boasting that he sees and wants to see no visions, and that he never theorizes,—he has not known how to be ignorant. He has let his ignorance master and overcome him. It has made him its slave. The man who, the more he becomes conscious of his hopelessness of great scholarship, has grown more and more sensible of what a great thing it is to be a scholar, and at the same time, by the same process, has grown more and more respectful toward his own side of life, more and more conscious of the value of practical living as a true contribution to the great final whole—the man, therefore, who has gone on his way, as most of us have to do, with little learning, but has also gone on his way doing duty faithfully, developing all the practical skill that is in him, and sometimes, just because their details are so dark to him, getting rich visions of the general light and glory of the great sciences, seen afar off, seen as great wholes, which often seem to be denied to the plodders who spend their lives in the close study of those sciences,—he is the man who knows how to be unlearned. It is a blessed thing that there is such a knowledge possible for overworked, practical men. The man who has that knowledge may be self-respectful in the face of all the colleges. He may stand before the kings of learning and not be ashamed; for his lot is as true a part of life as theirs, and he is bravely holding up his side of that great earth over which the plans of God are moving on to their completeness."

There is one other sermon to be mentioned here,—the companion of the sermon on "How to be abased" written at the same time, with only a week's interval, and from words in the same text, "How to abound." There are passages here to be remembered, words prophetic of those later years, in which, having learned to be abased, he reaped the fruit of abasement in the larger abundance of life:

"Many of the popular men have been tyrannized over and ruined by their popularity. Their principles have crumbled; their selfhood has melted away; they have become mere stocks and stones for foolish men to hang garlands on, not real men, real utterances of the divine life, leading their fellow-men, rebuking sin, inspiring struggles, saving souls.

"Ah, yes! Not merely to make men love you and honor you, but how to be loved and honored without losing yourself and growing weak,—that is the problem of many of the sweetest, richest, most attractive lives; and there is only one solution for it, which blessed indeed is he who has discovered! . . . If the much-loved man can look up and demand the love of God, if he can crave it and covet it infinitely above all other love, if laying hold of its great freedom, he can make it his, . . . then let him come back and take into a glowing heart the warmest admiration and affection of his brethren, the heaven that he carries in his heart preserves him. They cannot make him conceited, for he who lives with God must be humble. . . . He who knows that God loves and honors him may freely take all other love and honor, however abundant they may be, and he will get no harm.

In the robing-room of Trinity Church is a window given by Phillips Brooks in 1884, as a thankoffering to his people for their generous kindness. He gave it the name ΕΦΦΑΘΑ [Be opened]. It represents Jesus healing the "man that was deaf and had an impediment in his speech." Jesus stands at the left, stretching out his arm that his fingers may touch the lips of the man brought to him. The apostles and the friends of the man stand around; in the background the sail of a ship upon the sea of Galilee. Above are three angels holding a scroll with the words εἰς ἃ ἐπιθυμοῦσιν ἄγγελοι παρακύψαι ["which things the angels desire to look into"]. In the lower part of the window are two small pictures of the *Baptism* and the *Last Supper*. On the left the baptism—John upon the bank pouring the water upon the head of Christ, who stands in the stream, while above the dove is descending from heaven; on the right, Jesus breaking bread at the table with His disciples, and St. John leaning upon his breast. Of this window he wrote to a friend who admired it:

"I am glad you like the little window in the robing-room, because it was my own thought entirely and one in which I took the deepest interest. The makers did their work just as I wanted them to, and the result has already given me great satisfaction and inspiration. I hope that it will help a long line of the future rectors of Trinity to speak with free and wise tongues."

The return of Phillips Brooks to his work was an occasion for extending a formal welcome. A dinner was given him by the Clericus Club, at Young's Hotel, on the evening of September 24. The feeling was very deep and tender when once more he stood among them. He was silent, and the usual hilarity of his manner was wanting. Bishop Clark of Rhode Island remarked that we had a lion present, but a lion who would not roar. Another reception followed, given by the clergy of the diocese, which took the form of a breakfast at the Hotel Brunswick, on the morning of Thursday, September 27, and the bishop of the diocese presided.

The General Convention of the Episcopal Church, to which he was a delegate from the diocese of Massachusetts, was held in October, and, fortunately for Mr. Brooks, in the city of Philadelphia, for it enabled him to satisfy his longings to be with his friends in the place he had not ceased to love. In a letter to Mr. Cooper he indulges, as he often did, in expression of devotion to the city which was so much to him,—"Why did I ever leave Philadelphia!" It was his pleasure to talk of Philadelphia as if the glory and beauty of life, as he knew it in the freshness of his years, would have remained if he had never left there.

When the General Convention was over he was ready at last to resume his work as a parish minister. He had formed a great resolution to give himself henceforth more exclusively to the duties of his parish, and as far as possible deny himself to outside calls. He took up, of course, his duties as one of the chaplains at Harvard, going to Cambridge in November to conduct morning prayers. There came to him while in Philadelphia an invitation from the Evangelical Alliance to make an address in New York on the 13th of November, at the commemoration of the four hundredth anniversary of the birth of Martin Luther. He wrote at once declining it, but his tone was such that the invitation was renewed:

"I must not think of it. If there were six months in which to get ready for what would be to me a most unfamiliar duty I would try with trembling. But in a month, all crowded full as this next month is to be, I do not dare to do it, in justice to those who have asked me, or to Dr. Luther. I agree with you that it it is a most splendid opportunity to say things that we want said. It cannot be made a small or party celebration. It must open the whole relation of Christianity to human kind. But all that makes it the more necessary that the oration of the occasion should be no crude and hurried thing, but something well matured and thorough. I am very much afraid that I could not do it in any length of time. I am sure I could not do it in three busy weeks."

The invitation proved to be one which he could not decline.

He was alive to the significance of Luther to the modern world. The days he had spent in Germany at Luther's haunts had deepened his love and admiration for the great reformer. "I made a delightful journey [so he had written to a friend] down through the Luther land, stopping at every place I could find which had anything to do with him." He had watched the preparatory steps for the commemoration of the four hundredth anniversary in his own country. Much of the preparation for the address had already been made. He spoke therefore from a full heart:

"The name and fame of Luther coming down through history under God's safe-conduct has been full of almost the same vitality, and has been attended by almost the same admiration and abuse, as was the figure of Luther in that famous journey which took him in his rude Saxon wagon from Wittenberg to Worms when he went up to the Diet; and at Leipzig, Nürnberg, Weimar, Erfurt, Gotha, Frankfurt, the shouts of his friends and the curses of his enemies showed that no man in Germany was loved or hated as he was."

The force which Martin Luther exerted was distinctively a religious force:

"The consciousness of being sent from God with a mission for which the time is ripe, and the consciousness of eager return to God, of the great human struggle after Him, possessing a nature which cannot live without Him,—the imperious commission from above and the tumultuous experience within,—these two, not inconsistent with each other, have met in all the great Christian workers and reformers who have moved and changed the world. These two lived together in the whole life of Luther. The one spoke out in the presence of the emperor at Worms. The other wrestled unseen in the agonies of the cloister cell at Erfurt."

Luther was the exponent of religion, pure and simple, rather than the theologian,—a mystic and the highest representative of mysticism for all time. From this point of view he stood above Calvin the theologian, or Zwingle the politician, or the English ecclesiastics. But conjoined with the mysticism was morality: "He was the moralist *and* the mystic:"

"These are the universal human elements of religious strength and character. The theologian may be far separated from humanity, the mere arranger of abstract ideas. The ecclesiastic may be quite unhuman, too, the manager of intricate machineries. But the man who is truly moralist and mystic must be full of a genuine humanity. He is the prophet and the priest at once. He brings the eternal Word of God to man, and he utters the universal cry of man to God. Nothing that is human can be strange to him, and so nothing that is human can count him really strange to it. David, Isaiah, John the Baptist, Paul—nay, let us speak the highest name, Jesus, the Christ Himself—these elements were in them all. Grace and truth, faith and conscience, met in them and made their power. These elements united in our Luther, and so it was, as the result of them, that he inspired humanity and moved the souls of men and nations as the tide moves the waves."

In his comment on Luther's principle of Justification by Faith, he saw beneath the letter its correlated truths:

"However he may have stated it in the old familiar forms of bargain, this was Luther's real doctrine of justification by faith. It was mystic, not dogmatic. It was of the soul and the experience, not of the reason. Faith was not an act, but a being,— not what you did, but what you were. The whole truth of the immanence of God and of the essential belonging of the human life to the divine: the whole truth that God is a power *in* man and not simply a power over man,—building him as a man builds a house, guiding him as a man steers a ship,—this whole truth, in which lies the seed of all humanity, all progress, all great human hope, lay in the truth that justification was by faith and not by works. No wonder that Luther loved it. No wonder that he thought it critical. No wonder that he wrote to Melanchthon, hesitating at Augsburg: 'Take care that you give not up justification by faith. That is the heel of the seed of the woman which is to crush the serpent's head.'"

He takes up the question whether Protestantism has been a failure. If it is to be thought of as a power aspiring to take the place of Rome and to govern mankind after the same fashion, or if we think of it as a system of fixed doctrines, claiming infallibility, and refusing all prospect of development, seeking to hold men together by loyalty to confessions of faith, or in submission to some central ecclesiastical authority, then it has failed, as it ought to have failed.

"But there is more to say than that. These centuries of Anglo-Saxon life made by the ideas of Luther answer the question.

The Protestantism of Milton and of Goethe, of Howard and of Francke, of Newton and of Leibnitz, of Bunyan and of Butler, of Wordsworth and of Tennyson, of Wesley and of Channing, of Schleiermacher and of Maurice, of Washington and of Lincoln, is no failure. We may well dismiss the foolish question, and with new pride and resolve brighten afresh the great name of Protestant upon our foreheads. . . .

The time will come—perhaps the time has come—when a new Luther will be needed for the next great step that humanity must take, but that next step is possible mainly because of what the monk of Wittenberg was and did four hundred years ago. There is no failure there. Only one strain in the music of the eternal success,—fading away but to give space for a new and higher strain."

The address as written or as published is not quite what it was in the delivery. In sending the manuscript for publication he says: "I suppose it will do to let what I had written about Luther's life stand instead of the epitome of it; which I tried to extemporize on that tumultuous evening."

"I heard his Luther speech in New York [writes Bishop Lawrence], and then he did what I never knew him to do at any other time. He had a great audience in the Academy of Music, and it was a great occasion. He felt it. He read from his manuscript, but when it came to the burning of the Pope's Bull he left his manuscript, stepped to the side of the desk, then to the front of the platform, and launched forth on a most eloquent and impassioned description of the scene. He then returned to the desk and continued to read from the manuscript. My impression was that on the impulse of the moment he depicted it in extemporized language, or expanded what the manuscript contained."

In the fall of 1883 appeared the third volume of his sermons, published simultaneously in England and America, with the title, *Sermons preached in English Churches*. As he put the sermons in order for printing, having in view the reception given him by the English people, he dedicated the volume "To many friends in England in remembrance of their cordial welcome." No more genuine expressions of appreciation came to him than those from England.

"Your visit to us this summer [writes a high dignitary of the

Church of England] has left a mark, spiritual and intellectual, which, by God's help, will not soon be effaced from the Church which welcomed you and delighted to listen to you. And we, who have to preach and teach, feel that a prophet has been among us, and a new stimulus given to us, for which we are heartily grateful and solemnly responsible." "My gratitude [another writer says] has grown and deepened, and now cannot find the proper and suitable words in which to express itself." "I can assure you [writes a member of the legal profession who heard him in theTemple Church] I will never forget the lessons of charity you urged upon us. The older I get, and the more of the world I see, the more I am convinced that if Christianity is to lay hold on the higher order of intellects, it must be by such noble, broad, elevating preaching as yours."

In the notices of the book in the English papers Mr. Brooks was declared to be an exception to transatlantic eloquence. "The quality which will first strike the reader of these sermons," says one of these book reviews, "is their thoroughly English and Anglican tone." It was remarked by another critic that the sermons in reading did not suffer from the absence of the impressive manner of the preacher. "On every page we come across sentences which lend themselves readily to detached quotation, and they are of a quality which will stand examination and provoke thought; indeed, passages of this kind are so frequent that it is next to impossible to select quotations in illustration."

The estimate of these sermons which follows is from an English reviewer:

"We are disposed to assign to Mr. Brooks the rank of the first preacher of the day. Or, if that be too strong a statement, we shall mend it by saying that his printed sermons are the best we have read. They are, without exception, great sermons. Of the fourteen sermons in this volume, it may be said that they are great in all respects. Great in the gravity of their solemn eloquence, great in the felicity with which word is fitted to thought, and perfect simple expression is given to deep and profound thought, great also in the insight into character, motive, and action, and specially great in the act which fuses thought, speech, emotion, into one organic whole. Each sermon stands out clear and vivid before us, perfect in the one simple impression it makes on our mind. It is only as we proceed to analysis that we discover how much complexity and variety have gone to make the unity which is perfect as the unity of a true or of a living organism. There is boundless variety, manifoldness of many sorts, but all held together by a principle of life from within, and not of outward constraint as staves are held together by means of hoops in order to make a barrel."

Two of the sermons may be specially mentioned, as suited to the moment, although the immediate aim is buried beneath a form of adaptation to any age. One of them is entitled "The Mind's Love for God" from the words of Christ where He enjoins the divine love not only with the heart but with the intellect: "Thou shalt love the Lord thy God with all . . . thy mind." The preacher had in view the attitude of those who enjoined the intellectual formulas of other ages as final and authoritative and refused to allow to the present age the right to examine those formulas, or even to attempt to restate them in the language of the modern world, as though the mere action of the modern intellect were, in the nature of the case, either ineffective or else destructive and dangerous. He reviews the different religious attitudes,—those who cling to the Bible with the affection of the heart, but refuse to it the love of the intellect, declining to consider any questions as to where it came from, or from what parts it is made up, how its parts belong together, and the nature of its authority. He alludes to those who repel all questions about the nature of God, crying out: "You must not try to understand, you must only listen, worship, and obey"; or those who, when the incarnation of Christ is mentioned, and the question is raised, among other questions, of the way the sonship of Christ is related to the sonship of all other men in God, say in rebuke: "You must not ask; Christ is above all questions." Or again, when one would learn of the saint at Christ's sacrament what that dear and lofty rite means to him, must he be told: "You must not rationalize.—it is a mystery; the reason has no function here"! It is not only among devout Christians that this tendency appears, but among those who disbelieve the Christian faith:

"A curious way of talking, which seems to me to have grown strangely common of late among the men who disbelieve in Christianity. It is patronizing and quietly insulting; it takes for granted that the Christian's faith has no real reason at its heart, nor any trustworthy grounds for thinking itself true. At the same time, it grants that there is a certain weak side of human nature where the reason does not work, where everything depends on sentiment and feeling, where not what is true, but what is beautiful and comforting and reassuring is the soul's demand; and that side of the nature it gives over to religion. Because that side of the nature is the most prominent part, and indeed sometimes seems to be the whole of weaker kinds of men and women, it accepts the necessity of religion for these weak people, and does not desire its immediate extinction; only it must not pretend to be a reasonable thing. Theology must not call itself a science, and Faith must know it is a dream."

Against this one of many forms of exaggerated, provoking sentimentalism in the nineteenth century he protests in the name of religion and of historical Christianity:

"Think of David and his cry, 'Thy testimonies are wonderful. I have more understanding than my teachers, for thy testimonies are my study.' Think of Paul, 'O the depth of the riches both of the wisdom and knowledge of God.' Think of Augustine, Luther, Calvin, Milton, Edwards, and a hundred more, the men whose minds have found their loftiest inspiration in religion, how they would have received this quiet and contemptuous relegation of the most stupendous subject of human thought to the region of silly sentiment. They were men who loved the Lord their God with all their minds. The noble relation of their intellects to Him was the supreme satisfaction of their lives."

The other sermon in this volume which deserves mention as adapted to the age is called "Gamaliel," from the text, "Gamaliel, a doctor of the law, had in reputation among all the people" (Acts v., 34). It is a plea for absolute freedom in the search for truth, resting on faith in God as the final safeguard of the truth,— "If this work be of men, it will come to naught; but if it be of God, ye cannot overthrow it, lest haply ye be found even to fight against God."

"Every great teacher, every great scholar, ought to be aware of the mystery and of the mightiness of truth, and therefore he ought to be prepared to see Truth linger and hesitate and seem to be retarded, and even seem to be turned back, and yet to keep a clear assurance that Truth must come right in the end and that the only way to help her is to keep her free, so that she shall be at liberty to help herself. . . . The scholar of truth must trust truth. . . . The student must claim, for himself and for all men, liberty. . . . If you limit the search for truth and forbid men anywhere, in any way, to seek knowledge, you paralyze the vital force of truth itself. That is what makes bigotry so disastrous to the bigot."

Gamaliel was the type of such a teacher, broad-minded, inculcating earnestly his own views of truth, knowing at the same time that truth is larger than his view,—one of those men who give others the chance to make history, while they relegate themselves to obscurity. "There are few things finer than to see the reverence and gratitude with which the best men of active life look back to the quiet teachers who furnished them with the materials of living." With such an ideal of teaching, he contrasts the

"men who are set upon making all the world live in their own way, who have no real faith in God, and therefore no real faith in men. Human force and goodness seem to them to be not vital growths with real life in them, but skilfully arranged devices all artificially planned and pinned together, when, if you altered the place of any single pin, the whole must fall. Such men must blight the possibilities of any communities they live in. . . . To hold your truth, to believe it with all your heart, to work with all your might, first to make it real to yourself and then to show its preciousness to other men, and then—not till then, but then—to leave the questions of when and how and by whom it shall prevail to God: that is the true life of the believer. There is no feeble unconcern and indiscriminateness there, and neither is there any excited hatred of the creed, the doctrine, or the Church, which you feel wholly wrong. You have not fled out of the furnace of bigotry to freeze on the open and desolate plains of indifference. You believe and yet you have no wish to persecute."

It is remarkable that the last century, with its boasted freedom, had seen more attempts at religious ostracism, and caused more suffering for the sake of religious beliefs, than had been known for two hundred years. We must go back to the seventeenth century for an analogous moment in history since the Reformation. In the middle of the century Mr. Mill foresaw the danger and made his plea for liberty. Phillips Brooks, in this sermon, is occupied with the thought which he would later elaborate in his book on *Tolerance*. Now he closed his sermon with a great appeal, invoking the time when every "form of terrorism shall have passed away, when we shall frankly own that there is nothing for which God in any world will punish any of his children except sin."

The sermon on Gamaliel was preached in the Temple Church in London, rich with historical associations, its audience mostly made up of men, lawyers in large numbers among them. He was standing in Hooker's place, and his utterance was worthy of Hooker, and such as he would have welcomed. The sermon left an extraordinary impression. One who listened to him wrote him this letter:

"If I had obeyed my impulse last Sunday I should have written you after the service to tell you how deeply your words sank into my heart, and—may I say it?—with what pride I saw you in the old Temple, and knew that more noble words of truth had never resounded through its historic walls."

It was some time after Mr. Brooks returned to Boston before he settled down contentedly to work. So late as December 6th, he wrote: "I should not like to have the people here know how restless I am, and how hard it is to get to work again. London and Berlin and Delhi seem so much more real than Boston."

In response to an invitation to be present at an Interecclesiastical Church Congress he wrote:

"I wish nothing but good to the Interecclesiastical Church Congress. But I am of no use in such organized movements, nor have I any great faith in them. I think that the more freely the spirit of union works the better, and any attempts to put it into organic shape, or even to give it definition and expression, only do harm.

"I may be wrong. I probably am. I am not writing in any foolish idea of dissuading you, nor of throwing even a dipperful of cold water on the scheme; only to say why I myself cannot take part in it; and you will understand me, and if you don't we 'll talk it out the next time you get down your feet before my fire."

On receiving a copy of the translation of his *Lectures on Preaching*, Mr. Brooks wrote this letter:

"233 CLARENDON STREET, BOSTON, December 7, 1883.

"MY DEAR M. NYEGAARD,—I have just received the two copies of the *Conférences sur la Prédication* which you have kindly sent me, for which I thank you very heartily. I am sure I need not tell you that I value very highly the care and thought and labor which you have so generously bestowed upon my book. I wish the book to which you have given so much time were worthier of the pains which you have lavished on it. I fear there may be people who will say, 'Materiam superabat opus.' But none the less I thank you, and if any help or encouragement should come to any preacher in your country through this book, I shall feel that it is to you more than to me that the credit will belong.

"It is very strange to read one's own words in a foreign tongue. It is almost as if one's image in a mirror took a voice and spoke to one. The words are familiar and yet strange, and thoughts seem sometimes to put on new shades of meaning along with their new forms of expression. I have found myself reading my own book quite through with the attraction of the new interest which it gained from the new form. I have no right to speak about the merit of your work. I am too poor a French scholar to make my opinion of any value. I can only say that I have found it **very** smooth and easy reading. I do not doubt that critics who are competent to judge will find abundant reason to approve and praise the way in which the work of the translator has been done."

In a letter to Rev. Dr. W. N. McVickar, he speaks of the forty-eighth birthday:

"DEAR WILLIAM,—It was delightfully kind of you and your sister to remember that I was forty-eight last Thursday, and to send me this delicious little token of your good wishes, which I received to-day. Your kindness and the beauty of your little lamp almost reconciled me to the sadness of the event. The day passed calmly. There was no salute upon the Common nor any special form of prayer put forth by the Bishop; but Jim and Sallie came up from Salem and dined with me at my brother's, and we made believe it was good fun to be forty-eight years old. Wait till you try it, my good fellow, and see how you like it, to have your golden bowl and pitcher in this dilapidated condition."

Here follow a few extracts from the note-book for 1883:

"One feels there is great danger in the present attitude of multitudes of English people towards Christianity, accepting it without facing its problems, as the religion of their people, dwelling on its beautiful or comfortable features, and almost ready to resent as simply disturbing and unnecessary any effort to make its statements more reasonable. Not so common among us. It is closely mixed up with the loyalty and practicalness and institutionalism of the Englishman. The other temper also there."

"Let us never disparage the value of certain and sure belief about truth. Whatever compensations may come in its absence and delay, it is nevertheless, and we can never forget that it is, the ultimate purpose and ambition of the human soul, until it reaches which, it never can be satisfied."

"Sermon on the great revelation of the immanence of God in these days."

"As Columbus sailed to find the Old World and found the New, so possibly a reaction (like the Puseyite) may help the progress of truth."

"The ocean, ever defeated by man, and never conquered."

"The perpetual presence behind our life, with its temporary impulses, of God and His life."

"How old things may pass away without all things becoming new."

"As useless and provoking as it is to have one of those matches which won't light without the box, and you have n't got the box."

"No sooner *done than said*."

"French talk of a man having the danger of his qualities."

"Like the long zigzags up the hills, always coming back into sight of the same points, but viewing them from higher points,— so of theological progress."

"Thou shalt tread upon the lion and adder; the young lion and dragon shalt thou tread under thy feet"; "The sun shall not be thy light by day," etc.,—the universal Eastern prayers.

"Text: He was wandering in the field, and the man asked him saying, 'What seekest thou?' And he said, 'I seek my brethren;

tell me, I pray thee, where they feed their flocks.' The lonely soul wandering in doubt and personal experience, and craving the familiar ways of other souls which may be the very thing that will be his death.''

"The time for confirmation, I think, is not childhood, when others think for us; not middle age, when life grows weary, but just at the time when obedience to authority changes into personal responsibility,—in the period of youth when life is fresh and untried, but the way has to be trodden and the traveller just setting out needs a guide and a helper.''

"When I see how the real difficulty of multitudes of bewildered men is not this or that unsolved problem, but the whole incapacity of comprehending God—when I see this, I understand how the best boon that God can give to any group of men must often be to take one of them and, bearing witness of Himself to him, set him to bearing that witness of the Lord to his brethren, which only a man surrounded and filled with God can bear.''

"'The beauty of holiness.' It seems as if the good taste of goodness, the ugliness of sin, while it cannot be used as the first creative motive for a new life, must certainly come in by and by to certify and assure the work which conscience and obedience to the Law of God have done. Brought in at first it must create a feeble moral æstheticism and be fruitful in false and conventional standards. But it may apparently be recognized and enforced sooner with reference to the conditions of the world and society at large than with reference to the individual.''

A round of festivities awaited him in Washington. Lunches and dinners filled up the days. Among his hosts were Senator Bayard and the historian Bancroft. He met Senators Hoar, Dawes, Pendleton, Tucker, and Wade Hampton; Judges of the Supreme Court Field, Harlan, and Matthews. At a dinner given in his honor by Mr. Bancroft, he met, among others, General Sheridan and President Arthur. He called upon the President at the White House, and the President returned his call. He took the occasion while in Washington to revisit the Theological Seminary at Alexandria, and "grew very sentimental about old times."

In Pennsylvania the name of Phillips Brooks had been mentioned as a candidate for the bishopric in case Bishop Stevens should ask for assistance. He writes on the subject to Rev. Arthur Brooks:

"233 CLARENDON STREET, BOSTON, May 18, 1884.

"DEAR ARTHUR,—I thank you for your kind note, on which I have been pondering since it came. It is a funny feeling to be brought face to face with the question whether one would be a bishop if he were elected. But when I ask myself the question, I become quite sure that I would not. First, I feel confident that I do not want it, and second, I am sure that I am not made for it. . . . If anybody asks anything about me, tell them you believe—as I now assure you is the case—I would not accept it if I were chosen."

The summer passed without incident and rather dragged. Part of it was spent at Sharon Springs, New York. He went to a church where the ritual was not to his taste: "I sat in a pew at both services and enjoyed my mind." "What a dreadful time summer is! I long for Lent and its labor, or Christmas and its carolling, in contrast with this loungy, hot, dissipated life."

To a friend who was puzzled by the character of a person with whom both were thrown much in contact, he writes:

"SHARON SPRINGS, N. Y., July 9, 1884.

"Thank you for letting me see the remarkable epistle in which our friend pours forth his soul. It is a strange being. I doubt if he himself has any idea where sincerity ends and insincerity begins. And with this fulsome and unreal part of him there are mixed up such good qualities, so much energy and kindliness and desire to be useful, that it seems a perpetual pity that he should not be a great deal better than he is. He is a curious study of the way in which one's weakest and strongest qualities not merely lie side by side, but also are twisted in with one another, and get each other's strength and weakness."

In the fall, political issues were causing great excitement throughout the country. The nomination of Mr. Blaine for the presidency caused widespread dissatisfaction in the Republican party, giving rise to what was known as the "Mugwump" movement, by whose aid the Democratic candidate, Mr. Cleveland, was elected,—the first Democratic President in a period of twenty-five years. While Mr Brooks did not vote for Mr. Blaine, he positively refused to join in the revolt from the Republican party.

The Church Congress met at Detroit in October, where he read his paper on *Authority and Conscience*. He accepted an invitation to deliver lectures in the following year at the General Theological Seminary in New York, and fastened on the subject of Tolerance, which had long been in his mind. He now proposed "to give its history, and discriminate it from its counterfeits and anticipate its future."

The book on *Tolerance* is a very personal one, for he was vindicating his own position, his mental freedom, his superiority to narrow sectarian lines, his wide sympathies, his own tolerance for all sincere and earnest thought. He was guarding himself against "being travestied and misdescribed by bigotry, on the one hand, or by what is called "free thought" on the other. His tone is at times tender and pathetic. He was gentle and kind, for he had adversaries to conciliate if possible. He knew that his position was a difficult one to maintain, but he was determined to make it clear, and to enforce and recommend it by the fascination of his eloquence and his wide observation and experience of life. He took for his text, if we may call it so, a passage from the writings of Maurice, which he admits sounds like a paradox, but will come to be an axiom,—"It is the natural feeling of all that charity is founded upon the *uncertainty* of truth. I believe that it is found on the *certainty* of truth." He endeavored to meet that class of minds which are accustomed to think that strong, positive conviction is incompatible with

tolerance; that faith and tolerance can have no fellowship; that
"the only foundation for tolerance is a degree of scepticism."
He defined tolerance as "the willing consent that other men
should hold and express opinions with which we disagree until
they are convinced by reason that those opinions are untrue."
And again, "True tolerance consists in the love of truth and the
love of man, each brought to its perfection and living in harmony
with one another . . . and enfolded in the greater love of God.
The love of truth alone grows cruel. It has no pity for man. . . .
And the love of man alone grows weak. It trims and moulds
and travesties the truth to suit men's whims."

To Dr. Weir Mitchell he writes, speaking of his recent book,
In War Time:

"233 CLARENDON STREET, BOSTON, December 20, 1884.

"MY DEAR WEIR,—Just after I had finished *In War Time* there
came in the copy of it which you, in your kind thoughtfulness,
had sent to me. I should have sent a line anyway to say how
much I had enjoyed the story, but now I must also tell you how
very much I value the copy of it which you have given me yourself. I have not had enough to do with great people to have
ceased to feel a thrill at an author's gift of his own book. An
author, the man who can wave his wand and summon all these
people and make them behave themselves like folks for four hundred pages, is a mystery and a marvel to me. And to have him
open the door to me with his own wonderful hands is a surprise
and delight.

"I take it for a Christmas present, and send back swarms of
Christmas wishes for you and yours. God bless you, merry gentleman! "Ever affectionately yours,

"P. B."

This is a picture of Phillips Brooks worth preserving, as he
went to St. Paul's on Tremont Street, sitting in the pew where
he sat as a boy. He writes of it December 26, 1884:

"The Bishop had us all to talk to the other day in old St.
Paul's, and I sat alone in pew No. 60, and heard him, and used
Mother's old Prayer Book in the service."

The following letters were written to a lady who had thoughts
of entering a sisterhood in order that her life might be under
"rule" and subject to a "spiritual director."

"233 CLARENDON STREET, BOSTON, January 3, 1885.

"MY DEAR MISS ——,—Is there not very great danger that, in seeking to lose the worst part of yourself, its anxiety and oppression, you may lose the best which God has given you in the submission of your life to rule and machinery? I cannot help telling you once more how sad is the mistake which I feel sure that you would make if you gave way to the impulse which has taken possession of your mind.

"But may not this one thing have weight with you, the duty which you owe to your present work? Can you desert the souls which look to you for help? Can you give up your school-teaching into which God has allowed you to carry so much of life-giving power? Can you abandon your class in which you have gathered so many young hearts, all growing earnest under your inspiration? I do not see how it is possible. If ever God marked out one of his servants for a certain kind of work and showed His purpose for her by the blessing which He gave to her labors, He would surely seem to have done it for you. Can you disregard all this and give yourself up to a system in which you certainly do not thoroughly believe, and by your embracing of which you would assuredly seem to disown the method of the healthy, human, and spontaneous work in which you have accomplished so much?

"I need not tell you that you can make no change in your work which will change in the least degree my faith in your singleness of purpose and devotion to Christ. But, my dear friend, for your own sake, and the Church's sake, and the sake of the souls which you are training, may I not beg you to continue the work for which I have so often thanked God?

"May He give you His light abundantly.
"Your sincere friend,
"PHILLIPS BROOKS."

"233 CLARENDON STREET, BOSTON, January 8, 1885.

"MY DEAR MISS ——, —I am more glad than I can tell you. I do joyfully and solemnly thank God for your decision. Now may your whole life realize more and more in ever increasing usefulness and happiness that it is God whom you have followed, and that in His rich world is the place where He will give Himself to you most richly.

"May He bless you, my dear friend, always.
"Faithfully yours,
"PHILLIPS BROOKS."

It may have been partly in consequence of his repugnance to anything savoring of the monastic tendency that he sympathized with movements whose object was to give women a greater opportunity in the world of action. He felt the force of the circumstances begetting the two alternatives, one of which would send them to semi-monastic seclusion, and the other throw open to them the spheres of influence which had hitherto been closed. In municipal life, he felt that women could fill an important place which could not so well be filled by men. He gave his sympathy to those who were laboring to this end.

To the Rev. Heber Newton, who had incurred the danger of an ecclesiastical trial because of his views regarding the Bible, he writes:

"233 CLARENDON STREET, BOSTON, February 14, 1885.

"MY DEAR NEWTON,—I thank you very much indeed for your note, and I am glad to know from it that the impression which I formed this week in New York is correct, that the newspapers are making the mischief, and that we are not to see your real work hindered and the Church disgraced by a presentment and a trial. I am sure that the work which you have done is one for which you may well be thankful, and for which those who love our Church most wisely may rejoice. You have had a true message to many whom others' messages have failed to reach. You have done very much indeed to keep the mind of the Church open to the light. Whatever God may have to say to her, you have made it more possible for her to hear.

"That is a great work for any man to have done. In that, more than in the impression of his own exact ideas upon the Church's mind, any progressive man's best service to the Church must lie. We certainly cannot be surprised or angry that such a work excites anger and opposition. I, for one, believe that no opposition will exasperate you, and that you will be kept from any word which can hinder the best result of what you have seriously and devoutly undertaken.

"I wish you would rest yourself for a Sunday by coming on and staying with me and preaching in my church. Any Sunday that you will name I shall be delighted to see you.
"Ever sincerely yours,
"PHILLIPS BROOKS."

To his brother he writes as an officer of the Church Congress with reference to the fitness of one of the appointed speakers:

"233 CLARENDON, STREET, BOSTON, March 12, 1885.

"MY DEAREST ARTHUR,—The man who can say what side X—— will take on any imaginable topic is a dangerous member of society. He possesses a degree of insight and perspicacity which it is not safe to have about! On the whole, I think that X—— does n't like æstheticism in Christian worship. But I dare not say that his paper will not be a furious abuse of Puritanism and an assertion that only by altar lights and superfrontals can the Church be saved! Still, do put him on. Better, a thousand times better, X—— in the wrong than Y—— in the right! X—— will be interesting at any rate, which Y—— never was, nor is, nor will be for ever and ever, Amen. Honestly, I have no serious doubt that his talk would all be on the side of simplicity and sense, and I should think he would be a first-rate man for the place."

To the familiar complaint that the churches were incompetent to distribute the bread of life, or were "trying to dam up the water of life that it might be distributed only to regular subscribers," Mr. Brooks replied:

"Such speeches have just enough truth in them to make them pungent, but they are not really true. The churches to-day are honestly trying to bring the water of life to all men. They blunder and they fail, but they try. And I do not know, for myself, any other agency with which I can combine such poor effort as I can make in that direction, except with them."

Mr. Brooks strove to keep in view the situation as it actually was,—there were men whose aim was to be good and to be useful, but who no longer went to church or cared to do so. He alluded to the relation of the church to such men, whom the community might hold in the highest respect, in a sermon preached at Appleton Chapel April 26, when his text was: "Watch ye therefore, and pray always that ye may be accounted worthy to escape all these things that shall come to pass, and to stand before the Son of man" (Luke xxi., 36). The division between church-goers and non-church-goers was not to be explained by the operation of a "special" and a "common grace," as the earlier Puritan divines had taught. There was fault upon both sides to be removed, but a common ideal held both classes in the same responsibility,— worthiness to stand before the Son of man.

In a letter to his brother, written during Lent, he alludes to details of parish life:

"233 CLARENDON STREET, BOSTON, March 28, 1885.

"DEAR ARTHUR,—You letter talking about things to happen

after Lent is over sounds delightful, but very far away and mystical, very like the most glorious and mysterious passages of the Revelation. But it will all come to pass in good time. Indeed it is nearer now than it seems. Confirmation is over, and there is only one more Bible class after to-night. I wonder if those innocent boys have any idea how much I dread the meetings, and how awfully I am afraid of them. I am startled at the idea of holding a "mission." I don't know how, and, so far as I do understand it, I don't think that I have the right sort of power. I have an idea that there are mysterious methods of which I am profoundly ignorant, and, besides, I have made tremendous resolutions about staying at home next winter and working up my parish, which is running down."

Easter Day fell on the 5th of April, and from that time he gave himself to the preparation of his address before the Boston Latin School. What the prayer he made at Harvard on Commemoration Day in 1865 was to the University, this oration was to the Boston Latin School on the occasion of its two hundredth anniversary. It revealed his genius in a new light: his insight into the meaning of events, his power of characterizing historic personages, the large atmosphere wherein he environed an institution, the exquisite sentences, the humor and the satire, the directness, the simplicity, the naturalness of it all,—these characteristics of Phillips Brooks were here seen in their conjunction and at their best. The address was given on April 23, 1885. It elicited boundless enthusiasm from a constituency representing old Boston and without a shadow of adverse criticism. It was as a teacher in the Latin School that he had made his conspicuous failure, in his first start in life.

The President of Trinity College, Hartford, Rev. Dr. Pynchon, wrote:

"TRINITY COLLEGE, HARTFORD, April 27, 1885.

"DEAR DR. BROOKS,—I was very sorry not to find you at home on Saturday. I wanted particularly to express to you my very high appreciation of your Latin School address. To say that it was a masterly oration, powerful and interesting and full of humor, and worthy of the most famous of the old school of Boston orators, would be but small praise, because I think its greatest merit consisted in wise lessons and in its certainty of being very useful. I hope a very large edition will be printed, and that a copy will be placed in every famil, of young children in the entire city, and especially in the hands of the rich and well-to-do people. It is a very great misfortune to them as well as to the public that they no longer send their children to the city schools, and particularly to the Latin School. The reason they give for not sending them there is the very reason for sending them, viz., that they may come into contact with the sons of the people, and grow up with them as part of them. It would be of the greatest benefit to them all their lives. For myself, I feel under a debt to the city of Boston which I can never repay. . . . I have had all my life a consciousness of dignity, as having been educated by the city of Boston, and have nourished a strong desire to be able to do something, some day, in return. It was this feeling that drew me to Boston the other day. . . . Your delineation of Mr. Gardner was to the life. It was truly a masterly portraiture. . . . I was delighted to hear everybody in Boston, from President Eliot down, say that this was positively the finest thing you have ever done. If so, it was simply because it was the offspring of filial devotion to the old school and its master. May the oration of the five-hundredth anniversary be equal to it!"

On Saturday, May 8, Mr. Brooks sailed for England by the Cunard steamer *Etruria*, arriving at Queenstown the following Saturday, after a passage of six days, twelve hours, and twenty-five minutes, regarded at the time as the best record made in ocean travelling. There were many friends in England who were expecting his coming. He was inundated with letters, before he left home, asking him to preach in many of the most important churches in London and elsewhere. When his arrival in England was announced, the flow of letters increased, reminding him of conditional promises he had made to preach here or there, on his previous visit. His first sermon was at St. Margaret's, Westminster. At the Abbey, where he preached June 7, the crowd was vaster than ever that surged into the church before the service began. His Grace the Archbishop of Canterbury, Dr. Benson, was not among the early comers, and secured but a poor place, where it was difficult to hear. Mr. Brooks alludes to the occasion briefly in one of his home letters: "Preached in Westminster Abbey to a host of people. The great place looked splendid, and it was fine to preach there."

Mr. Brooks had preached notable sermons in the Abbey, but the sermon on this occasion, on "The Mother's Wonder," from the text, "Son, why hast thou thus dealt with us?"

enhanced his reputation and brought to him many letters of gratitude. On June 11 he went to Caterham Valley to preach the ordination sermon at the request of the Bishop of Rochester, when there were forty candidates to be presented. At the Chapel Royal, Savoy, whose chaplain, Rev. Henry White, was another friend, he preached, on June 21, from the text: "As free, and not using your liberty for a cloak of maliciousness, but as the servants of God." In its issue for June 25 the London *Truth* refers to the occasion:

"The Chapel Royal, Savoy, was densely crowded on Sunday to hear Dr. Phillips Brooks preach his last [*sic*] sermon in London during his present visit to England. The multitude was so great that Dr. Brooks might well have imitated the practice of a former chaplain of the Savoy, the renowned Thomas Fuller, and redelivered his sermon in the garden which surrounds the Chapel, to the disappointed audience outside."

On Thursday, June 25, he preached twice, in the morning at St. Mark's, Kennington, and in the evening at Lincoln Cathedral. The following Sunday he preached in Salisbury Cathedral. If he could have accepted all the invitations which came to him, it would have required a sojourn of several months. But he found time to go again to Harrow, at the urgent request of the head master, Dr. Montagu Butler, and roused the boys with his stirring appeal. He went to a meeting in behalf of the mission at Delhi, where he spoke out of a full heart and from a knowledge of the actual situation. He was asked by the Bishop of Winchester, Dr. Harold Browne, to preach the sermon at the opening of the Church Congress, but was unable to comply with the request.

Two events stand out in this visit,—his reception at the two universities of Oxford and Cambridge. Dr. Jowett, the Master of Balliol, had long been desirous that he should come to Oxford. On Trinity Sunday, May 31, he preached to a crowded congregation in St. Mary's Church, among them a large number of senior members of the University, from the text Proverbs viii., 1, 22, 23; the sermon was published in part in the *Oxford Magazine* for June 3, and in full in the *Oxford Review*. He was already known and "welcomed, as the author of much of the delicate analysis of human motive and aspiration which in American literature we have learned to love."

He remained long enough at Oxford to become a "familiar figure" to the students. On Monday night, June 1, he was a guest of Trinity College. On the next day he was present at a congregation in Convocation House. On June 16 he went to Oxford for a second visit, to receive the honorary degree of Doctor of Divinity, where he was the guest of the Vice-Chancellor, and of Dr. Hatch, the author of the Bampton Lectures on the *Organization of the Early Christian Churches.* In a convocation held in the Sheldonian Theatre, on Tuesday, for the conferment of honorary degrees, the Vice-Chancellor presiding, Dr. Ince, the Regius Professor of Divinity, presented Mr. Brooks, recounting the circumstances of his career: how, not long after his ordination, he had gained recognition in America for keen intellectual power and remarkable eloquence; as an eloquent expounder, also, of the true Catholic faith. Some years ago his fame as an orator and preacher had reached England. The University had now been given an opportunity to hear him preach, and he could, therefore, plead his own claim best for the honor of a degree.

That the Regius Professor of Divinity at Oxford should commend Phillips Brooks as a defender of the Catholic faith, and that, too, in Oxford, the home of ecclesiastical conservatism, is in harmony with the impression he had made by his sermon at St. Mary's. He had taken for his text verses from that chapter in the book of Proverbs which reveals the influence of Hellenic thought upon the Hebrew mind, where the complex life of Deity is suggested by the personification of Wisdom: "The Lord possessed me in the beginning of his way, before his works of old. I was set up from everlasting, from the beginning, or ever the earth was." The sermon was marked by the richness of imagination which had characterized his earliest preaching. Those vigils at the Virginia seminary, when for the first time he was reading Philo and Origen, had borne their fruit, as in the ancient Church they had prepared the way for the fuller Christian faith. The subject of his sermon was "The Life in God."

"I have known that I was to come here and speak to you to-day, while the whole air of the place and of the church in which I spoke was full of the great truth to which this day belongs,—the truth of the Trinity; and I have thought much of how I might best make what I desired to say seem fitted to the spirit of this lofty festival. It has not seemed to me best, even if it were in my power, to enter into dogmatic definition of the doctrine which tries to sum up in itself the Christian's faith in God. Rather I have chosen to preach to you of Life, its glories and its possibilities, to try to make the men to whom I was to speak feel with a deep enthusiasm the splendor and the privilege of life as the mysterious gift of God.

"It has appeared to me that, speaking so, I should not be speaking in a way inappropriate to Trinity Sunday. For what is the truth of the Trinity? It is the truth of the richness of the Divine existence. The statement of the doctrine of the Trinity is the attempt to tell in our poor human language how manifold and deep and various is the life of God. This is the special meaning of the Feast of the Trinity. Other festivals of the Christian year remember what God *has done*. Christmas, Epiphany, declare the manifestations of His love and power in the experiences of His Son. Good Friday makes real anew, from year to year, the tragedy in which mercy and righteousness triumphed over sin and death. Whitsunday bears witness to His perpetual presence with mankind. Once in the year, on Trinity Sunday, the Church dares to lift herself up, and think with awe and loving fear of what God *is*. That is the sublimest occupation of the human mind. If the human mind dares to think itself equal to that occupation, dares to believe that it has fathomed God or surrounded God with its adventurous thought, how weak it grows in its audacity. But if, as it thinks of Him, it finds itself filled with this one truth concerning Him, that He is Life, that He is infinite and endless Life, that not in one tight compact personality but in a vastness and variety of being, which reaches our human nature on many sides, making it vital on them all, that so God the Creator, the Redeemer, the Inspirer, comes with His manifold living influence to man,—if so the Church of God can think of God on Trinity Sunday, then what a blessed, what a glorious festival it is. How all of human living and thinking becomes the stronger for its devout observance!"[1]

One of the undergraduates who was present when the degree was conferred recalls "the hearty applause which the appearance of Phillips Brooks commanded":

"More than any man I have ever known, Phillips Brooks possessed that which commanded instant trust, complete confidence,

[1] Cf. *The Oxford Review*, June 3, 1885, p. 354.

—a power not only the outcome of a splendid physique, eloquent of strength and protection, of a broad, quick, and ever-sympathetic mind, but of a great heart filled with love for all his fellow-beings, a love blind to all differences of class and race, and which, shining ever from his kindly eyes, lit up his face with a sunny smile, and made him godlike. I was an undergraduate at Christ Church when Oxford conferred the degree of D.D. upon him, and I shall never forget him as he appeared before the Vice-Chancellor—Jowett, I think—clad in his gown of crimson and scarlet, nor the surprise with which many of my Oxford friends regarded his splendid athletic proportions, and his perfectly formed head. . . . In applauding Phillips Brooks, men did not merely applaud a famous preacher. The praise was not that of the scholar, the artist, the athlete, but of those who felt instinctively when they saw him that here was a man as God intended a man to be; and there were no hands that were not busy clapping—even the heads of colleges forgot for once to remain unmoved."

On June 13 he went to Cambridge, to fulfil his appointment as one of the Select Preachers before the University. During his stay he was the guest of the Vice-Chancellor, Dr. Ferrar, and of Professor Jebb, whose acquaintance he had made in the American Cambridge. He had the pleasure of witnessing a boat race on Saturday afternoon. Among those invited to meet him were the late Professor Freeman, and Dr. Westcott, the late bishop of Durham. On Sunday he preached in Great St. Mary's, and his subject was chosen well for the place and the time,—in substance the first of his lectures on *Tolerance*, already referred to. The occasion has been described by the late Dr. Hort, the eminent New Testament scholar, in a letter to his wife dated June 14, 1885:

"St. Mary's was a strange sight to-day. The scaffolding was prominent, now moved into the middle of the church. The crowds were enormous, at least downstairs. I do not think I have seen so many M. A.'s for many years, and the ladies swarmed and overflowed everywhere. The undergraduates alone put in a *comparatively* poor appearance. The labors of the week had probably been too much for them. The sermon itself did make me very sorry indeed that you missed it. I do not know how to describe the rather peculiar appearance of Mr. Phillips Brooks. He is very tall, with a marked face and manner. It is a shame to compare him to so very unlike a man as Thackeray, but there was a real likeness; something, also, of Mr. Hotham *and* of Sedg wick! In the Bidding Prayer it was startling to hear him, "as in private duty bound," speak of Harvard College, in Cambridge, Massachusetts. He began, as Mr. Litchfield had described after hearing his Oxford sermon. with quite extraordinary rapidity. It was a great effort to catch what was said, the voice being at that time rather low and by no means emphatic, and the manner, though interesting to an intelligent hearer, was not impressive to any one who needed rousing. But in all these respects he improved as he went along, though almost always too fast. But the simplicity, reality, and earnestness could hardly have been surpassed, and I should imagine that few ever let their attention flag. The matter was admirable,—a carefully thought-out exposition of Maurice's doctrine of tolerance, as the fruit of strong belief, not of indifference. There was no rhetoric, but abundance of vivid illustrations, never irreverent, and never worked up for effect, but full of point and humor. Altogether it was one of the sermons that it is a permanent blessing to have heard. If possible, I will get an extra copy of the *Review* before afternoon post on Wednesday, that you may be able to read it." [1]

The sermon excited so much interest, and so many persons expressed a strong desire to possess it, that Mr. Brooks was requested to give it for publication, the Cambridge Mission offering to take the responsibility of an edition. But the offer was declined, as the sermon only represented in part what he had in him to say on the subject of tolerance.

There was a continuous round of lunches and dinners marking each day of the month that he remained in England. The earl of Aberdeen gave him the opportunity of spending a Sunday with Mr. Gladstone. The Archbishop of Canterbury and the Bishop of London were among his hosts at dinner parties. Among those whom he met for the first time were Tyndall and Huxley, Professor Bryce, and Mr. Bosworth Smith. The artistic side of his nature was kept in view by Mr. Edward Clifford the artist, under whose guidance he looked at the work of Burne-Jones and Rossetti. He had many friends among the English clergy, and he made many calls. Dr. Vaughan, Dean of Llandaff, and formerly Master of the Temple, writes to him:

"June 30, 1885.

"It was a refreshment to look upon you in the church and

1 *Life and Letters*, vol. ii., p. 317.

pulpit at Kennington, and to feel assured that the old strength, the old grace, the old love, were fresh and young in you still. May it be so for many a long year on both sides of the great deep! To have known you, to have had your kind thought and your kind wish, will always be a memory, and a hope too, to

"Your respectful, admiring, and loving friend,
"C. J. VAUGHAN."

Clergymen and laymen, people of every grade, told him what he had done for them; how he had brought consolation and faith and hope to many who were walking in darkness. He had extended his pastoral office till it passed the limits of nationality. As he leaves England he writes: "Everything here has been delightful. People have been very kind and invitations flow in in far greater numbers than I can accept them. I have left England (July 15) after a most delightful visit. It was full of interesting occurrences, and I shall look back upon it with the greatest pleasure." In another letter he speaks of his visits to Oxford and Cambridge and contrasts the two universities:

"In Oxford I have had two delightful visits; staying first with Jowett, and then with Hatch, who wrote the Bampton lectures about the organization of the Church. It is a curious world, full now of the freest thought running in the channels of the most venerable mediævalism, which is still strong and vigorous and controversial. Almost everybody you see in Oxford believes either too much or too little. It is hard to find that balanced mind, so rational yet so devout, so clear and yet so fair, with which we are familiar in the Club. Cambridge, where I also had a pleasant visit, seemed to me to be freer, but less interesting. It is less burdened with the past, and also, it would seem, less picturesquely illuminated by it."

The remainder of the summer was spent on the continent in the company of Mr. Robert Treat Paine and his family, who joined him as he was leaving England. The party travelled through Germany, stopping at Bonn and then going through the Tyrol to Venice. He wrote numerous letters in a reminiscent mood, reminding his friends of the mutual associations they had with the place where he was tarrying. The return brought back memories in which there was no alloy. In this invisible companionship of his friends, he looked again at Bellini and Titian, Tintoretto and Carpaccio, lounged in gondolas, went from Venice to

Switzerland, gazing upon old scenes with fresh eyes, recalling his first visions. He wrote in these idle days some of his charming letters to children where he indulged his gift for arrant nonsense, and yet showing capacity to read the heart of a genuine child.[1]

To Rev. W. N. McVickar he writes:

"ST. MORITZ, August 2, 1885.

"I cannot bear to let the whole summer pass without sending you a word of greeting, and so—how are you, my dear boy? In what happy fields are you walking, with what happy girls? And what fragile country vehicles are you overloading with your preposterous weight? For myself, I was informed by the scales of a remote but entirely trustworthy Tyrolese village the other day that I had lost forty pounds, and now weigh only a contemptible two hundred and sixty. Since then I have not blushed to look the meek diligence horses in the face, nor trembled as I stepped into the quivering gondola. I was there last week, at Venice, I mean. Antonio and Giovanni still haunt the quay in front of Danieli's, and tempt you to go with them and smoke Minghettis on the Grand Canal. Not only there, but in many places which I have touched this summer, the fragrance of your footsteps lingers, and often, when I have fallen asleep in the railroad cars, I have stirred at some slight noise which seemed to me to be Jimmy feeling for his roll."

While in Venice he heard of the death of General Grant:

"What a blessed release, after his brave waiting, and what a fine, strong, simple figure he will make in our history! There could not be a more distinctively American life and character than his."

To Archdeacon Farrar he sends thanks for the address he had made in Westminster Abbey on the national loss:

"LUCERNE, August 8, 1885.

"You cannot know how deeply it will touch the hearts of our people, and how they all will thank you for carefully studying and valuing one to whom they owe so much, and whose character has in many respects appealed to them so strongly. You have done very much to bring the nations very near to one another at this time when the heart of America is softened to receive lasting impressions."

[1] Cf. *Letters of Travel*, pp. 325 ff.

29

On the return from Switzerland he stopped at Paris, where he met M. Nyegaard, and he also listened for the first time to M. Bersier. To M. Nyegaard, after he had reached home, he wrote this letter:

"233 CLARENDON STREET, BOSTON, October 17, 1885.

"MY DEAR FRIEND,—I look back to the hours which we spent together in Paris with sincere delight. Do you remember that we spoke of Emerson, our American philosopher, whom I ventured to praise, and whom you said that you would read? I took the liberty, the other day, of sending you a copy of his works, which I trust you will do me the favor to accept as a token of my affectionate regard. I think you will find much in him to like as well as much with which you will profoundly disagree.

"I saw M. Bersier on the Saturday after we were together, and spent a very pleasant hour at his house. I was delighted with him. There is a vigorous and healthy manliness about him, mind and body, which refreshes and inspires.

"The next day I heard him preach, and the preacher was the man. You added a new favor to the many for which I already am your debtor when you took me to him.

"I have received the Dutch translation of my Lectures, *Boodschap en Getuigenis*. Ponderous and incomprehensible name! With it there came a courteous note from M. Valeton. I cannot read the book, but I turn its pages with interest and awe. It is a most tantalizing tongue. It always seems as if you ought to be able to read it, and you never can. I shall dare to hope that something in it may help some far-away Holland preachers and congregations whom I shall never see."

To Mr. Cooper, who had furnished an introduction to a little book whose object was to improve the ways of life among the poorer classes:

"233 CLARENDON STREET, Sunday evening, October 4, 1885.

"DEAR COOPER.—I thank you very much for sending me the pretty little story about *Alice Dean*. I have read it with great interest, and shall profit by it all I can. I have also read your introduction to it, and shall put it in practice right away. I read the paragraphs on pages four and five, and straightway had my study carpet swept, and put a dictionary and a commentary on the table, and ordered some plaster figures of a boy in the street for the mantelpiece, and hung your picture and Willie McVickar's in a good light, and told Katie to wash the table cloth, and set the table for supper; but there I came to a standstill. Whatever shall I do for a bright, cheerful, tidy wife, with clean children! These I cannot beg, borrow, or steal, and it is too late now to come by them in the regular way. So this workingman's heart will never leap with joy, or at least only half way. But there are plenty of other workingmen whom your little book will help, and it was a capital idea to have it printed."

One of Dr. Brooks's sermons, written in the fall, was on the text, " Luke, the Beloved Physician." Already there were in the air symptoms of the movement known as Christian Science. In this sermon he touches upon the organic relation between good health and good morals:

"The duty of physical health and the duty of spiritual purity and loftiness are not two duties; they are two parts of one duty, —which is living the completest life which it is possible for man to live. And the two parts minister to one another. Be good that you may be well; be well that you may be good. Both of these injunctions are reasonable, and both are binding on us all. Sometimes on one side come exceptions. Sometimes a man must give up being well in order to be good. Never does an exception come on the other side. Never is a man under the necessity of giving up being good in order to be well; but the normal life of man needs to be lived in obedience to both commands."[1]

He goes on to compare the clerical and the medical professions. Both are apt to lose sight of their ends in their means.

"Theology has driven human souls into exquisite agony with its cold dissection of the most sacred feelings, and medicine has tortured sensitive animals in a recklessness of scientific vivisection, which has no relation, direct or indirect, to human good."

The reference to vivisection brought to him a protest from a physician who urged that the real correlative to the clerical sin he mentioned was the very common medical sin of attending to the disease and ignoring the patient's personal needs. "The few physicians who vivisect in this country are our most humane men, respected and loved by us all." To this letter and to its protest Dr. Brooks replied:

"You are right about the sermon. The true correlative of the clerical sin in medical life is the one which you named and not

[1] Cf. *Sermons*, vol. v., p. 230.

the one which I named. I shall make the change, but I must still somewhere put in my word about vivisection. I do not know how much of cruelty there is. I know that there is some."

During the fall he gave up much of his time to the preparation of a chapter for the *Memorial History of Boston*, entitled " A Century of Church Growth,"[1] where he reviewed the history of the Episcopal Church. His address before the Boston Latin School had shown that he could make history as real to the imagination as the passing event of the day. He now made thorough preparation for what was to be small in its seeming result. He sought for light on the personality of every name. He studied the data in the history of each parish, scanning its reports for the symptoms of life, however feeble its outward existence. Nothing seemed small or unworthy. But he kept in full view the larger life of the time in order to give the true setting. There breaks forth, now and then, a sense of humor at the situation. After going through the records of the episcopates of Bass, Parker, Griswold, and Eastburn, he sighs, "O for a touch of genius!"

Mr. Brooks had been requested by his brother to make some inquiries while in England in regard to clergy who were said to have accomplished successful results in holding missions. In carrying out the request he had become interested in the subject for himself. But it was with hesitation, and only after misgivings overcome, that he committed himself to approving the idea which the mission involved. For the mission seemed to imply that the regular work of the parish minister was not by itself sufficient to awaken an interest in religion, and that the pastor must go outside of his parish for aid. He deprecated the evils of the revival system, with wandering, irresponsible evangelists who caused ephemeral excitement by drawing crowds to whom the ordinary ministrations of the churches were dull. It was an effort to introduce into the Episcopal Church what many regarded as an element foreign to its ways. "On the whole," he writes to his brother Arthur, "I am very glad it [the mission] is to take place. It will at least break the rigidity of the church's ways, and strike the true keynote of preaching. Boston will be ready when New York has proved that it is the true thing to do."

[1] Cf. *Essays and Addresses*, where it is published in separate form.

The usual routine of work in the fall was varied by the visit to this country of Archdeacon Farrar, who during his stay in Boston was the guest of Mr. Brooks, and on All Saints' Day preached for him in Trinity Church. Mr. Brooks had been looking forward to the visit, and had done what he could to bring it about by urging it upon his friend. He was anxious that Dr. Farrar should see the country to advantage. He rejoiced in the cordial welcome everywhere given to Dr. Farrar, as helping to bring England and America to that better understanding of each other which should lead to international amity.

On Thanksgiving Day, he chose for his text the words describing the dream of Nebuchadnezzar: "I saw a dream which made me afraid, and the thoughts upon my bed and the visions of my head troubled me,"—where "the Babylonian king had summed up his realm in his feelings." The subject of the sermon was "The Temper of a Time," how one ought to feel in the days which were passing. For our own time this was the summary: (1) great sense of danger; (2) great expectation; (3) great hope in man; (4) great trust in God. He dwelt on the function of wonder as indispensable to any man or age. He passed in review the current feeling in regard to social changes, mechanical discoveries, and theological disturbances. It was indispensable for a man, if he would help his age, that he should be a man of the time. A value was to be set upon every movement which was in the right direction, however slight or unconnected, because no man could say how or where it would ultimate. There should be an earnest desire to get at the heart of things under their form,—yet keeping forms,—the mixture of conservatism and radicalism. He saw grounds for hope in the pursuit of mechanical discoveries and pointed out their true value. Everything should be valued which tended to increase true faith in and true hope for man in the reign of the coming democracy. Let religion grow deeper and more simple. Freedom was the word to be applied as a test in the political confusion which threatened to dissolve political parties. But the supreme need was for strong *moral* purpose, as the ground and basis of everything.

Although Phillips Brooks was an optimist, he was forced to wrestle in secret with the foes of hope. He could not assume that all was well until he had measured the motives which begot the pessimism. He found them in the theoretical philosophy of fatalism, in partial views of life, in personal disappointment, in an affectation of contempt. "Pessimism comes from and tends to the loss of individuality." While he was engaged in working up a sermon on the subject, texts of Scripture flashed upon his mind: "In the daytime he led them with a cloud, and all the night through with a light of fire." Every theist must be an optimist, but before one could say, "The Lord is good," he must take in the range of the divine activity: "See now that I, even I, am He, and there is no God with me. I kill and I make alive, I wound and I heal; neither is there any that can deliver out of my hand." He saw a truth in pessimism, something from which an inspiration for higher living could be obtained. He condemns the folly of vague optimism as of vague pessimism, or of vagueness anywhere. "Define yourself." Schopenhauer he designates as a "scared pessimist." Christ's view of man must be the true one—"not to condemn the world, but that the world through Him might be saved"; and yet He says, "For judgment have I come into this world." The salvation from pessimism is in the unselfish service of men. To get at the facts of life and place them in their true light is the first duty. Much of the pain in the world comes from memory and from anticipation, from the past and from the future, not from the present. He repeats the lines of Victor Hugo:

> "C'est le bonheur de vivre
> Qui fait la gloire de mourir."

He recalls, in a picture of Domenichino's, at Bologna, the little angel trying the point of one of the thorns in the Crown of Thorns with his finger. He notes the correspondence of general human good and ill, hope and despair, with the same in the personal life. "Progress must be seen as law, as well as fact. There remains, (1) the perpetual faith with which men trust each other; (2) the hopefulness with which they want to live; (3) the complacency with which they see their children start out in life. "The Lord is good.' The book Ecclesiastes gives the picture,—enjoyment with a background of judgment; neither wanton self-indulgence nor cynical pleasure and hatred; neither idle optismism nor wanton pessimism."

Among the sermons which issued from the inward process, weighing the materials of his own life as well as studying the world around him, there are three, written at this time or very nearly: the "Battle of Life" (1885),[1] the "Giant with the Wounded Heel" (1886),[2] and the "Sword Bathed in Heaven" (1886.)[3] In these sermons, the types of many others, there is the tone of a man in the thick of mortal combat, a giant in the toils, and yet in the process of escape, who discerns light and victory. The essential characteristic of human life, which the age is in danger of overlooking, is perpetual warfare,—of all life, whether in celestial regions or in earthly places. God is in the conflict as well as every man, and the battle is of Titanic proportions. There is victory for every man, though the type of human life at its best must be the giant with the wounded heel. There is victory for every man, but on one condition, that the sword with which he fights must have been bathed in heaven.

To the Hon. George F. Hoar, senator from Massachusetts, who wrote Mr. Brooks, asking why St. Paul, in the midst of his lofty statement of the great doctrine of immortality, in the fifteenth chapter of First Corinthians, should break the connection by the thirty-third verse, "Evil communications corrupt good manners," Mr. Brooks sends a letter, interesting and characteristic, as though he read the apostle through the knowledge of himself:

"233 CLARENDON STREET, BOSTON, DECEMBER 3, 1885.

"MY DEAR SIR,—I am sure that we must all have been struck, as you have been, by the curiously incongruous tone of the thirty-third verse of St. Paul's fifteenth chapter of his First Epistle to the Corinthians.

"I have been in the habit of finding the explanation, first, in the fact that the verse is a quotation (from Menander), and one, no doubt, so familiar to the people that it had become a proverb; and, second, that the Greek words had none of that particular tone which belongs to the words which our English translators used; particularly the word 'manners,' which surely has not either the dignity or the range of the Greek ἤθη.

"At the same time, it seems to me to be altogether characteristic of St. Paul to interrupt a glowing and lofty argument by a

---

[1] Cf. *Sermons*, vol. vi.
[2] Cf. *Ibid.*, vol. iv.
[3] Cf. *Ibid.*

few words of special and homely exhortation and warning suggested by what he is saying, then resuming his argument all the more loftily beyond. Such passages are not, I think, uncommon with him. Certainly they bring out very forcibly the way in which the two impulses, of high speculation and of care for men's behavior and character, were both always present with him; and I have come to feel that in this particular passage the two impulses add to each other's vividness and force.

"There are a few words on these verses in Dean Stanley's *Commentary on the Epistles to the Corinthians*, which seem to me to be suggestive, I am, my dear sir,
            " Yours most sincerely,
                        " PHILLIPS BROOKS."

On the 13th of December, 1885, Phillips Brooks crossed the line, the approach to which he had been dreading, and kept his fiftieth birthday. He seems to make light of the event, saying, "I reached the half century, and shook myself as I started out upon another half century." But this is on the surface. In reality he was beginning to assume that youth was over. He began to speak of himself as old. In addressing young men he would assume that he was a spectator of the scene in which they were the actors. When he was remonstrated with for taking such a tone, which only pained those who listened to him and who were surprised at his saying of himself what they did not believe was true, he would answer that he supposed he felt it or he would not say it.

To Rev. G. A. Strong he writes:

            " December 24, 1885.

"I was fifty a week ago last Sunday and you are—who can say how old? Well, no doubt it is all right, but there is getting to be a very 'John Anderson my Jo John' feeling about it all which I don't like nearly so well as the old cheery, hopeful feeling of the days when —— and —— were daily and hourly visions. I send you still with my own venerable hand, like Paul the aged, my best thanks and heartiest good wishes. . . .
            " Ever affectionately,
                        "P. B."

The following extracts are from his note-book made while travelling during the summer of 1885:

"Sermon on the impulse every now and then in every one to get loose from the despotic course of life and break things. The Radical in everybody. The love of camping out."

"Sermon on 'As he thinketh in his heart, so is he.' Cf. Descartes, *Cogito, ergo sum.* The relation of thought to life."

"As crossing a Paris or a London street, when we are half way over, we cease to look for danger on the one side, and begin to fear it only on the other, so of growing old."

"Some men make themselves God, without knowing what they are doing. The deity they appeal to is really their deeper, higher self. When they feel God's approval, it is really their own self-praise. When God reproaches them, it is their own self-rebuke. When they go apart from the world to hold communion with Him, it really is an entrance into their own self-consciousness. To other men some good fellow-man, more or less consciously and completely enlarged into an ideal of humanity, answers the same purpose, and is in reality their God. To still others, a vague presence of a high purpose and tendency felt in everything. Tennyson's 'one increasing purpose,' and Arnold's 'something not ourselves which makes for righteousness.' This fulfils the end and makes the substitute for God. But none of these supply the place of a true personality outside ourselves, yet infinitely near to us."

"Clear plea for search after *truth* in religion, as distinct from search for *pleasure* or for *safety*. Protest against æsthetic ritualism and against stubborn orthodoxy."

"Text: 'The summer is ended.' For most of us, the ship going *home*. A period of relaxation over. A touch of disappointment. It must be so wherever there is no real ideality and lofty hope. The summer a ripening of spring seed into autumn fruit. True value of foreign travel in ripening *home* affections and connections. The unity of a life is in *God*. His nearness. The summer and the whole year conception of life make it depend on God as *the sun*.
"There is a true and a false simplicity, and when the time comes that simplicity is desired it makes all the difference whether we choose the true.
"Such a time does come—hatred of all complication, in all deeper moods, in all mature life. Then shall you get simplicity by exorcism or by centrality?
"1. In civilization. Let us return to barbarism, let us cut

off elaborations? Not so! But let us get sight of the one increasing purpose.

"2. In the personal nature. Give us the simple man? Nay, so you get the meagre man. Give us the manifold man, with one great purpose.

"3. In thought. Let us stop this ranging of thought everywhere? But no, let us think devoutly.

"4. In action. Let us stop and come down to simple life? No, but men should be nobler by it all."

"Text: 'Be still, and know that I am God.' God's great assertion of existence, as if that were so much. 'Be still,'—the hush of this endless talk.

"The perplexities of life (labor, etc.), ignoring first principles and the deeper powers at work. The whole return to what seems pure theism. Battling in God."

CHAPTER XVIII.

1886.

ESSAY ON BIOGRAPHY. ELECTION AS ASSISTANT BISHOP OF PENNSYLVANIA. VISIT TO CALIFORNIA. VIEWS ON IMMIGRATION. ABOLITION OF COMPULSORY ATTENDANCE ON RELIGIOUS SERVICES AT HARVARD. NORTH ANDOVER. CHAUTAUQUA ADDRESS ON "LITERATURE AND LIFE." DEATH OF RICHARDSON. FOURTH VOLUME OF SERMONS. PROTEST AGAINST CHANGING THE NAME OF THE PROTESTANT EPISCOPAL CHURCH.

IN the spring of 1886 Dr. Brooks was elected Assistant Bishop of Pennsylvania, in succession to Rt. Rev. William Bacon Stevens, whose infirmities called for aid in his episcopal duties. When the question was brought before him he wrote to Rev. W. F. Paddock, of Philadelphia:

"February 26, 1886.

"My DEAR PADDOCK,—The idea of you writing to me like that! You, that have known me from my infancy, that have played with me on the pleasant slopes of Shooter's Hill, that have roamed with me in St. George's, that have preached side by side with me in Philadelphia! That you should think that now, in my declining years, I would be a bishop! No, my dear fellow, I was not made for such a fate. Stop, I beseech you, any movement that looks at all towards setting me up for that most unsuitable place. Kill it in the nest! Nip it in the bud! Blight it or ere it be sprung up! Yet let me not appear like a fool, declining and rejecting an office which I never have had offered me! This letter is for your own friendly eye alone, and I tell you, as if we sat upon the steps of St. George's and talked it over, that I am neither suited nor inclined to be a bishop, nor do I see how any thing could make me one. There!"

As the time for the election approached the feeling was universal among his friends that he must be chosen the Bishop of Pennsylvania. Phillips Brooks took a special interest in the subject because he hoped that Dr. McVickar, of Holy Trinity Church (now Bishop of Rhode Island), would be elected. Against Dr. McVickar, however, an objection had been urged that on a certain occasion he had gone to hear a lecture by the Rev. James Freeman Clarke, an eminent Unitarian minister of Boston. To a prominent layman in Philadelphia, who assured Mr. Brooks he could be elected, and urged him to accept, he wrote this letter in reply:

"CHICAGO, ILLINOIS, May 2, 1886.

"DEAR MR. C.,—Let me say how good I think you are to want me to be your bishop after all you have seen of me for this last quarter of a century. I cannot bring myself to think it best, partly because I do not think I would make a good bishop, and partly because I am so disgusted that McVickar should be so contemptibly thrown over for such an absurd reason. Why, my dear Mr. C., I would go and hear Freeman Clarke every week if I had a chance. If even you, who represent McVickar's friends, call that an 'indiscreet act,' why, I think the diocese deserves a Mr. X—— or worse! A man may go and hear mummeries at St. Clement's, or twaddle at a hundred churches, but if he goes to hear a great man and an old saint talk essential Christianity under another name, he is said to have denied Christ, and a thousand other foolish things. No. Gather around McVickar. Do not feebly apologize for him, but defend and approve him, and declare your manly contempt for this kind of opposition to him; and if he is defeated upon this ground, let him fall honorably in the midst of his friends, and let Mr. X—— have the diocese. I do not know why anybody should want it if that is the stuff it is made of."

When the convention met on May 5, after eight ballots had been taken without result, on the ninth ballot Dr. Brooks was elected, receiving eighty-two clerical votes,—a majority of two of the total number of votes cast, and a plurality of sixteen over the vote for the rival candidate. The clerical vote was at once ratified by that of the laity, the lay vote standing sixty-four to thirty-three.

The news of his election reached him by telegraph in the West, in the Territory of New Mexico. Although his decision was a foregone conclusion, he reserved his formal answer until he should have taken two weeks for consideration. There was no lack of pressure to induce him to accept. Among many letters was one from a clergyman who wrote:

"I am emboldened by what I believe is a fact which has several times appeared in your life, and which convinces me that you possess the rare power of revising and changing your purposes, even when most deliberately and conscientiously formed, provided sufficient reason to do so is made evident to you. You shrank back from the first work you were called to in Philadelphia,—in the Church of the Advent. You shrank back still more from the call to Holy Trinity, and again God mercifully led you to reconsider your refusal. When you went to Boston, it was only after you had said No, and had thought it your duty not to go."

Before sending his formal letter to the Convention declining the election he wrote to Dr. McVickar:

"SANTA FÉ, NEW MEXICO, May 9, 1886.

"How is it that you have allowed this thing to come about? Surely my declaration to Cooper was plain and positive enough. To that I hold, and when your letter comes I shall decline. My dear, dear Boy, I would do otherwise and be your bishop if I could, but I cannot. You will not think on such a question as this that I have been, or am, light or frivolous or prejudiced. I have considered it earnestly and solemnly. I did not think that there was any chance of my being elected, but I considered it exactly as if I thought there was, and conscience, soul, and judgment all said NO! I see no reason whatsoever for a change. I am sorry to compel another convention and election, but I cannot let myself take a place which is not mine simply to save that trouble. Besides, in some sense, it is the Convention's fault, for I said, clearly as I knew how, that I could not accept.

"You will not think I am ungrateful to you all. I love you dearly. That my old friends should have proposed me and elected me touches me more deeply than I can say, nor am I careless of the pleasure it would be to come and live in the old places with the old friends and new. Nor am I foolishly contemptuous of the episcopate. But simply *I must not.* I am not made for it. I can do better work elsewhere than *I* could do as bishop. So my decision is *absolute and final*, and when your committee's formal letter comes, I shall write and say that you must choose again. I am so heartily sorry that my telegram to Cooper did not come before the Convention had adjourned. Then you could have made your other choice at once."

On May 24 he wrote him again, from San Francisco:

"I have declined. I sent the letters yesterday. I told them all beforehand how it must be so, and said that if they chose me I could not accept,—and yet they chose me. I do not complain of that, I should be a beast if I did. They were very good, and I am proud of their regard. But this choice does not bring anything to change my previous judgment. It was by a bare majority, and after considerable struggle. It simply presents the chance to be bishop which I had considered in its possibility before, and yet I have carefully considered it again. Along the arid plains of Arizona I turned it over in the thing I call my mind. Under the orange trees of Pasadena I let it soak into me with the sunshine. Among the cataracts of Yosemite I listened to the tempting invitation. But it was no good. I could not see myself there doing those things that a bishop does, and so I wrote a formal letter (true, though, every word of it) to the committee, and declined; so now that is all over. . . .

"What a queer town this is, and who would live here if he could live anywhere else! But some of the beauty of this great Pacific slope passes one's dreams. I am ashamed some times to think what a Yankee I am, that all the beauty of the rest of the world makes me love our own ugly little corner of it all the more intensely."

From the Bishop of the Diocese of Massachusetts, he received this letter of congratulation:

"ASHFIELD, May 15, 1886.

"MY DEAR BROTHER,—Yesterday at our Diocesan Missionary Meeting at Amherst I saw the announcement that you had decided to remain at your present field of labor, and decline the honorable and great work to which you had been called in Pennsylvania. I rejoice that you can see it your duty to stay with us and still contribute so greatly as God has enabled you to do to the building up of His Church in our Diocese and of His kingdom in the hearts of men. May He increase and multiply your great influence for good in your present field, and justify by your abiding work and holy success your decision that your present field is your post of duty.

"I do not know what we should have done had you gone from us; and with many other considerable cares, I am truly thankful that I have not got to work out that problem.

"I am, dear Brother, yours sincerely,

"BENJ. H. PADDOCK."

It was thought by some that Mr. Brooks had scant respect

for the office of a bishop. He may have expressed himself carelessly on the subject, and given rise to the impression. He was alive to the incongruousness of the situation when the office was not adequately filled. But he had nothing of the Puritan dislike for the office in itself. Whenever personal criticism went so far as to suggest such a thought, he quickly and strongly resented it. The office was a high one, he would then assert, and it only needed to see the right man in its occupancy to bring out its charm and its efficiency. He hoped the day would come, as he remarked in one of his letters on the subject, when "the episcopate will stand not simply for the restraint and regulation, but for the inspiration of the Church."

While Mr. Brooks was in California, his attention was called for the first time to the question of the restriction of immigration to this country, particularly of the Chinese. To Mr. R. T. Paine he writes, June 1, 1886:

"One thing all the Americans say about the Chinamen,—that no more must come. All intelligent people own that they could not have done, and could not now do, without them, and would by no means drive out those that are here; but they would let in no more. The unanimity on this last point is striking. I have not met with an exception. And yet one is much struck also by hearing the best of qualities,—thrift, industry, self-control, and patience,—so often made a large part of the burden of indictment against the poor Mongolian. Certainly the look of Chinatown and its inhabitants is surprisingly prepossessing when one considers that he is seeing the very dregs and refuse of a race. If these are the lowest, the highest specimens must be something very good indeed.

"I have had a lot of correspondence about the episcopate in Pennsylvania. There was no moment when I thought of going. How could I, so long as I dared to believe that you all still wanted me to stay in Boston? Will you tell me, honestly and truly, and like a friend, when you think it is best to go away? Until you do, I shall rejoice to come back year after year and do the best I can. I am going back this year, taking it for granted that my work in Trinity is not yet done."

Among the motives holding him to his work in Boston was his relation to Harvard University. A change was now impending, when the University would rely upon his moral support. One of the chief difficulties which confronted the Board of Chaplains was the question of compulsory attendance on prayers. They encountered a feeling which had long been growing among the students, that it was not becoming that attendance on religious services should be required.

For several years the subject had been under discussion by the Faculty, the Overseers, and the Corporation. President Eliot and Mr. Ralph Waldo Emerson were among those who deprecated the growing opinion among the students, and were averse to the abandonment of a requirement which went back in its origin to the foundation of Harvard College, and was also established in other colleges and institutions of learning throughout the country. It was feared that " the abandonment of this time-honored custom would be fraught with serious consequences to the whole fabric of our civilization." Phillips Brooks had at first been firm in resisting the change. A petition of the students in 1885 had been referred to a committee of three, of which he was a member, to give the question thorough consideration, and return a final and exhaustive answer to the students' request. It was a relief to many when the answer came that Harvard remained true to the ancient ways. One of the reasons given for rejecting the petition was that "Harvard College can ill afford the loss of reputation which would ensue on its being the first of all literary institutions in New England to abandon religious observances." That the petition had a large number of signatures attached was regarded as of no significance seeing that "it is well known how easily such signatures are obtained." It was assumed that if students were not required to go to prayers they would not go.

Hardly, however, had Phillips Brooks signed the report than his mind began to go beneath the surface of both the petition and its answer. It might be possible that the students had better reasons for their request than they alleged. It was possible that they would continue their attendance, even if it were not required. If religion was natural for man and made its appeal to what was genuinely human, it might be thrown on its own native resources without being bolstered up by extraneous authority. It pained him to call in question the sincerity or earnestness of those who had signed the petition. The thing to do was to find out whether the sentiment of the students as a whole was averse to compulsory prayers, and then to trust and to honor their feeling in the matter as having some positive significance.

In February, 1886, the students renewed their petition. In May the first Board of Chaplains was appointed, and in June Phillips Brooks, in his place as one of the Board of Overseers, stood up and advocated the abolition of compulsory attendance on prayers, declaring further his unwillingness to officiate as a chaplain of the College unless the change were conceded. He did not argue for the change as a concession merely to the expressed wishes of the students, but as in itself the ideal arrangement, to be adopted because of its inherent fitness. There was surprise at the reversal of his attitude. But his influence was great; he was willing to take the responsibility; it could not hurt the College if it was known that he approved the change, and his name would be a guarantee of the success of the voluntary system; there was nothing else to do after his bold declaration of his faith in the new method. In taking this position Mr. Brooks had the support of the other chaplains associated with him. Their first joint act after their appointment was to recommend that attendance on prayers be voluntary, and the recommendation was approved by the Corporation and the Overseers. In the fall of 1886 the new arrangement went into operation. From this time he co-operated earnestly with the Rev. F. G. Peabody, who had been elected to the Plummer professorship and was president of the Board of Chaplains, to insure the success of the new scheme. He writes him, "Pray use me in any way, at any time, and do not let even Cambridge quench your hope."

With Mr. Brooks originated the brief address of three minutes. At the request of the students he said a few words before closing each service, and from this the custom grew until it became the general rule. It imposed a harder task upon the chaplains, but it tended to vitalize the occasion, to prevent it from becoming a religious formality.

Two characteristic addresses belong to this year, one on " Biography," delivered at Phillips Academy, Exeter, and published in pamphlet form "at the request of many teachers"; the other, entitled "Literature and Life," read before the Chautauqua Assembly at Framingham. In both addresses the interest centres

30

in human life and its interpretation. Every one, it is said, has his distinctive word. The ever recurring word with Phillips Brooks was "Life" with its epithets "rich," "large," and "full." The word appears in the titles of many of his best known sermons: the "Symmetry of Life," the "Withheld Completions of Life," the "Battle of Life," the "Shortness of Life," the "Seriousness of Life," the "Positiveness of the Divine Life," the "Liberty of the Christian Life," the "Eternal Life," "New Starts in Life," the "Sacredness of Life," "Whole Views of Life," the "Law of the Spirit of Life."

In the essay on "Biography" he appears as an omnivorous reader of biographies, so that when he came to speak it was from the fulness of knowledge combined with critical capacity for estimating the art of biography:

"I think that I would rather have written a great biography than a great book of any other sort, as I would rather have painted a great portrait than any other kind of picture.

"The New Testament is a biography. Make it a mere book of dogmas, and its vitality is gone. Make it a mere book of laws, and it grows hard and untimely. Make it a biography, and it is a true book of life. Make it the history of Jesus of Nazareth, and the world holds it in its heart forever.

"I believe fully that the intrinsic life of any human being is so interesting that if it can be simply and sympathetically put in words, it will be legitimately interesting to other men. There is not one of us living to-day so simple and monotonous a life that, if he be true and natural, his life faithfully written would not be worthy of men's eyes and hold men's hearts. Not one of us, therefore, who, if he be true and pure and natural, may not, though his life never should be written, be interesting and stimulating to his fellow-men in some small circle as they touch his life."

He condemns the statement of Ruskin that "the lives in which the public are interested are hardly ever worth writing." Notable and exceptional lives are entitled to biography, and "distinction is a legitimate object of our interest."

"Distinction is the emphasis put upon qualities by circumstances. He who listens to the long music of human history hears the special stress with which some great human note was uttered long ago, ringing down the ages and mingling with and

enriching the later music of modern days. It is a perfectly legitimate curiosity with which men ask about that resonant, far-
reaching life. They are probably asking with a deeper impulse
than they know. They are dimly aware that in that famous,
interesting man their own humanity—which it is endlessly
pathetic to see how men are always trying and always failing
to understand—is felt pulsating at one of its most sensitive and
vital points."

He gives the highest place to Boswell's *Johnson* and Lock-
hart's *Scott:*

"The streets of London and the streets of Edinburgh live
to-day with the images of these two men more than any others
of the millions who have walked in them. But in a broader way
the streets of human nature still live with their presence. The
unfading interest in Dr. Johnson is one of the good signs of English character. Men do not read his books, but they never cease
to care about him. It shows what hold the best and broadest
human qualities always keep on the heart of man."

He observes that there are some very great men who are unsuited for biography; among them Shakespeare, Shelley, and
Wordsworth. The lives of these men are in their poetry. The
more profound and spiritual the poet, the more impossible a
biography of him becomes. And finally the rule in reading
biographies should be to divest one's self of the literary sense as
far as possible, and read only to get the man. "Then you may
close and lose and forget the book. The man is yours forever."

Among the writings of Phillips Brooks the essay on "Literature and Life"[1] holds an important place, valuable in itself for its
suggestions admirable as an introduction to the study of literature; but also important because it gives the method of his own
work, revealing the springs of his enthusiasm and the sources of
his power. His theme is that "life underlies literature and is the
greater thing." "It is possible to treat almost any book so that
the literary quality will disappear and the pulsations of the
life beneath be felt." "Men must live before they can make
literature."

"Very impressive and mysterious and beautiful are these

[1] These essays, on "Biography" and on "Literature and Life," are included in the volume of his *Essays and Addresses*.

noble years in the life of a people or a man, which are so full of living that they had no time or thought for writing.

"How many of us can remember it in our own lives, the time when life claimed utterance and clumsily, shamefacedly, secretly, but with a dim sense of crossing a line and entering a new condition, we wrote something,—a poem, an essay, a story,—something which gave literary expression to life."

He was asking himself why it was that in the last years of the nineteenth century there seemed to be a falling away in the quality of high literature. He thinks that the relations between life and literature are very delicate and easily disturbed:

"Life may become too strong for literature. There is a question whether it be not so to-day, when the world is intensely and vehemently alive. It may be the former methods and standards are not sufficient for the expression of the growing life, its new activities, its unexpected energies, its feverish problems. If the social perplexities of the age could be set forth in a more competent literature, catching the true meaning of the situation, then the pent-up torrent of life would find easier vent and open into broader, juster, and more charitable thought. Under these circumstances a man must believe in the future more than he reverences the past."

After returning from his trip to the West, Mr. Brooks took up his residence at North Andover for the summer, where, as he writes, "there is peace and quiet to a terrible degree. I go down to Boston on Sundays and wake myself up with preaching to a miscellaneous summer congregation, and then go back to my bucolic cares." He tries to get his old friends to meet together with him there, and "talk over the universe," but the scheme was not realized. To Mr. Cooper he writes:

"July 3, 1886.

"Another journey is finished without accident. I have seen the Pacific, and now here I am, thankful and peaceful among my acres and bucolic cares at North Andover. The grass is to be sold this afternoon at public auction out behind the barn, and that makes me a little anxious and restless this morning. Except for that, I am very well and happy, and hope these few lines will find you the same.

"And you are coming week after next! I am sure you will not pass me by, but will look in and see my farming. There is nothing in the world to do. You shall not be bothered to go and see the cattle, for there are none; nor the kitchen garden, for there is n't any; nor even the chickens, for there is only one poor lone rooster, which the man who kept the place last winter could n't catch, but left behind him when he went away. No, you shall sit on the piazza and smoke, and sit in the study and smoke, and sit under the trees and smoke, and we will talk Pennsylvania and California, and you shall tell me all about the queer, queer things which have gone on in Philadelphia since the first of May."

His recreation at North Andover was in driving a quiet horse through Boxford and adjacent towns, when he dressed in a most unclerical garb and seemed to enjoy it as if it were the proper thing to enjoy. But in his manner he had grown more quiet and subdued. In the course of these excursions he came to the ancient town of Rowley, where the first Samuel Phillips, son of the George Phillips who was the founder of the family, had spent his long life. A call at the parsonage for the minister, who could have told him much that he wanted to know, was fruitless; for in the quiet of those summer afternoons, peaceful like a continuous Sabbath, the minister had the custom of retiring to the prophet's chamber on the wall, and was fast asleep while his distinguished visitor was knocking at the door. But there was a monument to be seen, erected to the memory of this distant ancestor. The only relic which survived of him in the town was a fragment of a sermon on the "sin of wearing long hair." But there were traditions to the effect that "he combined culture of mind, tenderness and sympathy of heart, and well-balanced Christian living."

In the retirement of North Andover Mr. Brooks was thinking much of Richardson, whose death had moved him deeply. He speaks of him in a letter: "Richardson is off alone on his long journey. I wonder how long it is." In an article for the *Harvard Monthly* (October, 1886), he paid a tribute to his character and genius. The qualities he discerned and selected for praise are those which the two men held in common, and which served to draw them together,—the instinctive and spontaneous character of his genius, expressing great ideas, based upon thorough study, and yet of which he could give no account as to how they came to him; he was "not a man of theories," but "his life passed into his buildings by ways too subtle even for himself to understand." "He grew simpler as he grew older." "Whoever came in contact with his work felt that the wind blew out of an elemental simplicity, out of the primitive life and qualities of man."

"The loss which his death brought to his friends it is not possible to describe.   It is a change in all their life.   When some men die it is as if you had lost your penknife, and were subject to perpetual inconvenience until you could get another.   Other men's going is like the vanishing of a great mountain from the landscape, and the outlook of life is changed forever.
"His life was like a great picture full of glowing color.   The canvas on which it was painted was immense.   It lighted all the room in which it hung.   It warmed the chilliest air.   It made, and it will long make, life broader, work easier, and simple strength and courage dearer to many men."

Mr. Brooks was occupied during the summer with the preparation for the press of his fourth volume of sermons, which appeared in the fall with the title *Twenty Sermons*, and was dedicated to the memory of his brother Frederick.   The book has a distinct character from his other volumes of sermons, and reflects the tone of his later preaching.   This is apparent in the sermon on "The Man with Two Talents," where his object was to show how the average man may become great and almost infinitely multiply his gifts by living in the consciousness of God. The power of the God-consciousness is also brought out in one of its most profound and far-reaching aspects in the sermon on "Standing before God," where he meets the difficulty which the mind encounters in thinking of immortality, because of the countless millions of human souls who have lived or are yet to live on the earth, till the insignificance of any one soul in the infinite throng overcomes the conviction of its priceless value. "The Knowledge of God" is the title of another sermon, where he makes his plea against what is called agnosticism.   His chief argument is built upon the fact of Christ's unconquerable conviction as in the words, "As the Father knoweth me, even so know I the Father":

"Surely it must forever stand as a most impressive and significant fact, a fact that no man who is trying to estimate the worth and strength of spiritual things can leave out of his account, that the noblest and most perfect spiritual being whom this world has ever seen, the being whom the world with most amazing unanimity owns for its spiritual pattern and leader, was sure of God. I cannot get rid of the immense, the literally unmeasurable, meaning and value of that fact."

There are sermons here which are the outcome of that consciousness of humanity in which he lived. The sense of sin, the evil in life, the conception of life as a tragic struggle between hostile forces where God and man seem to be arrayed against each other, the mystery of the conflict and its appalling proportions,— these things are brought out in sermons revealing the preacher's power. In a sermon entitled "Destruction and Fulfilment" he traces the beneficent evidence of human progress. When we read the sermon on "Going up to Jerusalem," it seems to have a prophetic character, as though the preacher, in urging upon his hearers to gain some clearer perception of the appointed result toward which the steady tendency of their lives was growing, was thinking and speaking of himself. Life was changing for him now to its last appointed phase. From this time his own face was set, like that of the Master before him, to go up to Jerusalem; and when friends remonstrated and would fain hold him back, he went steadily forward, and as they looked after him in his stride toward the end, they were amazed. "Do not pray for easy lives. Do not pray for tasks equal to your powers. Pray for powers equal to your tasks. If the life which you have chosen to be your life is really worthy of you, it involves self-sacrifice and pain. If your Jerusalem really is your sacred city, there is certainly a cross in it. Ask God to fill you with Himself, and then calmly look up and go on. Go up to Jerusalem expecting all things that are written concerning you to be fulfilled. Disappointment, mortification, misconception, enmity, pain, death— these may come to you, but if they come to you in doing your duty it is all right."

There is one other sermon in this volume to which a special importance attaches. Its subject is the "Church of the Living God." It was preached in 1885, on the third Sunday in Advent, when it was the custom at Trinity Church to take up the annual collection for domestic missions. In this sermon Mr. Brooks defined his position on the questions then agitating the Episcopal Church. In the first part of the sermon he gives his definition of the Church Universal:

"The Christian Church is the body of redeemed humanity. It is man in his deepest interests, in his spiritual possibilities. It is the under life, the sacred, the profounder life of man, his regeneration. Every human being in very virtue of birth into the redeemed world is a potential member of the Christian Church. His baptism claims and asserts his membership. . . .

"I cannot tell you, my dear friends, how strongly this view takes possession of me the longer that I live. I cannot think, I will not think, about the Christian Church as if it were a selection out of humanity. In its idea it is humanity."

He defends the custom of baptizing the dying child, which sometimes has seemed like the "blankest superstition." "Will the ceremony do any good?" "Will the child be any better for this hurried incantation?" He answers:

"Baptism is the solemn, grateful, tender recognition of that infant's life on earth, of the deep meaning of his humanity. It is the human race in its profoundest self-consciousness welcoming this new member to its multitude. Only for a few moments does he tarry in this condition of humanity. His life touches the earth only to leave it; but in those few moments of his tarrying, humanity lifts up its hand and claims it, . . . appropriates for it that redemption of Christ which revealed man's belonging to God, declares it a member of that Church which is simply humanity belonging to God, the divine conception of humanity, her own realization of herself as it belongs to God."

He exclaims what a world this would be if only baptism were universal, with this understanding of its significance. He turns to the sacrament of the Lord's Supper "as the rallying-place for all the good activity and worthy hopes of man. It is in the power of this great Christian sacrament, this great human sacrament, to become that rallying-place." It would be the evidence of the world's transformation if to this great "sacrament of man" all classes of people—the mystic, the seeker after truth, the soldier, the student, the schoolboy, the legislator, the inventor, men, women, and children—were to come, meeting in a great host at the table of the Lord, owning themselves His children, claiming for themselves His strength, and thence go forth to their work. "The communion service would lift up its voice and sing itself in triumph, the great anthem of dedicated human life."

He speaks next of the Christian ministry. The old sacerdotal

idea has not died away.   Sometimes it is distinctly proclaimed
and taught.   But the remedy does not lie in denying the priesthood of the clergy, but in asserting the priesthood of all men:

"We can have no hope, I believe, of the destruction of the
spirit of hierarchy by direct attack.   It may be smitten down
a thousand times.   A thousand times it will rise again.   Only
when all men become full of the sense of the sacredness of their
own life will the assumption of supreme clerical sacredness find
itself overwhelmed with the great rising tide."

The doctrine of the Church is not an end in itself but a means
to a greater end.   It is because life has been undervalued that
dogma has been magnified overmuch.

"The decrying of dogma in the interest of life, of creed in the
interest of conduct, is very natural, but very superficial.   It is
superficial because, if it succeeded, it would make life and conduct
blind and weak.   But it is natural because it is the crude, healthy
outburst of human protest against the value of dogma for its own
sake, of which the Church has always been too full.   Let us not
join in it. . . . I will not hear men claim that the doctrine of the
Trinity has no help or inspiration to give to the merchant or the
statesman; that it means nothing to the scholar or the bricklayer
whether he believes or disbelieves in the Atonement.
"I must summon all life to look up to the hills, . . . and so
make it cry out to the truths of the Trinity and the Atonement
to open the depths of their helpfulness, as they have never heard
the call to open them when only theologians were calling on them
to complete their theologic systems.   In the assertion of the great
human Church is the true adjustment of the relations of Doctrine
and Life."

This large human idea of the Church is a vision which yet lacks
fulfilment.   The Church and the world are now in conflict, and
those who are in the Church must keep watchful guard, and dread
and oppose the evil influence of the world.   But it is unnatural.
We must never lose sight of the vision,—the real Church and the
real world struggling each into perfection for itself and so both
into unity and identity with each other.   As the history of the
Church passes in review, there is encouragement: "Very interesting have been in history the pulsations, the brightening and
fading, the coming and going, of this great truth of the Church

and the world, really identical." He speaks of the Protestant Episcopal Church and of its relation to the church universal:

"We value and love our Communion very deeply. To many of us she has been the nurse, almost the mother of our spiritual life. To all of us she is endeared by long companionship, and by familiar sympathy in the profoundest experiences through which our souls have passed. When we deliberately turn our backs for a moment upon all these rich and sweet associations and ask ourselves in colder and more deliberate consideration why it is that we believe in our Episcopal Church and rejoice to commend her to our fellow-countrymen and fellow-men, the answer which I find myself giving is that our Church seems to me to be truly trying to realize this relation to the whole world, this sacredness of all life, this ideal belonging of all men to the Church of Christ, which, as I have been saying, is the great truth of active Christianity. I find the signs of such an effort in the very things for which some people fear or blame our Church. I find it in the importance which she gives to Baptism and in the breadth of her conception of that rite; for Baptism is the strongest visible assertion of this truth. I find it in her simplicity of doctrine. I find it in the value which she sets on worship; her constant summons to all men not merely to be preached to, but to pray; her firm belief in the ability and right of all men to offer prayer to God. I find it in her strong historic spirit, her sense of union with the ages which have passed out of sight, and of whose men we know only their absolute humanity."

But he makes a protest against those who are claiming for the Episcopal Church the exclusive title of "The American Church." That is a name to which she has no right, but rather it belongs to the total body of Christianity in America, under many divisions and different names, broken, discordant, disjointed, often quarrelsome, and disgracefully jealous, yet still bearing witness to the love of God, the redemption of Christ, and the sacred possibilities of man:

"If our Church does especial work in our country, it must be by the especial and peculiar way in which she bears that witness; not by any fiction of an apostolic succession in her ministry which gives to them alone a right to bear such witness. There is no such peculiar privilege of commission belonging to her or to any other human body."

He fears that the historic feeling in the Episcopal Church, while it makes part of the strength of the Church, may also constitute its weakness. It may be tempted "to treasure overmuch its association with the great Church of another land, the Church of England," importing customs and costumes, names and ways, and so become "what she has been in part of her history, what she is in many parts of the land to-day, an exotic, and not a true part of the nation's life." "The true apostolical succession . . . she must not boast that she has, but she must struggle more and more earnestly to win."

With thoughts like these in his mind—they had been in his mind from the beginning of his ministry—Dr. Brooks went as a delegate from Massachusetts to the General Convention of the Episcopal Church which met in Chicago in October, 1886. This convention is remembered as having set forth the "Quadrilateral,"—the terms on which the Episcopal Church would consider the question of Church unity. Dr. Brooks had been a member of the General Convention since 1880, but had not hitherto taken any important part in its discussions. At the session of 1886 he made himself heard upon various questions in debate. He offered the following resolution:

"*Resolved*, That the General Convention of the Protestant Episcopal Church sends cordial greetings to the assembly of the Congregational Church now in session in this city, and expresses its devout hope that our deliberations, though separately conducted, may minister together to the glory of God and the advancement of our common Christianity."

In supporting this resolution he spoke of the Congregationalists as representing "a large body of workers in the cause of Christianity alongside of us, who sometimes seem to me unnecessarily separated from us." The motion commended itself to the House of Deputies and was unanimously passed, with this amendment: "And we assure them that we earnestly pray for such real unity as is according to God's will through Jesus Christ our Lord."

The Convention of 1886 is remembered for the effort to change the name of the Church by dropping from its title the words "Protestant Episcopal." Various names were proposed as substitutes, such as "The Catholic Church," "The American Church," or "The Church in the United States of America."

In his speech against the proposed change Mr. Brooks urged the fitness of the existing name "Protestant Episcopal" as discriminating the church from the Roman Catholic on the one hand, and from Protestant churches which had not retained episcopacy. The name answered its true purpose. Such names as "American" or "Catholic" implied an assumption which was not true,—that this church was one of such large prominence, so largely representative of the Christianity of America, that all other denominations are practically insignificant. Until the Church identified itself more fully with the spirit of American institutions and ceased to support its claim by its relation to the Church of England, it was not entitled to be known as the American Church. But if this ground were untenable, upon what other ground could the Church take its stand as the American Church?

"It must stand before the country with the distinctive assertion of apostolical succession as the very substance and essence and life of the Church. Now there are those who believe the apostolic succession to be the essence and substance of the Church. There is no doubt about that. The position which they take in regard to the Church is absolutely clear. That there are other men in our Church who believe nothing of the kind, there is no doubt. I, for one, and I think that I am speaking for multitudes in this congregation this morning, do not believe in the doctrine of apostolic succession in any such sense as many receive it. I do not believe in the exclusive prerogative which gives to the Church which receives it any such absolute right of Christian faith. That is not the question before us; but there is no conceivable explanation of the desire to change the name of the Church except the distinct adoption of that theory as the absolute condition on which it lives. We have been told, sir, with great rhetorical flourish, that this Church, when it shall have taken its new name, is going to extend its area and take in all Christianity. I appeal to any reasoning man, whether, in any sense, this is to be considered an expansion of the power of the Church. It immediately dooms it. It dooms it to live in the corner and minister to men who are convinced of a certain theory with regard to the possession of the privileges of the Christian ministry. The passage of such a resolution as should fasten upon this Church the explicit title of the American Catholic Church dooms it to become distinctively the Church of those men who accept the theory which is based upon mere historical argument. Is that going to be the Church of America? Is tha going to be the Church for praying people? Is that the Church which is going to do a work worthy of the Church of Christ?"

On October 31, the first Sunday after his return to Boston, Dr. Brooks gave to his congregation an account of the Convention, and then denounced in vigorous language the attempt to change the name of the Church. The sermon created a popular sensation throughout the land. It was extemporaneous, but from the reports in the papers its drift may be gathered:

"He began by tracing the growing belief in the theory of apostolical succession, since the time of the Oxford Movement in 1833, till at last those who held the theory proposed to make it the cardinal feature of the Episcopal Church, and the warrant for changing its name. The name proposed as its substitute, which seemed most acceptable to those desiring the change, was "The American Church." Upon this name he commented to the effect that its adoption could only be justified on the ground that the Episcopal Church, even though one of the smaller Christian bodies, had a distinct and absolute right, through a divine commission from Christ and the Apostles not possessed by other churches, and entitling her, therefore, to claim for herself, and to be known as, the only true apostolic, catholic church in America. There was not a line in the Prayer Book which declares any such theory. It was simply a theory held by individuals, a theory which many both of the clergy and laity did not believe. He avowed for himself that he rejected the theory and would not consent to it for a single day. If this movement in behalf of a change of name were not checked, and the change were accomplished, he did not see how he or any one who did not believe in apostolical succession, could remain in the Episcopal Church. He was despondent as he considered that the proposition to change the name was defeated by what seemed a small majority; but there was hope in the circumstance that the laity were more numerously opposed to it than the clergy; unless the feeling and intentions of the laity should be asserted more strongly in the next few years, he feared the change would be accomplished. and the Episcopal Church be doomed in consequence to become a small fantastic sect." [1]

---

[1] In taking this attitude Phillips Brooks felt that he was not alone; that he was supported by eminent scholars: Dr. Arnold of Rugby, Bishop Lightfoot of Durham, Dr. Hatch of Oxford, in studies of early organization. Such had been the attitude of the Reformers in the English Church in the sixteenth century. In the American Episcopal Church there had been many bishops and clergy from the time of Bishop White, who held the

Having freed his mind on the subject Dr. Brooks refused to be drawn into controversy. He became the target for criticism, but, although the usual expositions were offered of the falsity of his position, he kept silence. He was familiar enough with the subject. He knew that the best scholarship in the Anglican Church and the best traditions in its history,—the traditions in this country as well, did not attach to the theory of Apostolic succession any such exclusive import. But he was annoyed by the way in which publicity had been given to his remarks. "A man," he said, "may go on all his life preaching the gospel and no one takes any notice of it, but when he speaks of some matter of church administration, he is treated as if he had made some marvellous discovery." Yet there was justification for the popular interest aroused by this sermon. How it impressed the congregation listening to him is evident from testimony of one who was present:

"It was the most thrilling, dramatic thing I ever heard. He was intensely stirred, and the stillness as people listened was painful. By and by the sound of sobs was heard in different parts of the church; the excitement was so great that tears came to relieve the tension."

For a long time Phillips Brooks continued to hear the echoes of his utterance. The letters began to come at once from every part of the country and from England, most of them thanking him for his sermon. There was a tone of excitement in them, or exhilarated gratitude. Many of the letters came from persons of distinction or of social position, but they came also from humble women and inquiring students, who thanked him for his words. It was the laity who were chiefly moved to thankfulness. It is not without its pathos and its deeper meaning that many who wrote him belonged to other denominations. Some of the letters were efforts to console and reassure him, expressing the

same view, valuing episcopacy, regarding it as having apostolic sanction, yet as not essential to the existence of the Church. Of some of these the lives have been written and their opinions placed on record: Bishop Griswold of Massachusetts, Bishop McIlvaine of Ohio, Bishop Meade of Virginia. Among them was his teacher in Virginia, Dr. Sparrow, with whose utterances on the subject he was in sympathy. Cf. *Life and Correspondence of William Sparrow*, by Walker, pp. 155, 195.

conviction that the change he feared would never be made, that any renewed attempt would never again come so near passing, that the laity of the Church were overwhelmingly of his way of thinking.

There were also letters of another kind, some of them anonymous, asking him to confine his attention to preaching the gospel and let the Church alone; he was renewing old controversies which would otherwise die out, and embittering party spirit. His attention was called to parts of the Prayer Book, which in his ignorance he had overlooked. An aged clergyman, who, with his wife, had found comfort and inspiration from his sermons, wrote to him in distress because of a report that he had become an "apostate," had "denied the truth of the Trinity, of the Incarnation, and of Apostolic Succession, and was about to leave the Church for Unitarianism." Others still thought it was not too late to labor with him, and to give him some light on the origin of the Christian ministry.

From the letters written by those belonging to other denominations it was evident it had not been without sorrow that they had seen the Episcopal Church withdrawing from the fellowship of the other Protestant churches, and erecting an impassable barrier between them by the theory of apostolic succession. This letter from the president of a New England college represents this feeling:

"I cannot refrain, after reading the report in yesterday's *Tribune* of the sermon on Sunday last, from expressing to you my gratitude at your frank repudiation of a doctrine which has been a great hindrance to the advance of the Protestant Episcopal Church, and, as I believe, to the progress of the kingdom of God in America.

"Thousands who have read your words hitherto with the deepest interest will henceforth feel towards you a loving loyalty that knows no limit. Not that before I have really believed that you held such a doctrine as that there are no other ministers of Christ but those in the supposed direct apostolic descent, but the frank rejection of this belief, and the loving brotherhood expressed by you for others, will certainly give the deepest joy to a great many."

The disturbance which this controversy caused to Mr. Brooks did not at once subside. In proportion to the depth and intensity of his feeling was the inward revolt through which he was passing. Meantime it was fortunate that, immediately after his return from the Convention, it fell to him to take up his work at Harvard, where his association with the young life brought its healing balm to a spirit that had been wounded.   He was also anticipating the great event at Cambridge when Harvard University was to commemorate its two hundred and fiftieth anniversary.   The festival began on the 5th of November and lasted four days.   Visitors came from foreign universities bearing congratulations.   The President of the United States, Grover Cleveland, was present on Alumni Day, when James Russell Lowell was the orator, and Oliver Wendell Holmes read the poem, and the honorary degrees were conferred.

One day, Sunday, the 7th of November, was consecrated to religion, when alumni of the college who were in the ministry had been requested to recall in their respective places the history of Harvard.   The sermon in the morning was preached by Professor Francis G. Peabody, at Appleton Chapel, and in the evening came the sermon by Phillips Brooks.   His subject had been assigned him,—the religious history of Harvard.   He took for his text the words of St. Paul, "Jesus Christ, the same yesterday, to-day and forever."   The changes through which the College had passed he refused to look upon in a negative way as a mere casting off of restraints, but as so many successive enlargements, wherein the partial was gradually reconciling itself to the universal, the temporary fulfiling itself with the eternal.   His brief summary reviewed the ground where momentous controversies had been waged:

"There was a discipline of the Christian Church larger than the discipline of the Puritans, in which the discipline of the Puritans had floated as the part floats in the whole.   The discipline of the Puritans felt that; was pressed on, was tempted by it, and at last broke open in the attempt to find it.   Experience was larger than Whitfield, dogma was larger than Calvin, life was larger than theology; and so, one after another, in these which are the concentric spheres within which human nature lives, the successive openings of the partial into the universal, and the temporary into the eternal came. . . .   What is this universal and eternal power within which these and all the temporary struggles of mankind are included?   We open the Sacred Book, we turn to the majestic letter written centuries ago to members of the great sacred nation,

and there we find our answer, 'Jesus Christ, the same yesterday,
to-day, and forever.'"

He was thus led to ask the question, What and who is Jesus
Christ? Theological curiosity was alert to know the answer he
would make. But he did not stand there for the purpose of putting himself on record, or of "bearing witness" as he has called
it in his *Lectures on Preaching* which has the tendency to
weaken the message. He gave the conditions, the atmosphere,
out of which the formula of the coequality of the Son with
the Father had originally grown, and left the inference to his
hearers:

"And what and who is Jesus Christ? In reverence and humility let us give our answer. He is the meeting of the Divine and
Human,—the presence of God in humanity, the perfection of
humanity in God; the divine made human, the human shown to
be capable of union with the divine; the utterance, therefore, of
the nearness and the love of God, and of the possibility of man.
Once in the ages came the wonderous life, once in the stretch of
history the face of Jesus shone in Palestine, and His feet left
their blessed impress upon earth; but what that life made manifest had been forever true. Its truth was timeless, the truth of
all eternity. The love of God, the possibility of man,—these
two which made the Christhood,—these two, not two but one,
had been the element in which all life was lived, all knowledge
known, all growth attained. Oh, how little men have made it,
and how great it is! Around all life which ever has been lived
there has been poured forever the life of the loving Deity and the
ideal humanity. All partial excellence, all learning, all brotherhood, all hope, has been bosomed on this changeless, this unchanging Being which has stretched from the forgotten beginning to
the unguessed end. It is because God has been always, and been
always good, and because man has been always the son of God,
capable in the very substance of his nature of likeness to and
union with his Father,—it is because of this that nobleness has
never died, that truth has been sought and found, that struggle
and hope have always sprung anew, and that the life of man has
always reached to larger and to larger things.

"This is the Christian truth of Christ. 'In Him was life, and
the life was the light of men.' This is the truth of man's redemption. As any man or any institution feels and claims
around its life, as the element in which it is to live, the sympathy
of God and the perfectibility of man, that man or institution is
redeemed; its fetters and restraints give way, and it goes forward

31

to whatever growth and glory it is in the line of its being to attain."

On December 15 Mr. Brooks took part in the commemoration of the two hundredth anniversary of King's Chapel, making an address which was felicitous under difficult circumstances. As the rector of Trinity Church, a daughter of King's Chapel, it was appropriate that he should be present; but recalling the theological divergence in consequence of which King's Chapel had been lost to the Episcopal Church, the occasion called for wisdom and moderation. He dwelt on the civic interests which united the two parishes, on their common relation to American history, on the deeper issues which underlay theological discussion and religious differences. "The present condition of the religious world was not a finality. There was to be a future for the Christian Church, bringing richer results than the past had attained. There were problems which had not yet been solved. To prepare for that future, it was not needful to revive old disputes, but, while recognizing their earnestness, to strive for a deeper consecration to Christ in personal obedience."

"It seems to me that any one who looks back on the past and recognizes in history the great providence of God in His dealings with men—so much deeper than men have begun to comprehend—simply wants to say to any church, speaking for his own as he speaks for others: Let us go and seek that Christ, that infinite Christ, whom we have not begun to know as we may know Him; that Christ who has so much more to show us than He has shown; that Christ who can show himself to us only as we give ourselves in absolute obedience to Him. May that Christ receive from us, in each new period of our history, more complete consecration, more entire acceptance of Him as our Master; and so may we receive from Him rich promises of new light, new manifestations of His truth, new gifts of His Spirit, which He has promised to bestow upon those who consecrate themselves to Him in loving obedience, unto the end of time and through all eternity! If one may turn a greeting to a prayer, may I not ask for you, as I know you ask for all of our churches, a more profound and absolute spirit of consecration to our Master, Christ, that in Him, and only in Him, we may seek after and come to His ever richer life?"

Among the books he was reading was the *Life of Longfellow*. "How charming it is! What a bright, happy, friendly existence he had!" He commemorated Christmas by going to a Sunday-school celebration of poor children, where a stereopticon exhibition was given, and commented on the different pictures. But on the Sunday before Christmas he could not refrain from reverting to the topic which had pained him. He preached a sermon on the apostolic commission, from the text St. Matthew xxviii., 20: "Lo, I am with you alway, even unto the end of the world," and brought out in more positive form the truth whose denial seemed to him to be fraught with grave danger. The sermon was heard from by an anonymous letter, reproaching him for higgling about a name and talking of a danger which no one saw but himself.

CHAPTER XIX.

1887.

INCIDENTS IN PARISH LIFE. INVITATION TO DE-
LIVER THE BAMPTON LECTURES. EXTRACTS FROM
NOTE-BOOKS. SERMON AT FANEUIL HALL. ST.
ANDREW'S MISSION CHURCH. TENTH ANNIVER-
SARY OF THE CONSECRATION OF TRINITY CHURCH.
SERMON AT ANDOVER. SUMMER IN EUROPE. ILL-
NESS. CORRESPONDENCE.

THE most important features in the life of Phillips Brooks
baffle description. It defies the imagination when we attempt
to reproduce the scene at Trinity Church, when every Sunday
seemed like the bridal of earth and sky. Of any one of these
years the same story may be told. There was no diminution in
the power of the preacher; there was no decline in the people's
interest. What was true of the Sundays in 1887 was true of the
preceding and of the following years: "Every Sunday crowds are
to be seen packing the vestibules and the corridors of Trinity in
vain efforts to enter." Whatever might be the subject of the
sermon, it was impossible for the preacher to be uninteresting;
it was impossible to be present and not to listen. Religion was
invested with perpetual freshness, as if therein lay the charm of
living. One Sunday a stranger was observed, who, after the
service was over, seemed to be confused, looking about in a distracted way. He was asked if he had lost anything. He replied: "I feel as if the gods had come down again to the earth.
I have come all the way from Canada just to hear him preach,
and I would come again." A person who went to Trinity for
the purpose of studying the congregation as well as the preacher
looked about him for a moment to find every face upturned to
the pulpit, and was unable to cast more than this furtive glance

for fear he would lose what the preacher was saying. We must not attempt to describe these occasions, or even to enumerate the sermons still remembered by those who heard them. But the mind seeks points on which to rest, as in a picture gallery, where nothing is seen if the attempt is made to look at everything. In the midst of this distraction a few incidents are taken as types of the rest.

It was a custom of Mr. Brooks through many years to speak of eminent persons who had died, whether in Church or State. One of his favorite hymns was, "Who are these in bright array?" When he announced it, the people knew that he had lost some friend, or was about to commemorate the departure of some one known for distinguished services. On the Sunday after Henry Ward Beecher died, he took for his text, "He that overcometh shall inherit all things." Part of the impressiveness of the moment lay in the feeling that it was the greatest of living preachers who was paying his tribute to the great preacher who had preceded him. This was in substance what was said at the close of the sermon, as recalled by an interested listener:

"I know that you are all thinking as I speak of the great soul that has passed away, of the great preacher—for he was the greatest preacher in America, and the greatest preacher means the greatest power in the land. To make a great preacher, two things are necessary, the love of truth and the love of souls; and surely no man had greater love of truth or love of souls than Henry Ward Beecher. Great services, too, did he render to theology, which is making great progress now. It is not that we are discovering new truths, but that what lay dead and dry in men's souls has awakened. The Spirit of the Lord has been poured into humanity, and no one more than Mr. Beecher has helped to this, pouring his great insight and sympathy and courage out upon the truths which God gave him to deliver. A great leader in the theological world, believing in the divine Christ and in eternal hope for mankind, foremost in every great work and in all progress, one of that noble band of men whose hands clutched the throat of slavery and never relaxed their hold till the last shackle fell off; inspiring men to war, speaking words of love and reconciliation when peace had come, standing by the poor and oppressed, bringing a slave girl into his pulpit and making his people pay her ransom. A true American like Webster, a great preacher, a great leader, a great patriot, a great man.

"We feel sure that Mr. Beecher knew these Revelation promises. Wonderful was the vitality given him. Surely he had inner communion with God. Truly was he a pillar of the temple. Rejoice in the dead who die in the Lord. They have overcome and shall inherit all things."

Mr. Brooks was reappointed a preacher to Harvard University for the year 1887-88, and continued to be reappointed until 1891. The degree of Doctor of Divinity was conferred upon him by Columbia University at its one hundredth anniversary. He declined a request from the editor of the *Contemporary Review*, asking him to describe the working of religion in America, about which the English mind was not clear. Any one who knew Phillips Brooks must be interested in the invitation he received to meet the late Mr. Ingersoll in joint debate on some question touching the essentials of the Christian religion. To enumerate the many invitations to occasions outside of his ministerial life is needless, but among them may be mentioned a speech made in 1887 before the insurance societies, where he turned over the principle of "safety" in its relations to a man's work in the world. He went to a meeting of Methodist ministers, where the subject of "Christian Unity" was discussed; and his address deepened the conviction that Christian unity already existed. During Lent he took for the subject with his Bible class the Apostles' Creed. The course was one of great interest, and was largely attended. He treated his theme in the manner of a systematic theologian, making formal definitions, stating objections and meeting them, dealing with modern theories. It was unlike his method in the pulpit, not wholly congenial, but no one could surpass him in this line when he chose to undertake it. The full analysis for each lecture is so admirable that one regrets he did not put his work into permanent form.

In April he received an invitation from Dr. Jowett, of Balliol College, Oxford, to deliver the Bampton Lectures, with the assurance that if he would comply with the terms of candidacy, by sending in a schedule of the lectures he proposed to give, there was no doubt of his appointment. He seems to have considered the request for some time before he dismissed it, as is shown by his note-book, where he went so far as to write out an analysis for five of the lectures, calling his subject tentatively the "Philosophy of Religious Teaching." But he did not complete the schedule, and finally wrote declining to become a candidate.

Mr. Brooks had been interested in the effort to import into the Episcopal Church the methods known as evangelistic, and had given his sanction to "holding missions." When an invitation came to him from the young men of the Trinity Club to preach on Sunday evenings at Faneuil Hall to the unchurched classes, he welcomed it and prepared himself, but with some fear of failure. It might be the verdict on the experiment that he could preach a comfortable gospel to those in easy circumstances, who knew nothing of the darker side of life, but could not reach the masses of men. He was putting his theology, his religion, to the final test. Before and after his sermons he walked the streets of old Boston, for encouragement, and then for relief,—High Street, where he was born, and Rowe Street (Chauncy Street), where he had grown from youth to manhood.

The first of these Sunday evening services at Faneuil Hall was held on January 23. It had been the task of the Trinity Club, of which Mr. Lorin F. Deland was president, to help make the experiment successful. It required no slight effort to get access to the people at the North End in Boston, and make it known that Phillips Brooks was to preach; to have it understood that the object in view was not a religious revival, but simply to increase the range of Mr. Brooks's influence, and to give those an opportunity to hear him who were unable to listen to him at Trinity Church. The announcement was altogether a sensation; the experiment was anticipated as an event in the ecclesiastical life of Boston. It forms an interesting picture, the association of Faneuil Hall with the memory of Phillips Brooks.

The text of the sermon was a verse from the Psalms: "Like as a father pitieth his own children, so the Lord pitieth them that fear him." A few extracts may indicate something of the power infused with tenderness and love, which went into his appeal:

"When fatherhood is spoken of, it means this love which takes the child simply because it is the child; not because of what the child has done, or what the child is in its character, but simply because it has been cradled in these arms in its infancy, and all the hopes and affections of the parent have gathered around that little life.

"Underneath all the approbation or disapprobation of God, is the great, patient, indestructible love of God for us because we are His children, the wickedest of us as well as the best of us. If you are ever going to understand the great enfolding life around us, and to trust in it and test its consolations, its encouragements, and its supports, the first picture of it must be in your own house. I almost hesitate when I talk to a multitude of people such as this, and ask them to consider their relations with regard to God from the way in which their own families are living. I hesitate and draw back and say, 'Do these people want me to talk to them in this way, to ask them to understand that God is to them just exactly what they are to their own children?' I should have to look round and think that I saw better men and women than I know that I do see here to-night. Where is the father who is willing to let his child draw his idea of God from the way in which his fatherly life is related to his child's life?

"I am struck, and I am sure you have been, by the way in which people think the basest moments of their lives the real and true moments, and are not willing to think of the grandest moments in their lives as the true ones. The noblest thing you ever did, the noblest emotion you ever felt, the deepest and tenderest and most self-sacrificing love ever in your soul, that is your self still, through all the baser life into which you have fallen.

"Men are continually preached to that they are a great deal wickeder than they think they are, that they must not value themselves so much, that they must not put so high a worth on their humanity. We want, along with that, another kind of preaching. Men are nobler than they think themselves to be. There is in every man something greater than he has begun to dream of. When he gives himself to Jesus Christ in consecration, then that begins to come forth. Break through the cross of your despair and ask Christ to let you see yourself as He sees you, all stained with sin but with the divine image in you all the time."[1]

The comments of those present indicate that they had been surprised at the fine congregation of non-churchgoers that had assembled to hear Phillips Brooks. One young man, not in the habit of going to church, said: "These people—and I live among them—have not been approached in the right way, and been made

[1] Cf. *The Spiritual Man, and other Sermons*, London, 1895, for a full report of the sermon.

to know the true meaning of religion and its place in their lives and homes. A preacher like Mr. Brooks will inaugurate a new era in their lives." An elderly man, who confessed that he did but "little in wearing out the carpets in church aisles," had gone for the purpose of seeing how Mr. Brooks would take hold of workingmen and their families. This was his verdict:

"He is in no sense a revivalist. He will not excite the emotions of people, but gives them a great many sound things to think about. He gives practical religion. That is what everyday men and women want. That was a very beautiful thought of his that men are apt to think that they are worse than they are, and that they should see that the true gauge of their character is the best that is in them. This is what shows a man his own possibilities; and the way in which Dr. Brooks spoke of the pity of God for those who had fallen short of the glorious possibilities of their natures was a helpful lesson; it kindled ambition, inspired hope, and warmed the heart with the love of God for His children. This is what people ought to hear, and this is what he is telling them."

Mr. Brooks was impressed by a man who approached him after the service, thanked him for coming, and asked if he could recommend anything for his wife's rheumatism. It was the human side of religion, as in the days when Christ was on the earth, after hearing the gospel people brought their sick to be healed. He promised the man to attend to his request.

On the 30th of January and on the 6th of February Phillips Brooks met the same large audience, with no diminution in attendance or interest. He preached great sermons also; one from the text, "He shall drink of the brook in the way; therefore shall he lift up the head " (Ps. cx., 7), where he dwelt on the sense of responsibility and the power of the forgiveness of sins; and another sermon from the text, "Lord, if thou wilt, thou canst make me clean" (Matt. viii., 2), when evangelical hymns were sung, " Come, ye sinners, poor and needy," and "Just as I am, without one plea." There were other efforts at this time to reach the people at the Globe Theatre. To these services Phillips Brooks went with the message that he had given in Faneuil Hall, and always met the same large concourse of the unchurched classes. It seemed as if a strong religious wave were passing over Boston.

During the weeks that cover the sermons at Faneuil Hall,

Trinity Church and its rector were absorbed in efforts for the extension of the parish life. In response to his appeal for fifty thousand dollars, the amount was raised with great enthusiasm for the purpose of establishing St. Andrew's Mission Church and equipping it with various helpful agencies. Under the guidance of the assistant minister at Trinity, Rev. Reuben Kidner, St. Andrews has continued to fulfil the large purpose in the mind of Phillips Brooks. Speaking of his dream of what it might be, he wrote to Mr. R. T. Paine:

"And now, St. Andrew's. Let that be conceived as generously as possible. Let there be nothing mean about it. If we need more money let us get it. Let us make it a home of which neither rich nor poor need be ashamed. Let us anticipate vastly more of work and life than we at present have to put in it. In all this I am with you heartily. The main hall of the parish building, I believe, will be above all our expectations in its usefulness,— a sort of Palace of Delight, like the one we read about in London four years ago, and which I saw in its partial realization the other day. It may be made the centre of all sorts of good influences for that whole region. O that I could see, on the 18th of September, as I turn into Chambers Street, the chaste and elegant façade of a finished building all ready for its work, with Kidner waving a St. Andrew's flag upon the doorstep, and the crowd waiting for the blessing at the open windows! I shall not quite see that, but something, I am sure, will have been done, and there is time left yet before we die, and other people are to follow us and take up what we leave undone."

St. Andrew's Church, the most elaborate mission church which had then been planned in this part of the country, became an offering, commemorating the tenth anniversary of the consecration of Trinity Church. Mr. Brooks made it the opportunity of saying a few words about the church and about his own work:

"I do not come to you to-night with statistics. I have not even counted how many have been baptized in these ten years, how many times the marriage service has been performed, how many times the beautiful burial service has been read over the dead, how many of you have been confirmed. I have not looked to see; I do not care. I care more for what these services have been to you and to many souls. I do know that some have come in to them and have gone out with no change in their faces; but there has been a change; there is something which they have got which they did not have before they came. I know that many of you have been helped, that many of you are the better for these years of services in this church. . . . Far be it from us to boast of what our church has done, but for some things we can be thankful that they have been done right. We welcome all those who come to worship with us. I know how heartily, and often at no little inconvenience to yourselves, this welcome has been given. There has not yet been turned away a person from our doors when there was a seat for him to occupy.

"And as your minister may I thank you for your help and sympathy during these years? You have made my task anything but a burden. As our church has grown and duties have increased, it has been impossible to keep up the personal intercourse which we had together in the first years. I appreciate the patience which you have shown to me. When a person gives up his whole life to such work, trying not to refuse to any the aid which he may be able to give, I think he may still ask for continued patience. I ask that you will bear with me in the future. We are thankful for the past years, but we want to make the coming years fuller and better, to consecrate ourselves more fully to God, and do more earnest work for Him."

At Andover, where he went on January 4, to preach the sermon at the consecration of the new Episcopal church, he made it the occasion for asserting more positively the faith that was in him regarding the Christian Church. The sermon glowed with the intensity of his emotions. He spoke of the place of the Episcopal Church in the Puritan town:

"Long before our Church came here this was a distinctly religious town. The Church of Christ in other forms, the experience of Christ in other forms, in deep reality was here. . . . It is not in arrogant presentation of herself as the only Church of Christ to which this old religiousness must conform before it can be really churchly. God forbid! It is as one distinct and valuable form of Christian thought and life—as one contribution to the Church of the future which is to be larger, deeper, wiser, holier than any Church existing in the land to-day."

The thought of Phillips Brooks on the nature of the Church, its doctrine and worship, has already been given; but he now spoke with a deeper emphasis and with great intensity of feeling:

"The Church is no exception and afterthought in the world, but is the survival and preservation of the world's first idea,—

the anticipation and prophecy of the world's final perfectness. The Church of Christ is the ideal humanity. Say not that it leaves out the superhuman. I know no ideal humanity that is not filled and pervaded with the superhuman. God in man is not unnatural, but the absolutely natural. That is what the Incarnation makes us know.

"The Church is the most truly human institution in the world; the church building is the most human institution in the town. It means the most human thing of all, the truest human fact of all facts, that man intrinsically and eternally belongs to God.

"Whatever mystic richness must belong to the Church's two perpetual sacraments, warm forever with the touch of the very hands of the dear Lord, deepened and filled with the countless holy experiences of countless souls, they must be ever pervaded, not in contradiction or in diminution, but in increase of their sacredness, by the simplicity and humanity which is in their very essence. The elemental substances,—water and bread and wine,—these keep the two sacraments forever broad and true. It is through earth's most common substances that Christ, the Son of man, symbolically gives Himself to man. The stream, the field, the vineyard, have their essential sacredness declared in those deep, venerable words, 'Baptize all nations.' 'This is My Body.' 'This is My Blood.'

"The Church whose fundamental truth is the essential sacredness of man must hold its doctrines humanly. . . . It will believe that no doctrine has been truly revealed until the human consciousness has recognized its truth. It will have nothing to do with the false awe of the *Credo quia impossibile*. The truths of heaven and the truths of earth are in perfect sympathy; every revelation of the Bible is clearer the more it is to be found in the speaking conscience, or in the utterance of history, or in the vocal rocks.

"The real authority of man to speak to brother man must rest in personal qualities and conditions. It is truth which cannot be carried save by the believing soul. It is God who can only shine through a soul luminous and transparent with His own divinity. Behind all other authorities lies forever the first authority of intelligence and sympathy and consecration. Without that all other authorities are worthless. With that, no man may disparage any ministry, however simple and unelaborate that ministry may be in other things."

A new pulpit was at this time placed in Trinity Church, in order that Mr. Brooks might be better heard in some parts of the building. He had hitherto preached from a lectern, the same that he had used in Huntington Hall, originally associated with

Holy Trinity Chapel in Philadelphia, whence it had been sent to him as a gift, at his own suggestion. What importance he attached to the associations connected with it is evident from the circumstance that the upper part of this lecturn was fitted to the new pulpit, for a sermon board. So he preserved the connection of his years.

To the Rev. Arthur Brooks, who was making the tour of Egypt and Palestine, he writes:

" Sunday (Sexagesima), February, 1887.

"At Cairo I lose you, for I have never been up the Nile, and it is a mysterious jumble of tombs and sphinxes and pyramids to me. If you see the veritable Rameses, with the magnificent head, tell him I salute him, and am quite sure that those Hebrews must have been terribly exasperating and disagreeable people. How strange it does seem that out of them should have come the world's religion!"

With reference to the "mind cure," in regard to which his opinion had been misrepresented, he writes:

" 233 CLARENDON STREET, BOSTON, March 25, 1887.

"I have never heard of these people who are disturbing Albany, and I have no sympathy with their kind. There is a truth in the fantastic performances and the confused philosophy of the 'mind cure,' but it and the notions which are related to it are capable of vast mischief in the hands of ignorant and self-seeking men and women. Such seem to be the folks of whom you speak. May those for whom you care be saved from them. I assure you they have no right to quote me as their endorser."

An incident occurred at the Diocesan Convention in May which is characteristic. In 1886 it had been voted to change the rule of order requiring a sermon at the opening of the Convention. When Mr. Brooks heard of it he was indignant at the idea of taking away the one chance which a man had of preaching to his brethren; it seemed like abolishing the first function of the ministry. At the Convention in 1887 he moved that the words be restored calling for a sermon by the appointed preacher. He made a short and vigorous speech in behalf of his motion, and carried the Convention with him. A member of the Convention writes: "The ease with which he swung the Convention back to the sermon was striking. I think no debate followed his speech. We all let him have his way."

On the 8th of June Mr. Brooks sailed for England, accompanied by his sister-in-law, Mrs. William G. Brooks, and her daughter, Miss Gertrude Brooks. His visit differed from previous ones in that he was mainly concerned to put himself at the disposal of the ladies, and share their pleasure at seeing what was so familiar to him. Among his English friends and admirers there was a rush to be early in the field of those claiming his services as a preacher. The Queen's Jubilee eclipsed every other event in national interest. One of his English friends wrote him that it seemed fitting he should be present as "a loyal subject."

"The Queen will come in great state to the Abbey. It will be a ceremony such as only occurred three times in nine hundred years (Henry III., Edward III., George III.), and will be a reminiscence of the coronation. Tickets of admission will be very hard to get. They are given to very few except the Houses of Lords and Commons, courtiers, and the great ones of the earth. But you shall have a seat; I pledge myself to get you one."

Mr. Brooks preached but a few times in England, at St. Margaret's, Westminster, as usual, and at St. Paul's Cathedral, where he met Dean Church. He also preached at Crosthwaite Church, in Keswick,—"the greatest sermon Crosthwaite ever listened to," wrote the vicar. He went down to the East End and made a speech to the workingmen. Among the invitations he was obliged to decline was one from the chaplain of the Royal Dockyard Church, with its large number of English soldiers and their officers. He met, through the kindness of Archdeacon Farrar, a large number of the clergy. The Nonconformists gave him a warm welcome.

After a few weeks in London, he went with his companions for a journey in rural England, visiting cathedrals and other objects of interest, and on the 19th of July left England, as he writes, "for the old commonplace Continental journey,—Brussels, Cologne, the Rhine, Heidelberg, the Tyrol, Venice, Milan, Switzerland, Paris,—all old and delightful, but no longer with the charm of novelty." He showed himself a restless traveller, impatient to be moving, unwilling to be idle when there was anything to be done; giving the friends who were with him no rest in his desire to show them what ought to be seen.

When the travellers reached Geneva, Phillips Brooks was called to know what physical suffering meant, in consequence of a felon on the thumb of his right hand. He seemed to bear it with heroic patience. Despite well-nigh unendurable agony he preserved his integrity. For weary days and sleepless nights he continued to suffer and endure. He was urged to call in a physician, but refused, in hope that the pain would subside, reluctant to admit that he could not overcome by strength of will an aberation of nature. At last he had almost waited too long. When the physician was summoned, he was alarmed on examining the arm, to find symptoms so dangerous that he despaired of saving it. Just before the finger was cut open, he advised chloroform, but it was declined; to his patient's request that he might light a cigar the physician consented, and he held the cigar in his mouth during the operation: "There was a moment," said the physician, "when he did n't draw."

The injury to his hand prevented Mr. Brooks for some time from the use of his pen, and no letters record his movements. On the 18th of September, he was again at his post in Trinity Church, and had resumed his connection with Harvard University. In October he went to the Church Congress at Louisville, Kentucky, where he made a speech on "Apostolical Succession," stating his position with the vigor which church congresses engender. There were hisses in the hall as he spoke. A prominent layman who heard him remarked it would have been a pleasure to assist in throwing him into the Ohio River. Again the speaker's words were caught up and carried throughout the country. No record of the speech remains, for the records of this congress perished by some accident in the flames. There is one brief allusion to the subject in a letter written by Mr. Brooks after his return to Boston, October 27, 1887:

"Only last night did I get back from this ecclesiastical junket, which began with the Congress in Louisville, and ended with the ministerial council in Philadelphia. The congress was ugly, but the saints had good rooms at the hotels and there were enough of them to praise each other's speeches."

With one other letter this phase in the life of Mr. Brooks comes to an end, and he no longer felt it incumbent on him to pursue the subject. Three times he had spoken his mind with all the fiery energy of his nature,—at the General Convention in 1886, at Trinity Church, and in the Church Congress. He had made his position known; there could be no doubt where he stood. In this letter to Dr. Dyer, for many years the honored leader of the Evangelical school, he shows himself still despondent, and expresses his misgivings. The letter is of further importance for its avowal that he no longer holds the system known as Evangelical:

"233 CLARENDON STREET, BOSTON, November 19, 1887.

"DEAR DR. DYER,—It does me good to hear your blessed voice again. Old scenes come trooping up with the sight of your handwriting, and I am a youngster again, sitting at the feet of my elders and betters. Yes, I will be an officer of the Church Missionary Society if they want me to,—most of all, if *you* want me to,—but it will not save the Church. Nothing will save it, I fear. It is fast on the way to become a small, fantastic sect, aping foreign ways and getting more and more out of sympathy with the great life of the country. I am sorry indeed, but I cannot think anything else. Look at the West and see what our Church means there. Where are the dioceses that you strove to build a quarter of a century ago? Well, well, the work will be done by somebody, even if our Church refuses to do it. But what a chance we had!

"I know no better place to work, and so I work on still in the old Church, growing more and more out of conceit with organizations,—more and more sure that the dogmatic theology in which I was brought up was wrong,[1] but more and more anxious for souls and eager to love God every year. The old days when we haunted Dr. Vinton's study and hammered out Constitutions for the Divinity School in Philadelphia, and took breakfast with the Volanses, look very bright, but far away and very young. Those days were earlier, but these are happier,—and, on the whole, the larger hopes which live on Christ and expect Him to do His work in His own way are more inspiring even than the hopes we used to have for E. K. S. and E. E. S."

[1] The points on which Mr. Brooks recognized his divergence from the dogmatic theology in which he had been brought up were these: 1. Its view of baptism as a covenant. 2. Its literal theory of inspiration and its conception of Scripture as a whole. 3. Its separation between things secular and sacred; its failure to recognize truth in other religions and in non-Christian men; its indifference to intellectual culture. 4. Its

To the Rt. Rev. Henry C. Potter he writes concerning the over-valuation of ecclesiastical domesticities:

"233 CLARENDON STREET, BOSTON, November 26, 1887.

"No, my dear Henry, I will not go back on what I wrote, or what the *Evening Post* says that I wrote, which is the same thing.

"I conceive the trimming of the altar, the cleaning of the candlesticks, the cutting out of artificial flowers, and the darning of the sacramental linen to be, on the whole, the noblest occupation of the female mind, the very crown and glory of the parish work of women. They correspond exactly to the sublime work of showing strangers to seats and playing checkers with loafers at the reading-room, which is what we have canonized as *men's* work in the same parish. How beautiful they both are! How worthy of the male and female topstones of Creation!

The following extracts are taken from his note-book for the current year:

"The true symmetry of the Intellectual and Spiritual in the religious teacher. The Seminary is the place to produce it. One-sidedness of College and other-sidedness of much popular religious life; the minister to restore the balance and to learn how in the Seminary."

"The present tendency to reduce doctrinal demands. Shall we insist on full requirements for the sake of consistency, or reduce faith to its barest terms for the sake of peace and conciliation? Either implies a power over truth which we do not possess. No, the duty of such times as these is to go deeper into the spirituality of our truths."

"The tendency of good people to object more to a dissenter

---

tendency to limit the Church to the elect. 5. Its view of salvation as escape from endless punishment. 6. Its insistence upon the necessity of acknowledging a theory of the Atonement in order to salvation. 7. Its insufficient conception of the Incarnation and of the Person of Christ. 8. Its tendency to regard religion too much as a matter of the emotions rather than of character and will. And yet he regarded these points as the accidents of the Evangelical theology, not its essence. Its essence lay in devotion to the Person of Christ. In his deep harmony with this feature of Evangelical teaching, he seemed to remain an Evangelical to the end.

than to an infidel; to hate another shade of truth more than error. (See Lord Falkland's Speech in Rushworth, vol. iii.)"

"The sense of sadness in life as one grows older, not wholly a sign of the badness and unsatisfactoriness of the world; partly a mere regret at leaving what is pleasant even for something pleasanter. Landing from a steamer. Partly the sense of vastness, which is always sad."

"The need of teaching sure religion; something definite. The fallacy of hoping to teach religion in general, to inspire mere devotional feeling."

"The different temperaments, intellectual, mystic, and practical; the different ways in which each receives truth. The real Church comprehends all. Dangers of asserting either solely as the office of the Church."

"The vague talk about the good in other religions as if it detracted from the value of Christ's teaching."

"The ink of the learned is as precious as the blood of the martyrs."

"It is the clear and constant feeling and presentation of the personality of the gospel that prevents its becoming monotonous. A person is endlessly interesting. You can tell men of him forever, men who care for him. But a truth once stated is not to be forever repeated.

"The faculty of perceiving what is needed; the way in which it belongs to some men and not to others. The presence of it makes the good preacher; the lack of it shown in men who argue endlessly for nothing."

"Jesus taught—by personal presentation, awaking conscience, reaching truth on moral side, and establishing church (John vi.). Paul taught by starting from old knowledge. Address at Athens. John Baptist taught by convicting of sin and arousing hope. They all went to work to break up dead satisfaction, and create lively desire."

"The way in which people listen. We say they listen stupidly, but really what they want is Religion. The sifting power of a congregation. It takes what it comes for: if poetry or science, then that; if religion, then that, throwing all else aside."

On November 26 Mr. Brooks laid the corner-stone of the

new St. Andrew's Church, in the presence of a large number
of people. On his fifty-second birthday he wrote this letter
to Mrs. Robert Treat Paine:

233 CLARENDON STREET, BOSTON, December 13, 1887.

"DEAR MRS. PAINE,—I want to write a word before the
birthday closes, to thank you for your kind word and the bright
flowers which made the birthday possible to bear. You and
yours will, I know, stand by me to the end, and give me your
friendship till I get safely through.

"God bless you for all you have been to me all these years.
"Affectionately yours,
"PHILLIPS BROOKS."

CHAPTER XX.

1888.

RAILWAY ACCIDENT IN PHILADELPHIA. INCIDENTS OF PARISH LIFE. LENTEN SERVICES. CORRESPONDENCE. SENTIMENT AND SENTIMENTALITY. COMMENTS ON "ROBERT ELSMERE." THANKSGIVING SERMON.

IN the first month of this new year Phillips Brooks encountered the vision of sudden death. Such was the report which startled Boston on the morning of January 27:

"Dr. Brooks had come on from Boston to visit his many friends in this city [Philadelphia], and to assist at the opening of the new chapel of the Holy Communion, at Twenty-seventh and Wharton streets. He was at the residence of Rev. Dr. Cooper, No. 2026 Spruce Street, during the afternoon, and later in the evening Rev. Dr. McVickar, with his sister, called in a carriage for the reverend gentlemen to convey them to the chapel.

"So bad was the condition of the icy streets that the driver had difficulty in keeping his horses on their feet. It was just 7.45 o'clock when they got to Greenwich Street, and the driver turned his horses' heads to cross the Pennsylvania Railroad. The spot is one of the most dangerous in the city, the high walls of the Arsenal building almost shutting the trains from the view of drivers of vehicles. The safety gate was not shut, in consequence of its being so encrusted with ice that it could not be worked. The driver, seeing that the gate was open and not seeing or hearing an approaching train, drove upon the tracks. Hardly had those in the carriage seen the dazzling headlight of the engine before it was upon them, catching up the heavy carriage like an eggshell, overturning it in the twinkling of an eye, and crushing a great hole in the side where it had struck.

"Along the track for fifty yards the engine pushed the cab and its affrighted occupants before it could be stopped. The engineer had seen the carriage before the locomotive struck it, and he at once reversed the lever. Had not this been done it is probable that some if not all would have been killed.

"Ready hands came to the rescue and helped the members of the party out of their perilous position. Rev. Dr. Cooper and Miss McVickar had been thrown violently against the side of the cab. Dr. McVickar was covered with broken glass and wood, and across Dr. Brooks's breast rested a heavy axletree. All considered their escape from instant death as marvellous. The driver fared worst. He was hurled from his box to the ground, and lay last night in a semi-conscious condition.

"The delay in the arrival of the party at the chapel caused some alarm, and a carriage was sent in search of them. The searchers found the clergymen by the railroad tracks, and conveyed them to the chapel, where the services proceeded as if nothing had happened."

There are allusions to the accident in his conversation and in his letters:

"I was not the least afraid to go; I know there are beautiful things God has to show us in the other world; but, I want to live to see what He has to show us that is beautiful and wonderful in the coming century in *this* world."

"You do not know the good which your letter has done me. If you did, you would be glad all your life for the blessed hour in which you wrote it. I have had all my share of happiness, and more. I have had friends such as are given to few men, and they have been constant and faithful to me in a way that fills me with gratitude and wonder when I think of it; but life is pretty lonely, after all, and so, when one of the oldest of the oldest of one's friends says kind, good things like this, it sort of breaks me down, and I am glad, like a true awkward Bostonian, that you are not here to see how much I feel it. This morning lots of people called, and I felt amazed and overcome to find how much people cared whether I lived or died. And so the thing goes into history, and we are safe for some years more of work. God knows how many! The more the whole event takes possession of me, the more I am willing to leave it all to Him, sure that it would have been all right if He had called us then, and sure, too, that every week of work He still allows us is a privilege."

The marvellous escape left its impression upon Phillips Brooks. He seemed to give himself even more unreservedly to the demands of the people. A visitor who spent several weeks at the rectory in 1888 was astonished at the frequency with which the door bell rang, from an early hour in the morning; he kept a record, and found that it averaged once for every five minutes. He declined to appoint hours when he would be at home to callers. Any one who went to call upon him at this time would be apt to find some one waiting for him in the reception-room, another in the dining-room, while he was closeted with a third in the study.

There were symptoms that his health was gravely impaired, but he continued to give himself, as if with the desperation of one who felt that his time was short. There was nothing that was so much wanted of him now as the man himself. A friend had an appointment to meet him at the rectory at eight o'clock one evening, whence they were to go to a reception. Not till nearly eleven o'clock did Mr. Brooks return to his house to keep the appointment. He had been detained at a hospital by a colored man who had been injured in some affray and had sent for him. A physician whom they met expressed some surprise that Mr. Brooks should not have sent his assistant, as any physician would have done. The reply was that the man had sent for *him*.

A workingman, living in one of the suburbs of Boston, was told at the hospital that he must undergo a dangerous surgical operation; that he could not live unless it were performed; that it was doubtful even then if his life could be saved, but there might be a chance. He returned with the information to his home and his wife. The operation was to take place the next day. They had the evening before them, and they proposed to spend it in a call on Phillips Brooks whom neither of them knew, nor had they the slightest claim on his attention. Mr. Brooks received them as they had expected he must, talked with them and soothed them, and promised to be with them at the hospital on the following day.

In other instances of a similar kind he kept the details of his kindness to himself. It is not that these incidents are peculiar in his experience. What strikes the imagination is the contrast they suggest, between the preacher who moved the admiration of the world and had received its honors, and the man claimed as their own by the humblest, the lowest. It would have been easy to have withdrawn himself, pleading that he was engaged in a higher work; that he had no right to be giving his days to ministrations which others could perform as well, while no one could do the greater work he was accomplishing. He might have gone to the opposite extreme of asceticism and have reasoned that the joy of social life was incompatible with daily ministrations to human suffering. But life in itself was never richer or more attractive; a social function still had its charm.

In the midst of many engagements, and when life was at its fullest, there are occasional complaints that he is lonely. Consciousness of isolation, lack of complete sympathy, or the unique position he occupied, the large demands for human love which no friendships could satisfy,—these may help explain his sense of increasing loneliness. He became more than ever dependent upon his friends. It was strange that with a world of friends he should ever find himself alone. What he dreaded at times was the return to the house at night where there was no one to welcome him. His face would light up in the evenings if fortunately, at ten o'clock, he found some friend awaiting him in the study. But the note of his life was one of hope and cheer for the world. "The richest gifts of God cannot be imparted at once, and man must wait in patience until the inward preparation to receive them is completed." "Life in the individual or the race follows the analogy of education, where the best is held in reserve." About this time was written the sermon entitled "The Good Wine at the Feast's End." It was born of an inward conflict in the adjustment of the changes of life.

"Christianity is full of hope. It looks for the ever richer coming of the Son of Man. It lives in sight of the towers of the New Jerusalem which fill the western sky. Therefore it has been the religion of energy and progress everywhere and always.

"There are ways in which the world grows richer to the growing man, and so the earliest years cannot be meant to be the fullest or the most glorious, but that privilege must belong rather to the ripest and the last.

"When what we vaguely call this life is done, there is to come the fulfilment of those things of which we have here witnessed the beginnings. This is the sublime revelation of the Christian faith. The words of Christ reach forward. They all own present incompleteness. The soul which uses them is discontented and lives upon its hope."

The accident at Philadelphia left no visible traces on his physical system. He took up his work as if nothing had happened. In the early part of the year he was making many addresses outside of his parish: at the Groton School, the Boston Latin School, the Little Wanderers' Home, the Harvard Vespers, the Workingmen's Club, and St. Mary's Church for Sailors, in East Boston,— a diversified list of calls upon his sympathy.

Lent came in on February 15. He commented on "the change to the great shadow." "There is much foolish talk about optimism and pessimism, but the highest and deepest, the brightest and darkest thoughts of life must go together." His sermon for Ash Wednesday was on the "Sin that doth so easily beset us." Another sermon is remembered on "David and the Shewbread," where he dwelt on the freedom of the Bible, the freedom of great men like David. "The needs of human nature are supreme, and have a right to the divinest help. The little tasks need divinest impulses. The secular woes are only to be relieved by God. In this use the shewbread is most honored."

In a sermon at Harvard vespers, March 8, he spoke on the text, "God's judgments are far above out of his sight." "There are judgments of our lives of which we are unaware, which we are not fine enough to feel. But the order of the universe feels the judgment as a jar between its wheels. Essential righteousness is busy condemning us and setting right the wrong which we are doing. It is awful to be thus judged at judgment seats too high for us to know. Our brother beside us is being judged at them and knows it; therefore the restless disturbance of his life. As we grow stronger we come into ever higher and higher judgments. Christ judged by them all: 'This is My beloved Son.'"

In his Bible class on Saturday evenings, he commented on the Psalms. He preferred those which he could associate with the experience of David, for David was one of the few whom he accounted great in the world, and the Psalms gained in vividness when associated with a great personality. "Only the experiences of a great soul accounted for such great utterances."

There were sermons dwelling on human sinfulness; one from the text, "He putteth his mouth in the dust, if so be there may be hope"; another, on the words of Jesus, "Neither do I condemn thee. Go, and sin no more," where he dwelt on the dilemma in

which sin places those who would fain deal with it. "How difficult it is to meet it rightly! The fear of cruelty and fear of
feebleness; the sense of one's own sinfulness; the danger of being
superior and patronizing; the fear of exasperating and condoning.
So we keep out of the way. The first thing about Christ is that
He never kept out of the way."

The prominence of Christ in these Lenten services overshadows
all the utterances. It seemed as if the speaker had known Him
in the flesh, or had other conversations with Him in the spirit,
enlightening him as to the deeper meaning of the Saviour's words.
Two sermons were given to the "Loneliness of Christ." On
Wednesday evenings he took up the relations of Jesus to some
of the problems of society and life. Of special interest were the
lectures on the Litany given on Friday afternoons. He analyzed
its structure and the significance of its various divisions, the
variety of its appeal, the emphasis in repetitions, its unvarying uniform cry for deliverance. The invocation of the Trinity
in the opening clauses was intended to expand the grounds and
motives of the infinite appeal. He dwelt especially on the phrase
"miserable sinners," as representing the human soul standing
in its emptiness and waiting to be filled with the profusion of God:

"On the threshold of the Litany sinfulness is encountered, as in
actual life,—the hindrance of sin. Its sources,—the very substance of our own nature; the remoter sources,—the offences of
our forefathers. The double cry to escape the punishment and
to be delivered from these palsying consequences, the guilt and
power of sin. (1) The sense of a universe against us, of external
foes, the assaults of the devil, and the feeling of the wrath of God;
(2) the defects within the soul, the passions and meannesses, the
spites and hatreds,—the soul deceitful and corrupt; (3) the triple
agency of evil,—the world, the flesh, and the devil; (4) the dangers of the physical life,—the cry to be spared from "sudden
death"; (5) the evils of corporate life, heresy, and schism."

One lecture was devoted to "The Great Appeals of the Litany,"
—"by the mystery of Thy Holy Incarnation, Thy passion,
Thy resurrection, and ascension." Then he turned to the public
means of grace, the Church, the Ministry, the Sacraments, the
State also, and suggested a new petition for "the world of
nations." He closed with an impressive summary: "*We sinners*,
what right—and yet what a right we have to pray!"

The Good Friday sermon was from Hebrews x., 20—"By a new and living way which He hath consecrated for us through the veil, that is to say, His flesh."

"It is strange how the great critical event of the world's life is a *Death;* not a battle, nor a coronation, nor a new institution, nor a birth, but yet all these summed up in this dying.

"Obedience unto death. This the only real approach to God. You may crowd upon Him any other way and you do not reach Him. Only the great submission of the will blends our life with His.

"The great silent bliss as soul joins soul,—the Son and the Father! But surely also those whose life He had gathered up into His own! He carried them through and in His obedience. Can we understand that? The human flesh has been always an *obstacle;* Christ made it a channel between God and man."

The sermon for Palm Sunday was on the cry of the multitudes that went before and followed after Christ as He entered Jerusalem. "The great future for the world and for the personal life" was the subject: "Up the broad pathway, lo, *He* comes rejoicing in the solemn crisis and the awful acquisition of life."

On Easter Even was revealed "the history that pauses. Here and there it seems to wait a moment. So with the world's history; so with a life's. There are moments when greater powers are more forceful than we can feel; greater truths are truer for us than we can know."

Exhausting as the Lenten services were, Mr. Brooks came to Easter Day with the culmination of his powers. The morning service at Trinity was attended by "the largest congregation ever gathered within its walls." The sermon was only another variation of the endless theme—

"the value and sacredness of life, the impossibility of man's creating it, the tremendous power with which man clings to life, and the imperishable hope with which man looks forward to the perpetuation of life.

> " No matter what crazy sorrow saith,
> No soul that breathes with human breath
> Has ever truly longed for death.

"In Christ there came rolling back the great flood of life, and into the harbor of life a flood of vitality. The thought of Easter is the Sea of Life, the ocean without bounds, flowing all ways and overflowing all, the Divine existence in its ocean-like extension."

An extraordinary scene was presented at Trinity Church during the Lenten services beginning with this year 1888. They were chronicled as public events of high importance. They reminded of "the flood of fiery eloquence poured forth by Savonarola." The preacher had made elaborate preparation, as evidenced by the note-books for the year 1888 and the following years to 1891. This last phase of the ministry of Phillips Brooks was marked by a deeper solemnity and an ineffable tenderness, where the heart alone was speaking and each individual present was the closest friend. Great throngs were always in attendance. The addresses reported and published were read with eagerness in all parts of the country. In one of his letters, March 13, 1888, he refers to the passing of Lent:

"The blessed Lenten days are fast slipping away from us, and before we know it we shall come out of the golden gate of Easter into that bewildering world where we do not go to church every day. How strange it will all be! But to-day, Winter is in our faces, and Lent is in our hearts."

As the months went by he continued to feel the influence of his wonderful escape: "How long ago it all seems, and yet what a shudder it sends through one's bones to think of it. Mr. —— sent to New York and got me a magnificent and mighty stick to replace that one that vanished on that awful night, so that I carry a memorial of the great accident on all my walks." He was engaged in getting signatures to an address to be made to James Martineau. On March 23, he went to Halifax to be present at the consecration of Bishop Courtney. He was projecting a larger work for Trinity but he felt also the need of an arrangement by which he should be relieved of some part of the burden of preaching. To all his suggestions the Proprietors of Trinity Church responded, with "grateful acknowledgment of his untiring and devoted services." He was withdrawing from some of the responsible positions he held, resigning his trusteeship on the Slater Foundation, to which he had been appointed by Mr. Slater in 1882, when he made his gift of one million dollars for Christian education in the Southern States. To the Rt. Rev. H. C. Potter he wrote:

"233 CLARENDON STREET, BOSTON, June 5, 1888.

"Can you really care about the infinitesimal question of 'non-communicating attendance'? It seems to me to be the very end and exhaustion of religion, a toy for the —— intellect to play with, but profoundly unworthy the consideration of any reasonable man.

"And then the way the disputants deal with it! The appeals to authority! The eager interest in the question whether the Early Fathers 'stayed to Communion'! Who cares?

"Are all the hard questions answered and the great wrongs set right that men are able to find time for things like these?

"I hope that you are well and idle."

At Trinity Church, on Sunday, the 10th of June, Phillips Brooks, in the course of his sermon, spoke of the death of Rev. James Freeman Clarke, a Unitarian minister who for many years had been held in the highest respect and reverence in Boston, for his intellectual and moral force and his saintly character:

"I cannot stand here to-day without a tribute of affectionate and reverent remembrance to Dr. James Freeman Clarke, the minister of the Church of the Disciples, the friend and helper of souls. How much that name has meant in Boston these last forty years! When I think of his long life; when I remember what identification he has had with all that has been noblest in every movement of the public conscience and the public soul; when I see how in the days of the great national struggle, from first to last, he was not only true to Freedom, but a very captain in her armies and a power of wisdom and inspiration in her councils; when I think what words of liberty the slave and the bigot have heard from his lips; when I think how his studies have illuminated not merely our own faith, but all the great religions; when I see how much of Christ was in his daily walk among us, in his unswerving truthfulness, his quiet independence, his tenderness and strength, his pity for the sinner, and his hatred of the sin; when I think how he loved Christ,—when all this gathers in my memory at the tidings of his death, the city, the country, the Church, the world, seem emptier and poorer. He belonged to the whole Church of Christ. Through him his Master spoke to all who had ears to hear. Especially he was a living epistle to the Church of Christ which is in Boston. It is a beautiful, a solemn moment when the city, the Church, the world, gather up the completeness of a finished life like this, and thank God for it, and place it in the shrine of memory to be a power and a revelation thenceforth so long as city and Church and world shall last. It is not the losing, it is rather the gaining, the assuring of his life. Whatever he has gone to in the great mystery beyond, he remains a word of God here in the world he loved. Let us thank our Heavenly Father for the life, the work, the inspiration, of his true servant, his true saint, James Freeman Clarke."

Part of this tribute, beginning with the words "He belonged to the whole Church of Christ," is now an autograph beneath the portrait of James Freeman Clarke in the church where he ministered.

Letters were constantly received, telling what his published sermons were doing to strengthen faith and inspire hope. This letter is from a person in England unknown to him, and represents the feeling, almost the expressions, of the many others who wrote:

" May 14, 1888.

"For the last five years I may say that I have read one of your sermons every Sunday, and the help and spiritual nourishment I get from them has been a very real source of strength and happiness in my life. . . . Often and often have I opened a volume of your sermons in hours of despondency and gloom, when the Unseen has seemed to be the non-existent, when all high ideals were slipping away, and the actual was pressing out faith and courage; and never did the reading of your words fail to encourage and strengthen me and send me back to suffering or action with fresh force and energy. I have been through the various phases of intellectual doubt and scepticism, and *you* have helped me out on the *right* side. The absence of all dogmatism and sectarian narrowness, combined with so inspiring a belief in God's revelation of Himself *to* us and of the Divine *in* us, is what I find so helpful in your books; and the large views you take of life are to me most educative and elevating."

The late Dr. Oliver Wendell Holmes was among those who admired and appreciated Phillips Brooks:

"296 BEACON STREET, MAY 23, 1888.

"MY DEAR MR. BROOKS,—I had the privilege of listening to your sermon last Sunday forenoon. I was greatly moved and impressed by it, and I came away very thankful that so divine a gift of thought and feeling had been bestowed upon one who was born and moves among us.

"My daughter would be glad to have me as her constant companion, and of course it would be a delight to listen to such persuasive and inspiring exhortations as those which held your great audience last Sunday. . . .

"I am ashamed to ask you to pardon this letter. You know the language of sincerity from that of flattery, and will accept this heartfelt tribute in the spirit in which it is given.

"Sincerely and respectfully yours,
"O. W. HOLMES."

He kept up his correspondence with friends in India, where he was held in affectionate remembrance. In his leisure at North Andover, where he was spending the summer, he wrote these letters to Rev. Mr. Lefroy, and to Mr. Robert Maconachie of the Indian Civil Service:

"July 5, 1888.

"MY DEAR MR. LEFROY,—It made me glad and proud to get your letter, now a long time ago. To be remembered for five years by one whose life is as full as yours is indeed something to be proud of, and to have the pleasant days which we spent at Delhi so pleasantly recalled is truly a delight.

"How long ago it seems, and what a host of things have happened since, and yet how clear it all is. I had a delightful letter from Maconachie the other day, which was like the thinning of a cloud which was very thin already. I saw the old scene perfectly, and could hear the tones of voices which I have not heard for five busy years. And that you and the friends I saw with you have been bravely and patiently going on at the good work ever since fills me with admiration. Do you still have your noon service in your chapel-room as you used to? That seemed to me always beautiful. And do the brown boys play cricket? And do you have school feasts and prizes? And is that region of the Kuttub as fascinating as it was when we drove out there one bright morning? I can hear the cool splash of that boy now, as he jumps down into the pool. It is a picture which never grows dim, and only needs the touch of a letter's wing to scatter the dust which lay collected on it.

"That you in your good work should care anything about my books touches me very much indeed. They were written for my people here, and nothing was farther from my thought than that they should be read by the Jamna and the Ganges. But how simple it all grows as we get older! The whole of what we per-

sonally have to live and what we go out to preach is loyalty to
Christ. It is nothing but that. All truth regarding Christ and
all duty towards His brethren is involved in that and flows out
from it. To teach Him to any one who never heard of Him is
to bring a soul into the sight of Him and His unspeakable friendship. To grow stronger and better and braver ourselves is to
draw nearer to Him and to be more absolutely His.

"And this seems to take off the burden of life without lessening the impulse of its duties. He is behind all our work. It is all
His before it is ours and after it is ours. We have only to do
our duty in our little place, and leave the great results to Him.
We are neither impatient nor reluctant at the thought of the day
when we shall have finished here and go to higher work.

"But, dear me! what right have I to say all this to you, who
know it so much better, who are putting it so constantly and
richly into your life and work? I grow stronger for Boston
when I think of Delhi. I hope that Allnut will come back to
you mightily refreshed. Give my best love to Carlyon, and tell
him how well I remember all his kindness. Your other mates
I do not know, but venture to send them my greeting as their
brother in the work. Be sure that I shall always delight to hear
from you. How hot you must be to-day! Would that you were
here in our New England coolness. God bless you always!
"Your friend,
"PHILLIPS BROOKS."

"July 6, 1888.

"DEAR MR. MACONACHIE,—It is long since anything has
made me so glad as your letter. That you, with all your busy
life, should think still of those two weeks which are an unfading
picture in my memory is indeed wonderful to me. I greet you
and your wife as if it were only yesterday instead of five long years
since we parted. What a life God has given you! To be His
minister to millions of His children, to touch their lives with
the new sense of justice and mercy which must bring them some
revelation of Him, and at the same time to care for the real life
which is the spiritual life of some of your fellow-workers—who is
there that has greater privilege? All that you say about your
friend touches me deeply. God help him! The great assuring
certainty is that God *is* helping him. I think we should all of
us long ago have given up trying to do anything for our friends
if we had not been spiritually sure of that. The things we do
are so out of proportion to what is to be done. But He is doing
it, and our work may well be content to be a bit.

"Since I saw you life has gone on with me in very pleasant
monotony. I came back to my work in the autumn of 1883.
Twice since then I have made summer visits to England and the

Continent. The winters have been given to preaching and working. I hope it has not been without result. But I grow less and less inclined to ask. The work itself is delightful, and, if it is faithfully done, it must do good. That is enough. Every year it seems to me as if not merely the quantity but the quality of Christian life grew better. Never was there an age when so many men had so high thoughts of God as now. And this I say in clear sight of the perplexing problems and discouraging spectacles to which no man can shut his eyes. We see dimly what your anxieties are. We, with our country swarming with the disturbed elements of all the world, have our anxieties and misgivings, which are yet not too much for faith. Is it not just in our two countries, yours and mine, India and America, that the meeting of strange races with one another is taking place, and so that the issues of the greater day of Christ are being mysteriously made ready? Would that we could sit either in your bungalow or in my study and talk of all these things! But this letter-writing is poor work. It is only like ships hailing each other at sea. But it is better than nothing. Your letter brought me the Indian sunshine and color and strength, and Boston for a moment seemed the unreal thing. Now I am reading it again, and answering it under my ancestral trees in the country twenty-five miles from Boston, where my forefathers have lived for a century, and where I retreat for summers. It is the very glory of a summer day. The trees are chattering Puritan theology, and I am rejoicing that the world is larger than they know, and that afar off in the Punjab there is some one who cares how it fares with me. May God bless him and his wife and his boys —so prays his friend,

"PHILLIPS BROOKS."

On Sunday, the 15th of July, Dr. Brooks preached at Trinity Church before the National Prison Congress. The sermon was noteworthy apart from its eloquence, for it contained the assertion of important theological and humanitarian principles, and as such was immediately published by the National Prison Association for gratuitous distribution. The text, "I was in prison and ye came unto me," led him to take up the deeper meaning of the words of Christ, who had suffered no imprisonment and yet had been in prison. "It must have been the deeper Christ,—the Christ which the theologies have tried to express when they have made Jesus the head of humanity,— Christ the typical manhood, Christ the divine and universal man, —this was the Christ who had lain in the prison waiting the

visitation of pitiful and sympathetic hearts." The great human
sympathy of the preacher flowed through the sermon like a
river. It closed with a fine passage drawing the distinction
between sentiment and sentimentality:

"In a word, sentiment is the health of human nature, and
sentimentality is its disease. Disease and health often look
strangely alike, but they are always different. He who would escape sentimentality must live in sentiment. He who would
keep sentiment true and strong must fight against sentimentality, and never let himself accept it for his ally. In these days,
when many men are disowning sentiment because they confound
it with sentimentality, and many other men are abandoning
themselves to sentimentality because they confound it with
sentiment, do not all men need to learn, and never to forget,
their difference? Do any men need more to learn and to
remember it than they who have to deal with prisoners and
prisons?"

In response to an invitation that he would deliver a lecture,
he writes:

"TRENTON FALLS, July 22, 1888.

"Your letter of last Wednesday has found me at this pleasant
place, where I am spending a peaceful Sunday without preaching
or any other clerical performance, only looking at the pretty
falls, and going this morning to a little village Methodist meeting,
where the sermon was very good indeed. And here comes your
request to lecture in your course next winter! If it were only
anything but lecturing! If you had only asked me to give a concert, or a ballet, or any of those things which are quite in my line!
But I have never lectured, and don't believe I can. I have not
a rag of preparation to cover the nakedness of my incompetence."

He gives his impressions of *Robert Elsmere*, which was the
literary sensation of the summer:

"I have finished *Robert Elsmere*, and found it very interesting,
mainly, however, with that secondary interest which belongs to
the circumstances of a book and its relation to its time, rather
than to its substance and absolute contents. It is a curious mixture of strength and weakness. It has the sharp definitions of
spiritual things, the fabrication of unreal dilemmas and alternatives in which the English mind, and especially the English clerical mind, delights. It is as unintentionally unfair as a parson,

33

only on the other side. It seems, as Matthew Arnold used to seem, to be entirely unaware of the deeper meanings of Broad Churchmanship, and to think of it only as an effort to believe contradictions, or as a trick by which to hold a living which one ought honestly to resign.

"It is not good to name a doctrine by a man's name, but there is no sign that this writer has ever heard of the theology of Maurice. But how interesting it is! what charming pictures of English life! and what description of mental conditions and evolutions whose real source and true issue we must still feel that she misses!"

Among the papers of Mr. Brooks there are rough notes indicating that he had been asked for some more formal expression of his opinion. The book had been so real in its portraiture that it had thrown people into mental and religious confusion.

"Thoroughly English. Weakness of the orthodox people. Preconceived idea that they *must not think*. Perhaps a return to the human Christ from which the disciples began. Thence to be led on through the mystery of manhood into His complete life. The whole question what is to become of his Brotherhood. Not be contemptuous about the new, extemporized, experimental character of it. By such experiments the great eternal stream of effort is constantly reinforced. The Christ-miracle; and then all else believable. Broad Churchmanship is not explaining away, but going deeper, embracing all nature. This is Matthew Arnold turned to prose. The incomplete story of the reasons of the change in Elsmere. The nineteenth century in the book. Elsmere between the Squire and Catharine. The necessary struggle of the new coming forth from the old, its exaggerations and distortions."

The attitude of Phillips Brooks in rejecting the tenet of apostolical succession, and his recognition of the Christian character and work of a Unitarian minister, the Rev. James Freeman Clarke, was followed by hostile criticism which continued through the summer, and indeed from this time was never intermitted. He had counted the cost when he took his ground, discounting the criticism which was sure to follow. The summer, on the whole, had been an agreeable one, broken up with short visits, but with no intermission of preaching. He started into the work of the fall with his usual apparent vigor.

To the proposal of some of his friends to nominate him for the presidency of Columbia University, in New York, he refused to listen, calling it "a wild suggestion":

"My only ambition is to be a 'Parish Priest.' I am not much of a P. P., but as a College President I should be still less. It would be good to be where I should see you all, and run perpetually in and out as seems to be you New York men's way. But it would not be Boston, and I should be lost in your vast town. So leave me here, and let another hold the college sceptre."

It was the custom of Phillips Brooks to reserve for his sermons on Thanksgiving Days such topics of general interest, political or religious, as afforded the opportunity to summarize the world's outlook in each successive year. In the preamble of one of these sermons, 1881, he alludes to this usage and justifies it, although aware of its dangers:

"Thanksgiving Day has fallen naturally into the habit of trying to estimate the tendencies and the present conditions of our current life. Such efforts have made a great literature which I think is almost peculiar to our time, the literature of an age's introspection; of the inquiry by living men into the nature and worth of the life of their own time."

His Thanksgiving Day sermons taken together present a picture of the time through which he lived. In 1888 he considered that passing mood of sadness which seems to have been widespread as the century drew to its close, when for a moment the world had grown subdued and thoughtful, with a sombre estimate of the future. Taking for his text Psalm lxxxix., 15, "Blessed is the people that hear the joyful sound," he spoke of the gratitude called for by the national festival, as in contrast with the prevailing mood of the hour.

"Let us think for a few moments about the tendency of the world with reference to this whole matter of joyfulness. Sometimes we hear, sometimes we certainly fear, that the world we live in is growing to be a *sadder* world, that happiness is less spontaneous and abundant as the years go by. Is that the truth, or is it a delusion?"

His method of meeting the inquiry is to reduce it to more exact terms. The world of realism is just as joyous as it ever was. The world of childhood knows no difference. The children have not found out that the world is old. Each new generation is still born into a garden. The world also of uncivilized, barbaric life keeps all the joy and freshness it ever had. It is only of the comparatively small world of adult human civilization of which it may be said that its sadness deepens its joy. And of this world it may be asked whether its growing sadness is a real decline and loss of that robustness and primitive simplicity of life, or whether the great world, like every man, is simply for the moment moody, and the stage of sadness is a temporary thing, not to be made too much of, sure to pass away, having no reasons which are deep; best treated, as the moods of a great healthy man are often best treated, by ignoring it. He turns to the reasons which may account for this existing mood:

"(1) The larger view of the world, the clearer atmosphere, so that we hear the groans of misery in Mexico or Turkey. The curtain has fallen between the rich and the poor; the poor look into our luxurious homes with their haggard faces, and we eat and talk and sleep in the unceasing sound of their temptation and distress. There has been nothing like it in any other day. No wonder the world grows sad.

"(2) The universal ambition; all who feel the spirit of the time are struggling for the unattainable. There is discontent everywhere, and discontent means sadness.

"(3) The vague way in which our complicated life puts us in one another's power. The strings of a man's destiny are held by a thousand hands, most of them unknown to him. Hence the burden of a conscious helplessness,—a nightmare which will not let him stir. He is sad with the vague loss of personal life.

"(4) Another reason for the sadness of which all are more or less aware is the presence of fear as an element in our life. Other ages knew at least what perils they were threatened with. The consciousness of our time is that it does not know. Vast, unmeasured forces hold us in their hands. Great, bleak, uncertain vistas open and appall us. We are like children in the waste of a great prairie. The mere vastness scares us. We fear we know not what. We only know we fear. And fear like that does not inspire and concentrate energy. It only breeds pervading and pathetic sadness.

"(5) The man on whom these causes of sadness act. Our modern human nature is *sensitive* as in no other time to such a degree. Things *hurt* more than they used to hurt. Once no one cared how much the beasts suffered by the lash or the surgeon's knife. Once men went home from an *auto da fé* and slept without uncomfortable dreams. The atmosphere has grown clearer and the perceptions within us finer. He who had foreseen it all years ago might have said prophetically, 'What a terrible capacity of sadness man is growing into and will reach!'"

In each one of these motives he had enumerated he then sought to show there was the possibility of contributing to joy; that they are the very elements and motives that must be mingled in the deepest joy. The large view of the world, the eager ambitions, the close complications of life with life, the outlook into future mystery, and the quickened sensitiveness,—these are essential to the final perfect happiness; they are permanent forces which have come to remain; it is only the first influence of them which is temporary; as the time goes on the first confusion and depression will pass away. "The life and character of Jesus is a perpetual illumination of the hopes of man. In Him behind the superficial and temporary sadness is revealed a profound and ultimate joy. No restless and impatient pessimist knows the deep tragedy of life as the Divine Sufferer knew it. All that lies undigested, unassimilated in the present condition of the world lay harmonized and peaceful in the soul of Christ."

"I have talked idly, almost wickedly, upon Thanksgiving morning, unless I have succeeded in making you see light shine out of the darkness, in making you hear a 'joyful sound' piercing through the complaints and wailings which besiege our ears. We take too little views. It is not the events of life, nor its emotions, or this or that experience, but life in itself which is good. The great joy is just to be alive. The fact of life is greater than what is done with it. So I answer confidently the question which I asked. No period of sadness can be other than temporary. The nature of the world is not changed. Nothing has happened to make it different from what it has always been. The essential tendency of life is towards happiness. Therefore we may wait confidently till the morning. Optimism tempered and sobered, nay, saddened, if you will, but optimism still is the only true condition for a reasonable man. I seem to see Christ stand over all making the world into His likeness. The promise issues fresh from the divine lips of the great Saviour, the great Sufferer, the Son of Man, the Son of God, that the pure in heart shall see God, and that He will lead all men to the Father."

On his fifty-third birthday he wrote to Mrs. Robert Treat Paine:

"December 13, 1888.

"DEAR MRS. PAINE,—I thank you again, as I have thanked you many times before, and always with a fuller and fuller heart. Few men have had such happy years and such kind friends as have been given me. I wish I had been more worthy of them, but at any rate I am grateful for them, most of all for you and yours. I dare to believe it will keep on until I am a hundred. At present, however, I am looking forward to next Saturday, when I shall thank you again. Gratefully,

"Your friend,

"PHILLIPS BROOKS."

CHAPTER XXI.

1889.

WATCH NIGHT. OCCASIONAL ADDRESSES. LENT SERVI-
CES AT TRINITY CHURCH. ILLNESS. SUMMER IN
JAPAN. EXTRACTS FROM NOTE-BOOKS. THE
GENERAL CONVENTION. SOCIAL AND POLITICAL
REFORMS. THE EVANGELICAL ALLIANCE. CORRE-
SPONDENCE.

THE peculiar service of "Watch Night" at Trinity had always
been an impressive spectacle and continued to grow more
impressive as the years went by.

"When the hour of eleven opened, Trinity Church appeared to
be filled in every part; yet for some time afterward there was a
constant stream of people entering and following the ushers, who
kept on providing seats in all possible places until not another
seat could be found; and then a multitude remained standing,
until the last hour of 1888 was ended, and the first hour of 1889
had come. As the hands of the clock that stood within the chancel railing pointed to one minute of midnight, the great congregation bowed in silent prayer until twelve strokes had been sounded
forth, and 1889 had begun. The united repetition of the Lord's
Prayer aloud ended this solemn stage of the service, after which
Dr. Brooks again spoke a few earnest words, expressing the hope
that all present might live stronger, purer, more manly, more
womanly, more Christlike lives in the year that had begun than
in the year that had closed."

An incident occurred in the early part of the year which illustrates the tolerance of Phillips Brooks. As a member of the
Standing Committee of the Diocese, he voted to confirm the election of a clergyman to a Western bishopric, writing letters also
in his behalf to other dioceses which were hesitating, urging that

the comprehensiveness of the Church should not be restricted by any personal or doctrinal prejudices. In a letter he remarks that he is surprised to find how earnest he has become in advocating the cause of one for whom nothing in the world would have induced him to vote.

He comments on his preaching in St. Paul's Church:

"I went to St. Paul's Church and preached there morning and evening the other Sunday, and had the usual curious and mixed sensations. I could n't help feeling as if Father and Mother were sitting over in Pew No. 60, and as if I were both the preaching minister and the tall boy in the congregation."

During January and February Mr. Brooks went again to Faneuil Hall for four successive Sunday evenings. He gave also one Sunday evening to a service in the Globe Theatre. There is the usual record of sermons at Appleton Chapel and of addresses at the Harvard Vespers. He was getting relief under the burden he was carrying through the aid of the assistant minister, Rev. Roland Cotton Smith. To Rev. W. N. McVickar, who was to make him a visit, he writes:

"You will preach for me, I hope, in the morning, and then we will make Roland Cotton Smith preach in the afternoon, so that neither of us shall be overworked. Cotton Smith is preaching excellently, and fast taking the work out of the hands of the old rector."

The sermons which Mr. Brooks delivered at Fanueil Hall or at the Globe Theatre required more preparation and a greater effort of strength than his ordinary sermon. He was not proposing to preach down to the congregations, but to lift himself above his highest level. He took for one of his texts the words of Christ, "I am among you as he that serveth." He did not urge upon his hearers the importance of goodness or righteousness in themselves; he struck a deeper note when he summoned up practical religion in the effort to make others good. "Christ in the Gospel never appears so much as one who is cultivating righteousness in Himself, but as one seeking to cultivate it in others."

In his sermon at the Globe Theatre he dwelt on the necessity of a feeling of "need" as lying beneath the world's life and the history of its civilization. No discovery was made or work done without it; imagine it removed and there would be a vast stoppage. "In the spiritual life the absence of the sense of imperious need is the great cause of sluggishness,—the dullness of the churches compared with the vitality of the streets." He wrestled like a giant with his theme, till it seemed as if every soul must have felt the need he portrayed. His text was the words of the centurion to Christ, "Sir, come down, ere my child die."

Turning from the sermons, we find him on the 15th of January at the dinner given to Professor Lovering on the completion of fifty years' service at Harvard, where he spoke for the ministry as bringing their tribute to the man of science. For himself, as he remarked, he had not been, while in college or since, a student who excelled in the natural sciences, and for mathematics, which Professor Lovering represented, he had shown no aptitude. And yet there remained "the value of forgotten knowledge, which has somehow passed into the blood. It was better to have known and lost than never to have known at all. At least the sense of the value of the sciences was something gained. It was like forgotten but effectual periods in the world's history." He recognized "the debt which we all owe to a man who has made any department of life more complete, the power of scientific study to enrich life and make it more youthful.

On the 21st of January he made the address on the occasion of the thirty-eighth anniversary of the Young Men's Christian Association, when they took possession of their building on Boylston Street. His subject was the value of the institution, and its significance for human life. As he went on he broadened his thought till it included religion and the changes it had undergone. He spoke of this organization as one of the necessary forms which the changed form of religion was demanding. He had no fear of its interference with the churches of Christ, for it is the Church of Christ. Liberty, he impressed upon the young men, had been the characteristic word of the last hundred years, but it was a negative term, the removal of obstacles in order that a higher order might come in, the reign of human sympathy under the recognition of human brotherhood. "Cultivate the power of sympathy because it is the spirit of your age and the coming age." Sympathy "is curing more and more the evils of social life, making harmonious the differences of our commercial life, entering more and more into the obstructed ways of secular life."

As we follow him into another Lenten season, we can only pause to note the topics with which he was concerned. Friday evenings he devoted to the versicles in the Prayer Book; as he expounded them, words which had become so familiar as to have almost lost their force were seen to be full of unsuspected depths of meaning. He dwelt on the "effect of a largely constructed liturgy like ours, constantly used, upon the progress of religious thought in an individual and in a church." They were mistaken who thought that he slurred the service in order to get to the sermon. The service took on new beauty and impressiveness when he read it. "He puts into his utterance of creed and litany and prescribed forms of prayer," said a writer not of his own communion, "such wealth of personal consecration that a person who should hear that and nothing more would remember the thrilling experience all his days."

On Wednesday evenings he dwelt on the "appeals to Christ," as given in the Evangelical narrative: "Come down ere my child die;" "Speak to my brother that he divide the inheritance with me"; "Give me this water that I thirst not, neither come hither again to draw"; "Remember me when Thou comest in Thy kingdom." He took up with his Bible class the evidences of Christianity,—what some have thought to be the most formal and perfunctory of subjects. His best thought was in his sermons, presented in such a living way that Christianity became its own evidence. It is evident from the preparation he now made that he was trying to reach the minds of the young men before him in ways that they would appreciate. The distinctive features of his theology appear at every turn, and the thoroughness of his mind, as he takes up in succession (1) Christianity, (2) Christ and the Trinity, (3) The Bible, (4) Miracles, (5) The Resurrection, (6) The Church, (7) Personal Experience, (8) Prayer. Although he did not value this kind of work, yet if his notes of these lectures could be published, they would form a valuable manual for Christian instruction.

One may detect a somewhat unusual tone in the Sunday morning sermons delivered during this season of Lent. The texts and their treatment imply a certain pathos in the mood of the preacher. The sermon for Ash Wednesday was from the text, "Who knoweth if He will return and repent and leave a blessing behind him?"

"The picture is of a departing God, once very near, now going away and going further. To some it is very real as a fact of experience. They did once have God nearer to them. The days of communion and obedience and realized love; the definite standards. And now the far-awayness of it all. Or to take the comparison, not of past and of present, but of idea and realization, God is close to us in His own revelation, but far from us in our actualization of Him. This the deeper historic meaning.

"Either way the withdrawing God and the soul crying after Him. Strange situation! Driving Him away and yet calling on Him to stay. The mixed mystery of our inner life. . . . He certainly will return, else what mean these promises? He is not going willingly, nor angrily, nor carelessly. He is going because He *must*, because you will not have Him.

"He will return if you seek Him rightly. The gift He will bring back with Him is an offering to Himself. Restoration to be sought that we may have a life to give Him.

"This puts a motive into our repentance. Repentance for safety, even for cleanness, is not complete. The true motive that God may be glorified in us.

"This implies a certain sense of the misery of sin. It is that our sinful lives do not belong to and redound unto Him. That is the felt misery of the best lives when they fall into sin. They have dishonored God. They have nothing to render Him. Then the delight of His return, that once more they may do Him honor.

"The sense of exhilaration which thus enters into repentance."

One of the sermons was on the text, in the Prayer Book version, "He brought down my strength in my journey and shortened my days." Another sermon was on a verse from a Psalm: "I shall find trouble and heaviness, and I will call upon the name of the Lord." And still another from the words of Christ: "It cannot be that a prophet perish out of Jerusalem." In this sermon he dwelt on the expenditure of energy for personal power and wealth and lower ends,—the giving of life for most unworthy things.

"The life *must* be given. You must expend it. You cannot keep it. It is going. What is there to show for it at the end? Is there the result of enlarged spiritual conditions in the world, so that first we and then our brethren are better for our having lived? He who perishes in Jerusalem claims Jerusalem for God."

Of the few letters belonging to this moment, there is one where he gives his opinion regarding the distinctive claims of the Episcopal Church:

"233 CLARENDON STREET, BOSTON, March 18, 1889.

"I do not know a single book about our Church which does not mingle with its exposition of what the Church is some notions, more or less erroneous, but certainly private and personal, of the author. Therefore, I am quite out of the habit of asking any one who is at all interested in our Church to study anything but the Prayer Book. The Prayer Book, without note or comment, interpreting itself to the intelligent reader,—that is the best thing. And histories of our Church are also written with a purpose. There is not one which is not colored with the intention of its writer. Bishop White's *History* is the best, and some of Frederick D. Maurice's *Lectures on the Prayer Book* have much light in them. Let your friends know that the only real "claim" of the Church is the power with which it claims their souls and makes them better men. Then offer them its privileges if they are humble and earnest enough to know their need."

It had now become apparent that Phillips Brooks was seriously ill. His friends noticed the change in his looks with alarm. The late Colonel Henry Lee spoke what many were feeling when he wrote to him:

"BOSTON, May, 3, 1889.

"I was shocked, as I have been several times of late, at your appearance. Who am I, to meddle in your affairs? Only one of many more thousands than you will ever know, to whom your existence is all-important; and as one of them I beg you earnestly to cease your incessant work this very day and depart, going by sea or land where you can find rest and recreation. I wish I knew who was your physician. I would urge him to order you off at once. If you knew of what importance, not only to your church, but to the college, to our city, to all of us, is your life, you would do what you can to preserve it."

The place to which he turned for rest and change was Japan. A conversation with Rev. W. E. Griffis, the author of *The Mikado's Empire*, encouraged him to make the venture. He read *The Soul of the Far East*, by Mr. Percival Lowell. As the scheme took possession of his mind he grew enthusiastic about its possibilities. It added to his pleasure in contemplating the journey that he had secured his friend McVickar for a travelling companion. To Mr. McVickar he writes:

"233 CLARENDON STREET, BOSTON, March 20, 1889.

"I went down to Salem and saw Professor Morse, who is the biggest authority on Japan to be found anywhere. And such a collection of bowls and basins, of cups and candlesticks, of jars and jimcracks as he has! My mouth is watering and my eyes are sparkling even now, in spite of several Lent services which have come in between. But what he says is this: that Japan is perfectly possible in summer; that it is very hot, but that the heat is not felt as much as it is here; that you must wear the thinnest of clothing and the strawiest of hats, and that it is as healthy as you please. He makes little or nothing of the rainy season. Says it rains worst in June and September, but declares that if we reach there about mid-July, and leave to come home about September 1, we shall have royal weather. . . .

"Isn't it sad about ——? Dear me, if that splendid fellow has indeed given way, who of us is there that can be sure of himself for an hour? And yet there are encouragements as well. Here is —— getting engaged and starting out on a new life when it seems as if he would think things were about through with him. He's like the fellow who lights up a new cigar just when it seems as if bedtime had really come. But there is a splendid courage about it, and it almost makes one ready to fling prudence to the winds and go in for it himself. But I guess I wont, on the whole.

"I can hear the chatter of Japanese tongues and the clatter of Japanese crockery in the distance, but just now I must get ready for service, and so must you."

Mr. Brooks left Boston on the 10th of June for the ride across the continent, breaking the journey at Salt Lake City, where he spent a Sunday, and visited the Mormon Tabernacle. He does not seem to have been impressed by the people, or their civilization. On the 20th of June he sailed from San Francisco for Yokohama. There were but two passengers on board besides himself and Dr. McVickar. The eighteen days passed quietly, the ocean was calm, and the only event which appealed to the imagination was the dropping of one day, Monday, July the 1st. "The lost day! Think what might have come of it! The undone deeds! The unsaid words!"

These are extracts from his note-book written on shipboard:

"Difference between 'a good fellow' and a good man."

"Preach on the tone of life, high or low, apart from special acts."

"Text, 'God hath laid on Him the iniquity of us all.' The way men bear each other's sins. The great sinful world on men's shoulders. Ah! there's the key! Imagine that complete."

"Those wise blinds, through which you can see out, but cannot see in."

"'Thou hast wrestled and prevailed.' The deeper life. The only question left, How to do one's duty?"

"'I will not do this wicked thing and sin against God.' The special definite resolve."

"'Unless the Lord build the house, their labor is but vain that build it.' The inner spiritual building of everything."

"'Then would I flee away and be at rest.' The deep impulse of escape and retirement."

"I would like to do one thing perfectly, and do only that the rest of my life. Yet, no!"

"A 'spent sea' in history, *e. g.*, the ages following the seventeenth century."

"Like the captain's view of things at sea, so different from the landsman passenger's."

"The question whether all life is to be drawn in,—its great expansion into the supernatural denied it. Intention for extension. The world it would make. Try to depict."

"'And the land had rest fourscore years.' The worth and dangers of rest."

"Awful the convulsion that *does nothing*. The beauty of our war—it killed Slavery."

"What is the greatest, noblest, finest deed ever done on this earth? What if we could put our finger on it!"

"Jehoram 'reigned in Jerusalem eight years and departed without being desired.' The being missed and its natural desire."

"'The Son can do nothing of Himself, but what He seeth the Father do.' Christianity all in the line of God's great first purposes."

"Coming in sight of a new land (Japan), with its mysterious multitudinous history, set in the ancient halls, like coming in sight of another man's life with its mystery. July 8, 1889."

During the long idle days of the ocean journey Mr. Brooks was writing Christmas and Easter carols, for which he had a peculiar gift. He wrote them with ease, as if they had long been singing in his heart.

> " The silent stars are full of speech
>   For who hath ears to hear;
> The winds are whispering each to each,
> And stars their sacred lessons teach
>   Of faith and hope and fear.

> "But once the sky its silence broke,
>   And song o'erflowed the earth;
> And Angels mortal language spoke,
> When God our human utterance took,
>   In Christ the Saviour's birth."

This was the first rapid sketch of one of the Christmas carols. Another begins with the lines:

> " The earth has grown old with its burden of care,
>   But at Christmas it always is young."

And a third:

> " Everywhere, everywhere, Christmas to-night!"

This Easter carol also, which has become widely popular:

> " Tomb, thou shalt not hold Him longer!
>   Death is strong, but life is stronger."

In the letters from Japan Mr. Brooks speaks of his journey as a great success:

"I don't think there can be a place anywhere in the world more suitable for pure relaxation. . . . Of all bright, pretty places, it is the prettiest and the brightest. . . . It is very fascinating: the merriest, kindest, and most graceful people, who seem as glad to see you as if they had been waiting for you all their years, and make you feel as if their houses were yours the moment you cross the threshold, . . . as if good manners and civility were the only ends in life. I never saw anything like it, and the fascination grows with every new street picture that one sees.

"We have had most hospitable welcome from American and English people; almost every night in Yokohama we dined out, and here we have been given rooms at the club, which is a Government affair and most comfortable. To-morrow night we are to dine with the English Bishop of Japan, and there is more of courtesy and kindness than we can accept."

While most of the time was spent in travelling, no opportunities were lost of meeting the missionaries, and learning of their work. He came across one of the missionaries engaged in translating into Japanese *Pearson on the Creed*, a learned work of Anglican theology in the seventeenth century; and thought it unwise to confuse the minds of the Japanese with the technicalities and processes through which the Western mind had passed. Once only did he preach.

He speaks of the impression which he and Dr. McVickar made upon the Japanese by their unusual size. He was afraid that the jinrikisha men would rebel at the burden, but that happened only once. The Japanese were curious to get the measurements of the head and hands and feet of their extraordinary guest. The children called him *Daibutsu*,—the image of the great Buddha.

"Kioto, August 1, 1889.

"I am anxious to send you all at least one greeting from this queer and interesting land, and I must do it quick or not at all, for our short time here is half exhausted and the next steamer but one will carry us to San Francisco. The journey has been a great success thus far, and here we are perched on a breezy hill just outside of the brightest and gayest of Japanese cities, with such a view of the confused and jumbled town and the high hills beyond as not many city suburbs can furnish. It is a hot, sweltering afternoon. All the morning we have been looking at Mikado's Palaces and Buddhist Temples, dragged in jinrikishas through picturesque and crowded streets by trotting coolies who must remember us and hate us all the rest of their miserable lives.

Now in the quiet afternoon there is a pleasant wind blowing across the hotel veranda, and all the time there comes the monotonous and soothing music of a Buddhist drum which a poor priest is beating at the Temple close to us, and which never seems to pause an instant from the sun's rising to its setting. It is all as calm and beautiful and different from Boston as anything can be. The bamboos are waving gracefully in the foreground and the pines are standing majestically behind. Japan is rich in both, and they are pictures of the way in which strength and grace meet in her history remarkably.

"We are now in our fourth week on shore, and indeed I do not know how any one could make for himself a more delightful summer than by doing just what we have done. A swift run across the continent, a slow and peaceful sail on the Pacific, and then this phantasmagoria of color and life and movement for six delightful weeks. And then the return over the familiar ways with much to think about and one's brain full of pictures. What could be better than that?"

On the return voyage he resumed his note-book:

"The strange personalness of a new land; becoming 'acquainted' with it."

"As the Japanese build their houses to suit their mats."

"The Japanese smiling as he tells of his mother's death."

"Japan strangely self-conscious. Lack of sense of individuality in the East."

"'Why pluckest thou not thy right hand out of thy bosom to consume the enemy?' The apparent indifference of God. What is God's enemy?"

"The thing which is done upon earth, He doeth it Himself."

"Both engine and brake. Conservatism and radicalism parts of the same machine."

"Sermon on a man's discovering a meanness in himself from which he thought he was free (coming from new circumstances, e. g., travelling)."

"Sermon on outgrowing temptations, falsely made cause for complacency. Like passing railway stations; the new ones are the old ones under new forms."

34

"The ultimate mystery of life is personality. All which stops short of that is partial."

"The spider spins his web in the rice-pot. Japanese phrase for poverty."

"You might as well think to help the moon fighting its battle with the clouds."

"The balance and co-operation of content and discontent."

"A law, a truth, an institution, a Person. Which is Christianity? There can be no doubt."

"The East haunted by the problems of reality and apparition as well as by that of personality and impersonality."

"The present with the future on its back, like a Japanese mother and her child."

"Sermon on the variety of aspect of religion in the various ages of life,—youth's activity and middle age."

"The rising tide catching one against a precipitous wall. Escape impossible."

"If we hope for that we have not, then we work for it."

"'Get thee behind me.' The everlasting word to the tempter. Who cannot say it, dies."

"Lives haunted like houses."

"The Shinto (ancestor-worship) of Boston."

"Losing a Tuesday going over and picking up a Thursday coming back,—August 28, 1889, lived twice on the Pacific."

"Pride before destruction. The great danger of boasting. Our liability to the sins from which we think ourselves most secure."

"A man's suffering till the consequences of his sin are exhausted."

"'There is nothing hidden that shall not be revealed' neither hid that shall not be known.' The kind of world that perfect light shall make, and the kind of life in waiting for it."

"The impressions of nature, the truths of science, all less than personal relations. The only final means of revelation. Reconciliation. The secret of Christ. God sent forth His Son. Two kinds of religion,—truth and person. All religions develop both. Love and faith are the powers."

"Houses for earthquake, built either very slight or very solid."

"R. S. V. P. So says nature with her invitations."

"A man behind whose closed eyelids light and darkness show their difference, though he can distinctly see no object."

"The latitude and longitude of life."

"'Lord, to whom shall we go? Thou hast the words of eternal life.' Christ the key of existence, not Buddha, nor any other."

"The Japanese giving a new name at the time of death. The new name of the new life kept hung up in the sacred place of the house."

"'While I am coming another steppeth in before me.' Competition,—its naturalness and unnaturalness; its advantages and horrors. Sure to be some day outgrown."

"Mark iii., 21. Christ's friends, not His enemies, said, 'He is beside Himself,' and wanted to restrain Him. The limitations that Christians put to Christ."

"Mark v., 7. The demoniac crying out, 'What have I to do with thee, Jesus?' But Jesus shows that he has something to do with the Son of God."

"He shall save his soul alive."

"Ashamed of himself. Filled with all the fulness of God."

"Evening and morning were the first day. Ending and beginning everywhere."

"A man in Christ."

By the middle of September Mr. Brooks was again in Boston,

and had resumed his work.   In Japan he had been far from well, and his enjoyment of what he saw, or of the hospitalities extended to him, had in consequence been diminished.   He was better, however, than if he had tried to spend "a lazy summer" at home, as he at one time proposed to do.   To the world he seemed vigorous and strong, or, as one of his friends abroad wrote to him, "the happiest and hopefullest man I know."

At Trinity Church, the first Sunday after his return, he spoke of God's ownership of the world, as giving it beauty and value: "The earth is the Lord's and the fulness thereof; the world and they that dwell therein."   With what interest he was followed is shown in this extract from a daily paper:

"As he passed quietly in to begin the service he looked and moved with all his old-time vigor, although some might fancy that his massive frame betrayed an appreciable loss of flesh.   A slight cough, too, was also noticed during the reciting of a portion of the service.   To the friends who embraced an opportunity to greet him, he manifested his unvarying cheerfulness and vivacity.   It was in the pulpit, as always, that he appeared with all the fulness of his personality and mental powers, and when he spoke it was with a torrent of language and abounding imagery that seemed to have gathered even more than the customary momentum from contact with the Oriental glow of life and scenes. Whether from association with these, or from the feelings evoked by return to the family of his congregation, he supplemented his unsurpassed rapidity of thought and utterance with more than his usual emotional quality."

On the second Sunday after his return he went to Cambridge to address the students at the opening of a new year of college life.   He spoke of the new system of voluntary prayers as no longer an experiment.   "Hitherto there had been a certain self-consciousness about it which it was now time to drop.   It was the legitimate successor of all the best religious influence."   He urged upon the students to give their best to the college if they would get its best in return; "treat it not as a playground or living-shop, but as a living being with a soul caring for spiritual nature, and it will bestow its riches, for *indeed it has them*."   The address was noticeable for its intense earnestness.   His love for Harvard came out in a few sentences at its close.   "Many noble men have rejoiced to live for the college, asking nothing as they grew old but to do something more for her before they died. Will you join their army? What she asks of you is to be as full men as you can, for so her life grows fuller."

The General Convention met in New York in October, when he was the guest of his brother Arthur. He took part in the discussions on the revision of the Prayer Book, urging the substitution of Psalm lxiv for Psalm lxix in the Evening Prayer for Good Friday. "We listen to Jesus crying, 'Father, forgive them, for they know not what they do,' and then proceed at once to say, 'Let their table be made a snare, to take themselves withal,'" etc.

In a proposed canon on marriage and divorce Mr. Brooks objected to a phrase forbidding "clandestine marriages": "If we are to forbid a thing, we must have some penalty for its disobedience, which in this case would obviously be exclusion from Holy Communion." He should feel himself unable to deny the sacrament to people who in their youth had been indiscreet enough to make a clandestine marriage. "There is a danger of making marriage too difficult." The subject of "divorce" had been in his mind as he was returning home from Japan. In his note-book he expresses hints of his opinion:

"The 'putting away' which Christ condemned was not the equivalent of our present divorce system; it was purely arbitrary, with no trial or opportunity of defence, the man's right only, while the woman had no corresponding power; it was originally for some cause which includes more than adultery, and it allowed remarriage (Deut. xxiv., 2). Our divorce is a different matter, involving different necessities. The Mosaic institution which Christ modified had reference to inheritance and preservation of purity of descent. There are strong objections to using the Holy Communion for enforcing a position on this subject, especially in the matter of its administration to the dying, in view of the perfect conscience with which divorces are obtained. It would be more consistent to deny divorces altogether. But the whole question is not a clear one, in view of the fact that Christian nations have so differed regarding it and so differ still. Circumstances have changed since the time of Christ. The spirit is more than the letter."

On his return from the General Convention, Mr. Brooks preached a sermon at Trinity Church more hopeful in its tone than his sermon in 1886. He reviewed its results in a kindly way, declaring himself not altogether in sympathy with the changes made in the Prayer Book, but speaking of the Convention as an inspiring one in its manifestation of high moral purpose, in its desire for Christian unity, its zeal for missionary work. He went to the Episcopalian Club, where the Convention was the subject of discussion, making a speech which pleased its members and was pronounced by some to be "churchly." He was apparently forgiven for what he had said of the Convention of 1886. He was so genuine, so rational, so human, that forgiveness was not difficult to grant.

Some of the sermons of Phillips Brooks at this time were notable for the advocacy of social and political reforms. On Fast Day he discussed the public schools and prohibition. In regard to the first he maintained that the state has incorporated its best ideas in the public schools, the three essentials of character without which a state cannot exist—freedom, intelligence, and responsibility. Not only the right of the state, but its duty in this matter of primary education, must be boldly maintained. If scholars were to be withdrawn from the public schools into private institutions, the state must assert its prerogative and enforce on them its principles, insisting that they shall be the equals of the public schools in cultivating freedom, intelligence, and responsibility.

On the subject of prohibition he declared his preference for restrictive legislation, on the ground that it gave the opportunity for self-control. But, on the other hand, his interest in the end to be attained was so real that he could say:

"I have no charge or reproach to make against the most extravagant temperance reformer. I can understand the intensity of his feeling, which urges the most sweeping laws which he can secure. But it seems to me that, instead of legal restriction, the great advance in this direction is to arouse the conscience of the people to live for the state and for their fellow-men, and not for themselves; to let no selfish desire stand in the way of any reasonable measure which shall help to overcome this evil. It does no good to champion this or that public measure while as yet our own hearts and consciences are untouched. In this as in similar matters it is very easy for intense earnestness to develop into mere partisanship, in which condition we oppose all plans which do not harmonize with our own, even though they may contain much good. Rather let us keep ourselves pure and broad, ready to accept any truest and best method by which at the time our purpose may be achieved."

He preached a sermon on Civil Service Reform, in response to a request that the clergy would treat the subject from their pulpits. The sermon showed his devotion to the cause of nationality and to the principles of a republican form of government. The text was from the Old Testament, "Ye shall be unto me a kingdom of priests and a holy nation. These are the words that thou shalt speak unto the kingdom of Israel" (Exodus xix., 6). That one should take a text from the Old Testament for civil service reform might appear to some, he said, as evidence of the incompetence of the clergy to deal with living political issues.

"The old reproach of ministers that they lived in the Old Testament and preached about the sins and virtues of the patriarchs, and not about the sins and virtues of the modern world, is perhaps obsolete. It is hardly worth while to ask how far it was ever deserved. That which it most concerns us to observe about it is the misconception which it indicated, on the part both of preachers and of hearers, of the true place and use of that wonderful portion of the word of God in which the story of God's dealings with his chosen people is related. The history of the Jews appeared to some men to be an utterly outgrown, uninteresting record of a people who perished as a nation centuries ago, and the constant recurrence to it seemed to be a hopeless effort artificially to keep alive the dead. To other men it seemed as if many, at least, if not all, of the details of Jewish life were of perpetual obligation, patterns to be mechanically copied and repeated to the end of time."

He spoke of the Old Testament as the "authoritative text-book of nationality," despite failures to enforce its teaching in Christian history, as in the notion of the divine right of kings, or in Puritan attempts to make the law of Moses the law of God for modern life. "God, may we not say, was too present with His modern world to let them treat Him as if He had died two thousand years ago." But the thought of the Old Testament lives on. The nation is sacred and struggles to assert its sacredness. "At the moment when it almost seemed as if the notion of the sanctity of the state had perished, and nations were coming to be regarded as only joint stock companies for mutual advantage, —there has come this wonderful thing, the sacredness of human life, standing up and demanding recognition ":

"Republican government is open to the influx of the essential sacredness of human life itself."

"The essential nature of humanity is so divine that every effort of man after self-government is a true echo of the life of God."

"The simplest republic is sacred as no most splendid monarchy could ever be."

"The divinity which used to hedge a king fills all the sacred life of a free people."

"Not down from above by arbitrary decree, but up from below, out from within by essential necessity, proceeds the warrant of authority."

"The sacredness of man, of the individual man; the cultivation, not the repression, of his personality; individualism not institutionalism; institutions only for the free characteristic development of the individual,—those are the tokens of healthy life, the watchwords of true progress."

"A state in which the people rule themselves is able to realize the sacredness of the nation more profoundly than any other."

"Popular government is not the last desperate hope of man, undertaken because everything else has failed. It is the consummation toward which every previous experiment of man has struggled. It is no reckless slipping down into the depth of anarchy. It is a climbing to the mountain top of legitimate authority."

"The public officer embodies the nation's character, expresses its spirit and its sanctity. The public servant is not simply a man hired by the state to do a certain work. He is the state itself doing that work and so making manifest at one point its intrinsic life and character."

"Is popular government naturally disposed to corruption and misrule, and so must you force upon it against its nature an integrity and unselfishness which it instinctively hates and despises, or is it the constant struggle of popular government to bring its best men to power, and have you only to work in confederation with that struggle and against the enemies which hinder its success?"

"To make America to be more truly American, with a profounder faith in and loyalty to herself, to resist any attempt to impose the will of a man or a party on the free action of Americans, this sums up the duty of every reformer who believes that, thus strengthened and set free, America will of her own nature send forth her own true governors."

He shared in the prevailing sense of anxiety about the country prevalent at the time:

"We cannot forget the *stress and strain* to which, as all men feel, the whole system of human government, popular government like every other, is evidently in the near future of the world to be subjected. We believe in our institutions as we believe in a strong ship in which we sail out upon the sea. But we cannot look forth upon the sea on which we are to sail and not behold it black with threatening storms. We are full of faith that the good ship will weather them, but what fools we are unless we look not merely to the soundness of the timbers which compose her structure, but also to the character of her officers and crew! In the great trial of popular institutions which is coming, the most critical of all questions concerning them will be as to their power to control their own leadership and to express the better and stronger, and not the worse and weaker, portions of their life through those whom the nation calls from the mass of her citizens and sets in public stations."

During the month of November Mr. Brooks was conducting prayers at Harvard, but he did not enjoy it as in previous years. He spoke of it as "distinctly an off-term," intimating that the sound of his voice had grown familiar and tiresome. For whatever reason he seemed disappointed, and at moments inclined to dreary forebodings about the future.

To an invitation from Rev. Lyman Abbott to take part in the services of his installation as pastor of Plymouth Church, he wrote the following letter:

"Wadsworth House, Cambridge, December 2, 1889.

"Dear Mr. Abbott,— . . . I thank you for the friendly impulse which made you wish that I should come and take any part in the most interesting service of your installation. I value that impulse of yours very deeply, and I always shall. I may most frankly say that there is no man from whom I should more joyfully receive such a token of confidence and affection.

"I should like exceedingly to come. I would make every effort to do so. There is nothing, I am sure, in any canon or rubric which would prevent my coming. I am not very wise in rubrics or canons, but I do not remember one which says a word about our ministers sitting in Congregational councils. . . . As to the function of a member of an ordaining council, I am disgracefully ignorant. I have been nothing but an Episcopalian all my life. What does an installer do, I wonder? And what would the Congregationalists say when they saw me there?

"Would it not be better that I should come, if possible, and utter the interest which I really deeply feel by giving out a hymn or reading a lesson from Scripture at the installation service? And then, if at the last moment, something here made it impossible for me to come, perhaps another man might do my important duty in my place, and I should be with you in spirit and bid you godspeed all the same. . . ."

"Ever faithfully yours,

"PHILLIPS BROOKS."

In the first week in December he took part in the meetings of the Evangelical Alliance, which held its session in Boston. One evening was assigned to him, when he made an address occupying nearly an hour in its delivery. His speech has been published in the proceedings of the society, where, in its intensity and tumultuousness, it still excites the reader. He travelled over the field of theology, co-ordinating his beliefs with the central truth that every man is the child of God. He was careful to have it understood in his opening remarks that he had not chosen his subject,—"The Need of Enthusiasm for Humanity"; but if he could have chosen, there was no subject upon which he would have desired more to speak. He recalled the origin of the expression by the author of *Ecce Homo*. It had originally been defined as "the love of humanity grounded in the conviction that Christ is the type and ideal of every man." This he had believed and had preached; but, according to his own definition, "the enthusiasm for humanity is based upon the conviction which Christ implanted, that every man is the child of God." He seemed to go beyond himself in the fiery zeal of his earnestness as he enforced this principle in all its implications. One passage may be cited:

"Do I believe that Jonathan Edwards, when he has told me about the power and the majesty of the divine will, has told me the whole truth? Do I believe, on the other hand, that Channing, when he has told me of the purity and dignity of human nature, has told me the whole truth? God, revealed to me by the deepest thoughts of those who have lost themselves in His existence; man, revealed to me by the deep and tender utterances of those who have lived in supreme sympathy with him! God and man, shall they stand separate? It is the Christ, the God-man that I see.   The great Christ-truth of the Sonship of man to God takes possession of these things which have been fragments, as we have heard this afternoon, and blends them in their glorious whole.   We have feared that man should be a traitor to God.   There is great danger also,—who shall measure dangers where they are all so tremendous?—there is vast danger lest man be a traitor to man.

We trace the working of his mind in some brief hints of his Christmas sermon on the text, "Hast thou not known, hast thou not heard, that the everlasting God, the Lord, the Creator of the ends of the earth, fainteth not, neither is weary?   There is no searching of His understanding."

"The greatest is the kindest and the dearest.   Tendency to run to the little in our religion.   The great landscapes, the great thoughts suitable for Christmas time.   Their belonging to all men makes them more and not less truly yours.   The dear earth and dear sky.   Dear humanity.   It is not relative size, but true relationship that makes the grip.   Ask yourself if your largest were not most sympathetic."

CHAPTER XXII.

1890.

SPEECH AT THE CHAMBER OF COMMERCE. LENTEN AD-
DRESSES IN TRINITY CHURCH, NEW YORK. CHANGE
IN MANNER OF PREACHING. CORRESPONDENCE.
ADDRESS AT THE CHURCH CONGRESS. THANKSGIV-
ING SERMON.

WITH the coming of 1890 we enter upon the last year in the
parish ministry of Phillips Brooks. All his years seem great,
yet this stands out in some respects the greatest of them all. It
was not that the incidents of his life were more striking than in
previous years, but the life itself seems greater and more impressive. He had reached the age of fifty-four, and had kept the
thirtieth anniversary of his ordination. Twenty-one years had
gone by since he became the rector of Trinity Church. He had
attained the simplicity for which he had aspired and struggled.
Intellectual difficulties about religion or the world process had
ceased to embarrass him. He had one theme, the sacredness,
the beauty, the glory of life, and that because all men were the
children of God, and Christ was the eternal Son. This one theme
ramified into a thousand variations, as the theme in nature is
simple, but inexhaustible in its beauty and variety. Whenever
he spoke, the subject was new, and this sense of freshness and
novelty was contagious. Wherever he went, whatever might be
the occasion, he lifted his banner whereon was written the sacredness and the possibilities of life. This was his work, to recall
men to their spiritual environment, to remind them of their spiritual heritage, and show them its content. He quotes in his
note-book the words of Schleiermacher: "Now this is just my
vocation,—to represent more clearly that which dwells in all
true human beings, and to bring it home to their consciousness."

But what seemed to rise above every other characteristic of his preaching or his conversation was the inextinguishable and boundless hope. He would not allow himself to be daunted by any circumstances of life in proclaiming the salvation by hope. Amidst voices of despair, or the wailings of misery, or the manifestations of indifference which surged about him striving to silence or drown his utterance, his voice rose above them all, proclaiming hope and the blessedness of life itself, the sacredness of humanity and its legitimate interests. Nor was it that he did not see the evil, the misery, and the sin. More than most men was he called into contact with suffering and with sorrow in their pathetic and tragic forms. Ministrations to the sick and dying, to those in mourning, filled up his days. His gift of consolation was in perpetual exercise. The more hideous forms of evil, the evidences of vice, lives from which the light had gone out,—with these things he was familiar. There were his own sorrows and disappointments, experiences of which he spoke to no one; the growing loneliness—"If any man knows what loneliness is, I do," he once said of himself; misgivings about his health; the feeling that youth was departing and with it might be lost the freshness of his outlook on life; the possibility that he might not live to see what life would soon reveal,—these combined to raise their varying strains of hopelessness and sadness; and still the faith that was in him soared above the discordance and confusion, proclaiming hope, and joy, and always cheerfulness as the word of God to man. He had to fight harder, it may be, to retain his faith, but for this reason it grew stronger and more secure. His conviction deepened that the world had been redeemed and glorified in Christ. In the light of this redemption it grew fairer and richer and life more attractive, till it almost pained him to address young men with the prospect before them of a vision he could not live to see. He was not a philosopher in the conventional meaning of the term, but in its larger and truer sense he had gained what philosophy could give. There was nothing in the line of philosophical thought beyond the range of his endeavor to comprehend and adjust in a large scheme of the world's order. What others were thinking he was feeling and living. He was not a professed student of philosophical systems, yet he inquired of them; and he seemed to know what they stood for in relation to the world problem. He was an idealist with Plato. With Aristotle he rejoiced in the world as it is. With Kant he lived in the human consciousness. There are hints of the Berkeleian principle, as well as reminders of Hegel's ruling idea. He retained his youthful devotion to Bacon in the glorification of the world of outward nature, while in Lotze he found a check for the one-sidedness of the purely intellectual estimate of things. He still retained the vision of his youth, when he saw the world transfigured as by Neoplatonic reverie; but he overcame its error and weakness by giving the central place in thought and life to the Incarnation, thus gaining unity and simplicity, the power of the personal Christ as the bond of union with God. He held the truth of the immanence of God, in nature and in humanity, uniting with it the personality of God in His distinctness from both, whose personal will was the final explanation of all the issues of life and thought.

In the various addresses he made, or in the sermons preached, these features of his thought may be traced. Thus, in January, he spoke to the merchants of Boston at a banquet of the Chamber of Commerce, when his speech was the amplification of the words of Bacon: "Not for gold, or silver, or precious stones was commerce instituted, not for silks or spices, nor for any other of those crude ends at which thou aimest, but first and only for the child of God, that is to say, for light." He began his address by remarking that it was a privilege "to sit in the midst of a multitude of merchants and see the modern look in their faces and catch the modern tone in their voices; it is the merchant to-day who holds the reins and bears the responsibility of life." This was the report of his speech:

"Let it be our place to rejoice that the world had not fulfilled itself,—that man, so marvellously mysterious as he was, evidently was beginning to realize that he had not begun to display the power that was in him. And let us take up boldly the responsibility which belonged to his enlarged outlook. The one thing that grew upon him as he grew older, he said, was the mysteriousness of human life and the absolutely unfulfilled powers that were in humankind. His one great assurance was that the world was bound to press onward and find an escape from the things that terrified it, not by retreat, but by a perpetual progress into the large calm that lay beyond. The very things that made men hesitate, fear, and dread were the things in which we most rejoiced, and which we could not possibly surrender. . . .

"Let us look forward and believe in men. Let us believe that every power of man put forth to its best activity must ultimately lead to the large consummation of the complete life to all the sons of men. To be in the thick of that seemed to be the glory of a single human life. It was for us to rejoice in the richness of the life in which we were placed,—the richness of thought and the richness of action,—to believe in it with all our hearts, to hesitate at nothing. But it seemed to him the very newness of our life, the very newness of business life and of scholarly life, compelled a complete loyalty to those great fundamental things which never changed. ". . . It was because those were being preserved, as he believed, most earnestly, most religiously, that we were able to look forward into the future without a fear. There never was a time for men to live like this time."

His imagination was working in the same line as he went in January to the Leather Trade dinner, noting down this point to be made in his speech:

"Each business touches the imagination. It stands between nature and man and turns the wonderful world to human use. Behind the carpenter, the waving forest. Behind the factory the sunny cotton field, and before both, *man*, human life, made stronger, happier by the transformation which they work. These the two great things of the earth, nature and man.

"Behind your business is the world of cattle on a thousand hills, the lowing herd in the pasture, the rush of buffaloes across the prairie, the bleating of flocks in the fold,—these bright and airy pictures; and in front of it man, with this tough element in his civilization which you bring there for his comfort."

He had taken offence at something he had heard uttered in disparagement of nature and of its study,—that the love of nature stood in the way of the spiritual life. His answer to it was a sermon at Trinity Church to "a great gathering," when his text was the words of St. Paul: "For the earnest expectation of the creation waiteth for the revealing of the sons of God"; and his subject was the relations of nature and humanity,—the waiting attitude of nature for the perfect man:

"How full were Paul's words of the spirit of our time! For what was Science doing to-day? Was she not building up and completing man so that he might be more and more able to ask of Nature what she means, and call forth from her the great forces of the world?

"The thing men were looking for was not that Nature should become more and more rich or full, but that man should become more worthy of the answers and the revelations which Nature could make to him of herself.

"This was also true of the poetry of the time, for it was a characteristic of the verse of the nineteenth century that it felt a soul in Nature.

"And it was the pain at the great soul of Nature that she could not do for man what she could do were he worthy as a son of God. The world was waiting to-day to do the things for man that it could not do so long as he had not in himself the son of God."

The question of the miracle, its actuality or its possibility, was one of the disturbing issues in the churches. There are many of Phillips Brooks's letters, many reports of conversations with him, turning on this point. Young men came to him with the difficulty. It was keeping them out of the Church, or preventing their whole-souled allegiance to Christ. He did what he could to help them by argument or by statement of the question in a new light. He received letters from those who rejected miracles, urging him to abandon what was unprofitable and men no longer believed. His answer to such protests was that the pulpit should be free, or that if all lived up to the truth they *did* believe, it would be well. He was troubled by an attitude in which he did not sympathize, and he seems to have kept his deeper conviction in the background as something others could not share. But in a sermon preached in 1889—one of the most characteristic he ever wrote—he gave full scope to his devotion. The text indicates his attitude toward this and every other conviction he held, "Rejoicing in the truth." It was one thing to *believe*, and another to *rejoice*. He enumerates the points of belief wherein he rejoiced, and in doing so comes to the miracle:

"There is the man who rejoiceth in the truth of the miracle, and for whom the earth he treads is always less hard, more soft and buoyant, because it has once trembled under the feet of Christ. He is glad through all his soul that the hard-seeming order of things has once and again felt the immediate compulsion of the Master soul. Critical as he may be in his judgment of evidence, he does not grudge assent because of any previous con-

viction of impossibility. He is *glad* to believe. Belief to him
is better than unbelief. Every sunrise is more splendid, every
sunset is more tender, every landscape has new meanings; the
great sea is mightier and more gracious; life has more fascination, death has more mystery, because Jesus Christ spoke to the
waters, and shone in the transfiguration glory, and called Laz-
arus out of the tomb, and stood himself in the bright morning
outside his own tomb door at Jerusalem."

There were so many addresses made by Phillips Brooks during
the early part of the year that it is useless to attempt to enumerate them. Wherever he was called he went, and he was
wanted everywhere. Among these multitudinous occasions,
these are two which stand out with greater prominence,—one
of them, the daily Monday addresses, during Lent at St. Paul's
Church, Boston. They were intended for business men, but
others took advantage of the opportunity, till the business men
were in danger of being crowded out. The following letter of
remonstrance sent to Mr. Brooks, indicates the estimate put upon
these services:

"BOSTON, March 13, 1890.

"DEAR SIR,—Will you inform me whether the Monday noon
services at St. Paul's during Lent are intended to be 'Business
Men's Meetings,' or not? There is a general impression on the
street that they are, and the lectures would seem to strengthen
the impression. Yet the preponderance of women in the audience would seem to belie the impression. If the meetings are
intended particularly for business men, would it be unjust to
others to reserve the central aisle for business men only until
12.05, for instance? That such a step would be approved I am
sure from conversations both at the church and on the street.
Business men feel, as far as my knowledge goes, that if it is
their service, it is keeping them out to have nine tenths of those
in the pews women, who can get there before twelve, and the
majority of whom can, and probably do, hear you on Sunday.
The business men from the suburbs or distant cities cannot hear
you on Sundays, we will assume, but can on Monday noon. I
know of many men who would attend the noonday service on the
Mondays in Lent but for the fact that they cannot get to St.
Paul's before twelve, and at that hour the seats are taken and
the aisles crowded, so they remain away. If the service is primarily for business men, they are at a great disadvantage at
present; if not primarily for them, of course they must take their

chances with the rest. A line will be appreciated by many friends."

A similar experience awaited him at Trinity Church, New York, where he went during Lent to give a course of addresses to business men on six consecutive days. The invitation came from the rector of Trinity, the Rev. Morgan Dix. The event was one of peculiar interest in the life of Phillips Brooks. He had been in the habit for many years of preaching at the Church of the Incarnation on the Sunday after Easter, and occasionally at Grace Church. But at Trinity he spoke to representative New York in the largest possible way. No effort was made to call attention to the services, no announcement in other churches, no advertisement in the newspapers. A simple placard was suspended to the iron fence on the day when the services were to begin, announcing that Rev. Phillips Brooks, of Boston, would speak to men at twelve o'clock each day of the week. The difficulty which had been experienced in Boston was not repeated. It had been proposed at first that one half of the church, divided by the middle aisle, should be assigned to women, and the other half to men. Mr. Brooks decided that the services should be confined to men. The following reports of these services are taken from the New York *Sun:*

"At 11.30 this morning [Monday, February 24], busy men began to file into Trinity Church. The great interior was dim by reason of the heavy rain outside, and the business men who entered carried umbrellas dripping wet, or shook the water from their gossamers as they stood in the entry. The seats were rapidly filled, and before twelve o'clock the benches in the aisles were occupied, so that, after that hour, the men who entered were obliged to stand in the broad space far in the rear.
" Before the lecture was completed a throng of men, whose business made it inconvenient for them to come at the beginning of the address, had pressed down the aisle at the end of which the pulpit stands, so that, when the lecture was half completed, there stood beneath the pulpit a great throng of men looking with the earnestness and steadiness which true eloquence begets up at the great preacher who was uttering simple words of Christian wisdom.
"It was an impressive sight to see this vast church filled to overflowing with a body of New York men, representatives of the professions, trades, commerce, and the financial energies of Wall

Street. For here were men who directed affairs involving millions, others who represent vast litigations, seated side by side with clerks and older men, who were employed, many of them, in subordinate capacities by the men beside whom they sat.

"The chimes in Trinity steeple, whose echoes were heard with dim resonance in the church, had scarcely ceased ringing for the hour of twelve when the door of the vestry room opened and the choir boys, with Dr. Brooks and Dr. Morgan Dix following, entered the chancel. Dr. Brooks wore the conventional surplice, while Dr. Dix wore no vestments. Dr. Brooks at once mounted the pulpit, where, as he stood, his giant stature was revealed to the great throng before him. In a low voice, which could be heard scarcely twenty feet away, he read the opening hymn, beginning, 'A charge to keep I have.' The great congregation rose, and it was a sight to see these busy men as they stood there singing the hymn to the familiar tune written for it. There were men who, a few moments before, had been plunged into the intricacies of trade and finance, now singing with devout manner the hymn, and the volume of music which arose from this great throng must have sounded sweetly to the ear of Dr. Brooks, for he paused in his own singing that he might listen to the glorious music made by this congregation of male voices.

"After a Collect and the repetition of the Lord's Prayer, which must have been pronounced by every member in the church, so great and distinct was the volume of sound, Dr. Brooks began the address. He started without a preliminary utterance right into the heart of the sermon, and his very first sentence was uttered with that mighty impetuosity of thought and speech which distinguishes him among American clergymen, which makes it impossible for the swiftest stenographer completely to report him, and which is a Niagara of thoughts and words maintained from the beginning to the end of the discourse. His voice is peculiarly sympathetic and sweet, even in his most impassioned utterances. His tones are mellow and a delight to the ear, and when he utters a sentence with the utmost speed of thought, and of great length, but with perfect symmetry and lucidity, his tones are so melodious that they seem almost like the intoning of his discourse.

"The first few sentences, however, were spoken in so low a tone that they were inaudible, and a silent gesture of protest went up all over the church, manifested by the holding of one hand to the ear that his words might be the better distinguished. He seemed to take the hint, and to have tested the acoustics of the church, for a moment later his voice was distinct and clear, and heard in the remotest corners. . . .

"As he finished his address he stopped for a moment and looked over the pulpit at that vast throng crowding the aisle beneath with upturned faces, listening for every word which came from his lips. When he turned to descend from the pulpit, the throng still stood there as though controlled by his presence and power, even after he had departed from the place where he had uttered these words of wisdom in a manner which seemed almost inspired."

On the second day, Tuesday, the hymn was "Rock of Ages, cleft for me," followed by the saying of the Lord's Prayer. The account of the service shows that the interest was growing:

"The heavy mist which palled the city this morning concealed the steeple which surmounts Trinity Church, and almost hid the clock at noon to-day, while the chimes rang out the mid-day hour in tones which seemed to be almost muffled. Yet a steady throng of men had been filing into the church for half an hour, ready to meet the discomfort occasioned by the packing together of a throng whose clothing was damp, and every one of whom carried a dripping umbrella. When the noon hour was reached, the great interior contained as dense a throng as were ever within its walls. After all the seats were taken, the crowd pressed down the aisles, and stood in a great mass of men in the passageway at the rear of the church. So dense was the throng that, after the exercises which called it together began, it was impossible for any to get in, and almost impossible for any to get out.

"Yesterday the church was comfortably filled, but the throng that gathered then was moderate in comparison with that which assembled to-day. In the aisles, too, there stood with perfect patience for nearly an hour men who command millions of money, and who direct affairs of colossal importance. Not one of these turned and left the building, although the discomfort was great by reason of the close packing of the throng and the dampness which was encountered on every side.

"Very many in the audience had never heard him before, and it was evident that they were, at the beginning, astonished at the rapidity of his utterance. He spoke with a voice better modulated to the acoustics of the church than was the case yesterday, and after the first sentence or two his words were heard with perfect distinctness all over the church. But, though he had increased the volume of his tone, and the distinctness of his utterance was evidently in his mind, yet the exquisite modulation of his tone was even more apparent than yesterday.

"The service closed with the hymn, 'Arise, my soul, and with the sun.' The impressiveness of this hymn as sung by the great body of men was very great, and not a few of those there assembled, who heard the volume of song, were so impressed that tears rolled down their cheeks."

As the days went on the interest continued to grow deeper, as the following comment shows:

"The services suggest none of the familiar scenes of the revival meeting. There is no excitement, but there is a majestic revelation of the power of eloquence used to illustrate the sublimest of all truths upon a vast body of business men.

"Each succeeding day has witnessed an increase in the attendance, till the chancel has been occupied, the preacher has found difficulty in wending his way to the pulpit, and hundreds have been turned away, unable to gain admittance. There have been clergymen present, a large number of young men, lawyers also, and the great throng of business men, till Wall Street and its vicinity seemed deserted. The women have pleaded to be admitted, but have been refused, for if women were admitted they would fill the church to the exclusion of those for whom the service is intended.

"Whatever the reason, the throng that has been drawn from the offices and stores in the lower part of the city to Trinity Church at the noontide has been something unprecedented. The wonderful success of the Lenten season at Trinity Church is an event about which merchants, bankers, and lawyers are talking."

We turn for a moment to the preacher himself, as he prepared for utterance. Several months before the time fixed upon, he decided upon his subject, and made a synopsis of each address. First he had taken rough notes in pencil, and then in ink drawn up the more matured plan. During the intervening time he was revolving the topics and their method of treatment in his mind. He spoke extemporaneously, without the assistance of notes, but each address meant an immense amount of preparation. Judging from the appearance of these analyses, it was no calm preparation that he made, but his soul was heaving with emotion, as he dug deep into the recesses of his theme. After he had made the final analyses he went over them in review with interlineations in almost every line. But in the presence of his audience he was set free and lifted up to say things with startling power, which are not mentioned in his plan. He never was more free, and therefore more himself, than when he stood in the pulpit of Trinity Church, New York. What he was endeavoring to do was only in more thorough manner that which he sought in every sermon. The occasion stimulated him with the possibility of presenting in complete though condensed form the total picture of life and of man in relation to the gospel of Christ. He was determined that nothing he esteemed of vital importance should be lost. He spoke as if the world were listening.

"Freedom" was his subject,—the one word most revealing men to themselves, in the presence and under the influence of an enfeebling fatalism, which had come in consequence of the decline of individualism, of the rise of socialism, of theories about heredity, and of the reign of universal law. He defined liberty in his first lecture, as the full opportunity to be one's best. In the second lecture he presented "Christ the Liberator." The third address, "The Process of the Liberation," was interesting as showing how he treated the endless controversy, as old in Christian history as the time of Pelagius and Augustine—the question of the relation of God's grace to human freedom. He combats lingering notions about election which still hamper men. He refers the whole work of salvation to God alone, as Augustine had done, and the freedom is God's gift. "God is working His side for you with His instruments. What are they? All your experiences. He is really the worker and He uses them all."

The subject of the fourth address had a distinct interest, for it concerned the "Freedom of Christian Thought." It stood out among the addresses as having made the most profound impression, and was referred to as having given character to them all. It cleared the intellectual horizon. Phillips Brooks was sensitive to a widely prevailing impression that the clergy were not free to speak the full truth, or even to think freely, because they were bound by subscription to theological tenets which were irrational, whatever their denomination or sect. This deep and widespread conviction was acting as a subtle barrier against the appeal of the Christian faith. There was the large body of Christian tenets, unintelligible to most men, which hung like a dead weight upon even the religious mind. Intelligent laymen who recited the creeds would in confidential moments admit that they did not know anything about it, whether they believed or did not believe.

The preacher had this advantage, that he had gained his own freedom, and knew that he was free, not by denying dogmas, but by entering into their spirit and discerning their relation to life. He devoted his time to the establishment of one supreme presupposition, which, if it were admitted, covered the whole ground.

"During all these days one thought must have arisen in many minds: 'All very well, but your boasted freedom stops with activity; it cannot reach to thought; that is all enslaved.' Such thought is common. It is sometimes assumed by churches and religious books that it is true.

"If true, the religion could not hold us by any means, and it could not really be an active force. Christ claims that it is not true : 'Ye shall know the truth, and the truth shall make you free.' It is the truth itself that is to bring freedom.

"What is the Christian faith? It is Christ the Leader. A thousand things besides attached to it. But that is it. It is the Being standing there in history and attaining the power of God to lead men into new life, so that the desires of richer life find fulfilment in Him. Am I hampering myself in that? Not unless electricity hampers itself when it gathers in lightning.

"But how do I get at Him? Just as the people in Jerusalem got at Him. Christ Himself, in His personal character, then faith in His words and their acceptance, the opening up of their possibility in life. Is a man not free with his world enlarged?

"Miracle, yes! That means that the world has larger answers to make to the greater power, as it says more to the civilized than to the savage. It bursts to larger music and diviner landscape. Miracle *does* happen when the miracle man appears.

"That Being claiming my confidence says He will be always here and will always lead. He promises the great extension of Himself,—the Holy Spirit. He gives one divine commandment.

"That is the Christian faith. The other things connected with it, character of books, forms of government, interpretation of His words, special injunctions, aye, His own nature, His scheme of penalties,—all of these are interesting, but Christianity behind them all. Let us not exclude Christians from Christianity. Whoever is His disciple and calls Him Master is a Christian.

"What does Christ do? He makes God real. The two reasons for believing God's existence,—*the world is intelligible with Him*, and a great puzzle without Him; and *Jesus believed Him*. I think He knew.

"I honor the sceptic. He will not enter this region unconvinced. Perhaps he is demanding conviction, which can only come when he is inside. Still, honor to him. Truthfulness is more than truth. But his is not a larger, 't is a smaller life."

The fifth address was entitled "The Christian is the True Man." The sight of men coming to these services raises the question

"Have they left one world for another, or have they mounted to the highest conception of their whole world?" In the last address, when the interest which had been daily increasing culminated, he began by expressing the sense and fear of too much talk lest he should have complicated what is simple, but also the rejoicing confidence that "when we plead with one another there is forever the great pleading power of God" standing behind the appeal, as the power of nature with the physician or the law of gravitation with the mechanic.

"I could never get hold of the theology of those who stand in perpetual amazement before the spectacle of God's love to his children. That love seems to me more and more natural. What I have tried to do is to make the whole seem natural.

"Do you say, What can I do? As your brother, let me try to tell you.

"(1) *Leave off your sin.* (2) *Do your personal duty.* (3) *Pray* simply, passionately, earnestly. (4) *The Bible;* read it till that Christ figure is before you. (5) *The Church*, which is the embodiment of all—if it is weak, make it strong.

"Unless you do these things you have no right to complain that the new life does not come in and you are not free. These are not a set of rules. They are windows of the soul.

"These are the great religious words ever deepening:

"(1) *Separation from the world;* not the desert or cell but independence by service.

"(2) *Salvation of the soul*, not from pain, but from sin.

"(3) *Prepare to meet thy God*, with glorious and glad welcome. He is always here.

"Be such a man that if all men were like you the world would be saved.

"Farewell, my friends. It is not for long, and yet it is so long. For the world will be here after we are gone, and after the world is gone we shall live forever. Whatever may come hereafter, not this particular opportunity to serve God will come again. Catch to-day. Be men; be men. Love God. Be brave. Be true. And at last may we say, as He said, 'Father, I have glorified Thee on the earth.'"

Those who were following Phillips Brooks at this time, as he pursued his wonderful career, felt that some mysterious change was passing over him, intensifying his power, producing effects upon his congregation which no words are adequate to represent. In this extract from a Boston paper is said what many thought:

"That quality which has entered into Dr. Brooks's sermons, especially of late, was felt in a marked degree by his New York audience. Always strong, earnest, and filled with the dignity of his words and work it has been a matter for comment in Boston that since his return from his last journey [the visit to Japan] he has brought to bear a deeper force than ever, a more impassioned delivery of thought, and an apparent burning conviction of the necessity of impressing upon the people the truth of which he is convinced. The repressed but tremendous effect of yesterday's sermon in New York confirms the belief that there is new power in his utterance, a sense of having been touched by the coal that the world's prophets have felt when they have spoken enduring words to those who 'hear indeed but understand not.'"

This "new power of utterance" was increasingly manifest in every sermon, but it cannot be described. One thing was apparent, however, that the whole man was visibly affected when he preached. It was not so in his earlier ministry, when he stood unimpassioned and unmoved, thrilling his audience till it took them long to recover their normal mood, but himself calm in the recesses of his spirit, and maintaining his self-composure. What struck his hearers now was the torrent of feeling within him, as he poured forth his burning words. The simple manhood in him had become a stronger appeal than any intellectual endowment.

One would like to linger over some of the sermons preached in a year which seems to have been among the most prolific in his ministry. The Lenten season was rich in these impressive sermons. His inclination was to dwell more on the passive side of the life of Christ, His sufferings and cross in their deeper relations to Christian experience. He preached the Baccalaureate Sermon at Harvard before the class of 1890, and performed the same service for the graduating class of the Institute of Technology. Two sermons stand out with peculiar vividness, where he seized the allegories of history and brought them home to the individual soul. They are both of them poems, with the tragic element supreme: "The Egyptians dead upon the Seashore" and "The Feast of Belshazzar." These were written sermons, while for the most part his preaching was extempore. In the year 1890 he wrote but six sermons. He was not satisfied with himself, and bemoaned the days when the sermon was the event of the week. He told one of his friends at this time that he intended to give up extempore preaching and go back again to the written sermon. He seemed to be reviewing his theological convictions, and giving them firmer expression. In a sermon on the text "Vengeance is mine; I will repay, saith the Lord," he speaks of the "blessedness" of "Eternal Hope" and of "our right to keep it."

How the mind of Phillips Brooks was working in other directions may be seen in an essay, already referred to, entitled "Orthodoxy," read before the Clericus Club, June 2, 1890. He saw the symptoms, as he believed, of an ecclesiastical reaction, waving this word on its banner. He challenges the coming storm in his own person. He denounces orthodoxy as "born of fear, and as having no natural heritage either from hope or love." He admitted that orthodoxy had its place and its importance, but they were both inferior.

"It is an arrogant, pushing thing, crowding itself into thrones where it has no right. . . . Is not the whole sum of the matter this, that orthodoxy as a principle of action or a standard of belief is obsolete and dead? It is not that the substance of orthodoxy has been altered, but that the very principle of orthodoxy has been essentially disowned. It is not conceivable now that any council, however œcumenically constituted, should so pronounce on truth that its decrees should have any weight with thinking men, save what might legitimately seem to belong to the character and wisdom of the persons who composed the council. Personal judgment is on the throne, and will remain there,—personal judgment, enlightened by all the wisdom, past or present, which it can summon to its aid, but forming finally its own conclusions and standing by them in the sight of God, whether it stands in a great company or stands alone."

At the beginning of the year 1890 he wrote to Archdeacon Farrar:

"233 CLARENDON STREET, BOSTON, January 12, 1890.

"MY VERY DEAR ARCHDEACON,—This New Year . . . starts well, I think, in spite of a thousand perverse things and people, which one would like to rectify or obliterate, and cannot. The thing which grows on me most is the splendid sense of liberty which is everywhere, which no sight of the extravagances and enormities to which it gives place can make to seem anything but splendid. I rather think that there has never been a time to which, if we were suddenly transferred, we should not feel as if we woke up in a stifling dungeon with chains at hand and heel. So let us rejoice and hope great things of 1890. I cannot picture your house with the changed look that it must have now that your children have, so many of them, gone. But be thankful that you are not a miserable celibate, whose being is bounded by the ground his two feet stand on. Browning and Lightfoot both are gone, and the world is vastly poorer. I think of both of them as you gave me the privilege of seeing them at your house, and their great work is nearer and more real to me because of your kindness. I will not believe that the new great Poet is not near at hand. I thought I met him in the street yesterday, but perhaps I was mistaken. But he will come soon!"

While staying in New York at the time when he was giving his addresses at Trinity Church, a gentleman called for the purpose of interviewing him and of publishing the results of the interview in a Philadelphia paper. The article appeared headed "Phillips Brooks's Broad Views about Modern Christianity— Truth, not Dogmas, Wanted." The report presented him as a radical reformer, eagerly awaiting some great religious revolution in the near future. To a friend disturbed at the unqualified, almost excited tone of the remarks reported by the interviewer, who wrote to know if he had been reported correctly, he replied:

"233 CLARENDON STREET, BOSTON, March 5, 1890.
"MY DEAR COOPER,—One day last week, when I was staying with Arthur in New York, a most respectable man called on me and introduced a friend whose name I did not catch. We talked for about half an hour. In the course of conversation he said that he had something to do with the New York *Sun*. I have not the slightest recollection of his mentioning any Philadelphia paper, or of his saying anything about reporting our conversation. If he had asked my consent I should certainly have refused it.

"This is the report which you have sent me in *The Press*. As to the matter of it, it follows the general line of our conversation, and I recognize a remark of mine here and there. I hope I do not wholly talk like that. The whole thing teaches me again not to talk freely with any living fellow-creature, unless you want to see what he thinks you said, or thinks that you ought to have said, in the next newspaper. Of course there is nothing to be done about it. It will die the quiet death which comes to rubbish, and the world will go on very much the same."

On May 14 Mr. Brooks was in Pittsfield, preaching the sermon on the occasion of the opening of the new church. People from far and near had come to Pittsfield, attracted by the occasion of the opening of the church and by the reputation of Phillips Brooks,—among them a Shaker brother, from a neighboring settlement, who was anxious to show him that his tenets were in sympathy with the Shaker creed. Failing to reach him, he wrote a long letter, expounding the faith as held by the Shaker community. The letter reached him with no other address than "Pastor Phillips Brooks, the Celebrated Preacher."

It had been Mr. Brooks's intention to spend the summer at North Andover, and he had so informed his friends; but he suddenly changed his mind and decided upon a visit to Europe. He was furnished with letters by his English friends, which enabled him to see what he wished in places not hitherto visited. He wandered through Devonshire and Cornwall, going also to the English Andover out of respect for its associations. While he was in London he was moved to the writing of sonnets. It was many years since his mood had tempted him in this direction. One of them was entitled

HAPPINESS AND CONTENT

Now will I find the traitor where he hides,
　　The culprit, Happiness, who did me wrong.
　　He came to me with trumpet and with song,
Even as he comes to Victory and to brides.
With rich delights he hung my sombre walls,
　　And taught gay dances to the serious hours;
　　His footsteps thronged the vacant mead with flowers,
His breath with music filled the silent halls.
And then he vanished. But, the day he went,
　　The central jewel of my house he stole,
The precious jewel which is called Content,
　　Without which no man keeps a living soul.
The thief I 'll find. The theft he shall restore,
Then he may go. I covet him no more.

In a letter to Rev. John C. Brooks he speaks of a visit to Tennyson:

"LUCERNE, August 25, 1890.

"I had a delightful little visit to Tennyson at his house at Aldworth. He has grown very old, but is bright and clear-headed, and may give us some new verses yet. Just after I left England Newman died, and all the pulpit and press have been full of the laudation and discussion of him ever since. He was a remarkable man, by no means of the first class, for he never got a final principle nor showed a truly brave mind; but there was great beauty in his character, and his intellect was very subtle."

In response to a letter asking his opinion on vested female choirs, he spoke his mind:

"Hôtel Clerc, Martigny, August 17, 1890.
"Not a surpliced female choir, my dear friend! Almost anything but that! But let us set ourselves against that most fantastic and frivolous affectation which has turned up in these days, when surely the Church is young-ladyish enough without putting young-ladyism decorated for a spectacle in the seat of prominence and honor. Surely it is amazing how much attention clothes enlist in all the operations of our great Communion. Let us keep our simplicity, and so, no vested female choirs! Almost anything but that!"

In his letters he makes allusion to the summer wanderings:

"I have had a bright, pleasant summer of the kind which makes no history, but leaves a pleasant taste in the mouth. And now even the door bell has a pleasant sound, because it means the old familiar life and work.
"It was a quiet little thing, the journey was, but very pleasant. Two placid voyages with interesting people enough on board; three weeks in England and three weeks in Switzerland; the old places which we knew so well,—Chamouni and Interlaken, and Lucerne, Paris, and London, all very delightful and refreshing. It went without an accident or disappointment, and when we stepped ashore on Saturday, it seemed easy enough to be thankful."

The burden of the familiar letters from 233 Clarendon Street, which went forth at once to his friends, was an urgent invitation to come and see him. He should be expecting them at every ring of the door bell. "Come at once." "I will put prohibitory marks against the calendar." Even the "precious fragments" of their time were besought amid many engagements, some of them "vexatious." The Church Congress was to meet in Philadelphia in November, when he was to read a paper entitled "The Conditions of Church Growth in Missionary Lands." But the prospect of a visit to Philadelphia loomed up more largely to his imagination than the subject of his paper.

Late in the fall Mr. Brooks published his fifth and last volume of sermons, dedicating it "To the memory of my brother, George Brooks, who died in the great war." Many sermons are here which must be counted among his best, such, for example, as "Backgrounds and Foregrounds" and "The Planter and the Rain," both written in 1889. An important sermon is "The Seriousness of Life," from the text, "Let God not speak to us lest we die," which has been mentioned in a previous chapter, where the impression it made was described. Another sermon, written from the depths of his own experience, is the "Silence of Christ," —"But He answered her not a word." "The Priority of God" was a sermon whose idea was the God-consciousness in which he lived and moved and had his being. He contrasts the phrase "the religious world" as employed popularly with the reality of the religious world as it should be:

"What a poor, petty, vulgar thing that old phrase, 'the religious world,' has often been made to mean,—a little section of humanity claiming monopoly of divine influences, and making the whole thought of man's intercourse with God cheap and irreverent by vicious quarrels and mercenary selfishness; the world of ecclesiastical machinery and conventions and arrangements. But look! See what the religious world really is in its idea, and shall be when it shall finally be realized. A world everywhere aware of and rejoicing in the priority of God, feeling all power flow out from Him, and sending all action back to report itself to Him for judgment,—a world where goodness means obedience to God, and sin means disloyalty to God, and progress means growth in the power to utter God, and knowledge means the understanding of God's thought, and happiness means the peace of God's approval. That is the religious world."

The sermon is also here which Principal Tulloch pronounced the finest he had ever heard, "The Opening of the Eyes." But Mr. Brooks gave the precedence to the sermon "The Light of the World," whence the volume takes its title. There is here also what seems like prophetic intimation, in the sermon which closes the book, "The Certain End."

On December 4 he went to Philadelphia to preach the sermon at the Church of the Advent, where he began his ministry over thirty years before. The occasion was the fiftieth anniversary of the establishment of the church. His text, "I will not let thee go except thou bless me," was suggestive of the mystery of the spiritual life,—the mystery of the withholding of spiritual gifts, when God is willing to give and man is desirous to receive, and yet the blessing does not come. "The meaning of it *must* be that there is some inability to take the gift." From the subject of his sermon he turned to the occasion, recalling to the congregation how he had kept the twentieth anniversary with them in 1860. He dwelt lovingly on the "little church," the "simple service," the "voluntary choir," the "great Sunday-school," the "people's love for the church," all still fresh in his memory. He enumerated the names of those with whom he had been associated. He touched on the war and its experiences. Then he reviewed the years that had passed since he left them, the new congregation, the more elaborate service, the freer thought, the new sense of God, personal liberty, greater work, and the truer missionary spirit. "And so, let the future come. It is better than the past, by the past."

So the year 1890 came to an end. He kept his twenty-first anniversary as rector of Trinity Church, which was to be also his last. His fifty-fifth birthday was commemorated as usual by some of his more intimate friends who met him at luncheon. He came to Christmas with its festivities, the last he should celebrate in the accustomed way, for a change was impending in his life, and "new experiences," of which he often spoke, were to open before him.

CHAPTER XXIII.

CHARACTERISTICS.

THE reserve which marked the early life of Phillips Brooks continued in his maturer years. He himself has spoken on the subject, but in his sermons to all who cared to listen, not to his immediate friends. From a sermon on the text, "The secret of the Lord is with them that fear him," these extracted sentences seem to have a personal bearing:

"Every living thing which is really worth the knowing has a secret in it which can only be known to a few.

"There is something that every man holds back from us; and the more of a man he is, the more conscious we are of this reserve. The more of a man he is, the more secret is the secret of his life, and the more plain and frank are its external workings. Anybody may know what he does and where he goes, yet all the while every one who looks at him will see that there is something behind all which escapes the closest observation.

"We all know how little other people know about us. The common saying that other people know us better than we know ourselves is only very superficially true. They do see certain tricks in us which we are not aware of; but if we are at all thoughtful and self-observant they do not get at the secret of our life as we know it."

The secret of his own personality he guarded to the end. Had some one known how to approach him it might have been unveiled. But the deep instinct which created the barrier of reserve passed into a settled habit, and what he might have told of himself remained unsaid. What the true method of approach should be he has also told us:

"When men try to get hold of the secret of your life, no friendship, no kindliness, can make you show it to them unless they evidently really feel as you feel that it is a serious and sacred thing. There must be something like reverence or awe about the way that they approach you. It is the way in which children shut themselves up before their elders, because they know their elders have no such sense as they have of the importance of their childish thoughts and feelings."

The following chapter of reminiscences and impression gathered from various sources deals with the external workings of his life in their frank simplicity. The career of Phillips Brooks always looked to those about him as one line of unbroken prosperity. There had been no check to his success, no halt in his triumphs. "Perennial sunniness," says one who crossed the ocean with him, was his characteristic. He was accustomed to say of himself that his life had been one of the happiest. In the later years, and after the death of his mother, the sense of loneliness increased. He hungered for human affection. This was the royal avenue to his soul for those who knew how to take it. He admitted that it had been the mistake of his life not to have married. Sometimes, in the homes of his younger friends, he seemed to resent their happiness. "The trouble with you married men is that you think no one has been in love but yourselves; I know what love is; I have been in love myself." He wanted to enter every great human experience. "To lose any of the legitimate experiences of a full human career is a loss for which one will be poorer forever." Life grew sad in the retrospect when he thought that he had been shut out from the greatest of all experiences,—marriage and wife and children. But he forced himself to look upon the brighter side of things. Out of his loneliness came consolation to himself and others.

Prominent among his personal characetristics was the power of making his residence home-like. This was evident in the rectory on Clarendon Street, where the personal adaptedness was apparent on entering. The ample study was the substitute for the drawing-room, whose massive fireplace, built of large blocks of unhewn stone, was the central feature. The room was luxurious in its appointments. The walls were lined with books on all sides of the room, halfway to the ceiling, and above the bookcases every available space was devoted to pictures. In the small reception-room next to the study the books overflowed and pictures abounded. He was particularly fond of portraits; he gave prominence to the portrait of Maurice. There were marble busts of Coleridge and Kingsley, replicas of those in Westminster Abbey, and a smaller bust of Stanley. He took pride in the image of Pico of Mirandola carved in wood. From India he had brought the image of Buddha. There was a cast of Cromwell's face and another of Lincoln's. There were interesting and beautiful objects, wherever the eye might turn.

His working-table, constructed for himself, was large and inconveniently high for any one else. Near it was the writing table of Dean Stanley, sent to Mr. Brooks after Stanley's death, on which, according to tradition, had been written the *History of the Jewish Church*. On another table, movable at pleasure, lay the latest books and magazines,—to many the most attractive feature of the room. It was a source of wonder how he seemed to secure in advance whatever was valuable in recent literature, and to have read it before others were aware of its appearance. Much of his work was done in a large alcove on the second story, above the front door, where the walls were lined with books of reference. His bedroom was over the study, corresponding to it in size, and opposite was the guest room, often occupied.

Those who enjoyed his hospitality knew what power of welcome he could offer. He had the capacity for mental concentration, so that the presence of others or the talk going on around him, even an interruption from a caller, were no disturbance. He rather looked down on ordinary mortals who were obliged to shut themselves up to their task. It was impressive to be with him on Sunday and watch him as he prepared himself for the afternoon service. There was no appearance of nervous anxiety, but a deep serenity, his face aglow with spiritual beauty. He would answer questions with a gentle refinement and sweetness of tone, but beneath the appearance was concentration upon the theme he was revolving, to whose power he seemed to be submitting himself. He held a scrap of paper which he would glance at quickly for a moment,—the only apparent aid in his preparation.

"I recall an incident [says a friend of Phillips Brooks] which happened on some occasion when he had invited a number of young men to his house. Among them was a theological student, whom I observed to be moving about in the study in a distracted manner, scanning the books, even getting down on his hands and knees in order to read the titles in the lower shelves. As Mr. Brooks was not in the room at the time, I took the liberty of asking him if there was anything he was searching for. He replied, 'I am trying to find out where he gets it from.' When I asked of him if he had found the source, he replied, tapping his forehead, 'He gets it here.'"

Among his relics were the sermon of Dean Stanley preached at Trinity Church, whose chirography it was impossible to decipher; the last sermon preached by Dr. Vinton; a sermon by Dr. Sears, of Weston, and another by Dean Farrar. When he was visiting Tennyson, he asked for the clay pipe just finished, about to be thrown into the fireplace. Tennyson had hesitated a moment, and, saying "Do you want it, mon?" had handed it to him. He called upon the widow of Rev. F. D. Maurice in London, and received from her a manuscript of one of Maurice's sermons, which he had bound up with *Maurice's Life and Letters*, in the richest of red morocco. Red was his favorite color. In ordering prayer books and hymnals for Trinity Church, he specified that they must be bound in red. He liked to collect autographs, pasting the autograph letter of authors in their books.

He had the gift of housekeeping. He was annoyed by signs of shiftlessness. He ordered the meals himself every morning, regulating in a few words the household affairs for the day. His hours were regular. He rose at seven and from the time he heard stirring in the morning he was singing to himself, and continued what was rather the effort at a tune until breakfast, which was at eight. Then followed a short interval of work before the crowd of callers came. He would have no office hours, nor would he refuse to see any one who called. Lunch was at one. After lunch came calls on the sick, or meetings of various kinds. He made few parochial calls. Six was the dinner hour. He sometimes found it hard to get out in the evening. Often there were callers. In the evenings when he did not go out and there were no callers, he was most delightful. At ten o'clock the house was shut, and at eleven he was in bed.

In the course of his life he often sat for his photograph and was quite willing to give his photographs to those asking for them. But he was averse to allowing them to be exposed for sale, giving the strictest injunctions to prevent it. Not until the last years of his life was this prohibition removed with his consent. Those taken in 1886, when he was about fifty, have been the most widely popular, representing him at his best, when he was still in unimpaired strength and vigor. The nervous tension and the harrassed look, caused by illness, which appear in the later photographs, have often been misconstrued since his death, as if they represented the spiritual yearning in his face when preaching in his later years. His own opinion of the photograph appears in his statement: "A portrait has a value of its own, entirely independent of its likeness to the man who sat for it; a photograph has none." He declined requests to sit for his portrait. The following letter is not to be taken too literally, and yet indicates what was more than a passing mood:

BOSTON, February 17, 1880.

"I thank you very heartily for your kind note. It is very pleasant to me to know that you would care to have my picture painted, and Mr. —— flatters me very much by wanting to paint it.

"But to have one's portrait painted has always seemed to me to be a very great and solemn thing, to be given as a privilege to very great people as they are getting to the end of life. I have almost a superstition about it. The modern promiscuousness of the cheap photograph seems to me to have taken the sacredness in large part from one of the most sacred things. Let us preserve the venerableness of the portrait. I am really serious about this, and I shall not think for twenty years yet, even if I dare to think then, that I have any right to be painted. . . .

"Yours most faithfully,

"PHILLIPS BROOKS."

There is one portrait of Phillips Brooks painted a few years later by Mrs. Henry Whitman, which has preserved a certain quality of expression his photographs do not give. Not only does it present the strength and grace of his stature, but the artist has caught what was, after all, the most distinctive quality of his nature, the eternal child-likeness,—something of that expression on his face, in those wonderful afternoon sermons in Trinity Church, which all remember and cherish, but no one can describe.

The years as they passed over him did not diminish the beauty of the countenance or the dignity and symmetry of form. In any company he carried the highest distinction in appearance. He stood head and shoulders above ordinary men, but so symmetrical were his proportions that, as was said of him by a lady with fine discrimination, it was not he that looked large but others that looked small. He stood for the type of the normal man. "He was the most beautiful man I ever saw," said Justice Harlan of the Supreme Court of the United States; "I sat opposite to him once at dinner and could not take my eyes off him." His photographs, after he allowed them to be published, were to be found everywhere. A commercial traveller, who had gone into almost every town in the State of Massachusetts, was struck with the fact that everywhere he found the portrait of Phillips Brooks, without regard to difference of race or of religion. A Roman Catholic Sister of Charity writes on receiving his photograph:

"I can't begin to tell you how grateful I am for that lovely picture of one of the loveliest men this world has ever known. . . . I like any one who likes Phillips Brooks. What a handsome face! His eyes seem to be looking for what has been much sought, but looking still, searching patiently, satisfied that beyond these 'mists and vapors' and 'darkened glasses' all is clear. The picture now hangs alongside of a beautiful photograph copy of Hoffmann's famous *Christ*, and seems at home there."

At times he appeared to rejoice in his stature; on coming into a friend's house he would easily place his hat on some tall bookcase or other object where any one else would have to mount on steps to reach it; or would light his cigar from a street lamp. Yet at times, also, he felt his height as an annoyance, saying that it made him feel awkward to be looking down on every one in the room.

Phillips Brooks always retained a lively impression of the call he made on Dr. Vinton, just after the failure in the Boston Latin School. He and Dr. Vinton would occasionally revert to the subject in later years, trying to straighten out each other's recollections. Dr. Vinton maintained that Brooks while in college had avoided him, in order to prevent any conversation on the subject of personal religion. When Brooks called on him for advice about possible openings in life, Dr. Vinton improved the opportunity. Brooks had resented at the time the attempt to introduce religion and, grateful as he was for what Dr. Vinton had done for him, could never recall the circumstance without the memory of a sense of injury done to his personality. He would say to Dr. Vinton when the subject came up, "It was *mean* in you to get a fellow in a corner and throw his soul at him." Dr. Vinton was fond of recalling that when he tried to get from Brooks some idea of what he would like to do in life, Brooks had replied: "I cannot express myself very clearly about it, but I feel as if I should like to talk."

He was careful in little things, in his dress observing great neatness, but avoiding, on principle, every badge of clerical dress. Conscientiousness marked his conduct, not only in dealing with others, but with himself. When he returned to his house, after an absence or journey, to find many invitations awaiting him, he followed the rule to accept them in the order in which he opened the letters, not allowing himself to choose which he would prefer. It was a principle with him never to decline an invitation to preach unless prevented by some previous engagement.

He was particular in the matter of correspondence, in the later years answering letters so promptly that one hesitated to write him for fear of increasing his burden. He wrote his letters with his own hand, and in most beautiful handwriting. He was severe upon illegible or even ungraceful handwriting.

"His reticence about his methods of work is shown by this anecdote. A clerical friend entering his study took up from the table the plan of a sermon just finished. 'Oh, is this the way you do it?' 'Put that paper down,' said Mr. Brooks sternly. 'No, I 've got the chance and I 'm going to know how it 's done.' '*Put that down or leave the room.*'"

His wit and power of repartee were great, but it would be difficult to illustrate. Here, however, are instances which may bear relating:

"A clergyman who was going abroad to study said in jest that when he came back he might bring a new religion with him. A person who was present said, 'You may have some difficulty in getting it through the custom house.' 'No,' said Mr. Brooks, 'we may take it for granted that a new religion will have no *duties* attached.'"

"He contrasted the ancient Church with the modern to the

effect that then they tried to save their young men from being thrown to the lions; now we are glad if we can save them from going to the dogs.''

"'Why is it,' said a friend to him, 'that some of these men who call themselves atheists seem to lead such moral lives?' 'They have to; they have no God to forgive them if they don't.' ''

His love of clear and simple humor was marked and emphatic, and he had a rippling way of describing ludicrous scenes which was like nothing so much as a bubbling, gurgling brook, laughing its way over rock and stone and moss. He had what has been called "the deep wisdom of fine fooling."

"He had his version of the 'Jonah' narrative. When some one was wondering at the possibility of Jonah being swallowed by the whale, he said, 'There was no difficulty. Jonah was one of the Minor Prophets.' ''

"The same charm which he exerted in the pulpit was felt in social festivities, or in the private room. No one else seemed to be present when he was there. He filled the room."

"I can remember [wrote Bishop Westcott] with highest pleasure a visit with which he honored me in my room at the Divinity School, Cambridge. His genial presence seemed to fill it, and spread around an atmosphere of energetic life."

"An English lady, an authoress and highly cultivated, spoke of him as the 'enchanter of souls.' ''

"He would have nothing to do with so-called psychological investigations, whose object was to communicate with the departed. 'Why is it,' he once said, 'that mediums always live at the South End?' ''

"He burst out once in talking of a person with rather affected manners, 'If only people would be simple!' Very reserved people he did not get on well with,—he was too reserved himself at once, and too sensitive to atmosphere. 'If they would only once express *themselves*,' he said. He loved people as people, and always wanted to 'hear about folks.' In one of his sermons he speaks of what he felt about the city streets. 'To prosperous men, full of activity, full of life, the city streets, overrunning with human vitality, are full of a sympathy, a sense of human fellowship, a comforting companionship in all that mass of unknown and, as it were, generic men and women, which no utterance of special friendship or pity from the best known lips can bring. The live and active man takes his trouble out on the crowded streets, and finds it comforted by the mysterious consolation of his race. He takes his perplexity out there, and its darkness grows bright in the diffused, unconscious light of human life.'"

"Sometimes Brooks displayed strange moods. He remained one night talking with Dr. Vinton in his study till it got to be twelve o'clock, when he displayed an unaccountable aversion to going back to his house. Dr. Vinton at once proposed that he should spend the night, and a room was made ready for him. But after waiting for some two hours longer he rose, and saying he would n't make a fool of himself he went home."

"In illustrating his preference for city over country life, he said: 'The Bible shows how the world progresses. It begins with a garden, but ends with a holy city.'"

"Commenting upon a meeting of the Church Congress, from which he had just returned, he said the speeches were like towing ideas out to sea and then escaping by small boats in the fog."

"Talking with an American gentleman one clear evening, in Japan, about some late discoveries in astronomy and the enormous number of the stars, the gentleman, who was engaged in a study of Buddhism, said, 'If we have a life to live in each one of the three hundred and fifty millions we have quite a row to hoe.' 'Ah, well,' said Mr. Brooks, 'if they are as beautiful as this I am willing.'"

In speaking of the histrionic art, he said that it demanded for success weakness rather than strength of character. The occasion which led him to speak on the subject was an effort he was making to prevent a young girl from going on the stage.

His presence in a house was so exciting that it seemed to penetrate every part of it, and the effect was long in subsiding after he had left. He threw family discipline to the winds. He would incite, or seem to do so, the children to disobedience, as though law and order in the household were a sham; like some picture from *Alice in Wonderland*, where things were reversed or lost their normal relations. To considerations of personal dignity of bearing he would become oblivious, romping on the floor or standing as Goliath for some small David of a boy to use his sling.

It was often annoying that he would not talk when he was expected to do so, maintaining his silence when people had been invited to meet him. On one of his visits to England, the American minister, Mr. Lowell, gave him a dinner, to which among others he had invited Mr. Huxley under the supposition that the two men would enjoy meeting each other. Mr. Huxley talked, and Mr. Brooks was silent, till Mr. Lowell feared he had made a mistake; but Mr. Brooks afterwards expressed himself as having found great pleasure in Huxley's conversation.

He had the gift for administration. He had his eye on everything, knew all that was going on, and seemed to be everywhere. When anybody wanted to do anything, he would make himself master of the situation in five minutes. But he dreaded machinery in a parish, and was fearful that organization might tyrannize over parishes. He did not at first welcome the St. Andrew's Brotherhood. He had already his Bible class, and thought that was enough.

He once said that he did n't like being fifty. He did n't want to be left behind. Some one had remarked to him, "Your generation was occupied with slavery; ours has taken up sociology." "And so," he remarked, "the inference is that I am to be thrown out."

He never could be alone except when he was travelling. "Travelling is the only place on this footstool where I can be by myself." "Why don't you have a prophet's chamber?" He said he did want one sometimes, but that his mission was to see people. That was what he was here for. After he had been two weeks by himself, he hungered for people. It was the possibilities in people that made them interesting.

He was always reading while he was travelling. The others might be looking out of the windows, the days might be hot and dusty, but he continued to read. He threw the books out of the window when he had finished them.

Once, when his carriage failed to come till it was too late to get him to a meeting, he expressed himself with considerable impatience, but the next morning went over to the livery stable office and apologized for his hastiness.

The moral character of Phillips Brooks stands out clearly in his sermons. Only the man who earnestly sought to realize in himself the ideal he was perpetually holding up to his hearers could have dared to enforce it as he did. He left the impression, by his appearance and his speech, of goodness and of inward purity. But "Phillips always hated," says his brother John, "to have people remark that he could n't help being good."

Very much to the point is this extract from a sermon entitled "The Sea of Glass:"

"You may go on through the crowded streets of heaven, asking each saint how he came there, and you will look in vain everywhere for a man morally and spiritually strong, whose strength did not come to him in struggle. Will you take the man who never had a disappointment, who never knew a want, whose friends all love him, whose health never knew a suspicion of its perfectness, on whom every sun shines, and against whose sails all winds, as if by special commission, are sent to blow, who still is great and good and true and unselfish and holy, as happy in his inner as in his outer life. Was there no struggle there? Do you suppose that man has never wrestled with his own success and happiness, that he has never prayed, and emphasized his prayer with labor, 'In all time of my prosperity, Good Lord, deliver me!' 'Deliver me!' That is the cry of a man in danger, of a man with an antagonist. For years that man and his prosperity have been looking each other in the face and grappling one another,—and that is a supremacy that was not won without a struggle than which there is no harder on the earth."

The intellectual constitution of Phillips Brooks puzzled some of his contemporaries. The following estimate is from a sermon by Rev. George A. Gordon, pastor of the Old South Church:

"The intellect of Phillips Brooks was as striking as the man. There was in it a platonic subtlety, sweep, and penetration, a native capacity for the highest speculations,—a capacity that did not always become apparent, because he passed at once like a flash of lightning to the substance of things, and because he believed that the forms of the understanding, into which the highest in man throws its findings, are at best only inadequate symbols. . . . There was in his mind a Hindu swiftness, mobility, penetrativeness, and mysticism. . . . Had he chosen, he could have been one of the subtlest metaphysicians, or one of the most successful analysts of the human heart, throwing upon his screen the disentangled and accurately classified contents of the soul. But he chose, as indispensable for his calling, to let the artist in him prevail, to do all his thinking

known no alien influence. In his freedom and his appeal to humanity he met the Unitarian. Free Religionists were desirous to secure him as a speaker at their assemblies. When he went to England he seemed to reflect the best type of Anglican theology. The rector of a large London church wrote to him, "The secret by which you make us High Churchmen enthusiastic about you remains unexplained to me." A lady who was a Swedenborgian in her religious belief, remarked as she came away from listening to him that Dr. Brooks was a Swedenborgian. She was told that others said the same thing of him, that Unitarians claimed him, that Methodists held him as one of their own, and so in other churches. She said in reply that she *knew;* Swedenborgians had certain unfailing tests of knowing, and she could not be mistaken. Indeed, so far did this conviction carry people, that they would sooner have believed that Mr. Brooks was mistaken, or did not understand himself, than that they could possibly be mistaken in their judgment about him.

A Roman Catholic wrote: "I feel a queer sort of soul kindred with him. I should like to have known and talked with him. Though we should not have agreed on all points, I am sure we would have been friends."

The situation was a puzzling one to many. It had also its dangerous side, for it was easily misunderstood. Few were capable of comprehending how any one mind could rise to the universality of the religious appeal, without disloyalty to his own household of faith. Criticism of this kind was not uncommon, and has its pathological aspect: "There is no question as to Mr. Brooks's honor, his sincerity, his devotion to truth as he sees it, to the church as he believes in it, and to God as he understands his duty to God. But his attitude is logically indefensible. Grant his premises, and there is no reasonable way for stopping where he stops." There was danger that a great religious genius would be entangled by these Liliputian snags of sectarianism.

But Phillips Brooks thought of himself primarily as a parish minister in the Episcopal Church. In every respect he was orthodox, judged by the formularies of the Book of Common Prayer, and to its rubrics he rigidly adhered. If he seemed out of harmony with prevailing popular opinions, it was because he had risen to the full height of Anglican orthodoxy where others had fallen short or departed from it. Objection was made sometimes to his conception of the Incarnation—that humanity as a whole, and not solely the Church, was the body of Christ,—but the doctrine finds its warrant in the Church Catechism, where it is said that Christ has redeemed the whole body of mankind. When it came to confirmation, his usage was strict in requiring unmistakable evidence that the candidate had experienced the sense of a conscious love toward God. Some thought it was enough in candidates for confirmation if they were ready to " renounce the devil and all his works," even if they had gone through no "religious experience." He fell back for his sanction on the Church Catechism, where in reply to the question, "What is thy duty toward God?" the child is taught to answer, "My duty toward God is to believe in Him, to fear Him, and *to love Him with all my heart, with all my mind, and with all my soul and with all my strength.*" He called for no conventional tests as evidence of the love for God, but in conversation with the candidate satisfied himself of the beginning of a new life. In these personal interviews he was gentle, yet searching, appreciative of the faintest signs of the awakening spiritual life. He never forgot that it was God's own child with whom he was conversing in order to know if the relationship to the Eternal Father were consciously felt and acknowledged. He preserved in a separate package the letters written to him by young boys and girls, where with inadequate language was expressed the desire to live for God.

In order that the significance of the Lord's Supper as the rite of Christian fellowship might not be obscured, he refused to multiply communion services, keeping the feast on the first Sunday in the month, at the mid-day service. When the number of communicants became inconveniently large, he made one concession, and allowed an earlier communion. A communion service at Trinity Church became a most impressive spectacle, when the congregation seemed to rise as a whole and surround the Lord's Table. To the influence of this service, a young Japanese student confessed that he owed his conversion to Christianity.

Another feature of the parish ministry of Phillips Brooks was his effort to make "Trinity Church the most hospitable church in Boston." This was an expansion of the parish ministry, for the number of those who sought access to Trinity was large and always increasing. Young men and young women from every part of the country came to Boston, and from England also, with letters intrusting them to his care, opening with the familiar formula: "May I introduce and commend to your confidence, as if he were my own son, my young friend," etc. His correspondence abounds with such requests from parents whose children were going out into the world, from ministers of churches of every denomination, concerned for the welfare of their young people, from personal friends who intrusted their sons and daughters to his solicitude. There were instances when other interests of his life were placed aside, in order that he might devote himself to one single case of need where his sense of responsibility had become to him the one absorbing duty of the moment. The popular faith in his power to work marvels is illustrated in the story of two poor women in Salem, belonging to the Roman Catholic Church, who had never seen or heard him, one of whom tells the other who is bemoaning her boy falling into evil ways— the thing to do is to take him to Phillips Brooks.

His relations with schools and institutions of learning of every kind form another line of the extension of his pastoral activity. The attempt cannot be made to give the list of those asking for his presence. Some of these invitations were most urgent. "Among all the inhabitants of the globe," so runs an invitation from Yale, "you are our first choice. If you can not write lectures, bring any of your old sermons." Next after Harvard came Yale and the Boston Institute of Technology, with which his relationship was most close. He went often to Cornell at the invitation of President White, and to Williams College under President Carter. In 1884 he was chosen president of the Harvard Alumni Association. The letter of invitation to give a course of lectures at Johns Hopkins University read: "You, better than any one else we can think of, can reach the minds of those who will be here assembled." He was one of the trustees of Groton School, of which Rev. Endicott Peabody was the founder and headmaster. In 1887 he wrote the Groton School Hymn, which has since been sung on the greater days in the school life.

He stood in intimate relations with theological schools, especially Andover and Cambridge; on the Methodist Divinity School connected with Boston University he made his influence felt for twenty years upon every class going forth from its walls. His interest in young men while in college, says Bishop Lawrence, surpassed the interest he felt in them after they had entered upon their course of professional study. So long as there was the undeveloped possibility, his interest was at the height, for his imagination was touched at the prospect.

His association with women's colleges should be mentioned, where he often went to preach. He was elected an honorary member of the class of 1889 at Wellesley College, of the class of 1890 at Mt. Holyoke College, and of the class of 1891 at Wheaton Seminary.

In 1886 a course of lectures was projected at Harvard on the different professions, each to be given by one who occupied the foremost rank. Phillips Brooks spoke for the ministry. One who was present describes the effect:

"I was there in Sever 11, and it was an occasion in the life of Brooks,—a great opportunity, and he realized it. The hall was never more crowded. Students stood and sat on the window-seats; they seemed to be on each other's shoulders. He tried to be cool and philosophical, and tell them what the ministry was like, as previous speakers had told of the other professions,—he started in that way, but the mass of the young men and the upturned faces and the subject got the better of him, till, throwing philosophy and cool statement to the winds, he broke out, 'I can't come here and talk to you of the ministry as one of the professions. I must tell you that it is the noblest and most glorious calling to which a man can give himself.' The torrent once loose, it did not cease till it reached the deep calm of his closing words. One was almost afraid that the whole body of young men would rise on the impulse and cry, 'Here am I, send me!' That was a great speech, for its feeling and its thought."

He was a defender of Harvard against any objection on the score of religious dangers to be encountered there. To a young man asking his advice, where he should go to college, he wrote:

"233 CLARENDON STREET, BOSTON, March 28, 1887.

"I think that it (Harvard) was never so good a place for the life and study of a young man as it is to-day. I have known it for the last thirty-six years, and watched it closely all that time. It has improved and ripened steadily, until it may be said to-day, with no disparagement to other colleges, that nowhere can a better education be obtained than at Harvard.

"There are young men there of every form of religious faith, and many who have no faith. There are scoffers, perhaps there are blasphemers. There are also earnest, noble, consecrated Christian men, and many souls seeking a light and truth which they have not yet found. You meet in the college what you will meet in the world. You will have to choose what you will be, as you will have to choose all your life. You will find all the help which Christian friends and Christian services can give to a young man whose real reliance must be on God and his own soul. I hope that you will come."

Any sketch of the pastoral activity of Phillips Brooks must include his relation to children. He read them by the power of his imagination and by close contact with child life. His love went forth from their infancy to the children of his brother William. He made it a rule to go to his brother's house on Sunday evenings. He had the children learn the poems which he liked, and, preserving the tradition of his father's household, he called for their repetition. He took the children with him when he went to buy the Christmas presents, enjoining them to forget all they knew about them until Christmas came. It was a rule that no presents were to be looked at until Uncle Phillips came to dinner on Christmas Day, after service in church was over. When Gertrude was old enough, he made her his companion, taking her with him on his journeys or when going to Cambridge, and often insisting on her being at the rectory for breakfast.

To be with children seemed to give him more pleasure than anything else in life. He was much in demand for children's schools. On one occasion he was disappointed when he went to a home for children in the suburbs of Boston one Sunday afternoon, expecting a good time in playing and romping with them, to find that advantage had been taken of his coming to invite an audience of adults, whose contribution to the support of the home it was desirable to obtain. He went to the window and stood there in silence, after having made his remonstrance. There were the children in various institutions whom he carried in his heart; there were the children in many households where he visited, who rejoiced at his coming and claimed him as a friend.

Helen Keller was intrusted to his care by her father, who wished that her first religious instruction should come from Phillips Brooks. He sounded the depths of that young soul, and gave to her the idea of God. He was impressed with the remark she made after the first conversation, that she had always known that there was a God, but had not known before His name. She continued to write letters to him as long as he lived. In one of his letters he tells her, "The reason why we love our friends is because God loves us."[1]

Still another sphere into which the ministry of Phillips Brooks expanded was among those, to be counted by the thousands, who had never seen or heard him but knew him by the reading of his books. Letters constantly came to him, telling him,—it almost seems in exaggerated strain,—how much he had done. These letters were to him like the staying up of Moses's arms when he engaged in prayer. A friend recalls his words: "Do not be chary of appreciation. Hearts are unconsciously hungry for it. There is little danger, especially with us in this cold New England region, that appreciation shall be given too abundantly."

The power of Phillips Brooks in the sick-room was recognized as something wonderful and rare. A mysterious influence went forth from him for good, for strength and life, even when he sat down by the bedside and no words were spoken. He had a gift for inspiriting people who were depressed or had lost heart for their work. A word from him would send them to their tasks again, with renewed energy. What he said to a young woman, tired with the care of an invalid mother, may illustrate, even without his voice and presence, how he dealt with the disheartened, "Go on taking care of your mother, and when she is gone, God will take care of you."

The letters he wrote to people in affliction, if gathered together, would form a considerable volume. He attracted them, as he did the poor, the sick, the outcast, by some force which he did not consciously exercise, and yet of whose existence he was aware. In the letters of condolence there is one sentence which reads, "God never takes away what he has once given."

So far as is known Phillips Brooks spoke rarely about his preaching, and even of his few references little can be recalled.

[1] Cf. *Letters of Phillips Brooks to Helen Keller*, Boston, 1893.

These personal reminiscences and comments which follow are worth preserving:

"In his morning sermons he was more formal and even violent; but as the day went on he came to himself and was more calm."

"I say many things [he once remarked] in the afternoon which I should never think of saying in the morning."

"He was always gathering hints [said one who knew him well], from those who had talked with him. He would take up their remarks in an impersonal way. It was always so in every sermon."

"He preached a sermon in Huntington Hall on the 'Martyrs beneath the Throne,' and was depressed because he had failed: 'I have n't told the people what was in that text.'"

"He was asked whether it was easier to preach extempore or written sermons. 'In preparation there should be no difference. But extempore preaching depends on moods.'"

"His tendency to stumble in preaching was partly owing to his habit of using a lead pencil to make corrections, especially before preaching a sermon a second time. These inserted words and phrases were in a fine handwriting, and looked somewhat dim compared with the bold manner of his manuscript. When he came to them in preaching they were like obstructions thrown across the track of the rushing engine.

"When he preached extemporaneously, he reminded one of a hound who does not at once catch the scent, but having caught it, goes off with a rush at his highest speed."

To the contemporaneous descriptions, already given, of the power of Phillips Brooks as a preacher, may be added these testimonies which express in better form what the people were saying. "He seemed," said the eminent New Testament scholar, Professor J. H. Thayer, "to have the leverage for moving the world." "He makes us feel strong," was the comment of Dr. Frazer, bishop of Manchester. "By common consent," said President Tucker of Dartmouth College, "no one has translated so much of the Christian religion into thought and life." The President of Syracuse University, Dr. Day, spoke of his universal sympathy:

"Marvellously did he bring, out of that wonderful gospel, teachings which appeal to the profound and the learned, and plain lessons which also help the unlettered; so that the deep-thinking were introduced to the profoundest philosophy, and the hurried man felt that somehow the hour and the lesson were for him, and that he could go out and work noble manhood out of the commonest callings of life. The scholar said, 'He is of us,' and the unlettered said, 'He is of us.' The poor said, 'He is of us,' and the rich said, 'He is of us.' To the young he was full of mirth and buoyancy; to the troubled he was a man deeply acquainted with grief. All men, of all classes and conditions, claimed him, because in his magnificent heart and sympathy he seemed to be all men, and to enter into their disappointments and into their successes, and to make them his own."

Of the many attempts to explain what was called the secret of his strength, it may be said that they were so many contributions to the problem, but the secret remained unsolved. It was said of him that he had "the genius for religion and for preaching. When he preaches, he becomes almost as completely the voice of the Spirit as Shakespeare is the voice of nature. He draws his illustrations not from his religious autobiography, but from the spiritual biography of the race." Professor Everett, of Harvard, said of him:

"We have to recognize that Phillips Brooks was a man of genius. He was as truly such as any of our great poets. It is not important, nor, indeed, would it be possible, to make a comparative estimate of his genius with that of any specified poet or artist. All that is to our purpose is to notice the fact of his wonderful genius, and to illustrate, as may be possible, its nature and its methods. . . . There are comparatively few in whom the special genius which marks the truest preacher as such makes itself felt. This genius was pre-eminently the gift of Phillips Brooks."

The late Professor A. B. Bruce, of Glasgow University, when asked how Phillips Brooks compared with great preachers in Scotland and England, said in reply, using a homely but striking figure:

"It is this way: our great preachers take into the pulpit a bucket full or half full of the Word of God, and then, by the force of personal mechanism, they attempt to convey it to the congregation. But this man is just a great water main, attached to the everlasting reservoir of God's truth and grace and love, and streams of life, by a heavenly gravitation, pour through him to refresh every weary soul."

An eminent scholar and writer, the Right. Hon. James Bryce (now the English ambassador to this country), spoke of him in comparison with other preachers,—Bishop Wilberforce, Dr. Candlish, Mr. Spurgeon, Dr. Liddon, and Henry Ward Beecher:

"All these famous men were, in a sense, more brilliant, that is to say, more rhetorically effective, than Dr. Brooks, yet none of them seemed to speak so directly to the soul. With all of them it was impossible to forget the speaker in the words spoken, because the speaker did not seem to have quite forgotten himself, but to have studied the effect he sought to produce. With him it was otherwise. What amount of preparation he may have given to his discourses I do not know. But there was no sign of art about them, no touch of self-consciousness. He spoke to his audience as a man might speak to his friend, pouring forth with swift, yet quiet and seldom impassioned, earnestness the thoughts and feelings of a singularly pure and lofty spirit. The listeners never thought of style or manner, but only of the substance of the thoughts. They were entranced and carried out of themselves by the strength and sweetness and beauty of the aspects of religious truth and its helpfulness to weak human nature which he presented. Dr. Brooks was the best because the most edifying of preachers. . . . There was a wealth of keen observation, fine reflection, and insight both subtle and imaginative, all touched with a warmth and tenderness which seemed to transfuse and irradiate the thought itself. In this blending of perfect simplicity of treatment with singular fertility and elevation of thought, no other among the famous preachers of the generation that is now vanishing approached him."

Mr. Bryce has also described one characteristic of Phillips Brooks's preaching, in some respects more extraordinary and inexplicable than any other,—his power of excitation over an audience:

"He rose in his first few sentences like a strong-winged bird, into a serene atmosphere of meditation, stilling and thrilling the crowd that filled the chapel like a strain of solemn music. Few have possessed in equal measure the power of touching what is best in men, and lifting them suddenly by sympathetic words to the elevation of high-strung feeling and purpose which they cannot reach of themselves, save under some wave of emotion due to some personal crisis in life."

Among those who followed the career of Phillips Brooks, no one was better fitted than the late Dr. R. S. Storrs of Brooklyn, himself a scholar and a preacher of the foremost rank, to describe the characteristics of the man which lay behind the force manifested in the pulpit. He has clothed the truth of his tribute to Phillips Brooks in these beautiful words:

"There was in him a majesty and strength of spirit, as of person, which all had to recognize, and were glad to recognize; but with this was the utmost, loveliest gentleness and tenderness which made a sunshine in the shadiest places, among the humblest families whom he visited. There was that unsurpassed affluence of nature and of culture, but with it there was the beautiful simplicity of spirit, as of the vital air, as of the sunshine which irradiates and bathes the earth,—a simplicity as childlike as one ever saw in a human soul. There was his utter devotion to the highest ideals of duty and of truth, and his keenest apprehension of the beauty and authority of these ideals; and yet there was with this the most sympathetic interest, habitual and spontaneous, in humble persons, and in the common affairs of life, his own or others. There was that marvellous eloquence, yet consecrated always, in its utmost reach and rush, to the service of the Master, to the giving of the message which the Master had given him for the souls of men. And with all the self-respecting consciousness which he could not but possess, and with all the admiration and love and honor which have surrounded him as almost no other of his time, there was that marvellous modesty which shrank from anything of self-assertion or assumption over others, and which showed to the last no more of either of these than when he had been a boy in school, or a freshman in college. It was this combination of qualities, interblending with each other, representing the golden hemispheres of the perfect globe, which gave a something unique and mystical to the spirit of Phillips Brooks."

From his youth Phillips Brooks had kept himself in close association with the lives of great men. The following extract is from his note-book, as he was preparing to speak in Trinity Church on Washington's Birthday, which in 1891 fell on Sunday. He took for his text, " Whosoever will be great among you, let him be your minister":

"It is the day of a great man to-day. This kind of festival nobler than the festival of an event. The latter is the presence of God's power, the former a presence of God himself. Great men are the treasures and inspirations of the nation. Let us think this morning of Great Men.

"The vague yet certain process of their discrimination. Let us admire the human instinct! No one can tell why this or that one stands out, but *he does*. The others fade away. Luther, Cromwell, Washington: the estimates vary, but the conclusion is clear. The sense of accident and circumstance comes in: the 'mute, inglorious Milton' theory; the subtle proof that the other man is greater. Yet still the element of timeliness to be regarded. There are men who are out of time; the need of getting a little distance off to see the prominence of some, to catch up with others. But the few great men stand. Others sometimes added, but almost never is one extinguished. Position cannot make or disguise.

"The question whether they are different in *kind* or in *degree* from other men. Both. *Difference of degree becomes difference in kind.* It is an affair of proportion of the elements of life. The simplicity of greatness; more elemental, more free, holding larger conditions in harmony. Comparison of a great city; how different its life! So of a great man.

"While greatness is ordinarily associated with prominence, we recognize its quality often in obscurity. There we see a person who has these two conditions: (1) He is at once exceptional and representative. He is unlike other men, and at the same time makes a revelation of them. Thus he haunts and fascinates. The moral and mental united. (2) He is not a mere expert, but a man; great, not in some special skill, but as a being.

"But enough of the effort to define greatness. We all know it. The real question whence it comes. Once great men were looked upon like meteors dropped out of the sky; now as if they grew out of the ground, expressing its fertility. The significance of the change. The greatest men make greatness possible to all. In a mysterious way it is we who did these things. Vicariousness. Personality is universal. Shall there come a time of high average with no great men? Surely not. They shall always be.

"Great men of the future. The world shall choose them better. They shall better know their places. Great men have not found their place, though they are always feeling after it. It is service. The conceit and jealousy of dignity must pass away. Who is greatest? He that sitteth at meat or he that serveth? Christ's appeal.

"Cultivate reverence for Greatness. Teach it to your children. Cultivate perception of it. The double blessing of pattern and power."

CHAPTER XXIV.

1891.

LENT AT TRINITY CHURCH.   NOON LECTURES AT ST.
  PAUL'S.   ELECTION TO THE EPISCOPATE.   THE CON-
  TROVERSY FOLLOWING THE ELECTION.   EXTRACTS
  FROM CORRESPONDENCE.

THE last of the Lenten ministrations was the most impressive
of all.   The scene in New York at Trinity Church was reproduced
in Boston at St. Paul's and it became the signal event that Phillips Brooks preached every Monday at 12 o'clock.   So great was
the interest that the addresses were reported at length in the
secular newspapers.   The preacher was at the height of his
power as he appealed to the crowd of eager listeners, whose gaze
was fixed upon him as though magnetized, with an intensity of
expression at times almost startling.

On Good Friday he took part in a union service at the Old
South Church, where the ministers of churches in the vicinity
of Copley Square were present.   On Easter Day he preached on
the text, " That through death he might destroy him that had
the power of death."   The sermon revealed the preacher in the
vast outreach of Christian faith, making it easier to understand
the mystery of St. Paul's theology:

"He was born that he might die.   The old sad story.   Can
anything be sadder?   So we talk to each other in our darkest
moods.   But the glory of Jesus is that He takes our old despairing
speeches and makes them glow.   The dirge becomes a pæan.
"'I am born that I may die,' becomes a cry of victory."

In the middle of Lent, on March 9, Bishop Paddock died and
the nomination of Phillips Brooks for the vacant episcopate was
immediate and spontaneous on the part of all the people.   During
the weeks which intervened before the diocesan convention

should meet on April 29, there were constant communications to the newspapers discussing the question in its various bearings— a thing unheard-of before—but it did not seem unfitting in the case of Phillips Brooks. The tenor of these communications varied, some maintaining that he would not accept the office, others, that it would not be right to take him from Trinity Church, where his influence was greater than it would be in the episcopate. Some thought he lacked the capacity for the administration of a large diocese. There were others still, a few sinister voices, suggesting that he was unfit for the office because he denied the articles of the Christain faith. As in the case of his call to Harvard, the discussion went on as if he were to have no voice in the matter, but it should be decided for him by the people. So many letters, however, were published opposing his election on the assumption that he would not accept the office, that his friends felt it necessary to get from him an authoritative statement.

"On April 2 [writes one who stood close to him], a few weeks before the meeting of the diocesan convention, it was my privilege to learn his views in a conversation which he himself opened by saying, 'Why have none of you spoken to me about the bishopric?' I replied that it was because in our ignorance of his wishes we thought it wiser to allow the matter to come before him for his decision when he should be elected, as we hoped he would be by a large majority. He answered: 'Why should I decline? Who would not accept such a great opportunity for usefulness, such an enlargement of his ministry?' At my request he then authorized all who desired his election to say that he would accept the office if offered to him."

The diocesan convention met on the 29th of April, and on the following day Phillips Brooks was elected bishop on the first ballot by a large majority of the clergy and a still larger majority of the laity. It was a personal election, where party lines ceased to be closely drawn. Some voted for him who were not in sympathy with his ecclesiastical attitude, and others voted against him who did not wish that he should be taken from Trinity Church. The enthusiasm over the election was unbounded. If the vote had been taken again, it would have been well-nigh unanimous, for many of those who had voted adversely were rejoiced at the result. It was a strange scene. As soon as the result was known, there was a rush from the hall where the convention was sitting to the house on Clarendon Street. He stood in his study to receive those who came, the large eyes filled with emotion, and not without a plaintive sadness.

The rejoicing in the land was so deep, so universal, that the occasion seemed like some high festival whose octave was prolonged in order that the full harvest of congratulations might be gathered in. His friends wrote to him—and their name was legion—expressing their joy. All took it for granted that the event meant the expansion of his influence. It was assumed that Christian unity would be assured by the enlargement of his power. It was "a perfect storm of congratulations," said one who was watching the scene. There had been other events in the life cf Phillips Brooks which had called out the popular applause, but this excelled them all. It was a day of personal rejoicing, as though each individual friend or admirer had been honored in the honor which had come to him. "It is one of the most encouraging events that has happened in the Church for years." "I cannot but feel," wrote one of his early parishioners in the Church of the Advent, "a sort of reflected honor on our own little Advent, and my heart is full of eager joy." From Philadelphia came these words:

"The gratification felt here over your election is unparalleled. I never saw anything like it. And those who knew you best have no words to express their joy. All our newspapers have had editorials on your election."

The colored people spoke through one of their representatives: "The negroes of the South rejoice with me in wishing you joy." A citizen of Boston who knew the city well writes, "Beautiful thoughts are thought of you in Boston, glorious things are said of you, and the noblest expectations cherished." Letters from the bishops who congratulated him—and a large number of them hastened to express their gratification— recognize the unique element in the situation: "No bishop of the American Church was ever called to his high office with such acclaim." Heads of universities and colleges wrote as if included in the universal benediction. Resolutions were sent from the students of theological seminaries of every name, from the institutions of learning with which he had been connected. To generalize on this amazing display of personal devotion, it might be said that all were inspired by a feeling that the moment had come when those who recognized his work, whether they knew him or not, had the right to speak, and express their deepest feeling to Phillips Brooks.

There was abundant recognition from his own household of faith; more than he could have imagined possible. What came to him from representative men in other communions was full of meaning. A distinguished Congregational clergyman wrote: "The event means a great deal for all our churches"; and another reminded him of the many thousands whom he did not know who were praying for him, and asking for him "life and health in order to do some great work." A prominent layman of the Congregational Church wrote:

"I want to add my voice to the general *Laus Deo, Deus vobiscum*. I am so thankful you are elected bishop, not of Massachusetts, but of the Church Universal. All of us who share in your scholarly liberality, of all denominations, will call you *our* bishop. May God make you Bishop of all souls, and may all humble and good men love and honor you more and more!"

A prominent Methodist clergyman writes to him, "I am now ready to intone '*Te Deum Laudamus*.'" An eminent lawyer, Unitarian in his religious faith, writes: "It is, indeed, a fine thing when a great body of Christians puts at its head one whom all Christians will gladly follow." A Universalist divine and leading educator:

"I do not so much rejoice in the immense forward movement that Episcopalianism has made in your election, though I trust I am broad enough *not* to be indifferent to that, as I do in the gain that has come, and that is sure to come more and more, to our common Christianity. In this feeling I know that I voice the general sentiment of clergy and laity alike of the entire Universalist Church."

The yearning in the soul of the common humanity for leadership had fastened upon Phillips Brooks as adequate to its demand. The well-nigh universal tribute from the newspapers throughout the country, was one of rejoicing because in some way he will now be a universal "bishop." The late James Russell Lowell gave utterance to the same feeling:

"ELMWOOD, CAMBRIDGE, MASSACHUSETTS, May 1, 1891.

"DEAR DOCTOR BROOKS,—Though I do not belong to the flock which will be guided by your crook, I cannot help writing a line to say how proud I am of *our* bishop.

"Faithfully yours,
"J. R. LOWELL."

In the Middle Ages, when the honors of canonization were in process, it was customary to hear the other side, in order that all which might be said against a man should be considered. That moment had now come, and come for the first time, in a public way, in the life of Phillips Brooks.

The process of making a bishop in the American Episcopal Church is longer and more complicated than in the Church of England. After the election has taken place the secretary of the diocese sends word of the election to the standing committee in each diocese in the United States, and also to the presiding bishop. As soon as the presiding bishop has received a reply from the majority of the standing committees in the affirmative he communicates the fact to the bishops and calls for their vote. After a majority of favorable replies from the bishops, the bishop-elect has been confirmed and the order is given for his consecration. The process is generally a formal one, requiring four or five weeks before the announcement of the result. In the case of Phillips Brooks ten weeks elapsed before the confirmation of his election was made known. The controversy which took place over his election was not important, nor were the sources influential or representative from which it proceeded; their importance was rather a reflected one, gaining significance from the unique greatness of the man. So sensitive was the public mind in everything relating to him that the slightest hint of opposition was magnified till it assumed unnatural proportions.

As to the final result, those who knew best the Episcopal Church had no misgivings. Their faith in its reserved wisdom, its comprehensiveness, and its freedom from doctrinaire tendencies gave them absolute confidence. Such also was the con viction of Dr. Brooks,—there was no doubt whatever of the confirmation of his election. To the efforts made to defeat it we now turn.

Hardly, then, had the election been made when a statement appeared in the newspapers, gaining wide circulation, that there was likely to be opposition among the bishops. Dr. Brooks, it was said, had expressed his disbelief in the historic episcopate, and as the bishops held strong convictions on that point they could not admit to their number one who differed from them. This statement in the newspapers was soon followed by a leaflet with the headline, "Ought Mr. Brooks to be Confirmed?" which was sent to bishops and standing committees, containing quotations from his sermons to the effect that he denied the apostolical succession. Another leaflet was widely distributed, giving the opinion of a Roman Catholic priest, who had formerly been a Baptist minister. When asked his opinion in regard to the propriety of Dr. Brooks becoming a bishop, he had shaken his head and seemed quite disheartened about the Episcopal Church. His words were quoted in the leaflet as follows:

"I regret to say they [the present movements in the Episcopal Church] indicate that the Episcopal Church is yielding to the rationalistic and agnostic tendencies of the age to a deplorable extent. . . . If its creeds and articles of faith no longer bind its clergy and people, the surging tide of infidelity will soon destroy its distinctive character as an organized and conservative form of Christianity."

A circular was sent to bishops and standing committees, addressed "To Whom it May Concern," containing an extract from an anonymous letter whose writer asserted that Dr. Brooks was a most unfit man to be a bishop, as he deemed the miracle to be unimportant and in the life of Christ unessential. "He will let everybody stand on their head if they want to, and avow that no doctrine is essential, not even the essential one of the Trinity and the divine Incarnation." One of the bishops sent to Dr. Brooks an "open letter" saying that his participation "in the so-called ordination services of Mr. Beecher's successor in Brooklyn required in the judgment of many honest minds an explanation or expression of regret, . . . assurances that what has pained so many of his brethren will not occur again." Another bishop wrote to him inquiring whether he were still true to his ordination vows, and whether he had ever united with a Unitarian minister in a public religious service; but he added, "On the absurd subject of apostolic succession I entirely agree with you."

On the other hand, a layman wrote:

"*My* questions are these: Do you consider that Apostolic Succession is indispensably necessary to the existence of Christ's Church?

"In your opinion, have the faithful followers of a Protestant creed which ignores the Succession an equal warrant with faithful Episcopalians in expecting, in the future life, the reward promised to the righteous?"

Among other questions he was called upon to answer were :

"Do you believe that the Protestant Episcopal Church alone represents in its integrity and purity, in the United States of America, Christ's Holy Catholic Church?

"Do you believe that episcopally ordained clergy alone have the right to exercise Christ's ministry,—to Baptize, to administer the Holy Communion, to pronounce God's declaration of absolution over repentant sinners, and to preach the Gospel?

"Do you believe that the Protestant sects in the United States constitute the American Church, and that the Protestant Episcopal Church is no more of a Church than any of these sects and has no more right to that title than any of them?"

Some were content with asking questions. Others were bolder and brought against him railing accusations. He was a Congregationalist, since he did not believe in apostolic succession. In theology he was an Arian, which meant that he denied not only the divinity but the humanity of Christ. He was a Pelagian, and held that man was sufficient for himself and that God had no connection with human salvation. The rumor went abroad that the Nicene creed was not recited at Trinity Church. To none of these questions or accusations did Dr. Brooks vouchsafe any reply. But there grew up a feeling of indignation in the Episcopal Church that it should be so misrepresented, or that any man in its fold should be subjected to such treatment. This feeling found expression in the following courageous and manly letter from Rev. John Henry Hopkins which appeared in the New York *Tribune* on June 1:

"Our Church is a comprehensive Church; and that means that there is room in her communion for a great variety of opinions on religious matters. We have three well-known parties, High, Low, and Broad. I am a High Churchman,—about as high as they make them. Had I been a member of the Massachusetts convention, I should never, under any circumstances, have voted for Dr. Brooks. But when he had been elected I should have signed his testimonials with pleasure, rejoicing in the elevation of one who is recognized on both sides of the Atlantic Ocean as a preacher now without a living superior, and whose high-toned, stainless life is acknowledged by all. As long as any one of our dioceses wants a Broad Church bishop or a Low Church bishop, it has a right to him; and the requiring of the consents of the standing committees and a majority of the bishops was never meant to give power to a majority to squeeze out a minority by refusing to let them have the kind of bishop they wanted. . . . To try now to return to a narrower basis in order to worry the most distinguished bishop-elect whom the American Church has ever known is all nonsense.

"When asked for 'explanations,' etc., I am delighted that Dr. Brooks had none to give. No bishop-elect ought ever to give any. If he can honestly make the answers put in his mouth at the time of his consecration, it is enough. The Church gives to no man the right to put to him any question beyond that. Especially is it uncalled-for in a case like that of Dr. Brooks, volumes of whose sermons are in print. Anonymous letters should be treated, in such a matter as this, with perfect contempt,— and all are anonymous whose writers are not named and known. . . . Especially is this the case when these anonymous writers display such abysmal ignorance of the very points in theology which they try to handle."

The election had taken place April 30, and by June 4 it was known that a majority of votes of the standing committees had been cast in favor of the bishop-elect. The question then went before the bishops. The presiding bishop, the Rt. Rev. Dr. Williams of Connecticut, had hoped that by the middle of June he should be able to report that the election had been approved. But the weeks went by, and the votes of the bishops had not been received. It began to be feared that the accusations and anonymous letters had influenced their opinion. One of the bishops had sent a circular letter to his Episcopal brethren warning them of the awful danger to the faith involved in the issue, of the "horrible consequences " which no one could forecast, if the election were confirmed. Dr. Brooks himself never had any doubts as to the final result, but he was annoyed by the unusual delay, and depressed by the anxiety of his friends and by the publicity given to the subject in the papers. He was urged by bishops and other friends to break his silence and assure the Church that he believed the articles of the Christian faith; but he refused to give any answers, or to define his position, or to make apologies or pledges.

"I have been for thirty-two years a minister of the Church [so he wrote, June 3, 1891], and I have used her services joyfully and without complaint. I have preached in many places, and with the utmost freedom. I have written and published many volumes, which I have no right to ask anybody to read, but which will give to any one who chooses to read them clear understanding of my way of thinking. My acts have never been concealed. Under these circumstances, I cannot think it well to make any utterance of faith or pledge of purpose at the present time. Certainly I made none to my brethren here, when they chose me to be their bishop, and I cannot help thinking that you will think I am right in making none now, when the election is passing to its final stages."

Had Mr. Brooks, however, met the wishes of those who advised him to make some utterance of a reassuring character, it would not have met the real difficulty. Had he affirmed his belief in doctrines he was falsely charged with denying, there would have been another question ready for him: How is it that believing these things, as you say you do, you could have taken part in the ordination of a Congregational minister? or how could you have allowed Unitarians to come to the Lord's Supper? or how could you have taken part in any religious service where they were present, or have spoken as you did, in the pulpit of Trinity Church, about an eminent Unitarian minister? Do you not see that your acts contradict your words, taking all meaning out of your language, so that you stand convicted by deeds which speak louder than words? He had maintained, in his book on *Tolerance*, that fellowship with those of different religious attitudes did not imply indifference to religious doctrines, but that true toleration should coexist with a deeper conviction of their truth and value. This was what his opponents refused to admit or understand. What they were in reality demanding was the retraction of his whole attitude—confession of wrong, contrition and promises of amendment. On that condition only could he be absolved from suspicion and accusation of false doctrine.

There may have been some danger of his being engulfed in the tragedy which has sometimes awaited those who depart from prevailing fashions in theological opinion. Samaritans and publicans were to orthodox Judaism in the time of Christ what the Protestant Churches are to modern "Catholic" ecclesiasticism. When Christ associated with Samaritans, He was reminded that the orthodox respectable Jews had no dealings with them. When He sat down to eat with publicans and sinners the principle was applied to Him that "a man is known by the company he keeps." Phillips Brooks was one of those who looked forward to some larger fulfilment of the words of Christ to the woman of Samaria: "The hour cometh when ye shall neither in this mountain, nor yet at Jerusalem, worship the Father, when the true worshippers shall worship the Father in spirit and in truth."

The votes were so slow in coming in that by the 1st of July a sufficient number had not been recorded. Those who knew the Episcopal Church had no serious misgivings. But the popular anxiety increased while it forecast what his defeat would mean, not only to the Episcopal Church, but to all the churches. Again he was urged to say a few simple words which would quiet the agitation.

"I had often begged him [says Bishop Clark, in a memorial sermon] to say a word or two, or to allow me to do it for him, which I knew would greatly relieve the minds of some honest people, who did not understand his position, and his uniform reply in substance was: 'I will never say a word, or allow you to say a word, in vindication or explanation of my position. I stand upon my record, and by that record I will stand or fall. I have said what I think and believe in my public utterances and in my printed discourses, and have nothing to retract or qualify.' And so through the whole of the trying campaign of his election to the episcopate his mouth was closed."

From July 1 to July 10 the uncertainty continued. On

38

the last-named day, the presiding bishop telegraphed to Dr.
Brooks that the election had been confirmed by a majority
of the bishops.   Then the congratulations poured in once more,
and there went up a shout of jubilation all over the country.
The confirmation of the election had been delayed too long.
But upon this aspect of the subject we need not dwell.   The
common feeling was expressed by one who understood the
situation:

"The persistent maintenance of your spiritual equanimity and
Christian temper has won for you the hearts of thousands of
God's people everywhere, during your recent persecution."

The scene in the little church at Northeast Harbor, Maine, on
July 12, is thus described in a letter to the bishop-elect by a
clergyman present:

"MY DEAR BROOKS,—I had a great comfort and happiness to-
day.   In church, Bishop Doane, with a few graceful words, announced that the news of your confirmation had just reached
him, and he asked us to join in that prayer in the service for the
Consecration of Bishops, 'Most merciful Father, we beseech Thee
to send down upon Thy servant Phillips Brooks Thy heavenly
blessing,' etc.   I never joined in a prayer with more fervor, nor
thanked God more devoutly that a great suspense was over. . . .
I was glad enough that our Church is broad enough to hold you
and ——.   I agree with neither, but what difference does that
make?   Accept my hearty congratulations."

The Rev. John Henry Hopkins had taken what part he could
in securing the confirmation of Dr. Brooks's election, and after
the result was reached wrote this letter to Phillips Brooks:

"July 11, 1891.

"REV. AND DEAR BROTHER,—At last the morning papers an-
nounce that the majority of the Bishops consent to your consecration, though they have been so slow about it that I began to
feel a little uneasy.   Not about you!   Your position is one which
Bishops can neither give nor take away.   Nor do I congratulate
you, for the burden of the Episcopate is too heavy to be a fit subject for congratulation.   But I rejoice that the American Church
has not been switched from its propriety by such a disgusting
mess of twaddle as the —— business even when backed up by so
light a weight as the name of Dr. ——.   I loathe this whole 'pri-

vate and confidential' business of stabbing a man in the dark, and only wonder that the miserable underground burrowing has affected as many good men as it has. Part of the opposition, however, is due (as with ——) to a conviction that you are an *Arian* of some shade! Of course, if you were *that*, I should do as he has done; but I have never seen any proof of it, and don't believe a word of it. I only wish I were well enough to attend your consecration; but I have an incurable disease, which renders it impossible, and have only a few weeks, perhaps months, to live. I shall be with you in *spirit* on that day. You and I do not agree about some things; but we can differ like honest men who respect one another; and I respect and honor you as the foremost preacher of our Anglican Communion, and shall rejoice to see you a member of our house of Bishops. I regard your elevation as the most important step yet taken in bringing New England into the Church.

"Your obedient servant in the Church,
"J. H. Hopkins."

One other circumstance remains to be mentioned illustrating the attitude of Phillips Brooks. Among those who voted for his confirmation there were some who were troubled with doubts as to the validity of his baptism. Now that he was free to speak without compromising his dignity, he was asked for the sake of peace and of quieting scruples to submit to what is known as "hypothetical baptism"; since his baptism by a Unitarian minister had raised the doubt whether "water were used, and in the Triune name." Others, he was told, who had been placed in similar circumstances had done so. With this request he refused to comply, assuring those who made it that the baptism had been by water, and in the name of the Father, and of the Son, and of the Holy Ghost. Of this he was as sure as that the name given him in baptism had been Phillips Brooks.

To Mr. Robert Treat Paine, who was in Europe, he wrote at great length:

"233 Clarendon Street, Boston, May 14, 1891.

"Yes, my dear friend, it has come, and I suppose it will move on to its completion, although there seems to be a little insignificant opposition to it. But that will not come to anything, and I shall be a bishop. Oh, how often have I wished that you were here, that we might talk it all over together, and I might have your counsel, as I have had it so abundantly all these happy years. But, indeed, there was nothing else to do but to accept the election when it came, and there was never any moment when one had the right or the chance to say, 'I cannot.' The thing became clothed with so much significance that one owed it to Truth and to the Church to stand, and so, the first thing I knew, I was bishop so far as the diocesan convention could make me one.

"Indeed I do not know wholly what to think about it, though the spirit and way in which the whole thing has been done seems to promise a beautiful and splendid chance for good. But at present I think that all my mind is running backward. What a twenty-two years this has been! How little I dreamed, when I came here in '69, of all the happiness that was before me! How good and generous everybody has been! And now, this great, splendid Church and Parish as the monument and token of it all! I sit and think it all over, and am very grateful,—I hope as grateful as I ought to be,—certainly as humble as ever any mortal was.

"And you know something, you cannot know all, of how this great happiness and delight in all these years has had the most sacred and close connection with you and yours. What you and your wife and your children have been to me it would be preposterous for me to try to tell. But the great years never could have been without you. How it all comes pouring on my recollection! What a million of little and big events. And how thankful I am you will never know. God bless you for it all!

"And now about the future. There surely is one. We are young fellows yet, and, much as there is behind us, there is more before, more in quality at least if not in quantity. The diocese is just a larger parish, with some things added which are full of interest. I feel as if the Episcopal Church and the State of Massachusetts needed to understand one another, and to be more to each other than they have been heretofore. If I can make them know one another at all, I shall be very glad. Then I look forward to much intercourse with young ministers, and to the effort to give them inspiration and hope and breadth of view. I expect to preach here and there and everywhere up and down the State, and the people will get tired of hearing me before I shall get tired of addressing them. The colleges and schools of Massachusetts are immensely interesting to me, and I shall know them all. And all the good work of every kind which one can touch with something of religious fire will have one's eager sympathy and service.

"Besides all this, I should be very sorry to think that personal pastorship would have to be entirely abandoned. Many people come to me now for the poor spiritual help which I can give who are in no way connected with Trinity Church. I know how vast a part of the population of our State is not connected with any church at all. I hope that there may be a good many of these

who in one way or another will find me out and give me the
privilege of hearing them and helping them.

"When I run over the opportunities of the episcopate thus, I
feel sure that it is no wooden and mechanical office to which I
have been summoned. It is all splendidly alive if one can make
it so. And there is no place so good to be bishop in as Massachusetts. Our Church here is sensible and broad. The people
about her are willing and glad to see her take her part in every
good work, and (what is a great satisfaction to me) those who
have chosen me know the worst of the man whom they have
chosen. They have summered and wintered me for twenty-two
years, and know pretty much what they will have to expect of
their new bishop.

"But I am sorry to say that I am sure it means the entire resignation of the rectorship of Trinity Church, and the election of a
new man who shall be absolutely master of that place. Nothing
else than that would be just to the diocese, or the parish, or the
new minister, or me. I shall have chance enough to preach in
Boston when I have the time to do so. And at first the larger
part of my time will be spent away from the city. The best
man must be found; would that we knew him! But he will be
found, and we will give him ungrudging welcome to the pulpit,
and he shall have for his own the best parish in the world. And
he and his family will live here in this house. I am trying to
fancy them in these rooms, and do not wish them anything but
good. And I shall come up into Chestnut Street,—26 is the
number,—and be as snug and comfortable as possible there. I
have read carefully all the good and thoughtful plans in your delightful letter, but, believe me, it is not good to think of anything except the entire separation of the church and the episcopate. You will give strength, I know, to both the parish and
the diocese, and I shall be close to all my old friends still. All
this about myself! You will forgive it, I am sure. You do not
know how I wish you were here! But the Consecration shall be
put off, if possible, till you get back."

As the excitement over the election was increasing he wrote
this letter to Rev. John C. Brooks:

"233 CLARENDON STREET, BOSTON, May 27, 1891.

"I thank you most heartily for your good letter. It is indeed
a ridiculous pother that is going on, but it has this advantage,
that it is bringing the whole matter out into broad daylight,
and the decision when it comes will have its full value, and when
a distinct Broad Churchman, thoroughly recognized and proclaimed as such, is made a bishop.

"The opposition has been thoroughly upon the grounds of admitted facts. Nobody has charged me with theft or murder. I do not believe the doctrine of apostolical succession, and I am sure that Lyman Abbott has the right to preach the gospel. I shall be confirmed with the clear knowledge of those positions in everybody's mind, and so it will be fully made known that they are no objections to a man's episcopate.

"And I *shall* be confirmed. There is no doubt of the result, and then I think the good bishops will find what a delightful member of the Upper House I am.

"What an excitement there is all through the theological world. It is all good, and in the end we are to have a larger Christian life. Certainly it is impossible to conceive of things going back to what they were twenty years ago."

In his correspondence, there are other allusions to the ordeal through which he was passing:

"These people who cannot sign the papers of the new man who will overlook everything and oversee nothing have a lot of sympathy from me. I can understand all their misgivings, and could give them a host more which they never guessed."

"There is no doubt, I take it, about my being bishop, but the matter moves on very slowly. I think the opposition have done everything in their power to clothe the election with significance, and when the final collapse of things does not happen upon Consecration Day, I do not see how they will explain the failure."

In acknowledging a wood-cut portrait of himself, which distorted his features, he sent these lines:

> " No wonder, if 'tis thus he looks,
> The Church has doubts of Phillips Brooks.
> Well, if he knows himself, he 'll try
> To give these dreadful looks the lie.
> He dares not promise, but will seek
> E'en as a bishop to be meek,
> To walk the way he shall be shown,
> To trust a strength that 's not his own,
> To fill the years with honest work,
> To serve his day and not to shirk,
> And quite forget what folks have said,
> To keep his heart and keep his head,
> Until men, laying him to rest,
> Shall say at least he did his best."

A few extracts follow from his private correspondence which disclose his feelings in view of the change in his life:

"I am glad of this quiet summer, and especially of the quiet days at North Andover, before the change comes. I have been thinking a great deal about it all and hoping and praying that I may be able to do my duty. The work looks very interesting, and I think the simplest view of it makes it most serious and sacred. I do not know why one should not carry into it the same simple faith by which he has always tried to live, that He whose the work is will give the strength; and so I do not dare to fear. Now that the matter is decided, and I am to be a bishop, I can only hope that I may so exercise my office that you and others, who do not think much of it, may see in it something more than they have suspected to be there."

He writes to Rev. C. D. Cooper, telling of the arrangements made for the Consecration, and urging his presence:

"MINNEQUA, PENNSYLVANIA, July 20, 1891.

"DEAR OLD COOPER,—The bishops have more or less reluctantly consented, and I am to be consecrated in Trinity, Boston, on the 14th of October. And you will come, won't you? I know you do not like such things, but this is *mine*. And we have loved each other all these years, and it will make the episcopate sweeter and easier always to remember that your kindly face looked on at the ceremony, and that your beloved voice joined in the prayers! I want you more than all the rest! I shall keep you a room under my own roof, and it is not likely I shall get you there again, for I must move into the old house where bishops live, on Chestnut Street, some time this autumn.

"So write me word that you will come. Let this be our token that no episcopate can break the friendship of so many years, and show the world that we belong together even if they have made their efforts to tear us from one another. I claim your presence as my right.

"I do not know that I feel right about it all; only it seems to me to be a new and broader opportunity to serve the Master whom we have been loving and serving all this long ministry, and with the opportunity I believe that He will give me strength; that 's all, and I am very happy. . . . God bless you, dear Cooper, and make us faithful, and give us the great joy at last.

"Your affectionate old friend,

"P. B."

And again, in urging his presence, he writes:

"The robes have just come in and stand beside me on the floor as I write. Poor things! they little know how they have got to travel up and down the land, and in what hundreds of pulpits they have got to stand. It is a pity that one has to wear them, and that the whole subject of the episcopate should be so involved with clothes, but one must make the best of that, and indeed, Cooper, the more I think of it the more it seems to me as if there were really no necessity in the nature of things that a bishop should be a fool."

To the Rev. Leighton Parks he writes:

"NORTH ANDOVER, Sunday afternoon, August 16, 1891.

"Let me write you once more before the summer is over, and you and the children set sail for home, and the new life which I cannot help dreading begins. You will do all you can to make it like the old life, won't you? You will not, either in jest or in earnest, behave as if there had come a break and a separation between us, because of what is to take place on the 14th of October! I hate to think of the pageant of that day. And what is to come after it I do not know. Sometimes I feel as if any good which my bishopric can do the Church were comprised in the mere fact of my election and confirmation, and now I had better resign or die. Certainly my kind opponents have done their best to make the selection of me significant. But I will try what I can do to show not that there was not what they called a great danger, but that what they chose to call a danger was really a chance and opportunity of good. You don't know how hard work attracts me in my better moments or how earnestly I pray for strength to do a hundredth part of what my imagination pictures. Only don't desert me."

October 14 had been appointed for the consecration. During the weeks that intervened he was occupied with the preparation that the event demanded. He resigned the rectorship of Trinity Church. He withdrew from the board of preachers at Harvard University. He resigned his position as president of the Clericus Club, which he had held since its formation, feeling that, while he was at liberty to retain his membership, it was no longer becoming that he should be so closely identified with any one organization of the clergy. At a meeting of the Club on October 5, when his resignation was to take effect, a silver loving cup was presented to him upon which were engraved the names of all its active members. Large schemes were in his mind for increasing the efficiency of the City Mission in Boston. He drew up the schedule for his first visitation of the churches in the diocese, which he proposed to begin among the Berkshire hills resplendent with their autumn foliage. He looked forward to his work with pleasure, but his heart was heavy under the changes that it involved. The review of his years was a sad undercurrent accompanying each step that he took. To one of his friends among the clergy he wrote with reference to the appointments he had made for Episcopal visits:

"NORTH ANDOVER, September 16, 1891.

"You don't mind my coming to you on an off day, say a Saturday, and giving the big days to men whom I know less well, do you? I must take liberties with some one; may I not take them with my friends who know that I love them and care for their work? It may be a big price to pay for the fruitless joy of my friendship, but such must be the penalty. At least, this first year I will try to stand by my appointments and let men first see that I want to know the men and the places which I now know least, and that I am not tempted by the prospect of fair Sundays in my good friend's rectory. Read this between the lines when the list comes out and forgive me for Saturday afternoon.

"I shall run in on you more than once during my Berkshire wanderings this autumn. There is no exhilaration about the new work yet, but it will come. At present, there is mostly a deep sense of what the past twenty-two years have been and of what I would make them if I could have them again, but I must not trouble you with that."

He speaks of the death of Lowell, at whose funeral he had officiated: "And Lowell is dead! It makes the world emptier and sadder. No man of letters has begun to do so much good work as he has done, and his whole bearing in the world has been a blessing. He was so brave and true and kind and simple." He joined the Sons of the American Revolution, of which he says in a letter to his brother Arthur: "We do not seem to be very rich in military ancestry, but our Phillips folks were certainly true patriots, and did their part in the council chamber, if not in the field, to set the new nation on its feet. So let 's go in for the assertion that our dear land at least used to be American."

Interesting invitations came to him, but he does not seem to have considered any of them as possibilities; he was shutting himself up more and more to his distinctive work. He was invited to make the address in New York before the society formed under the inspiration of General Sherman, to commemorate annually the birthday of General Grant on the 27th of April. He declined to take any part in the Parliament of Religions to be held in Chicago at the approaching World's Fair in 1893. He was asked by Dr. Montagu Butler, of Trinity College, of the English Cambridge, to allow his name to be placed in the list of "Select Preachers," and to fill the university pulpit on Whitsunday in 1892. The Regius Professor of Divinity, Dr. H. B. Swete, chairman of the Special Board of Divinity, urged him to accept a nomination to the office of Lecturer on Pastoral Theology for the year 1891-92, suggesting that the subject of the course should be "Preaching." He could not bring himself to accept an invitation from Mr. John Quincy Adams, president of the Harvard Alumni Association, to make a speech at the Commencement dinner. He accepted one honor which cost him no effort but gave him pleasure, honorary membership of the Alpha Delta Phi Club in New York. He also gave in his name after serious deliberation as a member of the Society of Friends of Russian Freedom.

He suffered through his sympathy with dear friends in their heavy bereavement; many were the letters of condolence which he wrote. He went out to Cambridge to officiate on the occasion of the death of a member of the University crew. Of the prayer which he made, Professor Peabody remarked, "It was the greatest illustration of the power of free prayer that I ever heard or read of."

On June 16 he was present at the alumni dinner of the Episcopal Theological School,—an occasion of unusual interest and enthusiasm, for the event which was to separate him to some extent from other institutions of learning was to bring him closer to its students. In the course of his address he remarked: "What this school seeks to do is not to turn out men of one school of thought or of a single stamp, but men great in every way—thinkers, scholars, preachers, saints."

Wherever Phillips Brooks went now, he went accompanied by a great concourse of the people. He preached at the Church of the Incarnation in New York on the Sunday after Ascension Day. "That is equivalent to saying," writes the correspondent of a New York paper, "that the Church of the Incarnation was the conspicuous attraction of the day." On October 4, the first Sunday after the opening of the college year, he was at Harvard, and the chapel was "jammed with more than fifteen hundred people." His sermon was from his favorite text, "I am come that they might have life, and that they might have it more abundantly." Though he had often preached on the text, this sermon was new, and, what was now most rare, a written sermon. It was also the last sermon that he would write, and this was to be his last appearance in Appleton Chapel as one of the officers of the University. The necessity of vitality and the glory of obedience was his subject. The sermon was simple, but beneath it lay an ocean of human experience. He closed with these words:

"If there is any man of whom this place makes a skeptic or a profligate, what can we sadly say but this: he was not worthy of the place to which he came; he was not up to Harvard College. But the man with true soul cannot be ruined here. Coming here humbly, bravely, he shall meet his Christ. Here he shall come into the fuller presence of the Christ whom he has known and loved in the dear Christian home from which he came, and know and love Him more than ever.

"'I am come to you here, where men have dreaded and said that I could not come. I am come to you that you may have life, and have it more abundantly.' So speaks the Christ to the students. Of such life, and of brave, earnest men entering into its richness, may this new year of the old College life be full!"

On Sunday, October 11, he stood in his place at Trinity Church,—the last Sunday when he should officiate as its rector after a ministry of twenty-two years. There had been great days at Trinity; this day also was now to be included among them. The intense feeling, the common bond of a sorrow that could not be measured, the sense of finality, combined to give every word of the preacher unusual significance and force. He must have felt more than any one the oppressive mood of the waiting congregation.

The sermon, without any formal farewell, had the essence of parting words. The text was, "Let your light so shine before men that they may see your good works and glorify your Father which is in heaven." From every text he now deduced one common message; these words, he said, "were words of hope, of splendor, and of life. Life is love; Christ is the great source of light and life. God is forever seeking His children; no depth is too deep for Him to go after you."

"For these twenty-two years I have preached this to you, and I have had no word to say to you but that you are God's, and that there is no depth of perdition into which you can sink from which God will not go after you to lift you up. Give yourself up to Him."

Again in the afternoon the same immense congregation came for the evening prayers, and another sermon of equal power was preached from the words: "The spirit and the bride say, Come. And let him that heareth say, Come. And he that is athirst, let him come. He that will, let him take the water of life freely."

"These words are full of exhilaration and hope, full of invitation and expectation. While they are filled with the great burden and sense of life, they are also anticipating the life that is to come. With every good healthy mind this is a necessity, that everything which has been bears in its bosom that which is to be, and fills him with expectation and hope."

Once more, in the evening, he preached at St. Andrew's Church, attended there by the same great throng of hearers. "He that overcometh shall inherit all things" were the words of his text. His life as a parish minister was closing with the utterance which had been his mother's prayer for him in almost every letter she wrote, as he was beginning his career in the little Church of the Advent in Philadelphia.

He had been speaking to himself all the day long while preaching to others. His words were brave and uplifting, but his heart was heavy. "In giving up Trinity Church, I know what it must be to die," was the language of his despondency. Through this waiting period of months, his life was passing in review before him. He inwardly groaned that he might live it over again, and how different it would be! What would he not make of it, could he have the opportunity! In the light of what it had been, or what it might have been, he condemned his life as a failure. In the searching self-examination things looked differently as one after another they were exposed in the strong searchlight of the reality. All that had been unreal, the conformity in any degree to the passing intellectual fashions of the hour, rose up before him for condemnation. He saw that he had not been wholly in sympathy with the age and the time, with its "burning questions," whose solution contributed nothing to life. In this mood he refused to identify himself with any attitude or purpose not vitally related to Christian living. But we may not intrude into the agony of a great soul. He was not given to speaking of his own religious experience. The mask of impersonality, with which he clothed himself in his youth as a garment and a panoply, he wore to the end. But there is one of his letters where he drops the mask, to tell us only what we know without his telling it. It was during the days of his trial, when his deeds and his words were misrepresented, and his truth turned into a lie; when the Spirit was bearing witness, "He is a chosen vessel unto me, and I will show him what great things he must suffer for my name's sake,"—it was during those days that he received a letter asking him to tell the secret of his life. He was moved by the request, and this was the letter he wrote in reply:

"233 CLARENDON STREET, BOSTON, June 30, 1891.

"MY DEAR ADDISON,—I am sure you will not think that I dream that I have any secret to tell. I have only the testimony to bear which any friend may fully bear to his friend when he is cordially asked for it, as you have asked me.

"Indeed, the more I have thought it over, the less in some sense I have seemed to have to say. And yet the more sure it has seemed to me that these last years have had a peace and fulness which there did not use to be. I say it in deep reverence and humility. I do not think it is the mere quietness of advancing age. I am sure it is not indifference to anything which I used to care for. I am sure that it is a deeper knowledge and truer love of Christ.

"And it seems to me impossible that this should have come in any way except by the experience of life. I find myself pitying the friends of my youth, who died when we were twenty-five years old, because whatever may be the richness of the life to which they have gone, and in which they have been living ever since, they never can know that particular manifestation of Christ which He makes to us here on earth, at each successive period of our human life. All experience comes to be but more and more of pressure of His life on ours. It cannot come by one flash of light, or one great convulsive event. It comes without haste and without rest in this perpetual living of our life with Him. And all the history, of outer or inner life, of the changes of circumstances, or the changes of thought, gets its meaning and value from this constantly growing relation to Christ.

"I cannot tell you how personal this grows to me. He is here. He knows me and I know Him. It is no figure of speech. It is the reallest thing in the world. And every day makes it realler. And one wonders with delight what it will grow to as the years go on.

"The ministry in which these years have been spent seems to me the fulfilment of life. It is man living the best human life with the greatest opportunities of character and service. And therefore on the ministry most closely may come the pressure of Christ. Therefore let us thank God that we are ministers.

"Less and less, I think, grows the consciousness of seeking God. Greater and greater grows the certainty that He is seeking us and giving Himself to us to the complete measure of our present capacity. That is Love, not that we loved Him, but that He loved us. I am sure that we ought to dwell far more upon God's love for us than on our love for Him. There is such a thing as putting ourselves in the way of God's overflowing love and letting it break upon us till the response of love to Him comes, not by struggle, not even by deliberation, but by necessity, as the echo comes when the sound strikes the rock. And this which must have been true wherever the soul of God and the soul of man have lived is perfectly and finally manifest in the Christhood of which it is the heart and soul.

"There is something very rich and true in the Bible talk about 'waiting for the Lord.' The waiting which is meant (and we know in our own lives what that waiting is) is having.

"Nothing but life can reveal Him who is the Life, and so we cannot be impatient but by and by we are satisfied, when everything that happens to us, without or within, comes to seem to us a new token of His presence and sign of His love.

"I have written fully and will not even read over what I have written, lest I should be led to repent that I have written so much about myself. I am not in the habit of doing so. But your letter moves me, and you will understand.

"Some day we will talk of all these things. I hope that you will give me the chance as soon as you can.

"Meanwhile, you know how truly I ask God to bless you, and how sincerely I am

"Your friend,

"PHILLIPS BROOKS."

CHAPTER XXV

1891–1892.

CONSECRATION AS BISHOP.   THE CHURCH CONGRESS AT
WASHINGTON.   ADMINISTRATIVE CAPACITY.   ILL-
NESS.   LENTEN ADDRESSES.   UNION SERVICE ON
GOOD FRIDAY.   CONVENTION ADDRESS.   CORRE-
SPONDENCE.   SUMMER ABROAD.   ENGLISH VOLUME
OF SERMONS.   RETURN TO BOSTON.   ST. ANDREW'S
BROTHERHOOD.   THE GENERAL CONVENTION IN
BALTIMORE.   DEATH OF TENNYSON.   CORRESPOND-
ENCE.

The universal interest in the election of Phillips Brooks to the
episcopate culminated with the consecration service at Trinity
Church.   Those who were present were but the smallest fraction
of the people without who were there in spirit.   It was something
phenomenal; nothing like it had ever been known before in
American religious history.   As an event it rivalled in importance
an exciting political campaign, or foreign news which touched
the problems of peace or war.   The popular feeling tended to go
beyond bounds in its expressions of devotion and gratitude.
The "Universal Church" was represented in the consecration
of Phillips Brooks as bishop.   "All of us might accept the 'historic episcopate' as he will define and embody it.   No denomination can wholly claim such a man.   He is a bishop for us all."
This was the feeling of the hour.

On the morning of Wednesday, October 14, the crowd took
possession of Copley Square long before the service began.   The
day which opened with clouds and threats of inopportune weather,
developed into one of sunlight and beauty.   In the robing-room
were gathered those who were to officiate: Bishop Williams, of
Connecticut, the presiding bishop, who was to act as consecrator;
Bishop Doane, of Albany; Bishop Littlejohn, of Long Island;

Bishop Howe, of Central Pennsylvania; Bishop Niles, of New Hampshire; Bishop Clark, of Rhode Island, and Bishop Whipple, of Minnesota, who had been chosen by the bishop-elect to act as his presenters; Bishop Potter, of New York, who was to preach the sermon; Rev. Arthur Brooks and Rev. John Cotton Brooks, who were to be the attendant presbyters. In the chapel were some four hundred clergy, of whom a third were visitors from other dioceses. Just before the procession started, there was a pause in order to allow the reading of a protest, signed by two bishops, against the consecration of Phillips Brooks. When the protest had been read, at once the signal was given for the organ, and the procession moved to the west entrance of the church, and the hymns sung were "Holy, Holy, Holy, Lord God Almighty" and "The God of Abraham praise." It was a state and civic event as well as an ecclesiastical: the governor of the Commonwealth, the mayor of Boston, and the president of Harvard College had been invited as honored guests, and the city of Boston had sent flowers for the decoration of the church within and around the portals. One incident in the service was noted—a reminder of the fiery trial through which he had passed: when, throwing back his head and expanding his figure to its full proportions, he made the promise of conformity: "I, Phillips Brooks, chosen Bishop of the Protestant Episcopal Church of Massachusetts, do promise conformity and obedience to the Doctrine, Discipline, and Worship of the Protestant Episcopal Church in the United States of America. So help me God, through Jesus Christ."

After the consecration, Bishop Williams took the new bishop by the hand and led him into the chancel. It seemed bewildering that Phillips Brooks should sit in his own church listening to the sermon of another, and then be conducted by another to the spot where for many years he had stood to administer the Lord's Supper. But all found consolation in the enlargement that opened before him. A peculiar effectiveness was given to the ceremonial under the superintendence of Mr. A. J. C. Sowdon, an acknowledged master in such things. The Proprietors of Trinity Church made arrangements by which he should retain the house on Clarendon Street as his Episcopal residence. On October 16, two days after the consecration, the new bishop wrote:

"The thing has drawn itself out so long that it is hard to believe that it is over. But the change of daily occupation reminds me constantly that I am a bishop, and is rapidly making the new name familiar.

"There is no wild exhilaration about it, but a quiet content that it is all right, and an anticipation of the work as full of interest and satisfaction.

In an address which he made to a large representative assembly of laymen on October 27, the bishop was deeply moved:

"I cannot tell you how full my heart is, and how earnestly I wish to do all in my power for the Church in this dear old State of Massachusetts. She gave me birth and education, and all that has gone to make a supremely happy life. I love her rugged landscape, her blue skies, her rich history; and out of her soil came the men who made her what she is. But I am no Massachusetts bigot. I am ready to welcome the new-comers among us. The Episcopal Church in Massachusetts must work in the line of Massachusetts people and the Massachusetts character. It must become a part of the New England life and make that life nobler,—so noble that we shall dare to say that there is nothing nobler in all the world, if only it may be touched with some finer radiance from this dear old Church of ours."

From this time Phillips Brooks plunged into the multiplicity of duties which appertain to a bishop's office. He was advised by a clergyman of large experience, Rev. Edward Everett Hale:

"I am older than you, can advise you. *Begin slowly.* Let things present themselves in order, and do not try to make an order for them. After you have thus accepted, for a little, what is,—you will be able to raise everything and see what may be."

Professor James Bryce, who saw in his growing influence some special significance for the future of American life, writes him how all his "English friends feel greater confidence in the future of the American Episcopal Church now that he will be officially connected with its guides." But he adds a caution:

"I hope the duties of an active kind may not, as happens with bishops here, trench too heavily on the time you have hitherto given to reading and thinking; for even the authority the office gives to guide church deliberations might be ill purchased by the loss of quiet times."

39

But he does not seem to have heeded the advice. From the first there was a tendency to overtax his strength, no longer what it was, or what at his age it should have been. Two weeks after entering upon his new work he wrote to a friend, "Life is so terribly convulsed and changed that it seems incredible that the old friends are there and are caring for me still."

On November 3 he went to the annual matriculation of the Episcopal Theological School, and spoke to the students:

"Here, in the seminary life, Christian truth and faith come into relation. There is no struggle between thought and work. Some abandon work for thought; others abandon thought for work. Never look upon your work as a refuge from thought, but express your thought in your work. Shrink from nothing God shall reveal to you. Trust yourself to Him wherever He shall lead you. He watches over mind and soul. He does not separate them and make them weak concessions of one to the other. Your seminary life is a going aside for three years with Christ, to drink in His spirit and to commune with Him. As you open your New Testament He says to you, 'This is who I am.' When you study church history, He says, 'This is but a history of me.' In psychology He says to you, 'I have saved this humanity by wearing it.'"

One of the first incidents of his new life was the call to preside as bishop at the Church Congress to be held in Washington in November, and to make the Communion Address at its formal opening. It was now suggested to him that he should avail himself of the opportunity to declare, as he might most germanely, his belief in the "miraculous Incarnation and real resurrection of our Lord." It would do much, he was told, to "convince the gainsayers." Scriptural precedent was adduced,—the apostle bids us comfort the feeble-minded. Bishop Clark, who was the go-between of those who wished to approach Phillips Brooks, wrote urging that he should follow this advice, but he firmly and even vehemently refused. It was impossible that he should do otherwise. To take the occasion of a Communion Address in order to speak "to the galleries," and be setting right his own reputation, was abhorrent. To have acquiesced would have neutralized the value of his silence while the question of his election was pending. It would also have been a failure in its object, and have quieted no one. What was really wanted from him was an apology for his association in religious services with Unitarians, and his promise to offend no more. So Bishop Clark found his protégé refractory. Several times had his good offers been declined. He had gently suggested to Phillips Brooks that as a bishop it might be more becoming if he adopted the conventional dress of the clergy. To this appeal Phillips Brooks had replied: "Now, Mr. Clark, you know very well it was Henry Potter who put you up to giving me that advice." The following letter of Bishop Clark shows at least he was not offended by the rejection of his good offices:

PROVIDENCE, November 4, 1891.

"MY DEAR BROTHER BROOKS,—I am a little bit sorry that you found my letter; not that it contains anything that I would revoke, for I still think it would be right and proper for you to say at the Church Congress the words you would be most naturally inclined to say, even if they did tend to allay the anxieties of certain good people, whose minds have been prejudiced by a persistent series of misrepresentations. As I intimated in my last letter, I was afraid that you would reply just as you have done, because I knew that you stand upon a very lofty moral pedestal and have a special aversion to all shams and pretences. As I happen to occupy a lower plane, perhaps I might be willing to do what you would decline doing.

"The *vehemence* of your first letter I admired very much; it was one of the chief attractions of the epistle. The lion always appears at his best when he is in a righteous rage. One lesson, however, I have learned, and that is to abstain from any further interference, and let other people roast their own chestnuts.

"And so, henceforth, beloved Brother, go thine own way. I will disturb thee no more. Prudent or imprudent, silent or outspoken, deliberate or not, thou art likely to come out all right in the end. I assume no longer the post of guide, philosopher, and friend, confining myself entirely to the latter function. But if, in thy comet-like sweep through the heavens, thou shouldest ever find thyself in a tight place among the suns, and the stars, and the planets, and the little ecclesiastical moons, I shall always be at thy service.

"Just as affectionately yours as ever, and a little more so,
"THOMAS M. CLARK."

The address for the Church Congress was prepared without any, the slightest, allusion that could be construed as explanatory or apologetic. He still felt about Church Congresses as in his earlier years. In writing to Rev. Arthur Brooks about the arrangement for trains, he adds:

"But the Congress is the great thing. Let us cast dull care away and go in for enjoyment. For the Church needs us radical old fellows to keep the conservatism of its young men from rotting, and we must take good care of our health."

The city of Washington was moved at his coming. Not even the drizzling rain deterred the people from waiting an hour before the doors of Epiphany Church were opened. The address was beautiful in its simplicity and adaptedness: "Jesus seeing their faith said unto the sick of the palsy, Son, be of good cheer, thy sins be forgiven thee."

Bishop Brooks had taken up his new work in a serene and happy mood. He was determined that all should be his friends among clergy and laity, and to allow no opening for enmities. His happiness showed itself in many ways,—in his note-books, where he begins again, as in his youth, to record his thoughts, as if life were opening anew before him. It was a vast relief, as he alone best appreciated, that he was free from the burden of the parish minister, which had become greater than he could bear. The task of preaching might now be reduced within limits that would no longer exhaust his physical vitality. It seemed at first, despite the multiplicity of engagements, that he had more time at his disposal for reading and quiet thinking. He carried books with him as he went on his episcopal visitations. He loved to travel, to go into new towns, to become acquainted with people, to visit a hundred homes where he had the privilege of being admitted as guest. He could not believe that his work would ever become perfunctory. When he was told that the recitation of the bishop's formula in the confirmation office tended to formality, he would not believe that he could ever be unsympathetic at the sound of those little words, "I do," coming from young hearts at a great moment in their lives.

He now showed that he possessed capacity for the administration of affairs which some had doubted. He soon mastered the details of the office. The affairs of the diocese, numerous and perplexing as they were, did not vex his peace of mind. There came hundreds of appeals from clergymen for admission to the diocese; he was called upon to adjust difficulties in parishes; to offer advice upon every conceivable subject. The church must have looked differently to him in this nearer view from what it had done when he gazed at it from the pulpit and saw only the crowds of eager listeners to his words.

He showed a tendency, says Bishop Lawrence, to be a strict canonist. This disposition was manifested in his dealings with candidates for Orders. He wished it to be understood that they were to go, when ordered deacons, where he should send them. There would be no relaxation of this rule. "I pity them, but they have got to go." He believed in government in church or state, and that government was a divine ordering, not the arrangement of a committee. In an address to the students of the Theological School in Cambridge, he was very practical in his suggestions. The first point he made was in regard to legibility of handwriting. "Small causes lead to great failures." But he soon sailed out on the ocean of principles: "Promptness must come from fulness. Get everything bigger." He talked, said Mr. Robert Treat Paine, "as if he had some large plans in contemplation for the extension of the Church's work and usefulness, and was not going into it vaguely." He sent to the State House for books or documents which would give information as to the population, and the character of the population, in the various towns and cities of the Commonwealth. He was studying the State of Massachusetts in its relation to the Episcopal Church, the causes which had hindered its growth, the motive of its strongest appeal. Of his three immediate predecessors in the episcopal office, not one had been a Massachusetts man by birth or education. He honored and loved Massachusetts, knowing how to read the beatings of its heart. To do what he was wanted to do, and to do it in the way to which people had become accustomed, was his rule. When he visited a town, he went to the Episcopal church, although the townspeople were expecting that the largest edifice would attract him, or some large hall where all might hear him. But he wended his way, as in duty bound, to the small "Gothic cathedrals," tucked away sometimes in a side street.

He was forced to overcome his habit of silence, of talking only when he chose to talk or had something special to say. Now he was expected to entertain the assembled company in rural parsonages. He had one resource, in giving himself up to the children. Beautiful accounts were written of his entrance into a household and establishing at once with the children a familiar footing, so that he and all in the family were completely at home.

"His modesty was conspicuous on his visitations. One day he was met at the station in Fall River by Rev. Mr. S——, who turned to help him with his valise. But he refused, saying he was able to carry it himself. As they came to a carriage Mr. S—— asked him to step in, but he stood back and said, 'Get in yourself first, S——, never mind me.' He had a way of refusing carriages. Once when he had been out to a service in a suburban town, and was leaving the church, Mr. C—— said, 'Bishop, there is a carriage for you at the door.' 'I sent it away,' he answered. 'It would have gratified our people if you had used it,' said Mr. C——. 'I preferred not to do so. I can go into town just as well in the horse cars.'"

In January Bishop Brooks was seriously ill with an attack of the grippe. From the despondency which accompanies the disease he was some time in recovering, nor did he ever recover from the effects of that lamentable illness. To a friend who called upon him, he remarked that there had been one bishop of Massachusetts who never performed an episcopal function, and he was afraid there would be a second of whom the same would be said. In answer to some request he said that the only thing he could not give was cheerfulness.

"233 CLARENDON STREET, BOSTON, January 21, 1892.

"DEAR ARTHUR,—How strange it all is, this being sick! I am not out yet except for necessary duties, when I go in carriages, wrapped up like a mummy and actually afraid of draughts, like an old woman. I hope it is most over, but the weather is beastly, and the doctor is so cautious and the legs so weak that I don't feel *very* sure of anything. Fortunately the doctor smiles on my going to Philadelphia next week, and thinks the change will do me good. . . . On Friday, the 19th of February, I am coming on to the dinner of the New York Harvard Club, and I shall count on you to take me in over night. I never saw a big New York dinner, and I expect to be delighted and dazzled in my provincial eyes.

"And you must send me the [episcopal] seal as soon as it is done. I am impatient for it,—not that I have suffered at all by the delay, but I want to get possession of the gem of the episcopate, and to show —— and —— that I have the finest seal of the lot."

On February 11 a meeting was held in Boston, where the laity, who had been invited to meet the city clergy, were present. The object of the meeting as stated in the bishop's circular letter, and more fully in his address, was to rouse the laity to individual and also concerted effort in order to meet people in sections of the city devoid of religious or moral influence who could not be reached by organized parochial work. This was the first step taken on a large scale by the bishop to carry out some more comprehensive plan for increasing the efficiency of the Episcopal Church.

Ash Wednesday fell on March 2, and, as Trinity Church was without a rector, Bishop Brooks consented to take the Friday evening lectures. He also gave during Lent the Monday noon addresses at St. Paul's. It need only be said of these latter addresses that they were a repetition of the scene in New York, or the previous year in Boston. The addresses were intended for business men, and they were there; but the clergy were there in large numbers and of every denomination, as though the addresses were *conciones ad clerum*.

The Friday evening lectures at Trinity were of another kind, full of the overflowing tenderness and love of a pastor still in relation to his people, unable to sever the tie which bound them together. The report of these talks is by an interested listener. At the Communion Service on the evening of Holy Thursday, April 14,

"He began by speaking of the Lord's Supper as an anniversary, not only of the Last Supper, but of the many times we have come together to celebrate it through all these years. The one thing we felt in reading about it was the love of Jesus for His disciples: 'with desire have I desired.' He named one disciple after another, and characterized each by a most masterly touch, so that each stood out a figure full of interest whom you felt you knew and loved. They were all, with their interesting varied personalities and experiences, gathered in that room and Jesus knew them all, every one, and loved each one of them. And as He looked into face after face, and moved about among them, His love filled all the place. He made it all most sacred, personal, the fire of His love transforming all their souls into perfect one-ness with Him. Then, while it was all so near and present, He looks forward and says, 'I will not drink of this again till I drink it new *with you* in the Kingdom.' The perfect assurance that their love reached forward, beyond, that they could never be separated, that their lives were all one, in Jerusalem then and afterwards in the heavenly city."

On Good Friday, he took for his text "It is finished," and be-gan by saying:

"Good Friday was the most important day in the whole year; it stood as the greatest of all days in its influence, in the event it commemorated. It was characteristic of human life that its greatest day should be its saddest, full of suffering and sorrow. It showed how life in its essential nature was sad, but it was a day of hope, its sorrow full of promise, and this too was characteristic of human life. He spoke about last words, how interesting even when they are a stranger's, how dear when they are a friend's. These last words of Jesus were sad. The end of any-thing is sad. No man leaves any experience without sadness, and the end of life is sad, even if it is the beginning of a richer existence.

> "For who, to dumb Forgetfulness a prey,
> This pleasing anxious being e'er resigned,
> Left the warm precincts of the cheerful day,
> Nor cast one longing, ling'ring look behind."

When the end of an experience comes, one gains a comprehen-sion of all that has gone to make up the experience. Details and complexity are untangled, and the real meaning is seen. So it was with Jesus. Galilee and the lake and the temple all came back to Him and stood out clear in those last moments. All these thoughts were in Jesus' mind because He was human. His life on earth had been an experience in His eternal life, one which was new and would never be repeated; it was as a man that He ended it now and passed from it into His unending, divine ex-istence; but the experience would be with Him always, making more perfect His perfect nature.

"Now what did these words 'It is finished' mean? What was finished? The answer, the rescue of humanity. Just as a father seeks for his child who has gone astray, and goes unresting day and night through vile haunts of sin and misery, and then finds her and places her again in the pure light of the old home life, and it is finished. As a diver plunges into the strange dark waters and wrestles with the hideous forms that grovel at the bottom, and finds the pearl and brings it to the land in triumph. Anything more? Yes, it was more than an act of redemption that was finished; it was a creative act. There are two creations, as we read in the Bible. The Spirit of God brooding over Chaos brings light and life and order and music out of it. That was the first creation. Then the Spirit of God brooded over human life so close and near and deep that it entered into human life and was incarnate, and wrought the mysterious change in the soul of man, —the change that brings order and beauty out of chaos and sin. And the power of the incarnation was sacrifice, and the power of the new creation is sacrifice. When once the spirit of sacrifice enters, sin is cast out, by the very entrance of this spirit, and old puzzles and doubts and evil thoughts flit away like hateful birds of night.

"One other point—the creative power is also the ministering power. In the natural creation more and more it is discovered that creation is not one act but a continuous process; so in the spiritual creation, Jesus creates and then abides in the soul and ministers to it until it is perfect even as the Father is perfect."

In the afternoon of Good Friday he commented on the words of St. Paul, "Always bearing about in the body the dying of the Lord Jesus, that the life also of Jesus may be made manifest in our body."

"St. Paul did not see Jesus die; perhaps his knowledge of that death, being removed from the actual sight of that anguish which for the time swallowed up the deeper meaning of a death, was in some ways more true and intelligent. When we see some one die we do not at the time catch the full significance of the event. Afterwards we remember and recognize the heroism, the patience, the triumph, that were in it. St. Paul says he bears this knowledge, the dying of Jesus, about in his body. It is interesting to notice how he speaks of his body. Poor, weak, small as it was, if tradition tells the truth, it was the scene, the theatre of all the great acts and experiences of his soul. He honors it, recognizes its mystery, its relation to his spirit, and so when he thinks of Jesus' death he says that it is in his body that he bears that knowledge. There are wonderful pictures in the Old World, everywhere, representing the descent from the cross, where the disciples touch the cold stiff limbs, though they know that the spirit of Jesus is no longer in them; tenderly and lovingly bearing in their arms the lifeless body. The pictures of the Virgin Mary, many of the girl-mother with her baby,—these have the unquenchable joy of youth and young motherhood,—but there are some of the Mother of our Lord in the fullness of mature life, splendid and august in the maturity of her beauty and her sorsow. She holds her Son dead across her knees, and as she looks down upon the cold, rigid limbs, there is in her face sorrow too deep for tears. You can see there the destruction of all her hopes; all the sacrifices she has made, the disappointments, the loneliness of His life. She has felt them all as mothers do the experiences of their children, and now He is dead, and she is dying too.

"He talked, in closing, about how people die,—living people. They die when those they love die. You die, something comes to an end. It is all over. Death was all about you and in you, death and sin, disappointment, failure, misery, injustice. All crowded around that cross, and the victim of it suffering there, and those who loved him dying too. That was what made the awful solemnity of life as we go on in it,—the bearing about in our body the dying of the Lord Jesus. We were left in the dark watching that figure, as it has been through the ages, suffering for all the sin ever since, and for all the sorrow and ignorance, and making us bear it about in our own bodies and never rest or cease to remember till we have done our part, have somehow carried this sacrifice to heal and bless some part of this weary world."

On the evening of Good Friday Bishop Brooks was present and took part at a union service in the Old South Church (Congregational), when a Unitarian minister was also present, Dr. A. P. Peabody, of Harvard College, for whom Phillips Brooks felt a filial reverence and affection. The event called forth the familiar protest within the diocese and woke up again the opposition without, which had been silent since his consecration.

On Wednesday, May 18, the diocesan convention met, when Bishop Brooks made his first convention address. So great was the desire to hear him that the occasion resembled a religious service with its throng of listeners. Like his other work, it had a literary quality, and reads like an interesting essay with artistic form. It contains his wisdom and experience brought to bear upon ecclesiastical matters, and placed at the disposal of his brethren. It more than fulfilled the expectations of the episcopal possibilities that were in him. It was comprehensive and statesmanlike, with suggestions of practical and immediate, but also of far-reaching importance. It breathed a spirit of universal charity, kindly and genial, and yet incisive to the last

degree. Its recommendations to clergy and laity are still remembered, still acted upon, as the legacy of a great bishop who
filled out the office in its highest ideal.

There was the usual reticence about making statements of
his work, and there was no comparative estimate. In the seven
months since his consecration the number of persons confirmed
by him was 2127. When to these was added the number confirmed by other bishops during the vacancy of the diocese, the
total was 2395. In 1890 the number of confirmations was 1743,
and in 1891, 1535,—figures which make apparent the modesty
of his remark, "The number of confirmations is a little larger
than ever before in the history of the diocese." There were
other signs of vigorous growth: the number of candidates for
orders had increased from 25 to 36, the number of clergy from
192 to 205, the number of lay readers from 16 to 70. There had
been a large increase in the Episcopal Fund, and the new Diocesan House had been purchased at No. 1 Joy Street, in Boston,
which offered ample accommodation compared with the "dreary
hospitality" of the Church Rooms in Hamilton Place.

But these items of growth showing the effect of the new
enthusiasm are not so interesting as the suggestions for the
future. The bishop and the man spoke out when outlining
the policy to be followed.

"Is it then true that our Church has worthily conceived her
whole relation to the whole people of this Commonwealth? Our
local history accounts for much of the defect of such conception.
We have been for two centuries counted an exception, almost an
exotic, in New England. It has seemed to those around us as if
we existed for the sake of a certain class of people of peculiar
character and antecedents. To others it has seemed as if we
were of value because we bore witness to certain elements of
Christian life which were in danger of being forgotten or neglected. Probably it was inevitable that we should come to take
somewhat the same view of ourselves which others have taken of
us. Certainly we have done so in some degree. With all our
self-appreciation we have lived in a limited notion of what it is
possible for us to do. We have been at once bold and timid.
We have been burdened with self-consciousness. We have dwelt
on what we have called the 'mission of our Church.' The real
mission of our Church is nothing less than the eternal, universal
mission of the Church of Christ, which is the preaching of right-

eousness, the saving of souls, the building of the Kingdom of God. All mere special commissions and endowments are matters of method, and ought to be much less kept before our consciousness and much less set before the world.

"And we are too much in the habit of asking, when a new town or city is offered as a possible field for an Episcopal church, whether there are any 'Church people' there, as if that name described a special kind or order of humanity to whom alone we were to consider ourselves as sent. The real question ought to be whether there are human creatures in that town. We are sent to the human race. That larger idea of our mission must enlarge our spirit and our ways, and make us fit to bear our part in the broad salvation of the world.

"Everything which I have to say tends to the strong assertion of the truth that the Church is bound to seek men; not merely to stand where men can find her if they wish, but to go after them and claim them. One application of this truth has forced itself upon my notice, with reference to the situation of our churches in some of the towns and villages of our diocese. The question of location is altogether the most important outward question which arises in connection with the establishment of a new parish. It is far more important than the question of architecture, important as that is. Better an ugly church in the right place than a gem of beauty where men have to search to find it. But, once more, we are driven to no such alternative. Rather, our alternative is apt to be this: Whether it is not best to wait and struggle a little longer and a little harder to set our church at last full in the centre of the town's life, on the town square, where men cannot help seeing it every day, where it shall perpetually claim its right to be recognized and heard,—than to take the pretty and retired lot down some side street, which we can have at once, which can be bought cheaply, or which some kind friend gives us for nothing, where the church we build will always seem to declare itself not a messenger to the whole people, but the confidant and friend of a few specially initiated people who know and love her ways, and who will find her, however she may hide herself. Here certainly we need more and not less boldness and assurance of what we are and what we have to do."

To a Candidate for Orders then in Germany, who had asked regarding the interpretation of the Creed:

"233 CLARENDON STREET, BOSTON, April 13, 1892.

"As to the question of your letter, I wish very much that I could have the privilege of talking with you, for writing is a most imperfect method of communication. But what I think is this:

"The Creed is drawn from the New Testament, and the New Testament declares and emphasizes the peculiar and supreme nature of Christ as outgoing while it fulfils the nature of humanity. It asserts that this, His higher nature, involved relations with the outer world more perfect and complete than those which belong to ordinary human lives. This assertion makes the story of what we call the supernatural. And both the entrance on and the departure from our human life are declared to have been in some way marked by circumstances which indicated his superior nature.

"In neither case is the exact character of the circumstances made clear, but in both there is the indication of something exceptional, and therefore wonderful, or, as we say, miraculous.

"Now this is what our Creed expresses, and the ability to repeat the Creed implies, therefore, the belief in the higher life of Jesus. That higher life is closely associated with the higher life of man. The divinity of Christ is not separate from His humanity. It is His total nature, which the Church tries to express in the large statements of His birth and death, which it takes from the New Testament.

"There is nothing in the results of modern scholarship which conflicts with the statements in the Apostles' and Nicene Creeds concerning the birth of Jesus. Those statements are variously understood by various believers, but they have this meaning always in them, that Christ bore a higher life than ours, and that that higher life manifested itself in the circumstances of His experience."

It was a new thing in the ecclesiastical world for a Congregational minister to request a bishop of the Episcopal Church to officiate at the consecration of his church. Such a request came from the Rev. Reuen Thomas of Brookline, where the enlarged and beautiful church was to be reopened, in which Phillips Brooks had often preached. He was obliged to decline the request on account of his appointments, but wrote that he would gladly have gone if he could, adding, "For Christian unity, such messages as yours prove not merely that it is to be but that it is."

To Mr. Cooper, who had promised a clergyman that he would write to the bishop of Massachusetts with reference to any vacancy in the diocese, Bishop Brooks replied:

"233 CLARENDON STREET, BOSTON, May 31, 1892.

"DEAR COOPER,—It is good to see your blessed handwriting.

"There is nothing here for Mr. —— now. The only vacancies are a few little country missions, generally without church buildings, where the salaries are very small and the prospects of growth are of the slightest, places like ——, and that sort of thing. Trinity Church, Boston, indeed, is vacant, but I do not believe he would like that. I was there myself for a while, and know what a queer sort of place it is. He would not like it.

"So all I can do is to keep my eye open for a place for Mr. ——. Our ministers here never die, and seldom resign, so that no man can tell what chances will occur.

"If he would like a place in London or the Tyrol, perhaps I could serve him better, for I am going there this summer."

The tone of his letters is genial and cheerful as ever, but there were moments when he was weary to exhaustion, and hardly seemed like himself. He suffered from the effects of the grippe. He had overtaxed his strength in fulfilling episcopal duties, but made no effort to reduce them, going everywhere at the beck and call of all who wanted him. That he was worried about his health might be inferred from the circumstance that before leaving home he caused a thorough examination of his house to be made. Unfortunately the examination failed to discover the actual situation. The report sent to him was to the effect that everything was in proper order. He sailed in the steamer *Majestic*, and Captain Purcell gave him the use of his deck-room during the day. On board the steamer he writes:

"The *Majestic* is a magnificent great thing, and could put our dear little *Cephalonia* into her waistcoat pocket. Her equipment is sumptuous and her speed something tremendous. . . . Yesterday [June 26] we had service, and I preached in the great saloon in the morning, and in the evening I held a service for the second-class passengers, of whom there is a multitude. . . . I should not have been disappointed if the *Majestic* could not have taken me, and if I had been left in North Andover, as I expected when I saw you last.

"Yours affectionately, and Majestically,
"P."

The month of July was spent in London. He was welcomed on his arrival by a telegram from Lord Aberdeen, asking for a visit at Haddo House in Scotland. He preached in the Abbey as usual, and at St. Margaret's; "there were a good many people in both churches." He preached also for Mr. Haweis, in his church at Marylebone, in return, as he said, for a fine sermon given by Mr. Haweis at Trinity years before. Other invitations, and they were many, he felt obliged to decline, with the exception of St. Peter's, Eaton Square.

The welcome from the English clergy was most cordial: "You do us much good by coming and preaching in England," writes Rev. J. Llewelyn Davies. A friend writes to him, speaking of his sermon in the Abbey on July 3: "It was such a blessing to hear your voice once more in that glorious place, and every heart was *very* full when you once more touched on the high thoughts and aspirations in which all can unite when recalling the birthday of your national life. Your visits to England are among the brightest gifts that come to cheer and encourage us." Invitations ecclesiastical and social were numerous and attractive; dinners and lunches filled up his days. He went to Brighton to review under the best guidance the scene of Robertson's ministry; to Winchester, in order that he might get the best impression of the Saxon metropolis. A few days were given to the Bishop of Winchester at Farnham Castle. In company with Archdeacon Farrar he made a visit to Lord Tennyson, whom he found "gentle, gracious, and talkative." That he greatly enjoyed his stay in London is evident, but he was not as well as he should have been. Archdeacon Farrar perceived some change:

"Every one noticed, during his last visit to England, that he looked much thinner than he had done two years before, but he always spoke of himself as perfectly well, and his great boyish heart seemed as full as ever of love and hope and joy. I noticed in him a just perceptible deepening of gravity in tone, but no diminution of his usually bright spirits. . . . I attributed the slightly less buoyant temperament of last summer—the sort of half-sadness which sometimes seemed to flit over his mind like the shadow of a summer cloud—to the exigencies and responsibilities of his recent dignity."

Phillips Brooks sat for his photograph while in London. In none of his portraits does the majesty of his personal appearance stand forth more distinctly; the effect of illness also; there is now sternness in the countenance, the inherited Puritan sadness.

A volume of his sermons had been published in England with

the title *The Spiritual Man and Other Sermons*. As it had been published without his knowledge or consent, he sent to the publishers this note to be inserted in all the remaining copies: "Bishop Phillips Brooks requests the publishers to state that the contents of this volume are printed from stenographic reports, gathered from various sources, and issued without his knowledge." The book has a singular charm. It contains sermons not to be found elsewhere, those which had most strongly touched the popular mind. And a certain pathos unites them in homogeneousness and unity,—the pathos, as it were, of a last will and testament.

To his friend the bishop of Rhode Island, keeping his eightieth birthday, he wrote:

"St. Moritz, Switzerland, August 10, 1892.

"Dear Bishop Clark,—When a man can write a letter such as this of yours, to tell the story of his eightieth birthday past and over, he is indeed snapping his venerable fingers in the face of Time. I am afraid it is not wholly right, and that you will have to be punished for it. There is a mossy quietude which people associate with your time of life, and whose absence they resent if it does not appear. If, indeed, you are eighty after all, and it is not a mistake, or a fraud. Are you quite sure?

"As to your legs, you must not worry yourself about them; they are not what interests your friends. It is not your walk, but your conversation, that we value. We will carry you in our arms so that your feet shall not touch the rough, coarse earth, if you will only stay with us, and brighten, and enlighten, and console, and strengthen, and amuse us. You will, won't you? I wish that you were here this morning. It is more bright and splendid than I know how to describe. I will not try, but your ever young imagination will tell you all about it, and I will tell you by and by.

"Need I say that I shall rejoice to be presented in the queer old House by you? It will crown your deeds and kindnesses in all this business.

"Good by. God bless you. Keep well. Be good.

"Your grateful friend,

"P. B."

From Chamouni he wrote to Rev. W. N. McVickar:

Chamouni, August 27, 1892.

"It is a superb day here. The great mountain was never

clearer nor more beautiful. The sky is cloudless, and the snow reaches up to heaven, and they are bringing down over the tremendous white slope the dead body of a poor fellow who died up there in the storm day before yesterday. You can see them through the telescope in the hotel yard. It is a wonderful funeral procession. It is as if he had gone up there to despatch his soul to heaven, and they were bringing the poor, done-with body down. He is an Oxford man, they say, named Nettleship."

On Thursday, September 8, Phillips Brooks sailed for America. His brother John Brooks recalls him, on that day in the Adelphi Hotel at Liverpool, where all was confusion and excitement around him, sitting on the lower steps of the stairway, with his arms resting on his walking stick and his head bowed low, remaining in that position for an hour or more, paying no attention to the scene before him. He seemed to be taking his leave of the Old World, as if he knew that he should come again no more. Among the letters which he wrote on board ship is one to Mr. Robert Maconachie in India:

"S. S. PAVONIA, September 10, 1892.

"MY DEAR FRIEND,—It must seem to you as if I never had received your letter, or as if I did not care about it. The truth is that I did receive it, and that I did care about it a great deal. I have read it often, and it lies before me now as, after all these months, I sit down on the steamship which is carrying me home, to send you a word of greeting and most grateful acknowledgment of your remembrance.

"I never forget the days we spent together. How can I? When one meets a fellow man and finds him simply and devoutly interested in the dear Master whom one loves and in the human creatures for whom the Master lived and died, there is no possibility of forgetting.

"All that you tell me of yourself and of the work which has been put into your hands is of the deepest interest to me. I know almost nothing of what the details of your daily life must be. It is enough that you are where your duty brings you into continual and intimate association with men and all their mysterious capacity. That cannot be without the Word of God finding expression, and the power of God coming into influence through you on them.

"It is all one constant Incarnation. All the spiritual meanings of the Gospel and the Church are renewed with every such active love and power of a Christian soul. The accident of for-

40

mal ordination is a trifle. 'As my Father hath sent me, so send I you,' is the unmistakable commission.

"I have been spending a summer abroad, much of it in your beautiful, delightful England. Would that I might have seen you there! I should not again have driven you to camp out in the yard while I took possession of your quarters, as I did in Delhi. But I have a strong feeling that, while we should have begun where we left off in sympathy and friendship, all these years which have come since would have opened a multitude of new subjects of thought and talk which would not easily have been exhausted.

"The new work which has fallen to me as Bishop of Massachusetts is all in the old lines and makes me more, I hope, but still the same. Certainly it makes me rejoice more than ever in such words as yours. May the time come when I shall hear them from your own mouth! I hope you can give my love to the dear Delhi men, Lefroy and Allnut and Carlyon. You will remember me most kindly to your wife, and you will be sure that I always delight to hear from you.

"God bless you bountifully.

"Your friend,
"PHILLIPS BROOKS."

THE HOUSE IN BOSTON

A pleasant house stands in a Boston street,
　　With wide-arched entrance opening to the west;
　　Of all earth's houses that to me is best.
There come and go my thoughts with restless feet;
There the quick years like hovering clouds have passed,
　　Catching the sunlight on their calm white breasts;
　　There Duty entered with her grave behests,
And there the shadow of my sin was cast.
Through this broad door my friends have brought their love,
　　Here need has sought what help I could bestow,
　　Here happy study finds its place below,
And peaceful slumber fills the room above.
Down these wide steps, all still from feet to head,
I shall be carried after I am dead.

S. S. PAVONIA, September, 1872.

Bishop Brooks reached Boston on September 19. A cholera scare during the summer led to precautions before landing. When the tug came up to take the cabin passengers, Phillips Brooks raised his hat to the steerage gathered on deck to watch the departure, and bade them good-bye. "He looked," said one who observed him, "the picture of perfect health," and in answer to an inquiry replied that he was well. That undoubtedly was the feeling of the moment, but a few weeks later he said that he was no better than when he went away.

After his return he resumed his work with great vigor. His time was filled with engagements. Sunday, October 2, was hardly an exceptional day, when four times he spoke from the pulpit of Trinity Church. At nine o'clock he gave the anniversary sermon before the St. Andrew's Brotherhood. He preached at the usual morning service at ten o'clock, and again in the afternoon before the congregation of Trinity Church. Then at nine o'clock in the evening he spoke at the farewell meeting of the Brotherhood. The church was filled with young men eager to hear the great preacher at both the services when he addressed them.

"He spoke with all the old-time brilliancy and power, and never was more impressive than in his parting exhortation in the evening. . . . In the early morning sermon, as he drew near the close of his sermon, he spoke more slowly than was his wont, and his voice trembled a little in places as he finished his glowing and earnest exhortation. As his voice sank, deathly stillness fell on the church, and the congregation hung on the last words as if listening to a celestial messenger."

At the evening service, when he said farewell to the young men before him, these were some of his words:

"It does not take great men to do great things, it only takes consecrated men. The earnest, resolute man, whom God works through, is the medium by which His greatest work is often done.

"Go, then, my brethren, to your blessed work. Be absolutely simple. Be absolutely genuine. Never say to any one what you do not feel and believe with your whole heart. Be simple, be consecrated, and above all things, be pure. No man who is not himself pure can carry the message of God.

"And never dare to hurt any soul. The most awful consciousness a man can have is that he has hurt a human soul years ago, and now has no power to repair the damage. He may have recovered from the injury to his own being, but the knowledge that he has ever injured the soul of another man or woman, who has gone out of his sight now, so that he cannot know how serious the injury may have been, is a terrible thing for any one to know."

From the anniversary of the St. Andrew's Brotherhood Bishop

Brooks went to Baltimore to remain for the greater part of the month in attendance on the sessions of the General Convention, also to take his seat for the first time in the House of Bishops. While there he learned that Rev. E. W. Donald of New York had accepted a call to the rectorship of Trinity Church. He was greatly pleased, for Dr. Donald had been his choice from the first, and he had done all in his power to bring about his election. Writing from the House of Bishops, he speaks of Tennyson's death:

"And so dear old Tennyson is gone! Nobody who has been writing for the last fifty years has won such deep affection of the best men and influenced so many lives. What days they were when we used to go spouting 'Locksley Hall' and 'The Two Voices' to the winds! And what has not 'In Memoriam' been to all of us! If I had never seen him, it would make me sad to know that he was no longer living on the earth. And to have seen him under his own roof, and to have had his personal kindness, will always seem to me to have been a great and precious privilege.

"Nothing is yet done here. I am quietly settled among the bishops, and no one has yet slapped my face."

Bishop Brooks spent Sunday, October 9, in Philadelphia, preaching in the morning at the Church of the Holy Trinity from the text, "Before Abraham was I am." There were some few of his sermons at this time in which he concentrated the essence of his thought and experience, and this was one of them,—the eternal consciousness of humanity as embodied in Christ. He took the occasion, also, to speak of the death of Tennyson, quoting the lines "Crossing the Bar." In the evening of the same day he preached for Mr. Cooper at the Church of the Holy Apostles, and then he took the same text on which he had written his first sermon while in the seminary at Alexandria, "The Simplicity that is in Jesus." Unwonted impressiveness hung about both these services. "But he looked tired" was the comment on his appearance.

"Philadelphia, October 9, 1892.

"Dear Arthur,—. . . This morning I go back to the House of Bishops. It is a queer place. There is an air about it which comes distinctly from their seclusion. They ought to open their

doors. They have a lot of good men among them, and there is a
great deal of good work done, but there is every now and then a
silliness which would not be possible if the world were listening.

"Ever affectionately,

"P."

"House of Bishops, Baltimore, October 8, 1892.

"Baltimore is a very pretty city, with a distinctly Southern
character, and no end of colored boys and girls about the street.
Everybody has been very hospitable; plenty of terrapin and
crabs, and all the lower luxuries of life. We meet every morning
at ten o'clock and sit till one. (It wants twenty minutes of one
now.) Then we go down into the basement and have a luncheon;
and then we go out into a tent in the yard and have a smoke.
At half past two we meet again and sit till five. At six we are
apt to have an invitation to dine with somebody. If nobody has
asked us, we dine at the Albion, and then have two hours of
evening sitting, and then go home and have a smoke and go to
bed. And then we do the same thing over again the next day.
The bishops are not very wise, but they think they are, and they
very much enjoy being bishops."

In the discussions in the House of Bishops he took but little
part, yet that little was significant. He opposed a proposition
to make the Sixty-ninth Psalm a part of the Evening Prayer on
Good Friday. The words of Christ upon the cross, "Father,
forgive them, for they know not what they do," were incompatible
with the imprecation of the psalm, "Pour out thine indignation
upon them; and let thy wrathful displeasure take hold of them."

The one event during Bishop Brooks's sojourn in Baltimore
was an address to the students of Johns Hopkins University.
Many invitations he had received to address its students, but
for some good reason had hitherto been prevented from accepting
them. When he was now invited, he wrote, "I find it very difficult to say Yes, but I find it quite impossible to say No." He
wished to know in advance what kind of a meeting it would be
proposed to hold. So many persons had expressed a desire to
hear him that a neighboring church had been suggested as a
suitable place. But his preference was "to speak to the students
by themselves, in one of their own halls, at an hour when they
are wonted to come together." His wishes were respected, and
but few were present except members of the University. The

time was Thursday, the 13th of October, at five o'clock in the afternoon. From the account written at the time these other particulars are taken:

"Many who were present found the scene unusually impressive. The eager attention of the crowded audience of students and professors; the intense earnestness of the speaker, expressing itself in an utterance even more rapid and impetuous that was his wont; the peculiar sympathy with students which was so characteristic of Bishop Brooks (and of which one was conscious from his first word to his last); his attitude and movements, walking back and forth behind the lecture desk, leaning forward over it as though to come into closer relation with his audience; the gathering darkness of the autumn afternoon,—all was singularly inspiring and affecting. Three gentlemen among the older persons in the audience, who happened to leave the room in company, agreed in remarking upon a certain unearthliness in the address, such as might be expected in the case of a man who had not long to live."

No report of the address was taken at the time, but the students jotted down sentences which struck them, and when these were put together, some idea was given of what seemed like farewell words. He quoted from "The Two Voices."

"'Tis life, whereof our nerves are scant,
O life, not death, for which we pant;
More life, and fuller, that I want.

"The great question underlying all the controversies between science and religion is whether Christianity proposes to restrain, prohibit, destroy, and then build up something new upon the old foundation; or whether it proposes to take humanity as it is, and, by opening up to it new and unthought-of possibilities, develop it into the measure of the fulness of Christ. What, then, is Christianity? It is not something added to us from without; it is not a foreign element in our souls; the Christian is not some strange creature, but a man developed to his normal condition. "Christianity is not the intruder, but sin. Christianity seeks not to cramp man's nature, saying to him constantly, Thou shalt not; but it leads on, up to freer air and wider space, wherein the soul may disport itself. It is God we follow. Obeying God is freedom. Our souls are like closed rooms, and God is the sunlight. Every new way we find in which to obey Him we throw open a shutter. Our souls are as enclosed bays, and God is the ocean. The only barrier that can hinder free communication is disobedience. Remember that each duty performed is the breaking down of a reef of hindrance between our souls and God, permitting the fulness of His being to flow in upon our souls. And so we, who in a peculiar sense are consecrated to Truth, are better students because we are Christians, and better Christians because we are students. It is when we remember the greatness of the nature which God has given us that we come into a full understanding of our relations to God. At some time every man comes to realize the meaning of the life he is living; the secret sins hidden in his heart rise against him. Then we would hide ourselves from God if we could. But the only way to run from God is to run to Him. The Infinite Knowledge is also the Infinite Pity. God is not an enemy seeking to catch us with cunningly devised schemes, but our sympathizer and friend. God wants to save us if we will let Him. 'I came not to judge the world, but to save the world.' And how shall we gain nearness to God, and power? We never become truly spiritual by sitting down and wishing to become so. You must undertake something so great that you cannot accomplish it unaided. Begin doing something for your fellow-men, and if you do it with all your power, it will almost immediately bring you face to face with problems you cannot solve; you need God, and you go to God. You may meet difficulties and trials; they call for no less devotion, but more. Hindrances are like the obstructions in a river's bed. Do not dam up the flow, but turn on a fuller flood till the current sweeps away the rubbish and runs under and around and over the stones, and flows smooth above them. Think of the fulness. 'I am come that men might have life, and that they might have it more abundantly.' So, in trying to win a man to a better life, show him, not the evil, but the nobleness of his nature. Lead him to enthusiastic contemplations of humanity in its perfection, and when he asks, 'Why, if this is so, do not I have this life?' Then project on the background of his enthusiasm his own life. Say to him, 'Because you are a liar, because you blind your soul with licentiousness.' Shame is born, but not a shame of despair. It is soon changed to joy. Christianity becomes an opportunity, a high privilege, the means of attaining to the most exalted ideal, —and the only means. Herein must lie all real power; herein, lay Christ's power, that He appreciated the beauty and richness of humanity, that it is very near the Infinite, very near to God. These two facts—we are the children of God, and God is our Father—make us look very differently at ourselves, very differently at our neighbors, very differently at God. We should be surprised, not at our good deeds, but at our bad ones. We should expect good as more likely to occur than evil; we should believe that our best moments are our truest.

"There are three conditions of human nature: first, the satisfaction of utter ignorance; second, the conflict, even misery, of the first stages of intelligence; third, the full fruition of a complete knowledge. To these conditions Christian experience is parallel. Therefore, when you encounter doubt, difficulties, push on; they will soon issue in the higher and more perfect understanding. Whatever happens, always remember the mysterious richness of human nature, and the nearness of God to each one of us."

At a meeting of the Episcopalian Club in Boston, October 31, to welcome the delegates to the General Convention, Bishop Brooks was present and spoke. Referring to the practice of the bishops sitting with closed doors, he said it was un-American, and sure to be amended some day or other. He reviewed the work of the convention,—the completion of the revision of the Prayer Book, the new Hymnal, the increase in the number of the missionary bishops. "One thing which we in Massachusetts," he humorously remarked, "are especially to be congratulated on, is that every proposition offered by the Massachusetts delegates was negatived almost without a division." November opened with an interesting event, the formal dedication of the Diocesan House on Joy Street. He had selected the building, given cheerfully to it, and had offered to give more if it were needed. He wanted it made attractive, and had sent many engravings for its walls. In his speech at the dedication, he expressed the hope that it would be "a place of friendly meetings, the cultivation of brotherly friendship and good will." He referred to its having formerly been a private residence and as possessing "a homelike atmosphere, sanctified by all the sweet and tender relations of family life."

And now the work of the diocese claimed the services of the bishop; the visitation of the parishes began; every day, every hour almost, had its fixed appointment. Henceforth there was hardly an opportunity for rest. It had been hoped that the change to a bishop's life would call for physical activity which would be beneficial. It might have been, but the pace which Bishop Brooks had set, or was set for him, was too rapid for any man to assume with impunity. He not only made the regular visitation of the parishes, but he was asked to grace with his presence and his words occasions of parochial interest of various kinds. He made no effort to spare himself, and indeed had he done so escape would now have been impossible.

"We all know [said Bishop Lawrence] the joy with which he undertook the work, and the undertone of joy that there was in it to the end. With all this, the physique was giving way. I am confident that, if he had had full strength and had lived a few years longer, it would have been impossible for him to keep up the pace. When a man is doing his work well, responsibilities always increase, and there would not have been hours enough in the day for him to get through what he had to do. I have said, and I believe, that it would have been almost impossible for him radically to change his methods and system. It was part of his nature to see everybody who wanted to see him and to help everybody who wanted help. Without that radical change, he must have gone under in a few years, as he did at the end of fifteen months."

Not until it was too late was it known that he carried a burden of his own creating too heavy for him, or any man, to bear.

"The very lavishness of his giving stimulated unconscious extravagance in demanding, so that all this community and all this people laid their claims upon him, and he honored them till the tension grew so strong that at last the strong man broke and he was laid low, a sacrifice to service, his life as truly given for his fellow-men as any life that was ever laid on the altar of sacrifice, from the day of Calvary to now."

There was one sermon often repeated in these last months, on the words, "I follow after if that I may apprehend that for which also I am apprehended of Christ Jesus." Whatever he now did seemed to be great and solemn beyond expression. The indefinable something in the man was apparent when he was administering the rite of confirmation, even in some small and obscure mission.

"I have seen the ceremony of confirmation hundreds of times, but never in its completeness before. . . . It was a never-to-be-forgotten sight. I have seen great sights in my life. I have seen all England welcoming the young Danish princess to her English home; the return of the guards from the Crimea. The great heart of the people throbbed on these occasions as I have never seen it since. I saw Napoleon and Paris welcome the African troops on their return from the desert fields of battle;

I have seen Grant and Sherman welcomed; I have witnessed the thrilling effect of war standards, with strips of the national colors still clinging to them, carried in the streets crowded with people. But what are these in memory compared to the touch of the divine I witnessed in the little church that Sunday evening, . . . which made this man seem something more than human in the eyes of many!"

He was lonely in these days and hungered for human companionship. People who would gladly have gone to him kept away for fear they would intrude on his time or interfere with important work. To a friend who was often with him after the day's work was over, he said, when entreating him to stay longer, "I need you more than any one else can need you." In conversation he talked more freely. He spoke of his mother, what she was and what she had been to him. He wished that he might hear again the sound of her voice speaking to him.

To Lady Frances Baillie he wrote:

"233 CLARENDON STREET, BOSTON, November 8, 1892.

"DEAR FRIEND,—When I came home last night from a week's wandering about my diocese, I found a letter from your son Albert on my table, for which I was very grateful. It told me about you, and almost seemed for the moment to set me in your room again and let me take your hand.

"At least it made me want to say, even across the stormy ocean, how much I am thinking about you, and how sorry I am that you are weak and ill, and how glad I am that you are yourself, full of the faith and strength of God, which no feebleness of body can subdue.

"People talk about how sadness and happiness pursue and give place to one another all through our lives. The real truth which we grow to see clearly is that they exist at the same time, and do not contradict each other. They really minister to one another. Christ was the saddest and happiest man that ever lived. And so am I thanking God for you while I am praying for you with all my heart.

"How beautiful the death at Haslemere has been. I owe it to you that I ever had the privilege of seeing Tennyson. For that, as for a thousand other goodnesses, I can never thank you. But it will be a treasure to me all my life. And what has he not been to all of us who began to hear him sing when we were boys! And what must life mean to him now when he is with God!

"Albert tells me that you have not forgotten about the picture and that he wants one too. Here they both are, and I wish that he would send me his. Yours I have had for years among my treasures. May the peace of God be with you always.

"Your sincere friend,

"PHILLIPS BROOKS."

The following letter was written by Phillips Brooks after reading a statement of the religious belief of a young man wishing to enter the ministry, and to know whether in the bishop's opinion he were eligible for the sacred office. Without the original document the reply may not be in every respect intelligible, but its general meaning is clear.

"233 CLARENDON STREET, BOSTON, November 10, 1892.

"MY DEAR MR. C ——, I have read your friend's paper with much interest. It is very strange how men's thoughts at any one time run in the same direction, are perplexed by the same difficulties, and tend to the same results.

"I do not know how much your friend has read of certain recent writings which discuss the relation between the formal and essential, the historical and spiritual in the Christian faith. But evidently the necessity for some adjustment and proportion between the two has pressed upon his mind as it has pressed upon so many others. The unquestioning acceptance of all that is written concerning the historical Christ and the almost exclusive value set upon the facts of His earthly life have given way to a larger estimate of what He eternally is, and of the spiritual meaning which the recorded facts enshrine.

"That the value of the historic fact may be depreciated, as it has in some other days been exaggerated, there can be no doubt; but that the disposition which your friend exhibits, to seek and dwell upon the spiritual meaning of the redeeming life, is good and true, I also thoroughly believe.

"As to his right to be a Christian minister I cannot hesitate. Our Church puts into the hands of her ministers the Apostles' and the Nicene Creeds, and asks them to repeat these symbols with the people. Of course there are various interpretations of many of the articles. But he who says them in good faith as an expression of his own religious thinking and believing has an unquestioned right within our ministry. Is not the same thing true substantially of yours, and would not your friend thus find that he really belongs where he very much wants to be?

"I must rejoice with him and for him in the spiritual earnestness which is evidently his. That is the great thing after all. He has life, which is what Christ came that we might have.

"Will you assure him of my heartiest good wishes?

"And will you believe me,

"Yours most sincerely,

"PHILLIPS BROOKS."

He preached on Thanksgiving Day, November 24, at Trinity Church. His text was "God saw everything that He had made, and, behold, it was very good." Again his subject was "Optimism." He defined it: "It is not merely a matter of temperament, nor does it mean that this is a thoroughly good world in which we live, nor is it simply a careless passing over of the evils of life, nor is it a way of seeing how everything is going to come out for good. But it is a great belief in a great purpose, underlying the world for good, absolutely certain to fulfil itself somewhere, somehow. That must have been what God saw when He looked upon the world and called it good."

To Dr. Weir Mitchell he wrote expressing his opinion of current poetic efforts:

"233 CLARENDON STREET, BOSTON, December 10, 1892.

"The verses are certainly fine. Some of them are exquisite and delightful. Of course they are fantastic and unhealthy— everybody is that, nowadays—and they are affected, and haunted always by recollections of somebody else's poetry, and wilfully and unnecessarily obscure, and awfully afraid of being commonplace. Sometime somebody will just dare to sing the first great simple things as all the great poets have sung them, and then, how the world will listen! and, instead of a few distorted connoisseurs of poetry like you and me praising it to one another, all men will be delighting in it as they delight in nobody to-day."

He went, on the 21st of December, to the dinner of the New England Society in Brooklyn, and made a speech, characteristic of him in every respect, noting with kindly satire their faults, yet praising greatly New England and the Puritans. He stayed with his brother while in New York, and in a letter describing Christmas Day he says: "We played childish games till midnight, and it was all very simple, and silly, and delightful." There were things which tried him greatly at this time, but he dismissed them on principle: "On Christmas Day one must be glad." That his thoughts were dwelling on Tennyson is evident from this letter to Lady Frances Baillie:

"233 CLARENDON STREET, BOSTON, December 30, 1892.

"DEAR LADY FRANCES,—The etching has arrived, after what I doubt not was a stormy and distressing experience on the Atlantic, for it seems as if the great ocean never had been so restless and uneasy-minded as in these last few weeks. But it has come, and brings its blessing to the end of the departing year. Surely the most touching and sacred thing to many of us during the year which goes out to-morrow will be that it opened the grave for Tennyson, and one of the first thoughts about 1893 as we bid it welcome will be that in it we shall not hear his voice.

"This picture of his grave is very good to have, especially from your kind hands. I do not think that my friends' graves mean very much to me. I do not find myself often going to them. I should not mind it if I did not know where my friend was buried, if only I knew that no dishonor had been done to his body. Death is so great and splendid, the wonderful emancipation which must come to the spirit is so exalting and inspiring, that it carries one's thoughts away from the body after we have once done to it the affectionate reverence which everything which has belonged to our friend suggests to us.

"It is only when a life has been monumental, like the great poet's, and his memory is part of the life of the earth, which he has richened, that his grave becomes a treasure for mankind. I am glad his body lies in the Abbey. The dear old place seems even dearer from this new association.

"And every token of your kind remembrance is very precious to me, as I am sure you know.

"And when you turn the page of the New Year, may you find some message of strength and good cheer written on the other side. You surely will, whether it be of sickness or of health. How one grows almost afraid to choose, or at least thankful that he has not to decide! The great simple truths, that God lives, that God loves, that Christ is our salvation, grow greater and simpler and dearer every year. May they flood this New Year with their light for you.

"I wish that I could see you. You will know, I am sure, that my thought and prayer are with you, and that I am always,

"Yours most affectionately,
"PHILLIPS BROOKS."

Among the last things Phillips Brooks wrote in his note-book is the following:

"THE FUTURE LIFE.

"How far we may get at a real conception of its essential nature by carefully observing the most spiritual moments of this life, in such particulars, for instance, as the following:

"1.   Relation to the bodily life, preserving it, but keeping it subordinate and servile.

"2.   Relation to our friends, getting at their true spiritual essence, not *minding*, *i. e.*, keeping in mind, their circumstances, poverty, wealth, etc.

"3.   Relation to God—true worship.   Communion more than petition.

"4.   Relation to time.   Essential timelessness, free drawing upon past and future.

"5.   Relation to ourselves.   Consciousness of our deepest ideality.   Fullest companionship with others, and proportionately deep sense of *self*.

"All these things we know in the highest moments of our lives; shall they not, clothed in fit scenery, make our Heaven?"

CHAPTER XXVI.

1893.

CONCLUSION.

WATCH-NIGHT was kept as usual at Trinity Church and the new year was ushered in by a fervent prayer from Phillips Brooks. Then rising and addressing the great congregation, he added: "I wish you all a Happy, a very Happy New Year." A lady who called upon him in his study during the day found him in depression, but rousing himself, he said: "It must be, it *shall* be, a happy new year." On the Sunday morning with which the new year opened he was at the Old North Church on Salem Street. He ate his New Year's dinner with the members of the Christian Union, as had been his custom for twenty years, and spoke to the young men as he had spoken during all those years.

"New Year comes to us with the presentation of the great things of life. Greatness and littleness are terms not of the quantity, but of the quality, of human life. If a man has a great conception of life, and is putting all of the little things which he is doing into that conception, he is a great man. There always is some great conception which makes for a man the interpretation of his life.

"Everything craves for manifestation. I believe that when Jesus Christ came and touched the earth, the earth had some response to make, which it does not make to you and me. Even now, Nature is saying something which she did not say to men that groped about five centuries ago. She says it in the lights which burn in our hall and in the cars that run by the door.

"The biggest truth that man knows is the most practical truth. Mankind only progresses as it progresses with the development of man's own personal character. Increased skill will come with increased goodness. Man is what man expects himself to be. Look at yourself and say, 'Am I a child of God?' Do that under any circumstances, and the circumstances immediately become sublime.

"Character, and character only is the thing that is eternally

639

powerful in this world. Character is the divinest thing on earth. It is the one thing that you can put into the shop or into the study and be sure that the fire is going to burn. Character now, and character forever!"

On Monday evening, January 2, he was at the Clericus Club for the last time. He began the next day the visitation of the churches in accordance with a list made out for six months in advance. Tuesday, January 3, he was at Wakefield; Wednesday, January 4, at Middleborough; Thursday, January 5, at Framingham; Friday, January 6, at Watertown; Sunday, January 8, he visited the three churches in Dorchester; Tuesday, January 10, he was at Belmont; Thursday, January 12, at Wellesley; Friday, January 13, at Canton. Minor appointments, commiteee meetings, etc., filled up the intervening time.

Into one event he entered with the zest of youthful happiness, —a reception at his residence on January 11, in honor of Miss Gertrude Brooks, when for the first time he threw open his house. It had been a promise made long before that such a reception should be given when the time came. He shared in the anticipation of the event and still more in its fulfilment; and as he stood by the side of his niece to receive the guests, with the sense of joy in kinship and proprietorship in her gladness, he seemed to be in the happiest, even the gayest of moods.

On Saturday morning, January 14, he preached at the consecration of St. Mary's Church for Sailors, East Boston. A window was open in the roof, which could not be shut, and the cold winter air blew on the heads of those present. Coming back on the ferry, he complained of feeling cold.

On Sunday he should have kept at home, for he was ill; but he went to Hyde Park, officiating there in the morning, and then in an open sleigh he drove to Dedham. A lady who was present has furnished an account of the morning of that day:

"The little church in Hyde Park was crowded with people. His subject was 'Life.' 'Thou shalt satisfy the king with long life.' 'Life forever and ever' was the burden. He read the words from *Saul*,

> "'How good is man's life! The mere living
>   How fit to employ
> All the heart and the soul and the senses
>   Forever in joy!'

"And even as he spoke, with Life upon his lips, I saw written plainly upon his face that other word, Death. I grew numb and faint, and thought that I would have to leave the church.

"After the confirmation he stayed and stayed. I have never seen him happier or gentler, never more childlike and lovable than he was that Sunday morning. He addressed the Sunday-school. When that was done he went about among the children. Women brought him their babies and their boys that he might look into their faces. He had a word for every one. When he sat down, a group of boys circled around him. One boy back of him noticed a speck upon his coat and went to brush it off. In a moment there were three boys brushing him altogether. He looked about and colored, his modesty overcome at being the object of so much attention. . . . He continued to talk with the children. It seemed even then that he was already entering God's kingdom as a little child.

"And still he did not go. He did not seem to want to go. Long after he had gone I stood in the church. Only a few were left. An old woman came to me and began talking. I had never seen her before, but she seemed to know me somehow, and began to talk about him. She remembered him as a boy, and began to tell about the old days at St. Paul's when the Brooks boys, as she said, used to spill over into another pew. I let her talk on and on. In the middle of it I looked up,—and there he was! Back again! I wondered what brought him. I was startled and could not speak. He looked at us a second and then he said, 'Good-bye,' and the smile that grew upon his face, the bright look in the eyes, I shall never forget. I did not say good-bye,—I could not. He looked so happy that I was glad too, and yet there was a sadness mingled with it deeper than words could say."

The next day, Monday, January 16, was apparently an off day, when he rested in his study, where callers found him:

"He came forth as usual with his arms extended in greeting in the old familiar way, but he was changed. During the hour which followed he was restless, walking the room, talking incessantly; it was hardly possible, so rapid and continuous was the talk, to put a question without interrupting him. When he was asked if he found any difficulty in conversation in making his episcopal visits, he said, 'Oh no; you only pull the spigot, and it comes.' He was full of reminiscences; referring to his early years and the absurd way he then had of selecting texts which no one had heard of. He spoke of one sermon which he got by asking a clerical brother what text he was going to preach on. The text was so striking that only one sermon could be

41

preached from it, and as he wrote on the text at once he made it impossible for the original suggester to use it. He talked of Watson's poems then just out, which he admired, especially the lines on Tennyson. Then he turned to the New England dinner, commenting on the difference between New York and Boston, how the exaggerated estimate of money was affecting even the clergy in New York. He told an incident of the New England dinner: A gentleman who sat beside him complained that he could not enjoy the dinner because of the speech he had to make. 'That,' said Phillips Brooks, 'is also my trouble.' 'Why,' said the gentleman, 'I did not suppose you ever gave a thought to any speech you had to make.' 'And is that your impression of the way in which I have done all my work?' 'It is,' said the gentleman; 'I have thought it was all spontaneous, costing you no effort of preparation.' The interview closed with his agreement to preach the sermon at West Point at the Commencement in the ensuing June."

The following narrative by Mr. William G. Brooks takes up the story and carries it to the end:

"On Tuesday, January 17, 1893, in the evening, Bishop Brooks made a visitation to the Church of the Good Shepherd, in Boston —his last visitation. I saw the notice in the evening paper, and went to hear him. He had a written sermon ready, but the pulpit desk was low and his glasses troubled him, and he laid it aside and preached an extemporaneous sermon on Christ feeding the multitude in the desert. He had a severe cold and was troubled with his throat. I went home with him and sat and talked till eleven o'clock. He was in good spirits and bright and interesting and spoke lightly of the soreness in his throat. When I bade him good-night he said he would come in and spend an evening with us soon.

"The next day, Wednesday, January 18, he walked out, and in the evening went to Newton to a choir festival and a dinner at the Woodland Park Hotel. There he made his last speech, with great difficulty on account of his throat. He was driven in a close carriage to the station in Newton, and also from the Huntington Avenue station in Boston to his home. During the night his throat grew worse, and in the morning was very much swollen. He sent for Dr. Beach, who told him he must keep his bed to prevent more cold and avoid a chill, but that he had only an 'old-fashioned sore throat.'

"I saw him in the evening. Dr. Beach was there, who stated the case the same as he did in the morning. He gave him a gargle and a Dover's powder to sleep on. But he had a poor

night, and was very restless in the morning.   I saw him in the
morning, afternoon, and evening.   This I did each of the days he
was sick, and Mrs. Brooks and Gertrude saw him each forenoon.
Dr. Beach each day told me of his condition, and constantly
spoke favorably and hopefully of it.   He objected to a nurse,
though the doctor suggested it, and, as the servants knew his
wishes and could prepare what he needed, there seemed to be no
occasion for one.

"His throat was so swollen that he could say but little, and
could take only liquid food.   He read his letters and papers and
dictated some of his correspondence.

"So it went on till Sunday, when he did not appear so well.
He seemed to be weaker and slept more.   Still Dr. Beach said
there was no cause for alarm.   At eight o'clock in the evening
he saw him and sent me word that he looked for a good night,
and he hoped to find him better in the morning.   So we went to
bed feeling easy and hoping for good results.

"But about one o'clock one of his servants came to our house
and said he was not so well.   It appears that he woke from a
light sleep about eleven o'clock, a little weak in his head, and
went out of his room and up the stairs a few steps, when the servants heard him and gently took him to his room and bed again.
He seemed to imagine he was in a strange house, perhaps on an
episcopal visitation, and said he was 'going home.'

"Dr. Beach was sent for and came at once.   He sent for me
and also for Dr. Fitz.   I was at the house before Dr. Fitz, and
Dr. Beach sent me at once to the Registry of Nurses for a nurse.
I got a man who was there in an hour or so, and on my return I
found Dr. Fitz at the house.

"The doctors had just examined his lungs.   They found them
sound and said they found nothing that was dangerous.   It seems
they suspected there might be a diphtheritic trouble below the
throat swelling, and had arranged to make an examination
at nine o'clock in the morning, with possibly Dr. Knight also
present.

"While the doctors were consulting together after their examination in the hall in the second story, I was alone with Phillips.
He knew me.   He looked up from his pillow with the sweetest
smile and held out his hand.   He pressed mine warmly and
strongly, smiled again and again, and once or twice said, 'Good-
night.'   Then he lay back on his pillow, put his great left hand
on his heart, and smiled and nodded his head with his eyes full
on mine.   Then he raised his right hand with the forefinger extended, and waved it round and round for several moments, as
he used to do when hearing music, or humming some tune himself.
It was all clear and bright and happy, full of the joy that was
in his heart, in harmony with the love that filled it and with

the heavenly melodies that he heard calling him to his eternal home, full of rest and life. This was about three o'clock.

"These were his last clear moments. After it he slept lightly, taking nourishment from time to time, and restless and uncomfortable when awake.

"About six o'clock he rose and insisted on getting out of bed, and as he was very decided, Dr. Beach said, as the room was warm, he might be wrapped in blankets and sit in a chair a little while. The doctor and the nurse covered him, and he stepped between them towards the door that opened into the hall as if he wished to go out of the room. Dr. Beach restrained him, saying a few words, when he said quite impatiently, 'Both you men cannot keep me from going through that door.' His attention was, however, diverted, and he was led to a large rocking-chair in the room, into which he was seated, the nurse in a chair by his side, and Dr. Beach and I in chairs near by.

"In a few moments the nurse called Dr. Beach, who went at once. His head had drooped, and he was breathing hard. We lifted him upon the bed. He still breathed, and Dr. Beach at once injected a strong dose of brandy into his arm. But it had no effect, and in two or three minutes the breathing grew fainter and then stopped. He had gone."

The funeral services for Phillips Brooks were held at Trinity Church on Thursday, January 26. At eight o'clock in the morning of that day the body, accompanied by a guard of members of the Loyal Legion, was borne to the church and placed in the vestibule, where it was viewed by a continuous procession of all classes of people, numbering many thousands, and there were thousands still waiting for the privilege when the hour of service, eleven o'clock, arrived. In the city were the evidences of mourning. The traffic seemed to cease in the streets, the Stock Exchange and places of business were closed, the flags were at half-mast. Within the church the scene resembled the day of his consecration to the episcopate. The governor of the Commonwealth of Massachusetts, the mayor of the city of Boston, and a delegation from the Legislature were there; representatives of many societies also, and of the congregation of Trinity Church; and many clergymen of other denominations. The white-robed procession of the clergy of the diocese and of visiting clergy in large numbers met the body at the west door of the church and passed up the aisle. The presiding bishop of the Episcopal

Church, Dr. Williams, who read the sentences, was followed by
the bishops of Rhode Island, New York, Western Virginia, New
Hampshire, Maine, and Central Pennsylvania. Eight Harvard
students bore the body aloft on their shoulders. Among the
honorary pall-bearers were the friends of many years. Bishop
Potter stood at the lectern to read the lesson. Bishop Clark led
in the recital of the Nicene Creed. The hymns were "Jesus,
lover of my soul," and "For all the saints who from their labors
rest."

When the service was over within the church, another service
was held without, for the larger congregation waiting in Copley
Square,—some said ten thousand, others twenty thousand, but
no one knew,—a vast concourse of people under the open heaven.
The body was borne from the church as it had been carried in,
on the shoulders of Harvard students, placed upon a catafalque
in sight of the multitude, when prayers were said and the hymn
was sung, "O God, our help in ages past." Then the long procession moved. When it reached Harvard Square at two o'clock,
the familiar college bell began to toll, announcing that the procession was entering the college grounds. "In a marvellously
short time the steps of University and Harvard halls were
crowded; men poured from the dormitories and recitation halls
in the quadrangle, and lined up two or three deep on both sides
of the driveway from University to the entrance gate between
Harvard and Massachusetts. There, with bared heads, they
stood in silence while the carriages passed one by one out of the
yard." Then they disappeared as silently and as quickly as they
had gathered, while the procession moved on to Mount Auburn
to meet another large assemblage of people about the open grave.
Here the committal was said by Rev. John C. Brooks, and the
prayers by Rev. Arthur Brooks, who gave the benediction. So
the body of Phillips Brooks was laid to rest, in the same lot with
the father and mother and the two brothers, George and Frederick. And the people went away again to their own homes.

When the awful intelligence that Phillips Brooks was dead
first fell upon the city of Boston and the country at large, it came
with "the crushing and stunning effect of unspeakable calamity,"
—a sorrow which at first could find no words. When the silence
was broken and utterance began, it seemed as though the re-

sources of the English language were exhausted to find fitting terms wherein to express the people's admiration and love. The sorrow and the mourning were exchanged for a song of triumph and spiritual exultation,—to the praise of God for Phillips Brooks. So it went on, as if it could have no ending, during the memorable months which are still recalled as something unwonted in human experience,—the afterglow of the great life. The "resolutions" adopted by countless societies and organizations, by the clergy in their associations,—clergy of every name; the thousands of private letters; the memorial sermons preached in churches everywhere, in this country and in England, and, indeed, wherever the English language is spoken the world over; the articles in every newspaper, editorial and contributed,—in this mass of expression, which no one can adequately measure, was the highest tribute to Phillips Brooks. Exaggerated, indeed, it was, for those who wrote seemed to vie with each other in the effort to say the strongest things in his praise,—exaggerated, for it went to the verge, and sometimes beyond it, of what it is lawful to say of mortal man in this world; and yet significant, not to be ashamed of, characteristic, in that it revealed, when taken together, what Phillips Brooks had been to his age, and also made known the age itself as it laid its inmost being open to the eye of God and man.

These are some of the texts of memorial sermons:

"There is a prince and a great man fallen this day in Israel."

"And Samuel died; and all the Israelites were gathered together, and lamented him."

"Whatsoever the king did pleased all the people."

"When he came near, the whole city was moved, saying, Who is this?"

"And they said one to another, Did not our heart burn within us, while he talked with us by the way, and while he opened to us the Scriptures?"

"Behold, I have given him for a witness to the people, a leader and commander to the people."

"God hath anointed thee with the oil of gladness above thy fellows."

At a service in Westminster Abbey, Canon Duckworth spoke these words:

"I think of the great American bishop, Phillips Brooks, that true king of men, whose sudden death has been mourned as an irreparable bereavement in the churches of the Old World as in those of the New. No more signal example has this generation seen of that deep, comprehensive work which the Holy Spirit accomplishes when He takes possession of the *whole man*. There was splendid natural faculty, transfigured, raised to its highest power, and dedicated to its highest use. There was the whole intellectual and moral being suffused with the flame of divine love, and aglow with those fervid convictions which found on his lips such matchless expression. And then there was the magnetic charm of personal intercourse, the pure teachings of the daily life, filled full of high interests, and still more persuasive in its unconscious humility, and self-forgetfulness, and sympathy, than those burning words which, wherever he was to be heard, drew thousands to listen, as one has truly said, 'with an intensity of expectation as if the very mystery of existence were at last to stand revealed.' Who could know him and remain sceptical as to the reality of that *divine life* which it is man's highest glory to receive?"

And these words, in which the Bishop of Winchester, the Rt. Rev. Dr. Thorold, dedicated a volume of sermons to Phillips Brooks, will find an echo in the hearts of all who knew and loved him:

TO THE DEAR MEMORY OF

PHILLIPS BROOKS

BISHOP OF MASSACHUSETTS

STRONG, FEARLESS, TENDER, ELOQUENT

INCAPABLE OF MEANNESS

BLAZING WITH INDIGNATION AT ALL KINDS OF WRONG

HIS HEART AND MIND DEEP AND WIDE AS

THE OCEAN AT HIS DOOR

SIMPLE AND TRANSPARENT AS A CHILD

KEEN WITH ALL THE KEENNESS OF HIS RACE

THIS VOLUME IS INSCRIBED

BY A BROTHER ACROSS THE WATER

WHO CHERISHES HIS FRIENDSHIP AS A

TREASURE LAID UP IN HEAVEN

AT THE RESURRECTION OF THE JUST

INDEX

Abbott, Rev. Lyman, letter to, 537.
Adams, C. F., Reminiscences of Phillips Brooks at Latin School, 21ff.
Agassiz, L., 271.
Ancient and Honorable Artillery Company, sermon before, 242.
Andover, 1, 2, 270, 272, 331, 491.
Andover Theological Seminary, 1, 5, 43, 207.
Apostolic Succession, 249, 590.
Arminianism, 2.
Arnold, Matthew, 58.
Atlantic Monthly, 60, 363, 364.
"Authority and Conscience," 436.

Baillie, Lady Frances, 362, 363, 634, 637.
Baptism, significance of, 472.
Beecher, Henry Ward, 485.
Berlin, 375ff.
Bersier, M., 450.
"Biography," essay on, 466.
Boston, account of fire in, 261.
Brahma Somaj, 393ff.
Brooks, Rev. Arthur, 142, 216, 254, 274, 393, 628, 645.
Brooks, Rev. Edward, 2, 3,
Brooks, Rev. Frederick, 84, 125, 223; death of, 276.
Brooks, George, 126, 130, 137; death of, 140.
Brooks, Rev. John Cotton, 253, 556, 597, 598, 625, 645.
Brooks, Mary Ann (Phillips), 2, 3, 6; letters to Phillips Brooks, 61, 62, 215; death of, 341ff.
Brooks, Peter Chardon, 3.
Brooks, Phillips, ancestry, 1ff; birth, 3; early years, 4ff; early education, 9; Boston Latin School, 10; enters Harvard College, 11ff; literary activity at Harvard, 12ff; religious attitudes, 14; reserve, 16; usher at Latin School, 19ff; resigns ushership, 21; first religious experience, 27ff; enters Virginia Theological Seminary, 37; first communion, 42; wide reading, 47ff; verse writing, 48, 49; note-books, 49; confirmation, 57; inward development, 58; studies in the Church Fathers, 69; reserve, 87, 88; first sermon, 89; essays in the seminary, 93; call to Church of the Advent, Philadelphia, 101, 102; ordination to diaconate, 103; ordination to priesthood, 110; call to Church of the Holy Trinity, Philadelphia, 113; resignation of Church of the Advent, 120; visit to Niagara Falls, 129; comments on general convention, 1862, 136; letter to his mother on the death of George Brooks, 141; Fast-day sermon, 1863, 143; vigorous advocacy of the Union, 143; visit to Gettysburg, 146; interest in the colored people, 150ff, 173, 176; sermon on "Mercies of Reoccupation," 152ff; call to Philadelphia Divinity School, 159; extracts from note-book on Mohammedanism, 163ff; attends Pennsylvania Diocesan Convention, 170; sermon on the Prayer Book, 170; advocates negro suffrage, 172ff; prayer in Philadelphia at the fall of Richmond, 178; prayer at Harvard Commemoration, 187; estimate of Lincoln, 179ff, 183ff; absence in Europe for a year, 190ff; call to Trinity Church, Boston, 212ff; comments on appearance of, 217, 218; second call to Trinity Church, 218; sermon on the Living Church, 220ff; begins his rectorship of Trinity Church, Boston, 231; interest in education, 243, 244; relation to evangelical party, 263; essay on Heresy, 273; method of pre-